Computer Concepts

Illustrated Series
Introductory

Ninth Edition

June Jamrich Parsons | Dan Oja | David W. Beskeen

CENGAGE
Learning

Australia • Brazil • Japan • Korea • Mexico • Singapore • Spain • United Kingdom • United States

CENGAGE
Learning·

Computer Concepts: Illustrated Series, Introductory, Ninth Edition

Computer Concepts: Illustrated Series, Introductory, Ninth Edition
June Jamrich Parsons | Dan Oja

© 2013 Cengage Learning. All rights reserved.

Microsoft Office 2013: Illustrated Introductory, First Course
David W. Beskeen

© 2013 Cengage Learning. All rights reserved.

Senior Project Development Manager:
 Linda deStefano

Market Development Manager:
 Heather Kramer

Senior Production/Manufacturing Manager:
 Donna M. Brown

Production Editorial Manager:
 Kim Fry

Sr. Rights Acquisition Account Manager:
 Todd Osborne

For product information and technology assistance, contact us at
Cengage Learning Customer & Sales Support, 1-800-354-9706

For permission to use material from this text or product,
submit all requests online at **cengage.com/permissions**
Further permissions questions can be emailed to
permissionrequest@cengage.com

This book contains select works from existing Cengage Learning resources and
was produced by Cengage Learning Custom Solutions for collegiate use. As such,
those adopting and/or contributing to this work are responsible for editorial
content accuracy, continuity and completeness.

Compilation © 2013 Cengage Learning
ISBN-13: 978-1-285-89724-0

ISBN-10: 1-285-89724-2

Cengage Learning
5191 Natorp Boulevard
Mason, Ohio 45040
USA

Cengage Learning is a leading provider of customized learning solutions with
office locations around the globe, including Singapore, the United Kingdom,
Australia, Mexico, Brazil, and Japan. Locate your local office at:
international.cengage.com/region.
Cengage Learning products are represented in Canada by Nelson Education, Ltd.
For your lifelong learning solutions, visit **www.cengage.com/custom.**
Visit our corporate website at **www.cengage.com.**

Printed in the United States of America

Brief Contents

Excerpted from:
Computer Concepts: Illustrated Series, Introductory
Ninth Edition
June Jamrich Parsons | Dan Oja

Excerpted from:
Microsoft Office 2013: Illustrated Introductory, First Course
David W. Beskeen

Contents

Preface

Welcome to *Computer Concepts Illustrated Introductory Ninth Edition!* This book is designed to help students learn and retain the most relevant and essential information about computers and technology in today's digital world. To enhance the teaching and learning experience, you can also bundle this text with CourseMate, our online digital companion site which includes a media-rich eBook, videos and interactive activities for reinforcement, and Engagement Tracker, a first-of-its-kind tool that monitors student engagement in the course.

Designed For All Users

The unique page design of the book makes it a great learning tool for both new and experienced users. Each concept is presented on two facing pages, so students don't have to turn the page to find an illustration or finish a paragraph. Also, because the text is organized in a question and answer format, students can choose to read all of the lesson material or only those questions and answers where they need to "fill in the gaps."

New to This Edition

Here are some highlights of what's new to this edition:

- **CourseMate**—The new CourseMate online companion for this book is packed with media-rich content to engage your students and to help you teach the course! CourseMate includes a **digital version of this book** that students can read and highlight online; brand new **videos** based on the book content that highlight the hot topics of each lesson; **Student Edition Labs** that provide hands-on learning and assessment activities for key concepts; interactive **games, flashcards,** and **puzzles** to reinforce what they've learned, and **practice tests** to assess mastery of content. The CourseMate also includes handy Independent Challenge worksheets adapted from the book that students can download, complete, and submit. CourseMate also includes a link to a **weekly podcast** on the hottest technology

Each two-page spread focuses on a single topic.

Introduction briefly explains why the lesson topic is important.

Lesson Objective in each lesson articulates key learning goal of the lesson.

Printers

UNIT B Concepts

Most output is viewed using a display device. This output is called **soft copy**. Sometimes, you want the output on paper. To create printed copy, you use a printer. Printed output is called **hard copy**. You can print hard copy on different media, such as paper, labels, or transparencies. Printers differ in resolution and speed, both of which affect the print quality and price. To find a printer that meets your needs, it is important to understand the different types of printers and their features.

Learning Objective 3:
Describe different types of printers, and explain the advantages and disadvantages of each type

- **What are the most common types of printers in use today?** The most common types of printers in use today are either ink-jet printers or laser printers. Both ink-jet printers and laser printers have features in common. For example, both are available as black and white or color printers. Both have trays for different paper sizes. You can print on 8" × 11" paper, 8" × 14" paper, envelopes, postcards, transparencies, and more. Both types of printers also have drawbacks to consider. For example, cost over the life of the printer, as well as the speed at which the printer produces hard copy.

- **How does an ink-jet printer work?** An **ink-jet printer** has a print head that sprays ink onto paper to form characters and graphics. Ink-jet printers usually use two cartridges: a black ink cartridge and a color cartridge that holds colored inks. See Figure B-9. Most ink-jet printers are small, lightweight, and inexpensive, yet produce very good-quality color output. However, the ink cartridges can be expensive and can add to the overall cost of printing.

FIGURE B-9: An ink jet printer

Color ink cartridges

Paper tray

Black ink cartridge

- **How does a laser printer work?** A **laser printer** uses a technology that produces dots of light on a light-sensitive drum. Instead of ink cartridges, laser printers use **toner** cartridges. See Figure B-10. Toner is the fine powder that is

applied to the drum, and then creates the image on the paper. Laser printers are popular for situations that require high-volume output or good-quality printouts. Laser printers are generally more expensive than ink-jet printers.

FIGURE B-10: A laser printer

Toner cartridge

Paper tray

- **What determines the quality of the printed images?** **Printer resolution** determines the quality or sharpness of printed images and text. Resolution is measured by the number of dots printed per linear inch, or **dots per inch (dpi)**. At normal reading distance, a resolution of about 900 dots per inch appears solid to the human eye. At 900 dpi, if you look closely, a dot pattern will be evident. Good-quality printers are rated from 2400 to 4800 dpi. If you want the printed images to have the quality of professionally printed books, use a printer with a resolution of 2400 dpi or higher.

- **How can I know if a printer is fast?** You can look at the pages per minute (ppm) and memory specifications provided by the manufacturer. Printer speed is measured by the number of **pages per minute (ppm)** output. Color printouts typically take longer to print than black-and-white printouts. Pages that contain mostly text tend to print faster than pages that contain graphics. Most printers for personal or small business use are rated from 15 to 30 ppm.
 Memory capacity is another factor to consider when evaluating printer speed. Printers often work in the background while you work on other computer tasks. If your printer has lots of

Concepts 32 Computer Hardware

Question & Answer format helps to engage students and make the content relevant.

- **Updated and Relevant Information**—each page of this book has been completely updated to reflect the most current and relevant information about computers and computing technology. New lessons include Communicating with Digital Devices and Protecting Your Privacy, Data, and Devices. In response to customer feedback, we also made a change to the table of contents; the unit on security is now Unit E, and the unit on Networks and Connecting to the Internet is Unit F.

- **Updated Design**—Our updated design and pedagogy make this edition more engaging for students. Each unit opener page now shows a large photograph of a student using technology related to that unit, and also lists learning objectives and lesson topics for the unit. Each lesson spread now displays the learning objective in a shaded box to help focus the student on the key learning goal for that lesson.

Exercises

Each unit features a wide variety of reinforcement exercises including Key Terms, Unit Review, and Concepts Review multiple choice questions. Other exercises include:

- **Talking Points**—Engage your students in lively discussions by assigning Talking Points, which provide information and discussion questions about computing topics that affect our everyday lives. Examples include Why Recycle Computers? and Who is Reading Your Email?

- **Independent Challenges**—Independent Challenge exercises are guided activities that students complete to reinforce what they have learned in that unit.

- **Buyer's Guide**—this activity lets student organize and record the important information learned in that unit to help them research options and make decisions about purchasing their own computer.

(Sample textbook page shown)

memory, you can send many print jobs to the printer. The print jobs will be in the printer's memory and not in your computer's memory. More memory is required to print color images and documents with graphics. You can work more efficiently if your printer has more memory.

- **Can a printer print on both sides of a page in one pass?** Yes, a **duplex printer** can print on both sides of the paper. This environment-friendly option saves paper. However, duplex printing slows down the print process on ink-jet printers because they have to pause to let the ink dry before printing the second side.

- **Does the number of pages I print affect the life of my printer?** Duty cycle determines how many pages a printer is able to print in a specified period of time. A printer's duty cycle is usually measured in pages per month. For example, on average, a personal laser printer has a duty cycle of about 3000 pages per month—that means roughly 100 pages per day. However, you wouldn't want to use it to produce 3,000 pages on one day. You can print more pages than the specified duty cycle, but this could shorten the usability of your printer. Also, a printer with a higher duty cycle will have a shorter useful life.

- **How does a printer connect to my computer?** A printer connects to your computer using one of the following connection options: USB port, serial port, parallel port, or network port. Usually a cable is used to connect a printer to a computer. However, a printer can also connect to a computer wirelessly if the printer and computer both have the wireless technology needed to connect.

You can connect a printer directly to your personal computer and use it only with that computer. But, sometimes, you might want to use a printer with more than one computer.

- **How do I use a printer with more than one computer?** If your computers are part of a LAN (local area network), you can share your printer with the other computers. In this situation, each computer on the network sends its print jobs to your computer's printer for output. This allows many computers to share one resource, the printer.

 Another way to configure network printing for multiple users is to purchase a **network-enabled printer** that connects directly to the network, rather than to one of the computers on a network. The network connection can be wired or wireless.

- **Do I need a different printer to print lots of photographs?** Yes, for more professional output, you want to use a **photo printer**. These printers have slower output speeds when compared to ink-jet or laser printers, but they do produce professional-quality images on specialized papers.

- **How do I know which type of printer is best for me?** The type of printer you need depends on several factors. For example: Do you need black and white hard copy or color hard copy Do you often need to print a lot of pages at one time? Are you working with a stand-alone or a networked computer? Do you want a wired or a wireless printer? Once you know the answers to these questions, you will know what type of printer best meets your needs.

Options for printing your photos

Do you print a lot of photographs? If so, you should compare the cost of printing the photographs using your printer to the cost of printing the photographs commercially. You can often have digital images printed over the Web using online services, such as Kodak Gallery, Snapfish, or Flickr. The printed photos are then mailed to you. You can also take the digital image files on a disc or flash drive to a store and have the photographs printed there. You can often shop while you wait for your photos. Some stores allow you to upload images to their Web site, where you specify your printing preferences, and then pick up the photos at your local store. Some stores even have self-service stations in the store. See Figure B-11. These printing services usually allow you to edit your digital images, for example, to remove red-eye or to crop an unwanted object out of the image. If you consider the cost of paper and ink to print large quantities of photographs, these services often are more economical. But for occasional use, a photo-printer provides quality images at a reasonable cost.

FIGURE B-11: Self-service photo printing

Computer Hardware Concepts 33

Unit B

Clues to Use yellow boxes relate the lesson material to real-world situations to provide practical information and context.

Large photos and graphics illustrate the lesson concepts.

CourseMate

Interested in a simple way to *complement* your text and course content with study and practice materials? **CourseMate** brings course concepts to life with interactive learning, study, and exam preparation tools that support the printed textbook. Watch student comprehension soar as your class works with the printed textbook and the CourseMate companion website. CourseMate goes beyond the book to deliver what you need! (CourseMate is sold separately.)

The following interactive activities and tools are included in CourseMate:

• ebook—A digital version of this text lets your students read, take notes, and highlight key content using their computer. Students can also search for information they want, and can view or print a PDF of any book page.

• Video Highlights—New videos highlighting the key points of each two-page lesson present the content to students the way they learn best.

• Concepts Review—Multiple choice questions from the Concepts Review exercises in the book are presented online. Students get immediate feedback on their results.

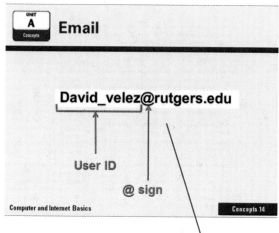

Video Highlights for each lesson bring book content to life

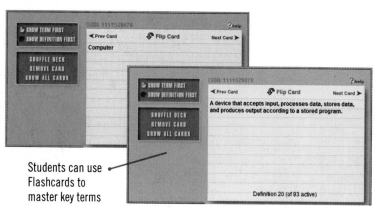

Students can use Flashcards to master key terms

• Glossary and Flashcards—Students can study and master key terms for each unit using the online glossary and Flashcard tools.

• Student Edition Labs—This collection of animations and hands-on activities help engage students and help them master key computing concepts.

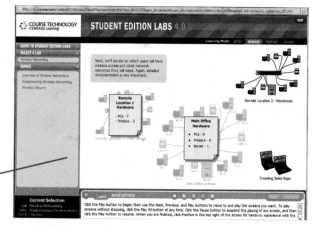

Student Edition Labs feature animations, guided steps, and reinforcement questions to help students learn key concepts

• Worksheets for Selected Exercises—Students can download worksheets based on the Independent Challenge and Guide to Buying a Computer exercises. The worksheets contain all the instructions they need to complete the exercises. Students can type their answers directly into form fields on the worksheet and submit to you for grading.

Students can download Independent Challenge worksheets

Students can type directly into form fields in the worksheet

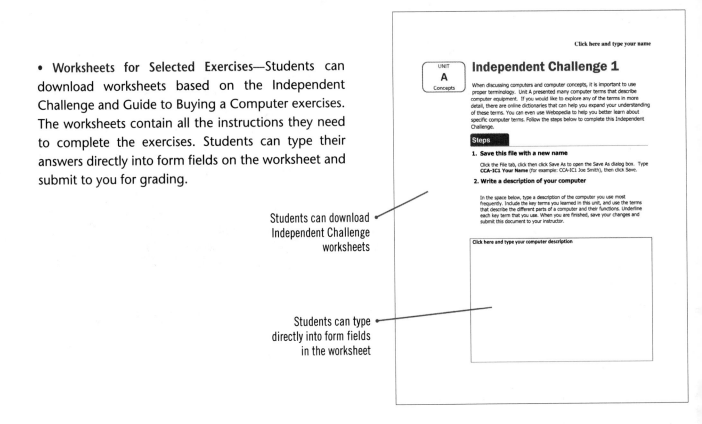

• **Games**—Crossword puzzles and a game let students test their knowledge of key terms and concepts in a fun, engaging way.

• **Practice Tests**—Students can prepare for exams by completing online practice tests on the unit content.

• **CourseCasts**—Keep your class up to date by assigning the CourseCast podcast each week. Hosted by Ken Baldauf of Florida State University, each podcast summarizes the hottest technology news from that week. Assign the CourseCast assignment to make sure that students listen to it! Students can listen on their computer, or they can download it to a mobile device to listen on the go.

• **Engagement Tracker**—Unique tool lets you monitor your students engagement in the course by tracking their usage of each CourseMate activity.

How Do Students Access CourseMate?

Instructions on how to access the CourseMate for this book are in the Getting Started with CourseMate Appendix. Note that students must purchase a CourseMate pin code to access CourseMate.

Instructor Resources

The Instructor Resources CD is Course Technology's way of putting the resources and information needed to teach and learn effectively into your hands. With an integrated array of teaching and learning tools that offer you and your students a broad range of technology-based instructional options, we believe this CD represents the highest quality and most cutting edge resources available to instructors today. Many of these resources are available at www.cengage.com/coursetechnology. The resources available with this book are:

• **Instructor's Manual**—Available as an electronic file, the Instructor's Manual includes detailed lecture topics with teaching tips for each unit.

• **Sample Syllabus**—Prepare and customize your course easily using this sample course outline.

• **PowerPoint Presentations**—Each unit has a corresponding PowerPoint presentation that you can use in lecture, distribute to your students, or customize to suit your course.

• **Figure Files**—The figures in the text are provided on the Instructor Resources CD to help you illustrate key topics or concepts. You can create traditional overhead transparencies by printing the figure files. Or you can create electronic slide shows by using the figures in a presentation program such as PowerPoint.

• **Solutions to Exercises**—Solutions to Exercises contains examples of the work in the end-of-unit material.

• **ExamView**—ExamView is a powerful testing software package that allows you to create and administer printed, computer (LAN-based), and Internet exams. ExamView includes hundreds of questions that correspond to the topics covered in this text, enabling students to generate detailed study guides that include page references for further review. The computer-based and Internet testing components allow students to take exams at their computers, and also saves you time by grading each exam automatically.

Content for Online Learning.

Course Technology has partnered with the leading distance learning solution providers and class-management platforms today. To access this material, visit www.cengage.com/webtutor and search for your title. Instructor resources include the following: video highlights, additional case projects, sample syllabi, PowerPoint presentations, and more. For additional information, please contact your sales representative. For students to access this material, they must have purchased a WebTutor PIN-code specific to this title and your campus platform. The resources for students might include (based on instructor preferences): topic reviews, review questions, practice tests, and more.

COURSECASTS Learning on the Go. Always Available…Always Relevant.

Our fast-paced world is driven by technology. You know because you are an active participant—always on the go, always keeping up with technological trends, and always learning new ways to embrace technology to power your life. Let CourseCasts, hosted by Ken Baldauf of Florida State University, be your guide into weekly updates in this ever-changing space. These timely, relevant podcasts are produced weekly and are available for download at http://coursecasts.course.com or directly from iTunes (search by CourseCasts). CourseCasts are a perfect solution to getting students (and even instructors) to learn on the go!

Acknowledgements

Author Acknowledgements

We sincerely appreciate all the members of the Illustrated team for contributing their vision, talent, and skills to make this book a reality. Special thanks to Rachel Biheller Bunin for her fast and efficient work as the adapting author, Pamela Conrad for her insights as the developmental editor, Heather Hopkins and Marisa Taylor for their solid work as production editors, Christina Kling Garrett for leading the project.

– June Parsons, Dan Oja, and MediaTechnics

I am forever grateful to Pam Conrad, the Developmental Editor on this book. Working with Pam is always a wonderful experience. As a personal friend and colleague, she contributes strength, knowledge, and intelligence to the project. My thanks to Marjorie Hunt, Executive Editor, for her encouragement and vision. Gratitude to Christina Kling Garrett, Senior Project Manager, for keeping all the components on track and providing endless support. Special credit to Emily Bunin for the stunning photos that begin each unit. Thanks to Abby Reip for her work collecting the stock photos and keeping it all straight. Thanks to Kathleen Ryan for her work on Web permissions. On the Production side, thanks to Marisa Taylor and Heather Hopkins for a beautiful book. Appreciation to Dan Oja and June Parsons for supporting the project. And finally, special thanks to David, Jennifer, Emily, and Michael.

– Rachel Biheller Bunin, Adapting Author

Advisory Board Acknowledgements

We would like to thank our Advisory Board for their honest feedback and suggestions that helped guide our development decisions for this edition. They are as follows:

Audrey Styer, Morton College

Sheila Sicilia, Onondaga Community College

Michelle Breitigan, Owens Community College

Sherry Lenhart, Terra Community College

Theresa Markovich, Everett Community College of Washington

Computer and Internet Basics

Learning Objectives

1. Define a personal computer and describe computer use in daily life
2. Explain the four basic functions of a computer system
3. Identify the main computer categories
4. Describe digital devices that can be part of a personal computer
5. Define software and give examples of operating systems
6. Define the Internet and explain how to navigate Web pages
7. Explain ways to use the Internet and digital devices to communicate with others
8. Explain how to protect your digital data and devices

LESSON TOPICS

- Computers in Your World
- How Computers Work
- Types of Computers
- Personal Computers
- Computer Software
- The Internet and the Web
- How to Communicate Using Digital Devices
- How to Protect Your Privacy, Data, and Devices

Talking Points: Who is Reading Your Email?

Courtesy of Emily Bunin

Computers in Your World

Whether you realize it or not, you already know a lot about personal computers and other digital devices. You've picked up information from advertisements and magazine articles, from books and movies, from conversations, and perhaps even from using a computer, smartphone, or other digital device. The digital revolution is the reason computers are all around you. See Figure A-1. This lesson helps you start organizing what you know about the digital revolution and computers.

Learning Objective 1:
Define a personal computer and describe computer use in daily life

- **What is the digital revolution and how does it affect me?** The **digital revolution** is an ongoing process of social, political, and economic change brought about by **digital technology**. Digital technology includes digital devices such as computers, portable media players, cameras, mobile phones, smartphones, tablet computers, global positioning systems (GPSs), DVD and CD players, e-book readers, digital voice recorders, and video games. Even cars and appliances, such as microwave ovens, refrigerators, and washing machines, use digital electronics. The digital revolution influences the tools you use to work, play, teach, and govern, especially when you use a computer.

- **What is a computer?** A **computer** is an electronic device that accepts input, processes data, stores data, and produces output as information. If a machine performs these four basic functions, it is a computer.

- **Why would I use a computer?** You might use a computer to access information on the Web, create documents, calculate a budget, change digital photographs, create music, and produce original graphics. Most likely, you will use a computer to communicate with people through the Internet.

- **Do all computers look alike?** No. Computers come in a variety of styles, models, and sizes. The way a computer looks depends on how the computer system is set up and what it will be used for. Usually, when people talk about computers, they are talking about a **personal computer (PC)**. A **computer system** includes hardware, peripheral devices, and software.

- **What is hardware?** **Hardware** refers to the electronic and mechanical parts of the computer. The **system unit** is the box that houses the most important parts of a computer system. The term hardware refers not only to the internal parts of the computer but also to its external parts, which are called peripheral devices.

FIGURE A-1: **Computers are a part of daily life**

- **What is a peripheral device?** A **peripheral device** is hardware that can be added to a computer system to expand what a computer can do. Popular peripheral devices include printers, media players, digital cameras, USB drives, scanners, and graphics tablets. Once your computer system is set up with its hardware and peripheral devices, it needs software in order to work as a computer.

- **What is software?** **Software** is a computer program that tells the computer how to perform tasks. You may have heard the terms word processing software, antivirus software, apps, or Web applications. These terms refer to some of the software that runs on your computer and other digital devices, such as your smartphone. There are many categories of software available for computers.

- **How do I use a computer?** To use a computer, you must input data or information. You use an **input device** (such as a keyboard, mouse, or touch screen) to input information. The input device and the computer work together to change the information into a series of electronic signals the computer can understand. Once the computer has the input, it processes the information and sends the processed information to an **output device**. Common output devices include monitors, printers, or speakers. As you work, you continue to input information and to use the output.

- **What is digitization, and why is it important in my daily life?** **Digitization** is the process of converting text, numbers, sound, photos, and video into data that can be processed by a computer. The advantage of digital images and sounds is that they can be easily stored, copied, and shared. Digital images have changed the photographic industry. Digital cameras have replaced film cameras. Digital imaging used in medical tests has had profound effects in the healthcare industry. Digital video is responsible for special effects in movies, new trends in 3D animation, portable video, and consumer interest in home video. Digital sound transformed the way music is marketed, sold, purchased, and played. Human speech can also be digitized. For example, when you call a business for help or information, digitized voice telephone systems understand and respond to your spoken words. GPS devices tell you the directions as your drive.

- **Is my smartphone a computer?** Yes, because a smartphone performs the four basic functions of a computer, it is considered a computer. For example, it accepts input—the phone numbers you type in. It processes the input, calling the number you entered. It stores data—keeping phone numbers in the address book. It outputs data—connects you to the phone you dial. When you think of a smartphone this way, it is a computer, but it is not a personal computer.

 Other digital devices, such as mobile tablets, video game consoles, and media players, also perform the four basic functions of a computer. These devices accept input, process data, store data, and output information in the form of text, spoken words, music, video, and images. These digital devices share other computer characteristics, as well. For example, many tablet computers feature a small keyboard, others accept handwriting input, and some work with touch screen icons. Many digital devices today are the result of digital convergence.

- **What is digital convergence?** **Digital convergence** is the trend to blend several technologies that have distinct functions into a single product. An early example of digital convergence is the multipurpose machine that worked as a fax, printer, scanner, and telephone. Today many devices, such as mobile phones, portable media players, cameras, and GPSs, include features that overlap each other. These devices are evolving into a single device. Most mobile phones are smartphones. Figure A-2 shows an HP smartphone and the Apple iPhone. They include voice communication and other features such as text messaging, email, Web access, removable storage, camera, radio, digital music player, and software options for games, financial management, personal organizer, GPS, and maps.

FIGURE A-2: **Smartphones**

Courtesy of Hewlett-Packard Company

Storage inside unit

Keyboard
(for input)

Processor
inside unit
(for processing)

Speakers
(for output)

Touch screen
(for input and
for output)

© amriphoto/iStockphoto

Microphone
(for input)

Computer and Internet Basics

How Computers Work

The parts of a computer system work together to accomplish these basic computer tasks—accept input, process data, store data, and produce output as information you can use. Most computers also are able to communicate to share information with other computers. Refer to Figure A-3 as you read more about how computers work.

Learning Objective 2:
Explain the four basic functions of a computer system

FIGURE A-3: **Basic computer parts and functions**

Display device for output

Speaker for sound output

CD/DVD drive for storing and getting data

System unit for processing and storing data

Hello!

Meet Polly

Printer for producing output

Camera for output and input

Mouse for input

Modem for communicating with other digital devices

Keyboard for typing input

Media for storing data

Top: Courtesy of MediaTechnics Corporation; © Sylvain Legare/Shutterstock.com; © Cengage Learning; Courtesy of MediaTechnics Corporation; bottom row: Courtesy of MediaTechnics Corporation; © Cengage Learning; © Tatiana Popova/Shutterstock.com; Courtesy of MediaTechnics Corporation; Courtesy of MediaTechnics Corporation

- **How do I turn on my computer?** A computer is often a computer system. You may need to press more than one switch or button to turn on the monitor, printer, speakers, and finally the computer. However, some computers, such as notebook or tablet computers, have one button or switch that turns on the entire computer system, including the computer, the monitor or display, and the speakers. Most computers take a few minutes to power up, and then you may be prompted to enter your **user ID** and **password**.

- **Why do I need a user ID and password?** You are assigned a user ID and password for security reasons. In a public setting, such as a school lab, you will usually be assigned a user ID and a password by the system administrator. If your personal computer asks for a user ID and password, you can create your own the first time you start the computer. You use that user ID and password every time you sign on to that computer and access the programs you have permission to use. Never share your user ID or password with anyone.

- **What does "run a program" mean?** It means to start a program. The instructions that tell a computer how to carry out the processing tasks are referred to as a **computer program**, or simply **program**. On mobile devices, such as tablets or smartphones, programs are called apps—short for applications. Once the program is running, it is ready for you to use.

- **How do I tell a computer what I want it to do?** You tell a computer what to do by interacting with it. You use a keyboard to type commands and other text. You use a mouse to access menus, as well as to click buttons and icons. On a computer with a touch screen, such as a tablet or smartphone, you touch and drag icons. Many digital devices today have on-screen keyboards. When you tell a computer what to do, you are providing input. Computer **input** is whatever is put into a computer system. Input can be supplied by a person, by the environment, or by another computer. Once information is input into a computer, it becomes data.

- **What do computers do with data?** Computers process—that is, they work with—data in many ways. In the context of computing, data refers to the symbols that represent facts, objects, and ideas. In a computer, most **processing** takes place in a **processor** (also known as a **microprocessor**). The main processor in a computer is called the **central processing unit (CPU)**, which is sometimes described as the brain of the computer. A computer does two things with processed data. It stores the data and it outputs the data as information.

- **Is there a difference between computer memory and computer storage?** Yes. **Memory** temporarily holds computer data waiting to be processed, stored, or output. **Storage** holds computer data on a permanent basis when it is not immediately needed for processing. While you are working on a document, it is in memory; it is not in storage until you save it for the first time. After you save the document as a computer file, it is stored on the hard drive or some other storage medium, such as a flash drive. It is also still in memory until you close the document, exit the program, or turn off the computer. You will learn more about storage and memory later in this book.

- **What are computer files?** A computer file, or **file**, is a named collection of data that exists on a **storage medium**, such as a disk drive, CD, DVD, or flash drive. Every file has a **filename**, which should provide meaningful information about the file contents. The filename has two parts: the filename and the file extension. An example of a filename for a photo is Bridge.jpg. The name that you give the file is to the left of the period. The **file extension** is the period and two or more characters to the right of the period.

- **What is output and how do I use it?** **Output** is the processed results produced by a computer. It is the information you want, such as reports, documents, music, graphs, and pictures. An output device (such as a monitor, a printer, or speakers) displays, prints, says, or otherwise transmits the results of processing.

- **Do all computers have network and Internet access?** Many personal computer systems include built-in technology for wired or wireless connections to a computer network. Networking technology is useful for constructing a home network, connecting one or more computers to share devices, or connecting to public networks such as the Internet.

- **How do I turn off my computer?** Usually, you turn off your computer by giving it a command, such as Shut Down. For a computer running Microsoft Windows, you click the on-screen Start button (see Figure A-4), and then click Shut Down. For an Apple computer, you click the Apple icon in the upper-left corner of the screen and then click Shut Down. For a tablet computer, such as an iPad, press and hold the Sleep/Wake button for a few seconds. When the red slider appears, slide the slider to turn off the device. After the computer powers down, you can manually turn off the printer and speakers, if necessary. Never turn off a computer by pressing the power switch, unless you are specifically instructed to do so.

FIGURE A-4: **Shutting down a computer running Windows**

Used with permission from Microsoft

Start button Shut down button

Understanding the importance of stored programs

Modern computers use stored programs, that is, the instructions for a computing task are stored on the computer so they can be loaded quickly into a computer's memory when needed. These instructions can easily be replaced by different instructions when it is time for the computer to perform a different task. The stored program concept allows you to use your computer for one task, such as writing a letter, and then easily switch to a different computing task, such as editing a photo, looking at a Web page, or sending an email message.

Programs can be stored locally on your computer. An emerging trend is to use programs stored in the cloud. The **cloud** is mass storage on remote computers. **Cloud computing** refers to working in the cloud. You will learn more about the cloud and cloud computing later in this book.

Types of Computers

Computers are electronic devices that perform many tasks. Some types of computers are better for certain jobs than others. Computers are categorized according to how they are used, what they cost, their physical size, and their processing capability. Knowing about computer categories can help you buy the computer that best meets your needs.

Learning Objective 3:
Identify the main computer categories

- **Which type of computer is right for me?** You will most probably use a personal computer. A personal computer is designed to meet the computing needs of an individual for home, school, or small business use. It typically provides access to a wide variety of software, such as word processing, photo editing, budgeting and financial management, email, and Internet access. Personal computers include **desktop computers**, and **portable computers** such as **notebook computers** (sometimes called **laptop computers**), **netbooks**, and **tablet computers**.

- **If I get a desktop computer, will it fit on my desk?** Probably, yes. That is why it is called a desktop computer. A desktop computer's system unit can be housed in a vertical case or a horizontal case. Most horizontal cases are placed under the display device to save desk space. A vertical case can be placed on the desk, on the floor, or in a space beneath the desk. The case for a vertical system unit is often referred to as a tower. Tower units are the system unit of choice for computer owners who want to upgrade their system, such as by adding additional storage devices or a more powerful graphics card. It is easy to get inside a tower case and swap parts. Some manufacturers of desktop computers create an all-in-one unit. These computers build the computer technology into the back of a flat-panel screen or into a keyboard. See Figure A-5.

FIGURE A-5: Examples of personal desktop computers

Left: Courtesy of MediaTechnics Corporation; Right: Courtesy of Gateway. Used with permission from Microsoft

Tower computer All-in-one desktop computer

- **What if I need to use my computer in different locations?** You will want to consider a portable computer. **Portable computers** include notebook computers, tablet computers, netbooks, and handheld computers. Examples of portable computers are shown in Figure A-6 and Figure A-7.

FIGURE A-6: Examples of portable personal computers

Notebook Convertible tablet

Netbook Mobile tablet

Top row, left: Courtesy of Hewlett-Packard Company; © Kathy Burns-Millyard/Shutterstock.com; Bottom row, left: PRNewsFoto/Radio Shack Corporation; Courtesy of MediaTechnics Corporation; Used with permission from Microsoft

- **What are the advantages of a notebook computer?** You might consider buying a notebook computer if you want to be able to move the computer from place to place, such as from home to school. Notebook computers have a clamshell design, which means they open and close on a hinge. When the computer is closed, the screen, pointing device, and keyboard are protected inside the case. Although notebook computers are much smaller than desktop computers, they are comparable when it comes to computing power. The two big differences between desktop and portable computers are their physical sizes and their cost.

● **Why should I consider a tablet computer?** A tablet computer is a portable computer that features a touch-sensitive screen. You can use this screen as a writing or a drawing pad. A tablet computer is similar in size to a notebook computer. The new mobile tablet computer is similar in size to a netbook computer. Most tablet computers can access the Internet or wireless networks. Most tablet computers are also configured to accept voice input. These capabilities are useful for people who use their computers while on the go.

● **What is a netbook?** A netbook computer offers more portability than a standard notebook computer. These small computers are scaled-down versions of standard clamshell-style notebook computers. They are typically only seven or eight inches wide and weigh about two pounds.

● **What if I just need a small portable computer that fits in my pocket?** Then, a **handheld computer** is just the answer. See Figure A-7. A handheld computer is one type of handheld digital device. There are a variety of handheld digital devices. These devices vary in how they can be used. Although these devices can be classified as computers, they are usually referred to by function, for example, as mobile phones, e-readers, or portable media players. The most popular handheld digital device is the smartphone.

FIGURE A-7: **Handheld computer**

Courtesy of Hewlett-Packard Company

Handheld digital devices usually have features such as removable storage, email, Web access, voice communications, built-in camera, and GPS. Handheld digital devices run computer programs, but, typically, they run special scaled-down versions of these programs. With its slow processing speed and small screen, a handheld computer is not powerful enough to handle many of the tasks that can be accomplished using desktop, notebook, tablet, or even netbook computers.

● **What are some other categories of computers I should know about?** There are three more general categories of computers you might hear people talk about.

■ **Workstations** are usually powerful desktop computers designed for specialized tasks that require a lot of processing speed, such as medical imaging, full-motion video graphics, and computer-aided design. Most are designed for creating and displaying three-dimensional and animated graphics.

■ A **mainframe computer** is a large and expensive computer capable of simultaneously processing data for hundreds or thousands of users. Mainframes are generally used by businesses, universities, or governments to provide centralized storage, processing, and management of large amounts of data where reliability, data security, and centralized control are necessary.

■ A computer is categorized as a **supercomputer** if, at the time it is built, it is one of the fastest computers in the world. Supercomputers can tackle tasks that would not be practical for other computers such as breaking codes and modeling worldwide weather systems.

● **What does it mean when I hear, "The server is down?" Is a server another type of computer?** The purpose of a **server** is to serve computers on a network (such as the Internet or a home network) by supplying them with data. Just about any personal computer, workstation, mainframe, or supercomputer can be configured to perform the work of a server. When you hear that a server is down, it means a computer connected to that server can't access the programs and files on that server.

Video game consoles

A videogame console, such as Nintendo's Wii, Nintendo's 3DS, Sony's PlayStation, or Microsoft's Xbox, is not generally referred to as a personal computer. Videogame consoles originated as simple digital devices that connected to a TV set and provided only a pair of joysticks for input. Today's videogame consoles contain processors that are equivalent to any processor found in a fast personal computer. They produce graphics, including 3D graphics, that rival those on sophisticated workstations. Many consoles include built-in Wi-Fi for easy connection to the Internet. Consoles can be used to watch movies, send and receive email, and participate in online activities such as multiplayer games. Despite these features, videogame consoles are not considered a replacement for a personal computer.

Personal Computers

The term **computer system** usually refers to a computer and all of the input, output, and storage devices that are connected to it. Despite cosmetic differences among personal computers (see Figure A-8), a personal computer system usually includes standard equipment or devices. These devices may vary in color, size, and design for different personal computers.

Learning Objective 4:
Describe digital devices that can be part of a personal computer

FIGURE A-8: **Personal computer systems don't all look alike**

From left: Courtesy of Gateway; © thesuperph/iStockphoto; © Cheng Xin/iStockphoto; © seaskylab/iStockphoto; Courtesy of Fujitsu Technology Solutions; Used with permission from Microsoft

● **What are the basic parts of a desktop personal computer system?** Figure A-9 shows the basic parts of a typical desktop personal computer system. Refer to the figure as you read about each part.

■ **System unit**: The system unit is the case that holds the power supply, storage devices, and the circuit boards. It houses the main circuit board (also called the motherboard), which contains the processor.

■ **Display device**: Most computers have a **display device** called a **monitor**. The monitor is the primary output device. The monitor for a desktop computer is a separate part connected to the system unit. Output is displayed on the monitor screen.

■ **Keyboard**: Most computers are equipped with a **keyboard** as the primary input device. It is used to enter text and numbers.

■ **Mouse**: A **mouse** is a common input device designed to move and select on-screen graphical objects and controls.

■ **Storage devices**: A **storage device** is used to store data on a computer or to share data among computers. Storage devices are both input and output devices. Data is read from a storage medium and often can be written to a storage medium. Most personal computers have more than one type of storage device. Each storage device uses a different storage medium. The primary storage device is the **hard drive** (also called **hard disk drive**). The hard drive is usually mounted inside the system unit.

Other storage devices can be used with a personal computer. A **USB flash drive** plugs directly into a USB port on the computer system unit. An external hard drive also plugs directly into a USB port. A CD drive, a DVD drive, a Blue-ray Disc (BD) drive, or a combination drive is usually mounted inside the system unit. These **optical drives** are storage devices that work with storage media such as CDs, DVDs, and BDs. They can be used to store computer data. Optical drives are also handy for playing audio CDs, DVD movies, and Blu-ray movies.

■ **Sound system**: A **sound system** is made up of speakers and a small circuit board called a **sound card**, required for high-quality music, narration, and sound effects. A desktop computer's sound card sends signals to external speakers. The sound card is an input and an output device, while speakers are output devices only.

■ **Printer**: A **printer** is an output device that produces computer-generated text, photographs, or graphic images on paper.

- **Web cam**: A **Web cam** allows you to capture video images using your computer. Software makes it possible to send and receive video in real time with another person to communicate with voice as well as images.
- **Peripheral devices**: There are many other peripheral devices that can be connected to a computer. For example, you can connect a portable **digital media player** and a **digital camera** in order to transfer music and photos between the devices and the computer system.

● **Does a portable computer have all these parts?** Yes, but a portable computer, such as a notebook computer, is a single unit that includes the system unit, a built-in flat-panel monitor, a built-in keyboard, and built-in speakers. Many new portable computers include a built-in Web cam. Other devices, such as a printer, can be connected to a portable computer in the same way they can be connected to a desktop computer. Portable computers can also be part of a network and can have Internet access.

● **How do I know if my computer has network and Internet access?** Many personal computer systems include built-in technology for wired or wireless connections to a computer network. Networking is useful for connecting to a home network or to public networks, such as the Internet. Internet connections require a **modem**. Modems can be built into portable computers. For tablets you can use an aircard or portable modem, which works like a mobile phone. For Internet access using a smartphone, the modem is built into the device. Modems for cable, satellite, and other types of Internet access from your home or office are usually separate devices.

● **What is a computer network?** A **computer network** consists of two or more computers and other devices that are connected for the purpose of sharing data and programs. For example, a **LAN (local area network)** is simply a computer network that is located within a limited geographical area, such as your home, a school computer lab, or a small business. If your computer is on a network, you can easily access files on other computers that are on the same network.

● **What parts of a computer system do I absolutely need?** You need a system unit for processing and storage, a monitor for output, and a keyboard and pointing device for input. Many people also want a printer and a portable storage device, such as a flash drive.

FIGURE A-9: Typical desktop computer system with examples of peripherals

Top: Courtesy of MediaTechnics Corporation; © Natalila Silverina/Shutterstock.com; Used with permission from Microsoft; Courtesy of MediaTechnics Corporation; Bottom row: Courtesy of MediaTechnics Corporation; Courtesy of MediaTechnics Corporation; © Norman Chan/Shutterstock.com; © Tatiana Popova/Shutterstock.com; Courtesy of MediaTechnics Corporation; Used with permission from Microsoft

Computer Software

A computer needs software to work. Software provides the instructions that tell a computer how to perform tasks. There are two main categories of software: operating system software and application software. Every computer has an operating system. But, as a computer user, you are probably most familiar with application software. You use application software to look at Web pages on the Internet, write reports, create budgets, view and edit photographs, play games, as well as other tasks you do using your computer. The operating system you have on your computer determines the software you can run on your computer.

Learning Objective 5:
Define software and give examples of operating systems

● **What is an operating system?** An **operating system (OS)** is the master controller for all the activities that take place within a computer system. An operating system is classified as **system software**. Its primary purpose is to help the computer system monitor itself in order to function efficiently. Most people have only one operating system running on their computer and most personal computers can run only one operating system at one time. There are several different operating systems available for personal computers, such as Windows, Mac OS, and Linux. The two most popular operating systems for personal computers are Windows and Mac OS. While these two operating systems look and even work in a similar way, they are different. Each is designed to run on different computer platforms.

● **What is a computer platform?** A **computer platform** determines the hardware and software of the computer system. Two of the most important factors that define a computer's platform are the processor and the OS. The Windows operating system was designed specifically for PCs. The PC platform is sometimes called the Windows platform. The Macintosh OS was designed specifically for Macintosh computers, which are based on a proprietary design and manufactured almost exclusively by Apple Computer, Inc. The Linux OS is usually used as an alternative to the Windows OS.

Today, many Mac computers use the same processors as PCs. If you have a Mac computer with an Intel processor (sometimes called an Intel Mac), you can install the Windows OS on that machine and run Windows software.

● **What is Windows software?** Windows software is software designed to run on a PC platform. Generally, software designed to run on a PC platform will not run on a Mac platform, and software designed to run on a Mac platform will not run on a PC platform. When shopping for new software, it is important to read the package to make sure that the software is designed to work with your computer platform.

● **How do I use the operating system?** Most of the time, you use the operating system without realizing it. See Figure A-10. You interact with the operating system for certain tasks, such as starting programs and finding data files. How you use the operating system depends on the user interface associated with the operating system. Operating systems use a **graphical user interface (GUI)**.

FIGURE A-10: **The operating system makes it possible to interact with the computer**

© Yuri Arcurs / Shutterstock.com

PCs and Macs

People generally refer to personal computers either as PCs, which run a version of Windows software, or as Macs, which run Macintosh software. PCs are manufactured and distributed by a variety of vendors. Macs are almost exclusively developed and distributed by Apple Computer Company.

FIGURE A-11: **Popular elements of a GUI**

Icon

Thumbnail

Taskbar

Application buttons

Gadget

Open windows

Desktop

Scroll bar

Notification area with icons

Show desktop button

Used with permission from Microsoft

See Figure A-11. A GUI displays on-screen icons, menus, buttons, and other graphical controls. These controls are manipulated by a mouse or other pointing device. For example, you might click an icon to start an application program, or drag time slots on a calendar to create appointments. If you are using a touch screen, you touch, tap, and drag icons with your fingers.

- **Does my mobile phone use the same OS as my personal computer?** No, mobile devices use an OS designed specifically for mobile devices, such as Android (see Figure A-12), BlackBerry OS, iOS for

FIGURE A-12: **Operating system for mobile devices**

Courtesy of Motorola Solutions

iPhones, or a mobile version of an existing OS, such as Windows Phone. Mobile OSs are also known as mobile software platforms or handheld operating systems.

- **How does the operating system help me do my work?** The operating system runs the software on your computer. **Application software** is a general term used to classify the programs that help you use the computer to carry out tasks. Word processing software, for example, helps you create, edit, and print documents. Browser software helps you view Web pages on the Internet. Each application software program has its own name, such as Microsoft Word or Internet Explorer. Your computer can run more than one application program at one time.

- **What are apps?** **Apps**, sometimes called **mobile apps**, are software programs designed to run on mobile devices, such as your smartphone. Apps are available for download from a variety of online stores. They are usually available for free or a small fee.

- **If my computer runs Windows and my friend's computer runs Mac OS X, can we share our files?** Sharing files depends on system compatibility. Some application software has been created so one version exists for the Windows platform and another for the Macintosh platform. You are able to share your files with your friend, as long as your friend has the same software installed on his or her computer.

The Internet and the Web

You can use the Internet to look for information. You can use the Internet to shop. You can use the Internet to share photos and videos. You can use it to communicate with friends, coworkers, or family. You can even use the Internet to buy products and services, look for a job, or plan a trip. The Internet offers abundant resources. This lesson will help you understand how you can use the Internet and the Web in your daily life.

Learning Objective 6:
Define the Internet and explain how to navigate Web pages

- **What is the Internet?** The **Internet** is the largest computer network in the world. It is a collection of local, regional, national, and international computer networks. These networks are linked together to exchange data and share processing tasks.

- **How do I access the Internet?** To access the Internet your computer must have special hardware and software. You need equipment called a router. The **router** connects to your computer and to the Internet. Computers connect to the Internet either with wires or wirelessly. To connect to the Internet you also need an **Internet Service Provider**. This is a company that provides the service of connecting the router to the Internet, usually for a monthly fee.

- **Is the Web the same as the Internet?** The **Web** (short for **World Wide Web**) is a collection of **Web pages** that are interconnected through the use of **hypertext** or links. The Internet is the network that carries Web pages to computers. Web pages can include text, photos, videos, animations, and sounds. The Web is the part of the Internet you will probably use most often.

- **Why would I use the Internet?** You might use the Internet to research, and then buy products and services. For example, you can buy airline tickets through the Internet. If you want to sell a product or service, you can use the Internet to help you run your own small business. See Figure A-13. You might use the Internet to share photographs with family and friends. At a job, you can use the Internet to work on documents with coworkers. Most banks have Web sites their customers use for bill paying and online banking. You might use the Internet to communicate with others.

FIGURE A-13: Using the Web to help run a business

Image courtesy of Photography by Toine

- **How do I view a Web page?** To view Web pages on your computer, you need a software program called a Web browser. Popular **Web browsers** include Microsoft Internet Explorer, Google Chrome, Mozilla FireFox, and Apple Safari. You enter a URL in the Address box of the browser window. If you are viewing a Web page, you can also click a link to view another Web page.

- **What is a link?** A **link** (also called a hyperlink) is text, a graphic, or other object on a Web page that is "linked" to another Web page or another area on the current Web page. You click a link to "jump" to another Web page, Web site, or place on the same Web page. Links are the main tool you will use to navigate among Web pages.

- **What is a URL?** Every Web page has a unique address called a **URL (Uniform Resource Locator)**. The URL for a Web page indicates the computer on which it is stored, its location on the Web server, the folder name or names indicating where it is stored, its filename, and its file extension. Most browsers provide a space near the top of the window for entering URLs. Figure A-14 identifies the parts of the URL for a

National Park Service Web page. A URL never contains a space, even after a punctuation mark. An underline character is sometimes used to give the appearance of a space between words.

FIGURE A-14: **Parts of a URL**

http://www.nps.gov/yose/index.htm

| Web protocol standard | Web server name | Folder name | Document name and file extension |

© Cengage Learning

● **What does it mean if I see http:// in the Address box?** Most URLs begin with http://. **HTTP (Hypertext Transfer Protocol)** is the technology used to transport Web pages over the Internet. You might also see https://, which is used for additional security at Web sites such as those that offer banking and shopping. When typing a URL, you do not have to type the http://. Typing www.cengage.com/coursetechnology/ works just as well as typing http://www.cengage.com/coursetechnology/. Be sure to use the correct type of slash—always a forward slash (/).

● **How do I navigate a Web site?** Web pages on a related topic are often grouped together to create a

Web site. Most Web sites have a main page, the **home page**, which acts as a doorway to the rest of the Web site pages. Usually, the Web pages have a navigation bar that contains links you click to move to other pages in the Web site. See Figure A-15. In addition, your browser has buttons to help you navigate the Web. For example, the browser's Back button lets you retrace your steps to view pages that you've seen previously.

● **How do I find information on the Web?** The term **search site** refers to a Web site that provides a variety of tools to help you find information on the Web. A **keyword** is any word or phrase that you type to describe the information that you are trying to find. Based on the keyword you input, the search site uses its **search engine** to provide a list of possible Web sites that may have the information you are looking for. The list is actually links (also called hits) to Web pages. So you can click each link to see if any Web site in the list has what you are looking for. You should try different variations on your keyword to improve your results. Also, search sites have different ways of ranking the search results. As a result, if you use two different search sites to search for the same keyword, you will probably get different results.

FIGURE A-15: **Navigating a Web page**

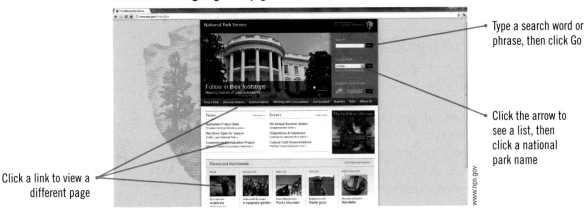

Type a search word or phrase, then click Go

Click the arrow to see a list, then click a national park name

Click a link to view a different page

www.nps.gov

Web apps and working in the cloud

A **Web application (Web app)** is software that you access through a Web browser. Instead of running on your computer, much of the program for the software runs on a distant computer, often called the **cloud**, connected to the Internet or other network. Web apps are available for many tasks, such as email, calendars, photo sharing, games, and even word processing. Web apps allow you to work on projects with people in multiple locations. Working with a Web app allows you to store your work in the cloud. When you use cloud storage, you can access your files from any computer that has a browser and Internet access.

Mobile Web apps are designed to work on mobile devices. Mobile Web apps have features designed for portability and a small screen.

The cloud has some risks. A security breach of a cloud provider could expose the data of all its users. Outages at the cloud provider, on the Internet in general, or locally at your computer can mean that you cannot get to your programs and files. If a cloud provider goes out of business without notice (and there are no regulations to prevent this from happening), all your data could become unavailable.

How to Communicate Using Digital Devices

Each year, countless email messages are sent around the world over the Internet. Millions of messages cross paths as instant messages. Even more text messages flow between smartphones. Social networks are buzzing with posts. This lesson will help you understand the many ways you can communicate digitally with family and friends.

Learning Objective 7:
Explain ways to use the Internet and digital devices to communicate with others

- **What is email?** **Email** (short for **electronic mail**) is a message sent electronically over the Internet. To send an email message, you must have an email account.

- **How do I get an email account?** You get an **email account** through an email provider. There are many providers, such as your Internet service provider, university, Gmail (through Google), or Hotmail (through Microsoft Windows Live). Your email account includes a storage area, often called a **mailbox**. Depending on who provides your email account, you will either be assigned an **email address** or you will create one. Figure A-16 shows the parts of an email address.

FIGURE A-16: Parts of an email address

David_velez@rutgers.edu
User ID "at" symbol Name of email provider

© Cengage Learning

- **Do I need a special computer to send and receive email?** No, but your computer or smartphone must be able to connect to the Internet and it must have email software installed. Email software usually includes an address book to help you maintain contact information, including email addresses of people you contact frequently.

- **What does an email message look like?** An **email message** has several parts. Every email message includes the recipient's email address, the address of anyone who is receiving a copy of the message, the message subject, the body, and the name of any file attachments. The body of the email contains your message. An email message is created in a form, which often includes buttons for formatting text, attaching files, or adding additional recipients as courtesy (Cc), or blind courtesy (Bcc) copies. Basic email activities include writing, reading, replying to, and forwarding messages.

- **Do I need to be at my computer when my friend sends me the email?** No. Email is based on store-and-forward technology. Emails that cannot be sent directly to their destinations are temporarily stored until they are forwarded to the email mailbox.

- **Can I send a file or picture through email?** Yes. In addition to the body text of an email message, you can send documents, spreadsheets, digital photos, video, and sounds. Any file that travels with an email message is called an **email attachment**.

- **Can I use the Internet to have real-time conversations with people?** Yes. One popular way you can do this is participating in a **chat group**, which consists of several people who connect to the Internet and communicate in real time by typing notes to each other. A private version of chat is called **instant messaging (IM)**. IM allows you to send text messages, images, and hyperlinks back and forth to another person instantly. If you are online at the same time as the person you want to chat or instant message, you can type messages back and forth in real time. There is no limit on the number of characters in your chat or IM.

 You can also use the Internet to talk to people in real-time thanks to **Internet telephony**, also called **Voice Over IP (VoIP)**. VoIP allows voice conversations to travel over the Internet. VoIP requires special software at both ends of the conversation. Instead of using a telephone, you have to use a headset with a microphone connected to a computer. VoIP providers, such as Skype, also offer video conversations. If you and the person you are talking with both have a Web cam connected to your computers, you can see each other while you are talking. Other popular ways of communicating are through forums, wikis, blogs, and social networking.

- **What are forums, wikis, and blogs?** An **Internet forum** is a Web site where you can post comments to discussion threads. Threads are simply topics. Comments can be read at any time by others who visit the forum. Most forums have a moderator who monitors the discussions, weeds out troublesome participants, and handles membership requests.

A **wiki** is a collaborative Web site that allows people to add to and modify material posted by others. Participants can post content on a topic, and others can change it. Wikis can also include discussion pages where people just comment on topic material. The best known is Wikipedia.

The term **blog** is derived from the phrase Web log. It refers to a personal journal focusing on a single topic or a variety of topics. The information in a blog is usually available to the public. Some blog sites allow you to restrict access to those you invite to read your blog. People often create blogs to share travel adventures, political views, or important events in their lives.

- **What is social networking?** **Social networking** is an online networking activity that allows registered members to communicate with others in the network. You can use online social networks, such as Google+, LinkedIn, MySpace, and Facebook. Twitter, another social networking option, uses 140 character messages for blogging. If you have a Twitter account, you can post or follow posted messages that can lead to more extensive information. See Figure A-17.

To become a member of an online social network, you fill out a questionnaire to create your profile and to identify

a list of friends. You can then interact with your friends or with friends of friends who are members of the same social network. This networking technique offers a level of security because members are interacting with friends or with friends of friends, rather than with strangers. Social networking sites provide private messaging options.

Social networking sites all have mobile apps to make it easy to follow and network from smartphones. In addition to using your mobile phone to social network, you can use it to send text messages.

- **What are text messages?** **Text messages** are typed messages you send using your smartphone, or mobile device. Depending on the service, text messages can be 140 to 160 characters or less. You can send text messages by using the Web sites of mobile providers but it is more common to use your mobile device to send text messages. If your mobile phone service has Multimedia Messaging Service (MMS), you can send pictures and video in addition to text. You do not need the added features of a smartphone to send text messages from a mobile phone.

The line between when to use your computer and when to use your smartphone to communicate is blurring. Computers and smartphones are allowing you to communicate in new and exciting ways with your circle of family, friends, and coworkers. See Figure A-18.

FIGURE A-18: Social networking with friends, family, and coworkers

FIGURE A-17: You can use Twitter for social networking

How to Protect Your Privacy, Data, and Devices

Whether you are surfing in the ocean or surfing on the Web. Whether you are buying an item in the mall or clicking to purchase airline tickets online, security and safety should always be the primary concern. Computers and digital communication have built-in dangers. You have to safeguard your health, safety, and personal data. You also need to take care of your digital devices so they work properly when you need them. This lesson will help you avoid potential pitfalls in the digital world so you can enjoy safe computing.

Learning Objective 8:
Explain how to protect your digital data and devices

● **What can go wrong?** Many things can happen. Someone might steal your computer, or you might misplace it. Your data might get damaged or stolen. A thief might steal your credit card numbers or, worse, your identity. You might drop your computer or spill coffee on it. See Figure A-19. The list of what can go wrong goes on and on. Fortunately, there are simple steps you can take to prevent things from going wrong.

FIGURE A-19: Be careful with your computer

©Mikael Damkier/Shutterstock.com

● **How can I prevent things from going wrong?** You can use common sense and tools to protect yourself, your data, and your digital devices. To protect yourself, you must safeguard your personal data. To protect your data, you must install an antivirus program, a firewall, and other programs that help keep your data safe. To protect your digital devices, you must treat them with care.

● **What is at risk if my computer is stolen?** Your identity is the biggest risk factor if your computer is stolen. Why? Because your computer contains data about you, such as your bank account information and credit card numbers, and PINs. A thief can use stolen data to assume your identity, empty your checking and savings accounts, run up debts, get into legal difficulties, ruin your credit rating, and cause you no end of trouble.

● **How can I keep my computer from being stolen?** You should never leave your computer unattended in a public

place. You should never leave your computer visible in a car, even in a locked car. If you live in a group situation, such as a dormitory, anchor your computer to your desk with a specially designed lock you can buy at most electronics stores.

In addition to these precautions, be sure to password-protect your computer. Then, if a thief steals your computer, he or she will need the password to access your data. Until the password is entered, your data is off limits. So, even if a thief is able to turn on the computer, he or she will not be able to get at the information on your computer.

● **What should I use for a password?** Use a **password** you can remember but that others cannot guess. Here are some tips for creating a unique password.
 ■ Use at least eight characters, mixing numbers with letters, as in m3p1e8.
 ■ Do not use your name, birthday, the name of a family member, or your pet's name.
 ■ Do not use a word that can be found in the dictionary.
 ■ Do not keep a written copy of your password near your computer.

While passwords keep your data safe from unwanted visitors, they do not keep your data safe from malware.

● **What is malware?** **Malware**, also known as **malicious software**, is a type of software that can do harm to your computer data. There are different types of malware, such as viruses, worms, Trojan horses, and spyware. On a personal level, malware can steal data or destroy files. On a larger scale, malware can create network traffic jams that affect Web sites or corporate computer systems. Malware is often installed on your computer without your knowledge. For example, malware can be installed behind the scenes while you download software. See Figure A-20. Malware is created by **hackers**, people that want to steal or damage your data or assume your identity.

FIGURE A-20: Know that your downloads are safe

© iQoncept/Shutterstock.com

● How can I protect my computer from malware?

You should install programs, such as an antivirus program, a firewall, or a malware detection program, that can stop malware from being installed. These programs can also find and delete any malware that slipped through the safety net and got installed. You can use these programs to scan files to be sure they are safe to download. These programs can keep your computer malware free and your data safe. You will learn more about malware later in this book.

Not only computers but all digital devices, including smartphones, can get malware. It is important to find and install programs to protect your device from malware. It is also important to keep the anti-malware software on all your digital devices up to date.

● Do I need to protect my privacy when using digital communication?

Yes. When you are social networking, posting to Web pages, chatting, IMing, sending email messages, or communicating in any way over the Internet, you have to protect your personal information. Table A-1 provides some guidelines to help you protect your personal information and your privacy.

● How can I limit who sees my digital communications?

Anything you write, or any photo you upload can be copied, posted, or forwarded around the Internet with just a few clicks. Anyone can read or see your digital communications unless you take some precautions. Here are some tips on how to limit who has access to your electronic messages.

When emailing…

- Click Reply to reply only to the person who sent an email message. Clicking Reply limits who sees your response. Click Reply All if you want your response sent to everyone who received the original email message (except the Bcc recipients).
- Use the Cc: feature to include people you want to read your email but that you don't want to respond to the message.
- Use the Bcc: feature to blind copy your email to people without revealing to the Send to and Cc: recipients who else got the message.
- Create a group if you have people you send messages to regularly. This will ensure all the people in the group get the same message. It will also save time because you only have to enter the group name and not type the email of each person in the group.

When posting…

- Check the options to identify those people or groups you want to see a message you post on a blog or wall of a social networking site. Some sites post to the general public if you don't specify otherwise.
- Be sure you have permission from anyone in a picture when you post or tag the photo; only post your own photos and graphics.
- Regard wall messages, posted photos, and chat messages as postcards that can be read and seen by anyone. Do not say or share anything you would not want repeated or broadcast to the world!

TABLE A-1: Ways to protect your privacy

Tips	Tips
Do not publish or post personal information, such as your home address, passwords, Social Security number, phone number, or account numbers.	Do not submit data to a social networking site until you've read its privacy policy and have made sure that you can remove your data when you no longer want to participate.
If asked for personal information, verify the Web site is legitimate, or make a phone call to confirm that you have to submit the information, and then confirm that the information will be securely transmitted and stored.	Avoid financial transactions when using a public computer. Never click the save my password box and make sure you log out from password-protected sites.
Be wary of contacts you make in public chat rooms and on social networking sites.	Never use a password-protected Web site on a public computer that doesn't give you the option to save the password.

© Cengage Learning

Talking Points: Who Is Reading Your Email?

When you drop an envelope into the corner mailbox, you probably expect it to arrive at its destination unopened, with its contents kept safe from prying eyes. When you make a phone call, you might assume that your conversation will proceed unmonitored by wiretaps or other listening devices. When you send an email, can you be sure it will be read only by the person to whom it is addressed?

In the United States, the Electronic Communications Privacy Act of 2000 prohibits the use of intercepted email as evidence unless a judge approves a search warrant. But, that does not mean the government is not reading your email. Heightened security concerns after the September 11, 2001 terrorist attacks resulted in the rapid passage of the Patriot Act, which became law on October 26, 2001. In an effort to assist law enforcement officials, the Patriot Act relaxes the rules for obtaining and implementing search warrants and lowers the Fourth Amendment standard for obtaining a court order to require an email provider to produce email logs and addresses.

> **Think of your email as a postcard, rather than a letter, and save your controversial comments for face-to-face or telephone conversations.**

To eavesdrop on email from suspected terrorists and other criminals, the FBI developed a technology that scans through email messages entering and leaving an email provider's email system to find email associated with a person who is under investigation. Privacy advocates are concerned because this software scans all messages that pass through an email provider, not just those messages sent from or received by a particular individual.

Although law enforcement agencies are required to obtain a court order before intercepting email, no such restriction exists for employers who want to monitor employee email. It is a known fact that many U.S. businesses monitor employee email; however, intentional eavesdropping is only one way in which the contents of your email messages might become public. For example, the recipient of your email can forward it to one or more persons—people you never intended it to reach. Your email messages could pop up on a technician's screen in the course of system maintenance, updates, or repairs. Also, keep in mind that email messages—including those you delete from your own computer—can be stored on backups of your email provider's email server. You also need to be aware that some email providers retain your email and gather information about you in exchange for the email service they provide.

You need to know what information your email provider collects via your email and what the email provider does with that collected information. For example, some Web-based email providers—particularly those that make you look at ads in exchange for free accounts—collect information on how often you log in and they monitor your keystrokes to find out which links you click. Email providers claim they gather this information to use internally so they can deliver the best possible service, prevent fraud, and select the ads for products that you are most likely to buy. Before selecting an email provider, find out what information the email provider collects, and then you can decide if that is acceptable to you.

You might wonder if such open access to your email and your ad-viewing habits is legal. The answer in most cases is yes. The United States Omnibus Crime Control and Safe Streets Act of 1968 and the Electronic Communications Privacy Act of 1986 prohibit public and private employers from engaging in surreptitious surveillance of employee activity through the use of electronic devices. However, two exceptions to these privacy statutes exist. The first exception permits an employer to monitor email if one party to the communication consents to the monitoring. An employer must inform employees of this policy before undertaking any monitoring. The second exception permits employers to monitor employees' email if a legitimate business need exists and the monitoring takes place within the business-owned email system.

Employees generally have not been successful in defending their rights to email privacy because courts have ruled that an employee's right to privacy does not outweigh a company's rights and interests. Courts seem to agree that because a company owns and maintains its email system, it has the right to monitor the email messages the system carries.

Like employees of a business, students who use a school's email system cannot be assured of email privacy. When a CalTech student was accused of sexually harassing a female student by sending lewd email to her and her boyfriend, investigators retrieved all of the student's email from the archives of the email server. The student was expelled from the university even

though he claimed that the email had been spoofed to make it look as though he had sent it, when it had actually been sent by someone else.

Why would an employer want to know the contents of employee email? Why would a school be concerned with the correspondence of its students? It is probably true that some organizations simply snoop on the off chance that important information might be discovered. Other organizations have more legitimate reasons for monitoring email. An organization that owns an email system can be held responsible for the consequences of actions related to the contents of email messages on that system. For example, a school has a responsibility to protect students from harassment. If it fails to do so, it can be sued along with the author of the offending email message. Organizations also recognize a need to protect themselves from false rumors and industrial espionage. For example, a business wants to know if an employee is supplying its competitor with information on product research and development.

Many schools and businesses have established email privacy policies that explain the conditions under which students or employees can and cannot expect their emails to remain private. These policies are sometimes displayed when the computer boots or a new user logs in. Court decisions, however, seem to support the notion that because an organization owns and operates an email system, the email messages on that system are also the property of the organization. The individual who authors an email message

does not own all rights related to it. The company, school, or organization that supplies an email account can, therefore, legally monitor the messages sent and received via that account. You should use your email account with the expectation that some of your email will be read from time to time. Think of your email as a postcard, rather than a letter, and save your controversial comments for face-to-face or telephone conversations.

> " An organization that owns an email system can be held responsible for the consequences of actions related to the contents of email messages on that system. "

Expand the Ideas

1. Do you believe that your email will probably be read only by your intended recipient? Knowing that your email is not private, will you be more careful in what you send via the email system? Why or why not?

2. Should the laws be changed to make it illegal for employers to monitor email without court approval? Why or why not?

3. Should the privacy laws governing an email account at your place of work differ from an account you purchase from an email service provider? Why or why not?

What is spam?

Spam is unwanted electronic junk mail that arrives in your email Inbox. A majority of today's proliferation of spam is generated by marketing firms that harvest email addresses from mailing lists, membership applications, and Web sites. Some spam messages advertise illegal products. Others are outright scams to try to get you to download a virus, divulge your bank account numbers, or send in money for products you will never receive. Beware of offers that seem just too good to be true—these offers are probably spam.

A **spam filter** automatically routes advertisements and other junk mail to either the Deleted Items or a spam folder maintained by your email provider. Spam filters can be effective for blocking spam and other unwanted emails, however, they sometimes block email messages you want. Be sure to examine your Deleted Items folder periodically to make sure the spam filters are not blocking emails that you want. If emails you want are in your Deleted Items or spam folder, reset your filters.

Key Terms & Unit Review

Key Terms

App
Application software
Blog
Browser
Central processing unit (CPU)
Chat group
Cloud
Cloud computing
Computer
Computer network
Computer platform
Computer program
Computer system
Desktop computer
Digital camera
Digital convergence
Digital media player
Digital revolution
Digital technology
Digitization
Display device
Email (electronic mail)
Email account
Email address
Email attachment
Email message

File
File extension
Filename
Graphical User Interface (GUI)
Hacker
Handheld computer
Hard disk drive
Hard drive
Hardware
Home page
HTTP (Hypertext Transfer Protocol)
Hypertext
Input
Input device
Instant messaging (IM)
Internet
Internet forum
Internet service provider (ISP)
Internet telephony
Keyboard
Keyword
LAN (local area network)
Laptop computer
Link

Mailbox
Mainframe computer
Malicious software
Malware
Memory
Microprocessor
Mobile app
Modem
Monitor
Mouse
Netbook
Notebook computer
Operating system
Optical drive
Output
Output device
Password
Peripheral device
Personal computer (PC)
Portable computer
Printer
Processing
Processor
Program
Router
Search engine
Search site

Server
Social networking
Software
Sound card
Sound system
Spam
Spam filter
Storage
Storage device
Storage medium
Supercomputer
System software
System unit
Tablet computer
Text messaging
URL (Uniform Resource Locator)
USB flash drive
User ID
Voice Over IP (VoIP)
Web (World Wide Web)
Web browser
Web cam
Web page
Web site
Wiki
Workstation

Unit Review

1. Make sure that you can define each of the key terms in this unit in your own words. Select 10 of the terms with which you are unfamiliar and write a sentence for each of them.

2. Explain how you use computers in your daily life.

3. Explain the basic functions of a computer: input, processing, storing, and output.

4. Identify and describe the purpose of each of the components of a basic personal computer system.

5. Describe the difference between an operating system and application software.

6. Explain why the stored program concept is important to computers.

7. List at least three activities that are not communications related and that you can accomplish using the Internet. If you have used the Internet, write a brief paragraph explaining how you benefitted from using it.

8. Make a list of at least three different ways you can use the Internet to communicate with other people.

9. Name the parts of a URL.

10. List the advantages and disadvantages of at least three types of computers as described in this unit and why you might choose one over the other.

Concepts Review

Select the best answer.

1. Which of the following is not a type of personal computer?
 a. mainframe
 b. notebook
 c. desktop
 d. netbook

2. The part that is considered the brains of the computer is called the _____ processing unit.
 a. main
 b. central
 c. operating
 d. local

3. The idea of stored programs means that instructions for a computing task can be loaded into a computer's _____.
 a. hard drive
 b. software
 c. operating system
 d. memory

4. The system _____ houses important parts such as the circuit boards, processor, power supply, and storage devices.
 a. processor
 b. memory
 c. drive
 d. unit

5. A device that expands a computer's capability is called a(n) _____ device.
 a. input
 b. peripheral
 c. output
 d. processing

6. A(n) _____ is a computer device that makes it possible to capture video.
 a. netbook
 b. scanner
 c. mp3 player
 d. Web cam

7. A(n) _____ system is the software that acts as the master controller for all of the activities that take place within a computer system.
 a. application
 b. processor
 c. digital
 d. operating

8. A computer _____ consists of two or more computers and other devices that are connected for the purpose of sharing data and programs.
 a. system
 b. network
 c. netbook
 d. hardware

9. Android is a type of _____ .
 a. power supply
 b. operating system
 c. blog
 d. network

10. A _____ is the system unit of choice for computer owners who want to upgrade because it is easy to get inside and swap parts.
 a. tower unit
 b. notebook
 c. netbook
 d. PDA

11. The _____ often provides a clue to the contents of a file.
 a. browser
 b. application
 c. filename
 d. operating system

12. A _____ computer uses a touch screen keyboard for typing.
 a. desktop unit
 b. notebook
 c. tower unit
 d. tablet

13. A(n) _____ is a personal journal posted on the Web for access by the public.
 a. chat
 b. email
 c. instant message
 d. blog

14. An email account has a unique address that typically consists of a user ID, the _____ symbol, and the name of the computer that maintains the mailbox.
 a. X
 b. *
 c. @
 d. #

15. Every Web page has a unique address called a(n) _____ .
 a. ARL
 b. URL
 c. RUL
 d. LUR

16. Facebook and LinkedIn are examples of Web sites that provide social _____ .
 a. chatting
 b. blogging
 c. networking
 d. email

17. To find information on the Web, it is best to use a _____ engine.
 a. Web
 b. home
 c. search
 d. program

18. A Web _____ is a series of Web pages on a specific topic.
 a. blog
 b. group
 c. site
 d. URL

19. Digital _____ is the trend in which several technologies with distinct functionalities evolve to form a single product.
 a. revolution
 b. electronics
 c. divide
 d. convergence

20. A(n) _____ is any word or phrase that you type in a search engine to describe the information that you are trying to find.
 a. keyword
 b. adjective
 c. verb
 d. Wiki

Independent Challenges

Independent Challenge 1

When discussing computers and computer concepts, it is important to use proper terminology. Unit A presented many computer terms that describe computer equipment. If you would like to explore any of the terms in more detail, there are online dictionaries that can help you expand your understanding of these terms. You can even use Webopedia to help you better learn about specific computer terms, for example, a tablet computer. See Figure A-21.

FIGURE A-21: Webopedia Web site

Provided by Webopedia.com

For this Independent Challenge:

1. Write a one-page paper that describes the computer you use most frequently.

2. Refer to the key terms used in this unit and use terms from this unit to describe the parts of your computer, including their functions.

3. Underline each key term that you used in your paper.

4. Follow your instructor's directions for submitting your paper either as an email attachment or as a printed document.

Independent Challenge 2

In 1982, the computer gained recognition in *TIME* magazine when it was named "Machine of the Year." That year, fewer than 10% of U.S. households had a computer. Maybe that is because working on a stand-alone computer wasn't for everyone. When computers first became available, people weren't tempted to spend the money to buy a computer and enter the digital revolution unless they were interested in typing up corporate reports or school papers, crunching numbers for accounting purposes, or playing computer games. But as interest in computers and in the Internet gained popularity, social scientists worried that people would become increasingly isolated as they focused on computer activities rather than social ones.

In 2010, Time magazine named Mark Zuckerberg the Person of the Year. He is the founder of Facebook, the social networking Web site that has arguably changed the way people throughout the world interact socially through computers. As of July 2010, Facebook had reached 500 million members—the equivalent of connecting with eight percent of the world's population.

Imagine that the producers for a television game show ask you to help them write computer-related questions for the next show. They want to know the impact of social networking. They want to find out how computer literate people have become. To help the producers, you will compose a set of 10 questions based on the information provided in Unit A. Each question should be in multiple-choice format with four possible answers.

For this Independent Challenge:

1. Write 10 questions that test a person's knowledge of the concepts covered in Unit A: two very simple questions, five questions of medium difficulty, and three difficult questions. Each question should be on an index card.

2. For each question, indicate the correct answer on the back of each card and the page in this book on which the answer can be found.

3. Gather in small groups and take turns asking each other the questions.

Independent Challenge 3

As a busy student, you are constantly on the go. When you are away from your home, you still need access to the Internet, your calendar, and contacts. For this independent challenge, assume that you have a basic mobile phone. You are considering upgrading your mobile phone to a smartphone. You are unsure if it makes sense to get a new smartphone or to invest in a tablet computer and keep your current mobile phone. You have heard about great apps for smartphones as well as tablet computers. It is time for you to start researching your options.

You can buy your digital device from a brick-and-mortar store (such as Best Buy), from an online communications company (such as verizonwireless.com, see Figure A-22), or from an online computer company (such as Dell.com). Each type of vendor has its advantages and disadvantages based on the kind of shopping experience you prefer. A brick-and-mortar store provides face-to-face service. A communications store provides the most up-to-date devices for its cellular service. A computer company often provides a wide selection of devices that are compatible with different cellular services.

In addition to purchasing the digital device, you will also need cellular service for the device. You will need to determine the network your digital device can access in order to receive and send data, as well as the price of the data service.

For this Independent Challenge:

1. Use the Internet or any magazines to research the latest offerings in smartphones and tablet computers.

2. Based on your research, list three different smartphones that you like. Be sure to compare the apps and features that come with each smartphone or that are available for each smartphone.

3. Based on your research, list three different tablet computers that you like. Be sure to compare the apps and features that come with each tablet or that are available for each tablet.

4. List the type of network required for each digital device, for example, Wi-Fi, 3G, or 4G. You do not have to understand the differences at this point, just list the type based on your findings.

5. Fill in the following table to help organize your findings.

6. Based on your research, write a concluding paragraph explaining your decision to purchase either a smartphone or a tablet. Support your decision based on your findings.

FIGURE A-22: A communications company that sells smartphones and tablet computers online

© 2011 Verizon

	Price	Operating system	Display size	Network carrier (Verizon/AT&T/Other?)	Memory	Weight	Features/Apps included	Connectivity (Wi-Fi? Bluetooth? 3G? 4G?)
Smartphone								
Tablets								

© Cengage Learning

Guide to Buying a Computer

As you prepare to buy a computer, there are a lot of decisions you have to make. This book is designed to help you build the knowledge base you need to purchase a computer. In this unit, you were introduced to the basics of computing and the Internet. Each subsequent unit covers topics that can help you understand the type of computer you need, the add-on parts you might want to buy, and the software and services that will enhance your computing experience, such as Internet access, software purchases, and so forth. After each unit, you will be asked to answer questions by completing a worksheet. By the end of the book, your Guide to Buying a Computer worksheet will provide comprehensive information about buying a computer.

To help you organize the information you will need when you are ready to buy a computer, you should complete the following activities.

1. Browse through computer magazines such as *Computer Shopper, PC Magazine,* and *Macworld* and online computer stores such as www.dell.com or www.compusa.com (see Figure A-23) to get a general idea of features and prices. Name three magazines and three online resources you reviewed.

2. Computer price points for a basic computer system (system unit, monitor, keyboard, mouse, sound system, Web cam, and printer) can be roughly grouped into three categories.
 - priced higher than $2,000
 - priced between $800 – $2000
 - priced below $800

 Think about how much you want to spend and whether you would be willing to buy older or used technology to meet your budget. Decide on a budget and stick to it. My budget range is _____.

3. Computers can help you perform such a wide variety of tasks that it can be impossible to predict all the ways you might use your new machine. You can, however, make a list of the ways you plan to use your computer and that list can help you think about the features you'll need. Some computer-based activities require more processing or storage capacity than others. If you have some ideas about your computer usage, you're more likely not to have to purchase expensive upgrades for it later.

 Make a list of three ways you plan to use your computer.

FIGURE A-23: A Web site that sells computers

4. As you continue to work through this book, you will learn more about personal computer systems. You will have the opportunity to answer more questions and complete other worksheets with information that will help you when it is time to buy a computer. To get started, fill in this worksheet to complete this portion of the Guide to Buying a Computer worksheet.

Guide to Buying a Computer: Getting started

Questions to consider	Pages where the topic is covered in this book (refer back to these pages to read more about the topic)	Notes (add additional comments, clarifications, or ideas about each topic)
What type of computer do you need?		
Desktop computer		
Portable computer		
If a desktop computer, what kind of case type?		
Tower (vertical)		
Horizontal		
No case (technology as part of flat-panel screen)		
If a portable computer, what kind do you want?		
Notebook		
Tablet		
Netbook		
Which computer platform?		
IBM-compatible PC		
Macintosh		
Will you need access to the Internet and the Web?		
Yes		
No		
Do you plan to email your friends, instructors, or family?		

© Cengage Learning

5. Write any questions you have about buying a computer on the lines that follow. As you continue to work through this book, check back to see if these questions have been answered.

My Questions

Visual Workshop

Today, more and more people use email to communicate. See Figure A-24 for one example of an email message.

To send and receive email, you need an Internet connection, an email account, and software that enables you to compose, read, and delete email messages. An email account consists of an email address, a password, and a mailbox. You can usually obtain an email account from your Internet service provider, your school, or a Web-based email provider, such as Hotmail, Yahoo! Mail, sor Gmail. To get a Hotmail account, you need to get a Windows Live ID.

To access your mail, you need a computer that has an Internet connection. Since Web mail can be accessed from any computer, you can send and receive email from public computers (such as those at a library or in a school lab). You do not need to own a computer. Once you are sure the computer is connected to the Internet, you simply open a browser and type the URL of the Web site that supports the email you signed up for (hotmail.com, yahoo.com, or gmail.com). As soon as you are logged in to your email account, you can begin sending and receiving email.

FIGURE A-24: Using email to communicate

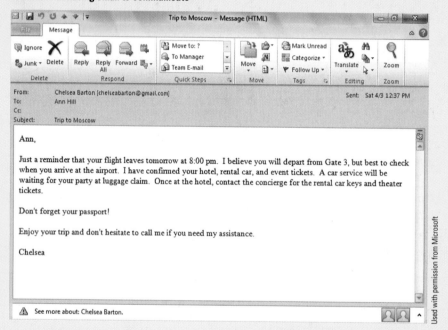

Used with permission from Microsoft

To get a Web-based Gmail account using your own computer, or a public computer if you do not own a computer, just follow these steps.

1. In the Address bar of your browser, enter www.gmail.com.

2. When the Gmail window appears, click the button labeled Create an account.

3. Follow the directions to enter your first name, last name, and login name.

4. Click the check availability button. If the login name you want is already in use, you'll have to try a different one, again clicking the check availability button.

5. When you've selected a valid login name, continue down the page to create a password. Try not to use a name, date, or any dictionary word as your password.

6. Continue down the page to complete the rest of the registration form.

7. Before finalizing your registration, review the information you've entered and jot down your login name and password.

8. Read the Terms of Service, and if you agree, click the I Accept button. That's it! You now have a Gmail account.

Computer Hardware

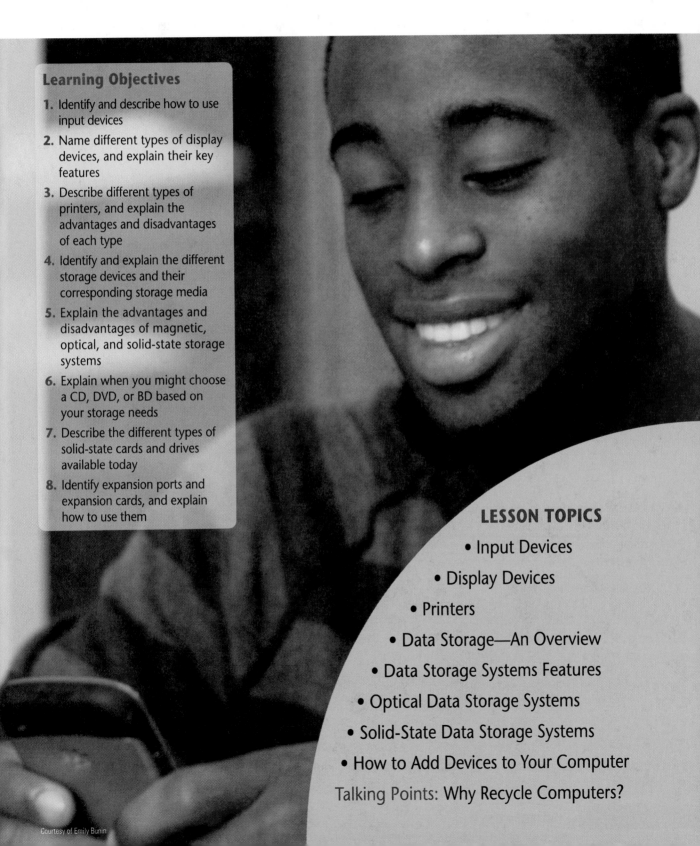

Learning Objectives

1. Identify and describe how to use input devices
2. Name different types of display devices, and explain their key features
3. Describe different types of printers, and explain the advantages and disadvantages of each type
4. Identify and explain the different storage devices and their corresponding storage media
5. Explain the advantages and disadvantages of magnetic, optical, and solid-state storage systems
6. Explain when you might choose a CD, DVD, or BD based on your storage needs
7. Describe the different types of solid-state cards and drives available today
8. Identify expansion ports and expansion cards, and explain how to use them

LESSON TOPICS

- Input Devices
- Display Devices
- Printers
- Data Storage—An Overview
- Data Storage Systems Features
- Optical Data Storage Systems
- Solid-State Data Storage Systems
- How to Add Devices to Your Computer

Talking Points: Why Recycle Computers?

Courtesy of Emily Bunin

Input Devices

When you use a computer or any digital device, you need to communicate with it. To tell a computer what to do, you input information. To input the information, you use an input device. An **input device** is computer hardware that can communicate with the computer. Most computer systems include a keyboard and a pointing device, such as a mouse.

Learning Objective 1:
Identify and describe how to use input devices

● **Are all keyboards the same?** Most keyboards are similar. In addition to standard keyboards, you might use on-screen keyboards on smartphones or tablets. See Figure B-1. A computer keyboard includes keys with letters and numbers. It often has keys with characters and special words to control computer-specific tasks. You use the keyboards to input commands, respond to prompts, and type text.

FIGURE B-1: **Keyboard examples**

on-screen keyboard built-in keyboard standard keyboard

Courtesy of Hewlett-Packard Company

© Eldad Carin/iStockphoto

© skajac/Shutterstock.com

● **Can I use the keyboard to move around the screen?** Yes, you can use the navigation keypad. See Figure B-2. The navigation keypad includes keys such as the Home, End, and arrow keys. You use these keys to move the **insertion point**

FIGURE B-2: **Navigation keys**

© skajac/Shutterstock.com

(also called the **cursor**) on the screen. An insertion point indicates where the characters you type will appear. The insertion point typically looks like a flashing vertical bar on the screen. You can change the location of the insertion point by pressing the navigation keys or by clicking a **pointing device**, such as a mouse.

● **Why do I need a mouse?** Often, you will find that it is easier to use a mouse to give some commands to a computer than it is to use a keyboard. A **mouse** allows you to control an on-screen pointer. A standard desktop computer uses a mouse as its primary pointing device. You can also use a mouse with many notebook computers. A typical mouse, shown in Figure B-3, includes one or more buttons.

FIGURE B-3: **Typical mouse features**

Scroll wheel

Left mouse button

Additional buttons

Right mouse button

Used with permission from Microsoft

● **How do I use a mouse?** You use a mouse by sliding a mouse along a hard surface. Some people use a mouse pad. As you move the mouse, a pointer on the screen moves. If you move the mouse to the left, the pointer on the screen moves to the left. In addition, you click the buttons on the mouse to give commands to the computer. Some mice have extra buttons for additional actions. For example, a scroll wheel can be used to scroll up or down a window. An extra button in the left side of the mouse can be pressed to undo a command. See Table B-1 for common mouse actions.

● **How do mice communicate with the computer?** Some mice are connected to a computer with a cable or wire. These wired mice communicate with the computer through the cable. Other mice are wireless. Wireless mice

communicate with the computer using radio signals. Many people prefer wireless mice because there is no cable to get tangled in when they move the mouse.

For both wired and wireless mice, you have several choices. An **optical mouse** uses an LED (an electronic light) and computer chip to track your mouse movements as a light beam bounces off a hard surface, such as a desk. A **laser mouse** uses a laser as the light source to track mouse movement. Both provide the flexibility to use the mouse on a wide variety of surfaces without a mouse pad.

● **What other pointing devices can I use?** Other pointing devices include touchpads, trackballs, and pointing sticks. These devices are typically used with notebook computers and other mobile devices and smartphones as an alternative to a mouse. A **touchpad**, also called a **trackpad**, is a touch-sensitive surface on which you can slide your fingers to move the on-screen pointer. See Figure B-4. A **trackball** is a roller ball on the top of a mouse. You use your fingers or the palm of your hand to roll the ball and move the pointer. A pointing stick, or TrackPoint, looks like the tip of an eraser embedded in the keyboard of a notebook computer. You can push the TrackPoint up, down, or sideways to move the on-screen pointer.

FIGURE B-4: **Other pointing devices**

Touchpad on a notebook

Trackpad on a smartphone

● **Why do some computers have touch screens?** Many smartphones and other mobile devices, tablet computers, and information kiosks use a touch screen. Special software works to accept the touch screen input.

Touch screen technology can interpret a single touch or more complex input, such as handwriting. You cycle through screens by swiping the glass. You zoom in and out by pinching and expanding two fingers. You rotate objects by twisting two fingers. Some touch screens use a stylus to provide input. See Figure B-5. Be sure to use the stylus intended for your touch screen because touch screens can be damaged by sharp objects.

FIGURE B-5: **Touch screen examples**

● **What if I want to input something I created on paper?** If you have data that exists on paper, you can use a **scanner** to input that data. The scanner captures the image, picture, or text and creates a digital graphics file.

● **Can I enter data by speaking?** Yes, a microphone is an input device that converts spoken words or sound information into a digital format. There are speech-to-text programs that can accept sound as input, which allows you to create a text file from the spoken words. Also, if you use your computer as an Internet telephone, you speak into a microphone and the telephone program sends it through the computer to the person you are speaking with.

● **Are digital cameras input devices?** Yes, a digital camera, creates photographic images as files. A web cam and a digital video camera capture moving images and sound as files. Image and video files can be transferred from a digital camera to any computer. Once these images or videos are on a computer, you can view, play, or change the images.

TABLE B-1: **Common mouse actions**

Action and result	How you do it
Click to select an object	Press the left mouse button once, and then immediately release it.
Double-click to activate an object	Press the left mouse button twice in rapid succession without moving the body of the mouse.
Right-click to display a shortcut menu	Press the right mouse button once, and then immediately release it.
Drag to move an object	Hold the left mouse button down while you move the mouse.

Display Devices

While working on a computer, you will want to see what's going on. You need to look at the data as you input it. You also want to look at the output. A display system is the main output device for a computer. Two key components of a computer display system are a display device or screen and a graphics card.

Learning Objective 2:
Name different types of display devices, and explain their key features

- **What is a display device?** A **display device** is the computer hardware that shows, or displays, the data. It shows the input as you enter data. It shows the output once the data has been processed. The main display device for a computer is either a monitor or a screen. Smartphones, tablet computers, and other mobile devices have screens.

- **Are a monitor and a screen the same thing?** Many people use the terms *monitor* and *screen* interchangeably, but they are not technically the same thing. A monitor is a stand-alone display device that connects to a computer. A screen is the area where output is displayed. A desktop computer has a monitor with a screen. A notebook, netbook, and tablet computer, as well as other mobile devices such as a smartphone, each have a screen.

- **What are my choices for a display device?** Two technologies are commonly used for computer display devices: LCD and LED. See Figure B-6. Your computer monitor will most likely have an **LCD (liquid crystal display)** screen. LCD monitors are also called flat-panel displays. LCD monitors produce an image by manipulating light within a layer of liquid crystal cells. The advantages of an LCD monitor include display clarity, low

radiation emission, portability, and compactness. Stand-alone LCD monitors are available for desktop computers. LCD screens are standard equipment for notebook computers. An LED (light emitting diodes) screen looks similar to an LCD screen but it uses light emitting diodes for the backlighting. LEDs are considered more environmentally friendly than LCDs.

- **What type of screen do mobile devices use?** Mobile devices such as mobile phones, portable media players, GPS devices, and digital cameras, use **OLED (organic light emitting diodes)** or LCD technology. See Figure B-7. Each technology has its advantages. For example, an OLED display device draws less power than an LCD screen. OLEDs have a crisp image and a fast response rate. OLED screens work well in direct sunlight. The image on an OLED screen can be seen from any angle.

FIGURE B-7: **Display technology for smartphones**

Example of an OLED screen Example of an LCD screen

- **What is a graphics card?** A graphics card is the another important component of your display system. A **graphics card** contains the technology used to display images on the screen. It also contains special memory, which stores images as they are processed but before they are displayed. The amount of available memory is the key to the overall performance, including response rate, of the display system.

FIGURE B-6: **Examples of monitors**

LCD

LED

- **What is response rate?** **Response rate** is how fast a screen updates the information being displayed. Display devices with fast response rates display a crisp image with minimal blurring or "ghosting" of moving objects. Response rate is an important factor for fast action games, 3D modeling, and graphics-intensive desktop publishing.

- **Where is the graphics card?** A graphics card can be built into a computer's motherboard or plugged into the motherboard. The graphics card is a chip built into the motherboard of a notebook or tablet computer, as well as other mobile devices.

- **What does a graphics card do?** Think of the computer screen as a grid. The rows and columns make cells in the grid. A graphics card sends an image to the screen to fill the grid. The graphics card sends the image at a specific resolution. **Resolution** is the maximum number of horizontal and vertical pixels displayed on the screen. A **pixel (picture element)** is a single point or the smallest unit in a graphic image. Each pixel fills one cell of the grid. As resolutions increase, the computer displays a larger work area on the screen with text and other objects appearing smaller. See Figure B-8. You can set the resolution on a Windows PC using options in the Control Panel. Higher resolutions are possible if your graphics card has enough memory to support those resolutions and if your display device is capable of displaying those resolutions.

- **Does it matter if my display device is square or rectangular?** No, but you should use a resolution that works best for your display device. Some monitors look square. For these monitors, a resolution based on a 4:3 aspect ratio works best. The 4:3 ratio matches the monitor since the width is slightly larger than the height. Some monitors have a rectangle shape. These are widescreen monitors. For widescreen monitors, a resolution based on a 16:9 aspect ratios works best.

- **What other factors besides resolution affect image quality?** In addition to resolution, image quality is determined by screen size, dot pitch, and color depth. These factors are all controlled by the graphics card.

- **What is screen size?** **Screen size** is the measurement in inches from one corner of the screen diagonally across to the opposite corner. Although large screens exist for commercial use, typical computer monitor screen sizes range from 15" to more than 20". In addition to screen size, you should also consider a monitor's **viewing angle width**, which indicates how far to the side you can still clearly see the screen image. A wide viewing angle indicates that you can view the screen from various positions without compromising image quality. A 170 degree viewing angle is preferable to a viewing angle of 150 degrees.

- **What is dot pitch?** **Dot pitch (dp)** is a measure of image clarity. A smaller dot pitch means a crisper image. Unlike resolution, dot pitch is not customizable. A display device's specifications include dot pitch.

- **What is color depth?** The number of colors that a monitor and graphics card can display is referred to as **color depth** or **bit depth**. Most PCs are capable of displaying millions of colors and photographic-quality images. On a Windows PC, you can change the color setting to customize the color depth by using options in the Control Panel.

- **Can I watch TV on my display device?** Yes, if your display system is equipped with NTSC (National TV Standards Committee) or HDTV (high-definition television) circuitry. Display devices rated for 1080i or 1080p are compatible with HDTV standards. Television signals are sent to the computer through an antenna or cable. You can even view computer data and television on the same display device at the same time using split-screen or picture-in-picture format.

FIGURE B-8: Comparing screen resolutions

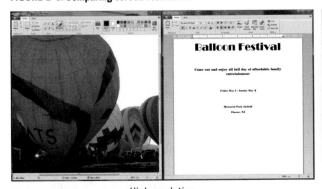

High resolution
Text and images fill the screen and more content can fit on a screen with a higher resolution.

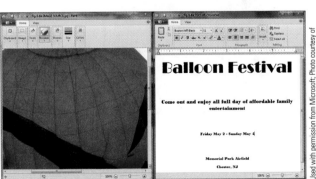

Low resolution
Text and images appear larger but less content can fit on a screen with a lower resolution.

Used with permission from Microsoft; Photo courtesy of Rachel Bunin

Printers

Most output is viewed using a display device. This output is called **soft copy**. Sometimes, you want the output on paper. To create printed copy, you use a printer. Printed output is called **hard copy**. You can print hard copy on different media, such as paper, labels, or transparencies. Printers differ in resolution and speed, both of which affect the print quality and price. To find a printer that meets your needs, it is important to understand the different types of printers and their features.

Learning Objective 3:
Describe different types of printers, and explain the advantages and disadvantages of each type

● **What are the most common types of printers in use today?** The most common types of printers in use today are either ink-jet printers or laser printers. Both ink-jet printers and laser printers have features in common. For example, both are available as black and white or color printers. Both have trays for different paper sizes. You can print on 8" × 11" paper, 8" × 14" paper, envelopes, postcards, transparencies, and more. Both types of printers also have drawbacks to consider. For example, cost over the life of the printer, as well as the speed at which the printer produces hard copy.

● **How does an ink-jet printer work?** An **ink-jet printer** has a print head that sprays ink onto paper to form characters and graphics. Ink-jet printers usually use two cartridges: a black ink cartridge and a color cartridge that holds colored inks. See Figure B-9. Most ink-jet printers are small, lightweight, and inexpensive, yet produce very good-quality color output. However, the ink cartridges can be expensive and can add to the overall cost of printing.

FIGURE B-9: An ink jet printer

Color ink cartridges

Paper tray

Black ink cartridge

Courtesy of Hewlett-Packard Company

● **How does a laser printer work?** A **laser printer** uses a technology that produces dots of light on a light-sensitive drum. Instead of ink cartridges, laser printers use **toner** cartridges. See Figure B-10. Toner is the fine powder that is applied to the drum, and then creates the image on the paper. Laser printers are popular for situations that require high-volume output or good-quality printouts. Laser printers are generally more expensive than ink-jet printers.

FIGURE B-10: A laser printer

Toner cartridge

Paper tray

Courtesy of Hewlett-Packard Company

● **What determines the quality of the printed images?** **Printer resolution** determines the quality or sharpness of printed images and text. Resolution is measured by the number of dots printed per linear inch, or **dots per inch (dpi)**. At normal reading distance, a resolution of about 900 dots per inch appears solid to the human eye. At 900 dpi, if you look closely, a dot pattern will be evident. Good-quality printers are rated from 2400 to 4800 dpi. If you want the printed images to have the quality of professionally printed books, use a printer with a resolution of 2400 dpi or higher.

● **How can I know if a printer is fast?** You can look at the pages per minute (ppm) and memory specifications provided by the manufacturer. Printer speed is measured by the number of **pages per minute (ppm)** output. Color printouts typically take longer to print than black-and-white printouts. Pages that contain mostly text tend to print faster than pages that contain graphics. Most printers for personal or small business use are rated from 15 to 30 ppm.

Memory capacity is another factor to consider when evaluating printer speed. Printers often work in the background while you work on other computer tasks. If your printer has lots of

memory, you can send many print jobs to the printer. The print jobs will be in the printer's memory and not in your computer's memory. More memory is required to print color images and documents with graphics. You can work more efficiently if your printer has more memory.

- **Can a printer print on both sides of a page in one pass?** Yes, a **duplex printer** can print on both sides of the paper. This environment-friendly option saves paper. However, duplex printing slows down the print process on ink-jet printers because they have to pause to let the ink dry before printing the second side.

- **Does the number of pages I print affect the life of my printer?** **Duty cycle** determines how many pages a printer is able to print in a specified period of time. A printer's duty cycle is usually measured in pages per month. For example, on average, a personal laser printer has a duty cycle of about 3000 pages per month—that means roughly 100 pages per day. However, you wouldn't want to use it to produce 3,000 pages on one day. You can print more pages than the specified duty cycle, but this could shorten the usability of your printer. Also, a printer with a higher duty cycle will have a shorter useful life.

- **How does a printer connect to my computer?** A printer connects to your computer using one of the following connection options: USB port, serial port, parallel port, or network port. Usually a cable is used to connect a printer to a computer. However, a printer can also connect to a computer wirelessly if the printer and computer both have the wireless technology needed to connect.

You can connect a print... puter and use it only... times, you might... one computer.

- **How do I ... compu...** area ... oth... the n... printer fo... share one res...

 Another way to ... ple users is to purchase ... that connects directly to th... of the computers on a network. ... can be wired or wireless.

- **Do I need a different printer to prin... photographs?** Yes, for more professional out... want to use a **photo printer**. These printers have ... output speeds when compared to ink-jet or laser printe... but they do produce professional-quality images on specialized papers.

- **How do I know which type of printer is best for me?** The type of printer you need depends on several factors. For example: Do you need black and white hard copy or color hard copy Do you often need to print a lot of pages at one time? Are you working with a stand-alone or a networked computer? Do you want a wired or a wireless printer? Once you know the answers to these questions, you will know what type of printer best meets your needs.

Options for printing your photos

Do you print a lot of photographs? If so, you should compare the cost of printing the photographs using your printer to the cost of printing the photographs commercially. You can often have digital images printed over the Web using online services, such as Kodak Gallery, Snapfish, or Flickr. The printed photos are then mailed to you. You can also take the digital image files on a disc or flash drive to a store and have the photographs printed there. You can often shop while you wait for your photos. Some stores allow you to upload images to their Web site, where you specify your printing preferences, and then pick up the photos at your local store. Some stores even have self-service stations in the store. See Figure B-11. These printing services usually allow you to edit your digital images, for example, to remove red-eye or to crop an unwanted object out of the image. If you consider the cost of paper and ink to print large quantities of photographs, these services often are more

economical. But for occasional use, a photo-printer provides quality images at a reasonable cost.

FIGURE B-11: Self-service photo printing

Courtesy of Hewlett-Packard Company

ta Storage—An Overview

...r, you will want to store or save your work. Once stored, you can use your work again or share it ...When you store your work, you save it using storage technology. The term **storage technology** ...ge systems that make it possible for a computer or digital device to store and retrieve data.

...s a data storage system? A data storage system is ...up of two main parts: a storage device and a storage ...um. A **storage device** is the equipment that stores ...d retrieves data from its storage medium. Storage devices ...clude hard drives, card readers, tape drives, flash drives, ...D drives, DVD drives, BD drives, and solid-state card read-ers. A **storage medium** is the technology that holds data. Storage media include hard drives, tape, memory cards, flash drives, CDs, DVDs, and BDs. Refer to Figure B-12 for examples of storage devices and storage media.

FIGURE B-12: **Examples of storage devices and storage media**

Flash drive

Removable hard disk drive

Card reader

Solid-state drive (SSD)

CD/DVD Drive

DVD

Solid-state cards

Top, left: © Dmitry Rukhlenko/Shutterstock.com; © Ruslan Ivantsov/Shutterstock.com; © Tatiana Popova/
Shutterstock.com; Kingston Technology Company, Inc.; Top, right: Kingston Technology Company, Inc.; BiTMICRO
Networks, Inc.

- **Are the storage medium and the storage device always two separate parts?** No. Some data storage sys-tems are self-contained, while others are two distinct parts. For example, a hard drive is both the storage device and the storage medium. A USB flash drive is both a storage device and the storage medium. But, a CD/DVD drive is a storage device and it uses CDs or DVDs as the storage media. And, a flash card reader is a storage device and it uses solid state cards as its storage media.

- **What is the main data storage system for a personal computer system?** The main storage system for a personal computer is a **hard drive**. Hard drives can be internal (permanently installed inside the system unit), removable, or external. Hard drives can be mechanical or use **solid-state technology**. Mechanical drives have moving parts. **Solid-state drives (SSD)** have no moving parts. The terms hard drive and hard disk drive are often used interchangeably.

- **Why are hard drives so popular?** Hard drives are the preferred type of main storage for most computer systems. They provide lots of storage, fast access to data, and are inexpensive. Most computers come with an internal hard drive that is installed in the computer and cannot be moved easily from one computer to another. You may not know what a hard drive looks like because it is usually found inside the system unit. Personal computer hard drive platters are typically 3½" in diameter with storage capacities ranging from 60 GB to over 2 TB. Refer to Figure B-13 to see what a mechanical hard drive looks like. Tablet computers, mobile devices, and some notebooks use a solid-state non-removable internal hard drive.

Courtesy of MediaTechnics Corporation

Spindle Read-write head Platter

● **What other storage devices can I use with my personal computer?** In addition to the hard drive just discussed, you can use additional storage devices such as CD/DVD/BD drives, USB flash drives, solid-state drives, and solid-state card readers.

● **Why would I want to use different storage devices?** Storage devices, such as hard drives, provide fast access to data. Some storage devices, such as CDs DVDs, and BVDs, are more dependable than others. Some storage devices, such as solid-state storage **USB flash drives** and external hard drives, are portable and can be moved easily from one computer to another computer.

● **How do these storage devices connect to my computer?** The system unit case for a desktop computer contains several storage device "parking spaces" called **drive bays** or **expansion bays**. Storage devices are installed in these drive bays. These bays are typically hidden from view with a faceplate. See Figure B-14. When you buy a computer, you will need to find out how many drive bays the computer has and what type of storage devices can be connected to the computer using the drive bay(s). Any drive that is mounted inside the system unit and that uses removable media or that has to

FIGURE B-14: **Drive bays**

DVD writer/CD writer drive

Courtesy of MediaTechnics Corporation

Expansion bay; another optical drive can be added here Button to open drive

be controlled manually by pushing a button or inserting the media into a slot, such as a CD/DVD/BD drive, must be able to be accessed from outside the system unit.

● **What if my computer doesn't have any empty drive bays?** In this case, you will want to add an external storage device. Some storage devices such as an external hard drive, a USB flash drive, or a card reader connect to your computer using a USB port. If you do not have enough USB ports for all the devices you want to connect, then you can use a USB hub. A USB hub adds ports to your computer, as shown in Figure B-15.

FIGURE B-15: **Drives connected through a USB hub**

USB flash drives

Self-powered USB hub

External hard drive

Courtesy of MediaTechnics Corporation

● **How do I connect storage devices to my notebook, netbook, and tablet computers?** These computers do not have drive bays. You will want to connect storage devices to these computers using an available USB port or a USB hub.

● **How can I increase my storage capacity?** You can increase the storage capacity of your computer by adding a second internal hard drive to an empty drive bay. You can also add an external hard drive that connects via a USB port.

● **Is my data safe on the hard drive?** In general, yes. But keep in mind that the read-write heads in a mechanical hard drive hover a microscopic distance above the disk surface. A head crash might happen if a read-write head runs into dirt on the disk or if the hard drive is jarred while it is in use. A head crash will damage some or all of the data on the disk. To help prevent dirt from contacting the platters and causing head crashes, a hard drive is sealed in its case. Although hard drives have become considerably more rugged in recent years, you should still handle and transport them with care.

● **Is there a hard drive in my iPod and other mobile devices?** Yes, although the physical sizes of the hard drives vary. Mobile devices use a miniature hard drive (sometimes called a microdrive). For example Apple's current iPod uses a 1.8" drive that can store 30 to 160 GB.

Data Storage Systems Features

Data storage systems for personal computers use magnetic, optical, or solid-state technology. Data storage systems can be compared based on their versatility, durability, capacity, and speed.

Learning Objective 5:
Explain the advantages and disadvantages of magnetic, optical, and solid-state storage systems

● **Why do I need versatility in a data storage system?** Most likely you will be working with other people. You will want to be able to store data on your storage medium and then give that storage medium to another person. That person can then use the storage medium to access the data. Or, you may have to use different computers. To move data among different computers, you will want data storage systems that are versatile. Some storage devices can access data from only one type of medium. More versatile storage devices can access data from several different media. For example, a DVD drive can access data on these storage media: DVDs, DVD movies, audio CDs, data CDs, and CD-Rs. A USB flash drive can plug into any USB port. Both a DVD and a flash drive are versatile.

● **Why do I need a data storage system that is durable?** Do you travel or carry your data files with you? If so, then you need a storage system that is durable. Most data storage systems can be damaged by mishandling them or by heat and moisture. Optical and solid-state technologies are more durable than magnetic technologies. They do not damage easily. This helps you prevent data loss. Solid-state storage devices are the most durable at this time.

● **Why is storage capacity important?** Different data storage systems hold different amounts of data. **Storage capacity** is the maximum amount of data (documents, photographs, songs, video) that can be stored on a storage medium. Storage capacity is measured in kilobytes (KB), megabytes (MB), gigabytes (GB), or terabytes (TB). Graphics and video require more storage capacity than text. You need more storage for photographs and video than you need for your school reports or letters. Before deciding on a data storage system, you need to be sure the data storage systems you use can hold all the data you need to store.

● **Do different data storage systems access and transfer data at different speeds?** Yes. There are two factors to take into account when considering access speed: access time and data transfer rate. **Access time** is the average time it takes a computer to locate data on the storage medium and read it. Access time is measured in **milliseconds** (thousandths of a second, abbreviated as **ms**). **Data transfer rate** is the amount of data that a storage device can move from the storage medium to the computer per second. So, if you are watching a movie on your computer, you want the fastest data transfer rate possible.

● **What does random access mean?** **Random access** (also called **direct access**) is the ability of a device to jump directly to the requested data. Hard drives, solid-state drives, CD drives, DVD drives, and BD drives are random-access devices. A tape drive, used with some business computers for long-term storage, must use slower **sequential access**, which means it reads through the data from the beginning of the tape to the end. As a result, accessing data on a tape is much slower than accessing data on a hard drive. The advantage of random access becomes clear when you consider how much faster and easier it is to locate a song on a CD (random access) or MP3 player (random access solid-state storage) than on tape (sequential access).

● **Which data storage systems use magnetic storage technology?** Hard drives and tapes use magnetic storage. **Magnetic storage** stores data by magnetizing microscopic particles on the disk or tape surface. The particles retain their magnetic orientation until that orientation is changed. Patterns of magnetized particles are interpreted as the 0s and 1s that represent data. Data stored magnetically can be changed or deleted simply by altering the magnetic orientation of the appropriate particles on the disk surface. Refer to Figure B-16.

FIGURE B-16: **Magnetic storage**

Randomly scattered particles | Magnetized particles | Read-write head | Disk surface

© Cengage Learning

● **Which storage systems use optical storage technology?** CDs, DVDs, and BDs use optical storage technologies. **Optical storage** stores data as microscopic light and dark spots on the disc surface. Low-power laser light is used to read the data stored on an optical disc. Patterns of light and dark are interpreted as the 1s and 0s that represent data. Figure B-17 shows the layers that make up an optical disc. You use an optical storage system because its storage media (CDs, DVDs, and BDs) are easy to transport and fairly durable. However, CDs, DVDs, and BDs do still require some special handling in order to be sure that data stored on these optical media is not lost or damaged due to environmental conditions or poor handling.

FIGURE B-17: **Optical storage**

Polycarbonate substrate
Reflective layer
Recording layer 1
Spacer layer
Semitransparent reflective layer

Laser beams | Recording layer 0 | Polycarbonate substrate

© Cengage Learning

● **Which data storage systems use solid-state storage technology?** Some hard drives, a variety of compact storage cards (also called memory cards or memory sticks) and flash drives (also called thumb drives or jump sticks) use solid-state technology. **Solid-state storage** technology stores data in a durable, erasable, low-power chip. Solid-state storage technology provides faster access to data than magnetic or optical storage technology because it includes no moving parts. Very little power is required, which makes solid-state storage ideal for battery-operated devices, such as a digital camera. Solid-state storage is very durable—it is usually not affected by vibrations, magnetic fields, or extreme temperature fluctuations—and very portable. Flash drives have become trendy stylish items that can be fun to carry. They can even be worn as a fashion accessory. See Figure B-18.

FIGURE B-18: **A flash drive can take many fun forms**

Left: © Fazakas Mihaly/Shutterstock Right, top: © andsem/iStockphoto; © Hasloo Group Production Studio/Shutterstock.com

● **What is tape storage?** **Tape storage** technology consists of a tape drive for the storage device and a tape for the storage medium. Tape drives are available in either internal or external models. The most popular types of tape drives for personal computers use tape cartridges for the storage medium. A **tape cartridge** is a removable magnetic tape module similar to a cassette tape. Tape storage is used mainly for back-up storage today, most often for backing up business or professional systems.

Non-technical words used to describe using a data storage system

You use certain words to describe what happens when you use a data storage system. When you want to retrieve data, you say the storage device is "reading," "loading," or "opening" a file. The storage device reads the file on the storage medium and loads the information into RAM. Once the file is loaded, it is open and ready for you to use. "Ripping" is the term used to describe copying files from CDs, DVDs, and BDs onto your hard drive. For CDs, DVDs, and BDs, you often use the term "burning" to describe when files are copied to a disc.

Optical Data Storage Systems

You may have used a CD to listen to music. You may have used a DVD or a Blu-ray Disc (BD) to watch a movie. But did you know you can also use these media to store computer data? **CDs (compact discs), DVDs (digital video disc or digital versatile disc),** and **BDs (Blu-ray Discs)** use optical storage technologies. Optical storage media use one of three technologies: read-only (ROM), recordable (R), or rewritable (RW).

Learning Objective 6:
Explain when you might choose a CD, DVD, or BD based on your storage needs

● **What are the parts of an optical storage system?** An optical storage system consists of a drive and the storage media used in that drive. The rest of this lesson provides more information about the types of optical drives available, as well as the type of storage media each drive can use.

● **What is the main difference between CD, DVD, and BD?** Today, most computers come equipped with one or more drives designed to work with CD, DVD, or BD discs. The basic difference between these technologies is the amount of data each disc can store. Current CD standards have the capacity to store 80 minutes of music or 700 MB of data. DVD standards offer 4.7 GB (4,700 MB) of data storage, about seven times as much capacity as a CD. A double layer DVD has two recordable layers on the same side and can store 8.5 GB of data. Currently, BDs have the highest storage capacity for optical storage media. They offer 25 GB capacity per layer. A double layer BD disc holds 50 GB of data.

● **What do the extra letters after CD, DVD, and BD mean?** The extra letters associated with a CD, DVD, or BD help you recognize how you can use the disc. Using CD as an example:

■ CD-ROM means read-only technology. A computer CD-ROM, DVD-ROM, or BD-ROM disc contains data that was stamped on the disc surface when it was manufactured, such as commercial software, music, and movies. Data cannot be added, changed, or deleted from CD-ROM, DVD-ROM, or BD-ROM discs.

■ CD-R means CD **recordable technology**. If you need to write data to the storage media, then you need to purchase recordable discs. You can usually write to a CD-R disc in multiple sessions. For example, you can store two files on a CD-R disc today, and add data for a few more files to the disc at a later time. This is also true for DVD-R/DVD+R and BD-R discs.

■ CD-RW means CD **rewritable technology**. If you need to write to the disc and rewrite to the disc, then you need to purchase the rewritable (multiple session use) discs. When you use these discs, you can record and erase stored data multiple times, which makes this a flexible storage option. This is also true for DVD-RW/DVD+RW. For Blu-ray Discs, you would look for BD-RE discs. BD-RE can be erased and re-recorded multiple times.

● **What type of optical disc should I buy?** When you purchase optical discs, be sure to purchase the type that works in your computer system's optical drive and meets your storage needs. To be able to write to the disc, you would need either the R or RW/RE format.

Understanding hard drive partitions

A hard drive partition is a section of a hard drive that is treated as a separate storage device. Many computers are configured with a single hard drive partition that contains the operating system, programs, and data. Some new computers come with two partitions. It is even possible to partition external hard drives. Partitions appear as independent hard drives but they are one physical drive in your computer. When you look at the single drive using Windows Explorer, each partition is labeled separately (such as C drive and D drive), These are sometimes called logical drives. The main partition is often labeled OS (C:), and it contains the operating system and other program and data files. The default folders for Windows are on the C drive. The second partition is often labeled Recovery (D):. This partition contains files that can be used to help restore the computer if drive C malfunctions. Partitions are not the same as folders. Partitions are more permanent, and a special utility is required to create, modify, or delete them.

- **Should my computer system have a CD, DVD, or BD drive?** Yes, it is a good idea to have a **CD drive**, a **DVD drive**, or a **BD drive**. You need to know your storage needs to know which type of optical disc drive is best for you. The most versatile, and at the moment the most expensive, optical storage device is a Blu-ray Disc writer/DVD writer. Optical drives can be built into your computer or you can use external optical drives that connect through USB ports. External optical drives can be moved as needed among your computers.

- **How do I insert a disc into an optical drive?** First, you must open the drive. Usually there is button that you push. When you push the button the drawer slides out. See Figure B-19. You hold the disc on the sides and place it in the drawer so the label or printed description of the disc is facing up. After the disc is set in the drawer, gently push the drawer or press the button and the drawer will close.

- **Can I use a CD, DVD, or BD drive instead of a hard drive?** No. A rewritable CD, DVD, or BD drive is a fine addition to a computer system, but it is not a replacement for a hard drive. Unfortunately, the process of reading data from and writing data to a rewritable disc is relatively slow compared to hard drive access speed. In addition, the storage capacity of CDs and DVDs is much less than the storage capacity of hard drives.

- **How does the optical drive work?** Figure B-20 illustrates how a CD drive works. Optical drives contain a spindle that rotates the disc over a laser lens. The laser directs a beam of light toward the underside of the disc. As the drive reads the disc, the light's reflections are translated into the 0s and 1s that represent data. Blu-ray Disc technology uses blue-violet colored lasers to read data. DVD technology uses a red laser. CD technology uses a near infrared laser.

FIGURE B-19: Inserting a disc in an optical drive

Courtesy of MediaTechnics Corporation

FIGURE B-20: How an optical drive works

Courtesy of MediaTechnics Corporation

Tracking mechanism positions a disc track over the laser lens

Laser lens directs a beam of light to the underside of the CD-ROM disc

Laser pickup assembly senses the reflections and translates the information into 1s and 0s

Drive spindle spins disc

Viewing your data storage systems using Windows Explorer

All of the data storage systems connected to your computer are named. You can view the data storage systems connected to your computer using a file management system, such as Windows Explorer. To view the contents of a disc or any media in Windows Explorer, open Windows Explorer and then click Computer to see all of the storage devices connected to your computer, including any external hard drives, any optical drives such as CD, DVD, or BD drives, any solid state drives such as flash drives, even cameras that you connect through a USB cable, and any network drives. Select the drive to see the contents in the right pane of the window. See Figure B-21.

FIGURE B-21: Viewing data storage systems connected to a computer

Used with permission from Microsoft

Computer Hardware

Solid-State Data Storage Systems

Have you ever used a cell phone? A digital camera? An MP3 player? If you have, then you have also used solid-state data storage. Solid-state data storage is portable and durable. It provides fast access to data, offers high-capacity storage, and uses very little power. It is an ideal solution for storing data on mobile devices and transporting data from one device to another.

Learning Objective 7:
Describe the different types of solid-state cards and drives available today

● **When would I use solid-state storage?** Solid-state storage systems are suitable for many storage needs. See Figure B-22.

FIGURE B-22: **Examples of solid state storage media**

Used mainly in cameras

Used mainly in mobile devices, such as GPS devices, MP3 players, PDAs

Used for portable storage through a USB connection

Used for portable storage through a USB connection; larger storage capacity than a flash drive

Used inside a computer for permanent storage

Counter-clockwise from top left: Courtesy of MediaTechnics Corporation; Courtesy of MediaTechnics Corporation; Courtesy of MediaTechnics Corporation; © Oleksiy Mark/Shutterstock.com; Courtesy of Iomega

You might use a solid-state memory card in your digital camera. A solid-state memory card in a digital camera can store hundreds of pictures. You can remove the card from the camera and insert it into a card reader that is connected to a computer. Once the card is connected to your computer, you can transfer the files to your hard drive so the photos can be edited using the computer's graphics software and transmitted via the computer's Internet connection.

You might use a solid-state memory card in your MP3 player. You can download MP3 music files using your computer and then store the files on a solid-state memory card. Next, you can insert the card into a portable MP3 player so you can hear your favorite tunes while you are on the go.

You might use solid-state storage, such as a flash drive or an external solid-state drive, for your portable computing needs, that is, for transporting data from one computer to another.

● **Why is solid-state storage so popular?** Solid-state storage uses a technology that stores data in a nonvolatile, erasable,

low-power chip. A **chip** is an electronic circuit. You will learn more about chips later in this book. Very little power is required to store the data. Solid-state storage is ideal for battery-operated devices, such as digital cameras or smartphones. Once the data is stored, the chip retains the data without the need for an external power source.

● **How do I know which solid-state cards to buy?** The type of card you buy depends on the device it will be used with. There are over 50 types of flash cards available. The device you buy should indicate the cards you can use with that device. Examples of several types of solid-state memory cards are shown in Figure B-23. The formats for these small, flat cards include CompactFlash (CF), Memory Sticks, Secure Digital (SD), Secure Digital High Capacity (SDHC), Micro SD, Micro SDHC, and Secure Digital Extended Capacity (SDXC). The micro cards are used in smartphones and portable media players.

FIGURE B-23: **Solid state cards**

Courtesy of Kingston Technology Company, Inc.

■ **CompactFlash (CF) cards** are about the size of a matchbook and provide high storage capacities and access speeds. CompactFlash cards include a built-in controller that reads data from and writes data to the card. CompactFlash cards use a card reader to transfer data from the card to your computer; the built-in controller

tells the card reader what to do. With their high storage capacities and access speeds, CompactFlash cards are ideal for use on high-end digital cameras that require megabytes of storage for each photo.

- **SecureDigital (SD) cards** are popular for digital images and MP3 storage. They use a card reader to copy data from the card to a computer. Newer SDHC cards have 32 GB maximum capacity; SDXC cards have a 2 TB maximum capacity. Although SDHC and SDXC cards fit in a standard SD slot, older devices might not be able to handle such high storage capacities.
- **Memory stick** technology was originally developed by Sony. Memory sticks are now developed in a joint venture with SanDisk. They have been expanded to include extended high capacity formats. Some can reach 2 TB of storage with very fast data transfer rates.

● Will my computer be able to read my solid-state storage cards? Solid-state storage cards require a device called a **card reader** to transfer data to or from a computer. A card reader can be built into a computer's system unit. Refer to Figure B-24. Sometimes referred to as 5-in-1, 7-in-1, or all-in-one card readers, these combination devices work with multiple types of solid-state storage formats. If your computer has one of these readers, it will be able to read your solid-state storage cards.

FIGURE B-24: **Card reader built into a system unit**

Memory card

5-in-1 card reader

● What if my computer system does not have a built-in card reader? You can use a stand-alone card reader. See Figure B-25. A stand-alone card reader usually connects to a computer via USB. To connect the stand-alone card reader to your computer, simply plug the USB cable into an available USB port.

FIGURE B-25: **Stand–alone card reader**

● Do I always need a card reader to read solid-state storage? No. USB flash drives and solid-state drives (SSD) (see Figure B-26) incorporate the memory and the reader into one device. Each has a built-in connector that plugs directly into a computer's port. USB flash drives plug into a USB port and internal solid-state drives plug into the motherboard. External USB solid-state flash drives that connect via a USB port are also available. SSDs have no moving parts so they are more durable than mechanical hard drives.

FIGURE B-26: **Examples of solid-state drives**

Flash drive Internal solid-state hard drive External solid-state hard drive

● What is the best choice for portability? USB flash drives are easy to take from one computer to another. When connected to your computer's USB port, you can open, edit, delete, and run files stored on a USB flash drive just as if though those files were stored on your computer's hard drive. USB flash drives are about the size of a large paperclip and so durable that you can literally carry them on your key ring. They are usually called flash drives, thumb drives, or jump sticks. They are also nicknamed pen drives, keychain drives, or UFDs (Universal Flash Drive). They come in a variety of shapes and sizes. Some samples were shown previously in Figure B-18.

How to Add Devices to Your Computer

You can expand or improve the capability of your computer by adding computer peripherals. Some peripherals you might want to add include a scanner, a different mouse, a joystick, a digital camera, a Web cam, a graphics tablet, and more. You typically plug the device into an expansion port on your computer. You can also expand or improve the capability of your computer by adding or upgrading expansion cards, such as sound cards, video cards, and so on.

Learning Objective 8:
Identify expansion ports and expansion cards, and explain how to use them

● **What is an expansion card?** An **expansion card** is a small circuit board that makes it possible for the computer to communicate with a peripheral device, such as a scanner, a joystick, or a digital camera. Expansion cards are also called expansion boards, controller cards, or adapters.

● **How are expansion cards connected to the computer?** An expansion card is plugged into an expansion slot on the motherboard. An **expansion slot** is a long, narrow socket on the motherboard into which you can plug an expansion card. Once an expansion card is plugged into the expansion slot, a peripheral device can be attached to the expansion card via the expansion port.

● **What is an expansion port?** An **expansion port** is a connector that passes data between a computer and a peripheral device. An expansion port is part of an expansion card. System units are designed with openings that make these ports accessible from outside the case. Common built-in expansion ports that come with a computer are shown in Figure B-27.
- Graphics ports: connect display devices
- FireWire ports: connect peripheral devices such as digital cameras and high-speed external data storage devices
- Ethernet network ports: connect the computer to a wired network
- eSATA ports: connect high-speed external data storage devices

- USB ports: connect peripheral devices such as mice, keyboards, flash drives, external drives, and cameras
- HDMI ports: connect high-definition video cables
- Audio ports: connect speakers, a headset, and/or a microphone

In addition to the ones shown in the figure, you can add other expansion cards and ports.

● **Why would I want to add more expansion cards and ports?** You might want to add more cards and ports to upgrade existing expansion cards or to install new expansion cards to enhance sound or communications functionality. For example, you can install a high-end graphics card (sometimes called a video card) if you want to use the computer for advanced graphics or gaming.

● **How does an expansion card work?** The computer controls the peripheral device by sending data over circuits called a **data bus**. One part of the data bus runs between **RAM (Random Access Memory)** and the processor; the other part runs between RAM and various peripheral devices. RAM is volatile storage used by a computer. You will learn more about RAM later in this book. The segment of the data bus between RAM and the peripheral devices is called the **expansion bus**. As data moves along the expansion bus, it may travel through expansion slots, cards, ports, and cables. See Figure B-28 on the next page.

FIGURE B-27: **Common expansion ports**

FireWire port

Graphics ports

eSATA port Ethernet USB ports Audio ports
 network port

Courtesy of MediaTechnics Corporation

Computer Hardware

FIGURE B-28: How the expansion bus works

Processor — Local bus — RAM — Expansion bus — Expansion slots and expansion cards — Ports — Cable — Printer or other peripherals

Expansion bus — Hard disk drive

● **How do I install an expansion card?** Usually, installing an expansion card requires you to open the system unit. Be sure to turn off the power to the system unit before opening a computer. An expansion card is inserted into an expansion slot in the motherboard. Expansion cards are built for only one type of slot. If you plan to add or upgrade a card in your computer, you must make sure the right type of slot is available on the motherboard. See Figure B-29.

FIGURE B-29: An expansion card slides into an expansion slot

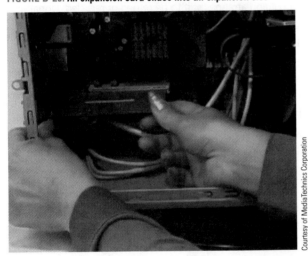

Courtesy of MediaTechnics Corporation

● **Once I install the peripheral device or expansion card, will it work automatically?** PCs include a feature called Plug and Play. This means that once you plug a peripheral device into its port, the device is ready to use. Each peripheral device or expansion card requires software called a **device driver**. This software program sets up communication between your computer and the device or card. The directions supplied with your new peripheral device or card will include instructions on how to install the device driver if it does not happen automatically when you start the computer.

● **How do I connect most peripherals to my computer?** Today, many peripheral devices connect to your computer using an external **USB (universal serial bus) port**. USB is currently the most popular technology for connecting peripherals. A USB connector is shaped like a flat rectangle. Make sure you know which side of the plug is up; the top is usually labeled with the USB logo. See Figure B-30. USB ports are conveniently located on the front or sides of the system unit for easy access. Notebook computers often have USB ports on the sides and back of the computer case. Several types of storage devices, such as USB flash drives, also use USB connections.

FIGURE B-30: Plugging in a USB device

USB logo

Courtesy of MediaTechnics Corporation

● **Can I just unplug the peripheral device when I am done using it?** When you connect a peripheral device while the computer is operating, you are hot-plugging. You can only do this with USB and FireWire devices. Before you unplug a device, such as a USB flash drive, however, your computer might require notification. In Windows, you can give notification using the Safely Remove Hardware icon in the notification area of the taskbar. With a Mac, hold down the Control key, click the device icon, and then select Eject.

Talking Points: Why Recycle Computers?

For some people keeping up with technology means replacing their computer every few years. This raises the question: What should you do with your old, outdated computer? All of this electronic waste is creating e-garbage or technotrash—unwanted and outdated computers, monitors, printers, cell phones, PDAs, disk drives, disks, CDs, and DVDs. According to Greenpeace, 50 million tons of it is discarded every year. In the United States alone, almost eight printer cartridges are discarded every second. U.S. landfills already hold more than 2 million tons of computer parts, which contain toxic substances, such as lead, phosphorus, and mercury. For example, a computer monitor can contain up to six pounds of lead, and on average, contains four pounds of lead. People need to find creative ways to reuse their obsolete computers, such as retrofitting a hard drive to be a clock (see Figure B-31) or a monitor to be a fish tank.

> " In this world of rapidly changing technology, disposal of computers and other electronic equipment has created a new and growing waste stream. "
>
> *Environmental Protection Agency (EPA) report.*

Many computers end up in landfills because their owners are unaware of potential environmental hazards and simply toss them in the garbage. In addition, PC owners typically are not provided with information concerning the options for disposing of their old machines. Instead of throwing away your old computer, you might be able to sell it; donate it to a local school, church, or community program; have it hauled away by a professional recycling firm; or send it back to the manufacturer.

With the growing popularity of Internet auctions and dedicated computer reclamation sites, you might be able to get some cash for your old computer. At Web sites such as www.earth911.com, you can post an ad for your old computer equipment. Off the Web, you can find businesses that refurbish and sell old computers. Goodwill stores in many communities accept old computer equipment and arrange for it to be reused or recycled. Donating your old computer to a local organization does not actually eliminate the disposal problem, but it does delay it. Unfortunately, finding a new home for an old computer is not always easy. Most schools and community organizations have few resources for repairing broken equipment, so if your old computer is not in good working order, it could be more of a burden than a gift. In addition, your computer might be too old to be compatible with the other computers that are used in an organization.

FIGURE B-31: **Creative use of old computer parts**

Courtesy of TECOART LLC

It helps if you can donate software along with your old computer. To provide a legal transfer, include the software distribution media, manuals, and license agreement. And remember, once you donate the software, you cannot legally use it on your new computer unless it is freeware or shareware. If you cannot find an organization to accept your computer donation, look in your local Yellow Pages or on the Internet for an electronics recycling firm that will haul away your computer and recycle any usable materials.

In recent years, about half the states in the U.S. have taken some legislative action to curtail the rampant disposal of obsolete computer equipment. For example, Massachusetts has banned televisions and computer monitors from its landfills. In Maine it is illegal to dispose of computers or monitors—they have to be recycled in an environmentally sound way. But recycling can be costly—equipment needs to be collected, sorted, disassembled, and shipped to processing or disposal plants.

When Californians were faced with the prospect of tax hikes to deal with alarming increases in electronic waste, activists questioned if tax increases were fair to individual taxpayers who generate very little electronic waste. Now, consumers buying computers in California have to pay a recycling fee at the time of purchase. Maryland requires computer manufacturers to ante up an annual fee for electronic waste disposal.

Other lawmakers propose making manufacturers responsible for recycling costs and logistics. "Extended producer responsibility" refers to the idea of holding manufacturers responsible for the environmental effects of their products through their entire product life cycle, which includes taking them back, recycling them, or disposing of them. Some manufacturers currently participate in voluntary producer responsibility programs. Some companies have instituted PC recycling programs, which allow you to ship any make of computer, including system units, monitors, printers, and optional attachments, to a recycling center for a nominal fee. Consumers who buy toner cartridges for laser printers, such as from Hewlett-Packard, are provided with a postage-paid shipping box so they can return the cartridges for recycling. Dell offers free recycling for all Dell-branded products. Just connect to the Dell Web site, enter the equipment serial number, and fill out a shipping label.

The EPA advocates a national plan in which consumers, retailers, and manufacturers can cooperate to reduce electronic waste. Its Plug-in To eCycling Web site makes the point that "No national infrastructure exists for collecting, reusing, and recycling electronics." With laws that differ from state to state, consumers are often confused about how to dispose of their unwanted computers, monitors, CDs, and ink cartridges. These programs and others are important steps in the effort to keep our planet green.

As stated in an Environmental Protection Agency (EPA) report, "In this world of rapidly changing technology, disposal of computers and other electronic equipment has created a new and growing waste stream." Basic to the issue is the question of "Who pays?" Should it be the taxpayer, the individual, or the computer manufacturer?

" U.S. landfills already hold more than 2 million tons of computer parts, which contain toxic substances, such as lead, phosphorus, and mercury. "

Expand the Ideas

1. Have you ever thrown away an old computer or other electronic device? If so, how did you dispose of it? Did you donate it, pass it along, or just throw it in the garbage? Write a short essay explaining what your options were at the time, any thoughts about recycling or donating you might have had, and exactly how you got rid of the old computer.

2. Research options for recycling electronic equipment in your local area. Create a chart showing ways to get rid of an old computer, and include the positive and negative aspects of each option. Include specific details for recycling or donating the computers, such as names and addresses.

3. Is it fair to ask consumers to pay a recycling tax on any electronic equipment that they purchase? Research the current trends. Include any important legislation or pending legislation in your area or around the world that you feel is relevant. Compile your findings in a short report. Include your opinion in the conclusion.

Key Terms & Unit Review

Key Terms

Access time

BD (Blu-ray Disc)

BD drive

Bit depth

Card reader

CD (compact disc)

CD drive

Color depth

CompactFlash (CF) card

Cursor

Data bus

Data transfer rate

Device driver

Direct access

Display device

Dot pitch

Dots per inch (dpi)

Drive bay

Duplex printer

Duty cycle

DVD (digital video disc or digital versatile disc)

DVD drive

Expansion bay

Expansion bus

Expansion card

Expansion port

Expansion slot

File

Graphics card

Hard drive

Ink-jet printer

Input device

Insertion point

Laser mouse

Laser printer

LCD (liquid crystal display)

Magnetic storage

Memory stick

Millisecond (ms)

Mouse

Network-enabled printer

OLED (organic light emitting diodes)

Optical mouse

Optical storage

Pages per minute (ppm)

Photo printer

Pixel (picture element)

Pointing device

Printer resolution

RAM (random access memory)

Random access

Recordable technology

Resolution

Response rate

Rewritable technology

Scanner

Screen size

SecureDigital (SD) card

Sequential access

Solid-state drive (SSD)

Solid-state storage

Solid-state technology

Storage capacity

Storage device

Storage medium

Storage technology

Tape cartridge

Tape storage

Toner

Touch screen technology

Touchpad

Trackball

Trackpad

USB flash drive

USB (universal serial bus) port

Viewing angle width

Unit Review

1. Make sure that you can use your own words to define the bold terms that appear throughout the unit.

2. Create a table to summarize what you know about different input devices discussed in this unit.

3. Create a table to summarize what you know about different printer technologies discussed in this unit.

4. Describe the advantages and disadvantages of magnetic storage, optical storage, and solid-state storage. Give an example of each type of storage. Summarize important uses for each type of storage technology.

5. List three facts that explain why a hard drive is the main storage device for a computer.

6. Describe the differences between the various CD, DVD, and BD technologies and why you would use one over the other.

7. Summarize the different technologies available for display devices. Be sure to include advantages and disadvantages.

8. List any peripheral devices that are attached to your computer. Describe what each one does. Be sure to identify each one as input, output, or storage. Identify how it is connected to your system unit.

9. If possible, identify USB ports on your computer and list any devices you have connected through USB ports. Are the ports on the front or back of the system unit?

10. Look at the front of your computer and identify the devices that are in the drive bays. List each device and explain what it does.

Concepts Review

Select the best answer.

1. A(n) _____ storage system uses lasers to read data.
 a. magnetic
 b. optical
 c. solid state
 d. tape

2. The _____ keys include the Home, End, and arrow keys.
 a. main
 b. numeric
 c. navigation
 d. function

3. A computer can move directly to any file on a(n) _____ access device.
 a. random
 b. optical
 c. laser
 d. sequential

4. A standard desktop computer uses a _____ as its primary pointing device.
 a. navigation pad
 b. track pad
 c. keyboard
 d. mouse

5. You should use a _____, which has the most storage capacity, if you want to store a full-length feature movie.
 a. USB drive
 b. CD
 c. DVD
 d. Zip

6. Most DVD drives can read _____ and DVD formats.
 a. Flash
 b. Compact Flash
 c. CD
 d. BD

7. If you want to input data that currently exists in print format, you need to use a _____.
 a. microphone
 b. scanner
 c. digital camera
 d. Web cam

8. A variety of compact storage cards and flash drives can be classified as _____ storage, which stores data in a nonvolatile, erasable, low-power chip.
 a. solid-state
 b. optical
 c. magnetic
 d. digital

9. The technologies used by mice to track motion are _____ and laser.
 a. flash
 b. random
 c. optical
 d. digital

10. A USB _____ drive is a portable storage device featuring a built-in connector that plugs directly into a computer's USB port and requires no card reader.
 a. compact
 b. Blu-ray
 c. optical
 d. flash

11. A _____ and a printer are the two main output devices for a computer system.
 a. mouse
 b. monitor
 c. keyboard
 d. storage device

12. _____ displays have a brighter image, better viewing angle, and faster response rate than standard LCD screens.
 a. LED
 b. DVD
 c. CRT
 d. PPM

13. People set the display settings for their monitor to a higher _____ to be able to see more on a screen.
 a. dot pitch
 b. resolution
 c. viewing angle
 d. access time

14. A(n) _____ is used to enter data in kiosks or on computers where a keyboard is not easily used.
 a. BD
 b. track pad
 c. mouse
 d. touch screen

15. If your computer and others are connected to a(n) _____ you can share a printer.
 a. group
 b. Internet
 c. network
 d. kiosk

16. Popular inexpensive printers for personal computers that produce quality color printouts are _____ printers.
 a. ink jet
 b. thermal
 c. plasma
 d. duplex

17. The front of the system case for a desktop computer contains several _____ where devices such as CD and BD/DVD drives are installed.
 a. ports
 b. expansion slots
 c. drive bays
 d. USB drives

18. An expansion _____, often located on the back of a desktop computer, is a connector that passes data between a computer and a peripheral device.
 a. port
 b. slot
 c. drive
 d. bay

19. Many peripheral devices connect to an external USB (universal serial _____) port.
 a. belt
 b. bed
 c. bay
 d. bus

20. A(n) _____ card is a small circuit board with a port that makes it possible for a computer to communicate with a peripheral device, such as a storage device.
 a. expansion
 b. add-on
 c. peripheral
 d. graphic

Independent Challenges

Independent Challenge 1

Storage technology has a fascinating history. Mankind has developed many ways to retain and store data. From the ancient days when Egyptians were writing on papyrus to modern day and futuristic technologies, societies have found ways to retain more and more information in permanent and safe ways.

For this Independent Challenge:

1. Research the history of storage technologies and create a timeline that shows the developments. Be sure to include such items as 78-rpm records, 8-track tapes, floppy disks (all formats including 8", 5.25", and 3.5"). Your research should yield some interesting technologies and systems. See Figure B-32 for some examples.

FIGURE B-32: **Old storage media**

2. For each technology, list the media, the device used to retrieve the information, two significant facts about the technology, the era in which it was used or was popular, and explain either what led to its demise or why it is still popular.

3. You can create the timeline using images or just words. This is a creative project. Your best research, artistic, and communication skills should come together to create this timeline.

Independent Challenge 2

It is important that you are familiar with the type of computer you use daily. If you do not own your own computer, use a typical computer in the lab at your school or use a friend's computer to complete this exercise. You may need to consult your technical resource person to help you complete this independent challenge.

For this Independent Challenge:

1. Identify the parts on your computer. What type of computer are you using? What kind of system unit do you have?

2. What display device is attached to the computer? What type of technology does it use? What is the screen size? Do you know the resolution?

3. Is there a printer attached to the computer? Is it a network printer? What type of printer is it (laser, ink-jet)? What is the brand, model?

4. What storage devices are part of the computer? Are there removable devices in use for the computer? What type are they? How big is the hard drive on the computer?

5. What peripheral devices are attached to your computer? List the name, manufacturer, and model number of each device, if available. How are these devices attached or connected to your system unit?

6. Draw a sketch of your computer. Label each component and identify what it does.

Independent Challenge 3

Technology is ever-changing so it can be impossible to predict all the ways you might use your computer in the future. But if you purchase a computer that is expandable, you will increase the possibility of using your computer for a long time.

For this Independent Challenge:

1. Refer to the ad in Figure B-33. Use one color marker to highlight all the components that come with this computer system that would make it possible for you to use this computer for video chatting, listening to music, and creating and editing photographs.

2. Refer again to the ad in Figure B-33. Use a second color marker to highlight all the parts of this system that are part of data storage systems.

3. Refer to the ad in Figure B-34. Review the system, the peripherals that come with it, and the possibilities for expansion. Use one color market to highlight all the components that can be used to expand the system with peripheral devices. Use another color to highlight the peripheral devices that come with the system.

4. Use the Internet to research three peripheral devices you would like to add to any computer system, then explain the following for each component:

 a. Why would you like to add this peripheral device?

 b. What is the cost to add this peripheral device?

 c. What technology would you use to attach this device to your computer?

FIGURE B-33: **Computer ad for laptop PC**

- Intel Core i5-520M processor 2.4 GHz 1066 MHz FSB
- 3 MB L2 cache
- 4 GB DDR3-800 MHz dual channel SDRAM
- 500 GB SATA HD (7200 rpm)
- 8x CD/DVD burner (Dual Layer DVD+/-R)
- 15.6" High Def (720p) LCD display screen
- 512 MB NVIDIA GeForce graphics card
- HD Audio 2.0 Support SRS Sound
- Integrated 1.3 megapixel Webcam
- 4 USB ports
- 1 IEEE 1394 port
- VGA and HDMI graphics ports
- 5-in-1 Media card reader
- Wireless networking 802.11 g/n
- Integrated 10/100 network card
- Windows 7 Home Premium 64-bit operating system
- Home/small business software bundle
- 1-year limited warranty

Courtesy of MediaTechnics Corporation; © Cengage Learning

FIGURE B-34: **Computer ad for desktop PC**

- Intel Core 2 Quad Q9650 processor 3.0 GHz, 1333 MHz FSB
- 12 MB L2 cache
- 4 GB DDR2-800 MHz dual channel SDRAM
- 500 GB SATA HD (7200 rpm)
- 16X max. DVD+/-R/RW SuperMulti drive
- 20" WUXGA monitor
- 512 MB NVIDIA GeForce graphics card
- Creative Sound Blaster X-Fi Xtreme Audio sound card
- Logitech speakers
- Mouse and keyboard
- Storage bay: Portable Media Drive Bay
- 6 USB ports: 2 front, 4 back
- 2 IEEE 1394
- 1 network port (RJ45 connector)
- 7 expansion slots
- Windows 7 operating system
- Home/small business software bundle
- Ink-jet printer
- 1-year limited warranty

Courtesy of MediaTechnics Corporation; Used with permission from Microsoft; © Cengage Learning

Guide to Buying a Computer

As you prepare to buy a computer, there are a lot of decisions you have to make. This book is designed to help you build the knowledge base you need to purchase a computer. In this unit, you were introduced to the basics of computer hardware. Each subsequent unit covers topics that can help you understand the type of computer you need, the software and services that will enhance your computing experience, such as Internet access, software purchases, and so forth. After each unit, you will be asked to answer questions by completing a worksheet. By the end of the book, your Guide to Buying a Computer worksheet will provide comprehensive information about buying a computer.

To help you organize the information you will need when you are ready to buy a computer, you should complete the following activities.

1. Storage devices are not the most expensive part of your buying decision. However, you should consider your options to make the best decisions for the data you want to store. Refer to the table below for an overview of storage technologies.

Storage device	Cost of device	Storage medium used with device	Capacity	Cost of media (Disk/Disc)	Technology	Is it portable?
Hard drive (Internal)			80 GB–2 TB		Magnetic	No
Hard drive (External)			80 GB–2 TB		Magnetic	Yes
CD-RW drive			700 MB		Optical	Yes
DVD+RW drive			8.5 GB		Optical	Yes
Blu-ray/DVD writer			50 GB		Optical	Yes
USB flash drive			512 MB–64 GB	N/A	Solid state	Yes
Solid-state drive (SSD) (Internal)			32 GB–256 GB	N/A	Solid state	No
Solid-state drive (SSD) (External)			32 GB–256 GB		Solid state	Yes

© Cengage Learning

2. Log on to the Internet and research each of the storage systems listed above. Use your research to complete the table.

3. Think of the way you might use storage. Select three of the storage devices listed above that meet your storage needs and explain why you chose them. Do you need only one of these three storage systems or do you need a combination?

4. Deciding on the printer you want to buy depends on the tasks at hand. Are you planning to use the printer for a lot of reports? Are you printing photographs? Do you need speed? Log onto the Internet and research the two main printer types: inkjet and laser. Write the price comparisons for each.

5. To continue what you started in Unit A, complete this portion of the Guide to Buying a Computer worksheet. Before beginning this part of the exercise, think about how you are planning to use the computer. You may be planning to use your computer for popular tasks such as email, browsing the Web, playing a few games, managing your checkbook, downloading digital music, and writing school papers. Another possibility is that you spend lots of time playing computer games. You might be purchasing the computer for someone who has special needs that must be considered.

As you continue to work through this book, you will learn more about personal computer systems. You will have the opportunity to answer more questions and complete other tables with information that will help you when it is time to buy a computer. To help you think about the hardware you need for a personal computer system, complete this portion of the Guide to Buying a Computer worksheet.

Guide to Buying a Computer: Hardware considerations

Questions to consider	Pages where the topic is covered in this book (refer to these pages to read more about the topic)	Notes (add additional comments, clarifications, or ideas about each topic)
What type of storage devices do you need permanently installed on the system unit?		
What size hard drive do you need?		
What types of removable storage do you need?		
Will you need to create or burn CDs? DVDs? BDs?		
What type of input devices do you need, such as a keyboard?		
What type of pointing devices will you need?		
Will you need to enter sound or voice data?		
Do you need a touch screen?		
What type of monitor do you want to buy? What are the main considerations that will help you make this decision?		
What type of printer do you want to buy?		
Do you need fast printing? Do you need to print in color? What are the main considerations that will help you make this decision?		
Do you need high-quality printouts? What are the main considerations that will help you make this decision?		
What peripheral devices will you need?		
If you choose a notebook, are these devices available?		
If you choose a desktop, is expansion possible?		
How many expansion slots should the computer system have?		
How many USB ports should the computer system have?		
If you choose a notebook or tablet computer, is expansion possible? How?		

Visual Workshop

The Talking Points section of this unit focused on the environmental impact of improperly discarded computers and other electronic devices. Some manufacturers are doing what they can to reduce the toxicity of components. Others are encouraging recycling. For this Visual Workshop, you will write a short paper about recycling computers based on information that you gather from the Internet. You will use the information you gather to create a poster for a campaign to promote Green Computing or responsible recycling in your community. Figure B-35 shows a possible theme for a poster.

1. Connect to the Internet and use your favorite search engine to search for and find Web pages to get an in-depth overview of the environmental impact and issues relating to the use and disposal of electronic devices and computers.

2. Determine the specific aspect of the issue that you will present in your paper. You might, for example, decide to focus on the toxic materials contained in computers that end up in landfills. You might investigate labor laws that protect those who dismantle computer parts for scrap. Current laws for shipping electronic devices such as monitors, printers, and computer parts to developing nations depend on the plan for the e-trash. If the plan is to use the computers, laws are more lenient. If the plan is to scrap the devices for their copper, lead, and gold, then the laws are more strict. Often people are hired to work in deplorable conditions without regard to the toxicity of the materials they are touching and breathing. You can investigate the government regulations that help to discourage the shipment of old computers across national borders or try to protect those who work in the scrapping industry.

3. Whatever aspect of the issue you decide to present, make sure that you can back up your discussion with facts and references to authoritative articles and Web pages. Place citations to your references (include the author's name, article title, date of publication, and URL) according to your instructor's directions, such as at the end of your paper as endnotes, on each page as footnotes, or in parentheses following the appropriate paragraphs. Follow your instructor's directions for submitting your paper via email or as a printed document.

4. After completing the paper, consider the main points that you want to convey in a poster to your community. Use paper to sketch out your ideas. Complete the poster using poster board. Follow your instructor's directions for submitting the poster.

FIGURE B-35: **Recycling poster**

e-waste + e-trash = toxic Environment

Get the picture? RECYCLE.

© Shipov Oleg/Shutterstock.com; © Cengage Learning

UNIT C
Concepts

Computer Software

Learning Objectives

1. List and describe computer software categories
2. Explain copyright law and define the different software licenses
3. Explain how to install and uninstall software
4. Identify the basic functions and features of operating systems
5. Compare operating systems
6. Describe utility software, including device drivers
7. Define office productivity software, and name examples in each major category
8. Define graphics software, and name examples in each major category
9. Name other categories of application software, and give examples in each major category

LESSON TOPICS

- Computer Software
- Licenses and Copyrights
- How to Install and Uninstall Software
- Operating Systems—An Overview
- Operating Systems—A Comparison
- Utility Software
- Office Productivity Software
- Graphics Software
- Other Application Software

Talking Points: What is the Downside to Software Piracy?

Courtesy of Emily Bunin

Computer Software

Software, also called **computer programs**, gives computers the instructions and data necessary to carry out tasks. Software is used to create documents or graphics. Software is used to help schedule classes or to listen to music. Software makes it possible to communicate using computers. Most software uses a **graphical user interface (GUI)**. This allows you to give the computer commands using pointing devices and graphics such as menus, buttons, icons, links, and more.

Learning Objective 1:
List and describe computer software categories

● **When do I use software?** You use software every time you use your desktop, notebook, or tablet computer. In addition, you use software when you use your mobile phone, digital camera, retail and banking machines, some home appliances, cars, some medical devices, and much more. Software carries out your commands anytime you press buttons or touch a screen to tell a machine what to do.

● **Are there different types of software?** Yes. Software is usually categorized as either system software or application software. **System software** is used by the computer for tasks that help the computer work. For example, you use system software to run your computer and all the programs on it. It can diagnose a problem with your hard drive, printer, or Internet connection. **Application software** helps you carry out tasks such as sending an email, getting you street-by-street driving directions, editing a photo, or writing a report.

Software can be grouped in subcategories according to how the software is used. System software can be grouped into subcategories for operating systems, utilities, and device drivers. Application software can be grouped according to tasks, such as producing documents, creating spreadsheets, or communicating with others. Figure C-1 shows common ways to categorize system software and application software. Some software can be in more than one category, so use these categories as a general guideline.

● **Are there other ways to group software?** Yes. Software applications can also be categorized according to their accessibility and where they are installed. These categories include local applications, Web applications, portable applications, or mobile applications.

FIGURE C-1: **Examples of software categories**

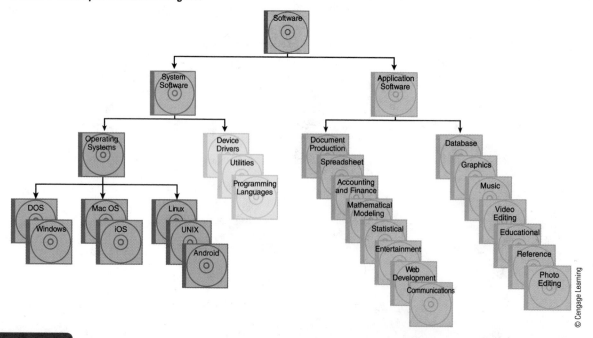

- **What is a local application?** A **local application** is software that is installed on a computer. When you install a local application, the program files are placed in the appropriate folders on the computer's hard drive. After the software is installed, the computer makes sure the program is ready to run.

- **What is a Web application?** A **Web application** (also called **Web app** or **cloudware**) is software that is accessed with a Web browser. Instead of running locally on a computer, much of the program code for the software runs on a remote computer connected to the Internet or other computer network. Web apps are available for many of the same applications that run locally. These include email, calendars, databases, photo sharing, project management, maps, games, and even word processing. Web apps make it possible for groups of people to collaborate on projects in multiple locations.

 The advantage of a Web app is that you can use it anywhere you have access to a computer connected to the Web. However, there are also disadvantages when using Web apps. For example, you don't have access to the Web app if you lose power to your computer or if you lose your Internet connection. And, you don't have access if the Internet server hosting the Web app goes down.

- **What is a portable application?** A **portable application** is designed to run from a removable storage device, such as a USB flash drive. Program files are not installed on the hard drive, and no configuration data is stored on the computer. When the media containing the portable software is removed from the computer, no trace of the portable application is left on the computer. Portable software can only be used when the removable storage device is connected to a computer.

- **What is a mobile application?** A **mobile application** (or **app**) is designed to run on mobile devices such as smartphones and tablet computers. Mobile apps include games, calendars, stock market trackers, tour guides, highway traffic monitors, news feeds, and more.

- **How do I know if a software program will work on my computer?** The **system requirements**, which specify the operating system and minimum hardware capacities, give you the information you need to know if a software program will work on a computer. You can find the system requirements on the software manufacturer's Web site or on the software packaging. See Figure C-2.

FIGURE C-2: **System requirements**

System Requirements

Operating Systems: Windows 7/Vista/XP
Processor: Intel Pentium or Core or equivalent
Memory: 1 GB or more
Hard Drive Space: 10 MB for installation
Network Protocol: TCP/IP
Network Connection: 10/100 Ethernet LAN/WAN, cable modem, DSL router, ISDN router, or dial-up modem

eCourse Internet Works

2012 eCourseWare Corp. All rights reserved. eCourse is a registered trademark of eCourseWare Corp.

Installed software that comes with new personal computers

Most computers are sold with the operating system installed so you can turn on the machine and use it right away. The operating system, Windows 7 for example, typically includes a Web browser, media player, and several simple programs. These include a simple text editor, a few games, and some gadgets. Some computers come with application software that you can use to create documents, manage budgets, and produce presentations. Your computer may come with antivirus software. Be sure to check the terms of the application software that is installed. The trend today is for manufacturers to install trial software that you can use free for a few months. To continue using the software beyond the trial period, however, you have to pay for it. If you're purchasing a computer to do a task that requires specialized software, you should factor its cost into the cost of your computer system. Check the specifications listed on the software box to make sure your new computer has enough memory and processing speed to run it.

Licenses and Copyrights

Just because it is easy to copy and share other people's documents, photographs, and music though email or post it on your Web site, doesn't mean it's legal to do so. Copyright and intellectual property laws, as well as the software license, govern how you can use **digital content.** This includes digital content you buy at a brick-and-mortar store or download from the Web using a computer. Understanding copyright law and software licenses for digital content will help you avoid legal troubles.

Learning Objective 2:
Explain copyright law and define the different software licenses

● **What is copyright? Copyright** is a legal protection that grants the author of an original work an exclusive right to copy, distribute, sell, and modify that work, except under special circumstances described by copyright laws. Exceptions include the purchaser's right to copy software from a distribution disc or Web site to a computer's hard drive in order to install it.

● **If I don't see the © symbol, does it mean the software is not protected?** Most software displays a **copyright notice,** such as "© 2014 Microsoft Corporation. All Rights reserved," on one of its starting screens. However, this notice is not required by law. As a result, even programs without a copyright notice are protected by copyright law. People who go around copyright law and illegally copy, distribute, or modify software are sometimes called **software pirates.** Their illegal copies are referred to as **pirated software.**

● **What is a software license?** A **software license,** or **license agreement,** is a legal contract that lets you know the ways in which you may use or share that computer program. Once you purchase software, or even if you get software for free, you can only use the software as defined by the software license. The type of license determines how the software is classified legally.

● **How is software classified legally?** Software is legally classified in two categories: public domain and proprietary. **Public domain software** is not protected by copyright because the copyright has expired, or the author has placed the program in the public domain making it available without restriction. Public domain software may be freely copied, distributed, and even resold. The primary restriction on public domain software is that you are not allowed to apply for a copyright on it.

Creative commons is an organization committed to freely sharing content on the Internet. See Figure C-3. Their Web site explains licensing options for distributing software.

FIGURE C-3: **Creative commons Web site**

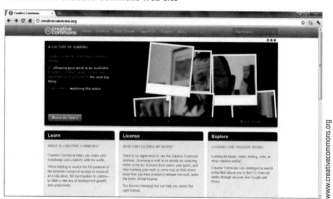

www.creativecommons.org

Proprietary software has restrictions on its use that are delineated by copyright, patents, or license agreements. Some proprietary software is distributed commercially, whereas some of it is free. Depending on the licensing rights, proprietary software is distributed as commercial software, demoware, shareware, freeware, or open source software. These classifications determine the software license.

● **What is commercial software? Commercial software** is typically sold in stores or on Web sites. Although you buy this software, you actually purchase only the right to use it under the terms of the software license. Some commercial software is available as a trial version, called **demoware.** Demoware is distributed free and often comes preinstalled on new computers. Demoware is limited in some way until you pay for it. Demoware publishers usually take steps to prevent users from overriding time limitations.

- **What is shareware?** Shareware is copyrighted software marketed under a try-before-you-buy policy. It typically includes a license that permits you to use the software for a trial period. To use it beyond the trial period, you must send in a registration fee. A shareware license usually allows you to make copies of the software and distribute it to others. If they choose to use the software, they must send in a registration fee. Registration fee payment relies on the honor system. Unfortunately, many shareware authors collect only a fraction of the money they deserve for their programming efforts.

- **What is freeware?** Freeware is copyrighted software that is available without a fee. Because the software is protected by copyright, you cannot do anything with it that is not expressly allowed by copyright law or by the author. Typically, the license for freeware permits you to use the software, copy it, and give it away, but does not permit you to alter it or sell it. Many utility programs, device drivers, and some games are available as freeware.

- **What is open source software?** Open source software makes the program instructions available to programmers who want to modify and improve the software. Open source software may be sold or distributed free of charge, but it must, in every case, include the source code. The Firefox browser is open source software. The Open Source Initiative is a non-profit corporation that advocates for open source software. See Figure C-4.

FIGURE C-4: Open Source Initiative

The OSI logo trademark is the trademark of Open Source Initiative.

- **Do I have to accept the license agreement to run the software?** Yes, usually before you install and run a program, you have to agree to the terms as stated in the EULA (end-user license agreement). The EULA displays on the screen when you install the software. You can indicate that you accept the terms by clicking a designated button or check box labeled OK, I agree, or I accept. See Figure C-5.

FIGURE C-5: Microsoft Office 2010 software license

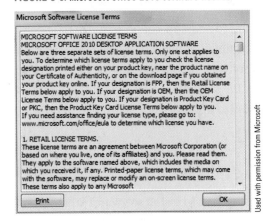

Used with permission from Microsoft

- **Since I didn't actually sign anything, am I still legally bound to this license?** Yes, while most legal contracts require signatures before the terms take effect, software publishers typically use two techniques to validate a software license. A shrink-wrap license goes into effect as soon as you open the packaging. Downloaded software has an installation agreement that goes into effect as soon as you click the option to accept the terms of the agreement.

- **What software licenses are available?** A single-user license limits use of the software to one person at a time. A site license is generally priced at a flat rate and allows software to be used on all computers at a specific location. A multiple-user license is priced per user and allows the allocated number of people to use the software at any time. A concurrent-use license is priced per copy and allows a specific number of copies to be used at the same time.

How does digital technology affect intellectual property laws?

Intellectual property refers to the ownership of certain types of information, ideas, or representations. It includes patents, trademarks, and copyrighted material, such as music, photos, software, books, and films. In the past, such works were difficult and expensive to copy. However, digital technology has made it easy to produce copies with no loss in quality from the original. Pirating software is simple and inexpensive. It has caused significant revenue loss for software publishers, as well as recording studios, and film producers. The fight against piracy takes many forms. Governments have passed strict anti-piracy laws. Technology is available that scrambles and encrypts content. Several companies use digital rights management technology that physically prevents copying. Organizations such as the Software & Information Industry Association have committed to consumer education and created anti-piracy videos that are shown to the public. See Figure C-6.

FIGURE C-6: Educating the public

Courtesy of the Software & Information Industry Association

UNIT
C
Concepts

How To Install and Uninstall Software

You often want to add application software or apps to your digital device. Software can be obtained in many ways, such as on distribution media (CD, DVD, or BD) or downloaded from the Web. Unless you are using Web apps, you must install software before you can use it. Installation procedures depend on your computer's operating system and whether the software is a local, portable, or mobile application. In addition to installing software, you should also know how to upgrade your software and how to uninstall software you no longer need.

Learning Objective 3:
Explain how to install and uninstall software

● **What does it mean to install software?** When you install software, you are copying the software from a distribution media, such as from a CD, DVD, BD or the Web, to your hard drive so you can use the program. You generally won't install the OS. It usually comes installed on the computer or mobile device when you buy it.

● **How do I start the installation process?** To install software from a CD or a DVD, place the disc in the CD or DVD drive. Once the disc is in the drive, you will see blinking lights on the drive and information will appear on your screen as a setup program starts.

To install software from the Web, read any information on the Web site about installing the software, then click the download link. See Figure C-7. The files you need will be downloaded and copied to a folder on your computer. Downloaded software files are usually zipped into one large compressed file. Compressed files are smaller so they download faster. Some compressed files are zip files, others are executable files. You will learn about file compression in the lesson on utilities. Once the files are downloaded, a setup program starts.

FIGURE C-7: **Downloading software**

If you are downloading from a trusted site and have antivirus software running, click the Run button in the File Download dialog box.

The files are downloaded to your computer.

● **What is a setup program?** A **setup program** is a series of steps designed to guide you through the installation process. You follow directions as prompted on the screen to complete the installation process. If you are installing software from the Web, the downloaded zip file is unzipped into the original collection of files and into a folder that you can specify during the installation process. As part of the installation process, you will be asked to accept the end user license agreement (EULA).

● **How do I know where the software is installed?** During the installation process, you will be prompted to specify the location where you want to store the program files. See Figure C-8. You can use the default folder specified by the setup program or a folder of your own choosing. You can also create a new folder during the setup process. Generally, when you install software, the new software files are placed in the appropriate folders on your computer's hard drive.

FIGURE C-8: **Select the location on the hard drive for the files**

● **What type of installation should I choose?** During the installation process, you are asked what type of installation you want: full or custom. If you select a full installation, the setup program copies all files and data from the distribution medium to the hard drive of your computer system. A full installation gives you access to all features of the software. If you select a custom installation, the setup program displays a list of software features for your selection.

Computer Software

After you select the features you want, the setup program copies only the selected program and data files to your hard drive. A custom installation can save space on your hard drive but limits functionality of the program because not all features are installed. Select the installation option that best meets your needs. See Figure C-9.

FIGURE C-9: **Select the type of installation**

⦿ **Full Installation**
◯ **Custom Installation**

© Cengage Learning

● **What else happens during the installation process?** As part of the installation process, your computer performs any software or hardware configurations necessary to make sure the program is ready to run.

● **How do I start the program?** When the installation is complete, you should start the program you just installed to make sure it works. Techniques for running applications depend on your computer's operating system. On most personal computers, you can double-click an application desktop icon, click a program icon on the taskbar or Dock, or you can select the application from a menu. See Figure C-10.

FIGURE C-10: **Many ways to start an application**

Double-click a desktop icon

Click the Start button, then click a menu item

Click a program button on the taskbar

Used with permission from Microsoft

● **Do I have to activate the software?** Yes. Although you may be allowed to run a program for a set number of times before activation, generally you need to activate the program for long-term use. To combat piracy, many software publishers require users to type in a validation code to complete an installation and activate the software. A **validation code** is a long sequence of numbers and letters that is typically supplied separately from the software itself. Validation codes can usually be found on distribution media packaging. If you download the software, the validation code is sent to you via email.

● **What is software registration?** Software registration collects your personal information, such as your email address. Generally, product activation is not the same as registration. A few software publishers tie activation and registration together. Activation is required but registration is voluntary.

● **Why would I want to register my software?** You register your software in order to receive product information and updates.

● **What are software updates?** After you install your software, several types of updates are usually available. These updates are patches, service packs, and software upgrades. **Patches** are small programs designed to correct, secure, or enhance an existing program. **Service packs** are a collection of updates, fixes, and/or enhancements to a software program delivered in the form of a single installable package. They are usually distributed over the Internet. Patches and service packs automatically install themselves when you download them. **Software upgrades** are available to consumers who already have a software program installed. Software upgrades are usually less expensive than buying the software package new.

● **How do I remove software I don't need anymore?** Most software programs come with an uninstall program. In addition, most operating systems, such as Windows and Mac OS, provide access to an uninstall program. Uninstall programs are designed to delete all the related program files from your computer's program and system folders on the hard drive and from the desktop.

Unit C

Installing portable software

Portable software is so simple to install that it is sometimes referred to as install-free software. Installation is simply a matter of transferring program files to the media on which they are supposed to run. For example, suppose that you want to run OpenOffice Portable from a USB flash drive. You can download the OpenOffice Portable zip file and then simply unzip it so that the files are saved on the USB flash drive. Other examples of portable applications include Thunderbird (email), Firefox (browser), and FileZilla (ftp upload and download). Each of these portable applications is designed to run from USB flash drives.

Operating Systems— An Overview

An **operating system (OS)** is system software. It is the master controller for all of the activities that take place in any computer system, including desktop, notebook, and tablet computers as well as smartphones and other mobile devices. The operating system determines how people interact with a digital device. It also controls how a digital device communicates with other computers on a network or peripheral devices such as printers and scanners.

Learning Objective 4:
Identify the basic functions and features of an operating system

● **How do I start the operating system?** The operating system starts each time you turn on your computer or digital device. The first task of the operating system when you turn on a computer is to start the **boot process**. This is why turning on a computer is also called "booting a computer." Six major events happen during the boot process. Refer to Table C-1.

TABLE C-1: **Six steps in the boot process**

Step	Description
1. Power up	When you turn on the power switch, the power light is illuminated and power is distributed to the computer circuitry.
2. Start bootstrap program	The processor begins to execute the bootstrap program that is stored in permanent memory called ROM.
3. Power-on self-test (POST)	The operating system performs diagnostic tests of several crucial system parts.
4. Identify peripheral devices	The operating system identifies the peripheral devices that are connected to the computer and checks their settings.
5. Load operating system	The operating system is copied from the hard drive to Random Access Memory (RAM).
6. Check configuration and customization	The operating system reads configuration data and the processor executes any customized startup routines.

© Cengage Learning

● **What does the operating system do?** Your computer's operating system ensures that input and output proceed in an orderly manner. It provides buffers to hold data while the computer is busy with other tasks. A **buffer** is an area of memory that holds data from one device while it is waiting to be transferred to another device. By using a keyboard buffer, for example, your computer never misses one of your

keystrokes, regardless of how fast you type. In addition, the operating system manages a computer's resources by interacting with your computer's software and hardware. See Figure C-11.

FIGURE C-11: **Example of how the operating system works**

1. You issue the Print command while using application software, such as a word processor.

2. The word processing application signals the operating system that a document must be sent to the printer.

Printer Driver

3. The operating system communicates the document data to the device driver for the printer.

4. The device driver controls the printer as it prints the document.

Courtesy of Media Technics Corporation

● **What is a computer's resource?** The term **resource** refers to any computer component that is required to perform work. For example, computer resources include the CPU (central processing unit), RAM, storage devices, and peripherals. While you

interact with application software, your computer's operating system is busy behind the scenes with resource management tasks such as those listed in Figure C-12.

FIGURE C-12: Resource management tasks

 Manage processor resources to handle simultaneous input, output, and processing tasks

 Manage memory by allocating space for all the programs and data that are in use during a computing session

 Keep track of storage resources so that files and programs can be found

 Ensure that input and output proceed in an orderly manner by communicating with peripheral devices

Establish basic elements of the user interface such as the appearance of the desktop, menus, and toolbars

Courtesy of MediaTechnics Corporation; © Sergei Devyatkin/Shutterstock.com; Used with permission from Microsoft

● **How does the operating system let you know there is a problem?** The operating system displays messages on the device screen if it encounters a problem. For example, if a device driver or a peripheral device is not performing correctly, the operating system usually displays an on-screen warning about the problem so you can take corrective action.

● **How do I know what programs are currently running on my computer?** When using Windows, you can open the Task Manager to see a list of programs. See Figure C-13. The operating system is **multitasking** when more than one program is running at one time. In addition to programs, many activities—called processes—compete for the attention of your computer's processor. Most processes are programs that run in the background to carry out tasks for the operating system, device drivers, and applications. You can see the list of processes that are running by clicking the Processes tab in the Task Manager.

FIGURE C-13: Windows 7 Task Manager

Used with permission from Microsoft

● **How do I use the operating system?** Although its main purpose is to control what happens behind the scenes of a computer system, many operating systems provide tools to make computing easier or more fun for you. You can use these operating system utilities to control and customize your computer equipment and work environment. The Windows Control Panel lets you personalize many features. See Figure C-14. For example, using options in the Control Panel, you can change your display properties, such as adjusting your screen resolution or setting a screen saver. Table C-2 lists some ways you interact with your computer's OS.

FIGURE C-14: Windows 7 Control Panel

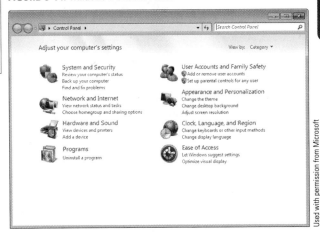

Used with permission from Microsoft

TABLE C-2: Ways you use an operating system

You can	Most operating systems
Launch programs	display graphical objects such as icons, a Start button, and the Programs menu that you can use to start programs
Manage files	include programs, such as Windows Explorer, that allow you to view a list of folders and files, move them to different storage devices, copy them, rename them, and delete them
Get help	offer a Help system that you can use to find out more about the OS, such as how various commands work
Customize the user interface environment	provide utilities that help you customize your screen display, system sounds, security and access
Configure equipment and install and uninstall programs	provide access to utilities that help you set up and configure your computer's hardware and peripheral devices, install and uninstall software

© Cengage Learning

Computer Software

Operating Systems—A Comparison

When you purchase a personal computer, it generally comes with the OS already installed. When you purchase a mobile device, it also usually comes with an operating system already installed. The operating system you use depends on the type of personal computer or digital device you use, as well as the type of processor running your personal computer or digital device. The operating system determines the user interface on your digital device.

Learning Objective 5:
Compare operating systems

● **What is a user interface?** A **user interface** is the combination of hardware and software that helps you communicate with a computer. Your computer's user interface includes a display device, mouse, and keyboard as well as software elements, such as icons, toolbars, menus, and command buttons. This combination of hardware and software determines how you interact with your computer. When a user interface has graphical elements, it is called a graphical user interface (GUI).

● **What are the main operating systems in use today for personal computers?** The three main operating systems for personal computers in use today are **Windows**, **Mac OS**, and **Linux**. The Windows operating system is installed on PCs. The Mac OS is installed on Apple computers. Linux can be installed on PCs. Each operating system has different versions, such as home or professional.

● **Why are there different versions of an operating system?** There are different versions to meet the wide range of consumer needs. For example, your home personal computer probably doesn't need as powerful an operating system as a computer used in a large business. You need your computer to perform basic tasks. A business may need its computers to perform basic tasks as well as network with other computers in the company. Different versions allow users to buy the operating system to best meet their needs. For example, Microsoft offers several versions, called editions, of the Windows operating system for various markets. As a consumer, you can choose from among these editions of Windows 7: Home Premium, Professional, and Ultimate. Each edition has features that meet specific markets or needs.

In addition to the desktop version, there are also server and embedded versions of Microsoft Windows. Server editions are designed for LAN, Internet, and Web servers. Embedded editions are designed for handheld devices, such as tablets and mobile phones.

● **Which version of Windows will probably be on my computer?** If you purchase a PC, it will probably be running the most current desktop version of Windows for personal computers. Windows 7 is a desktop operating system. See Figure C-15. Since its introduction in 1985, Windows has evolved through several versions. The latest version boasts easy personalization, enhanced security, flexible file management, and powerful search capabilities. A newer version, Windows 8, is currently being released. The Start button on the taskbar helps you recognize that the computer is running Windows.

FIGURE C-15: **Windows 7 User Interface**

Used with permission from Microsoft

● **What operating system is available for the Macintosh computer?** Mac OS X (the X can be pronounced either as ten or the letter X) is the operating system used on Apple Macintosh computers. Like Windows, Mac OS X has also been through a number of versions.

Versions of Mac OS X are named after big cats; the current version is named Lion. Previous versions include Snow Leopard, Cheetah, Puma, Jaguar, Panther, Tiger, and Leopard. The Apple logo at the top of the screen on the menu bar and the Dock at the bottom of the desktop help you recognize that the computer is running Mac OS.

● **What is Linux?** Linux is an operating system that is available as a free download. Linux was developed by Linus Torvalds in 1991. The Linux operating system is distributed under the terms of a **General Public License (GPL)**, which allows everyone to make copies for his or her own use, to give it to others, or to sell it. This licensing policy has encouraged programmers to develop Linux utilities, software, and enhancements. Linux is gaining popularity as a personal computer operating system. See Figure C-16.

FIGURE C-16: **The Ubuntu Linux operating system interface**

Courtesy of Canonical Ltd.

● **What operating systems run on tablet computers?** Leading tablet operating systems include Windows, BlackBerry®, Android, and iOS. Tablets running Windows include Lenovo, IdeaPad, and HP Slate. Tablets running the BlackBerry® Tablet OS include the BlackBerry®

PlayBook™ tablet. Tablets running Android are made by many manufacturers including Motorola, Samsung, and Toshiba. Apple tablets run the proprietary iOS Apple operating systems. See Figure C-17.

FIGURE C-17: **Tablet computer operating systems**

BlackBerry®, RIM®, Research In Motion® and related trademarks, names and logos are the property of Research In Motion Limited and are registered and/or used in the U.S. and countries around the world.; Used under license from Research In Motion Limited.; © Christine Glade/iStockphoto

● **What operating systems run on smartphones?** Smartphones are essentially communications devices so their operating systems need to accommodate voice as well as data on very small screens. These special requirements are met by several operating systems. Some manufactures produce smartphone models that use different mobile operating systems. See Figure C-18. For example, you can buy one Sony smartphone that runs Android and a different Sony smartphone that runs Windows Mobile 7.

FIGURE C-18: **Smartphone operating systems**

From left: Used by permission from Microsoft; Courtesy of Google Inc. Android is a trademark of Google Inc.; © amriphoto/iStockphoto

Comparing types of operating systems

Operating systems for computers, notebooks, and mobile devices provide many similar services, such as scheduling processor resources, managing memory, loading programs, managing input and output, and creating the user interface. But because mobile devices, such as smartphones and tablets, tend to be used for less sophisticated tasks, their operating systems are simpler and significantly smaller. By keeping the operating system small, it can be stored in ROM. Because operating systems for these mobile devices do not need to load the OS from the disk into RAM, these mobile devices are ready almost instantly when they are turned on.

Operating systems for mobile devices often provide built-in support for touch screens, handwriting input, wireless networking, and cellular communications. Touch screen input makes it possible to use fingers to swipe, squeeze, and expand content in order to control the size and placement of objects on the screen.

UNIT C
Concepts

Utility Software

As you use your computer, you will find it is important to keep it in good working order. Utility software can help you do just that. **Utility software** (also referred to as **utilities**) is a type of system software designed to perform a specialized task. Examples of utility software include diagnostic and maintenance tools, setup wizards, communications programs, security software, device drives, and gadgets.

Learning Objective 6:
Describe utility software, including device drivers

● **Why do I need utility software?** You need utility software to help maintain your computer and safeguard your files. Utility software helps you monitor and configure settings for your computer system hardware, the operating system, and application software. Utilities are used for backing up, securing, permanently deleting, and cleaning up files on hard drives. These utilities include security features for shredding files so they cannot be recovered. Other utilities can help you recover files deleted (but not shredded) by mistake. Utility software includes diagnostics that track down file errors and other problems that prevent computers from running at peak efficiency. These utilities can also give your PC a performance-enhancing tune-up. See Figure C-19.

FIGURE C-19: **Example of a utility to optimize your system**

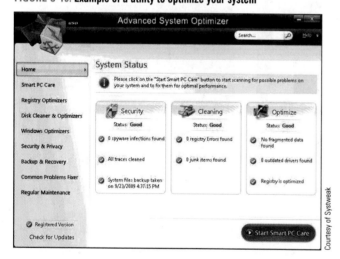

Courtesy of Systweak

● **Do any utilities come with the operating system?** Yes. A variety of utilities are included with your operating system. For example, Figure C-20 shows the System and Security utilities, which provides access to the many Windows operating system utilities. You use the Control Panel to access the System and Security utilities. You can access the Control Panel using the Windows Start menu.

FIGURE C-20: **Microsoft Windows System and Security utilities**

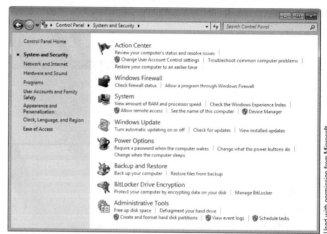

Used with permission from Microsoft

● **Do I always have to run the utilities or are some automatic?** There are operating system utilities that run in the background. For example, one Windows utility periodically sets a **restore point**, which is a snapshot of your computer settings. Restore points are created automatically every week, and just before significant system events, such as the installation of a program or device driver. If a hard drive problem causes system instability, you might be able to roll back your system to a restore point when your computer was operational. You can manually set restore points, too. For example, you might want to set a restore point before setting up a network. You do this so you can restore your system to the way it was before the installation if unexpected problems are created when you set up a network. This can save you a lot of time and aggravation.

● **Do I have to use the utilities that come with my operating system or do I have other choices?** You have choices. In addition to utilities that come with your operating system, other third-party utilities are available. You will typically use utilities from third-party vendors because operating system utilities are often not as comprehensive or

Computer Software

do not provide as many features as third-party utilities. Third-party utilities are designed by companies that specialize in system maintenance or security.

- **What are some utility programs I should know about?** If you work with large files, you might use a **compression utility** to reduce file size for quick transmission or efficient storage. The Windows operating system comes with a file compression utility. Many computer owners prefer to use a third-party utility, such as WinZip, IZArc, Quick Zip, or PKZIP.

 You will also want to use **security utilities**. These utilities can scan incoming and outgoing files to be sure they are safe. They can scan your applications to see if any are missing security patches. They can also help you control nuisance ads, intrusion attempts, and spam. Other security-related utilities include file-encryption software that scrambles file content for storage or transmission. You can also buy utilities that remove Internet history lists, files, and graphics from disk storage locations that can be scattered in many parts of the hard drive.

- **Can utilities help me customize my desktop?** Yes, for example, you can use utilities to customize your desktop with screen savers that display clever graphics when the machine is idle. Different themes can change the way fonts are displayed in menus and icons in programs. Themes can also customize sounds that are played when operating system events occur. For example, when an action doesn't work, you might hear a buzzer.

- **What is PDF?** PDF stands for Portable Document File. The PDF file format is used so that a document can be read by people regardless of what type of computers they are using or the software they have installed on their computers. To read a PDF file, you need a document reader utility, such as the popular and free Adobe Reader. Links to download Adobe Reader are available on many Web sites. See Figure C-21.

FIGURE C-21: Adobe Reader is a free utility to read PDF files

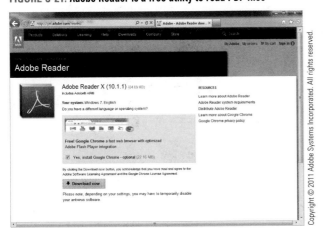

- **What is a device driver?** A **device driver** is a type of utility software that helps a peripheral device to establish communication with a computer. Device drivers are used by printers, monitors, graphics cards, sound cards, network cards, modems, storage devices, mice, and scanners. Once installed, a device driver starts automatically when it is needed. Device drivers usually run in the background, without opening a window on the screen. On a PC, the Windows Device Manager offers access to device drivers so you can check if they are working, change settings, and check the device driver's version number to compare it with the most recent version posted online. See Figure C-22.

FIGURE C-22: **Checking device driver details**

- **What is a desktop gadget or widget?** A **desktop gadget** or **gadget** (called a **widget** on Apple computers) is a utility program that is placed on a computer's desktop. It looks like a control and might display a snippet of information. Some examples of desktop gadget include clocks, calendars, calculators, news aggregators, sticky notes, and weather stations. Gadgets usually start automatically when a computer boots, and they remain on the desktop until the computer is shut down. Figure C-23 illustrates some popular gadgets on a PC desktop.

FIGURE C-23: **Desktop gadgets**

Computer Software

If you work in an office, you will use a computer to create documents, schedule meetings, send email, manage numbers, make presentations, and organize data. **Office productivity software** (also called **productivity software**) is generally defined as the software that allows you to be productive in an office setting. It integrates these major software categories: word processing, spreadsheet, presentation, database, and scheduling.

Learning Objective 7:
Define office productivity software, and name examples in each major category

- **What is word processing software? Word processing software** is used to produce documents, such as reports, letters, books, blogs, and manuscripts. If you are writing a paper, writing a blog, or organizing your résumé, you will probably use a word processor. Word processors allow you to apply a theme and styles to create a unified look across documents using the same word processing program. They give you the ability to create, check the spelling, edit, and format a document on the screen before you commit it to paper. See Figure C-24. Microsoft Word and OpenOffice Writer are examples of word processors.

FIGURE C-24: **Checking the spelling of a document in Microsoft Word**

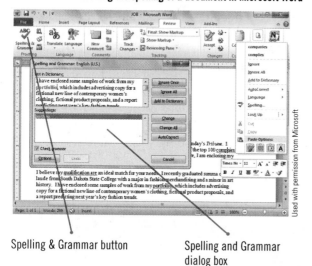

Spelling & Grammar button Spelling and Grammar dialog box

Used with permission from Microsoft

- **What is spreadsheet software? Spreadsheet software** is ideal for projects that require repetitive calculations, such as budgeting, maintaining a grade book, balancing a checkbook, tracking investments, and calculating loan payments. Because it is so easy to experiment with different numbers, spreadsheet software is useful for what-if analysis. Spreadsheet software can generate colorful graphs and charts based on the data in the spreadsheet. Spreadsheet software provides the tools to create electronic worksheets. A **worksheet** is a grid of columns and rows. See Figure C-25. Microsoft Excel and OpenOffice Calc are examples of spreadsheet programs.

FIGURE C-25: **A spreadsheet in OpenOffice Calc**

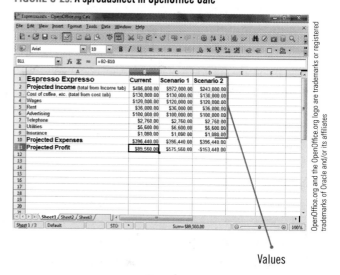

Values

OpenOffice.org and the OpenOffice.org logo are trademarks or registered trademarks of Oracle and/or its affiliates

Software suites

A **software suite** is a collection of application software sold as a single package. See Figure C-26. Purchasing a software suite is usually much less expensive than purchasing each application in the suite separately. Because all the applications in a suite are produced by the same software publisher, they tend to have similar user interfaces and provide an easy way to transport data from one application to another. The disadvantage of a software suite is that it might include applications you do not need. You should calculate the price of the applications you do need and compare that to the cost of the suite.

FIGURE C-26: **A software suite**

Used with permission from Microsoft

- **What is database software?** Database software provides the tools needed to create a database. A **database** is a collection of data that is stored electronically as a series of records in tables. See Figure C-27. Database software can help you print reports, export data to other programs (such as to a spreadsheet, where you can graph the data), and transmit data to other computers. A database can contain any sort of data, such as your music collection, a university's student records, or a company's customer information. Microsoft Access, FileMaker Pro, and OpenOffice Base are examples of database programs for personal computers.

FIGURE C-27: **Creating a table in Microsoft Access**

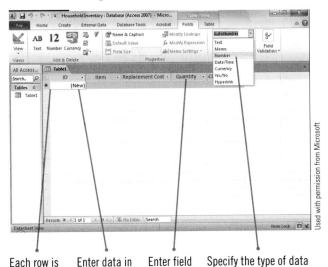

Used with permission from Microsoft

Each row is a record | Enter data in each field | Enter field names | Specify the type of data the field will hold

- **What is presentation software?** Presentation **software** provides the tools you need for combining text, graphics, graphs, animations, video, and sound into a series of electronic slides. See Figure C-28. You can display the electronic slides on a monitor for a one-on-one presentation, or you can use a computer projection device for group presentations. On-screen tools such as the highlighter or pen make it possible for you to annotate the slide during the presentation. How the slides advance is up to you. You can have the slides display automatically at set intervals, or you can advance the slides manually. Transitions between slides, such as checkerboard or wipes, create dramatic effect. You can also output the presentation as overhead transparencies, paper copies of the slides with or without notes, or 35-mm slides. Microsoft PowerPoint, iWork Keynote, and OpenOffice Impress are examples of presentation software programs.

FIGURE C-28: **A slide in a Microsoft PowerPoint presentation**

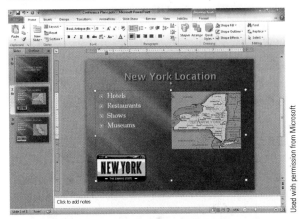

Used with permission from Microsoft

Other productivity software

Word processing, spreadsheet, database, presentation, and scheduling software are the five main types of office productivity software. Scheduling software such as Microsoft Outlook includes an email program. Two other office productivity software include Web authoring and desktop publishing software.

Web authoring software helps you design and develop Web pages that can be published on the Web. Web authoring software provides tools for generating HTML tags, which is the code used to display a document on the Web.

Desktop publishing (DTP) software provides both word processing and graphic design tools. Many of today's word processing programs offer page layout and design features. However, desktop publishing programs, such as Microsoft Publisher (Figure C-29), provide more sophisticated features to help you produce professional-quality publications. Most word processing software is page-oriented, meaning that it treats each page as a rectangle that can be filled with text and graphics. Text automatically flows from one page to the next. In contrast, most DTP software is frame-oriented, allowing you to divide each page into several rectangular-shaped frames that you can fill with text or graphics. Text flows from one frame to the next. You will want to use DTP to create complex documents, such as marketing brochures or magazines.

FIGURE C-29: **A page created using Microsoft Publisher**

Used with permission from Microsoft

Graphics Software

You may want to include images, such as digital photos or pictures you draw using the computer, in your work. These images are called graphics. The term **graphics** refers to any picture, drawing, sketch, photograph, image, or icon that appears on your computer screen or on your printed output. **Graphics software** is designed to help you create, display, modify, manipulate, and print graphics. Many kinds of graphics software are available, and each one is typically used with a particular type of graphic. Individuals who work with graphics will undoubtedly use more than one graphics program.

Learning Objective 8:
Define graphics software, and name examples in each major category

● **Can I use my computer to draw or create graphic images?** Yes. You can use **paint software** (sometimes called **image editing software**) to create more sophisticated images. Paint software provides a set of electronic pens, brushes, and paints for painting images on the screen. You can create these images from scratch, or you can use an existing image or photograph and add your own touches. See Figure C-30. A simple program called Microsoft Paint is included with Windows. More sophisticated paint programs include Corel Paint Shop Pro and Adobe Photoshop.

FIGURE C-30: **Paint software**

Tools on the Ribbon Different brushes Drawing canvas

Used with permission from Microsoft

You can also use **drawing software**, which provides tools, such as a set of lines, shapes, and colors. You can use these tools to create simple images, such as diagrams and corporate logos. The drawings created with drawing software, such as Adobe Illustrator and CorelDraw, tend

to have a flat cartoonlike quality, but they are very easy to modify and look good at just about any size.

● **Can I use my computer to edit my digital photographs?** Yes. You can use **photo editing software**, such as Adobe Photoshop and Corel PaintShop Pro. These programs include features that help you improve the quality of your photos. For example, using photo editing software, you can modify an image's contrast and brightness, crop unwanted objects, and remove "red eye." These programs often include photo organizers to help you locate and categorize your photos. See Figure C-31. Although photos can be edited using paint software, photo editing software typically provides tools that simplify common photo editing tasks.

FIGURE C-31: **Photo editing software**

Screenshot is © Copyright 2011 Corel Corporation and Corel Corporation Limited, reprinted by permission. Image courtesy of Rachel B. Bunin.

● **Is there a quick way to include art in my document?** You have several options. First, you can use clip art in your document, presentation, spreadsheet, or even database

table. **Clip art** is a collection of graphic images. These images might be drawn images or they might be photographs. These images are readily available. They are often included with some office productivity software. See Figure C-32. When using one of the Microsoft Office productivity programs, open the Clip Art task pane, and then search on a keyword to find an image that meets your needs.

FIGURE C-32: Inserting clip art in a presentation

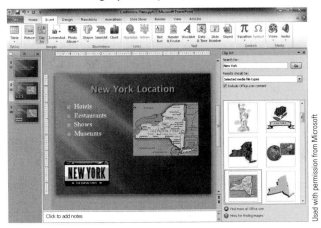

Used with permission from Microsoft

Collections of clip art focused on a particular theme can be purchased at a store or downloaded from a Web site. You can use your favorite search engine to find a wide variety of clip art that is ready to be inserted into your document. Before using any clip art, be sure to review its acceptable use statement to ensure you do not violate its copyright laws.

In addition to clip art, you can scan images, such as photographs, using a scanner. Once the image is scanned and saved, you have an electronic file of that image. You can insert that image and manipulate it in your document in the same way you would insert any picture in a document.

● **What software can I use to create three-dimensional graphics?** You can use 3D graphics software to create 3D graphics. **3D graphics software** provides a set of tools for creating wire-frame models

that represent three-dimensional objects. A wire-frame model is similar to the frame for a pop-up tent. In much the same way that you would construct the frame for the tent and then cover it with nylon fabric, you can use a 3D graphics program to cover a wire-frame model with surface texture and color to create a graphic of a 3D object. See Figure C-33.

FIGURE C-33: 3D graphics created using software programs

Courtesy of MediaTechnics Corporation; © Ralf Juergen Kraft/Shutterstock.com

● **What software is used to create technical drawings or blueprints? CAD (computer-aided design)** software is a special type of 3D graphics software. It is used by architects, engineers, and others who use computers to create blueprints and product specifications. You can purchase scaled-down versions of professional CAD programs. These programs provide simplified tools you can use for tasks such as redesigning your kitchen or drawing up new landscaping options. You may have used a CAD program at a home improvement store, where CAD is used to help customers visualize home improvement designs.

● **Do movie studios use computers to create graphics in films?** Computers and 3D graphics software are used extensively in the movie industry. Feature-length 3D animated films are responsible for stunning technology breakthroughs, such as the ability to realistically depict the movement of clothing on a moving animated character and animate individual strands of hair or fur. Graphics design companies such as Pixar Animation Studios and DreamWorks use 3D animation techniques to produce animated feature films as well as special effects.

Using data responsibly

Data can be numbers, text, or images. Whether you print, import, copy, save, or transmit the data in databases, worksheets, or documents, it is your responsibility to use the data appropriately. Here are some simple guidelines you can follow at work, home, or school to help you toward this effort. You should never introduce inaccurate information into a database, worksheet, or document. You should never alter the data in any way, such as to

digitally change a photograph or substitute words in a quotation. You should always respect copyrights and always be sure to give credit to the person or organization that compiled the data. You should always respect the privacy of the people who are the subject of the data. Unless you have permission to do so, do not divulge names, Social Security numbers, or other identifying information that might compromise someone's privacy.

Other Application Software

In addition to office productivity and graphics software, there are many other categories of application software. Some of the major categories are entertainment, gaming, music and video, education, business, and science. Application software in these categories can help you use your computer for entertainment, such as listening to music, playing games, and watching videos. They can help you use your computer for number-crunching tasks such as money management, mathematical modeling, or statistical analysis. This lesson looks at just a few of the many other types of application software.

Learning Objective 9:
Name other categories of application software, and give examples in each major category

● **Can I use my computer to play games?** Yes. Computer games are the most popular type of entertainment software. Computer games are generally classified into subcategories, such as simulations, multiplayer, role-playing, action, adventure, puzzles, and strategy/war games. Some games use game controllers that simulate musical intruments to interact with a computer. See Figure C-34. For example, you can use a guitar game controller to play lead guitar, bass guitar, and rhythm guitar across numerous rock music songs. Multiplayer games provide an environment in which two or more players can participate in the same game. Players can use Internet technology to band together in sophisticated virtual environments. Large-scale multiplayer games operate on multiple Internet servers, each one with the capacity to handle thousands of players at peak times.

FIGURE C-34: Playing a computer game

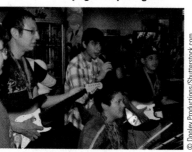

© Dooley Productions/Shutterstock.com

● **Can I use my computer to create music and sound?** You can use **audio editing software** to make digital voice and music recordings. You can store these files on your computer. Audio editing software typically includes playback as well as recording capabilities so you can preview your work and make changes as needed. Your operating system might supply audio editing software, such as Sound Recorder, or you can download open source software, such as Audacity. See Figure C-35.

Ear training software targets musicians and music students who want to learn to play by ear, develop tuning skills,

FIGURE C-35: Audio editing software

"Audacity" is a trademark of Dominic Mazzoni

Rewind to beginning Play Record Stop Fast forward to end

recognize notes and keys, and develop other musical skills. Notation software is the musician's equivalent of a word processor. It helps musicians compose, edit, and print the notes for their compositions. For non-musicians, **computer-aided music software** is designed to generate unique musical compositions simply by selecting the musical style, instruments, key, and tempo. MIDI sequencing software and software synthesizers are great for sound effects and for controlling keyboards and other digital instruments.

● **Can I use my computer to edit and create videos?** Yes. You can use **video editing software** and **DVD authoring software**. These programs provide tools for transferring video footage from a camcorder to a computer, deleting unwanted footage, assembling video segments in any sequence, adding special visual effects, and adding a sound track. See Figure C-36. Video editing software allows desktop video authors to transfer their productions to DVDs and watch them on standard DVD players connected to television sets or

projectors. Just like commercial movies, desktop videos can now include menu selections, such as Play Movie, Scene Selection, and Special Features.

FIGURE C-36: Video editing software

Used with permission from Microsoft; Courtesy of MediaTechnics Corporation

Preview your video to see how the clips, transitions, and soundtrack all work together

Add titles and transitions

Arrange the audio tracks to synchronize with each video clip

Import video clips, crop the footage, and arrange it in any order

● **How can I use my computer to learn new skills?** You can use **educational software** to learn and practice new skills. For the youngest students, this software can be used to reinforce basic skills. Instruction is presented in game format, and the level of play is adapted to the player's age and ability. When educational software is also entertaining, it is called **edutainment software.** For older students and adults, software is available to teach new skills, such as a foreign language, or to improve existing skills, such as keyboarding skills. **Reference software** spans a wide range of applications from encyclopedias and medical references to map software, trip planners, cookbooks, and telephone books. To find information in a reference program, you can search using keywords or you can click hyperlinks to access related articles.

● **What software is used to track business projects?** **Project management software**, such as Microsoft Project, is an important tool for planning and managing large or small projects. The software helps you with scheduling the project, assigning project tasks, tracking and allocating resources, and keeping an eye on project costs. See Figure C-37. Project management software is used to report progress and an overview of the project at any point to the main stakeholders and managers of a project.

FIGURE C-37: Project management software

Used with permission from Microsoft

● **What software is used to manage business finances?** **Accounting software** and **finance software** is used to keep a record of monetary transactions and investments. See Figure C-38. These easy-to-use programs do not require more than a basic understanding of accounting and finance principles. This type of software helps you invoice customers and keep track of what they owe. It stores additional customer data, such as contact information and purchasing history. Inventory functions keep track of the products that you carry. Payroll capabilities automatically calculate wages and deduct federal, state, and local taxes. **Tax preparation software** is a specialized type of **personal finance software** designed to help organize your annual income and expense data, identify deductions, and calculate your tax payment.

FIGURE C-38: An example of finance software

Courtesy of Intuit Inc.

● **Is there software specifically designed to analyze data?** Yes. **Mathematical modeling software**, such as MathCAD and Mathematica, provides tools for solving a wide range of math, science, and engineering problems. Students, teachers, mathematicians, and engineers like how this software helps them see patterns that can be difficult to identify in columns of numbers.

You can use **statistical software** to analyze large sets of data in order to discover relationships and patterns. Statistical software is a helpful tool for summarizing survey results, test scores, experiment results, or population data. Most statistical software includes graphing capability so that data can be displayed and explored visually.

Unit C

Talking Points: What Is The Downside To Software Piracy?

Software is easy to steal. For example, a customer does not have to walk out of a Staples or Best Buy store with a Quicken Deluxe box under his or her shirt to steal the program. Instead, the individual can simply borrow a friend's distribution discs and install a copy of the program on his or her computer's hard drive. Software piracy seems so simple that it could not be illegal; but it is! Software piracy takes many forms. Examples of end-user piracy include friends loaning distribution discs to each other and installing software on more computers than the license allows.

> " Counterfeit software is sold in retail stores and online auctions—often the packaging looks so authentic that buyers have no idea they have purchased illegal goods. "

Counterfeiting is the large-scale illegal duplication of software distribution media and sometimes even its packaging. According to Microsoft, many software counterfeiting groups are linked to organized crime and money-laundering schemes that fund a diverse collection of illegal activities. Counterfeit software is sold in retail stores and online auctions—often the packaging looks so authentic that buyers have no idea they have purchased illegal goods.

Internet piracy uses the Web as a way to distribute unauthorized software illegally. Some pirated software has even been modified to eliminate serial numbers, registration requirements, expiration dates, or other forms of copy protection. Web sites, peer-to-peer file sharing networks, and auction sites sell or distribute hundreds of thousands of pirated software products. In many countries, including the United States, software pirates are subject to civil lawsuits for monetary damages and criminal prosecution, which can result in jail time and stiff fines. Nonetheless, software piracy continues to have enormous impact.

According to a Business Software Alliance (BSA) and IDC Piracy Study, $130 billion dollars of software was legitimately purchased worldwide, but software worth a whopping $53 billion dollars was pirated. Figure C-39 shows piracy rates by region.

There is good news in this study, however. Progress was seen in a number of emerging markets, most notably in China, In China the piracy rate is 79%, down from 92% in 2003. In the

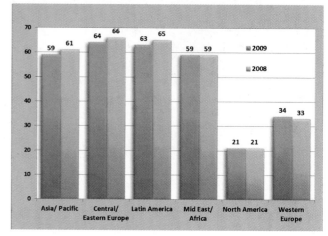

FIGURE C-39: Results of BSA/IDC Global Software Piracy study

Source: Seventh Annual BSA/IDC Global Software Piracy Study

United States, an estimated 20% of software is pirated. In Japan, the rate is 21%.

As justification for high piracy rates, some observers point out that people in many countries simply cannot afford software priced for the U.S. market. This argument could apply to China, where the average annual income is equivalent to about US $5,420, and to North Korea, where the average income is only US $2,820. A Korean who legitimately purchases Microsoft Office for US $250 would be spending about one-tenth of his or her annual income. Annual income rates do not necessarily correlate with piracy, however. Most countries with a high incidence of software piracy have strong economies and respectable per capita incomes. To further discredit the theory that piracy stems from poverty, India—which has a fairly large computer-user community, but a per capita income of only US $2,740—is not among the top 20 countries with high rates of software piracy.

Analysts believe that the Internet is a major factor in piracy growth. In fact, access to high-speed Internet connections makes it much easier to download large software files quickly.

Why should you care if someone uses Microsoft Office without paying for it? Is software piracy really damaging? Yes, without a doubt, it is damaging. Software piracy is damaging because it has a negative effect on the economy. Software production makes a major contribution to the United States economy, employing more than two million people and accounting for billions of dollars in corporate revenue. Software piracy in the

United States is responsible for tens of thousands of lost jobs, millions in lost wages, and lost tax revenues. A BSA economic impact study concluded that lowering global piracy from an average of 35% to only 25% would add more than 600,000 jobs and $141 billion in worldwide economic growth.

Decreases in software revenues can have a direct effect on consumers, too. When software publishers must cut corners, they tend to reduce customer service and technical support. As a result, you, the consumer, get put on hold when you call for technical support, find fewer free technical support sites, and encounter customer support personnel who are only moderately knowledgeable about their products. The bottom line—software piracy negatively affects customer service.

As an alternative to cutting support costs, some software publishers might build the cost of software piracy into the price of the software. The unfortunate result is that those who legitimately license and purchase software pay an inflated price.

The Software & Information Industry Association (SIIA) is an association for software companies whose mission is to protect, promote, and inform the industry. Part of its mission is to fight software piracy. See Figure C-40. To help with that effort, the SIIA provides an online form, as well as a toll-free number, for reporting piracy. SIIA also works hard to educate the consumer about piracy and its effects.

FIGURE C-40: SIAA Logos

Courtesy of the Software & Information Industry Association

Some analysts suggest that people need more education about software copyrights and the economic implications of piracy. Other analysts believe that copyright enforcement must be increased by implementing more vigorous efforts to identify and prosecute pirates.

> "As an alternative to cutting support costs, some software publishers might build the cost of software piracy into the price of the software. The unfortunate result is that those who legitimately license and purchase software pay an inflated price."

Expand the Ideas

1. Do you believe that software piracy is a serious issue? Write a two-page paper supporting your position. Include the opposing side's arguments in your report. Be sure to include your resources.

2. Do you think there are ways that software publishers can control piracy in the United States? In other countries? Do you know of any recent attempts at doing so? Work in a small group to brainstorm ideas and research recent trends or events. Compile your ideas and findings into a short presentation to give to the class. Include handouts for the audience and cite any sources you used.

3. Do you think that most software pirates understand that what they are doing is illegal? Design a marketing campaign that could be used to educate the public about the issue. Create a poster that could be used in the campaign.

4. Should software publishers try to adjust software pricing for local markets? How would you propose such a pricing structure? How would these policies be enforced? Can you think of any other industry that adjusts prices for local markets? Write a two-page paper discussing your proposals and explaining your findings. Be sure to cite your sources.

Software marketing and reviews

New software comes on the market frequently. At times, it can seem impossible to keep up with the flow of new software. However, publications and Web sites can help you keep up to date regarding software developments that might improve your computing experience.

Computer and technology magazines, such as *Wired*, *Macworld*, and *PC Magazine*, usually include software reviews in every issue. Most computer magazines have companion Web sites and some of those significantly extend the material offered in the magazine's printed pages. ZDNet and CNET (reviews.cnet.com),

for example, offer in-depth comparison reviews written by experts and tested under laboratory conditions.

Consumer-oriented Web sites also offer reviews. For example, the site toptenreviews.com contains easy-to-understand, in-depth checklists that make it easy to compare the features of popular software packages. User reviews and ratings can be found at download sites, such as download.com, cnet.com, as well as at comparison shopping sites, including bizrate.com, Amazon.com, and newegg.com. You might also find a blog or news feed that focuses on the type of software you typically use.

Key Terms & Unit Review

Key Terms

3D graphics software
Accounting software
App
Application software
Audo editing software
Boot process
Buffer
CAD (computer-aided design) software
Clip art
Cloudware
Commercial software
Compression utility
Computer-aided music software
Computer program
Concurrent-use license
Copyright
Copyright notice
Digital content
Database
Database software
Demoware
Desktop gadget
Desktop publishing software

Device driver
Drawing software
DVD authoring software
Educational software
Edutainment software
EULA (end-user license agreement)
Finance software
Freeware
Gadget
General Public License (GPL)
Graphical user interface (GUI)
Graphics
Graphics software
Image editing software
Installation agreement
Intellectual property
License agreement
Linux
Local application
Mac OS
Mathematical modeling software
Mobile application
Multiple-user license

Multitasking
Office productivity software
Open source software
Operating system (OS)
Paint software
Patch
Personal finance software
Photo editing software
Pirated software
Portable application
Presentation software
Productivity software
Project management software
Proprietary software
Public domain software
Reference software
Resource
Restore point
Security utility
Service pack
Setup program
Shareware
Shrink-wrap license
Single-user license

Site license
Software
Software license
Software pirate
Software suite
Software upgrade
Spreadsheet software
Statistical software
System requirements
System software
Tax preparation software
User interface
Utility software (utilities)
Validation code
Video editing software
Web app
Web application
Web authoring software
Widget
Windows
Word processing software
Worksheet

Unit Review

1. Use your own words to define each of the bold terms that appear throughout the unit. List ten of the terms that are the least familiar to you and write a sentence for each of them.

2. List at least five categories of application software and give an example of how you might use each type.

3. Explain the single-user, site license, multiple-user, and concurrent-user software licenses described in this unit.

4. In your own words, explain shareware, freeware, demoware, and open source software.

5. Describe the main activities you must perform when you install software on your computer. Explain the differences between downloaded software and software you buy in a store.

6. List three features of the Windows operating system discussed in this unit. Write a brief summary of each feature.

7. Name three resources managed by an operating system.

8. List three types of office productivity software that you might use, and describe how you might use each one.

9. List three types of software that you might use for creating and editing graphics, and describe how you might use each one.

10. Create a list of three utilities described in this unit and give an example of why you would use each one on the list.

Concepts Review

Select the best answer.

1. Software can be divided into two major categories: system software and _____ software.
 a. Web app
 b. application
 c. utility
 d. security

2. You should use _____ software for numerical calculations, such as tracking income and expenses.
 a. spreadsheet
 b. database
 c. document production
 d. utility

3. A software _____ is a collection of application software sold as a single package.
 a. operating system
 b. DVD
 c. suite
 d. productivity program

4. A(n) _____ is utility software that helps a peripheral device communicate with a computer.
 a. operating system
 b. desktop gadget
 c. connector
 d. device driver

5. To run more than one program at a time, the _____ must allocate specific areas of memory for each program.
 a. RAM
 b. operating system
 c. device driver
 d. ROM

6. When _____ software is used, program files do not exist on the hard drive and no configuration data is stored on the hard drive.
 a. demoware
 b. database
 c. portable
 d. freeware

7. _____ is distributed under the terms of a General Public License (GPL), which allows everyone to make copies for his or her own use, to give it to others, or to sell it.
 a. Linux
 b. Windows
 c. Mac OS
 d. Office

8. When using Windows, you can open the _____ Manager to see a list of processes that are being executed by the processor.
 a. Windows
 b. Program
 c. Explorer
 d. Task

9. The three main operating systems running most personal computers today are _____, Mac OS, and Linux.
 a. FileZilla
 b. Windows
 c. Office
 d. Internet Explorer

10. You can use _____ software to help organize information, such as library books and contacts.
 a. database
 b. spreadsheet
 c. document production
 d. finance and accounting

11. A desktop _____ is a utility program that may provide information, such as the weather or a calendar.
 a. icon
 b. gadget
 c. task
 d. menu

12. _____ software is a special type of 3D graphics software designed for architects and engineers who use computers to create blueprints and product specifications.
 a. DTP
 b. Statistical
 c. CAD
 d. Product Management

13. As part of the _____ program, you might be asked what type of installation you want: full or custom.
 a. Web app
 b. license
 c. setup
 d. demoware

14. To read a Portable Document File (PDF), you need to use _____ software.
 a. Microsoft Excel
 b. Microsoft Word
 c. OpenOffice Document
 d. Adobe Reader

15. To combat piracy, many software publishers require users to type in a(n) _____ code, a sequence of numbers and letters in order to complete an installation.
 a. EULA
 b. validation
 c. private
 d. pass

16. Snow Leopard, Cheetah, Puma, Jaguar, Panther, Tiger, and Leopard are all examples of _____.
 a. Windows programs
 b. Apple OSs
 c. license agreements
 d. Smartphone OSs

17. _____ laws provide software authors with the exclusive right to copy, distribute, sell, and modify their work, except under special circumstances.
 a. Copyright
 b. Software
 c. Shareware
 d. Piracy

18. _____ is copyrighted software that is marketed with a try-before-you-buy policy.
 a. Demoware
 b. Freeware
 c. Utility software
 d. Shareware

19. A(n) _____ license is priced at a flat rate so software can be used on all computers at a specific location.
 a. Single-user
 b. Shareware
 c. Multi-user
 d. Demoware

20. _____ software is not copyrighted, making it available for use without restriction, except that you cannot apply for a copyright on it.
 a. Demoware
 b. Productivity
 c. Public Domain
 d. Commercial

Independent Challenges

Independent Challenge 1

There are many software packages on the market today. Software is often dictated by the computer you are using and the installed operating system. Operating systems are updated every few years, giving you more options for newer features and new software.

Application software is also updated regularly. In addition, new programs come on the market frequently. In fact, the amount of software available in each category can be overwhelming, and no two packages offer all the same features. How can you make a decision about which software you need? How do you know which software to buy? Do you follow recommendations received by word of mouth? Do you read reviewer comments in professional magazines? Do you simply try it out? Do you go to the Web and find a software superstore and read all the reviews and descriptions? See Figure C-41.

FIGURE C-41: Software superstore

© Jorg Hackemann/Shutterstock.com

For this Independent Challenge:

Write a short summary answering each of the questions that follow.

1. Which operating system do you use?

2. What software is installed on your computer? How did you acquire the software? How would you categorize each program?

3. Identify one software program you want to download to your computer, such as an office productivity, a graphics, a Web development, an email, or a utility program. Locate vendor ads either on the Internet or in local papers or trade magazines that sell or discuss that program. Find two competitive products for the program you want to buy. Read comparison reviews of the products. Create a chart detailing the features and prepare a competitive analysis of the two products.

4. What are the system requirements for each program? Does your computer meet those requirements?

5. What kind of software license is required by each program? Do you have to pay for using it? Can you try it first, then pay after a trial period? Do you understand the licensing agreement? Write a short summary of your findings, indicating which program you would buy and why.

Independent Challenge 2

Copyrights and software piracy are relevant issues for software users, developers, businesspeople, and educators. There is constant debate among all stakeholders as to the best models for software distribution, as well as how developers, publishers, or programmers should be compensated.

For this Independent Challenge:

1. Log onto the Internet and use your favorite search engine to search for Web sites that discuss software piracy. Using information you have gathered through your research, select one of the following viewpoints and argue for or against it.

Discuss the topic of software piracy from the perspective of one of the following: a.) an advocate who believes in free software for all, b.) a librarian who believes that copyright laws, especially the Digital Millennium Copyright Act, minimize the needs of the public and go too far in their efforts to protect the rights of software authors, c.) a member of the Software Publishers Association who believes all software is protected by copyright law and the consumer should purchase all software and abide by the EULA.

2. Select one of the perspectives listed above or state your own perspective, then write a two- to five-page paper about this issue, based on information you gather from the Internet.

3. Be sure to cite your sources and list them as part of the paper.

4. Follow your instructor's directions for formatting and submitting your paper.

Independent Challenge 3

Smartphones and tablet computers are becoming the digital device of choice. Most people are turning in their cell phones to upgrade to smartphones with a data plan. As a result, more and more mobile apps are being developed to meet the growing consumer demand. Currently, there are apps that exist for fun and games. There are apps to help people navigate through their day. And, there are apps that are just silly. Whether or not you own a smartphone or a tablet computer now, you probably know at least one person who does. Learning about smartphones and tablets, as well as the mobile apps becoming so popular today, provides insight into the world of mobile computing.

For this Independent Challenge:

1. Log onto the Internet and search for information on the following mobile operating systems: Windows Phone, Android, iOS.

 Complete the chart shown in Table C-3 to learn more about each of the operating systems.

2. Go to a Web site that features Android apps, such as the Android market shown in Figure C-42. Explore the offerings and the different categories then answer the following questions:
 a. What is the most interesting free app that you can find to download? Why would you want this app? What made you select this app?

FIGURE C-42: **Android market**

©2011 Google.

 b. What is the most interesting app that you have to pay for? Why would you want this app? Why do you think it is worth paying for this app rather than getting a different free app?

3. Go to a Web site that features apps for Apple tablets or smartphones. Explore the offerings then answer the following questions:
 a. What is the most interesting free app that you can find to download? Why would you want this app?
 b. What is the most interesting app that you have to pay for? Why would you want this app? Why do you think it is worth paying for this app rather than getting a different free app?

TABLE C-3: **Comparison chart**

	Windows Phone	Android	iOS
Current version			
Latest features mentioned most in the marketing			
Three digital devices that can be purchased with this OS preinstalled			
Two game apps			
Two productivity apps			
One surprising fact			

© Cengage Learning

Guide to Buying a Computer

As you prepare to buy a computer, there are many decisions you have to make. This book is designed to help you build the knowledge base you need to purchase a computer, and then buy and install software on that computer. In this unit, you were introduced to the basics of the operating system and the different types of application software and utilities you might need to buy for your computer. Some software is provided with the operating system. Office productivity software can be expensive. However, you can take advantage of student discounts, competitive pricing, and various licensing options.

To be able to make decisions regarding buying a computer and the software you need, you have to do your homework. As an informed consumer, you should be aware of your options, research different software publishers, and compare features of each package. Computer and technology magazines, such as *Wired*, *Macworld*, and *PC Magazine*, usually include software reviews in every issue. Most computer magazines have companion Web sites and some of those significantly extend the material offered in the magazine's printed pages.

To help you organize the information you will need when you are ready to buy a computer, you should complete the following activities.

1. Research three productivity programs and three utility programs you might need. List the programs you selected, the cost, and a site where you read a review of each program. State whether you will buy the program or not.

2. Explore the idea of purchasing a software suite instead of individual software programs. Compare two productivity software suites, such as OpenOffice with Microsoft Office. What were the differences in features between the two software suites? What are the costs for each? Do you think the values are comparable?

3. Computers can help you perform such a wide variety of tasks that it can be impossible to predict all the ways you might use your new machine in the future. You can, however, make a list of the ways you plan to immediately use your computer and that list can help you think about the software you'll need. List some of the ways below.

Deciding whether to buy boxed software or download software

Boxed software can be purchased in a store or shipped to you by mail. The box usually includes distribution CDs and an installation manual. It might also include a user manual, but many software publishers supply user manuals online. The advantage of distribution CDs is their availability in case your hard drive fails and you have to reinstall your software. Boxed software can give you a physical record of your registration code, serial number, and certificate of authenticity, which might be necessary for reinstallation.

You can download software from a Web site instead of buying it in a box. Downloading can be convenient. It saves you a trip to the store and you don't have to wait for a mail order package to arrive. Depending on the speed of your Internet connection, however,

downloads can tie up your computer for a few hours. Even with a fast connection a download can be interrupted and you might have to call customer service to restart it without paying for the product again. Downloading can be risky. Some download sites display an irritating number of ads and are sometimes exploited by hackers. Software downloaded from less reputable sites might contain viruses. When possible you should download directly from the software publisher's Web site or from a download site operated by a reputable business, such as a computer magazine or retailer. In any case, it is good practice to scan downloaded files for viruses before installing them.

Prices for boxed software and Web downloads can vary, so if you have the time to shop around, you are likely to save some money.

4. As you continue to work through this book, you will learn more about personal computer systems. You will have the opportunity to answer more questions and complete other worksheets with information that will help you when it is time to buy a computer. To help you think about the software you need, fill in this portion of the Guide to Buying a Computer worksheet. Try to list the name of specific software programs you might buy or you would like to review further for each answer in the Notes column.

Guide to Buying a Computer: Getting started

Questions to consider	Pages where the topic is covered in this book (refer back to these pages to read more about the topic)	Notes (add additional comments, clarifications, or ideas about each topic)
Which operating system do you want?		
If you are considering Windows, which edition should you get?		
What browser are you considering?		
Do you plan to create documents? If so, what word processing program do you plan to use?		
Will you need to work with numbers? If so, what spreadsheet program or other numeric software do you plan to use?		
Will you need to create computer slide shows or presentations? If so, what presentation program do you plan to use?		
Will you need to work with graphics, such as original computer art? If so, what graphics program do you plan to use?		
Will you want to edit or organize photographs? If so, what image editing program do you plan to use?		
Are you going to use your computer to listen to music? To transfer music to your MP3 player? If so, what programs will you need? Do you need to consider any special hardware as well?		
What utility software will you need? Will you want to send compressed files? Customize your desktop? Maintain your disk's health?		
Rather than buying all individual programs, are there any software suites you might consider?		
What type of licensing works best for you for the software that you plan to buy?		
Do you have a tablet or smartphone? If yes, what do you use these devices for on a daily basis?		
What apps do you have on the mobile digital device? Do you plan to purchase any apps for your digital device? If so, which type? Any specific apps?		

© Cengage Learning

Visual Workshop

Mobile devices, such as tablet computers and smartphones now have the ability, through software and the different networks, to allow you to video chat or conference with other people directly from your device. Popular video chatting services include Tango, Fring, FaceTime, GoogleChat, and Skype. Figure C-43 shows the Tango home page. You will compare and contrast each option on its basic features.

FIGURE C-43: **Mobile video chatting**

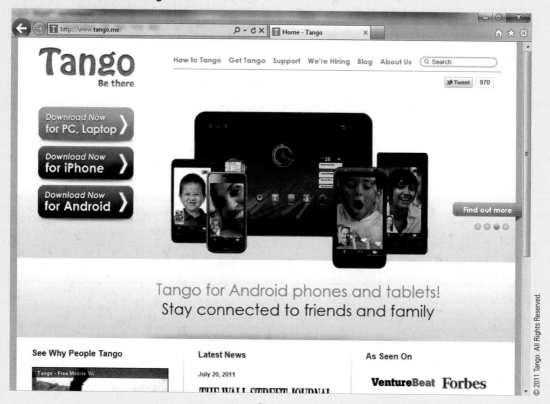

Log onto the Internet. Find Web sites that discuss each of these video chatting services listed above.

1. In your research, find three facts about each of the competing services.

2. What are the purchasing options, fees, and licensing options for each?

3. What operating systems are required for each? Are there limitations?

4. Which devices are supported by each of these video chatting services?

5. Are any interesting features built into these video chatting services?

File Management and Digital Electronics

Learning Objectives

1. Explain how file management programs help you manage your computer files
2. Explain how to create and use folders to store files
3. Identify the key elements of a computer file
4. Describe the file management steps for working with files
5. Describe how digital data representation produces numbers, text, images, video, and sound
6. Define integrated circuits and explain the role they play inside a computer
7. Explain how CPU factors affect computer performance
8. Define RAM and explain its importance to computers
9. Explain how a computer uses virtual memory, ROM, and EEPROM

LESSON TOPICS

- File Management Tools
- Computer Folder Basics
- Computer File Basics
- How to Manage Computer Files
- How Computers Represent Data
- Integrated Circuits—An Overview
- Processors—An Overview
- Computer Memory: RAM
- Other Types of Computer Memory

Talking Points: Is Your Computer Making You Sick?

File Management Tools

A typical personal computer stores thousands of computer files, usually in folders. You use file management tools to manage your files and folders. To organize your computer files and folders, you need to practice good **file management**. Good file management practices include how you create, open, save, delete, and rename files.

Learning Objective 1:
Explain how file management programs help you manage your computer files

- **What is a computer file?** A computer file, or simply file, is defined as a named collection of data that exists on a storage medium. The storage medium can be a hard drive, solid-state storage device, CD, DVD, BD, or tape. The content of the file is determined by the software program used to create the file and the data you enter. For example, you can use a word processing program to create a document file for your résumé.

- **What is a folder?** A **folder** is a logical representation of where you store your files on a computer. Folders help you organize your computer files.

- **How do folders help me organize my files?** By storing files in folders, you assign each file a place in a hierarchy of folders. Think of a data storage system as a filing cabinet. See Figure D-1. Each storage device is a drawer in a filing cabinet. Just like the drawers in a filing cabinet, a storage device is made up of folders and the folders hold files.

FIGURE D-1: **Files are stored in folders**

File cabinet storage Computer file storage

The file cabinet is a useful way to visualize how files and folders are organized on a storage device. The drive, folder names, and filename all work together to identify the file path.

- **What is a file path?** The location of a file on a storage device is defined by its **file path** (also called **file specification**). The file path begins with the drive letter and is followed by the folder(s), filename, and file extension. A folder name is separated from a drive letter and other folder names by a special

symbol. In Windows, this symbol is often represented on screen as an arrow head and written as the backslash (\). For example, the path to the folder Sarah uses to store Elvis music would be C:\Users\Sarah\My Music\Elvis\Hound Dog.mp3. This path tells you that Sarah stored an MP3 file called Hound Dog in the Elvis folder in the My Music folder on her hard drive. Its file path is shown in Figure D-2.

FIGURE D-2: **A file path**

C:\Users\Sarah\My Music\Elvis\Hound Dog.mp3

| Primary folder | Subfolder | Subfolder | Subfolder | Filename | File extension |

- **Who decides where my files are stored?** You decide where your files are stored. But to help you, Windows supplies a series of default locations. These locations include the four Libraries as well as default folders. See Figure D-3.

FIGURE D-3: **Windows default folders**

- **What is a library?** A **library** contains a set of links to similar files that are stored on various devices and in various folders. A library is similar to a folder. When you open a library in **Windows Explorer**, you'll see one or more folders and files. A library does not actually store files, but rather

provides a view of the files. A library can display folders that are found in several locations. A library can give you access to files and folders on your hard drive, an external drive, and also folders that have been shared over a network. You cannot use a library for removable storage such as a flash drive. In Windows 7, there are four default libraries: Documents, Music, Pictures, and Videos.

- **Where are my files stored if they are not stored in the libraries?** Your files are stored at the location you specify. For example, when you save a data file, you specify the location where you want to save the file. The default location for a file such as a letter or spreadsheet is the My Documents folder. The Document library tracks the saved file and you can access it through the library as needed. You can save your file to a default folder, or you can create a new folder and save your file to the new folder. However, avoid storing files in the root directory of your hard drive. Files should be stored in subfolders in the root directory.

 When you install a program, the installation process usually creates a new folder within the default Programs folder. This folder is not tracked by any of the libraries. Although you can change the suggested location when you install a software program, it is recommended that you don't.

- **What is the root directory?** The **root directory** is the main directory of the hard drive or other storage medium. So for a hard drive named C:, the root directory is also C:.

- **Do I name the root directory?** No, the root directory is the name of your storage device and it is assigned by your operating system. For example, the Windows operating system labels storage devices with letters, such as A: and C:. See Figure D-4.

A device letter is usually followed by a colon. The main hard drive is usually referred to as drive C or as Local Disk (C:). Additional storage devices can be assigned letters from D through Z.

The device letters for additional storage devices are not standardized. As a result, the file path for a file can change. For example, if you store a data file on a flash drive, the file path for the file will include the drive letter for the flash drive. The drive letter is based on which computer the flash drive is connected to. If you remove the flash drive and insert it in a new computer, the flash drive is assigned a new drive letter based on that computer. So, the file specification for a file might be F:\Cards\Birthday1.docx on a flash drive connected to one computer, but the file path for that same file might be H:\Cards\Birthday1.docx on the same flash drive connected to a different computer.

- **What should I use to manage the files on my computer?** Most operating systems provide a **file management program**. These programs contain the tools you need to organize your files. For computers running Windows, the file management program is called Windows Explorer. Using Windows Explorer, you can see the storage devices and a list of files and folders on those storage devices or on your network. You can find files, move files, make copies of files, delete files, view file properties, and rename files. Figure D-5 shows the Windows Explorer window.

 In addition, a file management program makes it easy to find the file or folder you are looking for by using the program's search capabilities. *TIP:* Do not confuse Windows Explorer (file management program) with Internet Explorer (a browser program you use to view Web sites on the Internet).

FIGURE D-4: Storage devices labeled with letters

FIGURE D-5: Windows Explorer showing contents of Sample Music folder

Hierarchy of devices and folders Details pane for selected file Selected folder Contents of selected folder

Computer Folder Basics

A folder is a logical representation of where you store your files on a computer. For example, you can use a folder called My Documents to hold reports, budgets, letters, and so on. If you understand how to use and manage folders, you will be able to organize the files on your computer successfully.

Learning Objective 2:
Explain how to create and use folders to store files

● **Why should I use folders to organize my files?** You can store thousands of files on one storage device. Without folders, it would be difficult to find the file you want. You create folders to hold folders and files. Folders within folders are **nested folders**, also called **subfolders**. You give folders descriptive names to help you remember what is in the folders.

● **How do I know which folder to use?** As you'll recall, Windows supplies default folders. When you save a file, you can use a default folder, you can create a new folder at the same level as the default folder, or you can create subfolders in any folder. You create folders and subfolders to meet your needs. For example, you might create a subfolder named TownProject in the default My Documents folder to hold documents related to a project in town. Within that folder you might create another subfolder named Budgets for all the spreadsheets containing budget data.

● **How do I create new folders?** To create a new folder, you can use Windows Explorer. With Windows Explorer open, you can navigate to the location on the storage device where you want to create the folder. Once you have selected the drive and folder location for the new folder, you click the New Folder button on the menu bar to create a new folder. Then, when it is created, a text box appears to the right of the folder. You type the folder name in the text box. See Figure D-6. Be sure to give the folder a meaningful name that will help you remember what files are stored in that folder. File and folder naming rules restrict you from using special characters such as a colon or a slash in folder names. Filenaming conventions are discussed in the next lesson.

● **Can I copy or move a folder?** In addition to finding folders, Windows Explorer provides a set of file management tools that help you organize your folders. To work with a folder, you must select it. See Figure D-7. Once a folder is selected, you can copy, move, rename, or delete it as needed.

FIGURE D-6: **Creating a new folder**

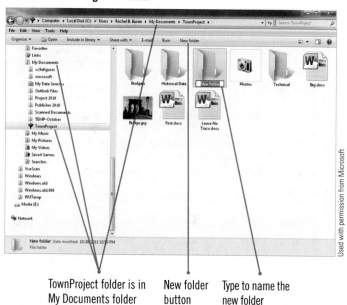

Used with permission from Microsoft

TownProject folder is in My Documents folder | New folder button | Type to name the new folder

FIGURE D-7: **Moving a folder**

Used with permission from Microsoft

Target location | Folder being moved

- **Can I copy or move more than one folder at a time?** Yes, if you want to copy or move more than one folder, you can select more than one folder and then perform the action. To select more than one folder, you press and hold the Ctrl key while you click each folder you want to copy or move. Once selected, you can work with the selected folders just as you would work with a single folder. If the folders are right next to each other in the list, you can click the first folder, hold the Shift key, and then click the last folder in the list to select the first folder, the last folder, and all the folders between the two selected folders.You can also use the Ctrl key or the Shift key to work with more than one file.

- **What are folder properties?** Folder properties include the size of the folder, the date it was created, the number of files and folders contained in the folder, and the location or path to the folder. Folder properties also carry security and sharing information to determine who can access the folder and whether or not they can make changes to the folder.

- **Is there a way to see or change folder properties?** Windows Explorer lets you work with a folder's properties. With Windows Explorer open, you can right-click any folder, and then click Properties to open the Properties dialog box for the selected folder. See Figure D-8. For example, the

General tab in the Properties dialog box provides general information about the files and folders that are stored in that folder. Each tab in the Properties dialog box includes additional information about the selected folder. You will see different tabs depending on the location and properties of the selected folder.

- **What are folder options?** When you work with folders you have options for how you can open and view the folders. These options are features of the operating system that can be customized to meet your needs. For example, you can see different icons depending on the contents of a folder. You can also decide if you have to double or single click to open a folder.

- **How do I change folder options?** Sometimes you might want to change the way you view and search for files and folders in Windows Explorer. For example, you might want to display file icons representing file types in a folder as folder thumbnails. You may also choose to include hidden files and folders in a search of the folder. To view or change a folder's options, open the Folder Options dialog box. To open the Folder Options dialog box, you open the Control Panel, click Appearance and Personalization, and then click the Folders Option. In the Folders Option dialog box, you select one of the three tabs, General, View, and Search. Refer to Figure D-9 to see the General tab options.

FIGURE D-8: **Properties dialog box for My Documents folder**

Used with permission from Microsoft

FIGURE D-9: **Folder Options dialog box**

Used with permission from Microsoft

Folders and subfolders vs. directories and subdirectories

Directories and subdirectories mean the same thing as folders and subfolders when talking about file management. The operating system on your computer maintains a list of files called a **directory**. There is a directory for each storage device. The main directory of a drive is referred to as the **root directory**. On a PC, the root directory is typically identified by the device letter

followed by a backslash. For example, the root directory of the hard drive would be C:\. A root directory is often subdivided into smaller **subdirectories**. When you use Windows, Mac OS, or a Linux graphical file manager, these subdirectories are depicted using icons that look like folders because subdirectories work like the folders in a filing cabinet to store related files.

Computer File Basics

There are several important elements that define a computer file. These include the contents of the file, the software that was used to create it, and the way the computer uses it. There are several categories of files, such as data files, executable files, configuration files, and drivers. Most of the files you create on your computer are data files. Although files can contain different data, they have several key elements, including filename, format, location, size, and date.

Learning Objective 3:
Identify the key elements of a computer file

● **What is a filename?** A **filename** is a set of letters, symbols, or numbers that identifies a file. A filename consists of a name followed by a period, followed by a file extension. Every saved file has a filename.

● **Are there rules I need to know for naming files?** Yes, the filename must follow specific rules, called **filenaming conventions**. Each operating system has a unique set of filenaming conventions. When you use the Windows operating system, you cannot use the symbols : * \ < > | " / and ? as part of a filename. If you try to save the file using one of the restricted symbols, you will receive a message telling you there is a problem with the filename. When you name a file, you should give it a meaningful name that can help you remember the contents of the file.

● **What are file extensions?** A **file extension** (or **filename extension**) is a set of letters and/or numbers added to the end of filename following a period that helps to identify the file contents or file type. A file extension helps describes the file contents. For example, the music files you listen to on your portable media player probably have the .mp3 file extension. A file extension is separated from the main filename by a period, as in BornToRun.mp3. In this example, the file extension .mp3 indicates that this is a music file.

You will also recognize that some file extensions are associated with a particular application program. See Table D-1 for a list of some common file extensions. Knowing the file extension can help you identify which application program was used to create the data file. Once you know the file format, you will know which application to use if you want to open the file. A software program can typically open a file that exists in its **native file format**, plus several additional **file formats**.

TABLE D-1: **Common file extensions**

File extensions	Application
xls, xlsx	Microsoft Excel
doc, docx	Microsoft Word
txt, rtf	Text editor (WordPad, Notepad)
ppt, pptx	Microsoft PowerPoint
mdb, accdb	Microsoft Access
gif, tif, jpg, bmp, raw, png	Graphic or photo viewer or editor
wav, mid, mp3	Music and sound player or editor
zip	Compressed file
pdf	Adobe Acrobat or Reader

© Cengage Learning

As you work with files, you will begin to recognize that some file extensions, such as .txt (text file) or .jpg (graphics file), indicate a file type (such as a document or a photograph). They are not specific to any one program. Understanding file extensions can help you if you receive a file but they don't tell you much about the file's contents.

● **Do I decide the file extensions?** Generally, no. As a user, you do not decide the extension. The software program assigns an extension to the file automatically when you save it. Some programs give you several options. For example, when you save a graphic you can decide if you want a jpg, tif, or some other graphic format.

● **Can I change the file extension?** Technically, yes, but you really shouldn't change file extensions because a file extension is usually related to the file format. Sometimes, a file extension is changed in error when you try to rename a file. Be careful to change only the name to the left of the period when you change a filename. If you change a file extension while renaming a file, the file will not be able to be opened.

- **Why can't I see the file extensions when I look at my files using Windows Explorer?** File extensions should be shown by default. If you can't see the file extensions, you can change the settings to show them. It is a good idea to show file extensions because they help you know the file type. To view file extensions, be sure the Hide extensions for known file types check box in the Folder Options dialog box does not have a check mark.

- **When do I name a file?** You name a file the first time you save it. You can rename a file any time after it has been saved. One way, you can rename a file is to use the Save As command.

- **How do I know when to use Save and when to use Save As?** The flowchart in Figure D-10 can help you decide whether to use the Save or the Save As command. When you try to use the Save command for a file that has not been saved, the program will open the Save As dialog box, even though you selected the Save command.

FIGURE D-10: Save or Save As?

© Cengage Learning

- **Why can't I open some files?** If you can't open file, you might see a warning message like the one shown in Figure D-11.

FIGURE D-11: Unrecognized file type

Used with permission from Microsoft

You might not be able to open a file for one of the following reasons:

- You do not have the software application needed to open the file.
- The file might have been damaged—or corrupted—by a transmission or disk error.
- The file extension might have been changed, perhaps while renaming the file, and so the file is no longer associated with its application program. In this situation, if you think you know the correct file extension, you can change the file extension again and try to open the file.
- The file might use a file format for a newer version of the software than you have. For example, Office 2010 files use a new file format that is not able to be opened by Office 2003 programs unless you have a special compatibility program.

Several Web sites provide lists of file extensions and their corresponding software. By looking up a file extension in one of these lists, you can find out what application software you'll need to open a file based on its file extension.

- **What other information is stored with each of my files?** The File Properties dialog box is a good way to find out information about a file. See Figure D-12. General information such as file size and file date can be helpful as you manage your files. **File size** is usually measured in bytes, kilobytes, or megabytes. Knowing the size of a file can be important, especially when you are sending a file as an email attachment. Your computer's operating system keeps track of file sizes. Your computer also keeps track of the date on which a file was created or last modified. The **file date** is useful if you have saved a file using slightly different filenames each time and you want to know which is the most recent.

FIGURE D-12: File Properties dialog box for Kalimba.mp3

Used with permission from Microsoft

How to Manage Computer Files

To manage files, you use the same file management tools you used to copy, move, rename, or delete a folder. As you work with programs, you will need to open and save files. You can open files while working with an application program or by using a file management program. You can also save files from within an application program such as a word processor.

Learning Objective 4:
Describe the file management steps for working with files

● **Do I have to remember all the information about where my files are stored?** No, you don't have to remember the details, but it is helpful to create a system for naming files and folders that is easy for you to use. Although file management programs, like Windows Explorer, help you locate your files, knowing the basics (the drive, the folder name(s), and the filename) will help you find your files faster.

Most application software provides access to file management tasks through the Save, Save As, and Open dialog boxes. Table D-2 lists additional file management tasks you will use when working with files and folders.

TABLE D-2: **Additional file management tasks**

File or folder command	Description and examples
Rename	Change the name of a file or folder to describe its contents better. For example, you might change the name of the file Letter.docx to Letter to Pam 10-6.docx. When renaming a file, be careful to keep the same file extension so that you can open it with the correct application software.
Copy	Create a copy of a file or folder; the file remains in the original location and a duplicate file is added to a different location. For example, copy a document file to a new folder so that you can revise the content in the copy and leave the original content intact.
Move	Move a file or folder from one folder to another, or from one storage device to another. For example, move a file to a new folder to organize your hard drive. When you move a file or folder, it is erased from its original location.
Delete	Remove the file from the folder and place it in the Recycle Bin. For example, delete a file or folder with files when you no longer need it. Note: most file management programs delete all the files (and subfolders) in a folder when you delete a folder.

● **What is a file tag?** Some applications also allow you to add tags to a file. A **file tag** is a short word or phrase that describes a file. It is useful when you search for a file. Tags appear in the Details pane in Windows Explorer, see Figure D-13, as well as on the Details tab of the Properties dialog box. For example, tags help you describe the location, camera settings, and people pictured in a photograph.

FIGURE D-13: **Tags provide additional information about a file**

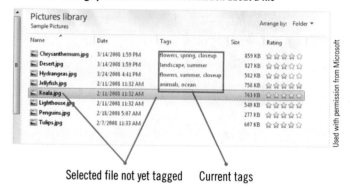

Selected file not yet tagged Current tags

● **Is it possible to convert a file from one format to another?** Yes. The easiest way to convert a file from one format to another is to find an application program that works with both file formats. Graphics programs can often handle most of the major file formats for graphics. For example, you can use a program such as Paint to convert a graphics file from the .tif file format to the .bmp file format. To do this, open the file using the Paint program. Once the file is open, click the File tab, then click the Save As command to see other possible formats. If you have a specific need for a format not listed, click Other formats to open the Save As dialog box. You then select a new file format, assign the file a new name if you want, and save it. See Figure D-14.

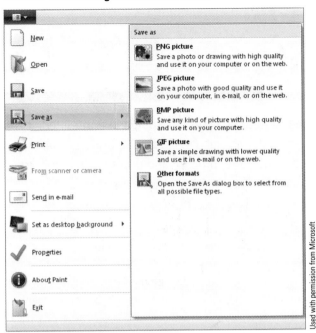

Used with permission from Microsoft

● **Are there rules and guidelines I should follow when managing files?** Yes. The following tips will help you manage your files:

■ Use descriptive names. Give your files and folders descriptive names when you save or create them, and avoid using cryptic abbreviations.

■ Maintain file extensions. When renaming a file, keep the original file extension so that you can open it with the correct application software.

■ Group similar files and consider using the default folders in Windows, such as Documents, Pictures, Music, and so on. Separate files into folders based on subject matter. For example, store your creative writing assignments in one appropriately named folder and your music files in another appropriately named folder.

■ Do not mix data files and program files, that is, do not store data files in the folders that hold your software. On computers running Windows, most software programs are stored in subfolders of the Program Files folder.

■ Do not store programs or data files in the root directory (C:\) of your computer's hard drive. It is better to create folders and store your files in those folders.

■ Be aware of storage locations. When you save files, make sure the drive letter and folder name specify the correct storage location.

■ Organize your folders from the top down. When creating a hierarchy of folders, consider how you want to access and back up files. A **backup** is a copy of your files made for safekeeping. You should back up your folders regularly. For example, it your files are stored in one folder, such as the My Documents folder, then it is easy to backup that folder and all nested subfolders. If your important data is scattered in a variety of folders, however, making backups is more time consuming.

■ Access files from the hard drive. For best performance, copy files from portable storage media to your computer's hard drive before accessing them.

■ Follow copyright rules. When copying files, make sure you do not violate copyright and license restrictions.

■ Delete or archive files you no longer need. Deleting unneeded files and folders helps keep your list of files from growing to an unmanageable size. One way to delete a file is to right-click the file name in Windows Explorer, and the click Delete on the shortcut menu. File archiving utility programs combine a number of files together into one archive file, or a series of archive files, for long-term storage.

Unit D

Deleting folders and files

The Windows Recycle Bin and similar utilities in other operating systems protect you from accidentally deleting folders and files from your hard drive. When you give the command to delete a folder or file, the operating system moves the folder or file to the Recycle Bin folder. See Figure D-15. The deleted folder or file still takes up space on the hard drive, but it does not appear in the usual directory listing. The folder file does, however, appear in the directory listing for the Recycle Bin folder. You can undelete any folders or files in this listing. It is important to remember that only folders or files you delete from your hard drive are sent to the Recycle Bin. Folders or files you delete from a removable storage medium, such as a USB device, CD, or DVD, are not sent to the Recycle Bin.

FIGURE D-15: Recycle Bin empty and full

Used with permission from Microsoft

Bin empty Bin full

How Computers Represent Data

Data representation refers to the way in which data is created, stored, processed, output, and transmitted. It is the technology that makes it possible for you to use digital electronic devices such as iPods, GPS devices, mobile phones, and computers. Data representation makes it possible to input, store, process, and display text, numbers, graphics, photos, or play music and videos. Digital data is represented using the binary number system.

Learning Objective 5:
Describe how digital data representation produces numbers, text, images, video, and sound

● **What is the binary number system?** The **binary number system** makes it possible for computers to represent data simply by using 0s and 1s. The 0s and 1s are translated into electrical on and off signals that the computer can understand.

Table D-3 compares the decimal number system with the binary number system. Notice that the decimal system, base 10, uses ten symbols (0, 1, 2, 3, 4, 5, 6, 7, 8, and 9) to represent numbers. The binary number system has only two digits: 0 and 1.

TABLE D-3: Comparing the decimal and binary number systems

Decimal	Binary	Decimal	Binary
0	0	7	111
1	1	8	1000
2	10	9	1001
3	11	10	1010
4	100	11	1011
5	101	1000	1111101000
6	110	1001	1111101001

© Cengage Learning

● **What is digital data?** **Digital data** is text, numbers, graphics, sound, and video that has been converted into the digits 0 and 1. All digital data is created from 0s and 1s. The 0s and 1s are electronic signals that represent on and off, or yes and no, respectively. The computer interprets these electronic signals as data.

● **How does the computer interpret these electronic signals?** The electronic signals are coded as a series of 0s and 1s. Each 0 or 1 is one **binary digit**, or **bit**. A series of eight bits is referred to as a **byte**. Each byte represents one piece of data, such as the letter g, the number 5, or one dot

in a picture. Bytes are coded using different coding schemes. Most computer coding schemes use eight bits to represent each number, letter, or symbol.

Digital computers use many different coding schemes to represent data. The coding scheme used by a computer depends on whether the data is numeric or character data. **Numeric data** includes numbers that might be used in arithmetic operations such as your annual income, your age, or the cost of dinner.

● **How can my computer process character data?**
Character data is composed of letters, symbols, and numerals that will not be used in arithmetic operations. Examples of character data include your name, address, and telephone number. Character data is represented by coding schemes, which use a series of 1s and 0s. For example, when you type the word dog, you press the key that represents each letter. As you press each key, an electronic signal is sent to the processor. The signal is the code for the letter you typed. See Figure D-16.

FIGURE D-16: Coding data

The letter g as digital code

© Cengage Learning

The most common coding schemes for coding character data are ASCII, EBCDIC, and Unicode. Unicode is the most flexible, and currently provides code for characters from all written languages, including languages such as Chinese, Russian, and Hebrew. Modern personal computers use the Extended ASCII (American Standard Code for Information Interchange) coding scheme.

● **How can my computer process numbers to be used in calculations?** Computers use the binary number system to represent numeric data. So, when you type the number you want to use in a calculation, such as 3, the number is converted to its binary representation, 11. The computer recognizes this digital data as the number 3.

● **How can my computer process images, such as the photos from my camera?** Images, such as photos, pictures, line art, and graphs, are not discrete objects like a number or letter of the alphabet. A computer must **digitize** the information that makes up the picture (such as the colors) into 1s and 0s. Digitized images are a series of colored dots, also called **pixels** (picture elements). See Figure D-17. Each pixel is assigned a binary number based on the color of that pixel. A digital image is simply a list of binary numbers for all the dots it contains. Each binary number in the list is associated with one pixel. The computer interprets the list of numbers to recreate the image.

FIGURE D-17: **Pixels in an image**

Each pixel is assigned a binary number based on its color.

© Cengage Learning

● **How are digital sound files created?** Sounds are continuous analog sound waves. In order for a computer to understand a sound, it must digitize the information that makes up the sound. Sound, such as music and speech, is characterized by the properties of a sound wave. An analog sound wave is digitized by sampling it at various points, and then converting those points into digital numbers. The more samples your computer takes, the closer the points come to approximating the full wave pattern. This process of sampling, as shown in Figure D-18, is how digital recordings, such as the music files on your portable media player, are made.

FIGURE D-18: **Digitizing sound**

An analog sound wave is a smooth curve of continous values.

To digitize a wave, it is sliced into vertical segments, called samples.

© Cengage Learning

More about bits and bytes

As discussed, a bit is one binary digit, and a byte is eight bits. The word bit can be abbreviated as a lowercase b, and the word byte can be abbreviated as an uppercase B. The terms used to quantify computer data are summarized in Table D-4. The prefixes **kilo-** (thousands), **mega-** (millions), **giga-** (billions), **tera-** (trillion), **peta-** (thousand trillion), **exa-** (quintillion), and **zetta-** (sextillion) are used for large amounts of data.

Bits and bytes are used in different ways. Data transmission speeds are usually expressed in bits, whereas storage space is usually expressed in bytes. Typically, kilobytes (KB) are used to refer to most common documents, megabytes (MB) are used to refer to RAM, and gigabytes (GB) are used to refer to hard drive, optical storage media, and solid-state drive capacities. In an iPod ad, you might notice that it can store up to 160 GB or 160 gigabytes of music and video. The Internet data transfer speed for your computer might be listed as 5 Mbps or 5 megabits per second.

TABLE D-4: **Terms used to describe digital data**

Term	Value	Term	Value
Bit	1 binary digit	**Byte**	8 bits
Kilobit (Kb)	1,000 bits (exactly 1,024)	**Kilobyte (KB)**	1,000 bytes (exactly 1,024)
Megabit (Mb)	1 million bits	**Megabyte (MB)**	1 million bytes
Gigabit (Gb)	1 billion bits	**Gigabyte (GB)**	1 billion bytes
Terabyte (TB)	1 trillion bytes	**Petabyte (PB)**	1,000 terabytes (2^{50} bytes)
Exabyte (EB)	1,000 petabytes (2^{60} bytes)	**Zettabyte (ZB)**	1,000 exabytes (2^{70} bytes)

(Note: All values are approximate unless noted otherwise.)

© Cengage Learning

Integrated Circuits— An Overview

Computers and digital devices are electronic devices that use electrical signals to process data. The electronic parts of a personal computer store, process, and transfer the data. In the beginning, the electronic parts were large and bulky. Over time, the electronic parts have become smaller and more efficient. The most significant technology that made the miniaturization of electronics parts possible is the integrated circuit.

Learning Objective 6:
Define integrated circuits and explain the role they play inside a computer

● **What is an integrated circuit?** An **integrated circuit (IC)** is a very thin slice of semiconducting material, such as silicon and germanium. ICs are packed with microscopic circuit elements. See Figure D-19. These elements include wires, transistors, capacitors, logic gates, and resistors, and are used to create miniature electronic parts and pathways. Electronic signals, the bits and bytes, travel over these electronic pathways. The terms **computer chip**, microchip, and **chip** are all synonymous with the term integrated circuit. Chips are manufactured in sterile environments to protect their parts.

FIGURE D-19: An integrated circuit

Courtesy of Intel Corporation; © Wetchawut/Shutterstock.com

● **Are there chips in all electronic devices?** Yes, chips are not only in a computer's system unit but also in other electronic devices, such as tablet computers, smartphones, and GPS devices. Chips are also embedded in appliances such as refrigerators, microwaves, and cars. In fact, electronic devices use integrated circuits for processors, memory, and support circuitry.

● **What protects chips from possibly being damaged?** Each chip is packaged in a protective carrier or chip package. Chip packages vary in shape and size. The **DIP (dual inline package)** chip package is small with caterpillar-like legs protruding from a black, rectangular body. The **PGA (pin-grid array)** chip package resembles a pincushion. The **DIMM (dual inline memory module)** chip package is long and slim. See Figure D-20.

FIGURE D-20: **Packaging for integrated circuits**

A DIP chip package

A DIMM chip package

A PGA chip package

© Arber/Shutterstock.com; Courtesy of MediaTechnics Corporation; © Richard Lister/Shutterstock.com

● **How are all these chip packages connected to the computer?** Chip packages are connected to the computer's motherboard. As you'll recall from Unit A, the **motherboard** is the computer's main circuit board. See Figure D-21. The DIP and PGA chip packages are plugged into sockets and connectors on the motherboard. DIMM chip packages and small circuit boards are plugged into slots on the motherboard. Some chips are soldered permanently in place. The motherboard contains the electronic circuitry that connects all these parts. As discussed in Unit B, expansion cards attach to the motherboard through expansion slots.

Because some chips can be inserted and removed easily, they can be replaced if they become damaged or need to be upgraded. Sometimes, multiple chips are required for a single function, such as generating stereo-quality sound. In this case, the chips might be housed on a separate small circuit board, such as an expansion card.

FIGURE D-21: **Chips on a motherboard**

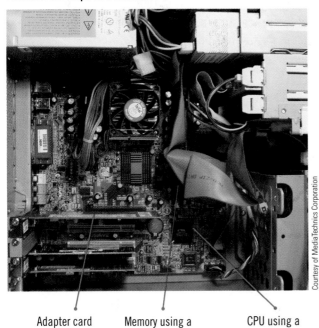

Courtesy of MediaTechnics Corporation

Adapter card with chips Memory using a DIMM chip package CPU using a PGA chip package

● **What is a processor?** A **processor** (also called a **microprocessor**) is one type of chip or integrated circuit. The main processor in a personal computer is the **CPU (central processing unit).** It is designed to process instructions. A processor is a very complex integrated circuit, containing hundreds of millions of miniaturized electronic parts. See Figure D-22. It is the most important and usually the most expensive single part of a computer. Looking inside a computer, you can usually identify the processor because it is the largest chip on the motherboard. Most of today's processors are housed in a PGA chip

FIGURE D-22: **Every digital device has a processor**

Courtesy of Intel Corporation Courtesy of NVIDIA

Desktop processor Smartphone processor

package. All digital devices have processors. As you might suspect, processors for mobile devices such as smartphones, cameras, and tablet computers are smaller than processors for desktop computers.

● **Which companies produce most of today's popular PC processors?** Intel is the world's largest chipmaker and supplies a sizeable percentage of the processors that power PCs. AMD (Advanced Micro Devices) is Intel's chief rival in the PC chip market. It produces processors that work just like Intel's chips but at a lower price. Processors for mobile devices are also made by companies such as ARM, Texas Instruments, Samsung, and NVIDIA.

A typical personal computer ad contains a long list of specifications describing a computer's parts and technical details. Most computer specifications begin with the processor brand, type, and speed. The processors that are marketed with today's computers will handle most business, educational, and entertainment applications.

● **How can I tell what CPU my computer uses?** You can use software to identify your computer's CPU and its specifications. If you are running Windows, you can access this information through the Windows Control Panel. See Figure D-23. If you have a Mac, click About This Mac from the Apple menu in the upper-left menu bar, and then click More Info to view the name of the processor.

FIGURE D-23: **Installed processor specs**

Used with permission from Microsoft

● **Can I replace my computer's processor with a faster or better one?** Yes, it is possible to upgrade your computer's processor, but computer owners rarely do. The price of the latest, greatest processor can often get you more than halfway to buying an entirely new computer system. Technical factors also discourage processor upgrades. A processor operates at full efficiency only if all parts in the computer can handle the faster speeds.

Processors—An Overview

As discussed in the previous lesson, the central processing unit (CPU) contains all the circuitry that performs the central processing tasks of the computer on a single chip. Different personal computers come with different processors. Processors have certain factors in common. Knowing how each of the processor's factors affects the performance of a computer can help you can make an informed decision when buying a computer.

Learning Objective 7:
Explain how CPU factors affect computer performance

● **What factors affect processor performance?** A processor's performance is affected by several factors, including number of cores, clock speed, bus speed, word size, and cache memory size. These factors combine to affect the processing speed, which determines the computer's performance. A processor's factors are described as part of a processor's specs (also called specifications). A processor's specs are available on its processor manufacturer's Web site and in processor documentation. You can also access this information about your computer through third-party software, such as CPU-Z. See Figure D-24.

FIGURE D-24: Specs for a processor using the CPU-Z program

Courtesy of CPUID

the specs for an Intel Core i7 quad-core processor in part of a sample computer ad. A processor that contains circuitry for more than one processing unit on a single chip is called a **multi-core processor**. Multi-core processors (such as dual-core and quad-core processors) are faster than processors with a single core. To gain maximum speed, however, your computer's operating system and software should be optimized for multi-core processing. Most operating systems support multi-core processing.

FIGURE D-25: Processor specs in an ad

Intel Core i7 2860QM processor 2.50 GHz 1600 MHz FSB 8 MB L2 cache

© Cengage Learning

● **What is clock speed?** The **processor clock** is a timing device that sets the pace (the clock speed) for executing instructions. The **clock speed** is specified in megahertz (MHz), which is millions of cycles per second, or gigahertz (GHz), which is billions of cycles per second. A **cycle** is the smallest unit of time a processor can recognize. The faster the clock, the more instructions the processor can execute per second. For the processor in the sample ad shown in Figure D-26, the clock speed is 2.50 GHz. This means the processor's clock operates at 2.5 billion cycles per second.

FIGURE D-26: Clock speed specs in an ad

Intel Core i7 2860QM processor 2.50 GHz 1600 MHz FSB 8 MB L2 cache

© Cengage Learning

● **What do processor specs tell me about the processor?** Computer ads typically include specs that determine a processor's performance. Figure D-25 shows

● **What is bus speed?** A **bus** is an electronic pathway that carries the electronic signals between the electronic parts of a computer. Bus speed identifies how fast the electronic signals move along the bus pathway. **FSB** stands for **front side bus**.

This term refers to the circuitry that transports data to and from the processor. See Figure D-27.

Currently, FSB speed is measured in megahertz (MHz). In the sample ad in Figure D-28, the FSB speed is 1600 MHz. When comparing processors, larger numbers indicate faster FSB speeds.

Wires transfer bits of information between the CPU and devices

Courtesy of Intel Corporation; © Cengage Learning; Courtesy of MediaTechnics Corporation

FIGURE D-28: Bus specs in an ad

Intel Core i7 2860QM processor 2.50 GHz 1600 MHz FSB 8 MB L2 cache

© Cengage Learning

- **What is word size?** Word size refers to the number of bits that a processor can manipulate at one time. A processor with a 32-bit word size, for example, has 32-bit registers, processes 32 bits at one time, and is referred to as a 32-bit processor. Processors with a larger word size can process more data during each processor cycle. Today's personal computers typically contain 32-bit or 64-bit processors.

- **What is cache?** Cache, also called RAM cache or cache memory, is high-speed memory that a processor can access more rapidly than memory elsewhere on the motherboard. The amount of cache memory, as well as its location, affects performance. A Level 1 (L1) cache is built into the processor chip, whereas a Level 2 (L2) cache is located on a separate chip, and so it takes a processor more time to get data from the L2 cache to the processor. Usually, cache capacity is expressed in megabytes (MB). The processor in the sample ad in Figure D-29 has 8 MB L2 cache.

FIGURE D-29: Cache specs in an ad

Intel Core i7 2860QM processor 2.50 GHz 1600 MHz FSB 8 MB L2 cache

© Cengage Learning

- **How can I tell which processor best meets my needs?** You can use benchmark results to compare the results to other processors. Benchmarking is a technique used across many industries to compare and measure performance. Testing laboratories run a series of tests called **benchmarks** to gauge the overall speed of a processor. The results of benchmark tests are usually available on the Web and are published in computer magazine articles.

All things being equal, a computer with a 3.8 GHz processor is faster than a computer with a 2.4 GHz processor—and a computer with a processor that has a larger word size can process more data during each processor cycle than a computer with a processor that has a smaller word size. Furthermore, all things being equal, a computer with Level 1 cache is faster than a computer with the same amount of Level 2 cache. But all things are not equal so you can use benchmark test results to compare processors before you buy a computer.

- **Is there a way for me to find out how my computer measures up?** Windows 7 offers a set of benchmarks called the Windows Experience Index. This index scores a computer's overall performance, as well as the performance of components such as its processor, memory, graphics, and storage system. You can see this on your Windows computer through the Performance Tools section of the Control Panel. See Figure D-30.

FIGURE D-30: Windows Experience Score

Used with permission from Microsoft

Subscores help you gauge performance for individual components

The base score provides an overall performance benchmark

How the processor gets instructions

Computer programmers write programs that control computers. These programs include the instructions that tell a processor what to do. These programs are usually written in a high-level programming language. The human-readable version of a program is called **source code**. Source code has to be converted into a digital format before the processor can use it. The procedure for translating source code into 0s and 1s is done by a compiler or an interpreter. A **compiler** converts all the statements in a program in a single batch. The resulting collection of instructions, called **object code**, is placed in a new file. Most of the program files distributed as software contain object code that is ready for the processor to execute. An **interpreter** converts and executes one statement at a time while the program is running.

Computer Memory: RAM

Memory is the electronic circuitry that holds data and instructions so it is available when needed by a computer. Computers use four categories of memory: random access memory (RAM), virtual memory, read-only memory (ROM), and EEPROM memory. Each type of memory is characterized by the type of data it contains and the technology it uses to hold the data. This lesson discusses random access memory, commonly called RAM.

Learning Objective 8:
Define RAM and explain its importance to computers

● **What is RAM?** In a personal computer, **RAM (random access memory)** is the waiting room for the computer's processor. RAM is usually several chips or small circuit boards that plug into the motherboard. RAM holds operating system instructions that control the basic functions of a computer system. These instructions are loaded into RAM every time you start your computer. These instructions are stored in RAM until you turn off your computer. RAM is also a temporary holding area for program instructions, as well as for data waiting to be processed, displayed, or printed. In addition, RAM holds the results of processing until they can be stored more permanently using a storage system. Refer to Figure D-31.

FIGURE D-31: **RAM is a a temporary holding area**

RAM

Courtesy of MediaTechnics Corporation; Used with permission from Microsoft

● **Does RAM matter?** Yes. The amount of RAM your computer has makes a difference in how well your computer can perform. Usually the more RAM your computer has, the better the performance. In fact, along with processor speed, RAM capacity is the other most important factor in determining and comparing the power of a computer system. The performance of your computer is directly related to how much RAM is available for your applications, data, and operating system. RAM is made by different manufacturers. Be

sure to read reviews about a RAM product before purchasing it because quality can affect performance.

● **How does RAM work?** In RAM, electronic parts called **capacitors** hold the bits that represent data. You can visualize the capacitors as microscopic lights that can be turned on or off. A charged capacitor is turned on and represents a 1 bit. A discharged capacitor is turned off and represents a 0 bit. You can visualize the capacitors as being arranged in banks of eight. Refer to Figure D-32. Each bank holds eight bits, or one byte, of data. Each RAM location has an address and holds one byte of data. A RAM address at each location helps the computer locate data as needed for processing. The content of RAM is changed by changing the charge of each capacitor. The capacitor charge is changed when you input data and the computer processes that data.

FIGURE D-32: **How RAM works**

Address: M1
0 1 0 0 0 0 0 1
Address: M2
0 1 0 0 0 0 1 0
Address: M3
0 1 0 0 0 0 1 1

© Cengage Learning

The two charged capacitors at this RAM address represent the letter A.

A different sequence of charged capacitors represents the letter B.

Another sequence of charged capacitors represents the letter C.

● **How does RAM differ from hard drive storage on my computer?** RAM holds data temporarily in circuitry that's directly connected to the motherboard. In contrast, the hard drive stores data on magnetic or solid-state media. Data in RAM is temporary storage. Data stored on the hard drive storage is more permanent. In some respects, RAM is similar to a whiteboard. You can use a whiteboard to write formulas, erase them, and then write an outline for a report. In a similar way,

RAM can hold the numbers and formulas you need when you use spreadsheet software to balance your checkbook, and RAM can hold the text of your English essay when you use word processing software. Unlike a whiteboard, however, RAM is volatile, which means that it requires electrical power to hold data. If the computer is turned off or if the power goes out, all data in RAM instantly and permanently disappears.

- **How much RAM should my personal computer have?** The amount of RAM your computer needs depends on the software that you use. The capacity of RAM is expressed either in megabytes (MB) or gigabytes (GB). Today's personal computers typically feature 2–8 GB of RAM. If you are using a Windows computer, you can view information about your computer, including how much RAM is currently installed, using the Control Panel. See Figure D-33.

FIGURE D-33: Installed RAM specs

RAM requirements are routinely specified on the outside of a software package. If you want to buy a new program that needs more RAM than is installed on your computer, you can purchase and install additional RAM. However, the amount of RAM is limited by the computer's motherboard, such as by the number of slots the motherboard has to hold RAM. The manufacturer of the motherboard sets the limits. Also, if you plan to upgrade, contact the manufacturer of the computer or motherboard so you can be sure to buy the correct type of RAM.

- **Why is it important to have the most RAM possible?** RAM capacity makes a difference you can notice. For example, if you are working on a spreadsheet, the program instructions and the worksheet are stored in RAM. See Figure D-34. With lots of RAM, you will notice that calculations happen faster and that many graphics operations take less time than with a computer that has less RAM capacity.

FIGURE D-34: RAM influences performance

- **Does RAM speed make a difference?** Yes. The amount of time that RAM takes to write or to read data once the request has been received from the processor is called the access time. So, faster RAM generally means faster performance. RAM speed is often expressed in **nanoseconds (ns)**, which are billionths of a second. Whenever referring to nanoseconds, lower numbers mean faster transmission and processing of data. For example, 8 ns RAM is faster than 10 ns RAM. RAM speed can also be expressed in MHz (millions of cycles per second). This measurement is used so RAM speed can be compared to clock speed. The way you interpret MHz rates is just the opposite of the way you interpret nanosecond rates. Higher MHz ratings mean faster speeds. For example, 1066 MHz RAM is faster than 800 MHz RAM.

- **How can I know if the computer I want to buy has enough RAM?** Most computer ads specify RAM capacity, speed, and type. The ad also provides important information about the maximum amount of RAM that can be installed in the computer. For example, a computer ad might list the specifications shown in the partial ad in Figure D-35.

FIGURE D-35: RAM specs in an ad

2 GB Dual Channel DDR2 SDRAM at 1066 MHz (max 4 GB)

© Cengage Learning

The specs in this ad mean the following: the computer currently has 2 gigabytes of installed RAM. The RAM uses dual-channel, double data rate 2 SDRAM. **SDRAM (Synchronous DRAM)** is a generic name for various kinds of DRAM that are synchronized with the clock speed for which the processor is optimized. Most of today's personal computers use SDRAM. Innovations such as dual-channel technology and double data rate (DDR, DDR2, or DDR3) have increased SDRAM speed. The ad indicates the RAM speed is measured at 1066 MHz. It also indicates that this computer can have a maximum 4 GB of RAM.

Other Types of Computer Memory

In addition to RAM, a computer uses other types of memory. Virtual memory, ROM, and EEPROM are the other main categories of memory commonly used in computers. This lesson looks at these types of computer memory and how all computer memory types work together.

Learning Objective 9:

Explain how a computer uses virtual memory, ROM, and EEPROM

● **What is virtual memory?** Although, technically, RAM cannot be full, it can reach near capacity. If you open several application programs and several large graphics or videos at the same time, you can push RAM to its limit. When this occurs, the computer slows down. You might notice that it takes longer to load a screen or respond to a command. To help solve this problem, the operating system uses an area of the hard drive to temporarily store data from RAM. This area of the hard drive is called **virtual memory**. The data that has been moved from RAM to virtual memory is called a **swap file**. See Figure D-36. Virtual memory stores parts of a program or data file until needed. By exchanging the data in RAM with the data in virtual memory, your computer gains almost unlimited memory capacity.

FIGURE D-36: **How virtual memory works**

Data is copied from RAM to the virtual memory area of the hard drive and back again as needed for processing.

RAM

Hard drive

Courtesy of MediaTechnics Corporation

Too much dependence on virtual memory can have a negative effect on your computer's performance. Getting data from a mechanical device, such as a hard drive, is much slower than getting data from an electronic device, such as RAM. Installing as much RAM as your computer system allows will help your computer improve its performance.

● **What is ROM?** ROM (read-only memory) is a type of memory that holds the computer's startup routine and other basic system information. ROM is housed in a single integrated circuit and is usually a large chip that is plugged into the motherboard. Unlike RAM, which is temporary and volatile, ROM is permanent and nonvolatile. The instructions in ROM are permanent and are not lost even when the computer power is turned off. The only way to change the instructions in ROM is to replace the ROM chip. To overcome this limitation, some newer computers use flash memory chips instead of ROM for storing the startup routine and other system information. Flash memory chips can be changed and they do not lose data when the power is turned off.

● **Does ROM control the boot process?** Yes. When you turn on a computer, the ROM circuitry receives power and begins the boot process by executing the bootstrap program. As discussed in Unit C, the boot process has six major events, including the power-on self-test (POST). See Figure D-37. During the boot process, the bootstrap program in ROM instructs the core operating system programs to load into RAM.

FIGURE D-37: **POST screen**

Péter Gudella/Shutterstock.com; © Cengage Learning

- **When I boot my computer, sometimes I see a message about BIOS. What is that?** When you turn on your computer, the processor receives electrical power and is ready to begin executing instructions. But, because the power was off, RAM is empty and contains no instructions for the processor to execute. Your computer needs to know how much memory is available so that it can allocate space for all of the programs that you want to run. This configuration information cannot be stored in RAM because no information is in RAM when the computer power is turned off. Instead, this configuration information is stored in ROM.

 ROM contains a small set of instructions called the **ROM BIOS (basic input/output system)**. When the computer is turned on, the BIOS message tells you that the operating system is reading the configuration settings. While ROM BIOS instructions are accomplished mainly without user intervention, the computer will not function without the ROM chip and the BIOS instructions. You know the boot process is complete when the operating system is loaded into RAM and your computer is ready to accept commands. See Figure D-38.

FIGURE D-38: **ROM and the boot process**

Courtesy of MediaTechnics Corporation

- **How does the computer recognize the devices connected to my computer?** When you turn on your computer, the boot program checks the configuration settings to see what hardware and which devices are connected to your computer. When you add new hardware, the computer needs information about the hardware in order to recognize the hardware you added. This information is stored in the configurations settings. Computer configuration settings include the date and time, hard drive capacity, number of CD/DVD/BD drives, and RAM capacity.

- **Are the configurations stored in ROM?** No. Remember that ROM holds data on a permanent basis. It cannot be used to store configuration settings because the data in ROM cannot be updated when new hardware is added. For example, if you add more memory modules, the computer could not update the memory specification information in ROM. This means the new memory would not be recognized by your computer system during the boot process. In order to be able to store and update basic system information, including configuration settings, your computer needs a type of memory that is more permanent than RAM but less permanent than ROM.

- **Where are configuration settings stored?** The configuration settings are stored in EEPROM. **EEPROM (electrically erasable programmable read-only memory)** is a nonvolatile chip that requires no power to hold data. So, when you change the configuration of your computer system—by adding RAM, for example—the data in EEPROM is updated. See Figure D-39.

FIGURE D-39: **Configuration settings**

Courtesy of Rachel B. Bunin

 Some operating systems recognize such changes and automatically perform the update. If this does not happen, you can manually change EEPROM settings by running your computer's setup program. To access the EEPROM setup program on a Windows computer, hold down the F1 key as your computer boots. But be careful! If you make a mistake with these settings your computer might not be able to start.

Talking Points: Is Your Computer Making You Sick?

More and more workers spend their entire eight-hour day in front of a computer screen. Many work longer than the typical 40-hour workweek of eight-hour days for five days a week. Road warriors are lugging notebook computers through airports and trying to get work done in the cramped confines of economy seats. As computers and other digital devices continue to infiltrate the workplace, worker advocates are concerned about health risks associated with computer use. They raise questions about how the use of digital devices affect ordinary consumers, too. The general population in most developed countries own more digital gadgets and spend more time using them than ever before. Studies have shown that the average American spends about two hours a day using a computer. The popularity of LAN parties has spawned intensive daylong competitions, and many serious gamers are still hunched over their keyboards in the wee hours of the morning. It is rare to go anywhere and not see someone talking on a cell phone or plugged into a portable music player. How does this digital lifestyle affect the health of our nation and world?

Radiation Risks

Although we tend to associate radiation with the fallout from nuclear blasts and debilitating cancer treatments, the term refers simply to any energy that is emitted in the form of waves or particles. Radiation streams out of the sun in the form of heat and out of your stereo system as sound waves. Even more radiation pulses out from electrical appliances, wireless networks, cell phone towers, and electrical power lines. Most of the radiation in your everyday world is considered safe, especially in moderation. A few types of radiation can be harmful. Gamma rays and X-rays, for example, contain enough electromagnetic energy to alter chemical reactions in the body and disrupt molecules in human tissue. Shielding against these types of radiation is an important safety factor.

Every electronic device emits some type of radiation; otherwise, they would not be functional. The light emitted by computer, mobile phone, smartphone, and portable music player screens is essential for their use. Cell phones emit sound waves so we can listen to the person at the other end of the connection. Wireless routers emit radio waves to carry data from one workstation to another. Although the radiation from most digital gadgets is considered harmless, researchers have raised concerns about radiation from cell phones and computer display devices.

" The available scientific evidence does not allow us to conclude that mobile phones are absolutely safe, or that they are unsafe."

U.S. Food and Drug Administration (FDA)

LCD, LED, and OLED display devices generate an image by illuminating a matrix of tiny lights. LCD, LED, and OLED technologies have no tubes, no electron sprays, and generate no X-rays. LCD and OLED devices do, however, emit low levels of radiation. Emission levels vary depending on manufacturer, brand, and model. Monitors that meet TCO or MPR standards have emission levels believed to be safe. Various devices designed to block radiation are on the market, but their effectiveness is questionable. Regardless of the type of display device you use, do not sit too close to it. Your exposure to radiation is reduced the farther away you sit from it.

A mobile phone is a radio transmitter and receiver. It emits RF (radio frequency) energy. High levels of RF energy can heat human tissue in much the same way a microwave oven heats food. Compared to a microwave oven, however, the amount of radiation emitted by a cell phone is miniscule. The amount of radiation emitted by a cell phone can be measured by its specific absorption rate (SAR). You can find the SAR level for your cell phone by entering its FCC ID number (look for it in the user manual) at www.fcc.gov/oet/ea/fccid/. See Figure D-40.

FIGURE D-40: Finding the SAR for a cell phone

www.fcc.gov

You can also find SAR information on the phone manufacturer's Web site. In addition, a quick Google search reveals that SAR levels for mobile phones are listed on several Web pages. You can use these sites to compare SAR levels for different phones.

The scientific community continues to study and debate the amount of RF radiation that should be considered safe for long-term use. A recent Swedish study found evidence that long-term, extensive cell phone use significantly increases the risk of developing a brain tumor. A contradictory study performed by the London-based Institute of Cancer Research and three British universities found that cell phone use does not increase the incidence of brain tumors in cell phone users. Research literature is full of similar conflicting studies. Even the U.S. Food and Drug Administration (FDA) admits, "The available scientific evidence does not allow us to conclude that mobile phones are absolutely safe, or that they are unsafe."

> **Most of the health risks associated with computer use are not caused by the equipment itself, but by how the equipment is set up and used.**

The easiest way to reduce your exposure to mobile phone radiation is to use a hands-free headset. Headsets offer the additional benefit of reducing your chance of becoming involved in a traffic accident. Today, many states require the use of headsets while driving, See Figure D-41.

FIGURE D-41: **Use a headset for mobile phone calls**

© iStockphoto/Ron Bailey

Repetitive Stress Injuries

Most of the health risks associated with computer use are not caused by the equipment itself, but by how the equipment is set up and used. Improper positioning of your keyboard and mouse can cause repetitive stress injuries to wrists, arms, neck, back, and shoulders. A repetitive stress injury is not a specific disease. Instead, it is a group of similar overuse disorders that affect the tendons, muscles, and nerves.

Symptoms include stiffness and minor pain in your hands, wrists, arms, or shoulders. See Figure D-42. Your symptoms might appear while you're working, or they might appear several hours or days later. With rest, these injuries tend to heal. Although there are some problems, such as carpal tunnel syndrome, that might require medical intervention.

FIGURE D-42: **Carpal Tunnel syndrome**

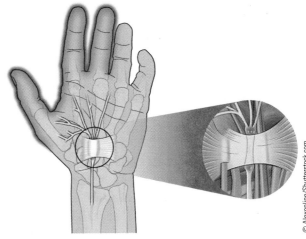

© Alexonline/Shutterstock.com

Your wrist contains eight carpal bones surrounding a large nerve that controls your thumb, index, and ring fingers. How you place your hands on the keyboard can affect the pressure on that nerve. See Figure D-43. Anything that compresses this nerve, such as arthritis or thickened tendons, can cause numbness, pain, or tingling in your fingers. This condition is called carpal tunnel syndrome. At one time it was generally accepted that keyboarding was a major cause of carpal tunnel syndrome. A recent Mayo Clinic study, however, concluded that keyboarding does not cause carpal tunnel syndrome. Although the study did find that keyboarding can make the condition worse.

FIGURE D-43: **Place your fingers correctly on the keyboard**

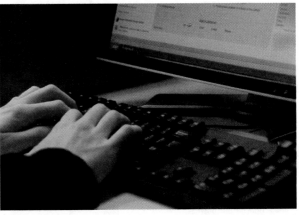

Courtesy of Emily Bunin

Most computer-related hand and arm injuries are repetitive stress injuries, which can be avoided by following ergonomic guidelines. Ergonomics is the study of safe and

efficient environments, particularly working environments. Ergonomics provides guidelines for making work environments safer and healthier. In the United States, the Occupational Safety and Health Administration (OSHA) sets and enforces standards for the safety and health of American workers. Although a federal law to enforce ergonomic standards in the workplace was repealed in 2001, many states have regulations designed to protect workers from repetitive stress injuries. You can review current OSHA policy by visiting their Web site at http://www.osha.gov/SLTC/ergonomics/index.html.

> **Most computer-related hand and arm injuries are repetitive stress injuries, which can be avoided by following ergonomic guidelines.**

To avoid future computer-related stress injuries, keep ergonomic principles in mind wherever you work. The key to avoiding uncomfortable stress injuries is in the placement and use of your keyboard, mouse, monitor, desk, and chair. Figure D-44 provides an overview of ergonomic workstation guidelines. Some specific tips for setting up your keyboard and mouse follow:

- Position the keyboard so that it is just above your lap and your elbows are able to extend past the 90-degree angle when you type.

- When shopping for a computer desk, make sure it has a keyboard tray. The tray should be adjustable if possible. Also, look for one with a small lip that reduces the distance between the tray and your thighs.

- Angle the keyboard so that your wrists are straight when typing.

- If you have a wrist rest, use it only when you are not typing. Resting your wrist or arm on a wrist rest while typing causes your wrist to be at an angle that is not efficient.

- Use a keyboard that fits the size of your hands and fingers. When you rest your fingers on the home keys (asdf and jkl;), there should be 1/8 to 1/4 inch of space between them. When you type, your fingers should not be cramped together or overextended.

- Make sure your mouse is positioned close by so that you don't have to reach for it.

- Keep the mouse at the same height as your keyboard to minimize arm movements.

- Use your mouse with a relaxed arm and wrist.

- When working at mouse-intensive activities, you should change mouse hands occasionally. You might also consider using an air mouse or trackball, each of which requires a different set of muscles.

FIGURE D-44: **Place your fingers correctly on the keyboard**

Mouse in plane or slightly above plane of keyboard

Top 1/3 of screen at or slightly below eye level

Monitor 18"–22" from body (arm's length)

Keyboard on slight negative tilt (back of keyboard lower than front)

Knee angle greater than 90 degrees with feet in front of you

Feet flat on the floor or on footrest

Lean back slightly with back supported from pelvis to shoulder blades

Elbow angle slightly more than 90 degrees

Thighs parallel to floor

Approximately 2"–3" of space between back of knee and chair

© Cengage Learning

Eye Strain

Studies have found links between computer use and eye problems. The most common symptoms are sore, tired, burning, or itching eyes; watery eyes; dry eyes; blurred or double vision; headaches; difficulty shifting focus between the screen display and printed documents; and increased sensitivity to light. For many computer users, eye problems can be avoided by proper monitor placement and adjustment.

> **"Studies have found links between computer use and eye problems."**

To position your monitor correctly, sit back slightly in your chair and stretch your right arm out straight ahead of you. Your middle finger should almost touch the center of your screen. See Figure D-45. Once the screen is set at the proper height, tilt it backwards just a bit. You should feel like you are looking down slightly at the screen. Your screen should be directly in front of you and parallel to your shoulders. A monitor that is tilted to one side or another makes your eyes focus at different distances, which is tiring.

FIGURE D-45: Positioning a monitor

© Cengage Learning

If you use two monitors, place your second monitor as close to the first monitor as possible, but angled so that when you turn your head slightly, you face it straight on. You might also consider moving it to the other side of your primary monitor periodically. When positioning your monitor, try to minimize the amount of glare from lights or windows that is reflected on the screen. Angle the screen away from windows. It is best not to end up facing a window where bright outdoor light can interfere with the way your pupils need to dilate for the brightness of your computer screen. If glare is a problem in your work area, you can purchase an antiglare screen that fits

over your monitor. Keeping the surface of your monitor free of dust can also cut down on glare. Notebook computers present an ergonomic problem because the screen and keyboard are typically attached to each other. Placement becomes a compromise between the best viewing angle and the best typing height. When possible, use an external keyboard and mouse with your notebook computer to achieve a more ergonomic work area.

People who wear bifocal and trifocal lenses tend to focus on the computer screen through the bottom of the lens. In order to do this, wearers raise their chins to view the screen. This puts stress on neck muscles and causes headaches. To avoid this situation, bifocal and trifocal wearers might have to lower their screens or ask their optometrist for eyewear dedicated to viewing the computer screen.

One of the most effective steps you can take to avoid eyestrain is to adjust the resolution of your monitor so that you can easily read the text displayed on your screen. Remember that you can make two types of adjustments. You can adjust the resolution of your monitor through the operating system. This adjustment affects window, icon, and text size globally. Refer to Figure D-46. LCD screens have a native resolution that displays one pixel for each tiny light in the display matrix. Selecting a resolution lower than a screen's native resolution forces the display device to interpolate pixels. This results in a slightly fuzzy display.

FIGURE D-46: Changing screen resolution

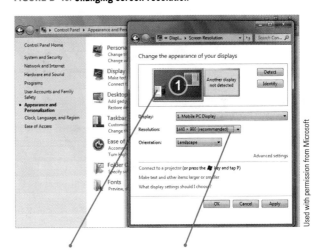

Used with permission from Microsoft

If you use more than one monitor, they will be shown here; select one.

The monitor's native resolution is usually the highest setting.

Once your monitor is set to its native resolution, you might find that the text on Web pages and in documents is too small to view comfortably. In that situation, you can adjust the zoom level within various applications. For example, you might set your browser to display larger text, and set your word processor to display text at 125 percent or 150 percent. Figure D-47 shows how a document in a word processor compares at two different zoom levels.

FIGURE D-47: Change zoom level to increase size of text on the screen

Zoom is set at 100%

To enlarge the text, Zoom to 130% but less text will be visible on the screen

Back Pain

Back pain can be caused by many factors, including poor posture and careless lifting of heavy objects. Doctors and physical therapists more commonly use the term *flex-forward position* to describe the sitting posture shared by many computer users. The layman's term *computer slump* refers to the posture of sitting hunched over a computer keyboard with your neck craned forward. See Figure D-48. Habitual slouching can lead to stiffness and muscle tenderness. Left uncorrected, the problem can cause nerve irritation that spreads down the arms and back. Back problems caused by habitual flex-forward posture are sometimes referred to as T4 syndrome, after the fourth cervical vertebra that is most affected.

FIGURE D-48: Incorrect posture

© Cengage Learning

The key to comfort while working on a computer is keeping your shoulders relaxed so that tense muscles don't generate headaches and stiffness. If the arm rests on your chair make your shoulders rise, you should remove the armrests or get another chair. Conventional wisdom about sitting straight has been challenged recently by a body of evidence that indicates the best position for computer work is with your upper torso leaning back slightly. With your torso at a 100-110 degree angle, the back of your chair helps to support your spine.

> "The key to comfort while working on a computer is keeping your shoulders relaxed so that tense muscles don't generate headaches and stiffness."

Carrying a heavy notebook computer can also contribute to back problems. To lighten your load, try to reduce the number of peripheral devices you carry. Consider toting your notebook computer in a backpack instead of a shoulder bag. Be sure the backpack provides the proper protection for your notebook computer. When traveling, place your notebook computer in a wheeled carrier.

Sedentary Lifestyle

People who live and work in digital cultures tend to spend many hours each day in sedentary pursuits, such as watching television and using computers. Many researchers believe that there is a link between our increasingly sedentary lifestyle and a steady climb in obesity and cardiovascular disease. To counteract the effects of a sedentary lifestyle, it is important to exercise and eat right. A good balance of stretching and cardiovascular exercise can help you keep physically fit and has the additional benefit of helping to prevent repetitive stress injuries and back pain. See Figure D-49.

FIGURE D-49: **Get exercise**

Sitting still for long periods of time, especially in positions that limit blood circulation, can be a health risk, similar to the risk of long-haul air travel. A condition called deep vein thrombosis is the formation of blood clots that commonly affect veins in the legs. Symptoms include pain, swelling, and redness in the affected area. Deep vein thrombosis requires treatment to prevent life-threatening complications if the clot moves to the heart. Although the condition is not common in young people, good work habits can help you maintain healthy circulation. For example, your chair should allow for good circulation to your legs. Make sure there are at least two inches of clearance between your calf and the front of your chair. Your thighs should be parallel to the ground to allow for good blood flow; if necessary, use a footrest to raise your feet and reduce the pressure on the backs of your thighs.

> " **Many researchers believe that there is a link between our increasingly sedentary lifestyle and a steady climb in obesity and cardiovascular disease.** "

To combat potential health hazards associated with computer use, you should try to take breaks periodically, say, every 20 minutes or at least once every hour. At minimum, try the 20/20/20 break: Every 20 minutes, take 20 seconds and look 20 feet away. Longer breaks of two to five minutes are more effective. During a longer break, stand up to change your circulation. Rest your eyes by focusing on distant objects. Gently rotate and stretch your wrists, shoulders, and neck. Break reminder software, such as RSIGuard and open source Workrave, can help you remember when it is time to take a break from your work. See Figure D-50.

FIGURE D-50: **An example of break software**

Courtesy of Workrave

> " **... try the 20/20/20 break: Every 20 minutes, take 20 seconds and look 20 feet away.** "

In conclusion, computer use can be hazardous to your health if you do not follow the guidelines set forth by health experts and described in this Talking Points section. But if you take proper care, you can work to improve your health and avoid computer-related health problems.

Expand the Ideas

1. Have you found that using computers has impacted your health in any way? Describe what you have experienced and any steps you have taken to improve the situation and follow good practices for healthy computing.

2. What steps have you taken to set up your computer so that it is ergonomically positioned? Explain how your actions have helped your situation and improved your health.

3. Do you make a habit of spending long hours in front of the computer? Do you try to take frequent breaks? How difficult is it to adjust your working habits to be healthier as you work at the computer? Do you believe that healthy habits will prevent computer-related injuries? Research current products and techniques for helping people work healthier at their computers.

Key Terms & Unit Review

Key Terms

Backup
Benchmark
Binary digit
Binary number system
Bit
Bus
Byte
Cache
Cache memory
Capacitor
Central processing unit (CPU)
Character data
Chip
Clock speed
Compiler
Computer chip
Computer programmer
Cycle
Data representation
Digital data
Digitize
DIMM (dual inline memory module)
DIP (dual inline package)
Directory
EEPROM
Exa-
Exabyte (EB)
File date
File extension
File format
File management
File management program
File path
File size
File specification
File tag
Filename
Filenaming conventions
Filename extension
Folder
Front side bus (FSB)
Giga-
Gigabit (Gb)
Gigabyte (GB)
Integrated circuit (IC)
Interpreter
Kilo-
Kilobit (Kb)
Kilobyte (KB)
Library
Mega-
Megabit (Mb)
Megabyte (MB)
Microprocessor
Motherboard
multi-core processor
Nanosecond
Native file format
Nested folder
Numeric data
Object code
Path
Peta-
Petabyte (PB)
PGA (pin-grid array)
Pixel
Processor
Processor cycle
RAM (Random Access Memory)
RAM cache
ROM (Read Only Memory)
ROM BIOS (basic input/output system)
Root directory
SDRAM (synchronous DRAM)
Source code
Subdirectory
Subfolder
Swap file
Tera-
Terabyte (TB)
Virtual memory
Windows Explorer
Word size
Zetta-
Zettabyte (ZB)

Unit Review

1. Review the bold terms in this unit. Then pick 10 terms that are the least familiar to you. Be sure that you can use your own words to define the terms you have selected.

2. Describe how the binary number system uses only 1s and 0s to represent numbers.

3. Describe three types of information that are stored with a file and the importance of a file extension.

4. Describe the difference between the Save and the Save As commands.

5. Describe three file management tasks that might best be accomplished using a file management program, such as Windows Explorer.

6. Using a sample file path from your own computer, describe a file path and how it describes the location of a file on the storage medium.

7. List five tips to follow when organizing files on your hard drive.

8. Explain the difference between bits and bytes, and the technical meaning of common prefixes, such as kilo, mega, giga, peta, and tera. What aspect of a computer system does each measure?

9. Make sure that you understand the meaning of the following measurement terms: KB, Kb, MB, Mb, GB, Gb, PB, TB, ZB, MHz, GHz, and ns.

10. List three different types of memory and briefly describe how each one works as you use your computer.

Concepts Review

Select the best answer.

1. The _____ is a unique set of characters that identifies a file and should describe its contents.
 a. folder
 b. file size
 c. file path
 d. filename

2. The main directory of a disk is sometimes referred to as the _____ directory.
 a. first
 b. root
 c. tree
 d. virtual

3. A file's location is defined by a file _____, which includes the drive letter, folder(s), filename, and extension.
 a. path
 b. extension
 c. name
 d. letter

4. A _____ further describes the file contents, and often lets you know which application can be used to open the file.
 a. file extension
 b. folder
 c. drive letter
 d. drive map

5. The main hard drive is usually referred to as drive _____ or as Local Disk.
 a. A
 b. B
 c. C
 d. D

6. Use the _____ command to specify a name and storage device for a file and then store it on a storage medium.
 a. Save As
 b. New folder
 c. Open
 d. Select

7. Which of the following is not a valid default folder supplied with Windows?
 a. Documents
 b. Pictures
 c. Budgets
 d. Music

8. Which of the following companies is a major manufacturer of computer chips?
 a. Yahoo
 b. Apple
 c. Intel
 d. Google

9. The _____ number system represents numeric data as a series of 0s and 1s.
 a. integrated
 b. decimal
 c. binary
 d. singular

10. _____ data is text, numbers, graphics, sound, and video that has been converted into discrete digits, such as 0s and 1s.
 a. Digital
 b. Number
 c. Multimedia
 d. Internet

11. Which of the following is not a valid term?
 a. Bigabyte
 b. Petabyte
 c. Exabyte
 d. Terabyte

12. A series of eight bits is referred to as a(n) _____.
 a. word
 b. byte
 c. megabyte
 d. kilobit

13. The terms computer chip, microchip, and chip are all synonymous with the term _____ circuit.
 a. digital
 b. chip
 c. integrated
 d. silicon

14. The _____ size refers to the number of bits that a processor can manipulate at one time.
 a. CPU
 b. bit
 c. cycle
 d. word

15. The chip _____ is what protects the chip and connects the chip to the motherboard.
 a. word size
 b. packaging
 c. power
 d. circuitry

16. A single processor that contains circuitry for more than one processing unit is called a(n) _____ processor.
 a. AMD
 b. semiconducting
 c. Intel
 d. multi-core

17. _____ is a temporary holding area for data, application program instructions, and the operating system.
 a. EEPROM
 b. ROM
 c. Virtual memory
 d. RAM

18. The decimal number 4 is represented as _____ in the binary number system.
 a. 40
 b. 1876
 c. 1
 d. 100

19. A computer specification with 2 GB Dual Channel DDR2 SDRAM at 1600 MHz (max 4 GB) currently has _____ of random access memory installed.
 a. 2 gigabytes
 b. 1600 megahertz
 c. 4 gigabytes
 d. 2DDR

20. If a program exceeds the allocated space in RAM, the operating system uses an area of the hard drive called _____ to store parts of a program or data file until they are needed.
 a. EEPROM
 b. virtual memory
 c. ROM
 d. RAM

Independent Challenges

Independent Challenge 1

How will you organize the information that you store on your hard drive? Your hard drive or other storage medium is your electronic filing cabinet for all your work and papers. You can create many different filing systems. The way you set up your folders guides your work and helps you keep your ideas and projects organized so that you can work efficiently with your computer. Take some time to think about the work that you do, the types of documents or files you will be creating, and then decide how you will organize your files and folders.

Windows provides a feature that allows you to customize the icons for your folder shortcuts. You can use these custom icons to help you organize your folders even more. Windows supplies a large collection of icons that you can apply to each folder. Start Windows Explorer and be sure you are viewing the folders listed under a user name and not the folders shown in the libraries. You must click the user name, and then drill down from there. Once you get to the folder, right-click it in the left pane of Windows Explorer, and then click Properties (click Customize if you are using Windows Vista). In the Properties dialog box, click Change Icon. See Figure D-51. Note: in Windows 7 you cannot change the folder icon if you access the folder through a library.

FIGURE D-51: **Changing folder icons**

Used with permission from Microsoft

If you are using a Mac, you can also customize the icons. Every volume (disk), application, file, and folder on your Mac appears as an icon. For example, your internal hard drive looks like a hard drive, removable drives look like removable drives, and optical discs such as CDs and DVDs look like discs. File icons generally show a document with an application logo that lets you know what application was used to create it or what can be used to open it, such as a graphic editor or Word. To make changes to the icons, you work through the File menu and use the Get Info command.

For this Independent Challenge:

1. Read each of the following plans for organizing files and folders on a hard drive or other storage medium and comment on the advantages and disadvantages of each plan.
 a. Create a folder for each file you create.
 b. Store all the files in the root directory.
 c. Store all files in the Documents folder.
 d. Create a folder for each application you plan to use and store only documents you generate with that application in each folder.
 e. Create folders for broad types of documents such as memos, flyers, letters, budgets, art, photographs, and data, then store all related files within the folders.
 f. Create folders based on specific topics such as business, personal, household, and school, then store all related documents and files within the respective folders.
 g. Create a new folder for each month and store all files or documents created in that month in the appropriate folder.

2. Write a summary of how you plan to organize the folders and files on your hard drive or other storage medium, and explain why you chose the method you did.

3. Refer back to Figure D-51 and describe how you might use icons to help you identify the types of files in the folders.

Independent Challenge 2

You can use Windows Explorer or any file management program on your computer to explore and find specific files and folders on your hard drive.

For this Independent Challenge:

1a. Start Windows Explorer, then click the Computer icon. List the devices under Computer. Identify each device as a Network Device, Hard Drive, or Removable Storage. Windows Explorer lets you organize and view applications, files, folders, discs, and memory cards located on the hard drive of your PC, and on shared drives on your network.

1b. If you are using a Mac, use the Finder program. The Finder is the blue smiling face icon on the Dock. Finder lets you organize and view applications, files, folders, discs, and memory cards located on the hard drive of your Mac, and on shared drives on your network.

2. Pick any five files on the computer that you typically use and write the full path for each one. Refer to Figure D-52. Identify the programs that were used to create each of the files you found.

| Primary folder | Subfolder | Subfolder | Subfolder | Filename | File extension |

© Cengage Learning

3. Open the Documents folder on the Local Disk C: (if not available, find the folder that has your documents). List how many folders are in the Documents folder (or alternate folder if you selected one) on your hard drive.

4. Open one of the folders in the Documents folder (or alternate folder), click Views, then display the Details view. Are file extensions showing? If so, list them and identify which programs would open those files. Look at the folder using at least two views. Explain the differences between the views.

5. How many different types of files can you find on your hard drive? List up to 10.

Independent Challenge 3

How powerful is your computer? Some computers are more powerful than others because they can store more data and process data faster. To find out how your home, work, or lab computer stacks up, you'll need to know a few of its specifications.

For this Independent Challenge:

Check your computer's specifications by doing the following:

1. Start your computer.

2a. If you are using a Windows computer: Click the Start button, then click Control Panel. Click the System icon or click the System link to open the System Properties dialog box. Depending on your version of Windows, you may have slightly different commands to open the System Properties dialog box or System and Security window. You might have to click System and Maintenance or System and Security to view this page. If you see a dialog box with tabs, make sure the General tab is displayed. If you see a page, be sure you are looking at the System page. You will see basic information about your computer system, including the operating system, the manufacturer and model, the processor, and the installed RAM.

2b. If your computer is a Mac running MAC OS X: click the Apple icon on the menu bar located at the top of the desktop, then select About This Mac. In the About This Mac window that opens, you will see the Mac OS version as well as the processor speed (in GHz) and the processor series (G4, G5) for your Macintosh. Additionally, it will list

the amount of memory (RAM) installed. Click More Info, and on the right side of the window that opens, click the arrow next to Hardware to view the list of devices.

3. Record information about your computer similar to the information listed in Table D-5.

TABLE D-5: **Computer specifications**

	Your computer	Notes
Computer model and manufacturer:		
Processor manufacturer and model:		
Processor speed:		
Number of cores in the processor:		
Installed RAM:		
RAM capacity:		
System type:		
Windows Experience Index: (for Windows PCs)		
Operating system version:		

© Cengage Learning

4a. Just to get an idea of other hardware you have attached to your Windows computer, click the link or icon for Device Manager. (You might have to click the Hardware tab first.)

4b. If you are using a Mac, open Finder. Expand the icons to see the display adapters, the disk drives, keyboard, pointing devices, ports, and processors. List five of the devices. Tell why each device is connected to the computer. For example, you might see a 3Com wireless network card and state it is used to connect the computer to the Internet, or you might see a Pioneer DVD-RW DVR-107D ATA device and state it is used to read files from and write files to a DVD.

5. When you're done, close all open dialog boxes.

Guide to Buying a Computer

As you prepare to buy a computer, there are a lot of decisions you have to make. This book is designed to help you build the knowledge base you need to purchase a computer. In this unit, you were introduced to file management and digital electronics. You learned that you can enhance the performance of your computer depending on the processor and memory that you include in your computer. The specifications can be referred to as the architecture of your computer.

Each unit in this book covers topics that can help you understand the type of computer you need, the add-on parts you might want to buy, and the software and services that will enhance your computing experience, such as Internet access, software purchases, and so forth. After each unit, you will be asked to answer questions by completing a worksheet. By the end of the book, your Guide to Buying a Computer worksheet will provide comprehensive information about buying a computer.

To help you organize the information you will need when you are ready to buy a computer, you should complete the following activities:

1. Review the specifications for the fictitious computer ad in Figure D-53.

 Referring to the computer in the advertisement, what type of processor and how much memory are included with this computer? Is this a powerful computer?

2. Refer again to the advertisement in Figure D-53. Based on what you learned about processors, who might use a computer with this power?

3. If you have an older computer, you might ask what makes more economic sense—to upgrade your older computer to make it more powerful or to buy a new computer. Some parts are easy to add or change, whereas others are not. Table D-6 summarizes the most popular computer equipment upgrades, and indicates their average time to install and the difficulty level of the installation.

4. Two columns have been left blank for you to complete. Log onto the Internet or go to the library and review recent computer magazines to complete the "Cost" column and the "Whether you would consider replacing this part" column?

FIGURE D-53: Fake computer ad

- Intel Core 2 Quad Q9650 processor 3.0 GHz, 1333 MHz FSB
- 12 MB L2 cache
- 4 GB DDR2-800 MHz dual channel SDRAM (max 8GB)
- 500 GB SATA HD (7200 rpm)
- 16X max. DVD+/-R/RW SuperMulti drive
- 20" WUXGA monitor
- 512 MB NVIDIA GeForce graphics card
- Creative Sound Blaster X-Fi Xtreme Audio sound card
- Logitech speakers
- Mouse and keyboard
- Storage bay: Portable Media Drive Bay
- 6 USB ports: 2 front, 4 back
- 2 IEEE 1394
- 1 network port (RJ45 connector)
- 7 expansion slots
- Windows 7 operating system
- Home/small business software bundle
- 1-year limited warranty

© Cengage Learning; © 300dpi/Shutterstock.com;
Used with permission from Microsoft

TABLE D-6: Popular computer equipment upgrades

Upgrade	Time	Cost (US$)	Difficulty	Would you consider replacing this part? (Yes/No) Why? Why not?
Replace processor	1–5 hours		Difficult and not Recommended	
Add memory	30–60 minutes		Moderate	
Add external hard drive	5–10 minutes		Easy	
Replace internal hard drive	1–2 hours		Somewhat difficult	
Replace graphics card	1 hour		Moderate	
Switch to wireless keyboard and mouse	5 minutes		Easy	
Add USB hub or digital camera memory card reader	5 minutes		Easy	
Add second display screen	30 minutes		Easy	
Add or replace speakers	5–10 minutes		Easy	
Replace internal CD, BD, or DVD drive	1 hour		Moderate	

© Cengage Learning

5. As you continue to work through this book, you will learn more about personal computer systems. You will have the opportunity to answer more questions and complete other worksheets with information that will help you when it is time to buy a computer. To help you think about the processor and RAM you need for a personal computer system, complete this portion of the Guide to Buying a Computer worksheet.

Guide to Buying a Computer: Processor and RAM considerations

Questions to consider	Pages where the topic is covered in this book (refer back to these pages to read more about the topic)	Notes (add additional comments, clarifications, or ideas about each topic)
PROCESSOR CONSIDERATIONS		
Processor manufacturer?		
Processor model		
Processor speed		
Details about the processor		
Word size?		
32 bit?		
64 bit?		
Bus speed?		
Clock speed?		
How many cores?		
Single-core processor		
Dual-core processor		
Multi-core processor		
RAM CONSIDERATIONS		
How much RAM?		
RAM cache type and size:		
Level 1 cache (L1)?		
Level 2 cache (L2)?		
RAM speed?		

6. Write any questions you have about buying a processor or RAM on the lines that follow. As you continue to work through this book, check back to see if these questions have been answered.

My Questions

Visual Workshop

Understanding the specifications listed for processors often seems overwhelming. When you buy a computer, you can now find processors by manufacturer (Intel or AMD), by brand (Atom and Xeon, or Phenom and Opteron), and by model names. You can choose from processor families, such as 2nd Gen Intel Core i7. More often than not, you will buy a computer, rather than buy only a processor. It is important to know about processors, however, so you can make an informed decision about the processor in each computer you are considering buying. Figure D-54 shows a Web page from the Intel.com Web site advertising high-end processors and a Web page from the AMD.com Web site advertising some Phenom processors. If you go to these Web sites, you can see that these two processor manufacturers have a very large selection of processors for many different applications.

FIGURE D-54: Web sites of popular processor manufacturers

© Intel Corporation

© Advanced Micro Devices Inc. AMD, the AMD logo, AMD Phenom, and combinations thereof are trademarks of, and used with permission from, Advanced Micro Devices, Inc.

1. Log on to the Internet or use any resource available to find these or similar Web pages describing current processors available for desktop and laptop computers. Find two featured processors at each site and list four key specifications for each. Write a brief statement, using the terms you learned in this unit, to explain each feature.

2. Find two computer ads on the Internet or in a local paper. Identify the processors for those computers. Can you find the processors on the Intel or AMD Web site? Explain your findings.

3. Both Intel and AMD also sell personal computer systems from their Web sites. Each has a "Help me find the right PC" feature (although the exact name may be different. Use this tool to find two computers from each manufacturer. Write a brief description of your search results and include the specifications for each computer.

Data Security

Learning Objectives

1. Identify factors that may damage your data, software, or computer hardware

2. Identify ways to protect computers from theft and physical damage

3. Define authentication and explain how to restrict access to computer systems

4. Define malware and explain its impact on computer systems

5. Explain how to guard against software security threats and malware

6. Identify network security threats and ways to protect your computer when working on a network

7. Describe Web and email security threats and how to guard against them

8. Explain ways to secure your files

LESSON TOPICS

- What Can Go Wrong
- How to Protect Computer Hardware
- Biometrics, Passwords, and User IDs
- Software Security Threats
- How to Protect Computer Software
- Network Security Threats
- Web and Email Security Threats
- How to Secure Files

Talking Points: Prosecuting Computer Crime

Courtesy of Emily Bunin

What Can Go Wrong

Your computer system is at risk for a variety of things that can go wrong. If your data is not secure, it could be lost, stolen, or destroyed. If you do not protect your computer hardware, the files on your computer and your personal data may be damaged or lost. **Risk management** is the process of identifying potential threats, avoiding as many threats as possible, and developing steps to fix whatever went wrong. You use risk management to help reduce downtime and maintain the best working conditions. A good risk management plan helps you protect your work, computer equipment, software, and data in a cost effective way.

Learning Objective 1:
Identify factors that may damage your data, software, or computer hardware

● **What can go wrong?** Any number of things can go wrong, such as power outages, hardware failures, software failures, human error, theft, and computer viruses. Liquid can destroy a smartphone or a computer (see Figure E-1) and result in losing important data. Less common threats, but ones that still create devastating effects, occur when computer systems are harmed by natural disasters, acts of war, security breaches, and malicious hackers.

FIGURE E-2: New York City during the summer 2003 blackout

James Patrick Cooper/Bloomberg via Getty Images

FIGURE E-1: Accidents can happen

© Milan Vasicek/Shutterstock.com

Power spikes (also called **voltage spikes**) and **power surges** can damage sensitive computer parts. Spikes and surges can be caused by malfunctions in the local generating plant or the power distribution network, downed power lines, power grid switching by the electric company, and faulty wiring. Lightning causes extremely large power surges and consequently poses a real threat to your computer equipment. Even large appliances like refrigerators and air conditioners powering on and off in your home or apartment can cause a surge. These events are potentially more damaging than a power failure. Smaller surges can slowly damage your computer's circuit boards and other electrical components. Both can destroy the circuitry that operates your hard drive or they can damage your computer's motherboard or circuitry in your printer.

● **Can power outages or fluctuations cause damage?** Yes, because most computers are powered by electricity. Devices that are plugged in are susceptible to power failures, spikes, surges, and power outages. A **power failure** is a complete loss of power to the computer system, usually caused by something over which you have no control. Power outages can be caused by natural disasters, overloaded power grids, planned brownouts, rolling blackouts, unexpected blackouts (see Figure E-2), and even human error. Even a brief interruption in power can force your computer to reboot and lose all data in RAM. Although a power failure results in loss of data in RAM, it is unlikely to result in loss of data stored on the storage media.

● **Why should I worry about hardware failure?** The effect of a hardware failure depends on which part fails. Most hardware failures are simply an inconvenience. For example, if your monitor fails, you can obtain a replacement monitor, plug it in, and get back to work. A hard drive failure, however, can be a disaster because you could lose all your data. Although an experienced computer technician might be able to recover some of the files on the damaged hard drive, it is more often the case that all programs and data files stored on the hard drive are permanently lost. The risk of a hardware failure increases as a hardware part ages.

● **What if there's a problem with my software?**
Software failure can result in lost data or inaccurate data, both of which can have serious consequences. Software failure can be caused by software bugs. A software bug is a general term for a mistake in the code or flaw in the design that creates an error or unexpected result when a program runs. A flaw can be disastrous on a computer network consisting of hundreds or thousands of computers. Software bugs have been responsible for systemwide outages of email networks for major mobile providers. Other bugs may cause security leaks. For example, hackers continue to discover bugs in software that allow unauthorized access to servers and the sensitive data these servers store.

● **Are many problems caused by simple human error?**
Yes. **Human error** (also called **operator error**) refers to a mistake made by a computer operator or programmer. Everyone has made mistakes while working on a computer, although most errors by individuals result in minor damage. Despite the press coverage of computer criminals and viruses, the most common cause of lost or inaccurate data is a mistake made by a computer user—such as entering the wrong data, deleting a file that is still needed, and failing to follow required procedures.

● **What are the chances that my computer will be stolen?** A thief might want the computer just to have a computer, or he might want to sell the computer on the black market. However, the thief might also want the computer for the data stored on it. Many security breaches have been traced to stolen computers. A thief can get data, such as your bank account and credit card numbers and PINs, from your computer. A thief can use that data to wipe out your bank accounts and can go on a spending spree with your credit cards. Even worse, a criminal can use stolen data to assume your identity, run up debts, get into legal trouble, ruin your credit rating, and cause you a lot of trouble. The portability of mobile computers makes them particularly easy for a thief to grab. You should never leave a computer unattended in a public space. See Figure E-3.

FIGURE E-3: **Unattended computers are easily stolen**

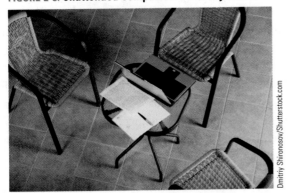

Dmitriy Shironosov/Shutterstock.com

● **How can I tell if something is wrong with my computer?** There are several obvious signs that your computer is in trouble. The most apparent one is if your computer fails to power up. A loud beep at start-up time can also indicate a problem. If your computer's screen remains blank or error messages appear, you might have a hardware problem. Hardware problems can also show up as unexpected restarts at random intervals or as a peripheral device that stops working. Some problems are intermittent and might seem to be resolved only to come back when they are least convenient to deal with. Hardware problems can quickly escalate and some can eventually make your computer non-functional or make your data impossible to access. A little time spent troubleshooting can save you lots of annoyance down the road.

● **How do I troubleshoot a hardware problem?** You might be able to solve many hardware problems by following the tips shown in Figure E-4.

FIGURE E-4: **Troubleshooting tips**

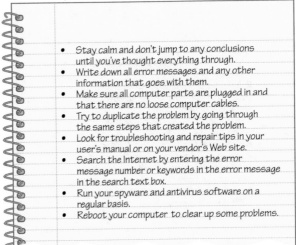

- Stay calm and don't jump to any conclusions until you've thought everything through.
- Write down all error messages and any other information that goes with them.
- Make sure all computer parts are plugged in and that there are no loose computer cables.
- Try to duplicate the problem by going through the same steps that created the problem.
- Look for troubleshooting and repair tips in your user's manual or on your vendor's Web site.
- Search the Internet by entering the error message number or keywords in the error message in the search text box.
- Run your spyware and antivirus software on a regular basis.
- Reboot your computer to clear up some problems.

© Cengage Learning

● **What is the blue screen of death?** Many Windows users have encountered the blue screen of death (also called the black screen of death, the blank screen of death, and BSoD). This is the sudden and unexpected display of an error message written in white text against a blue or black background that fills the screen. The computer no longer accepts any commands. The BSoD indicates that the operating system has encountered a critical error from which it cannot recover without some intervention. If this happens, you need might need to contact a technical support person.

● **Can terrorism affect my computer?** **Cyberterrorism** describes terrorist acts committed via the Internet. Cyberterrorism uses viruses and worms to destroy data and disrupt computer-based operations of critical national infrastructures, such as power grids and telecommunications systems. Cyberterrorism often results in security breaches, which might result in stolen or compromised data.

How to Protect Computer Hardware

No computer system can be completely risk free, but proactive procedures can protect computer systems from threats. This lesson discusses ways to protect your hardware such as from theft and power problems.

Learning Objective 2:
Identify ways to protect computers from theft and physical damage

● **How can I reduce the likelihood of someone stealing my computer?** The best way to protect your digital devices, such as your computer, tablet, or smartphone, from theft is to use common sense. See Figure E-5.

FIGURE E-5: **Tips to help prevent theft**

- Never leave your portable computer unattended, especially when you are at a coffee shop, the library, or the airport.
- If you have to leave your portable computer in your car, never leave it in plain view. Lock it up in the trunk or cover it up.
- Carry your portable computer in an inconspicuous carrying case.
- Record your portable computer's make, model, and serial number and store them away from the computer. Many recovered computers cannot be returned to their owners because this tracking information is not supplied to police.
- Consider securing your portable computer with an anti-theft device.

© Cengage Learning

If you have to leave your computer alone in a space that has public access, you should anchor your computer to your desk. You can use a specially designed lock attached to a cable and then fastened to a desk. Another option is a security plate that's affixed to the underside of the computer or to a desk. See Figure E-6 for ways to secure your computer in a public place.

FIGURE E-6: **Devices used to secure your computer in a public place**

Courtesy of Kensington Computer Products Group

Courtesy of AnchorPad Security, Inc.

A locking device A security plate

In addition, computer motion sensor alarms can be installed on PCs and armed so that any movement triggers audible alarm sounds or recorded verbal warnings. There are also several types of storage device locks designed to prevent unauthorized access to your computer's drives.

● **Is there a way to get my computer back if it is stolen?** Tracking and recovery software, such as CyberAngel and Lojack for Laptops secretly sends a message as soon as a thief uses a stolen computer to log onto the Internet. This message sends the computer's exact location to a monitoring center. The monitoring center shares the information with the local police so the computer can be recovered. Smartphones, which have built-in GPS capability, can also be tracked to help you locate your missing device. Once you log into the application Web site and identify the device as missing, the location of your phone is shown on a map with an address.

● **Is there a way to protect data if my computer is stolen?** Some tracking software can be configured to delete the data on a computer if it is stolen. The tracking system uses a trigger, such as a certain number of unsuccessful log-in attempts to delete the data. Be sure to change the manufacturer-assigned administrator password to a secure password as soon as you get your new computer. Also, be sure to either disable or assign a secure password to a preset guest account.

● **If my computer is stolen, is there a chance I'll get it back?** Your chances of recovering a stolen computer improve if you have installed tracking software. In addition, you should record unique information about your computer, such as its make, model, and serial number. You should store the information in a secure place away from the computer. Another option is to affix a STOP (Security Tracking of Office Property) plate, which contains a unique ID number, a warning message, and an 800 number to report a stolen computer. The plate leaves an indelible tattoo and is extremely difficult to remove.

- **How can I protect my computer from being damaged by power problems?** You can provide power protection by using a device such as a **UPS (uninterruptible power supply)**, which offers the best protection against power problems (see Figure E-7). A UPS is a device containing a battery that provides a continuous supply of power and other circuitry to prevent spikes and surges from reaching your computer. A UPS gives you enough time to save your files and exit your programs safely in the event of a power outage. Most UPSs have two types of sockets: one type offers battery backup plus surge protection, and the other offers only surge protection.

FIGURE E-7: **An uninterruptible power supply (UPS)**

Surge and battery backup outlets
Surge-only outlets

Courtesy of MediaTechnics Corporation

- **Why can't I just use a surge strip to protect my computer?** Because, unlike a UPS, a surge strip does not protect the data in RAM if the power fails. A surge strip does not contain a battery to keep the computer running. However, you can use a **surge strip** to protect electrical devices from power surges and voltage spikes. A surge strip is also called a **surge protector** or **surge suppressor**. You can plug your computer and printer into a surge strip rather than directly into a wall outlet. See Figure E-8. Some surge strips also have sockets for modem connections that prevent surges from traveling down telephone or cable lines

FIGURE E-8: **A surge strip**

Courtesy of MediaTechnics Corporation

and into your computer. A surge strip monitors the electrical current that passes from an outlet to all the devices plugged into the strip. When it detects a surge, it redirects the extra current to a grounded circuit.

A big power surge can burn out a surge strip while it tries to protect your equipment. Some surge strips have an indicator light that warns you if the surge strip is no longer functioning properly. When you shop for a surge strip, do not mistakenly purchase a power strip, which offers no protection.

- **Should I be concerned if my computer runs hot?** High-performance processors, hard drives, graphics cards, and several other computer parts generate a lot of heat. Overheating can shorten the lifespan of internal parts and chips. Most computers have fans that vent to the outside. See Figure E-9. Some fans run continuously to maintain the proper temperature inside the system unit. Some fans that come on only after the processor reaches a certain temperature.

It is important to be aware of the ventilation around your computer system. Do not block top and rear vents from releasing heat. Also, be sure not to leave a portable computer that is powered up on a soft surface that does not allow airflow.

FIGURE E-9: **Fans help cool a computer**

Courtesy of MediaTechnics Corporation

Fans vent outside the system unit

Fans blow cool air under a laptop

Courtesy of MediaTechnics Corporation

Courtesy of Targus Group International, Inc.

Tips for keeping your computer system in good working condition

- Clean your PC's parts and peripheral devices regularly to help keep your system in good working condition.
- Use extreme caution when you clean the inside of your computer's system case. First, make sure that you've turned off your PC, display device, and all attached devices. Second, do not touch the system board. Third, make sure not to loosen any cables.
- Always shut down your PC before you clean your keyboard.
- Avoid spills by not setting drinks too close to your keyboard.
- Use a flexible clear plastic keyboard cover to prevent damage from spills and sticky fingers.
- Flip the keyboard over and shake it gently to get rid of any small pieces of dirt between the keys.

- Use a vacuum cleaner designed for keyboard cleaning to clean your keyboard because a regular vacuum cleaner can pop off keys and suck them away.
- Use a can of compressed air or a computer vacuum cleaner hose regularly to clean out debris such as dust particles, dirt, and even your pet's hair from the keyboard, mouse, vents, and fans.
- Use cotton swabs just slightly moistened with a mild cleaning fluid to clean the sides of keys.
- Wipe the tops of the keys with a soft, slightly dampened cloth.
- Allow your keyboard to dry before you reconnect it to your PC.
- Clean your monitor regularly with a soft cloth or a dryer sheet that does not leave lint.

Biometrics, Passwords, and User IDs

UNIT E Concepts

User IDs, passwords, and personal identification numbers (PINs) are a fact of everyday life. They help protect you and your data. They are required for secure transactions. They help authenticate, or verify, who you are such as when you use ATMs and debit cards, log into your computer or smartphone, access wireless networks, access your online accounts (for example, email, eBay, or PayPal), or use instant messaging.

Learning Objective 3:
Define authentication and explain how to restrict access to computer systems

● **How can a computer system know that I am who I say I am when I use it?** A computer uses **authentication protocols** to confirm a person's identity when he or she tries to use a computer system. Three common ways to authenticate a user are discussed next.

■ *Using something a person carries:* A photo ID is an identity badge with a photo of a person's face. Because it can be lost, stolen, or duplicated, however, it works best when used on site where a security guard verifies that the face on the badge matches the face of the person wearing the badge.

■ *Using something a person knows:* User IDs, PINs, and passwords fall into this category of personal identification. Data security on a system that is guarded by user IDs and passwords depends on password secrecy. If users give out their passwords, choose obvious passwords, or store them in obvious places, hackers can break into the system, which means the data is no longer secure.

■ *Using a unique physical characteristic:* This third method of personal identification is called **biometrics**. Biometrics uses some physical trait, such as a fingerprint, handprint, or the pattern of blood vessels in the retina of the eye, to authenticate a person. See Figure E-10. Unlike passwords, biometric data cannot be forgotten, lost, or

borrowed. Technologies that can read biometric data include hand-geometry scanners, voice recognition, face recognition, fingerprint scanners, and retinal scanners.

● **Are there levels of security?** Authentication protocols that use more than one means of identification are more secure than others. **Two-factor authentication**, which verifies identity using two independent elements of confirmation, such as an ATM card and a PIN, is more secure than single-factor authentication, such as a password only. Generally, personal computer security is based on passwords associated with user IDs. However, some personal computers now include fingerprint technology to authenticate a user.

● **Why do I need a user ID?** A **user ID** (or username, screen name, or online nickname) is your unique identifier on a computer or Web page. User IDs are typically public and do not offer any level of security. You should have several user IDs, for example, your user ID for online banking should not be the same as your user ID for instant messaging.

● **Why do I need a password?** A **password** verifies a user ID and guarantees that you are the person you claim to be. Although you might be assigned a password, typically you are asked to create your own. Passwords provide the most protection if they are unique. In some situations, you might be given a temporary password, and then asked to change it as soon as you successfully log in for the first time. Passwords and user IDs are typically created on a registration or enrollment screen similar to the one in Figure E-11. You are often asked to pick a secret question, such as the name of a first pet, and then provide an answer that can help you get access to your information if you forget your password.

FIGURE E-10: Retinal scan and thumbprint biometric authentication

FIGURE E-11: Creating a user name and password

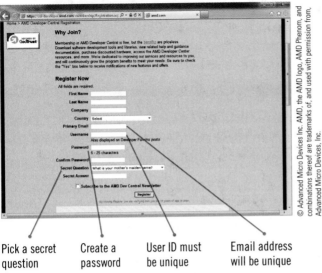

Pick a secret question | Create a password | User ID must be unique | Email address will be unique

● **Why do I need to type a verification code?** Web sites will often provide a verification code. One such code is provided by CAPTCHA.net. Captcha stands for Completely Automated Public Turing Test To Tell Computers and Humans Apart. See Figure E-12. Captcha displays a combination of letters and numbers that you must type. This code provides security for the Web site because computers cannot access this code to create phony registrations.

FIGURE E-12: Captcha

● **What is the difference between a password and a PIN?** Both passwords and PINs are based on the *something the user knows* authentication method. A PIN tends to be a short sequence of numbers that can be entered using a numeric keypad, whereas a password tends to be a longer sequence of letters, numbers, and special characters.

● **How can I manage all my passwords?** To help keep track of user IDs and passwords, you can use a password manager. A **password manager** stores user IDs with their corresponding passwords and automatically fills in login forms. For example, when you register at a Web site, click the "Remember me" check box so the browser stores your ID and password in an encrypted file. See Figure E-13. When you visit the Web site, your ID and password are filled in on the login screen automatically.

FIGURE E-13: Remember me box

Check the "Remember me" Box to save your user ID and password for the next time you log in, but you have to be using the same browser.

● **How can I reduce the number of passwords and user IDs I need?** You should maintain at least two levels of passwords. The top-level password is the most secure and it is used for accessing critical data, such as online banking or credit card information. The low-level password is for situations when you don't care if your security is compromised, such as for a Web site mailing list.

● **Are there other ways for me to limit who can use my computer?** You can establish user rights. **User rights** are rules that limit the directories and files that each user can access. They can restrict a user's ability to erase, create, write, read, and find files. Assigning user rights helps prevent both accidental and deliberate damage to data. If users are granted limited rights, a hacker who steals someone's password only has the same level of access as the person from whom the password was stolen.

Tips for creating secure passwords

DO
- Use passwords that are at least eight characters in length.
- Use a combination of letters, numbers, and special characters such as $, #, if permitted.
- Use uppercase and lowercase letters if the hosting computer is case sensitive.
- Create a passphrase based on a title, such as a song title, then insert special characters and numbers. The password makes sense to you but not to others.

DO NOT
- Use a password based on public information such as your phone number, Social Security number, driver's license number, birthday, and other personal facts such as the names of your spouse, children, or pets.
- Select passwords that contain your entire user ID or part of it.
- Use words that can be found in the dictionary, including foreign words or common words spelled backwards, such as drowssap instead of password.

Software Security Threats

One of the biggest security threats to your computer is the result of **malicious code**, called **malware**. Malware is created and unleashed by **hackers**, **crackers**, **black hats**, or **cybercriminals**. Many people use the term computer virus when they talk about malware. Although the term computer virus technically refers to a type of program that behaves in a specific way, it has become a generic term that refers to a variety of destructive programs including viruses, worms, Trojan horses, bots, and spyware. Security experts use the term **blended threat** to describe malware that combines more than one type of malicious program.

Learning Objective 4:
Define malware and explain its impact on computer systems

- **What is a computer virus?** A **computer virus** (also called a **virus**) is a set of program instructions that attaches itself to a file, reproduces itself, and spreads to other files on the same computer. A key characteristic of a virus is its ability to hide in a computer for days or months, quietly copying itself. While this takes place, you might not even know that your computer has contracted a virus.

- **How does a virus spread?** A common misconception is that viruses spread by themselves from one computer to another. A virus spreads when a person distributes an infected file. See Figure E-14. You can get a computer virus if you exchange or share infected files or if you download infected software from the Web. Once the virus is on your computer, you can pass it along if you put the infected file on a flash drive, a DVD, BD, or a CD that you share with others. You can also spread the virus if you send the infected file as an email attachment or if you exchange an infected file on a music or video file-sharing network. Usually the person sharing the infected file does not know the file is infected.

- **What can a virus do to my computer?** A virus can corrupt files, destroy data, display an irritating message, or otherwise disrupt computer operations. In addition, a virus might deliver a payload. Viruses that deliver their payloads on a specific date are called time bombs. Viruses that deliver their payloads in response to some other system event are called logic bombs. One type of virus, called a **boot sector virus**, infects the system files your computer uses every time the computer is powered up. This type of virus causes widespread damage to your hard drive and is very hard to remove.

- **What is a computer worm?** A **computer worm** (also called a **worm**) is a self-copying program designed to carry out some unauthorized activity on a victim's computer. Unlike computer viruses, worms can spread by themselves from one computer to another. Refer to Figure E-15. They can enter a computer through security holes in browsers and operating systems or as email attachments. A computer can become infected if a user clicks an infected pop-up ad or an infected link found in some emails. Worms can even infect mobile phones. A **mass-mailing worm** spreads by sending itself to every address in the address book of an infected computer. To make these worms difficult to track, the From line of the infected message sometimes contains a spoofed address of a randomly selected person from the victim's email address book. Hackers also spread worms over file-sharing networks and over instant messaging links.

FIGURE E-14: Viruses can spread quickly

© kenton/Shutterstock.com

1. The worm enters the host computer via the email system.

2. The worm copies itself over and over, fills up storage space, slows processing time, and looks for other hosts.

3. Copies of the worm attempt to use the email system to travel to other hosts.

5. Unprotected hosts are invaded.

4. Hosts protected by security systems do not let the worm enter.

© Cengage Learning

Unit E

● **What is a Trojan horse?** A **Trojan horse** (also called a **Trojan virus**) is a computer program that seems to perform one function while actually doing something else. A Trojan horse is not designed to copy itself or to spread itself to other computers. Trojan horses are stand-alone programs that pretend to be useful utilities or applications, which victims download and install unaware of their destructive nature. Trojan horses use a **keylogger** program to secretly steal passwords by recording keystrokes and sending the information to a hacker. Another type of Trojan horse called a **Remote Access Trojan (RAT)** has backdoor capabilities that allow remote hackers to transmit files to victims' computers, search for data, run programs, and use a victim's computer as a relay station for breaking into other computers. The Trojan horse virus is named after a Greek myth. Like the horse in the myth, the program appears to be something it is not. See Figure E-16.

FIGURE E-16: **Trojan horse was a trap**

© Ralf Juergen Kraft/Shutterstock.com

● **What is a bot?** Any software that can automate a task or execute a task when commanded to do so is called an **intelligent agent**. Because an intelligent agent behaves somewhat like a robot, it is often called a **bot**. Good bots perform helpful tasks, such as scanning the Web to assemble data for search engines. Bad bots are controlled by hackers and are designed for unauthorized or destructive tasks. They can be spread by worms or Trojans. A computer under the control of a bad bot is sometimes called a **zombie** because it carries out instructions without the knowledge of the computer owner. A **botmaster** is a person who controls many bot-infested computers and can link the bots together into a network called a **botnet**.

● **What is spyware?** **Spyware** is a type of malware program that secretly gathers personal information without the victim's knowledge, usually for advertising and other commercial purposes. Spyware can monitor keystrokes and relay information to cybercriminals.

● **What does malware do?** Once viruses, worms, bots, Trojans, and spyware enter your computer, they can carry out unauthorized activities, such as the following:

■ **Create network traffic jam**, which generates traffic on LANs and the Internet and/or causes service to deteriorate as download time increases for files, Web pages, and email messages.

■ **Initiate a denial-of-Service (DoS) attack**, which floods servers with useless traffic to overwhelm the server's processing capability and stops all communications.

■ **Reconfigure a browser**, which blocks access to some Web sites, changes the home page setting, and/or redirects the browser to infected Web sites.

■ **Delete and modify files**, which deletes files, downloads unwanted files, and/or modifies the Registry.

■ **Install ransomware**, which encrypts files, then demands payment for the decryption key.

■ **Access confidential information**, which steals passwords and credit card numbers, and/or sends spam to everyone in your email address book or your instant messaging buddy list.

■ **Disable antivirus and firewall software**, which leaves your system vulnerable to even more malware.

■ **Control your computer**, which spreads malware, allows hackers to access data on your computer remotely, and/or turns a computer into a zombie.

■ **Degrade performance**, which forces a computer to perform more slowly than normal, and/or sends annoying messages or pop-ups.

How to Protect Computer Software

Because malware is intended to be stealth, you may not know when your computer becomes infected. Although you should always use good computing habits, there are several software tools you can use to help avoid security threats. Security software can be classified as antivirus, antispyware, antispam, and firewalls.

Learning Objective 5:
Explain how to guard against software security threats and malware

● **How do I know if my computer is infected with malware?** Symptoms of an infected computer include the following: irritating messages or sounds; frequent pop-up ads, at times with pornographic content; the sudden appearance of a new toolbar; prolonged system start-up; slower than usual response to clicks and key strokes; application crashes; missing files; disabled security software that cannot be restarted; periodic network activity when you are not actively browsing or sending email; or the computer reboots frequently. Knowing these symptoms can help you recognize if your computer is infected and if you need to take immediate action.

● **How do I avoid security threats and malware?** Good habits can help you keep your computer safe. Install and activate security software. Keep software patches and operating system service packs up to date. Do not open suspicious email attachments. Get software only from reliable sources. Use security software to scan for malware. When you browse the Web, do not click pop-up ads and avoid suspicious Web sites. When using Windows Explorer, disable the option Hide extensions for known file types. Most importantly, consider using a security suite to help protect your computer.

● **What is a security suite?** A **security suite** integrates several security modules to protect against the most common types of malware, unauthorized access, and spam into one package. Security suites might include additional features such as Wi-Fi detection that warns of possible intrusions into your wireless network and parental controls for monitoring and controlling Internet usage.

● **What are the advantages and disadvantages of a security suite?** A security suite, like the one shown in Figure E-17, typically includes antivirus, firewall, and antispyware modules. A security suite costs less than purchasing stand-alone security modules. In addition, a single interface for accessing all of the security suite's features is less complex than having to learn how to configure and run several different products. Two disadvantages are that most security suites cannot run at the same time as stand-alone security products and that overlapping security coverage from two similar products can cause glitches. As a result, when installing a security suite, you are typically required to uninstall or disable all other antivirus, antispyware, and firewall software on your computer.

FIGURE E-17: **Norton Security Suite**

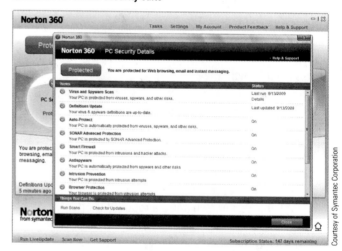

Courtesy of Symantec Corporation

Using Safe Mode

Safe Mode is a limited version of Windows that allows you to use your mouse, screen, and keyboard, but no other peripheral devices. To enter Safe Mode, you can press the F8 function key as your PC boots. If your PC shuts down unexpectedly due to a problem, you might be able to start it again in Safe Mode. While in Safe Mode, you can use the Control Panel's Add/Remove Programs to uninstall recently added programs or hardware that might be interfering with the operation of other parts.

- **What is antivirus software?** **Antivirus software** is utility software that looks for and removes viruses, Trojan horses, worms, and bots. It should be part of your data security plan. Most antivirus software also scans for spyware, although some security software publishers offer spyware detection as a separate module. Antivirus software is included in security suites or it can be purchased as a stand-alone module. Antivirus software is available for all types of computers and data storage media.

- **How does antivirus software work?** Antivirus software attempts to identify malware by searching your computer's files and memory for virus signatures. A **virus signature** is a section of program code that can be used to identify a known malicious program, much as a fingerprint is used to identify an individual. However, a stealth virus can temporarily remove the signature and hide in memory. Antivirus software scans for virus signatures in programs, data files, incoming and outgoing email, and instant message attachments. Antivirus software can also watch for unusual activity, such as a considerably large number of email messages being sent from your computer.

- **When should I run my antivirus software?** Installation and activation procedures vary for each virus protection product. However, once you have installed your antivirus software, the best and safest practice is to set it to start when your computer starts and to keep it running full time in the background so that it checks every email message as it arrives and scans all files the moment you access them.

- **How do I keep my antivirus software up to date?** Most antivirus products are preconfigured to check for, download, and install updates regularly and without user intervention. You can also update the software manually. See Figure E-18. These updates include the information your antivirus software uses to identify and remove malware. These updates allow your software to search for the most recent virus signatures. The information needed to find and remove malware is referred to as **virus definitions**. If your antivirus software is part of a security suite, the update might also include patches for other security software modules.

FIGURE E-18: **Status of installed antivirus features**

© 2011 AVG Technologies

- **How often should I do a system scan?** You should configure your antivirus software to scan all the files on your computer periodically. It's best to schedule a weekly system scan at a time when you are not usually using your computer, but it is powered on. At any time, you can also run a manual scan of your entire computer or of specific files that might be of concern to you.

- **What if I think my computer is infected?** If you suspect that your computer might be infected by a virus or other malware, you should immediately use security software to scan your computer. If your virus protection software identifies a virus, worm, Trojan horse, or bot in a file or attachment, it can try to remove the infection, put the file into quarantine, or simply delete the file. For your protection, most antivirus software encrypts the file contents and isolates it in a quarantine folder, so it can't be inadvertently opened or accessed. If the infected file ends up on a quarantine list, your antivirus software might give you the option of trying to disinfect the file or deleting it.

- **Can I count on antivirus software to protect my computer?** Today's antivirus software is quite dependable, but not infallible. So, you should always use security software as well as take additional precautions, such as making regular backups of your data.

Virus hoaxes

Viruses are very real, but you are likely to get emails about viruses that do not really exist. A **virus hoax** usually arrives as an email message containing dire warnings about a new virus that is on the loose. The message typically suggests some strategy for avoiding the virus, and recommends that you forward the email warning to all of your friends and colleagues. In most cases, the email message is a prank designed to send people into a panic.

Bogus virus email messages usually contain a long list of people in the To: and Cc: boxes; these messages have been forwarded many times. Most hoaxes include a recommended procedure for removing the virus, such as reformatting your computer's hard drive—a process that could cause more damage than the virus itself! Fake viruses are often characterized as being capable of bizarre acts.

When you receive an email message about a virus, check one of the many antivirus Web sites and look up the alleged virus by name to see if it is a hoax or a real threat. If the virus is a real threat, the Web site will provide the information that you need to check your computer and download an update to your antivirus software.

Network Security Threats

Networks can be wired or wireless; each type has its own risks. If a computer is on a network, security is a primary concern, especially if the network connects to the Internet. Networked computers can be accessed remotely. If a person gains unauthorized access to a computer, then that person can damage, steal, or destroy the data or programs on the computer. Methods for securing networks include password protection, encryption, and firewalls.

Learning Objective 6:
Identify network security threats and ways to protect your computer when working on a network

● **Can I tell if someone is using my network without my permission?** Yes. Network hardware, which you will learn about in the next unit, has built in protections to monitor who is on the network. The network router maintains a list of clients that are accessing the network using wired or wireless connections. You should look through the list of connected clients for unfamiliar users because they could be intruders. But remember, if you have a printer or other devices connected to the network, each of these devices will be listed, too. Those devices are legitimate connections. You can view a list of current connections, or you can set up your router software to maintain a log.

● **Is my wireless network at risk?** Yes, wireless networks are at risk for unauthorized access and use, especially if they are not secured. To gain access to an unsecured wireless network, an unauthorized person simply needs a wireless-enabled device within range of the wireless router. The device can access the wireless network and all unsecured data on that network. Another threat related to a wireless network is when users think they are logging onto a legitimate network, but the network's signals are being intercepted by hackers. Once hackers intercept the signals, they can extract passwords and even personal data such as credit card information from unsuspecting users. Hackers can intercept signals with a Wi-Fi enabled notebook computer, a practice called **LANjacking** or **war driving** (war stands for wireless access revolution). LANjackers can pinpoint the exact location of a wireless access point with the use of GPS (Global Positioning System) receivers. They can also use legitimate network-detecting and monitoring software, such InSSIDer and NetStumbler, which helps locate and identify secured and unsecured networks. See Figure E-19.

● **How can I secure my wireless network?** You can secure your wireless network by encrypting your data.

FIGURE E-19: Secured and unsecured networks

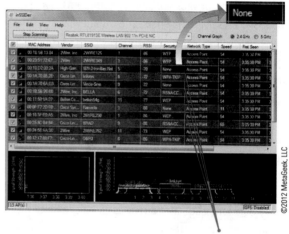

Unsecured networks can be easily identified

● **What is encryption? Encryption** scrambles (encrypts) data sent over wired or wireless networks and unscrambles (decrypts) data received to provide secure data transmissions.

● **What type of encryption should I use on my wireless network?** You should use **wireless encryption**, which encrypts the data transmitted between wireless devices and then decrypts the data only on devices that have a valid encryption key. There have been several wireless encryption technologies. One is **WPA (Wi-Fi Protected Access)**, which can encrypt data based on the user's password and implements message integrity checking. Currently, much better security is offered by **WPA2**, which uses the same kind of strong encryption required by government agencies and businesses. You should use WPA2 encryption if all the devices on your network support it. The Wi-Fi Alliance Web site provides a list of WPA- and WPA2-certified products.

- **How do I activate encryption for my network?** To activate encryption for your wireless network, you open the router's configuration software. You access the router's configuration settings by opening a browser and entering the router's IP number. You must enter the settings, including a wireless network key. See Figure E-20. A **wireless network key** (sometimes referred to as a network security key) is the basis for encrypting and decrypting the data transmitted between wireless devices. The key is similar to a password, only it is often longer. Be sure to remember the wireless network key or passphrase you use to configure the router. Later, when you set up computers and other network devices, you will enter the same wireless network key so that every device on your network can encrypt and decrypt the data flowing on the network.

FIGURE E-20: **Setting encryption for wireless security**

Enter a key or passphrase

Select an encryption protocol

- **Do I need a wireless network key for public networks I want to use?** Some wireless networks open to the public are not encrypted. See Figure E-21. You'll find these networks in coffee shops, hotels, airports and even in public parks. You should be wary of sending any sensitive data over an unsecured public network, or any unsecured network. Other public networks are secure because they are encrypted. For these secure public networks you will have to enter the associated wireless network key.

FIGURE E-21: **Wireless access in a public space**

- **How can people get on my network without permission?** One of the most common ways of gaining unauthorized access to a network-based computer is by looking for open ports. Hackers canvas the Internet probing ports to find their victims.

A **port probe** (also called a **port scan**) is the use of automated software to locate computers that have open ports and are vulnerable to unauthorized access. Port scanner software goes to a randomly selected IP address and systematically checks for a response from each port. Open ports can then be further tested to see if they are secure. You can check your computer for open ports using software tools or you can initiate an "innocent" port probe to discover if there are weaknesses.

- **What are the chances a hacker will find my computer or network?** You might scoff at your computer's vulnerability to port probes. After all, there are millions of computers on the Internet and a limited number of hackers. The chances of your computer becoming a target would seem to be slim, but the opposite is true. Port scanning software can examine more than 30,000 computers per minute. If you use security software to monitor port probes on an unprotected computer, you would see probes within seconds of going online.

- **How do I protect my ports?** One of the most effective steps you can take to secure your computer from intrusions is to install a router. Routers monitor and direct data being transported from one device to another. A router can also connect to the Internet and monitor IP addresses. When you use a router, data travelling with local IP addresses are kept within the LAN, and data with external IP addresses are routed out to the Internet.

- **Does a firewall keep intruders out of my network?** Yes, a **firewall** is software or hardware designed to filter out suspicious data attempting to enter or leave a computer. Firewall software makes sure that incoming information was actually requested and is not an unauthorized intrusion. It blocks activity from suspicious IP addresses and it reports intrusion attempts. Windows includes firewall software. See Figure E-22.

FIGURE E-22: **Windows Firewall settings**

Used with permission from Microsoft

Web and Email Security Threats

If you use the Web and if you send and receive email, you will have to protect yourself and your data from malware, scams, spyware, spam, and cookies designed to monitor your online activities and collect your confidential information. You need to minimize the risk these activities pose to your computer's security and your privacy. Viruses have already been discussed. This lesson focuses on other Web and email security threats.

Learning Objective 7:
Describe Web and email security threats and how to guard against them

- **What are cookies?** A **cookie** is a message containing information about the user sent from a Web server to a browser and stored on the user's hard drive.

- **Are cookies a security threat?** Generally, no because cookies have built-in safeguards designed to reduce their abuse. However marketers, hackers, and pranksters have discovered harmful ways to use them. For example, clicking a banner ad can create an **ad-serving cookie**, which is associated with a third party (usually a marketing company). This cookie is used to track your activities at any site containing the associated third party banner ads. The marketing firms that distribute ad-serving cookies claim that the cookie data is used to select and display ads that might interest you. Privacy advocates worry that shopper profiles can be sold and used for unauthorized purposes.

- **Can I see the cookies stored on my computer?** Yes, you can view a list of cookies stored on your computer. If you use Internet Explorer to browse the Web, you can see a list of cookies stored on your computer using the Internet Options dialog. Figure E-23 shows a list of cookies stored when browsing with Internet Explorer.

FIGURE E-23: A list of cookies

Used with permission from Microsoft

- **Can I delete cookies stored on my computer?** Yes. However, deleting all cookies does not solve the problem; it only creates a very temporary fix.

- **Can I control which cookies are stored on my computer?** Yes, you can block cookies so they are not stored on your computer. However, if you block all cookies, you will lose some benefits on some Web sites. If you decide to block cookies, you should block cookies from specific sites or third-party cookies, especially third-party cookies that do not have a privacy policy. See Figure E-24.

FIGURE E-24: **Blocking cookies**

Used with permission from Microsoft

Another way is to opt out. If a company offers the option to opt out and if you elect to opt out, then the company will not allow ad-serving cookies to be stored on your computer. In most cases, however, opting out creates an opt-out cookie. If you delete all the cookies on your computer, the opt-out cookie will be deleted, too. Once this happens, third-party cookies will again start to accumulate on your computer.

- **How do I protect my personal information when I am using a public computer?** Most browsers provide tools you can use to control how Web site providers receive and track information about your browsing sessions. If you work on a public computer, you probably don't want to leave evidence of your browsing or search history. The InPrivate Browsing feature in Internet Explorer, the Incognito mode in Google Chrome, and the Private Browsing feature in Firefox and Safari keeps the browser from storing any data, such as cookies, temporary Internet files, form data, or usernames and passwords about your browsing session. In Internet Explorer, you can start InPrivate Browsing from the Safety

menu, which opens a new browsing window. Close the window to end the InPrivate browsing session.

- **How can I avoid spyware?** A first defense is to avoid responding to pop-up ads, which often lead to downloading spyware or other malware. Most browsers include a pop-up blocking option. Spyware can piggyback on seemingly legitimate freeware or shareware downloads. Spyware also sneaks into your computer when you click infected pop-up ads or surf some insecure Web sites. You should install and use **antispyware** software. Antispyware is security software designed to identify and neutralize ad-serving cookies and other spyware. Antispyware programs include Spy Sweeper, Ad-Aware, Spybot Search & Destroy (Figure E-25) and Trend Micro AntiVirus Plus Anti-Spyware.

FIGURE E-25: AntiSpyware software

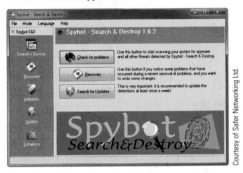

Courtesy of Safer Networking Ltd.

- **What is a fake site?** A fake Web site looks legitimate, but has been created by a third party to be a very clever replica of a legitimate Web site. See Figure E-26. Many fake Web sites are bogus storefronts designed exclusively for collecting credit card numbers from shoppers. When your data is received on a fake site, it is stored in a database that belongs to a hacker, who can use the data for unauthorized transactions. Always review the URL in the Address box to ensure the Web site is authentic before entering sensitive information on the Web site.

FIGURE E-26: A fake site

Courtesy of www.rantsandraves.co.uk

- **What is phishing?** **Phishing** is an email-based or IM scam designed to persuade you to reveal confidential information. In these scams, a hacker, posing as a legitimate representative of an official organization (such as your ISP or your bank), sends you an email and asks you to visit a Web page, which is actually a fake site. Once at the fake site, you are asked to confirm personal information, such as your billing information, or verify your account by providing your password, a credit card number, or your Social Security number. URLs in phishing emails are just slightly different from the official URL. Hackers depend on victims not paying close attention to the discrepancy when they click links. Even if the email message appears to be legitimate, do not click any links in the message. Instead, type the URL you know to be correct into your browser's address box, then access your account as you normally would. If in doubt, email or call a known representative. Do not use contact information in the email as that will probably direct you to the scammer.

- **What is pharming, and how can I protect myself?** **Pharming** is a scam that redirects users to fake sites by poisoning a domain name server with a false IP address. Pharming and phishing are similar in many respects; both take advantage of fake sites. Antipharming tools are emerging in response to the growing security threat pharming poses. Most browsers now include routines that compare IP addresses to a list of known fake sites and warn you of suspicious sites. The SmartScreen Filter feature available through the Safety menu in Internet Explorer should always be activated. The program works in the background. However, if you are concerned that a Web site might be fake, you can use the "Check this website" feature on the Safety menu to confirm whether the Web site is valid.

- **What is spam, and is spam dangerous?** **Spam** is unwanted electronic junk mail that arrives in your online mailbox. Spam is generated by marketing firms using email addresses from mailing lists, membership applications, and Web sites. Spam can be dangerous because it sometimes contains viruses, worms, or keyloggers. These unwanted programs can wreak havoc on your computer or steal personal information such as passwords.

- **Can I block spam before it gets to my mailbox?** Yes, you can use a **spam filter**, which is a type of utility software that captures unsolicited email messages before they reach your Inbox. It works by checking the text of email headers and messages based on a series of rules. You can train your spam filter. In addition, Internet service providers are using **email authentication** techniques to verify that email messages originate from the Internet domain from which they claim to have been sent.

How to Secure Files

Because you cannot always prevent disasters from happening, you need a backup plan that helps you recover data that has been wiped out by operator error, malware, or hardware failures. The exact steps you need to follow to make a backup depend on your backup equipment, your backup software, and your personal backup plan.

Learning Objective 8:
Explain ways to secure your files

● **What is a backup?** A **backup** is a copy of one or more files that has been made in case the original files become damaged. A backup is usually stored on a different storage medium from the original files.

● **Is there special software I can use to create a backup?** **Backup software** is a set of utility programs designed to back up and restore files. Backup software, such as the Windows backup utility shown in Figure E-27, usually provides options that make it easy to schedule periodic backups, define a set of files that you want to back up regularly, and automate the restoration process. If you purchase third-party backup software, make sure that you keep the original distribution CD and that you have a separate backup that contains any backup software that you downloaded from the Web.

FIGURE E-27: Backup software

Used with permission from Microsoft

● **Are there ways to back up my data?** Yes. Generally, you will use a combination of the ways described next.

■ A **full backup** (also called a **full-system backup**) contains a copy of every program, data, and system file on a computer.

■ A **differential backup** makes a backup of only those files that were added or changed since your last full backup session.

■ An **incremental backup** makes a backup of the files that were added or changed since the last backup—not necessarily the files that changed from the last full backup, but the files that changed since any full or differential backup.

● **What data should I back up?** You should make a full system backup regularly. Minimally you should back up all your data files, such as your documents, graphics, photographs, and music files regularly. In addition to data files, you should back up your Internet connection information, email folders, email address book, favorite URLs, downloads folder, validation codes, and all configuration data.

● **How do I choose a backup device?** The backup device you select depends on the value of your data, your current equipment, and your budget. Examples of backup storage media include writable CDs, DVDs, BDs, solid-state storage cards, tapes, or USB flash drives. For added security, some consumers use an external USB hard drive. These external drives can be disconnected when not in use and stored in a safe place. You can also use remote storage options, such as backing up to a network server or to a Web site.

● **Why would I want to back up my data to a network server?** One advantage to backing up to a network server is that all of your files are stored remotely. One disadvantage is that you must be connected to the network server in order to back up to or retrieve your files from the network server. Before backing up your data to a network server, you want to check with the network administrator to make sure that you are allowed to store a large amount of data on the server. Make sure that you have access to the backups in case you need to restore data to your local computer. If you want to limit those who can get to your data, ask the network administrator to let you store your data in a password-protected area.

- **Why would I want to back up my data on the Web?** One of the advantages to backing up your files on the Web is that your data is stored remotely. Your backup data is protected from any damage or theft to your personal computer. Several Web sites offer fee-based backup storage space. See Figure E-28. These sites are practical for backups of your data files, but space limitations and download times make them impractical for a full-system backup. You should not rely on a Web site as your only method of backup. If the Web site goes out of business or is the target of a denial-of-service attack, your backup data might not be accessible.

FIGURE E-28: **Web-based storage**

- **If something happens, how do I get my data back?** You **restore** data from a backup to the original storage medium or its replacement. The process that you use depends on your backup equipment, backup software, and exactly what you need to restore. After a hard drive crash, for example, you will probably need to restore all of your backup data to a new hard drive. On the other hand, if you mistakenly copy one file over another, you might need to restore only a single file from the backup. Most backup software allows you to select which files you want to restore. See Figure E-29. A **restore point** contains your computer

FIGURE E-29: **Restoring a system**

Select to use the most recent restore point

Click to open the System Restore dialog box

settings. If you experience a hard drive problem, you might be able to roll back to a restore point.

- **What is a boot disk?** A **boot disk** is a removable storage medium containing the operating system files needed to boot your computer without accessing the hard drive. If your hard drive fails or a virus wipes out the boot sector, you won't be able to use your normal boot procedure. It is essential to have a removable storage medium that you can use to boot your computer. With current versions of Windows, the Windows installation CD is configured as a boot disk and can be used if your computer does not boot normally.

- **What is a recovery disk?** A **recovery CD** (also called a **recovery disk**) is a bootable CD, DVD, or other media that contains a complete copy of your computer's hard drive, as it existed when shipped from the manufacturer. It contains the operating system, device drivers, utilities, and even software bundled with your computer. However, a recovery disk will not restore your data files, any software that you installed, or any configuration settings.

- **How do I decide what a good backup plan needs?** A good backup plan allows you to restore your computer to the way it was before the data loss. You must tailor your backup plan to your particular needs. Refer to the Figure E-30 to help you create a backup plan.

FIGURE E-30: **Create a backup plan**

- Decide how much of your data you want, need, and can afford to back up.
- Keep backup data files current so that you can restore them to your computer when necessary.
- Decide what kind of storage device you will use to make backups.
- Select software to handle backup needs.
- Create a realistic schedule for making backups.
- Make sure your computer is set to create restore points automatically.
- Make sure you have a way to avoid backing up files that contain viruses.
- Make sure you have a set of recovery disks either supplied by your computer manufacturer or created by you from a recovery partition.
- Make sure you have a procedure for testing your restore procedure so that you can successfully retrieve the data that you have backed up.
- Find a safe place to store your backups.

© Cengage Learning

Talking Points: Prosecuting Computer Crime

It doesn't take any special digital expertise to mastermind some computer crimes. Setting fire to a computer doesn't require the same finesse as writing a stealth virus, but both can have the same disastrous effect on data. Old-fashioned crimes, such as arson, that take a high-tech twist because they involve a computer can be prosecuted under traditional laws.

Traditional laws, however, do not cover the range of possibilities for computer crimes. Suppose a person unlawfully enters a computer facility and steals backup tapes. That person might be prosecuted for breaking and entering. But would common breaking and entering laws apply to a person who uses an offsite terminal to enter a computer system without authorization? And, what if a person copies a data file without authorization? Has that file really been stolen if the original remains on the computer?

Many countries have computer crime laws that specifically define computer data and software as personal property. These laws also define as crimes the unauthorized access, use, modification, or disabling of a computer system or data. But laws don't necessarily stop criminals. If they did, we wouldn't have to deal with malicious code. Computer crimes—costly to organizations and individuals—include virus distribution, data diddling, identity theft, salami shaving, and so much more. See the box that follows.

Data diddling: Unauthorized alterations to data stored on a computer system, such as a student changing grades stored in a school's computer

Identity theft: Unauthorized copying of personal information, such as credit card numbers, passwords, Social Security numbers, and bank account PINs

Salami shaving: Redirecting small, unnoticeable amounts of money from large amounts

Denial of service: An attempt to disrupt the operations of a network or computer system, usually by flooding it with data traffic

Information theft: Unauthorized access to a computer system, such as military or government computers, to gain restricted information

Virus distribution: Launching viruses, worms, and Trojan horses

Vandalism: Intentional defacement of Web sites

> "This world of bits is a strange one, in which you can take something and still leave it for its rightful owner. The theft laws designed for payroll sacks and motor vehicles just don't apply to a hacker."

One of the first computer crime cases involved a worm unleashed on the ARPANET in 1988 that quickly spread through government and university computer systems. The worm's author, Robert Morris, was convicted and sentenced to three years' probation, 400 hours of community service, and a $10,000 fine. This relatively lenient sentence was imposed because Morris claimed he had not intended to cripple the entire network. A 1995 high-profile case involved a computer hacker named Kevin Mitnick, who was accused of breaking into dozens of corporate, university, government, and personal computers. Although vilified in the media, Mitnick had the support of many hackers and other people who believed that the prosecution grossly exaggerated the extent of his crimes. Nonetheless, Mitnick was sentenced to 46 months in prison and ordered to pay restitution in the amount of $4,125 during his three-year period of supervised release. The prosecution was horrified by such a paltry sum—an amount that was much less than its request for $1.5 million in restitution.

Forbes reporter Adam L. Penenberg took issue with the 46-month sentence imposed by Judge Marianne Pfaelzer and wrote, "This in a country where the average prison term for manslaughter is three years. Mitnick's crimes were curiously innocuous. He broke into corporate computers, but no evidence indicates that he destroyed data. Or sold anything he copied. Yes, he pilfered software—but in doing so left it behind. This world of bits is a strange one, in which you can take something and still leave it for its rightful owner. The theft laws designed for payroll sacks and motor vehicles just don't apply to a hacker."

In 2005, an 18-year old German computer science student confessed to creating the Sasser computer worm that was blamed for shutting down British Airways and Delta Airlines flight check-ins, hospitals and government offices in Hong Kong, part of Australia's rail network, Finnish banks, British Coast Guard stations, and millions of other computers worldwide. The teen was given a suspended sentence of 21 months and was required to perform 30 hours of community service. Microsoft paid a $250,000 reward to the two people who provided German police with the

virus author's identity. He now holds a job at a computer company that creates anti-virus software.

Officials also made two arrests in connection with the Blaster worm. A 24-year-old Romanian citizen and an American teenager apparently downloaded copies of the worm source code, altered it slightly, and sent their versions back out again. The Romanian was allegedly angered by the way one of his professors treated him. The American teenager was just trying to see what he could get away with.

Under Romanian law, distributing a virus can mean a 15-year prison sentence. The U.S. Patriot Act and the Cyber-Security Enhancement Act carry even stiffer penalties—anywhere from 10 years to life in prison.

A CNET reporter questions the harshness of such penalties: "What bothers me most is that here in the United States, rapists serve, on average, 10 years in prison. Yet if, instead of assaulting another human being, that same person had released a virus on the Net, the criminal would get the same or an even harsher sentence." Lawmakers hope that stiff penalties will deter cybercriminals. Former U.S. Attorney John McKay is quoted as saying, "Let there be no mistake about it, cyberhacking is a crime. It harms persons, it harms individuals, and it harms businesses. We will investigate, track down, and prosecute cyberhackers."

> " Let there be no mistake about it, cyberhacking is a crime. It harms persons, it harms individuals, and it harms businesses. "

These cases provide a springboard to a discussion regarding computer hackers. On the one hand, they are viewed as evil cyberterrorists who are set on destroying the glue that binds together the Information Age. From this perspective, hackers are criminals who must be hunted down, forced to make restitution for damages, and prevented from creating further havoc. See Figure E-31.

From another perspective, hackers are viewed more as pranksters in our complex cybermachines—as moderately bothersome entities whose pranks are tolerated by the computer

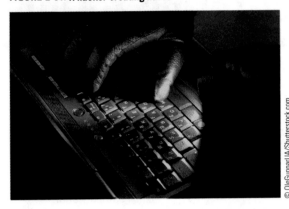

© OleGunnarUA/Shutterstock.com

community, along with software bugs and hardware glitches. Seen from this perspective, a hacker's pranks are part of the normal course of study that leads to the highest echelons of computer expertise. "Everyone has done it," claims one hacking devotee, "even Bill Gates (founder of Microsoft) and Steve Jobs (founder of Apple Computer)."

Which perspective is right? Are hackers dangerous cyberterrorists or harmless pranksters?

Expand the Ideas

1. Should a person who distributes a computer virus receive the same sentence as a person who commits manslaughter? Explain your position and back up your opinion with facts about current cases.

2. Should it be a crime to steal a copy of computer data while leaving the original data in place and unaltered? Why or why not? Support your position with examples of scenarios that justify your opinion.

3. Should hackers be sent to jail if they cannot pay restitution to companies and individuals who lost money as the result of a prank? If not jail, can you think of other, more fitting, punishments that might be more appropriate to fit the crime?

4. Do you think that a hacker would make a good consultant on computer security? Would you trust a hacker to work in such a position for a company that you were working for? Explain your position.

Identity theft through password theft

If someone steals your password, that person might have access to a wealth of personal information, including your Social Security number, credit card numbers, bank account numbers, health data, and other private details. When your personal data is used illegally, it is called **identity theft**. You don't have to give someone your password for your identity to be at risk because hackers have ways of stealing passwords. Some hackers use a **dictionary attack** to guess your password by stepping through a password dictionary containing thousands of the most common passwords. Others use a **brute force attack**, which exhausts all possible keys to decrypt a password. A brute force attack can run for as long as a week to crack some passwords. Still others use a technique called **sniffing**, which intercepts information sent out over networks. A good way to protect your data from these stealth attacks is to change your top-level password frequently and to keep an eye on your bank and credit card statements for suspicious activity.

Key Terms & Unit Review

Key Terms

Ad-serving cookie
Antispyware
Antivirus software
Authentication protocol
Backup
Backup software
Biometrics
Black hat
Blended threat
Boot disk
Boot sector virus
Bot
Botmaster
Botnet
Brute force attack
Computer virus
Computer worm
Cookie
Cracker
Cybercriminal
Cyberterrorism

Data center
Dictionary attack
Differential backup
Disaster recovery plan
Email authentication
Encryption
Firewall
Full backup
Full-system backup
Hacker
Human error
Identity theft
Incremental backup
Intelligent agent
Keylogger
LANjacking
Malicious code
Malware
Mass-mailing worm
Operator error
Password

Password manager
Pharming
Phishing
Port probe
Port scan
Power failure
Power spike
Power surge
Recovery CD
Recovery disk
Remote Access Trojan (RAT)
Restore
Restore point
Risk management
Safe mode
Security suite
Sniffing
Spam
Spam filter
Spyware
Surge protector

Surge strip
Surge suppressor
Trojan horse
Trojan virus
Two-factor authentication
UPS (uninterruptible power supply)
User ID
User rights
Virus
Virus definition
Virus hoax
Virus signature
Voltage spike
War driving
Wireless encryption
Wireless network key
Worm
WPA (Wi-Fi Protected Access)
WPA2
Zombie

Unit Review

1. Use your own words to define bold terms that appear throughout the unit. List 10 of the terms that are least familiar to you and write a sentence using each of them.

2. Create a chart to review the factors that cause data loss or misuse. List the factors you learned about in this unit in the first column. Then place an X in the appropriate column to indicate whether that factor leads to data loss, inaccurate data, stolen data, or intentionally damaged data. Some factors might have more than one X.

3. Summarize what you have learned about malware, including viruses, Trojan horses, bots, and software worms. Make a checklist of steps to follow if you suspect that your computer is infected with malware.

4. What devices exist to protect your computer from theft? What strategies should you follow to protect your data from unauthorized access or theft?

5. List three types of power problems that might affect your computer, and list what you can do to prevent damage to hardware from power problems.

6. Explain how passwords, User IDs, and biometrics work to protect a person's identity and his/her sensitive data. What are the differences between these methods and how can they work together?

7. Make a checklist of good practices to follow in order to protect your computer from malware.

8. Explain how pharming, phishing, and spyware are threats to your privacy. What can you do to prevent these threats from causing you harm?

9. What is a security suite? Explain why you might want one. Mention the advantages and the disadvantages of using a security suite.

10. Devise a backup plan for the computer you use regularly. What data would you want to be sure to include in your backup? Explain how you would implement your plan.

Concepts Review

Select the best answer.

1. A(n) _____ is a device that provides a continuous supply of power during a power failure and prevents spikes and surges from reaching your computer.
 a. power strip
 b. surge protector
 c. surge suppressor
 d. UPS

2. A(n) _____ contains multiple outlets but cannot filter out power spikes and surges.
 a. UPS
 b. power strip
 c. surge suppressor
 d. surge protector

3. A(n) _____ is a series of characters that a user creates to verify his/her user ID.
 a. protocol
 b. username
 c. password
 d. code

4. _____ is malicious code designed to disrupt a computer's normal operation.
 a. Spam
 b. Malware
 c. Phishing
 d. Router

5. A method of personal identification, called _____ , bases identification on a physical trait.
 a. authentication
 b. metrics
 c. biometrics
 d. scanning

6. A(n) _____ is software or hardware designed to filter out suspicious data attempting to enter or leave a computer.
 a. firewall
 b. virus
 c. encrypter
 d. spam filter

7. A computer _____ is a program that reproduces and attaches itself to a file so it can spread from file to file.
 a. encryption
 b. bug
 c. firewall
 d. virus

8. A spam filter will help you avoid unwanted _____ .
 a. bugs
 b. email
 c. software
 d. viruses

9. The _____ browsing feature in Internet Explorer keeps the browser from storing any data.
 a. antispam
 b. antiphishing
 c. history
 d. InPrivate

10. A(n) _____ attack floods network servers with useless traffic.
 a. spam
 b. denial of service
 c. mass mailing
 d. antivirus

11. A(n) _____ is a message containing information about the user sent from a Web server and stored on the hard drive.
 a. bot
 b. cracker
 c. cookie
 d. bug

12. A computer controlled by a bad bot is called a _____ .
 a. zombie
 b. spy
 c. botnet
 d. server

13. A(n) _____ is software that can automate a task when given a command.
 a. RAT
 b. port probe
 c. keylogger
 d. intelligent agent

14. Power _____ can damage sensitive computer parts.
 a. strips
 b. surges
 c. centers
 d. backups

15. A password uses a combination of letters and numbers, but a _____ uses numbers only.
 a. bot
 b. RAT
 c. PIN
 d. user ID

16. Virus experts use _____ threat to describe threats that combine more than one type of malicious program.
 a. blended
 b. hoax
 c. port
 d. zombie

17. A virus _____ is a section of program code used to identify a known malicious program.
 a. definition
 b. biometric
 c. filter
 d. signature

18. _____ is an email-based or IM scam designed to persuade you to reveal confidential information.
 a. Pharming
 b. Phishing
 c. Cyberterrorism
 d. Encryption

19. A _____ is a removable storage medium containing the files needed to start your computer without accessing the hard drive.
 a. CD
 b. botmaster
 c. restore point
 d. boot disk

20. A(n) _____ backup contains a copy of every program, data, and system file on a computer.
 a. incremental
 b. restore
 c. full
 d. protocol

Independent Challenges

Independent Challenge 1

Do you have a plan in place for data recovery in case something should happen to your computer? Are you working at a company that practices data backup and recovery on a regular basis? Is there antivirus software installed on the computer you use regularly? Assess the risk to the programs and data files stored on the hard drive of your computer.

For this Independent Challenge:

Write a brief essay that answers the following questions:

1. What steps, if any, have you taken to prevent data loss?

2. What threats are likely to cause your data to be lost, stolen, or damaged?

3. What measures could you use to protect your data from the threats you identified in Question 2? What is the cost of each of these measures?

4. What types of data files are critical and would need to be replaced if you lost all of your data? Make a list to refer to when you back up your files. See Figure E-32.

5. What would you need to do to reconstruct the critical files if the hard drive failed and you did not have any backups?

6. Taking into account the threats to your data, the importance of your data, and the cost of possible protective measures, what do you think is the best plan for the security of your data?

FIGURE E-32: List of files and folders to back up

Summary of data to back up

My Documents folder

My Pictures folder

My Music folder

My Videos

Programs folder

Download folder

© Cengage Learning

Data centers and disaster recovery plans

A **data center** is a specialized facility that is designed to house and protect a computer system and its data. A data center typically includes special security features such as fireproof construction, earthquake-proof foundations, sprinkler systems, power generators, secure doors and windows, and antistatic floor coverings. In general, data centers are not located in areas prone to earthquakes, floods, or tornadoes. Data centers typically include equipment to keep computers functioning during power outages. A data center must also protect and maintain its own power grid. Most data centers limit physical access via fingerprint identification systems, badges, or security guards. Motion detectors and automated alarm systems prevent unauthorized movement through the building.

A **disaster recovery plan** is a step-by-step plan that describes the methods used to secure data against disaster and explains how an organization will recover lost data if or when a disaster occurs. One of the most destructive disasters in history was the attack on the World Trade Center in New York City and subsequent collapse of the Twin Towers on September 11, 2001. Although the human toll was staggering, very few companies affected by the disaster experienced critical data loss. Most companies were able to rebuild their computer systems because they had developed and implemented disaster recovery plans that included remote offsite data backup servers or services.

Independent Challenge 2

Data loss can happen for many different reasons. You need to be aware of these reasons, as well as what preventative measures you can take to prevent data loss.

For this Independent Challenge:

1. The statements below list good email and computing practices to help prevent data loss or damage to a computer. Read each statement. Are there any practices you would add to the list? Select five practices and write a brief statement explaining why each of these defines a good practice.
 a. Never reply to spam when you receive it. If your email provider offers a way to report spam, use it.
 b. Don't click links telling you that your bank needs more information in email messages.
 c. Do not share your password or user ID with anyone.
 d. Give your email address only to people from whom you want to receive email.
 e. Be wary of providing your personal information at Web sites or posting it in public places such as online discussion groups.
 f. Use InPrivate browsing when viewing Web sites from a public computer.
 g. Use phishing filters and report suspicious Web sites to your ISP.
 h. Create a strong password for banking or credit card sites.
 i. Attach a UPS to your computer system.
 j. Have a backup plan and back up important data, files, and folders regularly.

2. Many times, damage to or theft of your computer is very avoidable. For example, you should never eat or drink near your computer because a spill could damage the computer. See Figure E-33. Make a list of five simple rules that you should follow in order to safeguard your computer from damage or theft.

FIGURE E-33: **Poor work habits**

Independent Challenge 3

You suspect that your computer has become infected with a virus, and you activate virus detection software to scan your files immediately. You find that your data has been corrupted and you lose several days work, not to mention the hours in locating and cleaning up the virus and restoring your system. This situation often results in frustration. See Figure E-34. Are you angry at the person who created the virus? The person who gave you the virus? Or, at yourself for not protecting your computer system better?

For this Independent Challenge:

Select one of the following statements and use library resources to learn more about each viewpoint. Write a two-page paper that argues for or against the viewpoint you selected using each case scenario below as a basis for your statements. Make sure that you support your viewpoint with facts and references from authoritative articles and Web pages, and include a bibliography of the resources you used.

1. People have the right to hone their computing skills by breaking into computers. As a computer scientist once said, "The right to hack is held higher than the right of someone to tell you not to. It's an inalienable right."

2. If problems exist, it is acceptable to use any means to point them out. The computer science student who created the Internet virus or worm was perfectly justified in claiming that he should not be prosecuted because he was just trying to point out that security holes exist in large computer networks.

3. Computer crimes are no different from other crimes, and computer criminals should be held responsible for the damage they cause by paying for the time and cost of replacing or restoring data.

FIGURE E-34: **Malware creates problems for users**

Guide to Buying a Computer

As you prepare to buy a computer, there are a lot of decisions you have to make. This course is designed to help you build the knowledge base you need to purchase a computer. In this unit, you were introduced to issues regarding data security. Personal, system, and data security were discussed. You learned that you can protect yourself as well as your data with a few simple steps, including installing and using security software and hardware protection devices. After each unit, you will be asked to answer questions by completing a worksheet. By the end of the book, your Guide to Buying a Computer worksheet will provide comprehensive information about buying a computer.

To help you organize the information you will need when you are ready to buy a computer, you should complete the following activities.

1. Take a security inventory of your computer system or of a computer system you use frequently. Complete the worksheet that follows to determine how secure this system really is.

Questions to consider	Answers	Is the protection sufficient?
Is your computer system protected against power failures: Is your system protected against power spikes or surges?		
If yes, how? UPS? Surge strip?		
Does your computer system have a hardware protection system in place? If yes, what kind?		
Is your computer kept in a locked room?		
Do you have a lock for your notebook computer?		
Do you have security software installed on your computer?		
If yes, is it a security suite? Which one?		
Do you have individual security modules installed on your computer system?		
If yes, does your system have firewall software?		
What security measures are in place on your computer system for protecting your Web activities? Do you use the safety features of your browser?		
Does your computer system have antivirus software?		
Does your computer system have spam protection?		
Does your computer system have antispyware software?		
Do you keep your antivirus, antispyware, and any malware programs up-to-date?		
Does your computer system have a password manager?		
Where do you store your passwords? Are they in a safe place?		
Does your computer system enforce user rights/restrictions?		
What backup systems does your computer system have in place? Backup devices? Backup media?		

© Cengage Learning

2. As you continue to work through this book, you will learn more about personal computer systems. You will have the opportunity to answer more questions and complete other worksheets with information that will help you when it is time to buy a computer and set it up to run securely. To help you think about the data and security needs for your computer system as well as your security needs as you use the Internet for shopping, banking, or general browsing, complete this portion of the Guide to Buying a Computer worksheet.

Guide to Buying a Computer: Data, hardware, and security needs

Questions to consider	Pages where the topic is covered in this book (refer to these pages to read more about the topic)	Notes (add additional comments, clarifications, or ideas about each topic)
What do I need to protect my system from power troubles? 　UPS 　Surge strip		
What do I need to protect my system from theft? 　Cable lock 　Tracking software 　Other locking device		
What do I need to protect my system from heat? 　Computer fan 　Computer stand		
What do I need to protect my system from malicious code? 　Antispyware security suite 　Antivirus software 　Spam filter 　Security suite		
What do I need to ensure I can back up my computer system and data adequately? 　Backup software 　Backup device		

© Cengage Learning

3. Write any questions you have about antivirus software and protecting your computer against hardware failure, as well as malicious software, on the lines that follow. As you continue to work through this book, check back to see if these questions have been answered.

My Questions

Visual Workshop

What security program or suite is on your computer? What options do you have for security? The most popular security suites include Norton Internet Security, McAfee Internet Security Suite, Alwil Avast AntiVirus!, and Trend Micro PC-cillin Internet Security. They can be purchased in most office, electronics, and computer stores, or downloaded from the Web. Some companies offer free versions. For example, you can download AVG Antivirus Free Edition from its Web site. See Figure E-35. AVG offers fee-based upgrades for more comprehensive coverage.

FIGURE E-35: AVG antivirus

© 2011 AVG Technologies

Research the various options you have for security software for your computer. It is also worth looking into your ISP's free security offerings. Write a brief paper that answers the following questions:

1. What is the security package currently offered to subscribers through these ISPs: Verizon? AOL? Comcast? Cox? AT&T? RoadRunner? What are the common features and offerings? Which package seems better to you?

2. Are open source software security packages available for download from the Web? What do you think might be the advantages or disadvantages to using open source security software? Compare annual subscription fees for these packages to the commercial offerings.

3. A security suite is often preinstalled on a new computer. However, usually it is demoware, so you have the option of purchasing it after the trial period, normally 60 days. Typically, there is also an annual subscription fee for continued use and regular updates. When you renew your subscription, you might have an option to upgrade to a newer version for an extra fee. Compare and contrast three of the offerings listed in the introduction to this Visual Workshop. Which package do you think you might buy? Why?

UNIT F
Concepts

Networks and Connecting to the Internet

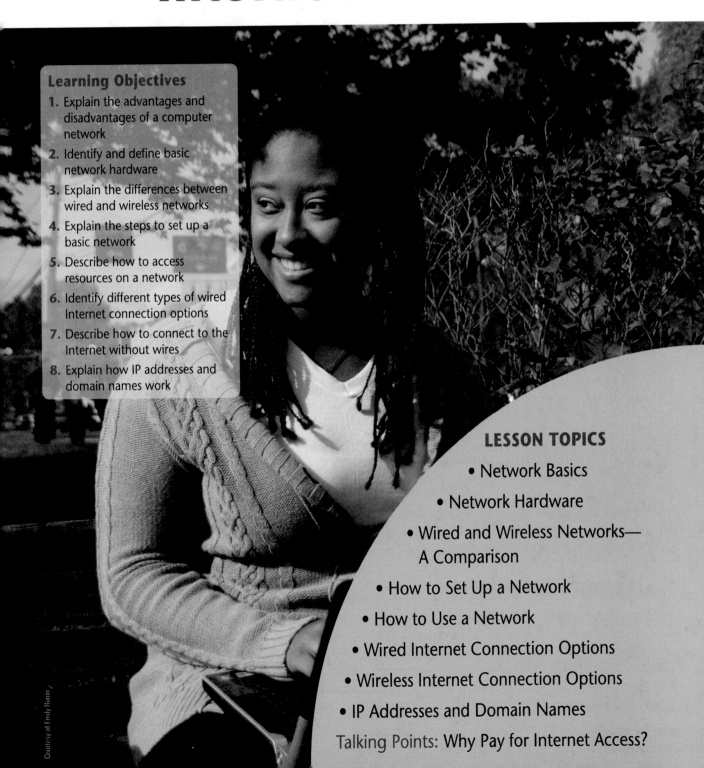

Learning Objectives

1. Explain the advantages and disadvantages of a computer network
2. Identify and define basic network hardware
3. Explain the differences between wired and wireless networks
4. Explain the steps to set up a basic network
5. Describe how to access resources on a network
6. Identify different types of wired Internet connection options
7. Describe how to connect to the Internet without wires
8. Explain how IP addresses and domain names work

LESSON TOPICS

- Network Basics
- Network Hardware
- Wired and Wireless Networks—A Comparison
- How to Set Up a Network
- How to Use a Network
- Wired Internet Connection Options
- Wireless Internet Connection Options
- IP Addresses and Domain Names

Talking Points: Why Pay for Internet Access?

Courtesy of Emily Bunin

Network Basics

A **computer network** (also called a **network**) is the combination of hardware, software, cables, and signals that transports data and allows computers to communicate with each other and other electronic devices. Networks allow users, such as you and your friends, to work together. Networks share resources. These include hardware, software, and data.

Learning Objective 1:
Explain the advantages and disadvantages of a computer network

● **Is my computer on a network?** If your computer can access other computers or share hardware (such as a printer or scanner) with other computers, then your computer is on a network. See Figure F-1. If your computer is connected to the Internet, then your computer is part of a network. As network technology continues to evolve, transporting data over networks becomes faster and more secure.

FIGURE F-1: **A network connects computers and peripherals**

Cable, DSL, or satellite modem for Internet access

Router

File server

Printer

Computer

Computer

Courtesy of MediaTechnics Corporation

● **What are the advantages of connecting my computer to a network?** Networks have several advantages because they share resources, such as hardware and software.

■ When you share networked hardware, you:

Spend less money. A network provides authorized users access to networked peripheral devices. For example, a single printer, scanner, or plotter can be attached to a network. This allows people working on networked computers to share the same device. This reduces costs because only one device, such as a printer, needs to be purchased for the entire network.

Have wider access to services. A network provides authorized users access to a range of Internet services, through a single Internet connection and specialized peripheral devices. VoIP is a technology that uses an Internet connection to use a computer to make telephone calls and video chat.

■ When you share networked software, you:

Spend less money. Software site licenses for network use are typically less expensive than purchasing single-user versions of a software program for each network user.

Share files. Networks provide authorized users with access to data files, such as documents, spreadsheets, and graphics, stored on network servers or network computers.

Work together with other people. Using groupware and other specialized network application software, several people connected to the network can work together on a single document, share calendars, communicate via email and instant messaging, and participate in online conferences and Webcasts.

Computing before networks

It has not always been possible for computers to connect to each other and share data, programs, and resources. In the early years of the computer revolution, most computers functioned as stand-alone units. Computing was essentially a solitary activity in which one person worked with a limited set of software tools. Some computer engineers, however, had the idea that personal computers could be interconnected or networked to one another. They understood that networked computers could provide advantages not possible with stand-alone computers. In 1976, Bob Metcalfe had an idea for transporting data between computers. His idea has become a key element in just about every computer network, including the Internet. He called his idea **Ethernet**.

See Figure F-2. Internet teleconference technology links participants with visual and audio real-time communications from multiple geographical locations.

FIGURE F-2: **Networks help people collaborate**

© 3Dstock/Shutterstock.com

● **Are there any disadvantages to connecting my computer to a network?** Yes. There are two significant disadvantages of connecting to an unsecured network:

Risk of unauthorized access. Whereas a stand-alone computer is at risk to theft or unauthorized use if a person sits at the computer, network computers are at risk of unauthorized access from many sources and locations. Intruders can access data stored on a network server or other network computers. Networks connected to the Internet are vulnerable to intrusions from remote computers. Unsecured wireless networks can be hacked through LANJacking.

Risk of malicious code. Whereas the greatest threat to stand-alone computers is a disk-borne virus, networks are susceptible to an ever-increasing number of malicious online attacks such as worms, Trojan horses, and other threats. Refer back to Unit E for information on what you can do to protect your computer from intrusions and viruses.

Despite the risks, most computer owners believe that the benefits outweigh the risks. They know it is safe to be connected to a network, especially if their computer is secured.

● **Are all networks the same?** Networks exist in many variations because each one is constructed from a collection of technologies. A network is several layers of technology. Table F-1 provides an overview of how networks are classified. For example, networks can be classified according to their size and geographic range or scope.

■ A **PAN (personal area network)** refers to the networking of personal digital devices within a range of about 30 feet (10 meters) and without the use of wires or cables. For example, a PAN can transmit data wirelessly from a notebook computer to a media player.

TABLE F-1: **Classifying networks**

Category	Description	Examples
Geographical structure	Area in which network devices are located	PAN, LAN, NAN, MAN, WAN
Organizational structure	Hierarchy of devices connected to a network	Client/server, peer-to-peer (P2P)
Physical topology	Layout and relationship between network devices	Star, ring, bus, mesh, tree
Communications channel	Technologies for cables and signals	Cable, RF signals, microwaves, laser and infrared light
Bandwidth	Capacity of a network	Broadband, narrowband

© Cengage Learning

■ A **LAN (local area network)** is a data communications network that typically connects personal computers within a very limited geographical area—usually a single building. LANs use a variety of wired and wireless technologies, standards, and protocols. School computer labs (Figure F-3), and home networks are examples of LANs. The focus of this unit is on LANs.

FIGURE F-3: **A computer lab**

© Ilja Mašík/Shutterstock.com

■ A **NAN (neighborhood area network)** provides connectivity within a limited geographical area, such as in a city's downtown area.

■ A **MAN (metropolitan area network)** is a public high-speed network capable of voice and data transmission within a range of about 50 miles. Examples of MANs include local ISPs, cable television companies, and local telephone companies.

■ A **WAN (wide area network)** covers a large geographical area and typically consists of smaller networks, which might use different computer platforms and network technologies. Networks for nationwide banks and large retailers are classified as WANs.

Network Hardware

You can think of a network as a spider web with many interconnecting points. Each connection point on a network is referred to as a node. A network **node** typically contains the network hardware, including computers, networked peripherals, or network devices. Even though networks come in many sizes and configurations, they all require similar basic network hardware parts.

Learning Objective 2:
Identify and define basic network hardware

● **Are all networks set up the same way?** Typically, networks are set up using either a client/server or a peer-to-peer structure. In a **client/server network**, the network must have at least one server and one or more clients. Figure F-4 shows the structure of a client/server network.

FIGURE F-4: **Structure of a client/server network**

Courtesy of MediaTechnics Corporation; Used with permission from Microsoft

● **What is the difference between a network server and a network client?** A network server, more commonly called a **server**, is a computer that provides services and distributes resources to other computers on the network, usually called **clients**. A server might provide a single service: An **application server** runs application software for network computers. A **file server** stores files and supplies them to network computers on request. A **print server** handles jobs sent to network printers. An **email server** is a computer that acts as a central post office for a group of people. More often, though, a server might provide several of these services.

A network client is usually a personal computer, although it is sometimes called a **workstation**. Each client is connected to the network and receives specific services by accessing the server. Each client has client software, such as a browser or email program, which it uses to access the server. A server can be accessed by more than one client at a time.

In a client/server network, network computers can function as clients or as servers, depending on the software installed on the computer and the computing power of the computer. However, servers are typically dedicated to the tasks they perform, which means they are not assigned to users to be used as clients.

● **Can a network function without a server?** Yes. Networks that use the **peer-to-peer (P2P)** structure do not have a server. In a peer-to-peer network, network computers serve as both clients and servers. In a peer-to-peer network, network computers share responsibility for processing, storage, printing, and communications tasks. See Figure F-5.

FIGURE F-5: **Structure of a peer-to-peer (P2P) network**

Courtesy of MediaTechnics Corporation; Used with permission from Microsoft

● **What is a network device?** A **network device** is any electronic device that broadcasts network data, boosts signals, or routes data to its destination. Network devices are discussed next.

- A **network interface card (NIC)** has the network circuitry needed to connect a device to a network. NICs send data over the network to and from networked devices, such as computers or printers.

- A **modem** is a network device that converts the digital signals from a computer into signals that can travel over a network, such as the telephone system or the Internet. Your modem modulates the signal that carries your data. A modem at the other end demodulates the signal.

- A **network hub** is a device that links two or more nodes of a wired network. On a typical network, the hub accepts data from one computer and then broadcasts it to all the other network nodes. Each device's NIC filters out any data that is not intended for that device. Two networks can be connected by a **bridge**, which simply transfers data without regard to its format.

- A **network switch** is a connection device that sends data only to the network devices specified as the destination. Using a switch instead of a hub can increase a network's performance and security because data isn't flowing to every network device.

- A **network router** is a device that can transmit data from one network to another network. A router is useful for connecting a home network to the Internet. Most routers are also switches that contain multiple ports. The router connects all the resources on a network.

- **Gateway** is a generic term for any device or software code used to join two networks. A gateway can be done using software, hardware, or using a combination of hardware and software.

- **What is Ethernet?** Today, most LANs are configured using Ethernet technology, see Figure F-6, which is a popular standard for transporting data between

computers and is used in most home and business installations. A NIC designed to support Ethernet is called an **Ethernet card** or an **Ethernet adapter**. The network devices in an Ethernet network are connected with network cables. The cables have a plastic RJ-45 connector at each end. You plug one end of the Ethernet cable into the port on your computer, and the other end into an Ethernet hub, a switch, or a router.

- **What if my computer doesn't have an Ethernet card?** You can purchase one and install it inside a desktop computer. Or, you can purchase a USB Ethernet adapter, which plugs into a USB port on the outside of your computer's system unit or your notebook computer. See Figure F-7.

FIGURE F-7: Ethernet adapters

Plugs into USB port

Ethernet adapter for USB port

Ethernet ports

Ethernet adapter for expansion slot

Plugs into motherboard

- **Are there other choices besides Ethernet?** Yes. Some computers also include a FireWire port. FireWire cables can be used to transport data at high rates of speed between a computer and another networked device.

- **What other equipment can connect to a network?** A **networked peripheral** is any device (such as a printer, a scanner, and a storage device) that has built-in network circuitry so it can connect directly to a network. A storage device that directly connects to a network is called **network-attached storage (NAS)**.

- **How many ports do I need for my network?** Your router, switch, or hub needs one port for each device you intend to connect to the network using a cable. It also has a WAN port that is only used to connect the router to the Internet. If you want to attach more devices to a network, you can purchase an inexpensive hub that provides additional ports and connects to the router.

- **Do I need special hardware for a wireless network?** Yes. You need equipment that can send and receive data wirelessly, instead of over cables.

FIGURE F-6: Ethernet ports and connector

Built-in Ethernet port

RJ-45 connector

Router with ports for connecting servers, computers, and peripheral devices

Unit F

Wired and Wireless Networks—A Comparison

A **communications channel**, or network link, is used for transporting data over a network. Communications channels are either wired or wireless. The type of communications channel used in a computer network determines how data travels over that network.

Learning Objective 3:
Explain the differences between wired and wireless networks

● **How does data travel over a network?** Data in a **wired network** travels from one device to another over cables or wires. Data in a **wireless network** travels between devices equipped with antennas, removing the need for most cables. Refer to Figure F-8. Wired and wireless networks have distinct advantages and disadvantages.

FIGURE F-8: **Cables and wireless router**

Courtesy of MediaTechnics Corporation

Courtesy of Belkin International, Inc.

Cables used for a wired network

Wireless router used for a wireless network

● **What are the advantages of wired networks?** Wired networks are fast, secure, reliable, and simple to configure. A wired network transfers data over cables. These cables have high bandwidth and are shielded against interference. Wired connections are generally reliable. Most computers are preconfigured with the hardware and software needed to join a wired network. You can plug the computer in to a router (or other network device) to connect the computer to a network.

● **If a wired network is so great, why use a wireless network?** Because the length of the cable limits the range of a device on a wired network. Wireless networks provide mobility. Notebook and tablet computers can be easily moved from room to room, or even outdoors. In addition to mobility, wireless networks are popular because of the absence of unsightly wires and cables.

● **Which is more secure, a wired or a wireless network?** Wired networks are more secure than wireless

networks because a computer can only join a wired network if it is physically connected by a cable. Wireless signals radiate through the air and penetrate walls. The signals that carry your wireless data can be accessed from outside your office or home. See Figure F-9. As a result, it is possible for your neighbor to access your files if your wireless network is not secured. If you use a wireless network, be sure it is secured.

FIGURE F-9: **Accessing a wireless connection outdoors**

© Luca Grandinetti/Shutterstock.com

● **Which is faster—a wired or a wireless network?** Wired networks are significantly faster than wireless networks for transferring files and sharing printers. The slower speed of a wireless network is generally not noticeable when transferring work or personal files. But, when games are being played over the network (such as a LAN or the Internet), then the fastest wired connection possible is needed.

● **How can I check the strength of my wireless signal?** You can check the signal strength of a wireless signal by using the Wireless network icon in the notification area on your computer screen. See Figure F-10. The range of a wireless signal can be limited by the type of signal, the transmitter strength, and the physical environment.

FIGURE F-10: **Wireless network signal strength**

SSID: LAN Services
Speed: 54.0 Mbps
Signal: Excellent
Status: Connected
Address: 192.166.1.337

2:07 PM

Courtesy of MediaTechnics Corporation

For example, signal range can also be limited by thick walls or ceilings. Also, a data signal fades as the distance between wireless networked devices increases. The signal strength limits the range of a device on a wireless network.

- **How does the data travel through my wireless network?** Wireless networks use radio waves, microwaves, or infrared signals to transport data. **RF (radio frequency) signals** provide data transport for small home networks, campus networks, and business networks. **Microwave signals** have more carrying capacity so they typically provide data transport for large corporate networks and form part of the Internet backbone. **Infrared signals** carry data only for short distances and with a clear line of sight, such as between a notebook computer and a printer.

- **What equipment do I have to buy for a wireless network?** Every network device requires a NIC or network adapter. If your computer is not pre-equipped with wireless circuitry, you can purchase and install a Wi-Fi card. A **Wi-Fi card** (also called a **Wi-Fi adapter** or a **transceiver**) is a wireless NIC that includes a transmitter, a receiver, and an antenna to transmit signals. Wi-Fi cards for notebook or tablet computers can plug into a USB port. Wi-Fi capability can also be added to a desktop computer. See Figure F-11.

FIGURE F-11: **Wi-Fi equipment**

Wi-Fi adapter in PCI slot

USB Wi-Fi adapter

Because a wireless network uses a centralized broadcasting device, you also need to purchase either a wireless access point or a wireless router. A **wireless access point** is a device that transmits and receives wireless signals. A **wireless router** is a wireless access point that also includes the circuitry needed to connect a Wi-Fi network to the Internet. Wireless devices that use **MIMO (multiple-input multiple-output) technology** have two or more antennas to send multiple sets of signals between network devices. See Figure F-12.

FIGURE F-12: **MIMO-equipped router**

Courtesy of Belkin International, Inc.

- **What is the most popular technology for wireless networks?** The most popular wireless LAN technology is **Wi-Fi (Wireless Fidelity)**. Wi-Fi technology refers to a set of wireless networking technologies defined by IEEE 802.11 standards that are compatible with Ethernet. A second wireless technology called Bluetooth is useful for short-range applications.

- **What about MiFi?** MiFi is a brand name for a small, mobile, wireless router offered by Novatel wireless. MiFi routers are battery operated, so they can make portable networks. With MiFi, you can assemble a small network just about anywhere. These routers are used with a cellular data plan, for example Sprint or Verizon, for accessing the Internet. Similar routers produced by other manufacturers can form a small network so you can connect notebook computers with cameras, media players, and other handheld devices. These small wireless networks transmit from one device to another creating mobile hotspots. See Figure F-13.

FIGURE F-13: **MiFi mobile router**

Courtesy of Verizon Wireless

Bluetooth technology

Bluetooth is a short-range (3–300 feet or 1–91 meters) wireless network technology that's designed to make its own connections between electronic devices, for example a printer, a mouse, keyboard, a PC, or a cell phone without wires, cables, or any direct action from a user. See Figure F-14. Bluetooth networks, called **piconets**, form automatically when two or more Bluetooth devices come within range of each other because a Bluetooth device can search for other Bluetooth devices within range. Bluetooth devices have to exchange passkeys, or PINs, to form a trusted pair. Bluetooth operates at the unlicensed 2.4 GHz frequency. Bluetooth can be used to link devices in a PAN, connect home entertainment system components, provide hands-free cell phone operation in an automobile, link a cell phone to a wireless headset, and synchronize PDAs with desktop base stations.

FIGURE F-14: **Bluetooth technology**

© A.S. Zain/Shutterstock.com

How to Set Up a Network

Networks, both wired and wireless, are easy to use and maintain. Ethernet equipment used in setting up a wired network is available from a variety of vendors. Ethernet hardware is not expensive or complicated. Likewise, you can easily buy the equipment needed to set up a wireless network.

Learning Objective 4:
Explain the steps to set up a basic network

● **Can I set up my wired Ethernet network?** Yes, it is easy to install a wired network. Once you purchase the basic hardware, you can follow the steps shown in Figure F-15 to set up a network.

FIGURE F-15: **Set up an Ethernet network**

1. Place the router in a central location and plug it into a surge-protected outlet.
2. Plug the cable into the router's WAN port, then run the cable from your router's WAN port to your Internet device, such as a modem.
3. Run cables from the router to the Ethernet adapter in each workstation.
4. Turn on network devices one at a time. Your operating system automatically detects the NICs and makes a connection to the network.

5. Use your computer's operating system network utilities to verify each connection. When using Windows, open Start menu to access Control Panel. From there, access Network Connections.

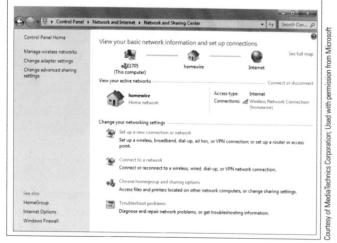

Courtesy of MediaTechnics Corporation; Used with permission from Microsoft

● **What are the basic steps for setting up a wireless network?** First, you place the wireless router, see Figure F-16, in a central location relative to the network devices. Next, you follow these basic steps: Set up the router, connect the computer to the router, access the router setup utility, configure the router, create a new router password, enter

FIGURE F-16: **Wireless router**

Courtesy of MediaTechnics Corporation

an SSID (service set identifier) which is the name that identifies a particular LAN, activate security and create an encryption key, and then set up the wireless workstations and wireless devices such as printers.

● **Can I connect both wireless and wired devices on the same network?** Yes. Most wireless routers include ports for Ethernet cables and a WAN port for a cable to an Internet device, such as a cable or DSL modem. The basic configuration for a network that includes both wired and wireless devices is shown in Figure F-17.

FIGURE F-17: **Basic configuration for a combined wired and wireless network**

— Wired connection
· · · · Wireless connection
File server
To an ISP and Internet
Cable, DSL, or satellite modem for Internet access
Router
Printer

Courtesy of MediaTechnics Corporation; © Ocean/Corbis; Used with permission from Microsoft

● **What is an SSID?** A wireless network requires an **SSID (service set identifier)**. In areas where there are

overlapping wireless networks, such as in a city or on a college campus, SSIDs help you log into the right network and provide a level of security. Most routers are shipped with a predefined SSID set by the manufacturer. It is a good idea to change the default SSID. When you name an SSID, think of it as a user ID rather than a password, and name your network something meaningful and easy to remember. You can change the default SSID when you configure the router.

● **How do I configure the router?** To access the router's configuration software, you have to connect a computer to the router. For a wireless network, the easiest way to make this connection is with a short Ethernet cable because the cable provides a direct link to the router without any preliminary setup. Once connected to the router with a cable, you can open your browser and type the LAN's address (usually http://192.168.1.1 or http://192.168.1.100) in the Address line. The LAN address and a default password are often supplied in the router's documentation. Enter the default password if one is required. The configuration utility might look like the one in Figure F-18. Be sure to change the default password by creating a new administrator password. This password is only used to configure the router; it is not needed by network users.

FIGURE F-18: **Set up the router**

Courtesy of MediaTechnics Corporation

● **How do I determine who can use my network?** Once your wired or wireless network is set up, you will need to create the workgroup, name the SSID if you are using a wireless network, and configure the router. A workgroup is a group of computers that communicate with each other to share resources on a network. You use the Control Panel Network and Internet utilities window to set up the workgroup. The operating system manages the workgroup. You can also set up and use a homegroup. A **homegroup** is a collection of trusted networked computers that automatically share files and folders. Access to the homegroup can be protected by a password. Windows 7 is preconfigured with a Homegroup that you can use to quickly link to other computers on your network and share files.

● **Once the network is set up, what happens next?** You need to be sure your computer is communicating with the network. Turn on your network computer, and wait for it to boot. Your computer's operating system should find the network automatically. For a wired network, no additional steps should be necessary. For a wireless network, enter the wireless network key or passphrase. If more than one wireless network is found, select the network you want to connect to from the list. Other networked devices should recognize and connect to the network once they are powered on.

● **How do I know when the network is ready to use?** The operating system usually displays a message or icon to let you know when you are connected to a network. Windows displays the Local Area Connection icon in the notification area on the taskbar. If that icon indicates the network is connected, it is ready for use. If you aren't sure, you can click the icon to see if the computer is connected to a network. See Figure F-19.

FIGURE F-19: **Network ready for use**

Used with permission from Microsoft

Network icon

How computers track devices on networks

Every node on a network has an address. Every packet of data that travels over a network also has an address, which helps to route a packet to its destination. A **physical address** is built into the circuitry of each network device at the time it is manufactured. In many cases a network device is also assigned a **logical address**. Network software keeps track of which physical address corresponds to each logical address. Two commonly used addresses are MAC (Media Access Control) addresses and IP addresses. A **MAC address** is a physical address, a unique number assigned to a network interface card when it is manufactured. MAC addresses are used for some low-level network functions and can also be employed to establish network security. An **IP address** (a logical address) is a series of numbers used to identify a network device. IP addresses are assigned to network computers, servers, peripherals, and devices.

How to Use a Network

Once your network is set up, you will be able to share files, folders, and hardware resources. It does not matter if the network is wired, wireless, or a combination of both, you can share resources easily on any network.

Learning Objective 5:
Describe how to access resources on a network

● **How do I access the network?** If you connect to the network using Windows, your computer automatically detects the network any time you power up your computer. Once the network is recognized, you might be asked to log in by entering a user ID and password, depending on your network setup. If you are not using Windows or if you want to switch networks, you can click the network icon and then click the workgroup name to access that workgroup.

● **Can I use a wireless network with my smartphone, notebook, or tablet computer?** Yes. When you are within range of the wireless network, turn on the device with wireless capability. When a wireless network has SSID broadcasting turned on, your device can find the network and connect to it. If the wireless network is secure, you will be asked to enter the wireless network key or passphrase.

● **How do I secure my network?** A wired network is very secure. Wireless networks, on the other hand, are much more susceptible to unauthorized access and use than wired networks. One reason is because wireless networks often broadcast their SSIDs so that legitimate users can easily find the network and connect to it. Some users turn off SSID broadcasting because they think this makes their wireless network more secure. Unfortunately, hackers can see the network even if the SSID is not being broadcast. Turning off SSID is a very weak form of security. You can review security measures for wireless networks discussed in Unit E.

● **How can I share and use shared resources on my network?** You can access shared resources on the network in a variety of ways. For example, Windows users can use the Connect To option on the Start menu to open the Network and Sharing Center to access and set up shared resources. These shared resources are listed as computers, folders, or drives when you view them in the Windows Explorer window. See Figure F-20. The name of a shared resource might indicate the computer on which it resides.

FIGURE F-20: **Shared resources on a network computer**

Network

Computers on the network

Printer on the network

Used with permission from Microsoft

● **What is drive mapping? Drive mapping** is a process that lets you create a shortcut to a shared folder, storage device, or computer on a network. Mapping assigns a drive letter to the computer, storage device, or folder. See Figure F-21. The Projects folder on the network computer MT is being mapped as drive M. Once mapped on the local computer, the files in the Projects folder can be accessed using Windows Explorer or through an Open dialog box in a program such as Excel or PowerPoint.

FIGURE F-21: **Drive mapping to share resources**

Used with permission from Microsoft

● **How do I share files and folders on the network?**
To allow other network users to access files or folders on your Windows computer, you have to designate the files as shared. You view the files in Windows Explorer, then right-click to access the file sharing menu. See Figure F-22. You can allow others to view, edit, and delete files, or restrict access to viewing only.

FIGURE F-22: File sharing

Used with permission from Microsoft

1. Right-click the file or folder you want to share, then select Share with.

2. Select a person or group that will be allowed to access the file or folder.

● **How do I share a printer over my network?** If you are using Windows, you enable printer sharing using the Windows Control Panel. Once printer sharing is enabled, you can connect a printer in one of three ways. The connection between network nodes can be either wired or wireless.

■ You can connect a printer to one computer on a network, see Figure F-23A, and then any computer on the network can send a print job to the printer. The job will print as long as the printer and the computer to which it is connected are both powered on.

■ You can use a **network print server device**, see Figure F-23B. By attaching a print server to a standard printer, any computer connected to the network can access the printer without going through a network computer. The print server and printer need to be powered on to print a job.

■ If you have a printer with built-in networking, you can connect the printer directly to the network hub or router, see Figure F-23C. Once the printer is configured and added to your list of printers, print jobs can be sent to the networked printer.

FIGURE F-23: Ways of connecting a printer to a network

Courtesy of MediaTechnics Corporation; Used with permission from Microsoft

(A) One-computer method

(B) Print-server method

(C) Direct-to-router method

Troubleshooting a network

Cables. Make sure all network cables are firmly connected. If only one network computer is not accessing the network, you can try swapping cables with another network computer.

Signal strength. In a wireless network, check the signal strength. If the signal is weak, move the network computer closer to the access point.

Security. Make sure you are using the correct password and that your password has not expired.

Interference. If you have intermittent network outages, look for sources of interference, such as cordless phones or baby monitors.

Network devices. Make sure your network hub, switch, router, or wireless access point is plugged in and functioning properly. Check the activity lights.

Settings. Make sure the network is enabled and then use the Control Panel to check the drivers for your network equipment.

Wired Internet Connection Options

The Internet is the world's largest network. It is made up of many smaller networks that are connected by the Internet backbone. The **Internet backbone** consists of high-speed fiber-optic cables. These cables connect high-capacity routers that direct network traffic and provide the main high-speed routes for data traffic. Backbone routers are maintained by **network service providers (NSPs)**. NSP equipment and links are tied together by **network access points (NAPs)**.

Learning Objective 6:
Identify different types of wired Internet connection options

- **How do I access the Internet?** To access the Internet, you connect your computer to a router that is connected to an **ISP (Internet service provider)**. The ISP is then connected directly to the Internet or it is connected to an NSP (see Figure F-24) that in turn connects to the Internet backbone. An ISP, such as AT&T, Sprint, and Verizon, operates network devices that handle the physical aspects of transmitting and receiving data from your computer. There are several fixed Internet access options for connecting to the Internet.

- **What is fixed Internet access?** **Fixed Internet access** links your computer to an ISP through a fixed point, such as a wall socket used in a cable Internet connection.

- **What are my fixed Internet access options?** You can connect to the Internet using a dial-up connection, a digital subscriber line (DSL) connection, a cable connection, a satellite connection, or a wireless connection.

- **How does my computer connect to the Internet using a dial-up connection?** Your computer's modem places a regular telephone call to your ISP. Your call is routed through the telephone company's local switch and out to the ISP because a **dial-up connection** uses POTS (**p**lain **o**ld **t**elephone **s**ervice) to transport data between your computer and your ISP.

- **How can phone lines carry data?** The signals in your computer that represent data are digital signals. The telephone system, however, works using analog signals. A **voiceband modem**, usually referred to as a **modem**, converts the digital signals from your computer into analog signals. Most computers have a built-in voiceband modem, which uses a standard telephone RJ-11 connector. Figure F-25 shows how a voiceband modem modulates the signal that carries your data.

FIGURE F-24: **Connecting your computer to the Internet**

Courtesy of MediaTechnics Corporation; © Ocean/Corbis; Used with permission from Microsoft; © Cengage Learning; ©2011 Google

FIGURE F-25: **How a modem works**

Courtesy of MediaTechnics Corporation

Your computer generates a digital signal.

Your modem changes the digital signal into an analog audio signal.

The receiving modem converts the analog signal back into a digital signal.

- **What is a DSL Internet connection?** A **DSL (digital subscriber line)** Internet connection provides high-speed, digital, always-on Internet access over standard telephone cables. DSL installations require a modem and a filter to keep

voiceband signals from interfering with DSL signals. You plug the DSL filter into the wall jack, and then connect the telephone line to the DSL filter. See Figure F-26.

FIGURE F-26: DSL equipment

Courtesy of Zoom Telephonics, Inc.

© Raymond Kasprzak / Shutterstock.com

DSL modem DSL filter

● **What is a cable Internet connection?** A cable Internet connection provides always-on broadband Internet access over the same infrastructure that offers cable television service. A cable Internet connection is faster than a dial-up Internet connection or a DSL connection. However, data transport speeds over cables are affected by subscriber use. When you set up your computer for cable Internet service, you are connecting your computer to the cable company's LAN. The LAN connects a neighborhood of cable subscribers. Your service might seem to get slower as more neighbors use the service.

● **Do I need special equipment for a cable Internet connection?** Most subscribers rent a cable modem from their cable company. However, third-party cable modems can be purchased. A cable modem can plug directly into a coaxial cable wall jack. You can use a cable splitter, as shown in Figure F-27. The splitter sends TV signals from your cable company to your TV and Internet signals from your cable company to your computer.

FIGURE F-27: Connecting to the Internet via cable service

Cable wall jack

Television or set-top box

Cable splitter

Cable modem

Stand-alone computer

© Cengage Learning; © ra3rn/Shutterstock.com; © Norman Chan/Shutterstock.com; © 2011 Google Corporation; © MishAl/Shutterstock.com; Courtesy of MediaTechnics Corporation; ©2011 Google

● **What is a satellite Internet connection?** A satellite Internet connection provides always-on, high-speed, Internet access by broadcasting signals to and from your satellite dish. Satellite Internet service only requires an unobstructed view of the orbiting satellite. In many rural areas, satellite Internet service is the only alternative to a dial-up connection. Satellite connections do not require wired infrastructure to connect to the Internet, but they do use wires to connect the computer to the required equipment, such as a cable from a computer to the satellite modem. See Figure F-28. One disadvantage to satellite transmission and reception is adverse weather conditions, which can result in unreliable data transfers and data transport.

FIGURE F-28: Connecting to the Internet via satellite service

PC Satellite ISP

Satellite modem Satellite dish Internet

Courtesy of MediaTechnics Corporation; © SSSCCC/ Shutterstock.com; © Helea/Shutterstock.com; Courtesy of MediaTechnics Corporation; © Ocean/Corbis; © Cengage Learning

● **How does access using a dial-up connection differ from access using an always-on connection?** With a dial-up connection, you must dial in each time you want to access the Internet. With an **always-on connection**, you are on the Internet and you stay connected as long as your browser is open.

● **Are all Internet connections the same speed?** No. The connection speeds offered by ISPs differ depending on the type of service you subscribe to. Connection speed refers to the amount of data that travels between a subscriber's computer and an ISP within a given time period. **Bandwidth** is the transmission capacity of a communications channel and it determines how fast data travels over a network. High-bandwidth communications systems, such as cable TV, fiber-optic, and DSL, are referred to as **broadband**. Systems with less capacity, such as dial-up Internet access, are referred to as **narrowband**. Bandwidth is measured in bits per second (bps), usually **Kbps** (kilobits per second) or **Mbps** (megabits per second). Maximum speed can differ from actual speed because links are susceptible to interference that can slow signals.

● **Is my connection speed the same for data I send as for data I receive?** Probably not. Upstream speed is usually slower than downstream speed. **Upstream speed** is the rate data is transmitted from your computer to the Internet. **Downstream speed** is the rate data arrives at your computer.

UNIT F
Concepts

Wireless Internet Connection Options

With so many people using notebook computers, iPads, smartphones, ereaders, and other portable digital devices, Internet users want the freedom to roam while accessing online information and services. Connecting to the Internet without wires gives mobile computer users the most flexibility.

Learning Objective 7:
Describe how to connect to the Internet without wires

● **What are my wireless connection options?** You have several options for connecting wirelessly to the Internet. **Mobile Internet access** allows you to access the Internet, such as using a mobile phone or tablet computer to check your email and browse the Web, while traveling. **Portable Internet access allows you** to move your network device, such as a notebook computer, and stay connected as long as you are within range of the fixed wireless signal. **Fixed wireless access** (also called **wireless broadband service**) provides Internet access to homes and businesses by broadcasting data signals over large areas.

● **What is the difference between portable and mobile Internet access?** Portable Internet access provides the ability to move your computer easily from one location to another without losing your connection to the Internet. If you connect to the Internet wirelessly at home and move your computer from room to room in your home, or even to your yard, without losing your Internet connection, then you are using portable Internet access. Portable Internet access services include Wi-Fi, portable satellite, and portable WiMAX. On the other hand, mobile Internet access offers a continuous Internet connection as you are walking or riding in a bus, car, train, or plane. Mobile Internet access includes mobile WiMAX and cellular broadband service.

● **What is WiMAX?** WiMAX (**Worldwide Interoperability for Microwave Access**), an Ethernet-compatible network standard, is one of the most well-known fixed wireless

standards. WiMAX can be used in rural areas. A WiMAX system transmits data to and from WiMAX antennas mounted on towers. See Figure F-29. WiMAX modems, usually provided by your wireless service provider, are easy to transport and can be plugged in anywhere within the coverage area of a WiMAX tower. WiMAX speed is affected by distance, weather, and usage.

FIGURE F-29: **A WiMAX tower**

Courtesy of Intel Corporation

● **What is a public Wi-Fi Internet connection?** A **public Wi-Fi network** is a wireless LAN that provides open Internet access to the public. Public Wi-Fi networks are now in places such as bookstores, restaurants, airports, hotels, airports, and coffee shops. See Figure F-30. The range of network coverage is called a **Wi-Fi hotspot**. You can access a Wi-Fi hotspot using a Wi-Fi-enabled notebook computer. Some Wi-Fi public networks offer free service; others require a subscription or one-time user fee.

FIGURE F-30: **A public Wi-Fi hotspot**

Used with permission from Microsoft

Public Wi-Fi hotspot

The "Eye-triple-E" and wireless standards

The nonprofit organization, IEEE (pronounced Eye-triple-E) is the world's leading professional association for the advancement of technology. Network technologies are standardized by the Institute of Electrical and Electronics Engineers (IEEE) Project 802- Local Network Standards. IEEE standards are available for most types of commercial networks. IEEE uses numbers to designate different

network standards. IEEE Wireless Communication Standards include 802.11, 802.15, and 802.16. An IEEE designation number, such as IEEE 802.3, is sometimes used in articles and advertisements. When you're shopping for equipment to connect your computer to a network, these designation numbers help you identify compatible network technologies.

- **What about speed and security when using a Wi-Fi hotspot?** The speed of a wireless hotspot is related to the speed of the wired line that connects it to the Internet. Speed can vary depending on the distance of the router to the access point, the number of people logged in, and interference from other networks. Hotspots, like any wireless connection, do not offer secure transmissions. So, it is important for hotspot users to secure their computers with antivirus software, firewalls, and encryption.

- **Can I use my cell phone to access the Internet?** Most cellular service providers offer data services, such as email and Internet access. See Figure F-31. These data services are referred as **mobile broadband**. Cellular technology used to provide mobile broadband is classified by generation or "G". For example, many of today's cellular service providers support digital transmission for both voice and data using 3G technologies, faster 4G access is available in some urban areas.

If you have mobile broadband service on your phone, you can plug your cellular phone into your computer to access the Internet (Figure F-32), or you can use a cellular wireless modem that plugs into a notebook computer's PC or USB slot.

You need a data plan to connect to the Internet through your cellular service. Prices vary and most cellular service providers

FIGURE F-31: **Using a phone for Internet access**

Courtesy of MediaTechnics Corporation; © 2011 Google

FIGURE F-32: **Using a phone as a modem**

© Victor Soares/Shutterstock.com

base price on the amount of data, measured in megabytes, you send and receive.

- **Do WiMAX and Wi-Fi work in remote areas?** Generally, no. WiMAX and Wi-Fi hotspots provide coverage in cities and small towns. To access the Internet wirelessly in sparsely populated areas, see Figure F-33, you have two options. **Mobile WiMAX** provides service to remote locations such as where you might want to hike, ski, or conduct research. **Portable satellite Internet service** provides service while you are on the move usually by mounting a satellite dish on a vehicle. The dish is stowed while the vehicle is in motion, but it can be deployed quickly when the vehicle stops. Like a fixed satellite dish, a portable dish transmits signals to and receives signals from a geostationary satellite which appears to remain in the same place because it orbits at the same speed as the Earth. Portable satellite systems have self-aiming hardware that automatically deploys the dish and rotates it until it locks onto the satellite signal.

FIGURE F-33: **Mobile access**

© Radu Razvan/Shutterstock.com

- **How do the computers on the Internet communicate with each other?** Whether your computer accesses the Internet using a wired or a wireless Internet connection, it must be able to communicate with the computers on the Internet. Computers on the Internet communicate with each other by following certain rules, known as **protocols**. Table F-2 lists some of the main protocols used on the Internet.

TABLE F-2: **Some of the main protocols used on the Internet**

Protocol	Name	Function	Protocol	Name	Function
TCP	Transmission Control Protocol	Creates connections and exchanges packets of data	SMTP	Simple Mail Transfer Protocol	Transfers email messages from client computers to an email server
IP	Internet Protocol	Provides devices with unique addresses	VoIP	Voice over Internet Protocol	Transmits voice and video conversations over the Internet
HTTP	Hypertext Transfer Protocol	Exchanges information over the Web	POP	Post Office Protocol	Transfers mail from an email server to a client Inbox
FTP	File Transfer Protocol	Transfers files between local and remote host computers	BitTorrent	BitTorrent	Distributes files using scattered clients

© Cengage Learning

Unit F

IP Addresses and Domain Names

Every computer connected to the Internet has a special name, known as its IP address. The format for an IP address is determined by the TCP/IP protocol.

Learning Objective 8:
Explain how IP addresses and domain names work

● **What is an IP address?** The IP address is used to identify a computer while it is connected to the Internet. It is a series of numbers, such as 204.127.129.001. When written, an IP address is separated into four sections by periods. The number in a section cannot exceed 255. The four sections are used to create classes of IP addresses. Each part of an IP address has specific meaning such as size, type of network, and other Internet functions. For example, an IP address that begins with a number between 128 and 191 corresponds to a Class B network, such as a large college campus. When delivering a packet of data, Internet routers use the first set of four numbers to get a general idea of where to send the packet. The rest of the IP address is used to drill down to the exact destination.

● **Are there enough IP addresses for all the Internet-enabled devices?** Actually, up until February 2011, there weren't. This is because IPv4, the standard used to assign IP addresses, allows only 32 bits for an Internet Protocol address, supporting 2^{32} (4,294,967,296) addresses. While this number is very large, it is not large enough to handle all the Internet-enabled devices expected to need IP addresses in the future. So a new version IPv6 is being used. IPv6 uses 128-bit addresses, which means it can provide 2^{128} (approximately 3.4×10^{38}) IP addresses. This extraordinarily large number allows for a seemingly unlimited number devices and users on the Internet.

● **Who oversees IP addresses?** An organization called ICANN is the global organization that coordinates the technical management of the Internet's domain name system, the allocation of IP addresses, and the assignment of protocol parameters.

● **How is my computer assigned an IP address?** IP addresses can be assigned by ISPs or network and system managers. Once assigned, the IP addresses are semipermanent and stay the same every time you boot your computer. Some IP addresses are permanently assigned. A permanently assigned IP address is called a **static IP address**. Computers with static IP addresses, such as ISPs, Web sites, Web hosting services, or email servers, usually are connected to the Internet all the time. For

example, the computer that hosts the Cengage Web site has a permanent address so that Internet users can always find it.

Most computers are assigned a temporary IP address called a **dynamic IP address**. Dynamic IP addresses are generally assigned to computers that are running client software that will access the Internet for activities such as surfing the Web, sending and receiving email, listening to Internet radio, or participating in chat groups. Dynamic IP addresses are obtained through **DHCP (Dynamic Host Configuration Protocol)**, a protocol designed to automatically distribute IP addresses. Most computers are preconfigured to get an IP address by sending a message to the network device acting as the DHCP server. A DHCP-assigned dynamic IP address is either good for a long time (sometimes called a sticky IP address) or good only for that session. Either way, a dynamic IP address is assigned automatically.

● **Is there a way for me to know the IP address assigned to my computer?** If you need to identify how your computer is connected to the Internet or troubleshoot your connection, you can see your computer's IP address by reviewing the Internet configuration settings. In Windows, you can use the Network and Sharing Center to open the Network Connection Details dialog box and view your computer's IP address. See Figure F-34. Most operating systems offer similar utilities.

FIGURE F-34: Network Connection Details dialog box

● **How is it possible that my computer is not assigned the same IP address as someone else's computer?** Every ISP controls a unique pool of IP addresses, which can be assigned to subscribers as needed. Your ISP keeps track of all

the IP addresses it assigns, including the one assigned to your computer. Your ISP makes sure that no two computers on its network have the same IP address.

- **What is a domain name?** While IP addresses work well for communication between computers, people often have difficulty remembering a series of numbers. As a result, many host computers have an easy-to-remember name that translates directly to the computer's static IP address. This name is the **fully qualified domain name (FQDN)**, but most people just call it a **domain name**. Every domain name corresponds to a unique IP address. Each domain name and its corresponding IP address have been entered into a database called the **Domain Name System**. Any computer that hosts this database is referred to as a **domain name server**. A domain name, such as cengage.com, must be converted to its IP address before packets can be routed to it. See Figure F-35. Once the IP address is identified, the request can be sent to the computer assigned that IP address, cengage.com in this example.

A domain name ends with an extension that indicates its **top-level domain**. See Table F-3. For example, in the domain name cengage.com, com indicates that the host computer is maintained by a commercial business, in this case, Cengage. Country codes also serve as top-level domains. Canada's top-level domain is ca; the Czech Republic is cz.

TABLE F-3: **Top-level domains**

Domain	Description
biz	Unrestricted use; usually for commercial businesses
com	Unrestricted use; usually for commercial businesses
edu	Restricted to North American educational institutions
gov	Restricted to U.S. government agencies
info	Unrestricted use
int	Restricted to organizations established by international treaties
mil	Restricted to U.S. military agencies
mobi	Available for sites that cater to mobile devices, such as tablets and smartphones
net	Unrestricted use; traditionally for Internet administrative organizations
org	Unrestricted use; traditionally for professional and nonprofit organizations

© Cengage Learning

FIGURE F-35: **How domain names work**

1. You type the address www.cengage.com in the Address box of your Web browser.

2. Your ISP routes your entry to a domain name server.

Domain name server

ISP

69.32.133.79

3. The domain name server returns the corresponding IP address and displays the associated Web page.

Courtesy of Media Technics Corporation; © Cengage Learning

- **How does my computer find the Web page so quickly anywhere in the world?** The Domain Name System is based on a distributed database. This database is not stored as a whole in any single location; it exists in parts all over the Internet. Because these parts are connected through the same network—the Internet—they can communicate quickly.

How to register a domain name

You might want a domain name if you plan to operate your own Web server or if you establish a Web site using servers provided by a Web site hosting service. Organizations or individuals can select a domain name and register it by using an online registration service. The first step in registering a domain name is to find out whether the name is currently in use or reserved for future use. See Figure F-36. Some domain names are not currently in use, yet they are not available because they are reserved. If a domain name is not available, consider using a different top-level domain, such as biz instead of com. After you have found an available domain name you like, you can continue the registration process by filling out a simple online form. You can register a domain name for a minimal annual fee.

FIGURE F-36: **Find and register a domain name**

© 1995-2011 by Register.com

Talking Points: Why Pay for Internet Access?

How would you like high-speed Internet access that requires no cables, no modem, and best of all—no subscription fees? Free community wireless access in cities as diverse as San Francisco, Miami, New York, Prague, and Amsterdam is made possible by free WLANs (wireless LANs). You can find free WLANS in airports, see Figure F-37, hotels, and coffee shops. Free wireless access is also offered by rogue WLANs operated by public-spirited individuals who are more than willing to share their bandwidth with passersby. Rogue WLAN operators typically subscribe to a high-speed Internet access service. They pay their monthly fees, but instead of limiting access to their own personal use, they distribute their connections over wireless LANs to friends, neighbors, and just about anyone who passes by with the right computer equipment. In addition, some users take advantage of unsecured wireless networks to obtain "free" Internet access.

FIGURE F-37: WLAN used in an airport

© Tyler Olson/Shutterstock.com

However, is free access always legal? The question is being debated, but at least one example has had its day in court. A Florida man was arrested and charged with unauthorized access to a computer network, a crime that's a third-degree felony and carries punishment ranging from probation to five years in prison. The accused man was allegedly piggybacking on his neighbor's wireless network to access the Internet. It was one of the first cases of its kind in the United States. Reporters and bloggers monitoring the case reported that the fault might actually rest with the network subscriber who failed to implement wireless security. An especially aggressive posting on one blog also suggested that the network equipment manufacturer could be at fault for not enabling encryption as the default security setting.

Another problem with wireless networks is data security. With the spread of home, school, and corporate wireless networks, hackers are expected to increasingly capitalize on unprotected household wireless systems to download child pornography, send threatening emails, and steal financial information. But what about casual interlopers who just want to borrow a little bandwidth from time to time? One tech-savvy reporter relates that "on a trip to Colorado, a fellow skier told me that, although the hotel we were both staying at did not have a wireless network, an apartment complex down the street did. So I sat on their doorstep in the freezing cold to check email with my laptop." He then wonders wryly if he should have rung the bell and asked if he could "please use their Wi-Fi."

What implications does this type of LANjacking have for you personally? Think about it. What if your neighbor sets up a free WLAN that becomes popular with customers in a nearby coffeehouse? Your previously sedate network neighborhood might suddenly become an overcrowded metropolis with major Internet access traffic jams.

> **Some free WLAN operators do not believe that sharing is the same as commercial use. "I'm sharing it with people," says one free WLAN provider. "I'm not selling it. I'm not making a profit off it."**

Free WLANs are based on Wi-Fi technology, which uses the 802.11b networking standard, to create wireless Ethernet-compatible LANs. Wi-Fi technology is used for many mainstream applications. Wi-Fi networks are popular in corporations and universities where users are mobile and the flow of information typically requires broadband capacity.

The 802.11b standard uses an unlicensed telecommunications spectrum, so it is perfectly legal to set up an antenna to transmit and receive Wi-Fi signals without obtaining a broadcast license or paying any fees to the Federal Communications Commission. Not only is it legal, setting up a Wi-Fi antenna is simple and inexpensive. A basic Wi-Fi antenna can be created with a few wires and an empty container.

Using a Wi-Fi network is even cheaper and easier than setting one up. Many notebook computers have built-in Wi-Fi transceivers and software. If a transceiver is not built into your computer, you can add one for less than $100. With a Wi-Fi-ready computer, you can literally walk down the street, and your computer will look for and connect to any available (that is, unsecured) Wi-Fi network. FCC regulations even prohibit landlords from limiting tenant use of or access to wireless networks. For example, network administrators at the University of Texas at Dallas attempted to prohibit students from installing private wireless access points in their

dorm rooms because the signals interfered with access to the campuswide wireless network. The university reversed its policy after reviewing FCC regulations. But some broadband providers, such as AT&T and Time Warner Cable, fear that every user of a free wireless network is one less paying customer.

Some free WLAN advocates envision a nationwide web of interconnected Wi-Fi networks that will form "a seamless broadband network built by the people, for the people." In this vision of a world connected by free WLANs, libraries could offer Internet access to people in low-income neighborhoods. Local schools could get Internet access without exorbitant cabling expenses. Parents, kids, and grandparents, as well as corporate executives, could exchange email and instant messages from locations that include the kitchen table, the corner coffee shop, and the Little League field. Many businesses, such as hotels, buses, trains, and restaurants, promote free Wi-Fi to attract customers. See Figure F-38.

FIGURE F-38: Wi-Fi Logos

© tuulijumala/Shutterstock.com

According to one industry analyst, "The telecom industries are addicted to the one-wire, one-customer philosophy." As you can see, sharing an Internet connection that is intended for single-user access does not coexist with this philosophy. Most subscriber agreements contain wording that limits use of a broadband connection to one user and perhaps immediate family members. Although wording varies from one provider to another, most agreements expressly prohibit subscribers from using their connections for commercial purposes. Some free WLAN operators do not believe that sharing is the same as commercial use. "I'm sharing it (the WLAN) with people," says one free WLAN provider. "I'm not selling it. I'm not making a profit off it."

Whether or not free WLANs are legal, their benefits are tempered by several potentially negative repercussions. For example, tightening up subscriber agreements to eliminate the sharing loophole could affect many broadband subscribers who currently operate private wired or wireless networks that link several computers to a single Internet connection. Broadband providers could force private network operators (such as those operating home networks) to purchase more expensive multiuser licenses—an option that might be too expensive for many individuals who maintain home networks.

Most free WLANs are operated as a hobby. Some operators are very conscientious, but others have a relaxed attitude toward quality of service. Consequently, free WLAN access

can be unreliable, but users cannot really complain when the network does not work if they are not paying for the service. In addition, if broadband providers threaten to pull out of areas where free WLANs are popular, community members might have to choose between unreliable free WLAN service offered by hobbyists and more reliable, but more costly, services supplied by for-profit providers.

The wisdom of unregulated network availability is called into question by resulting ethical, security, and privacy issues. A publicly accessible LAN that requires no passwords or accounts can be used anonymously for a variety of illegal and dangerous activities. In the same way that drug dealers can use public telephones to avoid taps and traces, terrorists and other criminals can simply walk into a free WLAN zone, tap into the Internet, and walk away without leaving a trace.

Despite possible repercussions, the free WLAN movement appears to be growing and becoming more controversial. The free WLAN controversy could pit a group of telecommunications giants against a grassroots alliance of free WLAN advocates. The outcome has the potential to affect broadband subscribers everywhere.

Expand the Ideas

1. Research Wi-Fi technology. Write a brief description of what it is and how it works. Then consider: Is it ethical to set up a free WLAN? Is it ethical to use one? Research two articles that present both viewpoints, for and against the unregulated use of free WLANs. Compare the viewpoints and then summarize the findings. Draw your own conclusion at the end of a short paper.

2. Do you believe that pirated WLANs can provide service alongside for-profit broadband ISPs? Why might a person prefer to use one service over the other? Might a for-profit broadband ISP consider offering free Wi-Fi service? How could that be beneficial for the consumer? Write a short description of your ideas.

3. Are broadband ISPs justified in limiting the terms of their service agreements to one subscription, one customer? Relate broadband ISP services to other services such as telephone, cable TV, software licenses, radio, and print media. How are the services similar? How are they different? Does the difference justify the "one subscription, one customer" service agreements? Should exceptions be made for the following: same family users, same dwelling users, or home network users? Explain your position in a media presentation.

Key Terms & Unit Review

Key Terms

Always-on connection
Application server
Bandwidth
Bluetooth
Bridge
Broadband
Client
Client/server network
Communications channel
Computer network
DHCP (Dynamic Host Configuration Protocol)
Dial-up connection
Domain name
Domain name server
Domain Name System
Downstream speed
Drive mapping
DSL (Digital Subscriber Line)
Dynamic IP address
Email server
Ethernet
Ethernet adapter
Ethernet card
File server
Fixed Internet access

Fixed wireless access
Fully qualified domain name (FQDN)
Gateway
Homegroup
Infrared signal
Internet backbone
Internet service provider (ISP)
IP (Internet Protocol)
IP address
Kbps (kilotbits per second)
LAN (local area network)
Logical address
MAC address
MAN (metropolitan area network)
Mbps (megabits per second)
Microwave signal
MIMO (multiple-input multiple-output) technology
Mobile broadband
Mobile Internet access
Mobile WiMAX

Modem
NAN (neighborhood area network)
Narrowband
Network
Network access point (NAP)
Network-attached storage (NAS)
Network device
Network hub
Network interface card (NIC)
Network print server device
Network router
Network service provider (NSP)
Network switch
Networked peripheral
Node
PAN (personal area network)
Peer-to-peer (P2P) network
Physical address
Piconet
Portable Internet access
Portable satellite Internet service

Print server
Public Wi-Fi network
RF (radio frequency) signals
Server
SSID (secure set identifier)
Static IP address
TCP (Transmission Control Protocol)
Top-level domain
Transceiver
Upstream speed
Voiceband modem
WAN (wide area network)
Wi-Fi (Wireless Fidelity)
Wi-Fi adapter
Wi-Fi card
Wi-Fi hotspot
WiMAX
Wired network
Wireless access point
Wireless broadband service
Wireless network
Wireless router
Workgroup
Workstation

Unit Review

1. Use your own words to define bold terms that appear throughout the unit. List 10 terms that are the least familiar to you and write a sentence for each of them.

2. Explain the advantages and disadvantages of using networks to share files and share resources; give three examples of each.

3. How can you determine which resources are shared on a network? How can you share files and data on a network?

4. List four network hardware devices discussed in this unit, and then briefly describe the purpose of each one of the devices.

5. Name three ways you can connect a printer to a network, then discuss the advantages and disadvantages associated with each method.

6. List the major steps required to set up and install a LAN in your home.

7. Define IP address, and then explain the differences between dynamic IP addresses and static IP addresses.

8. Explain what a domain name is, how you can get one, and why it is used.

9. What different options do you have to connect to the Internet? Organize your findings into connected by cables and wireless. Briefly describe each method that you can use to access the Internet and include its advantages and disadvantages.

10. Describe the advantages and disadvantages of mobile Internet access, and explain who would use the service.

Concepts Review

Select the best answer.

1. A(n) _____ is the combination of hardware, software, and connecting links that transport data.
 a. Internet
 b. domain
 c. network
 d. Web

2. From a geographic perspective, networks can be classified as LAN, _____, NAN, MAN, or WAN.
 a. PAN
 b. BAN
 c. CAN
 d. FAN

3. Each host computer has an easy-to-remember domain name that translates directly to the computer's _____ IP address.
 a. FTP
 b. FQDN
 c. static
 d. dynamic

4. _____ determines how fast data travels to your computer from the Internet.
 a. Protocol
 b. Broadband
 c. Narrowband
 d. Bandwidth

5. Drive _____ assigns a drive letter to a computer, storage device, or folder located on a network computer.
 a. mapping
 b. routing
 c. networking
 d. bridging

6. A public _____ network is a wireless LAN that provides open Internet access to the public in places such as bookstores, coffee shops, airports, hotels, and airports.
 a. Bluetooth
 b. WiMAX
 c. Ethernet
 d. Wi-Fi

7. A _____ is a device that makes it possible to send and receive data over telephone lines.
 a. bridge card
 b. network interface
 c. router
 d. modem

8. _____ is the leading technology for wired networks; it is also included in some printers and other peripheral devices.
 a. Intel
 b. Bluetooth
 c. Ethernet
 d. AMD

9. _____ is a short-range wireless network technology that is designed to make its own connections between electronic devices, without wires, cables, or any direct action from a user.
 a. Intel
 b. Bluetooth
 c. Ethernet
 d. AMD

10. Networks that use the _____ structure do not have a server.
 a. TCP
 b. static
 c. peer-to-peer (P2P)
 d. dynamic

11. A popular technology for wireless networks is Wi-Fi, which stands for wireless _____.
 a. fidelity
 b. freedom
 c. file server
 d. fixed Internet access

12. Data travels faster on _____ networks than on wireless networks.
 a. mobile
 b. regional
 c. wired
 d. local area

13. A network _____ is a computer that provides services and distributes resources to other computers on the network.
 a. client
 b. server
 c. node
 d. TCP/IP

14. A(n) _____ address is a physical address, a unique number assigned to a computer when it is manufactured.
 a. MAC
 b. Bluetooth
 c. IP
 d. domain

15. A(n) _____ address is a series of numbers used to identify a network device in virtually every type of computer network.
 a. MAC
 b. Bluetooth
 c. IP
 d. domain

16. DSL (_____ subscriber line) is a high-speed, always-on Internet access technology that uses standard phone lines to transport data.
 a. digital
 b. drive
 c. downstream
 d. domain

17. The database that keeps track of the names that correspond to IP addresses is called the _____ Name System.
 a. Internet
 b. Bluetooth
 c. Network
 d. Domain

18. _____ over IP refers to a technology that uses an Internet connection to place telephone calls instead of the regular phone system.
 a. Internet
 b. Bluetooth
 c. Voice
 d. Data

19. A wireless network uses _____ waves, not cables, to send data from one node to another.
 a. digital
 b. radio
 c. satellite
 d. air

20. The top-level domain _____ is primarily for use by businesses.
 a. gov
 b. edu
 c. com
 d. org

Independent Challenges

Independent Challenge 1

Wireless services are available in most regions of the country and are expanding. You can get mobile news, email, text messaging, and mobile access to the Internet. Wireless communication is already having an impact on the way people work. More and more people are working at least part-time from a remote location such as a satellite office, their car, while in airports or on airplanes, or from hotels. Look around any public space and you can see people checking email on handheld devices, such as smartphones.

The number of people who work from a home office has increased dramatically in the last decade to a point where almost everyone knows someone who works from home. See Figure F-39. As this becomes the emerging business model, employees are finding that being connected is a necessity, not just a nicety.

FIGURE F-39: **Working from home**

© Morgan Lane Photography/Shutterstock.com

For this Independent Challenge:

1. Write a brief statement explaining your position and opinions on each of the following:
 a. How do you think wireless email and wireless Internet access are changing the way business is conducted?
 b. How are they changing the relationship between employer and employee?
 c. How are they affecting personal relationships?

2. Portable Internet access and mobile wireless Internet access raise societal questions such as privacy issues, employer expectations vs. employee responsibilities, and impact on family life. For example, you can sit in a coffee shop and work on and transfer sensitive business documents. Or, you can get a budget with private personnel data, such as salary information, transferred to your cell phone.
 a. Choose one societal issue affected by portable and mobile wireless Internet access. Research the issue, and write a paper presenting your findings.
 b. Write a short summary of your findings. In your conclusion, compare your research findings with the opinions you expressed when you answered Question 1.
 c. Be sure to include references and resources from your research.

Independent Challenge 2

The Domain Name System contains a vast array of names for businesses, organizations, and institutions. When you see a URL in an advertisement or a book, you often know immediately what the company or organization is and what the site will be about when you get to the page.

For this Independent Challenge:

1. Use your favorite search engine to research top-level domains, or start by visiting the ICANN Web site.

2. Find out the latest information about domains and how to register a domain name. Sites are available to help you learn more about registering a domain name. See Figure F-40.

FIGURE F-40: **Research how to register domain names**

3. Think about a URL that you might want to register, for example, yourname.com or something else that is important to you personally. Also think about a business venture that you might want to begin. What URL would you want for that business?

4. Find out if these URLS are available. Find a Web site that offers a quick search. Track your research. If your first choice is not available, list how you went about finding a URL that you could use. For example, if your name is already taken, would you want to try using your first initial and last name instead? Or, a combination of both first and last names? If that is not available, would you go for something creative or descriptive?

5. Submit a paper detailing your quest and the results you achieved.

Independent Challenge 3

If you live in a home where more than one computer is being used by more than one person, you might consider installing a simple LAN in order to network the computers. Perhaps you want to share a printer, or a scanner. There are many good reasons for setting up a LAN in your home. It is not that difficult to install a LAN in your home. The LAN can be wireless or wired. You may have reasons for choosing one or the other.

For this Independent Challenge:

1. Consider your current living situation. Write a brief statement as to how computers are used in your home. How many computers do you, your roommates, or your family own. How many people use computers in the home? Is anyone using computers for a business? Do you have Internet access in your home?

2. Determine if you want a wired or wireless network. Perhaps you want both. Add that to the statement.

3. List the peripheral devices that you would want connected to the network.

4. Draw a floor plan, similar to the one shown in Figure F-41, for your home or apartment. Identify the rooms in which you would want to use a computer. Identify the best place to situate a wireless router, and mark it on the plan.

5. Submit your statement and floor plans detailing the results you achieved.

FIGURE F-41: **A floor plan**

Guide to Buying a Computer

As you prepare to buy a computer, there are a lot of decisions you have to make. This course is designed to help you build the knowledge base you need to purchase a computer. In this unit, you learned that networks are an integral part of computing. Most likely you will need to connect to a network. To do so, you will need to buy some hardware, some software, and subscribe to a service.

Each unit covers topics that can help you understand the type of computer you need, the add-on parts you might want to buy, and the software and services that will enhance your computing experience. After each unit, you will be asked to answer questions by completing a worksheet. By the end of the book, your Guide to Buying a Computer worksheet will provide comprehensive information about buying a computer, creating a network, and connecting to the Internet.

To help you organize the information you will need when you are ready to buy a computer, complete the following activities.

1. Think about your networking needs. Use computer magazines or the Internet to research three types of network hardware, such as routers, USB Ethernet cards, and wireless adapters. Find two sources for each. Are prices comparable for these devices? What features do each of them have?

2. Think about your Internet needs. What companies provide Internet service in your area? Internet service is often bundled with phone and television services. Companies are highly competitive when offering service to customers. You should be able to find advertisements in local papers, mailings, as well as on the Internet, for service in your area. What technology choices do you have for Internet service? Are the prices compatible? Write your findings on the lines below.

© tr3gin/Shutterstock.com

© zzoplanet/Shutterstock.com

© apostol_8/Shutterstock.com

© ARENA Creative/Shutterstock.com

3. As you continue to work through this book, you will learn more about personal computer systems. You will have the opportunity to answer more questions and complete other worksheets with information that will help you when it is time to buy a computer. To help you think about your networking needs, as well as how you will access the Internet, complete this portion of the Guide to Buying a Computer worksheet.

Guide to Buying a Computer: Installing a Network and Internet Access

Questions to consider	Pages where the topic is covered in this book (refer to these pages to read more about the topic)	Notes (add additional comments, clarifications, or ideas about each topic)
What requirements do you have for home networking?		
Can you run wires in your home? Or, do you prefer to set up a wireless network?		
What hardware will you have to buy for the network?		
What peripheral devices will you connect to the network? Will these peripheral devices require NICs?		
How will they connect to the network?		
What cables will you need if setting up a wired network?		
Which Internet service providers are available in your area?		
Does your ISP provide bundles with Television/Internet/Phone service? Is this package right for you?		
What is the fee?		
What is the bandwidth?		
What is the upstream speed?		
What is the downstream speed?		
What other options are available?		
Will you want portable Internet access? If so, what devices will you need to purchase?		
Will you need mobile Internet access? Does your cellular plan include data? Is there a monthly megabyte limit?		

© Cengage Learning

4. Write any questions you have about your networking and Internet needs on the lines that follow. As you continue to work through this book, check back to see if these questions have been answered.

My Questions

Visual Workshop

Bluetooth wireless technology is a standard for low-cost, personal area network connections among mobile computers, mobile phones, and other devices. Using a globally available frequency range, Bluetooth eliminates the need for cables and provides secure, radio-based transmission of data and voice. Many new devices include Bluetooth technology. See Figure F-42.

FIGURE F-42: Researching Bluetooth technology

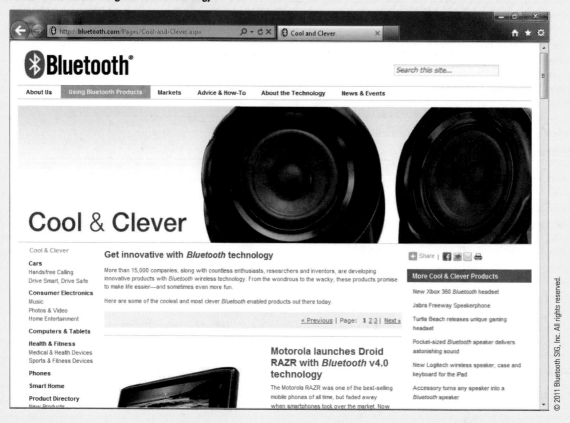

1. Log on to the Internet and go to the official Bluetooth Web site at www.bluetooth.com. You can also research Bluetooth technology on related sites. Answer the following questions: Who developed the Bluetooth wireless technology? When was it developed? What were the goals or reasons for developing the technology? What is the origin of the name "Bluetooth," and why is it named that?

2. Bluetooth technology is being included in many new applications. List two applications that are discussed on the Web site.

3. Bluetooth technology is being incorporated into many different products. Research some products that currently support Bluetooth. Name at least two products from three different categories. Describe how the products use the technology and how they benefit the user.

4. Find the Web site of one company using Bluetooth technology in its products. Describe one of the applications. Be sure to cite your sources.

The Web and E-Commerce

Learning Objectives

1. Explain the basic elements that make up the World Wide Web
2. Identify the main features and functions of a Web browser
3. Explain HTML and other tools used to display Web pages in a browser
4. Describe how to search the Web for information
5. Discuss several services provided by the Web and the Internet
6. Define e-commerce and explain how the Web is used for commercial transactions
7. Name systems used to secure e-commerce transactions
8. Identify several technologies used to enhance the Web

Courtesy of Emily Bunin

LESSON TOPICS

- The Web—An Overview
- Web Browser Basics
- Web Page Tools
- Search Tools and Techniques
- Web and Internet Services
- E-Commerce—An Overview
- Secure E-Commerce Transactions
- Ways to Enhance Web Sites

Talking Points: Regulating the Web

The Web—An Overview

The **Web** (also called the **World Wide Web** or **WWW**) is a collection of documents called Web pages that are accessed over the Internet. These documents are interconnected by links. The Internet is a communications network that transmits data, including email, videoconferences, phone calls, and messages. The Web is an Internet resource.

Learning Objective 1:
Explain the basic elements that make up the World Wide Web

- **What is a Web site?** A **Web site** is a collection of Web pages on a related topic. Each Web site is associated with a government, a business, an organization, or an individual. The Web is made up of millions of Web sites.

- **What is a Web page?** A **Web page** is a document that contains media elements such as text, graphics, video, and audio. These elements can contain links to related documents, graphics, sound, and video files. Common features of a Web page are shown in Figure G-1.

- **What is a browser?** A **browser** (as also called a **Web browser**) is software installed on your computer. It displays Web page elements and manages links between pages. Popular browsers are Microsoft Internet Explorer, Google Chrome, Mozilla Firefox, or Apple Safari. You use a browser

to view a Web page either by typing a URL in the Address bar or by clicking a link on the open Web page. Other ways to open and view a Web page include clicking a bookmarked link in your Favorites list and clicking a link in the History list. You can also click a link in a document, such as a report in Word, to open a Web page if the computer used to view the document has an active Internet connection.

- **What is a link?** A **link** (also called **hyperlink** or a **hypertext link**) is a navigation tool on a Web page. Clicking a link on a Web page—a word, a phrase, or a graphic—opens the related document. When you click a link, you move to another location on the same Web page or to a new Web page. The new Web page might be part of the same Web site, or it might be a new Web site. Links are what keep Web pages related.

FIGURE G-1: **A Web page in a browser**

© Cengage Learning

- **Where did the concept of linking Web pages come from?** Links are based on hypertext. The term started being used in the mid-1960s, when Harvard graduate Ted Nelson coined the term **hypertext**. He used this term to describe a computer system that could store literary documents, link them according to logical relationships, and allow readers to comment and annotate what they read.

- **Why does a Web page have a URL?** The **URL (Uniform Resource Locator)** for a Web page is the address for that Web page. Each Web page has a unique URL. The URL is used by the browser software to locate its associated Web page. For example, the URL for the Public Broadcasting Service (PBS) Web site is http://www.pbs.org. Most URLs begin with http:// to indicate the Web's standard communications protocol. When typing a URL, you do not have to type the http:// in the browser Address bar, so www.pbs.org works just as well as http://www.pbs.org.

- **Are there other rules to follow when typing a URL?** Yes. Be sure you do not type any spaces in a URL because a URL never contains spaces, even after a punctuation mark. Sometimes, an underline is used to give the appearance of a space between words, for example www.detroit.com/top_10.html. If a URL uses a slash, be sure to use the correct type of slash—always a forward slash (/). Always duplicate the URL's capitalization exactly because some Web servers are case sensitive. On these Web servers, typing www.cmu.edu/Info.html (with an uppercase I) will not locate the Web page that's stored as www.cmu.edu/info.html (with a lowercase i).

- **What is a Web server?** A **Web server** is a computer that uses special software to store and to transmit Web pages over the Internet. Web servers store Web pages as **HTML documents**. Web servers can also store data in databases. Data, such as product information, can be assembled into HTML format "on the fly" in response to Web page requests. A Web page can always display current data when it gets the data from a database that is updated regularly.

A Web server is configured to use HTTP software. **HTTP (Hypertext Transfer Protocol)** is the communications protocol used to transport data over the Web. A Web server listens for HTTP requests. When a request arrives, the server software analyzes the request and takes whatever action is necessary to fulfill it. The computer that runs Web server software might have other software running on it as well. For example, a computer might operate as a Web server, an email server, and an FTP (File Transfer Protocol) server all at the same time. To handle these diverse duties efficiently, a computer devotes a different port to each activity. For example, one port might listen for HTTP requests, another for SMTP or POP email requests, and a third for FTP requests.

- **How do Web pages get to my computer?** To view a Web page, you either type the URL into the browser's Address bar or you click a link. Your browser creates a request for the Web page file associated with the URL and sends that request to a Web server. The Web server interprets the request and sends the Web page back to your browser. The Web page is displayed in your browser. See Figure G-2.

- **How do my browser and the Web server communicate?** They use the HTTP protocol and the TCP/IP protocol to communicate. The browser uses HTTP to request the Web page, and the Web server uses TCP/IP to send Web resources to your computer. A **Web resource** is any data file that can be identified, such as an HTML document, a graphic, a video, or a sound file. HTTP and TCP/IP include commands or methods that help browsers and Web servers communicate.

- **What does it mean when I get a 404 error?** A Web server's response to a browser's request includes an HTTP status code. The code indicates whether or not the browser request could be fulfilled. A 404 error message or "Page not found" error means that the requested resource could not be found.

FIGURE G-2: How Web pages get to your computer

2. The browser sends the request to the Web server.

Address www.cengagelearning.com

3. The Web server receives the request.

Courtesy of MediaTechnics Corporation; © 2011 Google

© Cengage Learning

Courtesy of MediaTechnics Corporation

1. The URL is typed in the browser's Address box.

4. The Web server sends the Web page back to the Web browser.

Web Browser Basics

You use a Web browser, as also called a browser, to view Web pages. To navigate from page to page, you click the links on a Web page. In addition, a browser window contains menus and buttons to help you navigate from one Web page to another. There are a variety of browsers available for you to choose from.

Learning Objective 2:
Identify the main features and functions of a Web browser

● **What are the popular Web browsers that most people use?** Popular Web browsers include Microsoft Windows Internet Explorer (IE), which comes with Microsoft Windows and Apple Safari, which comes with Mac OS. Other common browsers are Mozilla Firefox and Google Chrome. See Figure G-3. Each browser has unique features that set it apart from the others. You should try different browsers to determine which one best meets your needs.

FIGURE G-3: Three popular browsers

Firefox

Internet Explorer

Google Chrome

● **How do I get a browser?** Browsers are free. Your operating system comes with a browser. If you do not like the default browser on your computer, you can go to the Web and download another browser. In fact, you can have several browsers installed on your computer at the same time and switch between them. However, you do have to select a default browser that will open when you click a link that is not in a browser, for example, a link in a Word document. Regardless of which browser you use, all browsers share common features and capabilities.

● **What are some common browser features?**
Most browsers have a navigation bar near the top of the window. A navigation bar typically includes buttons to navigate Web pages. Table G-1 lists common navigation buttons.

TABLE G-1: Common Web browser navigation buttons

Button	Use to...
Back	view pages you've seen previously
Forward	view the page you were viewing before you clicked the Back button
Refresh	redisplay the page you are currently viewing
Stop	stop a Web page from loading
Go or Search	start a search after typing a word or phrase in the Search box
Home	display your home page

In addition to buttons, the browser window might include a menu bar near the top of the window. The menu bar provides access to commands such as Print when you want to print a Web page. You should always preview the page before printing because a Web page on the screen may print out as several printed pages. A browser also provides commands that let you customize your browser by selecting a home page. The home page is the Web page that appears every time you start your browser or when you click the Home button. Most current browsers also provide tabs.

● **What are tabs?** Tabs are a way to view more than one Web page within one browser window, known as "tabbed browsing." You can display a different Web page on each tab. The name of the Web page appears on the tab. See Figure G-4. To move between Web pages, click the tab of the Web page you want to view. Using tabs makes it easy to keep your Web browsing organized.

FIGURE G-4: Tabs in a Web browser

Cengage Web site
is active tab

A different Web site is open in
each tab in one browser window

● **What is a favorite?** A **favorite** (or **bookmark**) is a saved link to a Web site. You create a favorite when you find a Web site that you want to revisit often. When you are on the Web page you want to save, you click the browser's Add to Favorites button to add the Web page's URL to the Favorites list. Later, when you want to go to that Web page again, open the Favorites list and click its URL. You can organize your Favorites list into folders. See Figure G-5. In addition to saving individual Web pages to your Favorites list, you can also save a set of open tabs. Simply click the option to Add Current Tabs to Favorites, type a folder name when requested, and click Add. The group of tabs will be saved in a folder to your Favorites list.

FIGURE G-5: Favorites

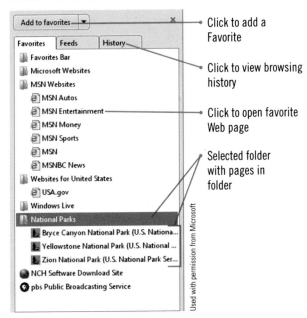

Click to add a Favorite

Click to view browsing history

Click to open favorite Web page

Selected folder with pages in folder

● **Does my browser keep a history of sites I have visited?** Yes, your browser provides a History list, which helps you revisit sites from previous sessions. To revisit any site in the History list, click its URL. You can specify how long a URL will remain in the History list.

● **Why do I have to download software to view some Web pages?** In addition to Web pages, browsers must handle many different file formats, such as multimedia graphic file formats to display video, animation, and other media. Some browsers do not have built-in support to view these file formats. If you click a link your browser cannot open, you will see a message that directs you to download the necessary software. The software, called an **add-on**, a **plug-in**, or a **player**, extends a browser's ability. Most add-on applications, such as the Adobe Flash Player, can be downloaded from the Web without cost. See Figure G-6. The Flash Player allows you to view animations and graphics created with Adobe Flash on a Web page. Or, to help with Web searching or pop-up blocking you can download and install the Google Toolbar. You can view a list of players installed on your computer. If you use Internet Explorer, look for a Manage add-ons option on the Tools menu.

FIGURE G-6: Add-ons for browsers

ADOBE® FLASH® PLAYER 11

Adobe® Flash® Player is a cross-platform browser-based application runtime that delivers uncompromised viewing of expressive applications, content, and videos across screens and browsers.

Flash Player is optimized for high performance on mobile screens and designed to take advantage of native device capabilities, enabling richer and more immersive user experiences.

For more information visit the Product Page.

● **Should I upgrade my browser when new versions become available?** Yes. Most browser updates are free, so you can get up-to-date functionality by spending a few minutes downloading and installing an update. Some Web pages depend on new features supported only by the latest browser versions. Without the latest upgrade, you might encounter errors when your browser tries to display a page or your browser might display the Web page without all the intended effects. Another reason to upgrade is to increase security; upgrades usually contain patches for known security holes.

● **How can I view a Web page on my smartphone?** Internet users can access Web pages and services while on the go by using smartphones and other mobile computing devices. See Figure G-7. WAP-enabled devices contain a micro-browser that displays Web sites specially designed for small screens. These devices cannot display most Web pages at their normal size. Some devices include specialized software to access popular Web sites.

FIGURE G-7: Web page on a smartphone

● **What is a Web cache?** When your browser gets the data it needs to form a Web page, it stores that data on your computer in temporary files called **Web cache** or **browser cache**. Your browser loads Web pages from the cache when you switch between pages. Files are deleted from the Web cache within the time period you specify in your browser's options dialog box.

Web Page Tools

Web pages today are usually visually appealing and often are filled with animations, sounds, videos, and graphics. Many programming languages are used to achieve the multimedia and interactive features of today's Web pages, but the foundation for all Web pages is HTML.

Learning Objective 3:

Explain HTML and other tools used to display Web pages in a browser

● **What is HTML?** HTML (Hypertext Markup Language) is a set of specifications for creating HTML documents. HTML is a **markup language**. Authors use HTML tags to mark up their documents. **HTML tags** specify how the document should appear when displayed on a computer screen or printed. The original HTML specifications that were developed by Tim Berners-Lee in 1990 have been revised several times by the **World Wide Web Consortium (W3C)**. Over the years, HTML has had several versions. The current version, HTML5, was introduced in 2010.

XHTML is a markup language very similar to HTML, but it can be customized with tags that describe the data in databases. XHTML is more rigidly structured than HTML and more complex. Other technologies, such as DHTML (Dynamic HTML) and Ajax (Asynchronous JavaScript and XML), offer tools and techniques for extending basic HTML and making Web pages more interactive, visually appealing, and media-rich. Today, the Web operates according to XHTML standards, even though people commonly refer to the technology simply as HTML.

● **Why don't I see HTML tags when I look at a Web page?** The term Web page refers to both the source HTML document and the corresponding Web page that is displayed by your browser. The HTML tags tell the Web browser how to display the Web page. The HTML tags are the source code for the Web page. Most browsers include a menu option that allows you to view the source HTML document with its HTML tags. The source code provides the information to create links, display graphics, play sound, and so on. See Figure G-8. HTML documents do not contain graphics. Instead, the tag contains the information used to display the graphic in the Web page. This information includes size, file location, and position on the Web page.

● **What do I need to know about links?** Links help you move around the Web page. The Web page author creates links by writing computer code that opens a location in the same Web page, a different Web page, or a different Web site. A Web page author can specify whether the linked page or graphic will

FIGURE G-8: **A source document and its Web page**

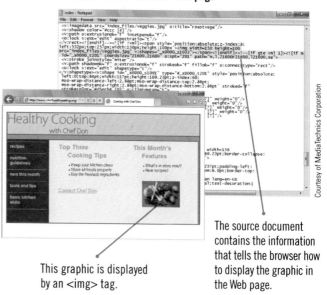

Courtesy of MediaTechnics Corporation

This graphic is displayed by an tag.

The source document contains the information that tells the browser how to display the graphic in the Web page.

appear in the current browser window, in a new tab in the current window, or in a new browser window. Whether they are text or graphics, links provide the fundamental tools for navigating Web pages or causing some other action to happen. Table G-2 provides some common link types.

TABLE G-2: **Common types of Web page links**

Link type	Used to
Interpage	jump to a different location within the current Web page; can be text or a graphic
Intersite	jump to a different location within the current Web site; can be text or a graphic
External	jump to a different location outside the current Web site; can be text or a graphic
Thumbnail	open a larger image of the thumbnail
Mailto:	open a preaddressed email form often used to provide a method for contacting the Webmaster, the Web site's author, or a customer service representative

© Cengage Learning

Typically, a link appears on a Web page as underlined, blue text, or as a graphic, such as a picture or a button. The arrow-shaped pointer changes, usually to a pointing hand, when it moves over any link in the browser window.

- **How are links on a Web page created?** HTML tags are used to create links. The HTML tag for a link contains the text that appears as a link or the information used to display a graphic as a link when the Web page is opened in a browser. It also contains the URL to the Web resource, such as a Web page, that the link is jumping to. Web authors need to be very careful when writing the HTML code or the result could be a broken link.

- **What is a broken link?** A **broken link** occurs when a Web page link cannot find the file, URL, or graphic file referenced in the link. For example, if a Webmaster moves, deletes, or changes the name of a file associated with a link, the link will not function properly when it is clicked. When a link points to a nonexistent graphic or other non-HTML format file, your browser typically displays a broken link icon, such as ⊠ or ⊠. It is the responsibility of Web page authors to check the links on their Web pages periodically to make sure they work. Broken links must be removed or edited to reflect the correct URL for a destination page or the correct location for a graphics file. To test links, an author can click through them manually or use the link checking feature of Web authoring software.

- **What other tools can I use to create Web pages?** You have several choices when it comes to Web page authoring tools. You can use a text editor such as Notepad to type the HTML tags along with the text that you want the browser to display on a Web page. However, this is very difficult and not recommended. A second option is to use an HTML conversion utility, which adds HTML tags to an existing document, spreadsheet, or other text-based file to create an HTML document that can be displayed by a browser. For example, you can work with Microsoft Word to create a standard document file and then you can use commands via the Save As dialog box to convert the document to a Web page (HTML) format. A third option is to use **Web authoring software** that provides tools specifically designed to enter and format Web page text, graphics, and links. Popular Web authoring products include Adobe Dreamweaver, and open source products such as KompoZer and Amaya. Another option is to use a set of online Web page authoring tools. These template-like tools are provided by some ISPs and other companies that host Web pages for individuals and businesses. Working with these tools is quite simple—you type, select, drag, and drop elements onto a Web page. See Figure G-9.

FIGURE G-9: **Online Web page authoring**

Courtesy of MediaTechnics Corporation; ©2011 Google

Text entry areas define the location for titles and subtitles.

Columns divide the page into areas for positioning text and graphics.

Tools allow you to choose a design, add photos, and format the elements of your Web page.

Unit G

HTTP status codes

A Web server's response to a browser's request includes an **HTTP status code** that indicates whether or not the browser's request can be fulfilled. If a link points to a nonexistent HTML document, your browser typically produces a 404 Page Not Found error. Common HTTP status codes are summarized in Table G-3.

TABLE G-3: **Common HTTP status codes**

Code	Message	Description
301	Moved Permanently	The resource was moved.
302	Moved Temporarily	The resource is temporarily unavailable.
303	See Other	The resource moved to another URL and should be automatically retrieved by the client software.
404	Not Found	The requested resource does not exist.
500	Server Error	An unexpected server error, such as encountering a scripting error, occurred.

© Cengage Learning

Search Tools and Techniques

There is an almost limitless amount of information in the form of text, video, sound, and graphics stored on the Web. To use this information, however, you have to be able to find it. To find the information you want, you need to use search tools. A search engine helps you link to pages that contain the information you seek.

Learning Objective 4:
Describe how to search the Web for information

● **What is a Web search engine?** A **Web search engine** (or **search engine**) is a program designed to help people find information on the Web. It does this by formulating queries based on keywords you enter. In response to a query, a list of results or **hits** is displayed, usually in the order of relevance. The list includes links to the Web pages and often short excerpts from each Web page containing the keywords used for the search query. See Figure G-10. Clicking a link connects you to the Web page. Sponsored links on Google are paid placements. Merchants pay to have their links listed on the site if a user's keyword matches those associated with the merchant's site. Merchants are charged for a paid placement only if a user clicks it.

FIGURE G-10: **Search results**

Keywords for search | More than 23 million hits to this query | Click link to go to this Web page | The list of results shows the most relevant first. | Sponsored links

● **What search engine should I use?** The search engine you use depends on the search site you use. Popular search sites include www.yahoo.com, www.ask.com, www.google.com, and www.bing.com. You can specify the default search engine that your browser uses. You can also allow a search engine to suggest search terms or results as you type them.

● **What is the difference between a search engine and a search site?** A search engine is the technology that powers searches on the Web. A search site, such as Google or Yahoo!, provides a variety of tools and services that allow a user to search the Web for information, images, video, or audio. When you perform a search, your search is powered by a search engine. Some sites, including Google, use their own proprietary search engines, but other sites purchase third-party search technology. For example, Yahoo!'s search engine is also used at search sites, such as AltaVista and AlltheWeb.

Although most search sites use automated search engines, a few sites such as www.mahalo.com and www.chacha.com specialize in human-powered searches, but within a limited range of topics. Some search sites offer separate searches for academic works, images, videos, news, e-commerce merchandise, and blogs. Some search sites use a **metasearch engine** that employs a series of other search engines and compiles the search results. Popular metasearch sites include www.dogpile.com and webcrawler.com.

● **Can I only use a search site to search the Web?** No. Many e-commerce, informational, and corporate Web sites offer tools or query controls, such as a search box, on their Web pages. See Figure G-11. The sites that offer these query controls are powered by a search engine, such as Google.

FIGURE G-11: **Search box on a Web page**

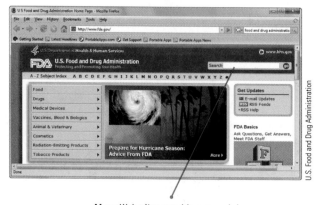

Many Web sites provide a search box

You can use the search box on any Web page to search that site or sometimes even the entire Web. You can also search the Internet directly from the browser's address bar and choose what search engine to use.

● **How do search engines work?** A search engine contains four parts: a Web crawler, an indexer, a database, and a query processor. The **Web crawler** combs the Web to gather data that's representative of the contents of Web pages. Web crawlers download Web pages and submit them to an indexer for processing. An **indexer** is a utility program. The indexer processes the information gathered by the Web crawler into a list of keywords and URLs stored in a database. The indexer makes pages easy to find based on their contents. A **query processor** looks for your search terms in the search engine's indexed database and displays a list of relevant Web sites in your browser.

● **How do Web sites get selected by search engines?** There are many different ways. First, a Web site can be discovered automatically by a search engine's Web crawler. Second, the URL can be submitted to a search engine by the Web master who manages the Web site. Third, it can be submitted for a paid placement. Or, fourth, it can be submitted as a banner or a pop-up ad. Manual submissions are added to the Web crawler's list of sites to visit. The site will be indexed once the Web crawler visits the site. Some search engines accept paid placements, which are bumped to the top positions on the results list.

● **Which Web sites are shown at the top of the results list?** The order in which Web sites are listed in response to a search depends on relevancy criteria, such as keyword matches and link popularity. **Link popularity** is a measure of the quality and quantity of the links from one Web page to others. Pages with links to and from popular sites tend to get high relevancy ratings. If a search is based on multiple keywords, pages that contain the most matching words are listed first.

● **Can I always trust the validity of results in ranking Web pages?** No, sometimes disreputable Web site operators manipulate meta keywords to move their Web sites to the top of search engine query results. A **meta keyword** is entered into a header section of a Web page when it is created and is supposed to describe the page contents. **Keyword stuffing** is an unethical practice in which meta keywords are manipulated to gain high relevancy rankings. Socially responsible search engine sites take steps to override practices that manipulate rankings and usually make their policies on paid placements clear to users.

● **What are some strategies for creating a good search?** Most search engines work with queries in which you enter one or more words, called **search terms** or **keywords**, related to the information you want to find. Narrowing a search can reduce the number of results and produce a more targeted list. When formulating queries, you can omit common words, such as "and," "a," and "the." To search for an exact phrase, enter it in quotation marks. Use the asterisk (*) as a wildcard character to find pages with any derivation of a basic word. If the results on the first two pages of your search are not what you are looking for, redo your search using different search terms.

● **How can I create better search terms?** A **Boolean operator** (or a search operator) is a word or symbol that describes a relationship between keywords and thereby helps you create a more focused query. Table G-4 provides a quick overview of how to use Boolean operators.

TABLE G-4: Boolean operators

Operator	Description
AND	When two search terms are joined by AND, both terms must appear on a Web page before it can be included in the search results. Some search engines use the plus symbol (+) instead of the word AND.
OR	When two search terms are joined by OR, either one or both of the search words could appear on a page.
NOT	The search term following NOT must not appear on any of the pages found by the search engine. In some search engines, the minus sign (–) can be used instead of the word NOT.

© Cengage Learning

● **What tools can help focus my search?** Many search engines provide forms designed to simplify the search process. See Figure G-12. To open a form, you click an Advanced Search link, which often is located on the main page of the search engine's Web site. You fill out the form to focus your search, such as whether to look for your search terms in the title, URL, or body of the Web page.

FIGURE G-12: **Advanced searching**

©2011 Google

Web and Internet Services

The Web and the Internet offer a variety of services and activities. Some of these services were already discussed in Unit A, such as social networking, blogging, creating wikis, instant messaging, VoIP, chatting, and text messaging. Other services include ftp, file sharing, online collaboration, financial management, and banking.

Learning Objective 5:
Discuss several services provided by the Web and the Internet

● **What is Web 2.0?** Web 2.0 refers to innovative ways of collaborating and using the Web and Internet services. Web-based applications, such as social networking sites, are sometimes characterized as Web 2.0. Web 2.0 uses the same Internet infrastructure as the original Web.

● **What is FTP?** FTP (file transfer protocol) provides a way to transfer files from one computer to another over any TCP/IP network, such as a LAN or the Internet. The purpose of FTP is to make it easy to upload and download computer files without having to deal directly with the operating system or file management system of a remote computer. FTP also allows authorized remote users to change file names and delete files. You access some FTP sites using a browser (see Figure G-13) and others with FTP client software. You may use FTP without even knowing it, such as when you download an updated device driver from a technical support site, when you

download a document in PDF format from a corporate Web site, or when you download an MP3 file from your favorite music site. Not every FTP server is accessible from a browser, and those that are might work only for downloading files, not uploading them.

● **Are there other ways to share files using the Internet?** File sharing, sometimes called **P2P file sharing**, uses peer-to-peer (P2P) protocols that allow users to exchange files from one computer directly with another computer over the Internet. File sharing became popular in the late 1990s when college students started using a Web site called Napster that provided free access to hit songs. Napster was closed down by court order in 2001 because most of the music was distributed without the permission of copyright holders. Free distribution of music without the copyright holder's permission is illegal, and file sharing server operators quickly encountered the legal ramifications. Today, there are sites that provide legal ways to download music. P2P is still used as a means of exchanging files.

● **How is FTP different than P2P?** FTP distributes files from a server. P2P distributes files using scattered clients, rather than a central controlled server. These P2P clients are a collection of personal computers located anywhere on the Internet. For example, **BitTorrent** is a peer-to-peer file sharing protocol that distributes the role of server to many computers. Unfortunately, file swapping networks are often used to illegally distribute copyrighted material. However, BitTorrent is a P2P network that is used legally for distributing music, images, videos, and software with the approval of copyright holders. A P2P network is designed to reduce the bandwidth bottleneck that occurs when many people attempt to download the same very large file, such as a feature-length film, application software, or an interactive 3D computer game. See Figure G-14.

FIGURE G-13: FTP government Web site

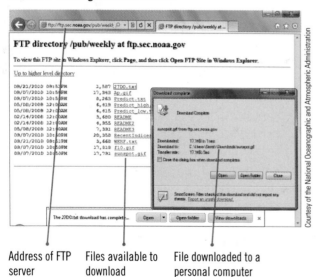

Courtesy of the National Oceanographic and Atmospheric Administration

Address of FTP server

Files available to download

File downloaded to a personal computer

FIGURE G-14: How P2P file sharing works

—— Networked computers
------ Files shared

Source Destination and source

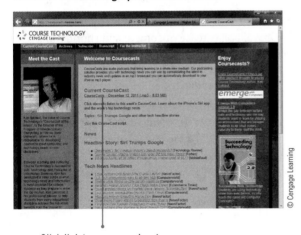

Partial files

Every user who downloads is automatically uploading to other users.

Courtesy of MediaTechnics Corporation, © 2012 Microsoft

Source Destination

● **What is a podcast?** A **podcast** (sometimes called a **Webcast**) is an audio file that is distributed through downloads or the use of a feed, such as RSS. You can download individual podcasts. See Figure G-15. Or, you can subscribe to a feed to make sure you automatically receive new podcasts as they are produced. Subscriptions are usually free. You subscribe at the host site (such as pbs.org), and then the podcasts are available to you via your media player. Podcasts are used to distribute radio shows, news, sports, educational tutorials, and blogs. **Videocasting** is similar to podcasting, but uses video files instead of audio files.

FIGURE G-15: Accessing a podcast via a Web site

© Cengage Learning

Click link to access podcast

● **What is RSS?** RSS (**Rich Site Summary** or **Really Simple Syndication**) is a format for feeding or syndicating news or any content from Web sites to your computer. Access to RSS content is free, but you have to subscribe to the RSS feed at a Web site that offers content you want to receive via RSS. RSS feeds provide subscribers with summaries that link to the full versions of the content. You might want to customize the home page of your browser to display your RSS links.

● **How can I collaborate using the Web?** You can use Web cloud services to work with others on the same files. For example, if you have a Windows Live SkyDrive account, you can post files to that account. Your files, such as documents and photographs are available from any computer with an active Internet connection. You can make these files available to others so you can collaborate on the file content. Once you share a file, you can work with your collaborators on the file remotely.

● **What Web and Internet services allow me to be more mobile?** Web-based applications, like the Office programs available via Office 365 or Google Apps, provide access to the most up-to-date software. If you use a Web-based application, you often do not have to have that application installed locally on your computer. You can work on a document on any computer with an active Internet connection. In addition, software programs like GoToMyPC, allow you to access your PC through the Web from a remote location using a computer with an active Internet connection. All of these services allow you to be more mobile because you no longer have to be tied to a computer in one location.

● **Can I use the Internet to communicate in real time?** Yes, in addition to text chatting and instant messaging, you can video chat. See Figure G-16. To video chat, you and each person you are communicating with need a microphone, a Web cam, and an active Internet connection. Video chatting can involve more than two people in more than two locations. Skype is a popular video chatting program.

FIGURE G-16: Video chatting

Photo courtesy Emily Bunin

● **Are Web and Internet services safe to use?** Yes, if you take precautions. For example, be sure you are working on secure or trusted sites. Do not share files via a P2P site unless you know the site is legal and the material is not copyrighted. Use common sense and be sure to follow all of the safety tips discussed in earlier units.

E-Commerce—An Overview

Shopping is one of the most popular activities on the Web. Most brick-and-mortar stores, like Target, Kohls, and Walmart, have Web sites where you can buy their products. In addition, smaller businesses and artists and craftspeople can sell their products on the Web, even if they do not have a brick-and-mortar store. This is all possible because of e-commerce.

Learning Objective 6:
Define e-commerce and explain how the Web is used for commercial transactions

● **What is e-commerce?** **E-commerce** is the term used to describe financial transactions conducted over a computer network. E-commerce activities include shopping, auctions, banking, and stock trading. E-commerce includes many kinds of physical products (such as clothing and books), digital products (such as music, video, and software), and services (such as travel and distance learning). Online information services sell subscriptions to news archives, databases, and online magazines. E-commerce technologies track shoppers' selections, collect payment data, guard customers' privacy, and protect credit card numbers. Most e-commerce businesses use as much automation as possible. For example, their order processing systems automatically update inventories, and then print packing slips and mailing labels. With e-commerce, when you shop online, you can shop at your leisure, in the privacy of your home, and without dealing with mall crowds. See Figure G-17.

FIGURE G-17: **Shopping online**

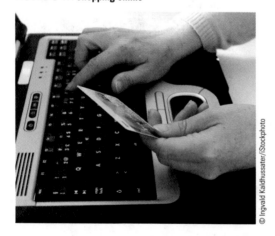

© Ingvald Kaldhussater/iStockphoto

E-commerce activities fall into different categories depending on the seller and buyer. Most e-commerce activities are classified as one of the following:
■ **B2C (business-to-consumer) e-commerce**. In the B2C model, businesses supply goods and services to individual consumers.

■ **C2C (consumer-to-consumer) e-commerce**. In the C2C model, consumers sell to each other. This model includes online auctions and craft sales.
■ **B2B (business-to-business) e-commerce**. In the B2B model, businesses buy and sell goods or services to other businesses.
■ **B2G (business-to-government) e-commerce**. In the B2G model, businesses sell to governments.

● **What are the advantages of e-commerce?** E-commerce works better than traditional business models by automating essential business tasks. E-commerce increases profit margins by cutting costs, allows the owner to sell to a wider audience, allows the owner to keep track of competitor prices, and more. For the consumer, e-commerce provides convenience, 365/24/7 availability, ease of comparison shopping, a wide variety of items to choose from, and more.

● **What are the disadvantages of e-commerce?** The biggest disadvantages are consumer concerns about security and privacy. Consumers want to be sure that their financial transactions are secure. They want to be sure information about them is kept private. They want to be sure they don't have to worry about fraud. Reputable e-commerce sites have safeguards to protect consumers against all these concerns. You will read more about these in the next lesson.

● **How do I shop online?** First, you enter the URL for an online store you want to visit in the Address bar of your browser. You can also click a link from search results or a link on another Web site. After you are connected to the online store, you can browse the online catalog and then select merchandise you want to buy. Once you have identified all the items you want to buy, you follow the on-screen directions to pay for them. Figure G-18 shows a Web site for an e-commerce site.

© 2011 Dell

Click to chat Click to view items Click for order information Search catalog Sign in

• How does the Web site track what I want to buy?

An **online shopping cart** (or **online shopping bag**) is a cyberspace version of the cart that you wheel around a store and fill with merchandise.

• What are cookies?

A **cookie** is data generated by a Web server and stored in a text file on your computer. Refer to Figure G-19. Cookies can also be used to store information necessary to keep track of your preferences

FIGURE G-19: **Shopping cart items stored as a cookie**

ITEM #B7655

1. When you click the Add to Cart button, the merchant's server sends a message to your browser to add that item number to the cookie, which is stored on your computer.

2. When you check out, the server asks your browser for all the cookie data that pertains to your shopping cart items.

3. Your browser sends those cookies along with a request for an order summary.

4. The Web server uses the cookies to look up products in its database and produce a Web page listing the items you want to purchase.

Your order:

1 Blender $29.95

1 Wok $38.49

© Richard Griffin/Shutterstock.com; © Jupiterimages; © Cengage Learning

and activities while visiting a Web site. The cookie information can include a customer number, a shopping cart number, a part number, the pages you viewed or the items you want to purchase, or any other data. An e-commerce site might use cookies as a storage bin for all of the items that you load into your shopping cart. Cookies can collect personal information you type into a Web page form and retain it for the next time you visit the Web site. It is your choice whether to allow cookies or not.

• Why is there so much advertising on Web sites?

E-commerce merchants gain income by hosting advertising space for banner and pop-up ads. A **banner ad** is an advertisement, typically embedded at the top of a Web page. A **pop-up ad** is an advertisement that appears in a separate window when you enter a Web site or connect to Web pages. See Figure G-20. When you click a banner or pop-up ad, your browser connects directly to the advertiser's Web site. Banner and pop-up ads earn revenue for hosting merchants based on the **click-through rate**—the number of times that site visitors click the ad to connect to the advertiser's site. The hosting merchant is paid a small fee for each click through. Click-through rates have declined in recent years because most consumers simply ignore the ads or install ad-blocking software to prevent ads from appearing on their screens. One disadvantage for consumers who click a banner or pop-up ad is that clicking a banner ad or a pop-up ad might install a third-party cookie on their computers.

FIGURE G-20: **A pop-up ad**

Courtesy of MediaTechnics Corporation

• How can I sell my personal belongings using e-commerce?

To sell your personal things, you can use an online auction site such as eBay or an online classified advertisement site such as Craigslist. These types of sites are the electronic equivalent to home-based yard sales. At these e-commerce sites, consumers offer goods and services to other consumers (C2C). The merchandise is typically individual items, such as a used boat, a collectible vase, or bicycle. The hosting site typically offers tools for sellers to auction or sell items or services facilitating the online bidding process and the transactions between buyers and sellers. Sellers are provided with a way to enter item descriptions, prices, and photos. They might also be provided with tools to track bids, purchases, and other activities. Buyers are provided with tools to locate products and contact sellers with questions. Host sites might also maintain ratings for buyers and sellers to help participants avoid shady deals.

Secure E-Commerce Transactions

After you finish adding all the items you want to purchase to your shopping cart, you click a button or link to take you to the checkout. At this time, you must verify the items you plan to purchase and you must pay for the merchandise online before your transaction can be completed. When making an e-commerce purchase, the buyer wants to be sure the merchant is reputable, and both the seller and the buyer want to make sure the transaction is secure.

Learning Objective 7:
Name systems used to secure e-commerce transactions

● **How can I be sure my online transactions are secure?** Many shoppers worry that hackers might intercept personal information, such as credit card numbers, traveling over the Internet. A **packet sniffer** (also called a **protocol analyzer**) is a computer program that monitors data as it travels over networks. Packet sniffers have legitimate uses in system maintenance, but hackers can also use them to pilfer data as it travels from customers' computers to e-commerce sites. That is why, when using an e-commerce Web site, you want to be sure you are using a secure Web site. A secure Web site, such as an online banking site, uses password security to prevent unauthorized access to pages on the site. You also want to be sure the secure Web site uses a secure connection.

● **What is a secure connection?** A **secure connection** encrypts the data transmitted between your computer and a Web site. **Encryption** is the science of coding data. To protect your credit card and all information you submit via an e-commerce site, you should engage in electronic transactions only over Web sites that provide a secure connection. Even if a hacker can capture the packets containing payment data, your encrypted information, such as your credit card number, is virtually useless for illegal purposes. Secure Electronic Transaction (SET) is a standard protocol for securing credit card transactions over the Internet. SET relies on cryptography and digital certificates to ensure that transactions are legitimate as well as secure. A **digital certificate** is a specially coded electronic attachment to a file that verifies the identity of the file's source. Technologies that create secure connections include SSL, TLS, and S-HTTP.

● **What are SSL, TLS, and S-HTTP?** SSL (**Secure Sockets Layer**) and its successor TLS (**Transport Layer Security**) are protocols that encrypt data traveling between your computer and the Web site you are using for your e-commerce transaction. **S-HTTP (secure HTTP)** is an extension of HTTP

that simply encrypts the text of an HTTP message before it is sent. Web pages that provide a secure connection start with *https://* instead of *http://*. Although SSL and S-HTTP both use encryption techniques to securely transmit data, they are technically different. SSL creates a secure connection between a client and a server over which any amount of data can be sent securely. S-HTTP is simply designed to encrypt and then transmit an individual message. Both technologies encrypt the data to create a secure connection.

● **How do I know a Web site I am visiting uses a secure connection?** Your browser helps you identify when a Web site uses a secure connection to submit data. Sites have different levels of security. See Figure G-21. To determine if a site is secure, look for https:// in the Address bar,

FIGURE G-21: **Identifying a secure connection**

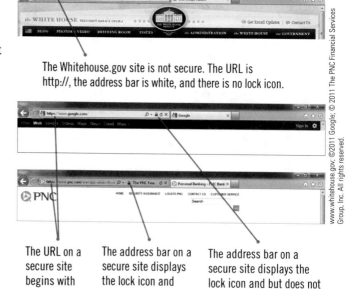

The Whitehouse.gov site is not secure. The URL is http://, the address bar is white, and there is no lock icon.

The URL on a secure site begins with https://.

The address bar on a secure site displays the lock icon and turns green if has a digital certificate.

The address bar on a secure site displays the lock icon and but does not turn green if it does not have a digital certificate.

a green background in the Address bar, the digital certificate, and/or a locked padlock. You can click the lock to access the digital certificate. Web sites that simply provide information do not need to be secure, but can be secure. Web sites that accept payments or manage your banking should be secure.

● **How should I pay for my online purchases?** Popular ways to make online payments include submitting your credit card number directly to a merchant or using a third-party payment service, such as PayPal. Other options include digital wallets and one-time-use credit card numbers. Any one of these methods of payments is acceptable if you are using a secure Web site and a secure connection.

● **What is a digital wallet?** A **digital wallet** (also called an **e-wallet** or an **electronic wallet**) is software that stores and handles the information a customer submits when finalizing an e-commerce purchase. It typically holds your name, shipping address, and the number, expiration date, and billing address for one or more credit cards. It might also hold a digital certificate that verifies your identity. Your e-wallet is protected by a password, which helps prevent unauthorized use. An e-commerce Web site that accepts a digital wallet displays a special checkout button. The term "digital wallet" is also used to describe smartphones or smartcards (Figure G-22) that store financial information and use wireless technologies for purchases such as at supermarkets and gas stations.

FIGURE G-22: A Visa payWave card

© Anthony Brown/iStockphoto

● **What is a one-time-use credit card number, and how can I get one?** A one-time-use credit card number is called a controlled payment number. One-time-use credit card numbers allow consumers to make purchases while keeping their actual card numbers hidden. A one-time-use credit card number works for a single online purchase. Your credit card company tracks the purchases you incur with one-time-use numbers and adds the charges to your monthly credit card statement. One-time-use numbers cannot be used twice, so, even if a hacker steals the number, it will not be accepted for any online or offline purchases. Banks and credit card companies offer this service.

● **What is person-to-person payment?** A **person-to-person payment** (sometimes called an **online payment**) offers an alternative to credit cards. See Figure G-23. It can be used to pay for auction items and to wire money over the Internet. PayPal pioneered person-to-person payments and has been copied by several other service providers. You open an account at a person-to-person payment service, and then you deposit money from your bank or provide your credit card information. You receive a user ID and password that allows you to access your account to make purchases and deposit additional funds. Money can be sent to anyone through email. One benefit of using a person-to-person payment service is that your credit card number is never given directly to the merchant.

FIGURE G-23: How to use a person to person payments

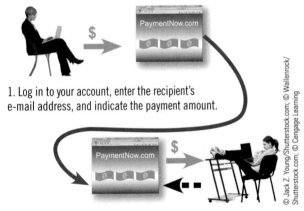

1. Log in to your account, enter the recipient's e-mail address, and indicate the payment amount.

2. The recipient receives an email notification of your payment, connects to the payment site, requests transfer of funds to his or her checking or payment account, requests a check, or sends the funds to someone else.

© Jack Z. Young/Shutterstock.com; © Wallenrock/Shutterstock.com; © Cengage Learning

● **What can I do to prevent becoming a victim of fraud?** Fraud is a serious concern to all consumers. Since computers store credit card and shopping information, you may find yourself a victim of fraud whether you shop online, shop using traditional stores, or shop using phone order services. To protect yourself, be vigilant and protect your personal information; conduct any transaction that includes your personal information over a secure connection.

Ways to Enhance Web Sites

Have you ever noticed that your Web browser fills in your username or password on some Web sites? Have you ever filled in delivery information on a form, and clicked a check box to say that same information can be used for your billing information—and then had the billing information filled in automatically? How can this be done? Quite simply, through the use of scripts. Scripts can do these tasks and much more. Scripts and other technologies enhance Web sites.

Learning Objective 8:
Identify several technologies used to enhance the Web

- **What is a script?** A script, or more accurately an **HTML script**, is a series of program instructions. A script can be embedded directly into the text of an HTML document or in a file referenced from an HTML document.

- **Why use scripts?** Scripts allow Web pages to be interactive. Scripts enable e-commerce sites to verify credit card information. Scripts enable Web sites to change based on your selections. They also make it possible to create interactive Web pages that include fill-in forms.

- **What is an HTML form?** An **HTML form** is used to collect user input for e-commerce orders, site registrations, apply for loans, opinion polls, and so on. See Figure G-24.

FIGURE G-24: **HTML form**

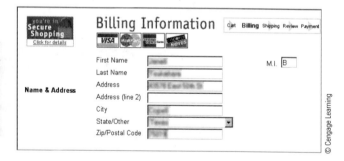

- **Are Web sites that run scripts safe to visit?** Many browsers turn off or disallow running scripts because they can pose a security risk. If you are using a secure Web site that uses a secure connection, it is usually safe to run the script while you are visiting that site.

- **Do scripts run on my computer or on a Web server?** Scripts can run on a client (your computer) or on a server. A **server-side script** consists of statements that run on a server. Server-side scripts accept data submitted by a form, like the one shown in Figure G-24, process that data, and then generate a custom HTML document that is sent to the browser for display. These Web pages, which are dynamically produced using information generated by the server-side script, can often be identified because they contain question marks (?) in the URL displayed in the Address bar of your browser. Server-side scripts can be written using a variety of programming and scripting languages, such as Perl, PHP, C, C++, C#, Java, and JavaScript.

 A **client-side script** consists of scripting statements that run on your local computer. The script is executed by the browser, which must have the capability to interpret the programming language used to write the script. Popular

The start of Web technologies

In 1990, a British scientist named Tim Berners-Lee developed specifications for three technologies: Hypertext Transfer Protocol (HTTP), Hypertext Markup Language (HTML), and URL (Uniform Resource Locator). HTTP is the communications protocol used to transport data over the Web. HTML is the set of specifications used to create Web pages. URL is the set of specifications used to create a unique address for each Web page. This group of technologies was designed to help researchers share information by creating access to a "web" of electronic documents. Berners-Lee's

free Web software appeared on the Internet in 1991, but the Web didn't take off until 1993. That year, Marc Andreessen and his colleagues at the University of Illinois created Mosaic, a graphical browser. Andreessen later formed his own company and produced a browser called Netscape, which put the Web into the hands of millions of Web surfers and made the Web accessible to all. Additional technologies, such as scripts, continue to enhance the Web experience for users.

languages for client-side scripts include VBScript and JavaScript. Client-side scripts often take the form of Flash objects, Java applets, or ActiveX controls. Most of today's browsers can run JavaScript, but only Windows Internet Explorer has the built-in capability to run VBScript and Active X.

● **What is Flash content?** Most people associate Flash with a popular video standard, but Flash objects can include interactive elements. **ActionScript** is a programming language used to create sophisticated applications that can be launched from Web pages and viewed using the Flash browser plug-in or the stand-alone Flash Player. See Figure G- 25.

FIGURE G- 25: **Web page that uses Flash**

Courtesy of the JFK Presidential Library and Museum and The Martin Agency

● **What's a Java applet?** A **Java applet** is an application written in the Java programming language. A programmer or Web page author places a reference to a Java applet in an HTML document. When you go to a Web page that contains an applet tag, your browser runs the applet when the Web page opens in your browser. Java applets are fairly safe. They cannot open, modify, delete, or create files on your computer. They cannot make network connections except to the originating site. They are not allowed to launch other programs. As a result, Java applets cannot contain malicious code.

● **What is an ActiveX control?** An **ActiveX control** is a compiled computer program that can be referenced from within an HTML document. When an HTML document that contains an ActiveX control is downloaded, the ActiveX control is installed on your computer and run within the browser window. You know you have encountered an ActiveX control when your browser displays a security warning and asks for permission to proceed with the installation.

● **Are Web pages that have ActiveX controls safe to visit?** Most Web pages that use ActiveX controls are safe to visit. However, an ActiveX control is a fully functioning program, which gives it the potential to include routines that alter or delete data on your computer's hard drive. Most browsers display a security warning before installing any programs that include ActiveX controls. ActiveX controls include digital certificates to increase their security.

Citing Web-based source material

Although it is easy to copy text and graphics found on Web pages, you have to consider the rights of the originator of the content. Presenting someone else's work as your own is plagiarism. In the United States, a fair use doctrine allows limited use of copyrighted material for scholarship and review without obtaining permission. For example, you can use a sentence or paragraph of text without obtaining permission if you include information that identifies the original source. Information that identifies the source of a quotation or excerpted work is called a citation. If you copy text, pictures, or other works from a Web page, make sure you give credit to the original author.

Most browsers provide Copy and Paste commands that allow you to copy a section of text from a Web page and then paste it into a document. To keep track of the source for cited text, you can copy the URL into your document. Written documents, such as reports and projects, typically include footnotes, endnotes, in-line citations, as well as a bibliography or works cited page, formatted according to a standard style. See Table G-5.

TABLE G-5: **Common styles for citing Web sources**

Style	Description and Example
Chicago Style and Turabian Style	Lastname, Firstname. "Title of Web Page." *Publishing Organization or Name of Web Site.* Publication date if available. URL.
	Jones, Edison. "Adventures in Electricity." *Electric Resources.* 2011. http://www.electricresources.org/electricity/adventures.html.
MLA Style	Lastname, Firstname. "Title of Web Page." *Name of Site or Online Publication.* Version number, posting date, volume or issue number if available. Page number. Method of access. Date you accessed material.
	Jones, Edison. "Adventures in Electricity." *Electric Resources.* Web. January 18, 2012.
APA Style	Lastname, Firstname. (Date of publication). *Title of Web page or document.* Retrieved from URL.
	Jones, Edison. (2011). *Adventures in Electricity.* Retrieved from http://www.electricresources.org/electricity/adventures.html.

© Cengage Learning

Talking Points: Regulating the Web

The Internet offers instant access to information across national and cultural borders, but along with helpful information the Internet hosts a significant amount of provocative and disturbing material. Militias and hate groups use Web sites to recruit new members and spread their views. Pornographic sites make a business of selling lewd images, and their material can be accessed by anyone—even children. Criminals, anarchists, and dissenters post guidebooks and tips on how to do all kinds of illegal activities, from making suitcase bombs to spreading computer viruses.

Some concerned "netizens" (a combination of the words net and citizen used to describe members of the online community of the Internet) advocate cybercensorship to curtail irresponsible Web sites, blogs, and discussion groups. Cybercensorship typically means blocking access to Web sites, but it can also mean closing sites and removing them from host servers.

> "Cyberspace is malleable. Thus, it is possible to construct barriers in cyberspace and use them to screen for identity, making cyberspace more like the physical world and, consequently, more amenable to zoning laws."

Censorship advocates are opposed by free-speech supporters who believe that the right to free expression should be unshackled by any laws or regulations. The controversy over censorship is not new. Guidelines from the pre-Internet era also shape the debate over cybercensorship versus free-speech debate. In most cases, words are acceptable, whereas actions can be punishable. Writing a mystery novel that describes how the main character cultivates botulism and then uses it to poison another character is acceptable; actually carrying out such an act is against the law. This concept was applied to cyberspace when the U.S. Supreme Court upheld a law that pornography featuring real children was illegal, but ruled that child pornography featuring computer-generated children is not illegal because children were not harmed when it was created.

Cyberlaw is not yet totally consistent on the words versus actions precedent, however. In some cases, words are punishable. For example, the Digital Millennium Copyright Act makes it illegal to disseminate information on how to bypass software, CD, and DVD copy restrictions. A second censorship guideline hinges on local standards of morality. Local communities can apply their own standards to determine whether material is obscene. As a result, a raunchy magazine that you might find on a supermarket news stand in New York City might be limited to adult bookstore shelves in a conservative Tennessee community. Local standards, however, are difficult to sort out on the Internet, where a Web surfer in Tennessee can easily access Web sites, bulletin boards, and chat groups that originate from anywhere in the world.

Judges upheld the conviction of two system operators (sysops) whose California-based porn site distributed obscene material to individuals in Tennessee. The sysops claimed that the Internet required a more flexible definition of "community" to account for the Internet's global accessibility; otherwise, Web sites would be forced to eliminate all materials objected to by anyone. Judges denied that claim, saying that technology could be used to filter out objectionable material based on age and location information provided by member registration data.

Underlying a group of decisions on cybercensorship, the U.S. Supreme Court seems to support the concept of cyberzones that limit Net access to certain materials in a way similar to how the adult sections of newsstands restrict children from browsing through certain magazines. As now-retired Justice Sandra Day O'Connor explained, "Cyberspace is malleable. Thus, it is possible to construct barriers in cyberspace and use them to screen for identity, making cyberspace more like the physical world and, consequently, more amenable to zoning laws." For example, AOL is trying to develop a family-friendly Internet portal by enforcing policies against offensive speech, but AOL has been criticized by free-speech advocates for its policies. AOL responds that it is a private company, and members who disagree with AOL terms of use are free to terminate their subscriptions.

In some countries, however, netizens have no choice but to use a government-controlled ISP. In many countries, free speech is not a basic right conferred to all citizens. Many dictatorial regimes want their citizens to receive news from the outside world only after it has been screened by a government censor. Rather than depend on legislation, officials in more than 20 countries use sophisticated tools to block sites, filter email, and censor discussion groups.

China has some of the most rigorous Internet censorship restrictions in the world. Like the Great Wall of China (Figure G-26), the "Great Firewall of China," as it is sometimes called, blocks Internet content by preventing IP addresses of objectionable sites from being routed through its gateways into China. The blocking system also selectively engages in DNS poisoning, a technique that tricks a DNS server into believing it has received authentic information when, in reality, it has not. So Web surfers in China who attempt to access the Electronic Frontier Foundation's Web site that advocates free speech might instead see a Chinese government site on social responsibility. In addition to blocking Web sites, the Chinese government filters email, message boards, chat rooms, and blogs. In Iran, government censors monitor political and news Web sites, and block access to many pornographic Web sites, anonymizer tools, sites with gay and lesbian content, politically sensitive sites, and women's rights sites. If you tried to access *Rolling Stone* magazine's Web site from Saudi Arabia, you would find that access has been denied. The Saudi government claims it censors the Internet to preserve Islamic culture and heritage. This is an argument that in many ways reflects the concept of cyberzones that conform to local standards of ethics and morality. Even free-speech activists at the OpenNet Initiative (ONI) seem to agree. "We do think that information should be free," states one ONI technician, "but we do need to find a balance for respect for sovereign states to preserve their own culture."

Technology giants such as Microsoft, Yahoo!, Google, and Cisco Systems have been criticized for providing foreign governments with tools for blocking culturally objectionable sites. Critics question whether companies in a free society should aid foreign governments' attempts to censor cyberspace. For some people it is astonishing to realize that ideas such as liberty, equality, and women's rights would be subject to the same censorship attempts as pornography and hate speech. The solution to online censorship is still evolving as free speech comes into balance with cultural, ethical, and moral concerns in the global realm of cyberspace.

FIGURE G-26: **The Great Wall of China**

© Hung Chung Chih/Shutterstock.com

> **We do think that information should be free, but we do need to find a balance for respect for sovereign states to preserve their own culture.**

Expand the Ideas

1. Do you believe that access to certain Web sites should be restricted in any way by government regulators? Do you think that public access facilities, such as public libraries, should have filters that restrict Web site access based on certain parameters? Would you use filtering software that was preprogrammed to block pornographic and nuisance Web sites at your home? Your office? Are they in use at your school? If so, what types of access regulations or restrictions are in place, and why? Write a brief paper explaining your findings and viewpoints on these questions.

2. Should companies like Microsoft, Yahoo!, Google, and Cisco Systems provide blocking technology to foreign governments? What other industries provide products they develop in one country but which are not in use or distributed for use in other countries?

3. Do you believe that a privately held Internet service provider has the right to censor the data posted on Web sites it hosts? If so, should access be blocked based on local religion, politics, and customs? How should the regulators be regulated? Who would determine the "acceptable" content that can filter through? Write a one-page dialog between two people with opposing viewpoints on this topic.

4. On the Web, some sites contain pornography, bigotry, and terrorist rhetoric that many people would rather not be public. One of the cornerstones of democracy, however, is freedom of speech. Where do you draw the line when it comes to censoring and filtering on the Internet? Make sure you consider questions such as: Do parents have the right to monitor, screen, and filter their children's Web use? Are governments ever justified in regulating what their citizens can access? Should anyone be responsible for policing the Internet? Write a one-page paper explaining your views.

Key Terms & Unit Review

Key Terms

ActionScript
ActiveX control
Add-on
B2B (business-to-business)
B2C (business-to-consumer)
B2G (business-to-government)
Banner ad
BitTorrent
Bookmark
Boolean operator
Broken link
Browser
Browser cache
C2C (consumer-to-consumer)
Click-through rate
Client-side script
Cookie
Digital certificate
Digital wallet
E-commerce
E-wallet (electronic wallet)

Encryption
Favorite
FTP (file transfer protocol)
Hit
HTML (Hypertext Markup Language)
HTML document
HTML form
HTML script
HTML tag
HTTP (Hypertext Transfer Protocol)
HTTP status code
Hyperlink
Hypertext
Hypertext link
Indexer
Java applet
Keyword
Keyword stuffing
Link
Link popularity
Markup language

Meta keyword
Metasearch engine
Online payment
Online shopping bag
Online shopping cart
P2P file sharing
Packet sniffer
Person-to-person payment
Player
Plug-in
Podcast
Pop-up ad
Protocol analyzer
Query processor
RSS
Search engine
Search term
Secure connection
Server-side script
S-HTTP (secure HTTP)
SSL (Secure Sockets Layer)
TLS (Transport Layer Security)

URL (Uniform Resource Locator)
Videocasting
Web
Web 2.0
Web authoring software
Web browser
Web cache
Web crawler
Web page
Web resource
Web search engine
Web server
Web site
Webcast
Wiki
World Wide Web (WWW)
World Wide Web Consortium (W3C)
XHTML

Unit Review

1. Use your own words to define bold terms that appear throughout the unit. List 10 of the terms that are least familiar to you, and write a sentence for each of them.

2. In your own words, explain the purpose of each of these three key Web technologies: Hypertext Transfer Protocol (HTTP), Hypertext Markup Language (HTML), and URL (Uniform Resource Locator).

3. In a short paragraph, explain three different services provided through the Web and the Internet.

4. List three features common to browsers and provide a brief description of each.

5. Name and explain the four classifications for e-commerce.

6. Explain how each of the following payment methods work and why you would use each one: a person-to-person payment and a one-time-use credit card.

7. Why would you search the Web? What are some strategies for creating a good search? Write a keyword search phrase that uses a Boolean operator to find information about something of interest to you.

8. Explain the tools available in a browser that you can use to search the Web and navigate Web pages.

9. Locate an e-commerce Web page, print it out, and then identify elements that make it a good or poor site for shopping. How can you be sure your shopping transaction is secure on this site?

10. Describe why it is important for Web authors to be sure all links are active and current for Web pages and graphics on the Web pages. Explain what happens if a user clicks a link that is not active.

Concepts Review

Select the best answer.

1. The Web is a collection of _____ that can be related by links.
 a. networks
 b. documents
 c. technologies
 d. graphics

2. _____ is the original markup language that specifies how a Web document should appear when printed or displayed on a computer screen.
 a. TCP/IP
 b. HTML
 c. HTTP
 d. URL

3. You can identify a secure Web site if you visit the Web site and your browser displays any of the following elements in the Address bar, except:
 a. the color green
 b. a lock icon
 c. an ActiveX control
 d. https://

4. A Web _____ is a software program that runs on your computer and helps you access Web pages.
 a. site
 b. server
 c. resource
 d. browser

5. When a broken link points to a nonexistent HTML document, your browser typically produces a _____ Page Not Found error.
 a. 303
 b. 301
 c. 500
 d. 404

6. A digital _____ is a specially coded electronic attachment to a file that verifies the identity of the file's source.
 a. certificate
 b. add-on
 c. bookmark
 d. status code

7. A plug-in, such as _____, is a program that lets a browser display a particular file format.
 a. Flash Player
 b. Google
 c. HTTP
 d. Safari

8. Each of the following is a navigation tool available in a typical Web browser, except:
 a. Home button
 b. text link
 c. Favorites list
 d. status code

9. A Web server's response to a browser's request includes a(n) _____ code that indicates whether or not the browser's request can be fulfilled.
 a. status
 b. HTML
 c. hypertext
 d. cache

10. Most search engines work with queries in which you enter one or more words, called search terms or _____.
 a. hypertext
 b. links
 c. keywords
 d. benchmark

11. A broken link icon looks like _____ and occurs when a Web page link cannot find the file, URL, or graphic file referenced in the link.
 a. `##`
 b.
 c. `@@`
 d. `**`

12. A _____ is an audio file that is distributed through downloads or the use of a feed.
 a. cookie
 b. link
 c. podcast
 d. favorite

13. _____ is a peer-to-peer file sharing protocol that distributes the role of file servers across many computers.
 a. Chatting
 b. BitTorrent
 c. Podcast
 d. Boolean operator

14. _____ allow(s) Web pages to become more interactive and to incorporate activities that would otherwise require a computer program, such as to enable e-commerce sites to verify credit card information.
 a. Hypertext
 b. Scripts
 c. HTML
 d. Links

15. The typical way to get a plug-in application, such as the Adobe Reader, is to _____.
 a. download it for free
 b. buy it online
 c. get it in a store
 d. get it with the OS

16. _____ is the broad term used to describe all shopping for goods and services over the Internet.
 a. Cookies
 b. E-commerce
 c. Encryption
 d. Protocol analyzer

17. An HTML _____ is a series of program instructions that can be embedded directly into the text of an HTML document.
 a. player
 b. script
 c. keyword
 d. cookie

18. Some search sites use _____ to employ a series of other search engines and compile the search results.
 a. link popularity
 b. Boolean operators
 c. metasearch engines
 d. indexers

19. When creating a Boolean search, the minus sign (–) can be used in some search engines instead of the word _____.
 a. NOT
 b. OR
 c. AND
 d. AND/OR

20. Web pages that provide a secure connection start with _____.
 a. httpx://
 b. https://
 c. httpt://
 d. httpz://

Independent Challenges

Independent Challenge 1

Shopping on the Web has benefits for consumers as well as merchants. You will take a quick shopping tour of the Web and compare a few sites to see how they differ. You do not have to make any purchases to complete this independent challenge.

For this Independent Challenge:

1. Find three retailers on the Web. If possible, find e-commerce retailers that also have brick-and-mortar stores, such as Sears; Target; Bed, Bath, and Beyond; or Home Depot.

2. In addition to the name of the Web site, what clues on the Web page help you identify the products or services being offered?

3. For each of the retailers, search for two items and place them in a shopping cart. Do not complete the purchase, and do not enter any credit card or personal information.

4. Create a chart with three columns, one for each retailer. Complete the chart by answering the questions that follow:
 a. What procedures did you go through to find the merchandise?
 b. Was there a shopping cart or comparable way of gathering your purchases? (See Figure G-27.)

FIGURE G-27: **Sample shopping cart logos**

 c. What methods of payment did the sites offer?
 d. Were there any warning dialog boxes that opened in your browser during the shopping trip?
 e. Was the Web page designed and organized well? Were the colors and graphics pleasing? Overwhelming? Did they encourage you to stay and shop at the Web site?
 f. Select one of your choices that also has a brick-and-mortar counterpart: Would you prefer to shop online or at the brick-and-mortar store? Write a brief summary supporting your response.

Independent Challenge 2

Search engines provide different results for different reasons. Some hits are displayed based on the accuracy of your query, and some hits are based on the amount of money the Web sites paid the search engine. The hits you see might also vary by time of day the search was conducted and by the search engine used.

For this Independent Challenge:

1. Select three search Web sites that you want to compare. Popular search engines include www.google.com, www.bing.com, www.msn.com, www.yahoo.com, and www.ask.com.

2. Search for the following: a product, a historical fact, a geographical fact, a political event, and a scientific fact. Use Boolean operators in at least two of the queries.

3. Notice that search sites sometimes offer suggestions as you begin to type your keywords. Are the hints provided by the search site helpful? Refer to Figure G-28 for an example of suggestions provided while typing a search at one search site.

FIGURE G-28: **Google search results**

4. Perform each search using each of the three search Web sites. Compare the first page from each search. How many hits were common across the search Web sites?

5. Were any results surprising? Write a brief summary of your findings.

Independent Challenge 3

This unit focuses on the World Wide Web, or "Web" for short. The most important software tool for accessing Web pages and Web sites is a browser. A default browser is provided with a computer's operating system: people who buy Windows computers will find Internet Explorer on their computers; Mac buyers will find Safari on their computers. Browsers can also be downloaded for free from the provider's Web site; in fact, PC owners can download Safari for their Windows machines. You can install more than one browser and use the one that suits you best.

For this Independent Challenge:

You will learn about the browser on your computer, and, if you feel adventurous, you will have a chance to try a new browser.

1. Which browser do you typically use to access the Web? If you don't know, look for browser icons on your desktop. Popular browsers include Internet Explorer, Safari, Firefox, Chrome, and Opera.

2. The home page is the first Web page displayed when you open your browser and the one displayed when you click the Home button. What is the URL that your browser uses as its home page? You can change your browser home page.
 a. To change your browser's home page on a Windows computer running IE, start your browser and navigate to the page you want to be your home page (such as your favorite search engine). Once the Web page opens in your browser window, click the Tools icon, then click Internet Options to open the Internet Options dialog box with the General tab active. The selected URL in the Home page list box should match the URL of the active page in your browser. See Figure G-29. Click OK to set the selected URL as your browser's home page.

FIGURE G-29: Setting the Home page in IE

Used with permission from Microsoft

b. You follow similar steps to change the home page on a Windows computer running Google Chrome. Click the Wrench tool, and then click Options to open the Basics pane in the Options window. In the Home page area of the Basics pane, be sure that the Open this pane option button is selected and that the URL you want to open as your home page is listed in the text box. See Figure G-30.

FIGURE G-30: Setting the Home page in Chrome

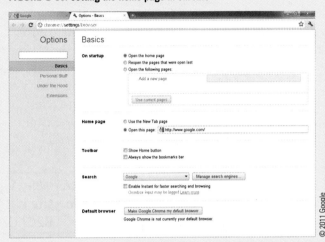

© 2011 Google

3. What is the version number for the browser that is installed on your computer? To find your browser's version number on a Windows computer using IE, start your browser, click the Tools icon, then click About Internet Explorer. For Google Chrome, click the Wrench icon, then click About Google Chrome. For a Mac, click your browser's name on the Mac title bar and then select About. Your browser's version number should be displayed in a dialog box. After you write down the version number, close the dialog box. Is it the latest version? Log onto the Internet and research your browser to find out.

4. If you are working on your own computer or if you have permission to add programs to the computer you are working on, download the most recent version of your browser. Do you notice any changes?

5. Which add-ons are installed on your browser? Can you view PDF files? Can you view Web sites that require the Flash player? Is there any adware installed on your computer? Any spyware?

6. Research two other browsers. Which ones did you select? Are the features similar? What distinguishes one browser from the other?

7. Based on your findings, would you consider changing browsers? Trying a new one?

Guide to Buying a Computer

As you prepare to buy a computer, there are a lot of decisions you have to make. This course is designed to help you build the knowledge base you need to purchase a computer. In this unit, you learned about the Web and how to take advantage, in a secure way, of all that the Web has to offer. If you buy a new computer, you will most likely use the computer to view Web pages, shop online, and take advantage of the Internet and Web services. After each unit, you have been asked to complete a worksheet. By the end of the book, your Guide to Buying a Computer worksheet will provide comprehensive information about buying a computer. The worksheet in this unit focuses on what you need to know as a user and consumer of the Web and the Internet.

To help you organize the information you will need to know when you are ready to use your computer to view Web sites, shop, or use Internet services, you should complete the following activities.

1. When you go to the Web for e-commerce, chances are you will visit a Web site with a .com top-level domain. There are many Web sites that exist using other top level domains. Log onto the Internet and find two Web sites that use the different top-level domains shown in the table below. List them in the table below with a brief description of each site.

Top level domain	Web site URL	Is it a secure site? How do you know?	What type of e-commerce site is it? B2C? C2C? B2B? B2G?	Description
org				
org				
gov				
gov				
net				
net				
biz				
biz				
edu				
edu				

© Cengage Learning

2. What commonalities did you find between the sites with .edu domains? Between the sites with .gov domains? Why do you think a site used the .biz domain rather than the .com domain?

3. As you continue to work through this book, you will learn more about personal computer systems, the Internet, and the Web. You will have the opportunity to answer more questions and complete other worksheets with information that will help you when it is time to buy a computer and set it up to run securely. To help you think about your Web surfing needs as you search the Internet to shop, to bank, or simply to browse for information or enjoyment, complete this portion of the Guide to Buying a Computer worksheet.

Guide to Buying a Computer: Web browsing needs

Questions to consider	Pages where the topic is covered in this book (refer back to these pages to read more about the topic)	Notes (add additional comments, clarifications, or ideas about each topic)
What do you use the Web for? Information? Education (online classes?) Shopping?		
Do you access the Web using a mobile device?		
If you use a mobile device, do you shop using a mobile device?		
Will you be using a digital wallet? Person-to-person payment service? If so, which one?		
What options are available for you to use to pay for online shopping?		
Do you plan to do online banking? How can you know that your bank provides services online that are secure?		
Do you plan to participate in social networking?		
What type of security will you need to have on your computer or mobile device when you do these activities?		
What browser do you use?		
Do you have the latest version of your browser?		
Do you participate in video chatting? Do you have a Web cam? If so, which one?		
Do you use any software add-ons?		
Do you find that you might need to purchase additional software to meet your needs as you use the Web?		

© Cengage Learning

4. Write any questions you have about security on e-commerce Web sites. As you continue to work through this book, check back to see if these questions have been answered.

My Questions

Visual Workshop

The Internet has opened up small business development to anyone with a computer, an Internet connection, and the willingness to spend some time designing and creating a Web site to enhance their business. See Figure G-31. Not only can small businesses now have a national reach, they can even attract international clients! In addition to attracting small businesses, Web sites are available for politicians and citizens to discuss issues. Web sites can be created by anyone with a cause, idea, or product or service to sell or promote. As a citizen, you can shop, explore, and learn using the Web. As a concerned citizen, you can participate in government using the Web. Political action committees as well as environmental organizations all have Web sites promoting their agendas and providing information to citizens.

FIGURE G-31: **Running a small business with the help of the Web**

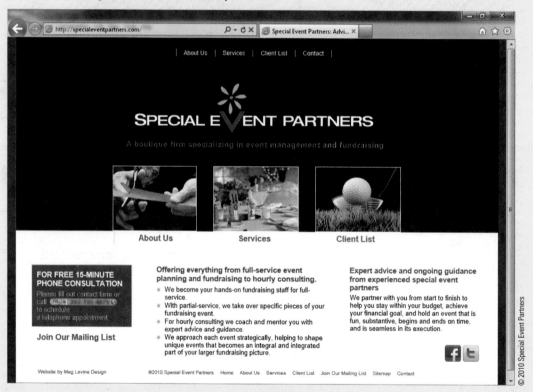

1. Select a current political event or issue that interests you. Create a list of important facts about your topic that you will research on the Web using skills you learned about in this unit. You should incorporate the influence of technology on your topic. For example, you might want to research what influence Web technology has had on e-commerce for small businesses.

2. Log on to the Internet, and then use your favorite search engine to search the Web and research your topic. Then use another search engine and compare resulting hits on the topic.

3. As you browse the Web, maintain a log describing the Web sites you visit. For each site, include its URL, the name of the organization that maintains the Web site, a brief description of the site's content, and your assessment of the reliability and validity of information on the site.

4. Write a short essay describing your findings. If you copy information from any Web site, be sure to cite your sources. Copy and paste each URL from the Web sites you used into your essay. Your essay should include a well-rounded discussion of the topic you originally formulated. Include a summary paragraph on how the Internet and computers influenced the topic and how the Internet facilitated your research.

UNIT H Concepts

Digital Media

Learning Objectives

1. Explain how computers record, store, and play sounds
2. Define, then give real-world examples and practical uses for synthesized sound
3. Define bitmap graphics and explain ways to capture, store, print, and transfer bitmap images
4. Explain how image resolution, density, and file size affect bitmap graphics
5. Explain how color depth affects file size and how you can compress images to reduce file size
6. Describe the features and benefits of vector and 3D graphics
7. Define digital video and explain how to create video files
8. Identify and describe how to use digital video equipment and video editing software

Courtesy of Emily Blain

LESSON TOPICS

- Digital Audio—An Overview
- Synthesized Sound
- Bitmap Graphics—An Introduction
- Bitmap Graphics—Features
- Color and Compression
- Vector and 3D Graphics
- Digital Video—An Overview
- Video Equipment and Software
- Reference Tables for Media Files

Talking Points: Who Owns the Rights?

Digital Audio—An Overview

Computers can record, store, and play sounds, such as narration, sound effects, and music. Digital audio makes it possible for you to use your computer and any portable digital audio player, including a smartphone, to listen to your favorite songs, podcasts, and personal compositions. See Table H-1 in the Reference Tables for Media Files section near the end of this unit for a list of audio file formats.

Learning Objective 1:
Explain how computers record, store, and play sounds

● **What is digital audio?** **Digital audio** is music, speech, and other sounds represented in binary format for use in digital devices, such as computers and portable media players. Sound is produced by vibrations, which create analog sound waves. To create digital audio that a computer can play, samples of the analog sound wave are collected at periodic intervals and stored as numeric data. This process of sampling creates the sampling rate associated with a digital audio file.

● **What is sampling rate?** **Sampling rate** refers to the number of times per second that a sound is collected or measured during the recording process, and it is expressed in hertz (Hz). One thousand samples per second is 1,000 Hz or 1 KHz (kilohertz). Higher sampling rates increase the quality of the sound recording, but they require more storage space than lower sampling rates. The audio clips associated with Figure H-1 illustrate how sampling rate affects file size and ultimately the sound quality.

FIGURE H-1: **Sampling rate affects file size**

Low sampling rate:
File size = 66 KB

Medium sampling rate:
File size = 124 KB

High sampling rate:
File size = 235 KB

Courtesy of MediaTechnics Corporation

Regardless of sampling rate, digital audio file size can be reduced using audio compression techniques. Audio compression reduces the size of a sound file by removing bits that are beyond the frequencies of normal hearing. A compressed audio file requires less storage space than the same uncompressed file. Popular online music stores supply files that use a compressed audio file format, and popular portable music players work with compressed audio file formats.

● **How does my computer play digital audio?** Your computer uses a sound card or sound card circuitry and software. A computer's **sound card** has audio-processing circuitry that transforms the bits stored in an audio file into music, sound effects, and narration. A sound card contains a digital signal processor. See Figure H-2. The **digital signal processor** transforms digital bits into analog waves when a waveform audio file is being played, transforms analog waves into digital bits when a sound recording is being made, and handles compression and decompression, if necessary.

FIGURE H-2: **How a sound card converts signals**

Courtesy of MediaTechnics Corporation

The microprocessor sends compressed digital data to the sound card.

The sound card's digital signal processor decompresses data and converts it to analog signals.

The sound card sends analog signals to speakers.

A desktop computer's sound card usually is plugged into an expansion slot inside the system unit. Alternatively, sound card circuitry might be built into the motherboard. Portable computers usually have sound circuitry built into the motherboard. Sound card circuitry, called **integrated audio** is built into the motherboard. In addition to the circuitry, a sound card is typically equipped with input and output jacks, which allow it to accept input from a microphone and provide output to speakers or headphones.

● **What devices can play a digital audio file?** You can play a digital audio file on your computer as well as portable devices, such as a portable audio player, a mobile phone, and a gaming device. In fact, you can play a digital audio file on any device that has a sound card and appropriate hardware and software.

What hardware do I need to hear digital audio?

Your computer outputs sound to speakers or headphones. Portable computers and handheld devices typically include built-in speakers. Ports for external speakers are usually on the system unit. Speakers come in several configurations, such as the system shown in Figure H-3.

FIGURE H-3: **An external speaker system**

© Alexander Kalina/iStockphoto

What hardware do I need to record digital audio?

A computer or portable digital device gets sound input from a microphone. Although smartphones typically include a built-in microphone, you connect most standard microphones, or a headset with a built-in microphone, to your computer through the microphone socket, also called a jack, or USB port. Many Web cams include a microphone to capture your voice or other sound during video chatting. Almost all sound cards use standard color codes for input/output connector jacks. See Figure H-4.

FIGURE H-4: **Audio ports are also called jacks or sockets**

© Shcherbakov Sergei/Shutterstock.com

© Tootles/Shutterstock.com

Microphone jack for a laptop Headset jack

Computers with just two audio channels have green (output), blue (input) and pink (microphone) jacks.

What type of software do I need to play digital audio files?

To play an audio file on your computer or portable player, you must use player software, such as audio software or media software. Player software usually supports several audio file formats. In the Windows environment, for example, you can use Windows Media to play audio formats such as WAV, WMA, and MP3. Software that plays and records various audio file formats is generally included with your computer's operating system, with your sound card, or with your portable player. You can also find software on the Web. Popular audio and media players include iTunes, Windows Media Player, and open source offerings such as QuickAudio and Audacity.

In addition to playing digital audio files, audio player software typically includes features that help you organize and modify your audio files. For example, the software often provides the ability to create a playlist, which is a list of songs from your music library that you can arrange to play in any order. The software often provides links to online music stores, as well as options for transferring music files to a portable audio player.

How does the Web deliver audio?

Digital audio files can be embedded into a Web page using the HTML5 <audio> tag. WAV, a popular audio file format, is supported by most Web browsers. Other audio formats can be transported over the Web, but might require plug-ins to play in a browser. Web-based digital audio is often delivered in streaming format to avoid lengthy delays while the entire audio file is downloaded. **Streaming audio** plays as the file is downloaded. Streaming audio provides the technology for real-time Internet radio broadcasts, podcasts, and voice chat sessions. See Figure H-5.

FIGURE H-5: **Streaming audio**

www.npr.org

Where can I get digital audio?

Digital audio, such as music, is available from a variety of sources including online music stores, such as the iTunes Music Store, the Zune Music Pass, and Amazon.com MP3 Downloads. Individual songs can be downloaded for about $1 each, entire albums typically cost less than $10. Some music artists post sample tracks on their Web sites. You can digitize music from your CD collection by using iTunes or CD ripper software that converts CD-audio music into computer-friendly digital audio format. You can also find free digital music posted by artists trying to encourage fan loyalty. Other digital audio files, such as podcasts, can be downloaded from the Web site hosting the podcast.

Synthesized Sound

Audio can be analog, digital, or synthesized. As explained in the previous lesson, digital audio is created by sampling an analog sound signal. In contrast, **synthesized sound** is artificially created sound. Synthesized sound is classified as MIDI music or synthesized speech. This lesson explores MIDI music and synthesized speech.

Learning Objective 2:
Define, then give real-world examples and practical uses for synthesized sound

● **What is MIDI?** **MIDI (Musical Instrument Digital Interface)** specifies a standard way to store music data for synthesizers, electronic MIDI instruments, and computers. MIDI is a music notation system that allows computers to communicate with music synthesizers. While digitized sound files contain digitized recordings of real sound passages, MIDI files contain instructions that sound like various musical instruments.

● **How does my computer store and play MIDI files?**
The computer encodes the music generated by a MIDI device as a **MIDI sequence** and stores it as a file with one of these file extensions: .mid, .cmf, or .rol. A MIDI sequence contains instructions specifying the pitch of a note, the point at which the note begins, the instrument that plays the note, the volume of the note, and the point at which the note ends. Most computer sound cards are equipped to generate music from MIDI files, and many can capture music data from a MIDI instrument as well. A MIDI-capable sound card contains a **wavetable** (sometimes called a patch set), which is a set of prerecorded musical instrument sounds. The sound card accesses these sounds and plays them as instructed by the MIDI file. For example, if a sound card receives a MIDI instruction for a trumpet to play middle C, it accesses the trumpet's middle C patch and routes it to the speaker until it receives a MIDI instruction to stop the note.

● **How can I create MIDI tunes?** You can use MIDI software to compose your own tunes, or you can get permission to use MIDI files that you find on the Web. For composing your own MIDI music, you can input the notes from a MIDI instrument, such as an electronic keyboard, directly to your computer. See Figure H-6. The input is typically handled by music composition software, which provides tools for entering notes, specifying instruments, printing sheet music, and saving compositions. You can also use it to edit the notes and combine the parts for several instruments.

● **Why would I choose to use MIDI?** MIDI files are much more compact than digital audio files. Depending on the piece of music, three minutes of MIDI music might require only 10 KB of storage space, whereas the same piece of music stored in a high-quality, uncompressed digital audio file might require 30 MB of storage space. MIDI is a good choice for adding background music to multimedia projects and Web pages. Most browsers include built-in support for MIDI music. One of the big disadvantages of MIDI is that it does not produce high-quality vocals. Another disadvantage is that it does not have the full resonance of real sound.

FIGURE H-6: **Music composition software**

Most musicians can easily identify MIDI recordings because they lack the tonal qualities of symphony-quality sound.

● **How can my computer produce spoken words?**
Your computer uses a speech synthesizer to output spoken words. For example, a speech synthesizer can read your email messages to you when you call for messages using your cell phone. Or, a speech synthesizer can read a computer screen aloud, which provides access to computers and the Internet for individuals with vision impairment. Most speech synthesizers use **speech synthesis**, which is the process computers use to produce sound that resembles spoken words. Speech synthesizers string together basic sound units called **phonemes**. A basic speech synthesizer consists of **text-to-speech software**, which generates sounds that are played through your computer's standard sound card; other speech synthesizers are special-purpose hardware devices. Windows comes with a program called Microsoft Narrator that reads all commands and activities happening on screen and says each keystroke as you type. This program is helpful for visually impaired users. See Figure H-7.

FIGURE H-7: **Microsoft Narrator**

● **How does a computer understand the words I speak?** Your computer uses a speech recognition system to understand words you speak into a microphone. See Figure H-8. **Speech recognition** (also called **voice recognition**) refers to the ability of a computer to understand the spoken word. A speech recognition system typically collects words spoken into a microphone attached to the sound card. The sound card's digital signal processor transforms the analog sound of your voice into digital data, which is then processed by speech recognition software.

Speech recognition software analyzes the sounds of your voice and breaks them down into phonemes. Next, the software analyzes the content of your speech and compares the groups of phonemes to the words in a digital dictionary that lists phoneme combinations along with their corresponding English (or Chinese, Spanish, and so on) words. When a match is found, the software displays the correctly spelled word on the screen.

FIGURE H-8: **Speech recognition input requires a microphone**

© Yo-ichi/Shutterstock.com

● **Can I use speech to issue computer commands?** Yes. For example, speech recognition can be used to activate Windows controls. Most speech recognition software also works with your browser. Windows 7 includes a speech recognition module. The first steps in using speech recognition are setting up a microphone and training the computer to recognize your speaking style. See Figure H-9. Training consists of reading a series of short text passages into a microphone attached to your computer. Tips for successful voice recognition training include the following:

■ Speak at a consistent volume.
■ Speak at a steady pace, don't speed up or slow down.
■ Speak naturally, without exaggerated pauses between words or syllables.
■ Work in a quiet environment so that the computer hears your voice instead of the sounds around you.
■ Use a good quality microphone and keep it in the same position.

FIGURE H-9: **Setting up Windows Speech Recognition**

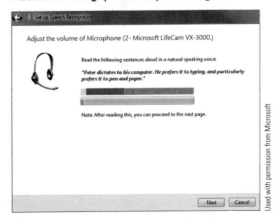

Used with permission from Microsoft

● **Is speech recognition available on other devices?**
Yes. Today, you can find speech recognition on devices such as mobile phones and GPS (global positioning system) devices. Speech recognition will no doubt become even more widespread, as consumers demand more hands-free computing applications.

Bitmap Graphics—An Introduction

Digital graphics are images that have been created as or converted to a digital format. Many graphics file formats exist, and most graphics software offers a choice of popular formats, such as BMP, RAW, TIFF, JPEG, GIF, and PNG. See Table H-2 in the Reference Tables for Media Files section near the end of this unit for a complete list of graphic file formats. Some digital graphics are classified as bitmap graphics.

Learning Objective 3:
Define bitmap graphics and explain ways to capture, store, print, and transfer bitmap images

● **What is a bitmap graphic?** A **bitmap graphic**, also called a **raster graphic**, or simply a **bitmap**, is composed of a grid of dots. Think of a grid superimposed on a picture. See Figure H-10. The graphic is mapped to a grid. The grid divides the picture into cells, called pixels. Each **pixel** is assigned a color, which is stored as a binary number in a file.

FIGURE H-10: **A bitmap graphic**

Used with permission from Microsoft; Courtesy of MediaTechnics Corporation

Bitmap graphics are used to create realistic digital images. There are many sources for bitmap graphics, for example, images converted by a scanner or photos created using a digital camera or a camera-enabled cell phone. Bitmap graphics can be sent as email attachments, and they are used often as Web page graphics.

● **How can I create a bitmap graphic?** There are a variety of ways you can create bitmap graphics.

■ You can create a bitmap graphic using the tools provided by graphics software—specifically paint software such as Adobe Photoshop, Corel Painter, and Microsoft Paint (included with Windows). Paint software provides tools for freehand sketching, filling in shapes, adding realistic shading, and creating effects that look like oil paints, charcoal, or watercolors.

■ You can use a **scanner** to convert a printed image, such as a newspaper or magazine article, photo, or a drawing, into a

bitmap graphic. See Figure H-11. Essentially, a scanner converts the visual information you see into digital information the computer can understand. A scanner digitizes printed images. A scanner divides an image into a fine grid of cells and assigns a digital value for the color of each cell. These values are transferred as a file to your computer. The file is processed so the image can be displayed, printed, modified, sent via email, or saved as a bitmap graphic file to a storage medium.

FIGURE H-11: **A scanner**

© Feng Yu/Shutterstock.com

■ You can use a **digital camera** to take a photograph when you want a picture of an object, a landscape, or a person. A digital camera creates digitized images of real objects, converting the images into digital information that can be stored as bitmap graphics files. The lens focuses light from the image onto a small image sensor called a **CCD (charge-coupled device)**. A CCD contains a grid of tiny light-sensitive diodes called photosites. A CCD's **photosites** correspond to pixels. The more pixels used to capture an image, the higher its resolution, and the better the resulting picture.

Cameras with larger CCDs produce higher quality images. Some cameras contain multiple CCDs, which enhance the color quality of a camera's output. Digital single-lens reflex (DSLR) cameras, such as the one in Figure H-12, have removable lenses. With a DSLR camera, you look through the lens while taking the image.

Courtesy of MediaTechnics Corporation

Courtesy of Learning Technology Services, University of Wisconsin-Stout

Shutter release button Lens CCD

- Point-and-shoot digital cameras are generally smaller and lighter and either use a view finder or have an LCD screen for viewing images during and after shooting. See Figure H-13. Almost all digital cameras feature high resolution, optical digital zooms, and digital image stabilization to guarantee a good picture even if the camera shakes. Digital cameras use a sensor array to capture an image. The sensor is packed with millions of light sensitive cells that record color and brightness for millions of points in the image grid. User interface options include image management menus and options for saving various image formats. Many cell phones have integrated digital cameras that take good quality images.

FIGURE H-13: Using a point-and-shoot digital camera

Courtesy of Emily Bunin

- **Where does a digital camera store the photographs?** Some digital cameras store photos on mini CDs, or microdrives. The most popular digital camera storage is solid state memory cards, which can be erased and reused. This means you can preview images while they are still in the camera and delete those that you do not want. Solid state storage uses no power, so it doesn't lose data when the camera is turned off. Your computer treats memory cards as any other storage device. You can use Windows Explorer or Finder to copy photo files from the SD card to your computer's hard drive.

- **How can I transfer images from the digital camera to my computer or printer?** You can transfer photographs directly to some printers. Typically you will transfer the photos to your computer's hard drive. This transfer can be achieved in several ways, depending on your camera.

- **Direct cable transfer.** If your computer and your camera have FireWire ports (also called IEEE-1394 ports), you can connect a cable between these two ports to transfer the photos. You can use a similar transfer method if your computer and camera have USB ports. See Figure H-14. Both ports provide good transfer speed. Some cameras come with a USB connector that can be connected directly to the computer so the camera is seen as another storage device. You can transfer your digital images in the same way you transfer files from any storage device connected to your computer.

FIGURE H-14: Transferring images from a camera to a computer

© A.S. Zain/Shutterstock.com; Courtesy of Rachel B. Bunin

- **Infrared port.** Some cameras can beam the data from your camera to your computer's infrared port. This method eliminates the need for a cable but is much slower than using a FireWire or USB.

- **Media transfer.** If your camera stores data on mini CDs or another type of media, you can simply remove the media from your camera and insert it into the appropriate drive of your computer.

- **Docking station.** Some camera manufacturers offer a camera docking station that connects to a computer by cable. A camera can be placed in the docking station to transfer photos to the computer's hard drive.

- **Email.** Cell phone photos can be transferred to a computer by emailing the photo to your email account. The photo arrives as an attachment, which can be saved as a separate file.

- **Card readers.** A **card reader** is a small device designed to read data contained in a solid state memory card. Card readers can be connected to your computer's USB port, built into a computer system unit, or built into a photo printer. To transfer photos from a memory card, you remove it from the camera and insert it into the card reader.

Regardless of the technology that you use, transferring photos from your camera to your computer requires software, which may be supplied along with your camera, with your card reader, or by a stand-alone graphics software package, such as Adobe Photoshop. This software allows you not only to transfer and save the file but also to select a file format, specify a filename, and determine the location for each image file.

Unit H

Bitmap Graphics—Features

Because bitmap graphics are stored as bits that represent pixels, you can use software to modify or edit them. In order to modify bitmap graphics, you need an understanding of image resolution, density, and file size.

Learning Objective 4:
Explain how image resolution, density, and file size affects bitmap graphics

● **What is resolution?** **Resolution** refers to the dimensions of the grid that forms a bitmap graphic, and it is usually expressed as the number of horizontal and vertical pixels that it contains. For example, a graphic for a Web page might have a resolution of 150 × 100 pixels: 150 pixels across and 100 pixels up and down. Bitmap graphics are **resolution dependent**, which means that the quality of the image depends on its resolution. A high-resolution graphic contains more data and looks better than a low-resolution graphic. Why? Because each pixel contains data, the high-resolution graphic contains more data that defines the image than the low-resolution graphic.

Camera manufacturers sometimes express resolution as megapixels. A **megapixel** is 1 million pixels. A camera that can capture an image with a resolution of 1600 × 1200 has the capability of producing photographs containing 1.9 megapixels (1600 multiplied by 1200). A camera that can capture images with a 3888 × 2592 resolution is technically a 10.1 megapixels camera, but it is sold as a 10 megapixel camera.

● **How does resolution relate to the size of an image?** A bitmap graphic is simply a collection of data. Unlike a printed photograph, a bitmap graphic has no fixed physical size. The size at which a bitmap graphic is displayed or printed depends on the density as well as the resolution (dimensions) of the image grid. Imagine that each bitmap image and its grid come on a surface that you can stretch or shrink. As you stretch the surface, the grid maintains the same number of horizontal and vertical cells, but each cell becomes larger and the grid becomes less dense. As you shrink the surface, the grid becomes smaller and denser. The graphic retains the same resolution (grid dimensions) no matter how much you stretch or shrink the graphic's physical size, as shown in Figure H-15. This concept of stretching and shrinking without changing resolution is important for

understanding what happens when bitmaps are displayed and printed. The denser the grid, the smaller the image will appear. The **density** of an image grid can be expressed as dots per inch (dpi) for a printer or scanner, or as pixels per inch (ppi) for a monitor.

FIGURE H-15: Resolution and image size

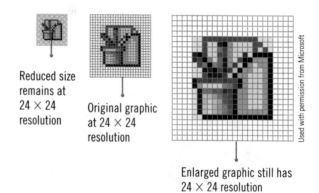

Reduced size remains at 24 × 24 resolution

Original graphic at 24 × 24 resolution

Enlarged graphic still has 24 × 24 resolution

Used with permission from Microsoft

● **Why are some graphic files so large?** As already discussed, bitmap graphics are made up of pixels. Each pixel holds bits of information about the image. More pixels in a bitmap graphic means more bits are needed to store the image as a file. So, while a large bitmap graphic contains the data needed to display a high-quality printout, these files take up space on your hard drive, can require lengthy email transmission times, and make Web page downloads seem sluggish. The file size of a bitmap graphic depends on its resolution and color depth.

● **How can I reduce the size of an image?** Sometimes the resolution and corresponding file size of a graphic are too large for your needs. One way to reduce the size of a bitmap graphic is to crop it. **Cropping** refers to the process of removing part of an image. Cropping decreases file size by reducing the number of pixels in a graphic.

The image changes to reflect the cropped changes. For example, the image in Figure H-16 has been cropped to include some, but not all, of the food. Information has been removed from the image, which means the file size for the cropped image is smaller.

FIGURE H-16: Cropping an image

Courtesy of Rachel B. Bunin

Another way to reduce file size is to use graphics software to reduce the resolution by eliminating pixels from the image based on settings you specify. This will reduce the size of the image grid as well as the file size. For example, if you use graphics software to reduce the resolution from 2160 × 1440 (3.1 megapixels) to 1080 × 720 (.8 megapixels), the image grid becomes one quarter of its original size. The file size is reduced by a similar amount.

- **What is the relationship between file size, resolution, and image quality?** Image quality is affected by resolution, which in turn affects file size. So, reducing file size only should not affect the image quality. For example, cropping an image reduces the file size but does not affect the resolution or the image quality. However, reducing file size by adjusting the resolution does compromise the image quality. Why? Because the quality of the image depends on its resolution, and if the resolution is reduced, then pixels and data are lost.

- **Does file size affect storage media?** High-resolution photographs use more storage space than low-resolution photographs. A typical RAW image file from a professional DSLR camera might be 10 MB, whereas a lo-res image from a point-and-shoot digital camera might be 200KB. Only a few hundred high-resolution photographs might fit on a 16 GB card, whereas the same card might hold thousands of low-resolution photographs.

- **How can I modify my photographs?** You can use graphics software to modify your photographs. Using graphics software, you can enhance or change bitmap graphics with a variety of effects. You can retouch or repair old photographs to eliminate creases, spots, and discoloration. Graphics software tools include many creative effects including tools to fix red eye, remove unwanted elements or objects, apply artistic filters, add text, and change the contrast or brightness. See Figure H-17.

FIGURE H-17: Modifying a bitmap graphic

Courtesy of MediaTechnics Corporation

Before After

- **Can I increase the quality of an image?** You can increase the resolution of a bitmap graphic using graphics software. When you do this, your computer must somehow add pixels because no additional picture data exists. Most graphics software uses a process called **pixel interpolation** to create new pixels by averaging the colors of nearby pixels to create the additional pixels. See Figure H-18. For some graphics, pixel interpolation results in an image that appears very similar to the original. However, images that contain strong curved or diagonal lines may develop an undesirable pixelated, or bitmap, appearance.

FIGURE H-18: Pixel interpolation

The figure above has a resolution of 130 × 130.

Courtesy of MediaTechnics Corporation

The figure above was enlarged to 260 × 260, but notice it has a pixelated appearance.

Color and Compression

Without color, viewing video, photographs, Web pages, or even menus and icons on your computer would be a very dull experience. To display the full range of colors, computer display screens use a complex storage scheme.

Learning Objective 5:
Explain how color depth affects file size and how you can compress images to reduce file size

● **How does my screen display color?** Each screen pixel displays a color based on the intensity of red, green, and blue signals that it receives. Each red, green, and blue signal is assigned a value ranging from zero to 255, from absence of color (0) to the highest intensity level (255) for that color. A pixel appears white if the red, green, and blue signals are set to maximum intensity (255, 255, 255), and black if set to the minimum intensity (0, 0, 0). If red, green, and blue signals are equal but at a lower intensity, the pixel displays a shade of gray. If the red signal is set to maximum intensity, but the blue and green signals are set to 0, the pixel appears a brilliant red. See Figure H-19. A pixel appears purple if it receives red and blue signals, and so on. These values (0 to 255 for red, blue, and green) produce a maximum of 16.7 million colors. For monochrome (black and white) screens, the bitmap is displayed by manipulating the pattern of "off" and "on" pixels displayed on the screen. Windows users can calibrate their monitor's color settings using Control Panel options.

FIGURE H-19: Setting colors by assigning color values

Range of colors available

Color values

Color displayed based on color values

● **How do graphics store color information?** A graphic stores data about color in each pixel. A graphic that uses the full range of colors is referred to as a **True Color bitmap graphic** or a **24-bit bitmap graphic**. The data for each pixel in a True Color bitmap graphic requires three bytes of

storage space: eight bits for red, eight bits for green, and eight bits for blue, for a total of 24 bits per pixel. True Color bitmap graphics produce photographic-quality images, but they also produce very large files. A **32-bit bitmap graphic** displays 16.7 million colors just like a 24-bit bitmap. The extra eight bits are used to define special effects, such as the amount of transparency, for a pixel. As a result of the extra byte of data for each pixel, 32-bit bitmap graphics files are even larger than 24-bit bitmap graphics files.

● **How can I reduce the size of these large files?** In addition to the techniques discussed in the previous lesson (such as changing an image's resolution and cropping an image), you can adjust an image's color depth. **Color depth** refers to the number of colors available for use in an image. As the color depth increases, image quality improves and file size increases.

● **How can I adjust color depth?** You can reduce a graphic's color depth by using graphics software. A **color palette** holds the selection of available colors. You select a group of colors from the color palette to use for a bitmap graphic. If a palette contains only 256 colors, the data stored for each pixel is eight bits instead of 24 bits, which reduces the file to one-third the size required for a True Color bitmap graphic.

● **How does a color palette work?** A color palette is stored as a table within the header of a graphics file. Each palette contains a list of 256 color numbers. This information is used to translate the color data stored in the bitmap graphic. Each of these numbers is mapped to a 24-bit number that corresponds to the actual levels of red, green, and blue required to display the color. Most graphics software offers a selection of ready-made palettes that you can use to select colors.

● **What ready-made palettes are available?** Ready-made palettes usually include a grayscale palette, a system palette, and a Web palette. A **grayscale palette** displays an image using shades of gray. Most grayscale palettes consist of 256 shades of gray. Figure H-20 illustrates a grayscale bitmap graphic and a grayscale palette.

A **system palette** is the selection of colors used by the operating system for the graphics that represent desktop icons and controls. Windows, for example, uses a system palette that contains 20 permanent colors and 236 colors that can be changed, depending on the application. A **Web palette** contains a standard set of colors used by Internet Web browsers. Because most browsers support this palette, it is typically regarded as a safe choice when preparing graphics for Internet distribution. Figure H-21 shows the collection of colors used by a system palette and a Web palette. Your graphics software might offer additional palettes. They are likely to include a "woodsy" palette that works well for outdoor photographs and a flesh-tone palette that's designed to work nicely for portraits.

FIGURE H-21: **Other palettes**

Windows system palette

Web palette

- **In addition to adjusting color depth, is there another way to reduce the file size of bitmap graphics?** Yes, for some types of graphic files, you can reduce file size by using data compression.

- **What is data compression?** **Data compression** is the general term used to describe the process of recoding data so that it requires fewer bytes of storage space. During data compression, bytes are removed, which reduces the file size. Compressing a file is also called zipping or archiving a file. Because data compression is reversible, bytes previously removed from a file can be restored. The process of reversing data compression is sometimes referred to as unzipping, uncompressing, decompressing, extracting, or expanding a file. The amount of shrinkage produced by data compression is the **compression ratio**. A compression ratio of 20:1, for example, means that a compressed file is 20 times smaller than the original file. Data compression is based on a **compression algorithm**.

- **Can any file be compressed?** Technically, you can compress any kind of file, including program and data files, graphics, and document files. Some graphics file formats automatically compress file data. GIF, JPEG, PNG, and TIFF file formats support compression. Many programs that work with these file formats allow you to select compression levels before saving or even emailing the file. For example, when saving an image in JPEG format, you might have the option of selecting compression settings from 1 (worst quality) to 99 (best quality). When emailing an image, your program might ask you to select the picture size as original, large, medium, small, or smaller in order to reduce the file size to lower resolutions. You can also use file compression software to compress files.

- **What is file compression software?** **File compression software** is a utility program that allows you to compress files. Using a file compression program, you might be able to compress a BMP file by as much as 70 percent, and other non-compressed file formats, such as Wave, by about 20 percent. However, file formats such as GIF, PNG, MP3, MPEG, and JPEG hardly shrink at all when you compress them using a file compression program because these file formats are already stored in a compressed format. File compression software allows you to compress one or more files, such as several graphic files, into one file, often referred to as an archive. See Figure H-22.

FIGURE H-22: **A file compression archive**

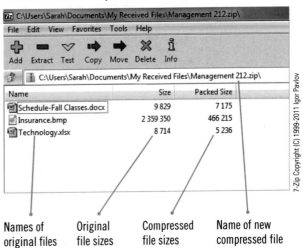

Names of original files

Original file sizes

Compressed file sizes

Name of new compressed file

- **Which file compression program should I use?** PKZIP and WinZip are popular shareware programs that compress and decompress files; these programs produce compressed files with .zip extensions. A popular open source compression utility is 7-Zip. Some operating systems come with a compression program. For example, if you are a Windows user, you can use the compression utility feature of the Windows operating system to create compressed (zipped) folders.

Vector and 3D Graphics

If you have played any computer games recently or watched an animated hit movie, you have seen the result of computer-generated, animated graphics. Many of the images used in these games are vector graphics or 3D graphics.

Learning Objective 6:
Describe the features and benefits of vector and 3D graphics

● **What is a vector graphic?** A **vector graphic** consists of a set of instructions for creating an image. Vector graphics are suitable for most line art, logos, simple illustrations, and diagrams that might be displayed and printed at various sizes. The parts of a vector graphic are created as separate objects. For example, the vector graphic image in Figure H-23 was created with a series of rectangular objects for the stones and a circular object for the sun. A vector graphic file contains the instructions needed to create the shape, size, position, and color for each object in an image. Each instruction requires storage space. The more lines, shapes, and fill patterns in the graphic, the more storage space it requires. Vector graphics usually require less storage space than bitmap graphics and resize better than bitmap graphics. When you change the physical size of a vector graphic, the objects change proportionally and maintain their smooth edges.

as realistic-looking as bitmap images. For example, clip art images, which are typically stored as vector graphics, are a good illustration of what vector graphics tend to look like. The cartoon-like characteristic of vector images results from the use of objects filled with blocks of color.

● **What software do I need to create a vector graphic?** Vector graphics are created using vector graphics software, referred to as **drawing software**. Drawing software is sometimes packaged with bitmap software to create a graphics software suite. Popular drawing software includes Adobe Illustrator, Corel DESIGNER, OpenOffice Draw (Figure H-24), and open source Inkscape. Vector graphics software provides an array of drawing tools that you can use to create objects, position them, and fill them with colors or patterns.

FIGURE H-23: **Resizing graphic images**

Vector graphic at 200% (above) and 50% (left)

Bitmap graphic at 200% (above) and 50% (right)

Photo courtesy of MediaTechnics Corporation

● **How do I edit a vector graphic?** Vector graphic objects are layered, so you can stretch, shrink, distort, color, move, or delete any object without disrupting the rest of the image.

● **How can I recognize a vector graphic?** In general, vector graphics produce images that are flatter and not

FIGURE H-24: **Drawing a vector graphic**

OpenOffice.org and the OpenOffice.org logo are trademarks or registered trademarks of Oracle and/or its affiliates; Photo courtesy of MediaTechnics Corporation

● **How can I apply color to a vector graphic?** There are several ways to apply color to vector graphics using drawing software. You can simply fill a shape with a solid color, or you can use tools for creating a gradient. A **gradient** is a

smooth blending of shades from one color to another or from light to dark. Gradients can be used to create shading and three-dimensional effects. Some tools apply bitmapped textures to vector graphics objects, giving them a more realistic appearance. For example, a vector drawing of a house with a bricklike texture. Graphics that contain both bitmap and vector data are called **metafiles**.

- **Can I create a bitmap graphic from a vector graphic?** You can create a bitmap graphic from a vector graphic using graphics software and a process called rasterization. **Rasterization**, superimposes a grid over a vector graphic and determines the color for each pixel. It is important to output your rasterized images at the size you will need. If you rasterize a vector image at a small size and then try to enlarge the resulting bitmap image, you will likely get a poor-quality pixelated image.

- **What are 3D graphics?** Like vector graphics, 3D graphics are stored as a set of instructions. For a 3D graphic, however, the instructions contain the locations and lengths of lines that form a **wireframe** for a three-dimensional object. The wireframe provides a framework for the 3D graphic. A 3D wireframe can be covered with surface texture and color to create a graphic of a 3D object. The process of covering a wireframe with surface color and texture is called **rendering**. The rendering process outputs a bitmap image. A fast processor, lots of RAM, and a fast graphics card with its own video RAM all speed up the rendering process.

- **What makes 3D graphics look realistic?** **Ray tracing**, which is the technique used for adding light and shadows to a 3D image, adds realism to 3D graphics. Ray tracing adds highlights and shadows that are produced by a light source. Before an image is rendered, the artist selects a location for one or more light sources. The computer applies a complex mathematical algorithm to determine how the light source affects the color of each pixel in the final rendered image.

- **What special software do I need to create 3D graphics?** You can create 3D animations on a standard PC or Mac with commercially available 3D graphics software, such as Autodesk AutoCAD or Caligari trueSpace. 3D graphics software has tools for drawing a wireframe and viewing it from any angle. It provides rendering and ray tracing tools, along with an assortment of surface textures that you can apply to individual objects. See Figure H-25.

FIGURE H-25: Creating a 3D graphic

Courtesy of MediaTechnics Corporation

3D graphics are based on a wireframe... ...which can be rendered into a bitmap image that looks three-dimensional

- **How are 3D graphics in films or computer games animated?** 3D graphics can be animated to produce special effects for movies or to create interactive, animated characters and environments for 3D computer games. Animated special effects are created by rendering a sequence of bitmaps in which one or more objects are moved, or otherwise changed, between each rendering. In traditional hand-drawn animation, a chief artist draws the key frames, and then a team of assistants creates each of the in-between frames, which includes changes to the images in the key frame. For 3D computer animation, the computer creates the in-between frames by moving objects and rendering each necessary image. It is common practice to create 24 frames for each second of animation. All of the frames are then combined into a single file, creating essentially a digital movie.

- **How are game animations different from movie animations?** Special effects and animation can be accomplished during the production phase of the movie and incorporated into the final footage. In contrast, 3D computer game animation happens in real time. See Figure H-26. Each frame that makes the image seem to move must be rendered while you are playing the game—a process that requires an incredible amount of computer power.

FIGURE H-26: Playing an animated computer game

© Barone Firenze/Shutterstock.com

Digital Video—An Overview

Animated 3D graphics are typically created from scratch by an artist with the help of a computer. In contrast, digital video is based on a movie of real objects filmed and then stored as bits. Digital video encompasses several technologies, including those that produce theater-quality DVD movies, desktop videos, and Web-based videos.

Learning Objective 7:
Define digital video and explain how to create video files

● **What is digital video?** A **video** is a series of frames projected at a rate fast enough to fool the human eye into perceiving continuous motion. **Digital video** uses bits to store data, including color and brightness data for each video frame. The process is similar to storing the data for a bitmap image in which the color for each pixel is represented by a binary number. Videos in digital format can be easily manipulated on a personal computer. Digital video retains image quality no matter how many times it is copied.

● **How do I create digital video?** You can create digital videos using a video camera, a smartphone, or a Web cam. You can use your personal computer to edit digital video into videos for personal and professional uses, such as video wedding albums, product sales or training videos, and documentaries for organizations. These videos can be stored on a hard drive or distributed on CDs, DVDs, BDs, videotapes, memory cards, or the Web.

● **How can I view digital video?** You can view digital video using videotape, television, DVD, Web cam, or even a **digital video recorder (DVR)**, such as TiVo. You can view digital videos on your computer, smartphone, tablet (see Figure H-27), or digital media player. Popular video player software, such as the RealMedia player, Windows Media Player, or Apple's QuickTime player, is used to view the video. How you view a digital video is determined by its platform.

FIGURE H-27: Mobile video

© ra2 studio/Shutterstock.com

● **What is a digital video platform?** A digital video platform is defined by the tools used to create the digital video. Some common digital video platforms are desktop video, Web-based video, and DVD video. The term **desktop video** refers to videos that are created and displayed using a personal computer. Web-based video is incorporated in Web pages and accessed

with a browser. DVD-video refers to a DVD format used for commercial DVDs that contain feature-length films.

● **What digital video file formats are available?** Many video file formats are available. The format you use should be compatible with the devices on which it is played and its browser or player software. Digital video file formats are sometimes referred to as container formats because they hold the compressed video and audio data streams that form a video. Some popular video container formats are AVI, MOV, MPEG, WebM, ASF, Flash video, VOB, and Blue-ray Disc Movie. Table H-3 in the Reference Tables for Media Files section near the end of this unit provides some basic information about each format.

● **How are desktop videos created?** You use digital video equipment and software to create desktop videos. See Figure H-28. Desktop videos are typically stored on a hard drive or DVD, and they are sometimes sent as email attachments.

FIGURE H-28: Steps for creating a desktop video

1. Produce video footage. Select equipment for filming videos and use effective filming techniques.

2. Transfer video footage to a computer. Use a cable, a video capture card, or an SD card to move video footage from cameras, videotapes, television, and DVDs to your computer's hard drive.

3. Edit video footage. Use software to select video segments, arrange them into a video, and add a soundtrack.

4. Store and play. Select digital video file formats for playback on desktop, Web, portable, and DVD platforms.

Courtesy of MediaTechnics Corporation

How do Web-based videos work? A video for a Web page is stored on a Web server in a file. Usually, a link for the video file appears on the Web page. When you click the link, the Web server transmits a copy of the video file to your computer, often using **streaming video technology**. This technology sends a small segment of the video to your computer and begins to play it. With streaming video technology, your computer essentially plays the video while continuing to receive it. As the video is received, it appears on your computer screen if you have the correct video player installed on your computer. Usually a digital video file is delivered via **streaming video**.

How does my Internet connection speed affect how I view Web videos? Web video is best viewed using a high-speed Internet connection. Until everyone has a high-speed connection, however, many Web sites provide one video file that is optimized for slow Internet connections and a better quality video file that is optimized for high-speed connections.

How do I post a video to YouTube or a similar file-sharing site? YouTube is a video-sharing Web site that allows registered members to upload, view, and rate video clips. YouTube and similar sites typically accept most popular video file formats directly from digital cameras, camcorders, cell phones, and Web cams. See Figure H-29. YouTube automatically converts all submitted files into Flash Video format. Most video-sharing sites have a length and file limitation, so you should check those before you finalize your video.

Are digital video files large? Yes, video files are large. Despite the use of real time compression to filter out unnecessary data as you record with your camera, digital video contains lots of data, which creates large files. Video files produced from digital tape typically are largest, whereas videos stored on memory cards are somewhat smaller, and videos from cell phones and Web cams are usually small enough to e-mail.

Are there ways to reduce the size of video files? Yes, most video capture software offers a variety of compression options to reduce the size of video files. Video compression can be achieved by decreasing the **frame rate** (number of frames per second) and reducing the frame size. Other techniques include using a smaller video window and decreasing the resolution.

Which compression techniques should I use? If you decide to store your video for desktop viewing, you can compress the video stream using various codecs. A **codec (compressor/decompressor)** is the software that compresses a video stream when a video is stored and decompresses the file when the video is played. Codecs allow you to specify the compression ratio or bit ratio. A **compression ratio** indicates the ratio of compressed data to uncompressed data. Compression can be measured by **bitrate**, the number of bits required to display one second of video. Higher bitrates produce better quality video. The codec used to compress a video also must be used to decompress the video when it is played.

FIGURE H-29: Creating movies for YouTube

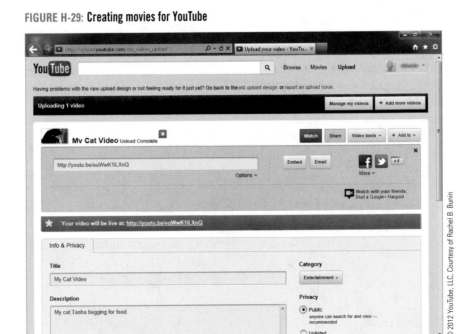

© 2012 YouTube, LLC. Courtesy of Rachel B. Bunin

Digital Media

Video Equipment and Software

At a very simple level, you can take digital video using a mobile device such as a smartphone or a Web cam. For higher-quality digital video, you use a digital video camera. Once you capture video, you use equipment to transfer the video to a computer for editing or viewing. If you edit video, you use video editing software.

Learning Objective 8:
Identify and describe how to use digital video equipment and video editing software

● **Can I use a mobile device to capture digital video?**
Yes. Many mobile devices, such as a smartphone, include a camera that stores video footage on the device's internal hard drive or memory card. The video quality produced by these cameras is not as high as the footage produced by dedicated digital video cameras. Video from handheld devices can be emailed directly to friends or to yourself, which is an easy way to get it to your computer for editing. Alternatively, your mobile device might store video footage on a memory card that you can use to transfer the footage to your computer. Most mobile devices also allow you to upload videos directly to YouTube and other video sharing sites.

● **When would I use a Web cam?** Web cams are most often used for video chatting. Typically, they produce low-quality video. Most Web cams must remain tethered or are built into your computer. Web cams are controlled by various software applications, including instant messenger clients, video chat clients, and specialized Web cam software that is bundled with new computers and add-on Web cams.

● **What equipment do I need for filming digital video?** Usually, you can use a digital video camera to capture digital video footage. See Figure H-30. A **digital video (dv) camera** stores footage as digital data. Most of today's dedicated digital video cameras store data on solid state memory cards, but storage options also include solid state drives, miniDVDs, digital tape, or built-in hard drives. Because a digital video camera captures video data in digital format, video can be transferred directly to a computer for editing.

FIGURE H-30: Digital video cameras

Courtesy of JVC America; Carlos E. Santa Maria/Shutterstock.com; Courtesy of RED Digital Cinema-product illustration is a design concept subject to change

You can also use an analog video camera to shoot analog video footage that you must convert the analog video footage to a digital video format before you can work with it on a computer. There is software available to help you do this.

● **How do I transfer digital video footage to my computer?** To digitally edit and process digital video, you must transfer the video footage from its source to your computer. The basic method for transferring video footage to your computer is to either place the memory card in a card reader on your computer or send the data over a cable that connects your video source to your computer (Figure H-31).

FIGURE H-31: Transferring video to a computer

Courtesy of MediaTechnics Corporation

- **How do I control the transfer process?** Some video editing programs have the controls you need to transfer your video from your camera to your computer. Some video editing programs also include video capture software. Video capture software allows you to start and stop the transfer, select a file format for storing your video footage, and specify the filename for each video clip. A **video clip** is a small video file in a video format. Large video files are often composed of many video clips. Some video capture software automatically creates clips. It is easier to edit a video if it is divided into several files, each containing a one- or two-minute video clip.

- **How do I edit a video?** After your video footage is transferred to your computer, you can edit your video by using video editing software. As you edit, you can arrange your video clips. You can add transitions. You can add audio, such as voice and music. The video tracks and the audio tracks can be arranged on a timeline. The video editing software combines the data from all of the selected tracks into a single file. Most video editing software allows you to set the file format, frame rate, color depth, and compression levels as you are saving the video in its final form.

 There are two types of video editing. **Linear editing** moves footage from one videotape to another. **Nonlinear** editing uses a random-access device, such as a hard drive, to hold both the original footage and finished video. Today, nonlinear editing simply requires a computer with **video editing software**, such as Adobe Premiere, Apple Final Cut Pro, Windows Live Movie Maker (Figure H-32), or Corel VideoStudio. The advantage of nonlinear editing is that you can edit and arrange video clips easily. Video editing requires lots of hard drive space, so make sure your computer has several gigabytes of available storage space before you start editing.

- **How can I make my own professional-looking DVD video?** You can use DVD authoring software which provides the tools you need to package completed video footage into a professional-style DVD. Using DVD authoring software, you can include interactive menus on your video with options, such as Play Video, Select a Scene, and Special Features, that viewers can select using their DVD remote controls. To do this, you need a writable DVD drive (DVD burner) plus DVD authoring software, such as Windows DVD Maker (Figure H-33), to design menus and buttons that viewers can use to navigate to specific parts of your video. Be sure to test your project, and then burn it to DVD.

FIGURE H-33: **DVD authoring software**

- **Will my DVD video play on a stand-alone DVD player?** To create a DVD that can be viewed on a stand-alone DVD player, you have to output your video in DVD Video format, which requires video encoded with MPEG2 and stored in VOB (video object) files. Most DVD authoring software can accomplish the MPEG encoding as it burns the DVD. This process takes time, however, so you might want to consider creating a DVD image. A **DVD image** (also called a DVD volume) is essentially a prototype of your DVD stored on your computer. You can use a DVD image for testing. You can also use the image to burn multiple DVDs without waiting for your software to prepare the files for each burn.

FIGURE H-32: **Video editing software**

Preview window Storyboard area

Unit H

Reference Tables for Media Files

TABLE H-1: **Popular file formats for audio**

Audio Format/Extension	Advantages	Disadvantages
Advanced Audio Compression (AAC) .aac	Very good sound quality; compressed format, used on files available via the iTunes music download site	Files are copy protected and use is limited to approved digital devices
Audio Interchange File Format (AIFF) .aif	Excellent sound quality; supported in browsers without a plug-in	Audio data is stored in raw, uncompressed format, so files are very large
MP3 (also called MPEG-1 Layer 3) .mp3	Good sound quality even though the file is compressed; can be streamed over the Web	Requires a stand-alone player or browser plug-in
RealAudio .ra, .ram	High degree of compression produces small files; data can be streamed over the Web	Sound quality is not up to the standards of other formats; requires a player or plug-in
Wave .wav	Good sound quality; supported in browsers without a plug-in	Audio data is stored in raw, uncompressed format, so files are very large
Windows Media Audio (WMA) .wma	Compressed format, very good sound quality; used on music download sites	Files can be copy protected; requires Windows Media Player 9 or above
Ogg Vorbis .ogg	Free, open standard; supported by some browsers; supplies audio stream for Google's WebM format	Newer format so not commonly used

TABLE H-2: **Popular file formats for graphics**

Format/Extension	Description
BMP .bmp	Native bitmap graphic file format for the Microsoft Windows environment; supports True Color; used for GUI elements, and for a wide variety of graphics applications
TIFF .tif	Tagged Image File Format is highly flexible and supported by most photo editing software packages; supports True Color; used for high resolution scanned images and digital photos
JPEG .jpg	Joint Photographic Experts Group; a graphics format with built-in compression that stores True Color bitmap data efficiently in a small file; used for photographic or scanned images
GIF .gif	Graphics Interchange Format; specifically designed to create images that can be displayed on multiple platforms, GIF graphics are limited to 256 colors; used for Web graphics; uses a built-in compression algorithm patented by Unisys
PNG .png	Portable Network Graphics format used as an alternative to GIF for Web graphics; can display up to 48-bit True Color; is a public domain format without any restrictions on its use
RAW .raw	Used by professional and semi-professional photographers to capture images before they are stored in other formats
SVG .svg	Scalable Vector Graphics format is designed specifically for the Web; automatically resized when displayed on different screens such as handheld computers and cellular phones or when printed
SWF .swf	Flash graphics format; they require less storage space than SVG graphics and require the Flash Player plug-in to be viewed in a browser

TABLE H-3: **Popular file formats for desktop video**

Format/Extension	Players/Platform; Description
AVI (Audio Video Interleave) .avi	Microsoft Media Player/PC; format for storing digital clips from video cameras
QuickTime Movie .mov	PC, Mac, UNIX, Linux; one of the most popular formats for desktop and streaming Web videos
MPEG (Moving Pictures Experts Group) .mpg, .mpeg	PC, Mac, UNIX, Linux; versions include MPEG1, MPEG2, and MPEG4; used for desktop video, and streaming Web video
RealMedia .rm	PC, Mac, UNIX, Linux; produced by RealNetworks, a popular format for streaming Web videos
ASF (Advanced Systems Format) .asf, .wm	PC; container format for Microsoft's Windows Media Video (WMV) desktop and streaming video
Flash Video .flv	PC, Mac; popular for Web-based video; requires Adobe Flash Player
VOB (Video Object) .vob	Stand-alone DVD players, PCs, Macs, Linux; industry-standard format for stand-alone DVD players
Blu-ray Disc Movie .bdmv	PC, Mac; format used for storing HD video clips to Blu-ray disc
WebM .webm	PC, Mac: UNIX, Linux: Royalty-free, high-quality open format for use with HTML5

Talking Points: Who Owns the Rights?

Suppose you purchase a music CD of your favorite recording group. Now you want to transfer the music to your computer, rip the best tracks, and transfer these songs to your portable media player. As you attempt to copy the music files, you discover that the CD is copy protected and your computer CD drive will not copy the disc. Since you purchased the disc, shouldn't you be able to listen to the music on any device you choose? The answer depends on a concept called fair use and is often limited by technology called digital rights management.

First, let's take a look at the language and words that are important to the discussion of digital rights management.

Copyright is a form of legal protection that gives certain exclusive rights to the author of a program or the owner of the copyright. Disobeying copyright is against the law and can result in legal action such as imprisonment and fines. See Figure H-34. Copyright law gives you the right to make copies for your personal use and transfer works into a format that can be used on your equipment.

FIGURE H-34: **FBI anti-piracy warning**

Used with permission, www.fbi.gov

Digital rights management (DRM) is a collection of techniques used by copyright holders to limit access and use of digital content. In the context of DRM, digital content (or simply content) usually refers to movies, music, e-books, and computer games because DRM is primarily used to protect products associated with the entertainment industry. Digital content is accessed by means of a player. Keep in mind that the term player can refer to a hardware device or software. Software players include familiar media players, such as iTunes, Windows Media Player, and QuickTime. Hardware players include stand-alone devices such as CD players, VCRs, DVD players, Blu-ray players, e-book readers, smartphones, and portable media players. Computer devices, such as CD, DVD, and Blu-ray drives, are also considered players, though they require software to play back content. DRM applies to both the content and player used to deliver the content.

Copy protection refers to technologies designed to prohibit consumers from copying content. CDs with copy protection cannot be duplicated and music that is ripped to another format does not play back correctly.

Signal scrambling is a term commonly used for obscuring cable or satellite television images until they are unscrambled by a set-top box or other authorized mechanism. With digital content, scrambling encrypts the digital bits of the signal. It is technically possible to build a device to unscramble signals, but it is illegal to use one.

DRM technologies such as digital watermarks, however, can further limit the use of unscrambled content. A **digital watermark** is a pattern of bits inserted at various places in an image or a content stream that can be used to track, identify, verify, and control content use. Watermarks, such as broadcast flags, are usually imperceptible to viewers or listeners, but can be picked up by compliant devices.

A **broadcast flag** is a set of bits inserted into the data stream of digital television or radio programs that specifies how the stream can and cannot be used. Broadcast flags can prohibit a program from being unencrypted or copied. They can limit copies to low resolution, such as by reducing high-definition video to the resolution of a standard television. In addition, broadcast flags can prevent fast-forwarding past commercials.

Copy generation management is a digital watermark that specifies the number of times a content stream can be duplicated. Compliant players recognize the watermark and abide by it. With the watermark set to no copy, for example, a video stream cannot be copied to other compliant devices. If a content stream carries a one-copy-only watermark, compliant devices can make one copy and then change the watermark to no-copies-allowed. As a result, second generation copies cannot be used to make additional copies. See Figure H-35.

FIGURE H-35: **How watermarks work**

Original DVD with one-copy-only watermark Compliant DVD burner DVD copy now contains do-not-copy watermark Compliant DVD burner will not copy the DVD

Courtesy of Media Technics Corporation

Digital Media

Fair use is the right to use portions of copyrighted material without the permission of the copyright holder for purposes such as review, criticism, or parody. Fair use is a successful defense under certain circumstances for practices, such as time shifting. However, exactly what does or does not constitute fair use is only sketched out in copyright law. The precise nature of fair use is shaped by a somewhat amorphous cloud of court decisions covering situations and devices as disparate as player piano rolls, printer toner cartridges, video tape recorders, and file-sharing networks.

Time shifting is the process of recording a broadcast, such as a television show, so that it can be played back at a more convenient time. As one of the original time-shifting technologies, video cassette recorders (VCRs) made it possible to set a recording time to capture movies and shows broadcast on television or cable channels. Digital video recorders (DVRs), such as TiVo, make time shifting possible by saving content to a digital storage device, such as a hard drive. The legal precedent for time shifting is the landmark 1984 Betamax case in which Universal Studios attempted to hold Sony Corporation of America liable for copyright infringement by people who used video recorders to tape movies from their televisions. The U.S. Supreme court sided with Sony and concluded that some instances of time shifting were legal. The court's decision, however, was based on a definition of time shifting as "the practice of recording a program to view it once at a later time." Note the word "once." The Betamax case did not offer legal precedent for copying and saving content for viewing multiple times. The Supreme Court was influenced by testimony from copyright holders, such as the host of the well-known children's show *Mister Rogers' Neighborhood*, who welcomed the practice of time shifting. At the time, some TV guides even listed shows that networks permitted viewers to copy.

Place shifting allows media that originates in one place to be accessed from another place without changing the device on which it is stored. Place shifting is often achieved using computer networks, such as when you view a cable television broadcast sent from your Wi-Fi equipped set-top box to your Wi-Fi equipped notebook. The proliferation of computer networks and streaming media has made place shifting a reality. For example, a Slingbox, see Figure H-36, is a place-shifting device that redirects video content from a cable box, satellite receiver, or digital video recorder to a remote computer, tablet, or smartphone. Content is delivered over a LAN or the Internet so you can watch your recorded content or live TV anywhere in the world. The television broadcast or recorded content is sent from your Wi-Fi equipped set-top box in your home to your Wi-Fi equipped device. Your

FIGURE H-36: **Slingbox**

Courtesy of
Sling Media, Inc

Wi-Fi network, however, is transmitting a copy of the broadcast, which is a use of copyrighted work that is explicitly not allowed by copyright law in most countries. Therefore, place shifting would be considered to be a questionable practice unless a user agreement extends the basic rights granted by copyright law.

Format shifting is the process of converting media files from a format suitable to one device to a format suitable for a different kind of device. A common use of format shifting is ripping audio tracks from a CD and converting them into MP3 format for playback on a portable audio device, such as an iPod. Surely, it must be legal to rip tracks from a CD that you own, save them as MP3 files, and play them on your iPod. Many consumers believe that format shifting is a legal form of adaptation. Perhaps they base this belief on the fact that it is true for computer software. According to the Copyright Law of the United States of America and Related Laws Contained in Title 17 of the United States Code section 117, "...it is not an infringement for the owner of a copy of a computer program to make or authorize the making of another copy or adaptation provided:

(1) that such a new copy or adaptation is created as an essential step in the utilization of the computer program in conjunction with a machine and that it is used in no other manner, or

(2) that such new copy or adaptation is for archival purposes only and that all archival copies are destroyed in the event that continued possession of the computer program should cease to be rightful."

It might seem that digital content, such as an MP3 file, is similar to a computer program because both are in digital formats that can be manipulated by computers. The courts, however, do not agree that the two are the same, so consumers do not have a right to format shift movies and music. Copyright holders, however, can allow format shifting for specific works if they choose to do so.

It is interesting to consider the basis for the widely held belief that once a song or video has been purchased, consumers have a right to use it in any manner they please short of redistributing it for profit. Precedents for this belief exist in the music and publishing industries. Although it is not well known, no U.S. law protected recorded music until 1971. Sheet music and the underlying composition could be copyrighted, but a particular artist's performance was not. So-called record pirates could freely copy, say, an Elvis Presley recording without violating U.S. Federal law until an amendment to the copyright law was passed in 1971. A statement accompanying the 1971 amendment seemed to approve of copying music for personal use: "Specifically, it is not the intention of Congress to restrain the home recording, from broadcasts or from tapes or records, of recorded performances, where the home recording is for private use and with no purpose of reproducing or otherwise capitalizing commercially on it."

> **Specifically, it is not the intention of Congress to restrain the home recording, from broadcasts or from tapes or records, of recorded performances, where the home recording is for private use and with no purpose of reproducing or otherwise capitalizing commercially on it.**

Now that you have an understanding of the key terms used in this discussion, let's discuss what consumers know about copyright restrictions on printed books and the expectation that digital media can be legally used in parallel ways. Readers expect to be able to carry a book with them to any location, read it at any time they like, use any type of reading light or reading glasses, loan the book to friends, and sell the book when they have finished using it. No wonder consumers are peeved when e-book vendors and other digital content providers use DRM technology to limit how much of an e-book can be viewed, whether the text can be printed or shared, and for how long it can be viewed.

Although it is convenient to focus on the "once I buy it I can use it as I like" rationale, we tend to ignore situations in which our expectations about content use are more limited. From rock concerts to theaters, consumers are familiar with the idea that different venues and formats might require separate payments. For example, we do not expect that after attending a Bruce Springsteen concert, we are entitled to a free DVD or video of the performance. If we pay to see a movie at a theater, we don't then expect not to pay for the DVD or soundtrack CD when they are released. Digital rights management technologies simply enforce this idea in practice. Advocates of DRM even contend that it broadens the scope of what consumers can do with digital content because End User License Agreements (EULAs) often provide consumers with more flexibility than today's copyright laws. However, opponents of DRM fear that the growing pervasiveness of digital rights management may curtail consumers' abilities to exercise these rights, such as place shifting, time shifting, and format shifting.

> **Advocates of DRM even contend that it broadens the scope of what consumers can do with digital content because End User License Agreements (EULAs) often provide consumers with more flexibility than today's copyright laws.**

Circumventing DRM is possible and it would seem okay to do so for legitimate reasons, such as making backup or archival copies. However, the Digital Millennium Copyright Act makes it illegal to circumvent any technological measure that controls access to a work. The current status of DRM seems to conflict with consumer fair-use expectations for manipulating and copying music, video, and other digital content. DRM technologies are still evolving, however, as are copyright laws. The Digital Millennium Copyright Act undergoes a formal review every three years, and a bill is circulating in Congress to revise the DMCA ban on circumventing DRM protection for non-infringing activities. To date, all DRM systems have failed to meet the challenge of protecting the rights of the rights holder while also allowing the use of the rights of the purchaser. None has succeeded in preventing criminal copyright infringement by organized, unlicensed, commercial pirates. It will be interesting to see whether the future produces a shift that creates a balance among fair use, digital rights management, and copyright law.

> **Opponents of DRM fear that the growing pervasiveness of digital rights management may curtail consumers' abilities to exercise these rights, such as place shifting, time shifting, and format shifting.**

Expand the Ideas

1. Do you believe that it is or it is not against the law to download music from the Web and create CDs or to copy purchased music for personal use? Why or why not? Write a short paper supporting your position.

2. Research three current music-sharing networks. Are their policies stated on their Web sites? What restrictions, if any, do they impose on music downloaded from their sites? Create a table to compile your findings. Write a brief summary comparing and contrasting the trends that you found.

3. Can you envision any way to create a system for digital rights management that not only protects the rights of the artists and publishers but is fair to consumers? Use the Internet to research the current state of DRM for music and video. Are new technologies being developed? Have any existing technologies generated controversy? Write a short paper discussing your findings. Be sure to include your sources.

Key Terms & Unit Review

Key Terms

24-bit bitmap graphic
32-bit bitmap graphic
Bitmap graphic
Bitrate
broadcast flag
Card reader
CCD (Charged coupled device)
Codec (compressor/decompressor)
Color depth
Color palette
Compression algorithm
Compression ratio
Copyright
Copy generation management
Copy protection
Cropping
Data compression
Density
Desktop video

Digital audio
Digital camera
Digital graphics
Digital rights management (DRM)
Digital signal processor
Digital video
Digital video (dv) camera
Digital video recorder (DVR)
Digital watermark
Drawing software
DVD image
Fair use
File compression software
Format shifting
Frame rate
Gradient
Grayscale palette
Integrated audio
Linear editing
Megapixel

Metafile
MIDI (Musical Instrument Digital Interface)
MIDI sequence
Nonlinear editing
Phoneme
Photosites
Pixel
Pixel interpolation
Place shifting
Raster graphic
Rasterization
Ray tracing
Rendering
Resolution
Resolution dependent
Sampling rate
Scanner
Signal scrambling
Sound card
Speech recognition

Speech recognition software
Speech synthesis
Streaming audio
Streaming video
Streaming video technology
Synthesized sound
System palette
Text-to-speech software
Time shifting
True Color bitmap graphic
Vector graphic
Video
Video clip
Videoconferencing camera
Video editing software
Wavetable
Web palette
Wireframe

Unit Review

1. Use your own words to define bold terms that appear throughout the unit. List 10 of the terms least familiar to you and write a sentence for each of them.

2. Explain the hardware necessary to create sound in a digital device. How is the hardware different for a laptop, tablet, or desktop computer?

3. Make a list of three types of software mentioned in this unit, indicate the type of media that you would use with this software and the task that it helps you accomplish.

4. Describe ways to transfer photos from a digital camera to a computer.

5. Describe how resolution and color depth contribute to the file size of a graphic file.

6. Explain how a computer creates different colors, and how a color palette creates the colors you see in images.

7. Explain ways you can create a bitmap graphic, a vector graphic, and a 3D graphic. Make a list of the advantages and disadvantages of bitmap and vector graphics.

8. Explain the difference between speech synthesis and speech recognition.

9. Give two examples of why you would use MIDI sound and two examples of why you would use digital audio.

10. Name the equipment you would need to create a desktop video, and then give the steps for creating the desktop video.

Concepts Review

Select the best answer.

1. A _____ digitizes printed images.
 a. card reader c. scanner
 b. media player d. video camera

2. _____ specifies a standard way to store music data for synthesizers, electronic instruments, and computers.
 a. DRM c. Vector
 b. Wave d. MIDI

3. _____ is expressed as the number of horizontal and vertical pixels that the grid of a bitmap graphic contains.
 a. Resolution c. Depth
 b. Specification d. Pixelation

4. A(n) _____ graphic is resolution dependent, which means that the quality of the image relies on its resolution.
 a. digital c. analog
 b. bitmap d. vector

5. Color _____ refers to the number of colors available for use in a bitmap graphic.
 a. depth c. resolution
 b. map d. pixels

6. A color _____ holds the selection of available colors and allows you to select a group of colors to use for a bitmap graphic.
 a. palette c. resolution
 b. grid d. pixel

7. A _____ graphic contains the instructions that a computer needs to create the shape, size, position, and color for the graphic.
 a. bitmap c. wireframe
 b. rendered d. vector

8. Speech _____ is the process by which computers produce sound that resembles spoken words.
 a. recognition c. compression
 b. synthesis d. notation

9. _____ rate refers to the number of times per second that a sound is collected or measured during the recording process, and it is expressed in hertz (Hz).
 a. Digital c. Sampling
 b. Bit d. Audio

10. Ray _____ is the process of adjusting the colors in a rendered image to coincide with the highlights and shadows that would be produced by a light source.
 a. tracing c. digitizing
 b. synthesis d. rendering

11. _____ video plays the video while continuing to receive it.
 a. Digital c. Streaming
 b. Synthesis d. Rendering

12. A _____ is a smooth blending of shades from one color to another or from light to dark.
 a. vector c. bitmap
 b. gradient d. rendering

13. File _____ software is a utility program that allows you to manually reduce the size of files.
 a. digitizing c. synthesis
 b. shrinking d. compression

14. A _____ compresses a video stream when a video is stored and decompresses the file when the video is played.
 a. codec c. player
 b. synthesizer d. vector

15. Each _____ in a picture is assigned a color, which is stored as a binary number in a file.
 a. element c. digit
 b. byte d. pixel

16. Audio can be _____ , digital, or synthesized.
 a. sound c. sampling rate
 b. analog d. waves

17. You can transfer images from a digital camera to a computer using any of the following except a(n) _____ .
 a. docking station c. infrared port
 b. cable d. codec

18. Which of the following devices is never used to capture digital video?
 a. scanner c. smartphone
 b. digital camera d. Web cam

19. AAC, AIF, MP3, Wave, and WMA are formats for which types of files?
 a. graphics c. video
 b. text d. audio

20. RAW, gif, tif, jpeg, and bmp are formats for which types of files?
 a. graphics c. video
 b. text d. audio

Independent Challenges

Independent Challenge 1

Digital graphics are fun—fun to create, fun to modify, and fun to share. There are many ways to create digital graphics. You can draw your own using graphics software. You can create photographs using a digital camera. You can get images from friends or colleagues, or you can buy or download images from the Web. Learning to use Paint software to modify and enhance your photos can be enjoyable, as well as challenging. You can use your computer to work with many types of media, such as photos, music, and videos. Your computer stores media that you've created and downloaded.

For this Independent Challenge:

1. What kinds of graphics, audio, and video files are on your computer? Did you create the files using software? Import them from a digital device? Did you download them from the Web? Give two examples of each type of media file that you found on your computer, and list how each came to be on your computer.

2. Modify a graphic you own.
 a. Select a photo or graphic that you own, one that either you took or someone gave to you, that you have the right to modify. If you have a Windows computer, open the file using Paint. If you are working on a Mac, open the file using Paintbrush or any other graphics editing program on your computer.
 b. Save the file with a new name so you still have the original.
 c. Use the various Paint tools to create a new masterpiece. See Figure H-37 for an example of what can be done to an ordinary photograph.

FIGURE H-37: **Using Paint to enhance a photo**

Courtesy of Rachel B. Bunin

Independent Challenge 2

Do you own a portable media player (one that plays not only songs but also video)? Do you know someone who does? Do you share music with a friend? See Figure H-38. If you look at the advertisements that come with the local papers, you will see that most consumer electronics retailers and even mobile phone providers are selling a variety of portable media players. How can you know which is best for you?

For this Independent Challenge:

1. Research the latest offerings in portable media players. Find three leading manufacturers of portable media players. Research the latest offerings by cell phone companies regarding their smartphones phones with multimedia capabilities, as well as any portable media players they sell that are not phones.

2. For portable media players, what is the range of prices? How is price related to features? Storage?

3. List any accessories that you might want to purchase with the device. For example, can you use it to play music through your home stereo? Can you use it to play music in your car?

4. Create a table comparing features and prices. Determine which device has the best value. Write a summary of your findings and which portable media player you might purchase.

FIGURE H-38: **Listening to digital music**

© Lev Olkha/Shutterstock.com

Independent Challenge 3

The hardware used for digital media is evolving at a very rapid pace. Technology that was once the toolbox of professionals is now readily available for the consumer market. You can research and, eventually, purchase scanners, digital cameras, digital video cameras, digital video recorders, and a variety of portable media players that combine audio, video, and now even Web connectivity in local electronics shops, and even at online stores on the Web.

For this Independent Challenge:

1. Form a group with several of your classmates.

2. Use the local paper or Internet advertisements to research and then select up to five different digital media devices, such as a scanner, professional microphone, digital camera, Web camera, digital video camera, or digital video recorder. If some of the members of your group own a device, ask them to bring it in.

3. If a member of your group owns a digital camera, create a series of photos for each of the products. If possible, post the images on an image management Web site such as www.kodakgallery.com, www.dotphoto.com, or www.flikr.com. You can even create a print advertisement from the photos using photo editing software or even a presentation program like PowerPoint.

4. Create materials for a tradeshow booth featuring your products. Create a poster and marketing materials. See Figure H-39 for a sample ad. You might include a product photo, list of specifications, and short instruction manual. Be sure to research and include technical specifications as well as a list of applications.

5. If possible, create a 2- to 3-minute video commercial for the product. If you cannot film the commercial, create a storyboard for it. If possible, post the video on a Web site, such as YouTube. Refer to the tips that follow for creating good videos.
 - Use a tripod to maintain a steady image.
 - Move the camera slowly to pan from side to side.
 - Zoom in and out slowly.
 - Direct your subjects to move slowly, when possible.
 - Position your shot to eliminate as much background detail and movement as possible.
 - Ask the subjects of your video to wear solid-colored clothing, if possible.

6. If time permits, your instructor might ask your group to present your sales presentation to the rest of the class.

FIGURE H-39: **Sample advertisement**

Courtesy of Emily Bunin

Guide to Buying a Computer

As you prepare to buy a computer or other electronic device, such as a portable media player, digital camera, or video camera, there are a lot of decisions you have to make. This course is designed to help you build the knowledge base you need to make these purchases. In this unit, you learned about digital media—images, sound, and video. Each unit in this book covers topics that can help you understand the type of computer you need, the software and services that will enhance your computing experience, such as Internet access, digital media options, and so forth. After each unit, you are asked to answer questions by completing a worksheet. By the end of the book, your Guide to Buying a Computer worksheet will provide comprehensive information about buying a computer.

There are a wide variety of portable media players available today. When purchasing a portable player, you should consider which music formats you are likely to use, and then be sure to purchase a player that supports that file format. The specifications for a player include a list of the compatible file formats that can be played on that device. With the popularity of players, new models appear frequently. Most players include a screen, storage, personal organizer software, a few games, and a way to connect an external microphone and a memory card reader. You can use these versatile players to store a large collection of digital music, and you can use their hard drives as portable mass storage devices for document, photo, and video files. With some of these players, you can even use them as voice recorders and as personal organizers for storing contacts and appointments. As you can see, the current players do a whole lot more than play music. In fact, when the capability of a portable audio player extends beyond just audio, the device is called a portable media player. Portable media players are a good example of digital convergence since many are also mobile phones and include Wi-Fi Internet access.

To help you organize the information you will need when you are ready to buy a computer, you should complete the following activities.

1. Research the latest technology in smartphones that have digital media capabilities. Make a list of three smartphones. Compare the features by completing the following table:

Features	Phone 1	Phone 2	Phone 3
Does it have a digital camera? If yes, which of the following features does it include: flash, megapixels, image stabilizer, zoom, file formats, filters, other?			
Does it have a digital video camera? If yes, which of the following features does it include: megapixels, zoom, file formats, filters, other?			
Does it have a media player for audio? If yes, which features does it include?			
Does it have a media player for video? If yes, which features does it include?			
What other media capabilities does it have?			

© Cengage Learning

2. File compression programs generally use one of two methods for compressing data. One compression method, known as lossless compression, reduces the file size without any data loss and provides the means to compress a file and then reconstitute all of the data into its original state. Various techniques exist for lossless image compression. As a simple example, consider a type of lossless compression called run-length encoding. Run-length encoding (RLE) replaces a series of similarly colored pixels with a code that indicates the number of pixels and their colors. Suppose that a section of a picture has 167 consecutive white pixels, and each pixel is described by one byte of data, as in a 256-color bitmap image. RLE compresses this series of 167 bytes into as few as two bytes. In contrast, another compression method, known as lossy compression, throws away some of the original data during the compression process. Lossy compression can be applied to graphics, videos, and sounds because, in theory, the human eye or ear will not miss the lost information. Most lossy compression techniques provide adjustable compression levels so that you can decide how much data you can afford to lose.

If you have access to two cameras, create a scene, such as books on a table, and then take the same image with each camera. Transfer the images to your computer. Save the images in different formats, use different compression techniques for each version of the saved files. Name each file with a unique name. View each image in a photo viewer on your computer.

Compare the files based on compression techniques and different cameras used to create the files. What can you conclude?

3. As you worked through this book, you learned about personal computer systems and supporting devices. You have had the opportunity to answer questions and complete other worksheets with information that will help you when it is time to buy a computer, purchase the supporting devices, and set up the system to run securely. To help you think about your digital media needs, as well as your software needs to work with, listen to, or view the media that you create or purchase, complete this portion of the Guide to Buying a Computer worksheet.

Guide to Buying a Computer: Digital media considerations

Questions to consider	Pages where the topic is covered in this book (Refer to these pages to read more about the topic)	Notes (Add additional comments, clarifications, or ideas about each topic)
Portable Media Player Questions Do you own or plan to buy a portable media player? What features do you want in the player—audio? video? both? Do you want the player to include mobile phone technology? Will you need contact management software? Web browsing capability? Email software?		
Digital Camera Questions Do you own or plan to purchase a digital camera? What features do you want in the camera? What type of storage media? How much storage? What type of power or battery? What number of megapixels? Autofocus? Auto zoom? Single-lens reflex? Software included?		
Scanner Questions Are you buying a scanner? Do you want a multi-function scanner, one that also transmits images?		
Digital Video Camera Questions Do you own or plan to buy a digital video camera? What features do you want in the digital video camera? What type of storage media? How much storage? What type of power or battery? What number of megapixels? Autofocus? Auto zoom? Software included? Type of transfer to PC technology?		
Digital Video Recorder Questions Do you own or plan to buy a Digital Video Recorder (DVR)? Type of features? Amount of storage?		

© Cengage Learning

Visual Workshop

Digital photography and digital cameras have changed the way we view and manage images. Without having to incur the cost of film or the cost and time of developing images, you can enjoy the freedom of taking as many pictures as your digital camera memory card will permit. You can send and share pictures instantly with friends and family in your home or across the world. Online photo sites, such as www.flickr.com, www.kodakgallery.com, www.Shutterfly.com, and www.Snapfish.com, make it possible to upload and organize the images. Once on the Web, these sites provide features for sharing the photos with friends and colleagues. Viewing the photos online is free and you can create communities to comment on the photos. People who view your online photos can order prints or a variety of products such as albums, t-shirts, and mugs with printed images.

Digital image manipulation is readily available at the consumer level with affordable software packages that put professional tools right on the desktop. Adobe Photoshop and Corel PaintShop Pro are two of many commercial packages that are available. The free Paint program (Figure H-40) that comes with Windows offers some excellent tools to manipulate your image. Most photo editing software includes professional digital editing tools for your photos. Most digital cameras come with some kind of proprietary software that you can use to not only download and save files but also to erase lines and reduce red eye.

FIGURE H-40: Editing a photograph in Paint

1. Log on to the Internet and search for information on digital photography. List three interesting facts that you find about camera and software manufacturers, new trends in digital photography, and image processing.

2. Use your favorite search engine to find three online photo sites. Create a comparison chart for the three sites. List and compare features such as services offered, products offered, pricing, and various options.

3. Review current digital image manipulation software packages. Make a comparison chart for at least three software packages. Write a summary paragraph indicating how the packages are alike, how they are different, and why a consumer might purchase one over the other.

Technology, Careers, and Job Hunting

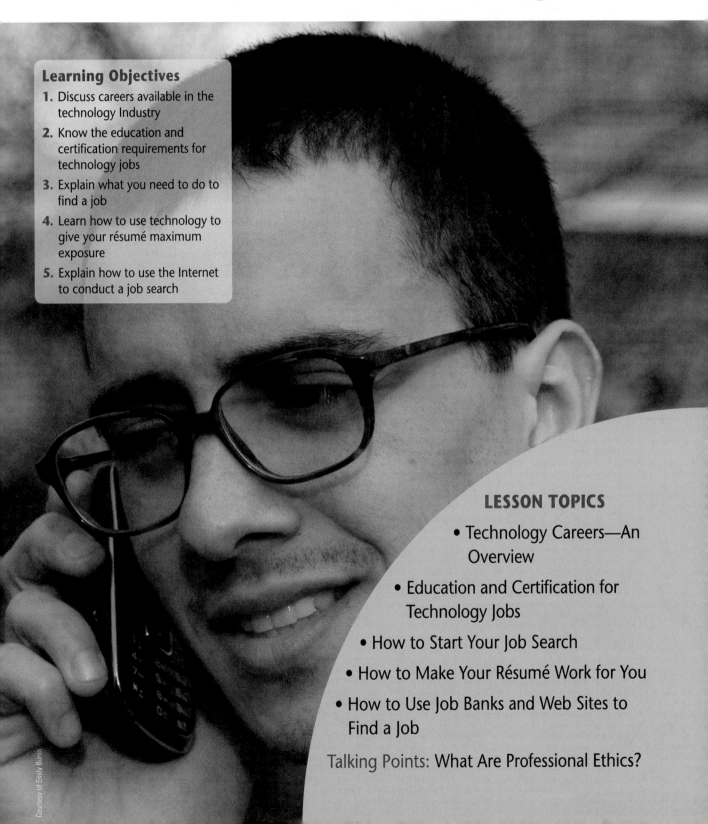

Learning Objectives

1. Discuss careers available in the technology Industry
2. Know the education and certification requirements for technology jobs
3. Explain what you need to do to find a job
4. Learn how to use technology to give your résumé maximum exposure
5. Explain how to use the Internet to conduct a job search

LESSON TOPICS

- Technology Careers—An Overview
- Education and Certification for Technology Jobs
- How to Start Your Job Search
- How to Make Your Résumé Work for You
- How to Use Job Banks and Web Sites to Find a Job

Talking Points: What Are Professional Ethics?

Courtesy of Emily Bunin

Technology Careers—An Overview

Even if you work in a fast food restaurant, you need to know how to use a computer. But who writes the software that all these workers use? Who designs the hardware, sets up the networks, and helps with technical problems? If you are considering a career as a computer professional, you will need to know about the computer industry and the types of computer jobs that are available.

Learning Objective 1:
Discuss careers available in the technology industry

● **What is the computer industry?** The term **computer industry** includes companies that manufacture computers and computer components, software publishers, and peripheral device manufacturers. The term **information technology (IT) industry** is used to refer to the companies that develop, produce, sell, or support computers, software, digital communications, and computer-related products.

● **What is a computer professional?** A **computer professional** is any person who designs, configures, analyzes, develops, tests, or ensures the security of computer hardware or software.

● **Where do computer professionals work?** Many computer professionals work in a company's **Information Technology (IT) department**, which is responsible for a company's computers, data, software, and support services. This group determines an organization's information needs, as well as creates, maintains, and updates its information systems. The IT Department is sometimes called the **Information Systems (IS) department** or the **Management Information Systems (MIS) department**.

● **How is an IT department organized?** A **chief information officer (CIO)** heads most IT departments. Under the CIO is a staff of computer professionals whose members are often grouped under programming services and computer operations. Figure I-1 shows the structure of a typical IT department in a mid-sized business. Table I-1 shows IT jobs grouped into eight clusters along with a sampling of job titles in each cluster.

● **What are some examples of IT jobs?** The following lists brief descriptions of some IT jobs:

■ A **systems analyst** investigates the requirements of a business or organization, its employees, and its customers in order to plan and build new or improved computer services. This job requires good communications skills for interacting with managers and other employees.

FIGURE I-1: **Structure of a typical IT department**

© Cengage Learning

- A **computer programmer** (sometimes called a **programmer/analyst**) designs, codes, and tests computer programs. In addition, programmers modify existing programs to meet new requirements or fix bugs.

- A **security specialist** analyzes a computer system's vulnerability to threats from viruses, worms, unauthorized access, and physical damage. They install and configure firewalls and antivirus software. They develop policies and procedures to protect computer equipment and data.

- A **database administrator** analyzes a company's data to determine the best way to collect and store it. They create databases, data entry forms, and reports. They supervise day-to-day database use.

- A **network specialist/administrator** plans, installs, and maintains one or more local area networks. These specialists also provide network accounts and access rights to approved users. They troubleshoot connectivity problems, respond to network user requests for new software, and may be responsible for maintaining the security of a network.

- A **computer operator** typically works with servers, mainframes, and supercomputers. They monitor computer performance, install software patches and upgrades, perform backups, and restore data.

- A **technical support specialist** troubleshoots hardware and software problems. Some work in-house with company employees, while others provide phone support to customers.

- A **Web site designer** creates, tests, posts, and modifies Web pages. This job requires a good sense of design and artistic talent, and an understanding of how people use graphical user interfaces. Familiarity with Web tools, such as HTML, XML, and JavaScript and knowledge of programming and database management is important.

● **What are some examples of computer professionals who work outside of IT departments?** The following jobs represent some of the positions available at computer hardware and software companies:

- A **technical writer** creates documentation for large programming projects and writes the online or printed user manuals that accompany computers, peripheral devices, and software. Some technical writers write columns about the latest hardware and software. Good writing skills are essential, as is an ability to quickly learn how to use new computers and software.

- A **computer salesperson**, or **sales rep**, sells computers. Sales reps might visit potential corporate customers or staff the order desk of a mail-order computer company. Effective sales reps have good people skills, and they can understand business problems and solutions.

- A **quality assurance (QA) specialist** participates in alpha and beta test cycles of software, looking for bugs or other usability problems. This job title sometimes refers to assembly-line workers who examine and test chips, circuit boards, computers, and peripheral devices.

- A **computer engineer** designs and tests new hardware products, such as computer chips, circuit boards, computers, and peripheral devices.

- A **manufacturing technician** participates in the making of computer chips, circuit boards, system units, or peripheral devices. Some of these jobs require special training.

● **Are there IT jobs where I can work from my home office?** Workers in many industries prefer to **telecommute**. They use technology to work from home or another off-site location. Employees work together remotely through virtual private networks, email, Web apps, groupware, messaging, chatting, and videoconferencing.

TABLE I-1: Information Technology Association of America (ITAA) job categories and sample job titles

ITAA job category	Sample jobs	ITAA job category	Sample jobs
Database Administration and Development	Database Administrator Database Analyst Database Developer	Programming/Software Engineering	Applications Analyst; OS Programmer/Analyst; Program Manager
Digital Media	2D/3D Artist/Animator Audio/Video Engineer Media/Instructional Designer	Technical Support	Call Center Support Rep; Customer Service Rep; Help Desk Specialist/Technician
Enterprise Systems Analysis and Integration	Application Integrator Data Systems Designer Data Systems Manager	Technical Writing	Desktop Publisher; Documentation Specialist; Instructional Designer
Network Design and Administration	Communications Analyst Network Administrator Network Analyst	Web Development and Administration	Web Administrator Web Architect/Designer; Web Master

Unit I

Education and Certification for Technology Jobs

For most IT-related jobs, you need some type of higher education, certification, or computer experience. A bachelor's degree in a computer-related area is a common requirement, but some employers accept a two-year associate's degree. A master's or doctoral degree can lead to an advanced position. Certification can also help you advance.

Learning Objective 2:
Know the education and certification requirements for technology jobs

● **What skills do I need to get a job in the computer industry?** The IT industry contains workers with many different skills. Jobs exist for highly focused programmers as well as outgoing sales reps and technical support specialists. Most of these jobs require a wide-ranging knowledge of computers. Many IT positions require you to plan efficient ways to make a computer perform specific jobs and to identify problems and research technical solutions. You should have good interpersonal skills, good writing and communications skills, and an understanding of business problems and solutions. Computer professionals have to continue learning new skills to work with emerging technologies.

● **If I want a job in the IT industry, what degree programs and courses should I consider?** Colleges and universities offer many computer-related degrees:

■ **Computer engineering** focuses on computer hardware and peripheral device design at the chip level. At a university such as MIT (Figure I-2), courses toward the degree cover calculus, physics, computer architecture, chemistry, engineering, physics, computer organization, logic design, signal processing, computer architecture, and microprocessor design.

FIGURE I-2: **MIT offers many computer-related degrees**

© Jorge Salced/Shutterstock.com

■ **Computer science** focuses on computer architecture and how to program computers. Course topics include calculus, physics, programming, computer architecture, data representation, logic design, calculus, discrete math,

physics, and software development. You will study how to write application and system software, computer languages, and device drivers.

■ **Information systems (IS) degree programs** focus on applying computers to business problems. IS programs are typically offered by a university's college of business. Students take courses in business, accounting, computer programming, and systems analysis. For students who want to become computer professionals but lack strong math aptitude, most academic advisors recommend the information systems degree.

■ **Information technology (IT) degree programs** focus on securing, upgrading, and maintaining the computer equipment and software businesses use. In IT programs, you work hands-on with hardware, networks, Web pages, and security.

■ **Software engineering degree programs** focus on developing reliable, user-friendly, and affordable software. Such programs include courses from computer science and information systems (IS) programs.

● **Besides a four-year degree, what other degree choices do I have?** Colleges, community colleges, and technical schools offer several computer-related associate's degrees, ranging from computer programming to graphic design, networking, and telecommunications. Graduates of two-year programs usually find jobs as entry-level technicians, programmers, or support staff. Advancement might be limited without additional education or certification.

● **Can an advanced degree help me?** Master's degrees in software engineering are available at large research universities. Master's degree programs in computer science are available at most four-year colleges and universities that offer graduate degrees. A master's degree qualifies you for management. Doctoral degrees in software engineering, applications software engineering, and management information systems qualify you for advanced

technical research or for a position as a college professor.

- **What is certification, and how can it help me in my career?** Along with a college degree or lengthy experience, certification can help you get a better job at a higher salary and increase your standing in the workplace. Certification falls into two broad categories: certificates of completion and certification exams.
 - A **certificate of completion** verifies that you have successfully completed one or more courses on a specific topic. Community colleges and technical schools offer certificates of completion in areas such as information technology specialist, user support specialist, and PC support specialist.
 - A **certification exam** verifies your knowledge level about a particular technology or subject. You can choose from about 300 computer-related certification exams in areas from desktop publishing to network installation. Most of these exams cost money.

- **What kinds of certification exams are there?** Certification exams fall into the following categories:
 - **General computer knowledge**. IC3 certification, offered by Certiport, covers basic computing knowledge and skills. See Figure I-3. General certification is also offered by the College Board's Computer Skills Placement (CSP). The Institute for Certification of Computing Professionals (ICCP) offers several generalized certification exams in accounting and banking, education, manufacturing, and many other fields.

FIGURE I-3: **Certification exams verify your knowledge of a particular subject**

© DAJ / Getty Images

 - **Software applications**. Many certification exams test knowledge of a specific software application. The Microsoft Office Specialist (MOS) certification is most useful for entry-level secretarial and clerical positions as well as help desk staff. Autodesk offers the AutoCAD Certified User exam on the use of its 3D design software. You can also get certified to use Adobe software applications such as Illustrator, InDesign, Photoshop, Premiere, Dreamweaver, Flash, and ColdFusion.
 - **Database administration.** Databases require a high level of skill, not only in the use of database software, but in database concepts and design. Many computer professionals are certified in database systems, such as Access, Sybase, and DB2. The most popular database certification exams include Oracle Certified Professional and Microsoft Certified Database Administrator (MCDBA). See Figure I-4.

FIGURE I-4: **Certification logo**

Microsoft
C E R T I F I E D
Database Administrator

© 2012 Microsoft

 - **Networking**. Among IT workers, network certification might be the most useful. Novell offers certification in the NetWare network operating system. Microsoft offers a corresponding Microsoft Certified Systems Engineer (MCSE) certification. Cisco Systems offers the Cisco Certified Network Professional (CCNP) certification. Wireless network certification, such as Wireless CWNP certification, is also available.
 - **Computer hardware**. One of the most popular hardware certification exams is the A+ Certification, sponsored by the Computing Technology Industry Association (CompTIA). It qualifies entry-level computer service technicians to install, configure, upgrade, troubleshoot, and repair computers and related equipment. A+ Certification provides good credentials for jobs in computer stores or repair shops.
 - **Computer security**. With the increasing number of computer viruses and worms, analysts predict that computer security will become a hot job area for IT workers. CompTIA offers the Security+ Certification exam. The (ISC)[2] offers a Certified Information Systems Security Professional (CISSP) exam.
 - **How can I study for a certification exam?** You can use books, online courses, or exam preparation classes. Visit Web sites to find educational programs and testing services. You can also locate more information on technical school, community college, and university Web sites.

Finding information on computer-related degree programs

Peterson's is a comprehensive resource for educational services. Its Web site at www.petersons.com has become a primary resource for locating educational programs. The College Board, www.collegeboard.com, is another source. Both the College Board and Peterson's maintain a searchable database of two-year, four-year, and graduate programs that prepare you for a variety of IT jobs. You can find additional information at the Web sites of various technical schools, community colleges, and universities.

How to Start Your Job Search

You might be a computer professional looking for work in the IT industry. Or, you might want to find a job in another industry. In either case, you should know how to use technology tools in your job search. You also need to show potential employers that you are capable and comfortable with technology and the Internet.

Learning Objective 3:
Explain what you need to do to find a job

● **How do I begin to find a job?** Begin by looking carefully at your qualifications and decide what you want to do. Find job titles related to your skills and seek out potential employers in the city or area where you want to work. Create a carefully worded résumé. Then look for job openings and contact employers. Work with school placement offices, employment agencies, and recruiting firms, and check the newspaper's Help Wanted section. Job hunting strategies are not the same for all industries, careers, or jobs. For example, looking for a job as an actor or perhaps as a civil servant might require auditions or elections. However, most jobs require that you follow a general strategy. Figure I-5 shows general steps in a typical job hunt.

FIGURE I-5: **Job hunting steps**

1. Define the job you want
2. Create your résumé
3. Look for job openings
4. Supply potential employers with résumé
5. Prepare for interviews
6. Evaluate job offers
7. Accept a new job

© Cengage Learning

● **What is a résumé?** A résumé is a written document that lists your career objective, skills, education, and work experience. It provides a written snapshot of you to potential employers, who use it to see if your skill set matches their needs. Potential employers often use a candidate's résumé to determine if they want to offer the candidate a job interview.

● **Should my résumé contain any special features?** Yes, your résumé should be written to match the job you want. For

example, your résumé should emphasize skills and experience related to the job you are pursuing. But, no matter which industry you want to work in, your résumé must be clear, correct, and easy to read. It is a good idea when preparing your résumé to ask friends, coworkers, and career counselors to read it and suggest improvements. See Figure I-6 for a checklist of résumé writing guidelines.

FIGURE I-6: **Résumé writing tips**

Tips for an Effective Résumé

Be clear and concise
✓ Eliminate unnecessary words, phrases, and sentences.
✓ Be economical with words when describing tasks, duties, titles, and accomplishments.
✓ Be brief and to the point without selling yourself short.

Place the most important point first
✓ List your qualifications by importance to the job you seek.
✓ Summarize skills at the top of the résumé.
✓ Use bold font to emphasize skills and accomplishments that are required for the position you seek.
✓ Include key information about training, certification, and professional affiliations, but avoid personal information, such as religion and hobbies, that is not directly related to the job.

Use language effectively
✓ Target terms and wording to prospective employers.
✓ Use industry jargon wherever appropriate.
✓ Use action verbs to maintain the reader's interest.
✓ Use past and present tenses consistently.
✓ Double-check grammar and spelling.
✓ When posting information in a database, use nouns that describe your skills.

© Cengage Learning

● **How should I prepare my résumé?** To show that you can take advantage of technology, format your résumé for a variety of different computer platforms and delivery methods such as for printed output, email delivery or Web site posting. Figure I-7 shows a sample résumé as a Word document, as an email message, and in a browser.

FIGURE I-7: **Ways to post a résumé**

Word document format

Email message format

HTML format

Used with permission from Microsoft

■ **Print.** You should save one version of your résumé as a well-formatted word processing file. Consider using desktop publishing software to put the finishing touches on your résumé before you print it on high-quality paper. Make sure the résumé file converts easily into a format such as PDF that can be read on Mac, PC, and Linux computers, in case a prospective employer asks you to send it as an email attachment.

■ **Email.** Before sending your résumé as an attachment, try to learn the format that your prospective employer wants. The Microsoft Rich Text Format produces files with .rtf extensions, which many word processing programs can read. Many people use the Adobe PDF format or the Microsoft document format. Some career counselors advise against using email attachments. They say that many employers never open attachments because they might contain email viruses. Instead of attaching your résumé, you can paste it into the body of an email message. To make sure many people can read it, especially those who might get and read your email message on a smartphone, you might create a plain text version of your résumé, without fancy fonts, bullets, or symbols. You can also use this text version for online job posting sites that store your résumé information in a searchable database.

■ **HTML and XML.** You might also want to create HTML and XML versions of your résumé. You can paste the HTML version into an HTML-formatted email message or post it on a Web site provided by your school or ISP.

● **Are formatting and paper choice important for my résumé?** Paper color, fonts, and wording are still important for hard-copy résumés. But today, résumés are often stored in online databases. These résumés are initially scanned not by human eyes, but by a computer.

Contract workers

The IT industry, as well as other industries, has many contract workers. **Contract workers** are usually hired as consultants and are not official employees of a company. They might be paid by the project or by the hour instead of being salaried, and they are not eligible for a company's health insurance benefits, vacation pay, or retirement plan. Businesses benefit because they can hire from a pool of contract workers temporarily, usually for the length of the project. Using contract workers means that employers can choose from a wide variety of people with specialized skills. If you are looking for a job as a contract worker, be sure your résumé emphasizes any special knowledge that will benefit the project. You also should include specific examples promoting your organizational skills, ability to stay focused, and drive as a self-starter. If you are offered a contract job, read your contract carefully so you fully understand the terms of employment.

Unit I

How to Make Your Résumé Work for You

Your résumé does you no good sitting on a hard drive or printed on your desk. You have to get it to potential employers and get it noticed.

Learning Objective 4:
Learn how to use technology to give your résumé maximum exposure

● **How can my résumé get maximum exposure?**
Because your résumé will likely be part of a computer-searchable database, experts recommend that you focus on nouns, not verbs. At one time, the trend was to pepper your résumé with action phrases and power verbs, such as "implemented successful solutions" and "created innovative algorithms." When employers use a job site's search engine to locate potential employees, however, they typically search for particular skills by entering nouns associated with programming language names, software, computer equipment, analysis methodologies, and business sectors. They might also enter buzzwords and acronyms, such as HTML5, B2B, and AJAX, which relate to specific IT tools and methods. Job seekers should try to envision the search terms that employers might enter, and then include applicable terms in their résumé.

In addition to computer-related terms, employers sometimes search for words that indicate a job applicant's personality, communication skills, and work ethic. When appropriate, adjectives such as enthusiastic, team player, industrious, honest, capable, and experienced can be effective in helping an online recruiter pull your résumé from those submitted by thousands of other applicants. To improve your chances of landing an interview (Figure I-8) and the job, you should review your résumé frequently to make sure the information is up to date.

FIGURE I-8: **A successful interview**

© Goodluz/Shutterstock.com

● **What is an ePortfolio?** A simple **ePortfolio** (also called **electronic portfolio** or **Web portfolio**) is a hypertext version of your résumé. But an enhanced ePortfolio can also contain links to Web sites of past employers, schools you have attended, and samples of your work. Similar to the way an artist shares a portfolio of works of art, an ePortfolio can be used to share samples of projects you have worked on. You can personalize your ePortfolio with photos or even videos that show your communications skills and your technology skills. You can share the URL to your ePortfolio with potential employers in order to showcase your talents. Remember, however, to keep the content of your ePortfolio professional. It should not contain any personal information or links to personal information, such as family photos, that you do not want to share professionally. There are several programs as well as Web sites (see Figure I-9) out there that can help you create and post your ePortfolio.

FIGURE I-9: **Web sites can help you create an ePortfolio**

© silver tiger/Shutterstock.com

● **Where do I post my ePortfolio?** You can post your ePortfolio on a professional network, such as LinkedIn. You can also post to a personal Web site. Just remember

that your personal Web site is an open book to prospective employers. If you don't want them to know the details about your spring break, you should remove such extraneous material from your Web site. Even if you don't mention your Web site to prospective employers, they can find it easily simply by entering your name in a search engine, such as Yahoo! or Google.

● **Can I use social networking to get my résumé noticed by potential employers?** Yes. If you have a Facebook page or other social networking page, employers can quickly find that page and view its contents. However, if there is content you do not want potential employers to see, be sure to share those with a limited audience and not publicly. Also be sure to search for photos that your friends might have posted and tagged as you. Ask them to remove the tags or even the photos.

● **Should I enhance my ePortfolio with multimedia?** Current technology gives you the ability to personalize your ePortfolio with photos, your favorite music, or even video portraits that demonstrate your speaking and communications abilities. However there are important points to consider before adding multimedia. For example, unless you are looking for a job in the music business or as a singer, you should probably not include music. It will be difficult to find tunes that please everyone. As a result, background music is more likely to irritate prospective

employers than impress them. In addition, photos and videos that indicate an applicant's age, gender, ethnicity, or physical characteristics also have potential drawbacks. While decisions based on such characteristics could be viewed as discriminatory, it would be difficult to prove. Therefore, you might want to keep multimedia presentations on hand but supply them only when requested.

● **What if I'm looking for work and don't want my current employer to know?** Many job seekers are hesitant to post their résumé or advertise their ePortfolio for fear that their current employers will learn they are considering changing jobs. If you post your résumé online, there are ways to limit who can see your posting. You will learn about job bank features in the next lesson. You should also review links for Help, Privacy, and Terms of Use on any site you post your résumé to.

● **Are there any risks involved with using the Internet to help distribute my résumé?** Yes, so be sure to follow the security and privacy tips provided throughout this book anytime you are on the Web. Remember that once information is on the Web, it is available to anyone, not just potential employers. Employers will search the Web and use information about you to get a picture of the person you are. So, you want to be vigilant and take care that information about you on the Web always shows you with your best foot forward. You would hate to be fired before you are even hired.

Examining outsourcing and offshoring

Increasingly, computer companies use **outsourcing**, which is buying parts and labor from outside suppliers. For example, a company might get its microprocessors from Intel, its hard drives from Seagate, and its LCD panels from Samsung. Why would a computer company do this? Because the source companies specialize in those components and can make them more cheaply and with better quality. They help computer companies keep prices low and stay competitive. Companies also outsource manufacturing, engineering, call centers, and software development. Software publishers also make use of outsourcing by hiring outside firms to develop products and manufacture packaging. Outsourcing offers economies of scale and expertise to companies in the highly competitive computer industry.

When companies began outsourcing to U.S. firms, people thought it was a good idea. But companies then started outsourcing jobs to other countries. See Figure I-10. This practice is known as **offshoring**. U.S. computer companies have established manufacturing and development facilities in countries such as China, India, Malaysia, Thailand, and Mexico, where labor is inexpensive but reliable. Companies such as Microsoft and Oracle often use programmers based in India. These workers telecommute, when nec-

essary, using the Internet. Computer manufacturer Dell Inc. has a staff of offshore technicians in its customer call centers. But some companies find that cost savings don't balance out the problems of offshoring, which can include language barriers, cultural differences, miscommunication, and bad service. Yet they know that U.S. consumers won't pay higher prices for U.S.-made products. So the use of offshore resources has become increasingly mainstream and, for some, controversial.

FIGURE I-10: Outsourcing jobs

© Michael D. Brown/Shutterstock.com

Technology, Careers, and Job Hunting

How to Use Job Banks and Web Sites to Find a Job

Not long ago, people used newspaper want ads, employment agencies, and head hunters to find a job. Today, using word processing, email, and job search Web sites, you can control your job search more than ever before.

Learning Objective 5:
Explain how to use the Internet to conduct a job search

- **How can I use the Internet to find a job?** You can use the Internet to research potential jobs and employers, and to post your résumé. The Internet can help you locate job leads and write to potential employers. But don't do all of your job searching online. Job-hunting experts advise IT job seekers to spend no more than 50 percent of their total job-hunting efforts online. They say to spend the other 50 percent contacting placement agencies, career counselors, and mentors. But your job needs, geographic location, and current job situation may also determine how much you use the Internet in your job search.

- **Where do I start?** You begin by defining the jobs for which you qualify. As you do, note that in the IT industry, job titles are not standardized. For example, the job title for a person who provides employee or customer support over the phone might be Help Desk Operator, Customer Support Technician, Support Specialist, Technology Support Specialist, or Inbound Telephone Service Consultant. Nonstandard titles for the same job can be a problem, especially if you are using search engines to find jobs. Not entering a particular job title might cause you to miss a good opportunity. Many job search sites have lists of equivalent job titles, but it is best to compile your own lists of job titles and search terms. To create your list, enter the search phrases *job titles* and *computer industry* into a search engine such as Google. When you visit the sites the search finds, you can make note of any job titles that seem right for you. You can then use these terms to continue refining your job search. In addition to searching the Web using search engines, you can search company Web sites and online job search banks.

- **How can company Web sites help me with my job search?** Many companies have Web sites with links to information about their job openings. If you have a list of companies that you'd like to work for, check out their Web sites. While visiting a company Web site, look for information about job openings.

 Once you are asked to interview with a company, you can visit the company Web site to get information about the company. A potential employer will take notice if you are knowledgeable about the company, its mission, its products, and so on during an interview. It is important to go into a job interview knowing about the company and how your skills can help support the company's mission. The company Web site can help you prepare for the interview.

- **What is an online job bank?** An **online job bank** is a database of thousands of job openings posted by employers, each with unique job announcements. The largest job banks cover almost every industry. Others are devoted to specific industries. Several online job banks, like the one in Figure I-11, specialize in the IT industry.

FIGURE I-11: **Online job bank**

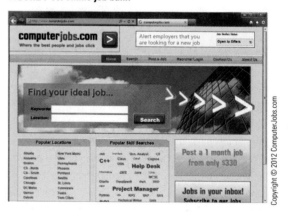

You can search most online job databases by job title, location, or company. These searches are typically free, although you might need to register before searching. You might want to automate your search to save time.

- **How can I automate my search?** Search agents and metasearch tools let you automate the search process across many sites. A **job search agent** is a program that automatically searches databases and notifies you when it finds any jobs that match your requirements. To use a job search agent, add keywords that describe the type of job you want, your preferred location, and salary requirements. When you launch the agent, it searches for matching jobs.

When it finds a match, the search agent sends you an email message with the information you need to view the job posting. Most job banks provide access to free job search agents. The key advantage of using a job search agent, like the one shown in Figure I-12, is that you do not have to be online while it works.

FIGURE I-12: **Job search agent**

A **metasearch engine** is a software program that searches the Web across more than one job database at a time. Instead of notifying you by email, a metasearch tool works like a standard search engine and supplies a list of links to applicable job postings. As a result, you must stay online when using a metasearch tool to research jobs.

- **How can I protect my privacy when using an online job bank?** When you register at an online job bank, be sure to use common sense to protect your privacy. For example, do not provide your Social Security number (SSN) online. You should only give your SSN to your employer once you receive a job offer and only then in person. You might consider removing most of your contact information, such as your address, phone number, or your business email address at your current job, from your online résumé. Some job banks might distribute your personal information to advertisers without asking you, so be sure to read the job bank's privacy policy and terms of use. Some job banks let you set an expiration date for your résumé. It is important to use this feature, just in case you forget to remove it when your job search is complete.

- **What other types of Web sites can help me find a job?** You can use Web sites that have classified advertisements, such as Craigslist. Classified advertisements are grouped into categories or classes such as *Items for sale*, *Housing-rent or sale*, or *Jobs*. Employers often list jobs on these Web sites. These Web sites sometimes focus their opportunities geographically. In addition to employers posting job opportunities, these sites often let you post your résumé and the type of job wanted.

- **Are there other ways to network using the Internet?** Yes, some social networking sites, such as LinkedIn (Figure I-13), are dedicated to linking employees and employers and discussions about jobs and careers. These sites offer personal and business profiles, groups, discussion forums, event coordination to help you reach others in your current or anticipated career field. If you have created an ePortfolio, you can include its URL as part of your LinkedIn profile. Others, including potential employers, who visit your LinkedIn page, will be able to view your ePortfolio. This is a great way to get your name out in the field.

FIGURE I-13: **Using LinkedIn to search for a job**

- **How will potential employers contact me?** You can open a Web-based email account specifically devoted to job hunting. By the way, consider your email user ID carefully. Employers might respond better to an email address such as SidneySimone@hotmail.com than to an address such as couchpotato@hotmail.com.

Keeping healthy in your career

Whether you work inside or outside the IT industry, you will probably spend a lot of time at a computer. So you should understand the effects that computer work can have on your body so you can have a safe and healthy work environment. **Ergonomics** is the study of safe and efficient environments, particularly working environments. The U.S. Occupational Safety and Health Administration (OSHA) describes ergonomics as "the science of designing the job to fit the worker, rather than physically forcing the worker's body to fit the job." OSHA has developed ergonomic guidelines to follow when setting up computer, desk, and lighting equipment to avoid potentially disabling musculoskeletal injuries. Be sure to review the Talking Points in Unit D, "Is Your Computer Making You Sick?"

Talking Points: What Are Professional Ethics?

Defining Ethics

The term **ethics** refers to the study of moral standards and how they affect our conduct in daily life. The term **professional ethics** refers to our on-the-job choices and actions that reflect our values. Professional ethics include standards of conduct that specify how workers should behave, particularly in situations where doing the right thing might not seem to have short-term benefits, or when doing something that might not be legal seems to offer attractive benefits. Situations where you ask yourself, "What is the right thing to do?" often require you to make ethical decisions. Professional ethics come from principles of right and wrong. In most modern societies, ethical decisions and actions are based on values such as impartiality, fairness, objectivity, honesty, regard for privacy, commitment to quality, and respect for others.

Society's ethics are based on laws, which define permissible behavior according to the society that created the laws. As computers and digital technologies play a more important role in every aspect of daily life, laws are being created to deal with ethical issues related to computer uses and abuses. While it is important to consider applicable laws as you make decisions, it is also important to remember that not all ethical behavior is regulated by laws. Indeed, some actions that are unethical, such as lying about what time you arrived at work or claiming a sick day to go shopping, are not illegal.

Ethical values such as honesty, fairness, respect, responsibility, and caring are universal. You encounter decisions involving these values every day. Some decisions are easy to make, and you make them without even giving the decision a second thought. Other decisions are more difficult, perhaps because the consequences of the decision can be negative. In the workplace, you must regularly make decisions that challenge ethical values.

Ethics and Computers

Situations that require computer professionals to make ethical decisions often involve software copyrights, privacy, conflicts of interest, use of work computers, software quality, hacking, and social responsibility. Every day, computer professionals must cope with ethical dilemmas in which the right course of action is not entirely clear—or in which the right course of action is clear, but the consequences (such as getting fired) are not easy to face. Suppose, for example, that you are hired to manage a local area network in a prestigious advertising agency. On your first day of work, your employer hands you a box containing the latest upgrade for Microsoft Office and asks you to install it on all the computers in the business. When you ask if the agency owns a site license, your boss responds, "No, do you have a problem with that?" What would you reply? Would you risk your job by insisting that the agency order enough copies for all the computers before you install it? Or would you go ahead and install the software, assuming that your boss would take responsibility for this violation of the software license agreement? What is the ethical thing to do? How is it that software copyrights can become an ethical issue?

As this example points out, sometimes computer professionals are pressured to engage in activities that are clearly unethical and that can even be illegal. These activities are sometimes justified with statements such as "Everyone does it," or "No one will know." Employees might be assured, "You won't be responsible," or "It's for the good of the company." Such justifications are not, however, always true or appropriate. And even if these statements were true, would the action in the example be any more justified because of these excuses?

> "...sometimes computer professionals are pressured to engage in activities that are clearly unethical and that can even be illegal. These activities are sometimes justified with statements such as 'Everyone does it' or 'No one will know'."

Workers in corporate IT departments and individual entrepreneurs sometimes get caught up in unethical activities because they make bad judgments or they have not done their homework regarding applicable laws and regulations. These individuals frequently face ethical decisions relating to software copyright laws. The software installation scenario above is a classic example of how not understanding software copyright law and bad judgment might lead to unethical activities. As computer professionals, it is critical to be familiar with the general principles of copyright law and the

provisions of the Digital Millennium Copyright Act. See Figure I-14. It is critical to understand that it is illegal to make unauthorized copies of software and other copyrighted media, such as commercial music and movies. And, in fact, it is critical that programmers, Web designers, and other computer professionals respect intellectual property and follow copyright laws and license agreements as they are called upon to use intellectual property, such as installing software or using other people's graphics in their own work.

FIGURE I-14: **Computer professionals should be familiar with U.S. copyright law**

www.copyright.gov

As an employee, however, you might find yourself in a software copyright dilemma like the one previously described in the advertising agency example. Business managers are not always familiar with current copyright restrictions, or they might choose to ignore them. Because computer professionals are required to carry out the requests of management, they should stay up-to-date on current copyright law that applies to software and other digital media. It is important for companies to develop strict guidelines and to let management know the guidelines *before* the guidelines need to be used.

Consider another example that raises ethical questions. Imagine that you are hired as a programmer for a local public school system. One day, the superintendent of schools calls you into her office and asks if you can write software that will monitor online access and provide reports to management. From your understanding of the school's network and Web access, you realize that it would be easy to write such monitoring software. You also realize, however, that the superintendent could use the software to track individual teachers and students as they visit Web sites. You ask the superintendent if faculty and students would be aware of the monitoring software, and she replies, "What they don't know won't hurt them." Should

you write the program? Should you write the program, but start a rumor that monitoring software is being used to track faculty and student Web access? Should you pretend that it would be technically impossible to write such software? Having clear, detailed, written user guidelines of how the school network can be used by staff and students would help in the decision making.

Acting on Ethical Issues

When confronted with a difficult ethical decision, you should consider ethical guidelines, but also consider the policies of your workplace and relevant laws. You might also seek legal advice, consult the human resources advocate at your job, or ask advice from your union representative. Sometimes even talking to a trusted friend helps you recognize the correct course of action.

You might find yourself in the position of becoming a **whistleblower**. A widely accepted definition of **whistleblowing** is the disclosure by an employee (or professional) of confidential information that relates to some danger, fraud, or other illegal or unethical conduct connected with the workplace, be it of the employer or of fellow employees. A whistleblower is someone in an organization who decides to speak out against on-the-job activities that are contrary to the mission of the organization or threaten the public interest. Generally, a whistleblower is making an ethical decision to address a situation or activities that are troubling to him or her.

> " Although whistleblowing might seem effective, the consequences of whistleblowing can often be extreme. "

Recently, whistleblowers, like those who focused public attention on corporate abuses at large corporations such as Enron and WorldCom, have revealed major problems in the way the FBI investigated potential terrorists prior to 9/11, and they have uncovered defects in the body armor supplied to the U.S. combat troops. Although whistleblowing might seem effective, the consequences of whistleblowing can often be extreme. Whistleblowers are often fired or forced out of their jobs. If they keep their jobs, they might be excluded from promotions and shunned by coworkers.

Whistleblowing is risky under any circumstance, which is why the decision to blow the whistle is often grounded in ethical principles. But what one person considers ethical might not be viewed the same way by others. Employee advocates offer

Talking Points: (continued)

the following suggestions for reducing the risk of career repercussions so often experienced by whistleblowers:

- **Examine your motives.** Make sure your cause is significant. Do not act out of frustration or because you feel underappreciated or mistreated.

- **Try the normal chain of command.** Before you blow the whistle, try to correct the problem by reporting up the normal chain of command. Consider every possible way to work within the system before you take your concerns public.

- **Collect evidence to back up your accusations.** Gather evidence that proves your case and keep it in a safe place before you draw attention to your concerns. Do not break any laws while collecting evidence.

- **Record events as they unfold.** Keep detailed, dated notes about events before and after you report the incident. Keep in mind that your notes might become public if the information is used as evidence in a trial.

- **Act ethically.** Do not embellish your case and do not violate any confidentiality agreements you may have. Engage in whistleblowing activities on your own time, not your employer's.

- **Be ready to accept repercussions.** Think through the effect your actions might have on your family. Be prepared for unemployment and the possibility of being blacklisted in your profession.

- **Establish a support network.** Seek out potential allies, such as elected officials, journalists, and activists that can support your cause.

- **Consult a lawyer.** Make sure you understand your rights as an employee.

- **Consider your strategy.** You might reduce the risk of repercussions if you lodge your complaint anonymously or as part of a group.

Privacy and Confidentiality Issues

As you learned in the above school system example, computers can be used to monitor employee activities. Software that captures screen shots over a period of time can be used to view what employees are seeing on their computer screens. RFID (Radio Frequency Identification) chips can be embedded in ID badges and used to keep track of employee locations in an office or manufacturing facility. Keystroke monitors, random samples of active programs, Web browsing history, network logs, and email logs all can be used to track what employees are doing on their computers. Management defends the use of these monitoring systems as a way to make sure their employees are working productively. Privacy advocates question if these systems are ethical.

Because surveillance is often set up by a programmer or network administrator, it is important for computer professionals to be familiar with laws and company policy applicable to privacy. Privacy laws differ from one country to the next, and most companies have unique privacy policies. Rather than assume you know the rules, make an effort to check applicable documents before you take action. Having this information in writing (both laws and company policies) will help guide you in making ethical and legal decisions.

> " Before you blow the whistle, try to correct the problem by reporting up the normal chain of command. Consider every possible way to work within the system before you take your concerns public. "

Computer professionals also must be concerned with confidentiality issues. Confidentiality is the obligation not to disclose any information obtained in confidence. Confidentiality rights apply to individuals and organizations. For individuals, confidentiality means not disclosing names and associated data from databases and other stored information. Laws in most countries restrict the disclosure of an individual's medical or financial information. In addition to the medical or financial professionals working with the individual, computer professionals often have access to this information. It is ethically necessary that all parties keep this information confidential. For organizations, confidentiality means protecting private information about company finances, procedures, products, and research that competitors would find valuable. Computer professionals can find themselves in compromising situations where they are asked to disclose confidential information gathered while employed in previous jobs.

Staying Ethical

So, how do computer professionals stay grounded in their ethical judgments? One way is through the use of a code of ethics, which is a document designed to help computer professionals thread their way through a sometimes tangled web of ethical decisions. These codes are published by many professional organizations, such as the Association for Computing Machinery (ACM), the British Computer Society, the Australian Computer Society, and the Computer Ethics Institute. See Figure I-15.

FIGURE I-15: Professional organizations, like ACM, publish codes of ethics

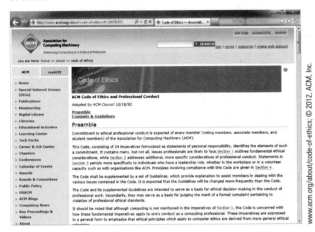

www.acm.org/about/code-of-ethics; © 2012, ACM, Inc.

Each code varies in detail, but supplies a similar set of overall guiding principles for professional conduct. One of the shortest codes, listed below, is published by the Computer Ethics Institute.

1. Thou shalt not use a computer to harm other people.

2. Thou shalt not interfere with other people's computer work.

3. Thou shalt not snoop around in other people's computer files.

4. Thou shalt not use a computer to steal.

5. Thou shalt not use a computer to bear false witness.

6. Thou shalt not copy or use proprietary software for which you have not paid.

7. Thou shalt not use other people's computer resources without authorization or proper compensation.

8. Thou shalt not appropriate other people's intellectual output.

9. Thou shalt think about the social consequences of the program you are writing or the system you are designing.

10. Thou shalt always use a computer in ways that ensure consideration and respect for your fellow humans.

Not all codes of ethics are short and snappy. For example, the ACM's Code of Ethics and Professional Conduct contains 21 guidelines.

A code of ethics can provide guidelines, but it might not offer ready answers to every dilemma that arises in the course of your career. Ethical decisions can be tough, and sometimes the results of your decision—good or bad—are not clear right away. Ultimately, a decision about the right course of action is yours, and you must be willing to take responsibility for the consequences of your decision.

Expand the Ideas

1. What might the conversation be regarding the following scenario involving ethics? You are a new employee at a company and your boss asks you to install software that you know is not properly licensed. Write a one-page dialog between you and your employer that reflects how this scenario might unfold.

2. Who is responsible for illegally installed software? Is it the organization or the individual? Are there any legal precedents to determine this? Research cases where action might have been brought against companies or individuals who illegally installed software. Summarize the case, then write a short paper supporting your opinion and the facts.

3. Do you agree with the code of ethics listed in this Talking Points? If you were responsible for writing the code, what would it be? Write a code of ethics that you think is fair for computer users.

4. What is your opinion about whistleblowers? Do you believe that there should be strong legal protection in every field for whistleblowers? Do you think it is possible to protect those who are whistleblowers from the inevitable backlash from those who are reported? How important is it to provide legal protection for whistleblowers? Write a short paper explaining your position.

Key Terms & Unit Review

Key Terms

Certificate of completion
Certification exam
Chief information
 officer (CIO)
Computer engineer
Computer engineering
Computer industry
Computer operator
Computer professional
Computer programmer
Computer salesperson
Computer science
Contract worker

Database administrator
Electronic portfolio
ePortfolio
Ergonomics
Ethics
Information systems (IS)
 degree programs
Information systems (IS)
 department
Information technology (IT)
 degree programs
Information technology (IT)
 department

Job search agent
Management information
 systems (MIS) department
Manufacturing technician
Metasearch engine
Network specialist/
 administrator
Offshoring
Online job bank
Outsourcing
Professional ethics
Quality assurance (QA)
 specialist

Security specialist
Software engineering
Systems analyst
Technical support specialist
Technical writer
Telecommute
Web portfolio
Web site designer
Whistleblower
Whistleblowing

Unit Review

1. Use your own words to define the bold terms that appear in this unit. List 10 of the terms that are least familiar to you, and write a short sentence for each one.

2. List at least five computer professional job titles and write a brief description of each job.

3. Explain the term *contract workers* and why companies might hire them. Explain the term *telecommuting* and why workers might use this practice.

4. Write a short paragraph about which ITAA job category (see Table I-1) you think would be most appropriate for you and why, considering your strengths and skills.

5. Explain in a short paragraph the focus of these degree programs: computer engineering, computer science, and information systems.

6. Describe the steps you would follow to find a computer-related job and how you would actively pursue it.

7. Describe three ways you can use the Internet in a job search. List two risks of using the Internet in a job search and how you might protect yourself from these risks.

8. Describe the purpose for a résumé and the three main categories it should present.

9. Explain how an ePortfolio can enhance your résumé.

10. Write a short paragraph describing ways you might use social networking to find a job.

Concepts Review

Select the best answer.

1. The term _____ industry is used to refer to the companies that develop, produce, sell, or support computers, software, digital communications, and computer-related products.
 a. IT
 b. ITAA
 c. MIT
 d. ethics

2. A _____ analyzes the needs of a business, its employees, and its customers in order to plan and build new or improved computer services.
 a. computer engineer
 b. database administrator
 c. technical writer
 d. systems analyst

3. A _____ analyzes a company's information to determine the best way to collect and store it.
 a. computer scientist
 b. systems analyst
 c. database administrator
 d. security analyst

4. A _____ typically works with servers, mainframes, and supercomputers to monitor computer performance.
 a. computer operator
 b. computer scientist
 c. technical writer
 d. security analyst

5. A _____ creates, tests, posts, and modifies Web pages.
 a. security analyst
 b. Web site designer
 c. technical writer
 d. systems analyst

6. _____ focuses on computer hardware and peripheral device design often at the chip level.
 a. Information systems (IS)
 b. Computer engineering
 c. Database administration
 d. Systems analysis

7. Online classified advertisements, such as those you might find on _____ , are helpful when looking for a job.
 a. LinkedIn.com
 b. fcc.gov
 c. Craigslist.org
 d. copyright.gov

8. Which of the following computer degrees focuses on applying computers to business problems?
 a. Computer science
 b. Information systems
 c. Computer engineering
 d. Information technology

9. Which of the following certification exams covers basic computing knowledge and skills?
 a. MOS
 b. MCDBA
 c. IC3
 d. A+

10. The job description for a _____ includes designing, coding, and testing software; as well as modifying software to meet new requirements or eliminate bugs.
 a. network specialist/ administrator
 b. computer programmer
 c. database administrator
 d. security specialist

11. A _____ exam verifies your knowledge level about a particular technology or subject.
 a. certification
 b. computer
 c. database administrator
 d. security analyst

12. You can receive a certificate of _____ when you successfully complete one or more courses on a specific topic.
 a. certification
 b. completion
 c. database administrator
 d. security analyst

13. _____ workers are not official employees of a company.
 a. IT
 b. Systems
 c. Contract
 d. Database

14. A _____ engine is a software program that searches the Web across more than one job database at a time and supplies a list of links to applicable job postings.
 a. metasearch
 b. database
 c. hypertext
 d. simple

15. An enhanced _____ version of your résumé is called an ePortfolio.
 a. email
 b. printed
 c. hypertext
 d. docx

16. A _____ search agent is a program that automatically searches databases and notifies you when it finds any jobs that match your requirements.
 a. metasearch
 b. job
 c. hypertext
 d. simple

17. An online job bank is a database of thousands of job openings posted by _____ .
 a. employees
 b. Web specialists
 c. employers
 d. engineers

18. To show that you can take advantage of technology, you should format your résumé for _____ .
 a. different computer platforms
 b. Web site posting or e-mail delivery
 c. printed output
 d. all of the above

19. Which of the following file formats would not be a good choice for your résumé.
 a. DOCX
 b. RTF
 c. PDF
 d. XLSX

20. Certification falls into two broad categories: certificates of _____ and certification exams.
 a. acceptance
 b. specialists
 c. completion
 d. engineers

Independent Challenges

Independent Challenge 1

When you read about careers that put you in the heart of a company's technology needs, you might have found some job areas interesting because they seem to match your skills. For example, perhaps you are a good writer and can understand computers easily; if so, you might make a good technical writer. Or, perhaps you have both technical and design skills; if so, you might make a good Web site designer. To find out if you like Web site design, you can even test your talents and skills by using one of the many self-publishing tools available on the Web.

For this Independent Challenge:

1. Review the job descriptions and the job titles listed in Table I-1. Choose one job that you think might be a good match with your skills.

2. Search the Web for information to answer the following questions about the job:
 a. What are the job's responsibilities?
 b. What education and certification is needed to be qualified for the job? Review possible certification options at the Microsoft Certification Web site. See Figure I-16.
 c. What education and/or certification is needed to qualify for the job you chose?
 d. What information can you find about job availability?

3. Write a short paper explaining your findings.

FIGURE I-16: Review certification options

Independent Challenge 2

You are planning to use the Internet to conduct a job search. You also intend to use the Web as a way to publish your résumé so prospective employers might see it. You decide to set up your job-hunting strategy and create an effective online résumé.

For this Independent Challenge:

1. List four ways in which you plan to use the Internet in your job search.

2. Make a list of job-hunting resources on the Internet. Describe each one and indicate how it might help you find a job.

3. Use the Web to locate information and tips about creating effective online résumés. Using the guidelines that you find, create a résumé using word processing software or Web page authoring software.

4. Show the initial draft of your résumé to several friends, colleagues, or instructors. Collect their feedback and make any necessary revisions. See Figure I-17.

5. Submit your completed résumé to several friends, colleagues, or instructors in the default format of your word processor documents, as a PDF file, as an RTF file, and as an HTML or XML file. Ask them for any additional feedback.

6. Explain the circumstances under which you would use a version of your résumé in PDF, DOC, DOCX, RTF, ASCII, HTML, or XML formats.

7. Write a brief description of the features or keywords that you included in your résumé in order to make it easy to find once it is posted on the Web.

FIGURE I-17: Review your résumé

Independent Challenge 3

Industry analysts often use market share as a gauge of a company's success. Market share is a company's percentage of the total market pie. Industry analysts organize computer manufacturers into market tiers, or categories. The concept of tiers helps explain price differences and changing market shares. The first (top) tier in any segment of the computer industry consists of large companies, such as Dell. These companies have been in the computer business for many years and have an identifiable market share, usually more than two percent of total sales. The second tier includes newer companies with sales volume just below the cutoff level for identifiable market share. They have fewer financial resources than companies in the first tier. The third tier consists of smaller start-up companies that sell primarily through mail order. Computers from top-tier vendors generally are more expensive than those offered by second-tier or third-tier vendors. First-tier companies are more likely to provide continuing support, honor warranties, and maintain an inventory of replacement parts.

Computer hardware and software are sold through outlets called marketing channels. See Figure I-18. These channels include computer retail stores, mail-order/Internet outlets, value-added resellers (VARs), and manufacturers direct. Some channels supply hardware and software at lower prices than other channels, which can save you money.

For this Independent Challenge:

You will review market tiers and marketing channels.

1. Examine the computer you use most frequently. It might be a laptop or desktop computer you use at home or at work. Answer the following questions about the computer:
 a. Note the manufacturer, if available. Can you identify which market tier this company is in?
 b. If you know the source of the computer, what market channel was it purchased from: a manufacturer? a retail store? a VAR?
 c. Locate the computer model number, which might be located on the bottom or back panel. Look up the model number on the Internet and try to determine the age of the computer.

2. Choose a software product on this computer that you use frequently. Determine the version of the software. Search the Internet to determine if there is a newer version available.
 a. If a new version exists, what would be the cost, if any, to upgrade to that version? (Note: If you are using a shared computer, do not perform upgrading procedures without permission from the computer owner.)
 b. What advantages, if any, would the new version provide, such as new features that might be useful to you?

3. Write a short paper containing the results of your research. Include a short assessment of how, if at all, this information might affect your plans for your computer needs in the next year.

FIGURE I-18: Marketing channels

Distribution centers stock products from many different manufacturers and then sell the products to retailers.

Computer retailers stock products from several manufacturers and sell these products to customers.

Some manufacturers ship products directly to customers.

Distribution centers

Retail stores

Customers

Manufacturers produce products and ship them to resellers, distribution centers, computer retailers, and mail-order suppliers.

Manufacturers

VARs

Mail-order suppliers

Value-added resellers generally modify products or assemble them into complete hardware and software solutions targeted at specific businesses.

Mail-order suppliers specialize in taking phone orders and shipping products to customers using U.S. mail or courier services.

© LWA/Dan Tardif/Jupiterimages; © Steve Rosset/Shutterstock.com; © Comstock/Getty Images; © Ken Davies/Masterfile; © Konstantin Chagin/Shutterstock.com; © Samuel Acosta/Shutterstock.com

Guide to Buying a Computer

As you prepare to buy a computer, there are a lot of decisions you have to make. This course has been designed to help you build the knowledge base you need to purchase a computer. In previous units, you listed information about the type of computer system that would meet your needs. When you buy computers or software, it is helpful to know the process hardware manufacturers use when they create and release products as well as how they market and sell products. Why? Because it will help you know what questions to ask so that you get the best product for your money. In this exercise, you can consolidate the information about the type of system you need and then shop for it to determine availability and price.

Complete the table on the next page about the computer you need. In column two, enter the components of your desired system, based on your notes in the Guides to Buying a Computer in Units A–H. Then research a system price using three sources, which can be computer stores (Figure I-19), a current computer magazine buyer's guide or product evaluation chart, or a company that allows you to shop for a custom computer online, such as www.dell.com, or www.apple.com.

You can also consider using an online computer shopping site.

Note: If you use an online site, do not enter any personal or financial information, including credit card numbers, into any site, unless you actually intend to purchase a computer. This exercise is for informational and pricing purposes only; you should be able to obtain system prices without making a purchase of any kind. If not, try another site.

For each source, make any necessary notes about factors that might influence the price. Enter prices for individual components where necessary, and a total price, from each source, for the complete system in the last row.

FIGURE I-19: **Shopping for a computer**

© Yuri Arcurs/Shutterstock.com

© 1000 Words/Shutterstock.com

Ordering custom computers on the Web

Dell Computers pioneered Web-based direct sales to individual customers. Its Web site allows customers to select from a variety of standard models or to design and order their own custom machines. A "just-in-time" inventory model allows Dell to build each customer's computer as it is ordered. This eliminates costly inventories that quickly become outdated. By cutting out the retailer, a manufacturer such as Dell can make more profit on each unit sold. But the manufacturer still must provide customers with technical support—a costly service that requires large teams of workers.

As you worked through this book, you learned about personal computer systems and supporting digital electronic devices. You have had the opportunity to answer questions and complete several worksheets with information that will help you when it is time for you to buy a computer, purchase the supporting devices, and set up the system to run securely. To help you summarize the information you entered in your previous worksheets, complete this portion of the Guide to Buying a Computer worksheet.

Guide to Buying a Computer: Comparing computer systems

System Components from your Units A–H Buying Guide notes	Specification (name, model, capacity, etc.)	Source #1	Source #2	Source #3
Computer type, platform, case (Unit A)				
Storage, pointing and data entry devices, screen type, monitor, printer, peripheral device(s), expansion slots, USB ports (Unit B)				
Operating system, productivity software, utility software (Unit C)				
Processor type, clock speed, bus speed, amount of RAM, RAM cache and speed (Unit D)				
Data security, power protection, hardware protection, security software; firewall, antivirus, antispam, antispy software; backup devices and media (Unit E)				
Networking hardware and peripheral devices, cables, Internet service and fees (Unit F)				
Software add-ons, Web services and capabilities (Unit G)				
Portable media device, scanner, digital camera, graphics software, audio/ video player, audio/video editing (Unit H)				
	Total System Price	$	$	$

© Cengage Learning

Visual Workshop

Computer- and IT-related jobs have many job titles and career paths. As the IT industry continues to change and the technologies become more specialized, the need for training and ultimately certification will continue to grow. Employers need to know that the people they hire have the skills for the job. As a consumer of training materials and certification exams, you have to know which courses will teach you what you need to know, which exams will be valued by employers, and how you can prepare yourself for the current job market. Figure I-20 is a career information site sponsored by the U.S. government. This site provides information about computer jobs in the geographic location of your choice, necessary training and certification, and opportunities.

FIGURE I-20: **USA JOBS Web site**

1. Log on to the Internet and visit the the USAJOBS Web site at http://jobsearch.usajobs.gov. Search the Web site for information about a job that interests you. Write a brief summary of the type of help and information the site offers.

2. Cisco offers certification in many levels and career paths. Use your browser to go to www.cisco.com. Read through the pages on training and certification. What certifications are available? What types of courses are available? How is the courseware delivered?

3. Go to www.microsoft.com, then search for training and certification. What certifications are available? What types of courses are available? How is the courseware delivered?

4. Write a short paper comparing the certification and training programs offered by Cisco and Microsoft, and any jobs you found for which they might be helpful.

Getting Started with CourseMate

Learning Objectives

1. Explain why you would use a CourseMate
2. Know how to access the CourseMate for this book
3. Know how to use CourseMate study tools

LESSON TOPICS

- CourseMate Overview
- Accessing CourseMate
- Using CourseMate
- Student Edition Labs Reference

CourseMate Overview

Cengage Learning's CourseMate brings course concepts to life with interactive learning, study, and exam preparation tools that support the printed textbook. CourseMate includes an integrated eBook, and interactive teaching and learning tools. These include quizzes, flashcards, videos, and Student Edition Labs, which are an engaging collection of hands-on training activities and animations. In order to use CourseMate, you must have purchased a CourseMate access code for this book. You also need a Web browser and must be connected to the Internet. This lesson reviews the key elements of the CourseMate for this book.

DETAILS

The CourseMate for this book includes the following elements for each unit:

- **Interactive eBook**
 The eBook lets you read each unit of the book on your computer screen. You can search for specific topics or keywords, highlight text, and take notes.

- **Videos**
 The CourseMate includes short "highlight" videos for each two-page lesson in the book. Each video runs about 2 to 3 minutes long and presents highlights of the key points covered in the lesson, to help draw you into the topic. See Figure CM-1.

- **Glossary and Flashcards**
 Use the Glossary and Flashcard features to help you master the key terms in each unit. The Glossary provides a list of key terms and their definitions; the Flash Cards present key terms on one side of a digital card and definitions on the other. See Figure CM-2.

- **Concepts Review**
 The CourseMate includes an online version of the Concepts Review questions from the end-of-unit exercises; you can answer the questions online and get your results instantly.

- **Student Edition Labs**
 The Student Edition Labs are hands-on interactive activities to help you learn, understand, and retain key concepts about computers. The Student Edition Labs include animations, guided activities, and reinforcement questions. See Figure CM-3.

- **Games**
 Beat the Clock and Quiz Bowl games let you test your knowledge in a fun game format.

- **Practice Test**
 Interactive practice tests for each unit help you prepare for your exam.

- **And More!**
 CourseMate also has exercises from the book that you can access online and submit to your instructor. There is also a link to **CourseCasts**, which are podcasts on hot technology news. Hosted by Professor Ken Baldauf of Florida State University, CourseCasts are updated weekly so you will stay up to date with the latest technology developments.

FIGURE CM-1: **Videos for each lesson bring key topics to life**

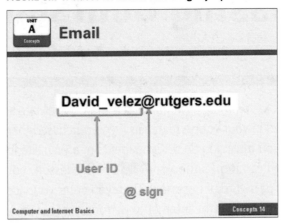

FIGURE CM-2: **Use Flashcards to master key terms**

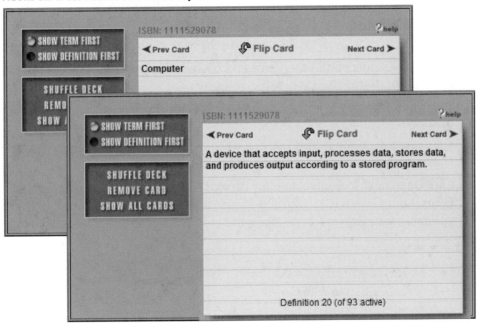

FIGURE CM-3: **Student Edition Labs feature animations, guided steps, and reinforcement questions to help you learn and master key concepts**

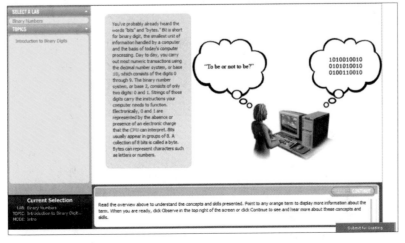

CourseMate

Accessing CourseMate

To access the CourseMate for this book, you must have purchased the CourseMate access code for this book. The access code might have been included in your course materials if you purchased them at your school's bookstore. Then, with your access code handy, you must log on to CengageBrain, a Web site for accessing various student resources that accompany Cengage Learning textbooks. In this lesson, you set up a CengageBrain user profile and establish a username and password, if necessary. Then you enter your access code to access the CourseMate. (Note: You must be connected to the Internet to perform these steps.)

STEPS

1. **Open your browser, type** http:// login.cengagebrain.com **in your browser's address bar, then press [Enter]**
 The Login page for the CengageBrain site opens. See Figure CM-4.

TROUBLE

If you don't have a CengageBrain user-name and pass-word, click Create an Account, then follow the prompts to create one.

2. **Type your CengageBrain username and password in the Log In section of the screen**
 The Find your Textbook or Materials page opens.

3. **Type your access code in the box below Have Another Product to Register?, then click Register**
 The CengageBrain site accepts your access code and the Computer Concepts Illustrated 9th Edition cover and title appear under My Courses & Materials. See Figure CM-5.

4. **Click Open next to CourseMate for Parsons/Oja Computer Concepts Illustrated 9e CourseMate**
 The CourseMate page opens. See Figure CM-6.

FIGURE CM-4: CengageBrain Log In screen

Log in by typing your username and password here.

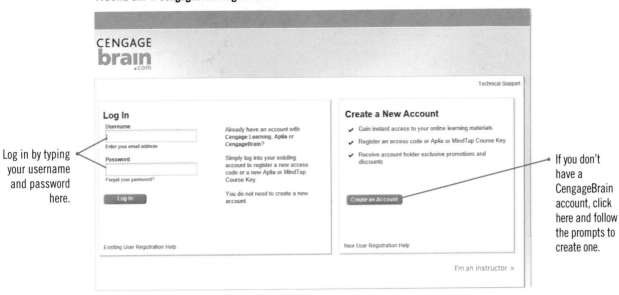

If you don't have a CengageBrain account, click here and follow the prompts to create one.

FIGURE CM-5: My Home page, with Computer Concepts Illustrated CourseMate added

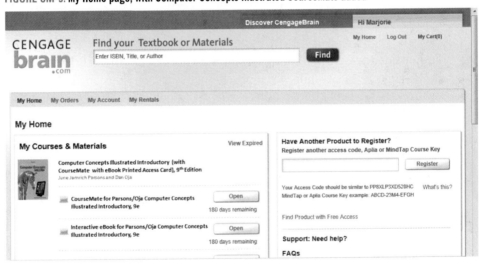

FIGURE CM-6: CourseMate Welcome page

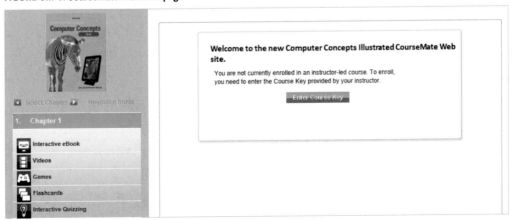

Using CourseMate

CourseMate is a great study tool that will help you learn and master the content you need to succeed in this course. In addition to interactive learning and study aids, CourseMate comes with Engagement Tracker, a tool that lets your instructor monitor student engagement in the course. Your instructor might provide you with a Course Key, which you will need to enter in order to use Engagement Tracker. (If your instructor chooses not to use Engagement Tracker, you can still access all the content on CourseMate.) ▄▄▟▟▛ In this lesson, you learn the basics of using CourseMate.

STEPS

TROUBLE
Skip to Step 3 if your instructor did not provide you with a Course Key.

1. **If your instructor provided you with a Course Key, click Enter Course Key**
 The Enter Your Course Key dialog box opens, as shown in Figure CM-7.

2. **Type your Course Key, then click Submit**

3. **Click Select Chapter, just below the book cover on the left side of the screen**
 The full table of contents for the book appears in the Select Chapter window. You can open this window anytime you want to access the content for a particular unit.

4. **Click outside the Select a Chapter window , click eBook, then click Access the eBook**
 After a moment, a new window opens and displays an eBook version of this book. You can navigate through the eBook content using the Table of Contents, glossary, or index. You can search for words or phrases, and you can annotate the text.

5. **Click the Close button on the eBook title bar**
 The eBook closes, and your screen displays the CourseMate window again.

6. **Click Videos in the Navigation pane**
 The main window displays a series of video windows. You can click any video window to start that video. Figure CM-8 shows a snapshot from a sample video.

7. **Explore the other CourseMate elements by clicking the remaining items in the navigation pane**

8. **Click the Close button in your browser's title bar**
 Your browser and CourseMate close.

FIGURE CM-7: Enter Your Course Key dialog box

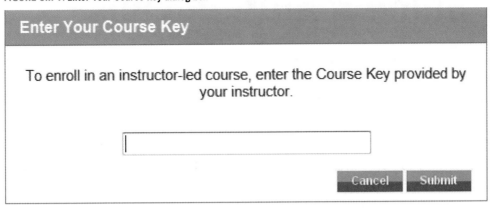

FIGURE CM-8: Videos provide animations on key concepts covered in each lesson

Student Edition Labs Reference

The Student Edition Labs provide hands-on interactive activities to help you learn, understand, and retain many of the concepts presented in the book. These hands-on interactive activities include animations, activities, and reinforcement questions. This page lists all the Student Edition Labs that are available in this book's CourseMate.

Student Labs Available in CourseMate

E-mail
Using Input Devices
Peripheral Devices
Maintaining a Hard Disk Drive
Understanding the Motherboard
Using Windows
Word Processing
Spreadsheets
Databases
Presentation Software
Working with Graphics
Working with Video
Working with Audio
Project Management
Installing and Uninstalling Software
Advanced Spreadsheets

Advanced Database Lab
Binary Numbers
Managing Files and Folders
Networking Basics
Wireless Networking
Connecting to the Internet
Keeping Your Computer Virus Free
Protecting Your Privacy Online
Backing Up Your Computer
Getting the Most Out of the Internet
Creating Web Pages
Web Design Principles
E-Commerce
Careers and Technology: Getting Ahead
Visual Programming
Computer Ethics

Glossary

24-bit bitmap graphic A True Color graphic that requires 24 bits for each pixel, used for photographic-quality images that can include any of 16.7 million colors. *Also called* True Color bitmap graphic.

32-bit bitmap graphic A True Color graphic that requires 32 bits for each pixel, used for photographic-quality images that can include any of 16.7 million colors. *Also called* True Color bitmap graphic.

3D graphic A type of digital graphics format that represents a three-dimensional image in a two-dimensional space.

3D graphics software A category of software that provides a set of tools for creating wireframe drawings to represent three-dimensional objects.

802.11b A popular wireless network standard that operates between 200 and 400 Kbps, with a range of up to 300 feet.

AAC *See* Advanced Audio Compression.

Access time The estimated time for a storage device to locate data on a disk, usually measured in milliseconds.

Accounting software A category of software that helps you keep a record of monetary transactions and investments.

ActionScript A programming language used to create sophisticated applications that can be launched from Web pages and viewed using a browser plug-in.

ActiveX control A compiled computer program that can be referenced from within an HTML document, downloaded, installed on your computer, and executed within the browser window to add interactive features to Web pages.

Add-on Software that extends a browser's ability to work with file formats. *Also called* helper application, plug-in, or player.

Ad-serving cookie A cookie distributed by marketing firms that is used to track activities at any site containing banner ads from that third party.

Advanced Audio Compression (AAC) An audio format with very good sound quality; used on the iTunes music download site; has the .aac file extension.

Adware Software bundled with a program that automatically displays or downloads advertising material to a computer after the program is installed or while the program is being used.

AIFF *See* Audio Interchange File Format.

Always-on connection A permanent connection to the Internet, as opposed to a connection that is established and dropped as needed.

Analog data Data that is represented using an infinite scale of values, in contrast to digital data, which is represented as discrete digits, such as 0s and 1s.

Analog video camera A device used to collect, store, and process video in an analog format on a magnetic tape.

Animated GIF A type of graphic image file, in GIF format, that displays a sequence of frames to create the appearance of continuous motion.

Antispyware Security software designed to identify and neutralize Web bugs, ad-serving cookies, and other spyware.

Antivirus software A computer program used to scan a computer's memory and disks to identify, isolate, and eliminate viruses.

App Typically used to describe a software program on a smartphone or tablet computer.

Application server A server that runs application software for network computers.

Application software A category of software programs that helps you perform a specific task such as word processing. *Also called* application programs, applications, or programs.

Archive The process of moving infrequently used data from a primary storage device to a storage medium, such as a DVD or CD.

ASCII (American Standard Code for Information Interchange) A code that represents characters as a series of 1s and 0s, making it possible to transfer data between computers.

ASF A PC video format that acts as a container format for the Microsoft Windows Media Video (WMV) desktop, PDA, and streaming video.

Audio editing software A category of software that includes sound playback as well as recording capabilities. Menus provide additional digital editing features, such as speed control, volume adjustments, clipping, and mixing of sounds.

Audio Interchange File Format (AIFF) A popular cross-platform audio format developed by Apple; has the .aif file extension.

Authentication protocol A way to restrict access to computer systems; used to positively identify a person as an authorized user by verifying the person through one of three methods: something a person carries, something a person knows, or some unique physical characteristic.

AVI (Audio Video Interleave) A video file format developed by Microsoft that is the most common format for desktop video on the PC.

B2B (business-to-business) An e-commerce transaction involving products, services, or information between businesses.

B2C (business-to-consumer) An e-commerce transaction involving products, services, or information between businesses and consumers.

B2G (business-to-government) An e-commerce transaction involving products, services, or information between businesses and governments.

Backdoor Concealed software flaw that allows unauthorized access to victims' computers by bypassing normal computer authentication systems, providing a way for hackers to harm a computer system in some way.

Backup A duplicate copy of a file, disk, or tape. Also refers to Windows utility backup software that allows you to create and restore backups.

Backup software A category of software used to copy program and data files to a storage medium for backup purposes; most provide options that make it easy to schedule periodic backups, define a set of files that you want to regularly back up, and automate the restoration process.

Bandwidth The data transmission capacity of a communications channel.

Banner ad An advertisement typically embedded at the top of a Web page.

BD (Blu-ray Disc) A high-capacity disc for storing large quantities of digital content, such as high-definition video.

BD drive A drive that plays Blu-ray discs.

Benchmark A test used to measure computer hardware or software performance.

Binary digit The smallest unit of information handled by a computer; can hold one of two values, either a 0 or a 1. Eight bits make up one byte, which can represent a character, such as a letter or number. *See* Bit.

Binary number system A method for representing numbers using only two digits, 0 and 1; contrast this system to the decimal system, which uses ten digits: 0, 1, 2, 3, 4, 5, 6, 7, 8, and 9.

Biometrics A method of personal identification based on some unique physical trait, such as a fingerprint or the pattern of blood vessels in the retina of the eye.

Bit The smallest unit of information handled by a computer; can hold one of two values, either a 0 or a 1. Eight bits make up one byte, which can represent a character, such as a letter or number. Short for binary digit.

Bit depth The number of bits that determines the range of possible colors that can be assigned to each pixel. For example, an 8-bit color depth can create 256 colors. *Also called* color depth.

Bitmap graphic An image, such as a digital photo, that is stored as a grid of colored dots.

Bitmap image *See* Bitmap graphic.

Bitrate A measure of compression, the number of bits required to display one second of video.

BitTorrent An Internet protocol that distributes files using scattered clients rather than a server.

Black hat *See* Hacker.

Blended threat A threat that combines more than one type of malicious program, such as a Trojan-horse/virus combination or a worm/virus combination.

Blog Derived from the phrase "WeB LOG," refers to a personal journal focusing on a single topic or covering a variety of issues posted on the Web for access by the general public.

Bluetooth A wireless technology used in conjunction with standard Ethernet networks that allows peak data transfer rates between 1 Mbps (version 1.2) or 3 Mbps (version 2.0+EDR), up to a maximum range of 300 feet.

Blu-ray Disc *See* BDs.

Blu-ray drive *See* BD drive.

BMP The native bitmap graphic file format of the Microsoft Windows OS.

Bookmark A link to a Web page; a list of saved URLs in a browser; you click the URL to return to the page. *Also called* favorite.

Boolean operator A word or symbol that describes a relationship between keywords and thereby helps you create a more focused query. *Also called* search operator.

Boot disk A DVD or CD that contains the essential instructions needed to boot your computer without accessing the hard drive.

Boot process The sequence of events that occurs within a computer system between the time the user starts the computer and the time it is ready to process commands.

Boot sector virus A computer virus that infects the sectors on a disk containing the data a computer uses during the boot process.

Bootstrap A program stored in ROM that loads and initializes the operating system on a computer.

Bot Any software that can automate a task or autonomously execute a task when commanded to do so. *Also called* intelligent agent.

Botmaster A person who controls many bot-infected computers.

Botnet Many bot-infected computers linked together into a network to provide combined computing power of their zombie computers for many types of illegal and unethical tasks.

Bridge A device that connects two networks using the same communications protocol; it transfers data without regard to its format.

Broadband A term used to refer to communications channels that have high bandwidth.

Broadcast flag A set of bits inserted into the data stream of digital television or radio programs that specifies how the stream can and cannot be used.

Broken link A non-functioning hyperlink on a Web page.

Browser A program that communicates with a Web server and displays Web pages.

Browser cache A stored collection of temporary files from previously viewed Web pages. *Also called* Web cache.

Brute force attack *See* Brute force method.

Brute force method A method whereby hackers use password-cracking software to exhaust all possible keys to decrypt a password. *Also called* brute force attack.

Buffer The area of computer memory that holds data from one device while it is waiting to be transferred to another device.

Bus An electronic pathway that carries the electronic signals between the electronic parts of a computer.

Bus topology A network topology that uses a common backbone to connect all network devices. The backbone functions as a shared communication link, which carries network data, and stops at each end of the network with a terminator.

Byte An 8-bit unit of information that represents a single character.

C2C (consumer-to-consumer) An e-commerce transaction involving products, services, or information between consumers.

Cable A wire used to connect a peripheral device to a computer through a port.

Cable modem A communications device that can be used to connect a computer to the Internet via the cable TV infrastructure.

Cache Special high-speed memory that gives the CPU rapid access to data that would otherwise be accessed from memory elsewhere on the motherboard. *Also called* RAM cache or cache memory.

Cache memory *See* Cache.

CAD software A special type of 3D graphics software designed for architects and engineers who use computers to create blueprints and product specifications.

Capacitor The electronic parts in a chip that hold the bits that represent data.

Card reader A device that transfers data to or from a computer.

CCD (charged coupled device) The image sensor used by the lens in a digital camera to focus light from the image onto a grid of tiny light-sensitive diodes called photosites.

CD (compact disc) An optical storage medium that can store up to 700 MB of data. There are a wide variety of CDs including CD-ROM, CD-R, and CD-RW.

CD drive A storage device that uses laser technology to read data from a CD-ROM.

CD-R disc An optical storage medium that allows the user to write data once onto a CD, once the data is recorded it cannot be re-recorded; an acronym for compact disc-recordable.

CD-ROM disc An optical storage medium that is read-only and that can store up to 700 MB of data.

CD-RW disc An optical storage medium that allows the user to write data onto a CD, then change that data; an acronym for compact disc-rewritable.

CD-writer A general term for recordable CD technologies such as CD-R and CD-RW.

Central processing unit *See* CPU.

Certificate of completion A certification offered to students who successfully complete one or more courses on a specific topic.

Certification exam An objective test that verifies the level of the test-taker's knowledge about a particular technology or subject.

Character data Letters, symbols, or numerals that will not be used in arithmetic operations (name, Social Security Number, and so on).

Chat A networked-based, real-time messaging system that allows people in groups to exchange short messages while they are online.

Chat group A discussion in which a group of people communicates online simultaneously.

Chief information officer (CIO) The highest-ranking executive responsible for information systems.

Chip *See* Computer chip.

Click-through rate The number of times that site visitors click an ad on a Web site to connect to the advertiser's site. The hosting merchant is paid a small fee for each click through.

Client A computer or software that requests information from another computer or server.

Client/server network A network where processing is split between workstations (clients) and the server.

Client-side script A series of scripting statements that runs on your local computer; it is executed by the browser, which must have the capability to deal with the programming language used to write the script. Popular languages for client-side scripts include VBScript and JavaScript.

Clip art Graphics designed to be inserted into documents, Web pages, and worksheets, usually available in CD-ROM or Web-based collections.

Clock speed The pace for executing instructions as set by the processor clock specified in megahertz (MHz) or gigahertz (GHz).

Cloud Mass storage for programs and data on remote computers connected to the Internet or other network.

Cloud computing A method of offering Internet-accessible computing services ranging from office productivity applications to complex corporate data processing.

Cloudware Software applications that are not installed locally on your computer but rather installed on the Web and used while online through a browser. *Also called* Web apps.

Coaxial cable A type of cable with BNC connectors made of a center wire surrounded by a grounded shield of braided wire and used to connect nodes on a network. *Also called* coax cable.

CODEC (COmpressor/DECompressor) Hardware or software routine that compresses and decompresses digital graphics, sound, and video files.

Color depth The number of bits that determines the range of possible colors that can be assigned to each pixel. For example, an 8-bit color depth can create 256 colors. *Also called* bit depth.

Color palette The selection of colors used in graphics software.

Commercial software Copyrighted computer applications sold to consumers for profit.

Communications channel Any pathway between the sender and receiver; channel may refer to a physical medium or a frequency.

Communications protocol A set of rules for ensuring orderly and accurate transmission and reception of data.

CompactFlash (CF) card A solid state storage device that is about the size of a matchbook and provides high storage capacities and access speeds; includes a built-in controller that reads and writes data within the solid state grid; ideal for use with high-end digital cameras.

Compiler Software that translates a program written in a high-level language into low-level instructions before the program is executed.

Compression algorithm The steps required to shrink data in a file and restore it to its original state.

Compression ratio A measurement of the amount of shrinkage when data is compressed.

Compression software A type of software, such as WinZip, that effectively reduces the size of files. *See also* File compression software.

Compression utility Software used to reduce file size for quick transmission or efficient storage.

Computer An electronic device that accepts input, processes data, stores data, and produces output.

Computer-aided design software (CAD) *See* CAD software.

Computer-aided music software A category of software that helps musicians compose, edit, and print the notes for compositions. For non-musicians, designed to generate unique music simply by selecting the musical style, instruments, key, and tempo.

Computer chip An integrated circuit consisting of a thin slice of silicon crystal containing microscopic circuit elements, such as transistors, wires, capacitors, and resistors. *Also called* integrated circuit, chip, or microchip.

Computer engineer A computer professional who focuses on the design and development of hardware and peripheral devices.

Computer engineering A career field that focuses on the design and development of computer hardware and peripheral devices.

Computer file A named collection of data (such as a computer program, document, or graphic) that exists on a storage medium such as a hard drive, flash drive, CD, or DVD. *Also called* file or data file.

Computer language Tools that allow a programmer to write instructions or software that a computer can execute. *Also called* programming language.

Computer network A collection of computers and related devices, connected in a way that allows them to share data, hardware, and software.

Computer operator A computer professional who works directly with and maintains mainframe computers.

Computer platform A computer system's underlying hardware and software, in particular, its processor and operating system; the two dominant computer platforms today for desktop and notebook computers are PC, which is sometimes called the Windows platform, and Mac, which is the Macintosh OS by Apple Computer, Inc.

Computer professional Any person whose primary occupation involves one or more aspects of computer technology.

Computer program Detailed, step-by-step instructions that tell a computer how to solve a problem or carry out a task. *Also called* program.

Computer programmer A person who codes or writes computer programs. *Also called* programmer/analyst.

Computer projection device An output device that produces a large display of the information shown on the computer screen.

Computer salesperson A person who sells computers, visits corporate customers, or staffs the order desk of a mail-order vendor. *Also called* sales rep.

Computer science A career field that focuses on developing fast and efficient computers, from their construction to their programming and operating systems.

Computer system The hardware, peripheral devices, and software working together to input data, process data, store data, and produce output.

Computer virus A program designed to attach itself to a file, reproduce, and spread from one file to another, disrupting computer operations.

Computer worm A self-copying program designed to carry out unauthorized activity on a victim's computer.

Concurrent-use license A software license agreement that is priced per copy and allows a specific number of copies to be used at the same time.

Contract worker A computer professional who does not work directly for one company and often is paid by the job instead of a salary.

Cookie A message sent from a Web server to a browser and stored on a user's hard drive, usually containing information about the user.

Copy protection Technologies designed to prohibit consumers from copying content.

Copyright A form of legal protection that grants certain exclusive rights to the author of a program or the owner of the copyright.

Copyright notice A line such as "Copyright 2014 ACME Co." that identifies a copyright holder.

CPU (central processing unit) The main processing unit in a computer, consisting of circuits that processes data. *Also called* the "brain" of a computer.

Cracker *See* Hacker.

Cropping The process of selecting and removing part of an image.

Cryptographic algorithm A specific procedure for encrypting and decrypting data.

Cryptographic key A specific word, number, or phrase that must be used to encrypt or decrypt data.

CSS (Content Scramble System) A DRM technology designed to encrypt and control the use of content stored on DVDs.

Cursor A symbol that marks the user's place on the screen and shows where typing will appear. *Also called* insertion point.

Cybercrime A crime that uses a computer, such as transmitting trade secrets to competitors and reproducing copyrighted material. Also a crime targeted at computers, such as denial-of-service attacks on servers, Web site vandalism, data theft, and destructive viruses.

Cybercriminal *See* Hacker.

Cyberterrorism An act that attacks or threatens to attack computer systems using viruses and worms to destroy data and otherwise disrupt computer-based operations, including critical national infrastructures, such as power grids and telecommunications systems.

Cycle The smallest unit of time a processor can recognize. For example, 2.8 GHz means that the processor's clock operates at a speed of 2.8 billion cycles per second.

Dashboard widget A term used to define a utility program on an Apple computer's desktop used to display information such as a clock, calendar, calculator, news aggregators, notes, and weather. *Also called* widget or control.

Data In the context of computing and data management, the symbols that a computer uses to represent facts and ideas.

Data bus An electronic pathway or circuit that connects the electronic components (such as the processor and RAM) on a computer's motherboard.

Data center A specialized facility designed to house and protect computer systems and data.

Data compression The process of condensing data so that it requires fewer bytes of storage space.

Data diddling Unauthorized alterations to data stored on a computer system, such as a student changing grades stored in a school's computer.

Data file A named collection of data (such as a computer program, document, or graphic) that exists on a storage medium, such as a hard drive, flash drive, CD, or DVD. *Also called* computer file or file.

Data representation The use of electrical signals, marks, or binary digits to represent character, numeric, visual, or audio data.

Data security Techniques that provide protection for data.

Data transfer rate The amount of data that a storage device can move from a storage medium to computer memory in one second.

Database A collection of data that is stored electronically as a series of records in tables.

Database administrator A person who supervises database design, development, testing, and maintenance.

Database software A category of software designed for tasks associated with maintaining and accessing data stored in data files.

Decryption key The code needed to unscramble encrypted data that was sent over wired or wireless networks to provide secure data transmission.

Demodulate The process of restoring a received signal to its original state; for example, when a modem changes an audio signal back to a digital pulse.

Demoware Commercial software available as a trial version and distributed for free. Often comes preinstalled on new computers, but it is limited in some way until paid for.

Denial-of-Service attack The result of hackers sending malicious software that is designed to overwhelm a network's processing capabilities, shutting it down.

Density The number of dots per inch (dpi) for an image or the number of pixels per inch (ppi) for a monitor.

Desktop computer A category of computer small enough to fit on a desk but is too big to carry around and has attached, rather than built-in, keyboard, display, and pointing device.

Desktop gadget A term used to define a utility program on a computer's desktop that is used to display information such as a clock, calendar, calculator, news aggregators, notes, and weather. For Apple computers, called a widget. *See also* Gadget.

Desktop publishing software (DPT) A category of software used to create high-quality output suitable for commercial printing. DPT software provides precise control over layout.

Desktop widget *See* Widget.

Device driver The software that provides the computer with the means to control a peripheral device.

DHCP *See* Dynamic Host Configuration Protocol.

Dial-up connection A connection that uses a phone line to establish a temporary Internet connection.

Dictionary attack A method used by hackers to guess a password; involves stepping through a dictionary containing thousands of the most commonly used passwords.

Differential backup A backup of only those files that were added or changed since your last full backup session.

Digital Any system that works with discrete data, such as 0s and 1s, in contrast to analog.

Digital audio Music, speech, and other sounds represented in binary format for use in digital devices.

Digital camera A peripheral input device that records photographic images in digital format.

Digital certificate A security method that identifies the author of an ActiveX control.

Digital content Any text, graphics, video, audio, or any data and information stored in a file and available for transmission, viewing or playing, and storage via a computer.

Digital convergence The trend to blend several technologies that have distinct functionalities into a single product, such as smartphones that combine voice communication, text messaging, email, Web browsing, cameras, and GPS.

Digital data Text, numbers, graphics, sound, and video that have been converted into discrete digits, such as 0s and 1s.

Digital device A device that works with discrete (distinct or separate) numbers or digits.

Digital electronics Circuitry that is designed to work with digital signals.

Digital graphics Images that have been created as or converted to a digital format.

Digital media player A peripheral device that can be attached to a personal computer system to transfer and play music and photo files.

Digital revolution An ongoing process of social, political, and economic change brought about by digital technology, such as computers and the Internet.

Digital Rights Management (DRM) Technology that has evolved to protect copyright holders as well as software and media developers.

Digital Satellite Service (DSS) An Internet connection option that uses a geosynchronous or low-earth satellite to transmit television, voice, or computer data directly to and from a satellite dish, or base station, owned or leased by an individual.

Digital signal processor Circuitry that is used to process, record, and playback audio files.

Digital technology Technologies that work using digital electronics such as computers, communications networks, the Web, and digitization.

Digital versatile disc *See* DVD.

Digital video Filmed sequences that are stored in one of several different digital formats, including AVI, QuickTime, MPEG, RealMedia, MMV, and VOB.

Digital video (dv) camera A device used to collect, store, and process video in a digital format.

Digital video recorder (DVR) Used to record and store footage for digital videos.

Digital wallet Software that stores and processes customer information needed for an e-commerce transaction. *Also called* electronic wallet or e-wallet.

Digital watermark A pattern of bits inserted at various places in an image or a content stream that can be used to track, identify, verify, and control content use.

Digitization *See* Digitize.

Digitize To convert text, numbers, sound, photos, and video to a digital format that can be processed by a computer, through the use of a scanner, camera, or other input device.

Digitizing tablet A device that provides a flat surface for a paper-based drawing and used with a "pen" to create hand-drawn vector drawings.

DIMM (dual in-line memory module) A long, slim memory chip package that has gold pins that provide the electronic connection between the chip and other computer parts.

DIP (dual in-line package) A chip configuration characterized by a rectangular body with numerous plugs along its edge.

Direct access The ability of a storage device (such as a hard drive) to go directly to a specific storage location without having to search sequentially from a beginning location. *Also called* random access.

Directory A list of files contained on a computer storage device.

Disaster recovery plan A step-by-step plan that describes the methods used to secure data against disaster and explains how an organization will recover lost data if and when a disaster occurs.

Disk partition *See* Hard drive partition.

Display device The main output device for a computer; presents visual information on a screen such as a computer monitor.

Distribution media One or more discs, CDs, or other storage media that contain programs and data, which can be installed to a hard drive.

Document reader utility Computer program, such as Adobe Reader, that transforms files into a portable format that can be created and read by any computer on which the document reader utility is installed.

Domain name An identifying name by which host computers on the Internet are familiarly known; for example, cengage.com. *Also called* fully qualified domain name (FQDN).

Domain name server Computers that host the domain name system database.

Domain Name System A large database of unique IP addresses that correspond with domain names.

DOS (disk operating system) The operating system software shipped with the first IBM PCs and used on millions of computers until the introduction of Microsoft Windows.

Dot pitch The diagonal distance between colored dots on a display screen. Measured in millimeters, dot pitch helps to determine the quality of an image displayed on a monitor. A smaller dot pitch means a crisper image.

Dots per inch (dpi) A measure of screen resolution and printer quality. A higher number of dots per inch indicates a higher resolution and better-quality output.

Downloading The process of transferring a copy of a file from a remote computer to a local computer's hard drive.

Downstream speed The rate at which data from the Internet arrives at your computer.

Dpi (dots per inch) *See* Dots per inch (dpi).

Drawing software A category of software that provides tools to draw lines, shapes, and colors that can be assembled into diagrams, corporate logos, and schematics that tend to have a flat cartoon-like quality, but are very easy to modify.

Drive bay Storage device "parking spaces" on the system unit case for a desktop computer; until these are used, they are typically hidden from view with a faceplate. *Also called* expansion bay.

Drive mapping In network terminology, assigning a drive letter to a network drive.

DSL (digital subscriber line) A high-speed Internet connection that uses existing telephone lines, requiring close proximity to a switching station.

DSL modem A device that sends and receives digital data to and from computers over telephone lines.

DSS *See* Digital Satellite Service.

DTP software *See* Desktop publishing software.

Dual-core processor A single chip containing the circuitry for two processors; faster than a processor with a single core.

Duplex printer A printer that has the capability of printing on both sides of a page in a single pass.

Duty cycle Determines how many pages a printer is able to print out; is usually measured in pages per month.

DVD (digital video disc or **digital versatile disc)** An optical storage medium similar in appearance and technology to a CD but with higher storage capacity.

DVD authoring software A category of software that provides tools for transferring video footage from a camcorder to a computer, deleting unwanted footage, assembling video segments in any sequence, adding special visual effects, adding a sound track, and creating a DVD.

DVD drive An optical storage device that reads data from CD-ROM and DVD discs.

DVD image A prototype of your DVD stored on your computer. Used for testing and to burn multiple DVDs. *Also called* DVD volume.

DVD+R (digital versatile disc recordable) A DVD disc that stores data using recordable technology.

DVD-R (digital versatile disc recordable) A DVD disc that stores data using recordable technology.

DVD-ROM (digital versatile disc read-only memory) A DVD disc that stores data that has been permanently stamped on the disc surface.

DVD+RW (digital versatile disc rewritable) A DVD disc that stores data using rewritable technology.

DVD-RW (digital versatile disc rewritable) A DVD disc that stores data using rewritable technology.

DVD writer Device that can be used to create and copy CDs and DVDs.

Dynamic Host Configuration Protocol (DHCP) A protocol designed to automatically distribute IP addresses.

Dynamic IP address A temporarily assigned IP address usually provided by an ISP.

EBCDIC **(Extended Binary-Coded Decimal Interchange Code)** A method by which digital computers, usually mainframes, use 0s and 1s to represent character data.

E-commerce (electronic commerce) Business conducted over the Internet, including online shopping, online stock trading, and electronic auctions; characterized in one of four segments: business-to-business (B2B), business-to-consumer (B2C), business-to-government (B2G), or consumer-to-consumer (C2C).

E-wallet (electronic wallet) A category of software that stores and handles the information a customer submits when finalizing an e-commerce purchase. *Also called* digital wallet.

Educational software A category of software that helps you learn and practice new skills.

Edutainment software A category of software that is both educational and entertaining.

EEPROM (electrically erasable programmable read-only memory) A nonvolatile chip that requires no power to hold data and holds computer configuration settings, such as the date and time, hard drive capacity, number of CD/DVD drives, and RAM capacity.

Electronic mail *See* Email.

Electronic portfolio *See* ePortfolio.

Electronic wallet A category of software that stores and processes customer information needed for an e-commerce transaction. *Also called* e-wallet or digital wallet.

Email (electronic mail) A single electronic message or the entire system of computers and software that handles electronic messages transmitted between computers over a communications network.

Email account A service that provides an email address and mailbox.

Email address The unique address for each mailbox on the Internet, which typically consists of a user ID, an @ symbol, and the name of the computer that maintains the mailbox.

Email attachment A separate file that is transmitted along with an email message.

Email authentication Techniques, such as Sender ID and Domain Keys, that verify that email messages originate from the Internet domain from which they claim to have been sent.

Email client software A category of software that is installed on a client computer and has access to email servers on a network. This software is used to compose, send, and read email messages.

Email message A computer file containing a letter or memo that is transmitted electronically via a network.

Email server A computer that uses special software to store and send email messages over the Internet.

Email software A category of software that is used to compose, send, and read email messages. Usually includes an address book to help you maintain contact information.

Email system The collection of computers and software that works together to provide email services.

Encryption The process of scrambling or hiding information so that it cannot be understood without the key necessary to change it back into its original form.

ePortfolio A hypertext version of a résumé that contains links to information and details referenced in the résumé, such as Web sites of former employers or schools and online projects. *Also called* electronic portfolio or Web portfolio.

Ergonomics The study of safe and efficient environments, especially working environments.

Ethernet A type of network on which network nodes are connected by coaxial cable or twisted pair wire; the most popular network architecture, it typically transmits data at 10 or 100 megabits per second.

Ethernet adapter *See* Ethernet card.

Ethernet card A type of network interface card (NIC), or network adapter, designed to support Ethernet protocols sending data to and from network devices, such as workstations or printers, over the network usually using cables. *Also called* Ethernet adapter or NIC.

Ethics *See* Professional ethics.

EULA (end-user license agreement) License agreement that is displayed on the screen when you first install software; you accept the terms of the license by clicking a designated button.

Exa- Prefix for quintillion.

Exabyte Used to identify vast amounts of data; approximately equal to 1 billion gigabytes.

Executable file A file, usually with a .exe extension, containing instructions that tell a computer how to perform a specific task.

Expansion bay Storage device "parking spaces" on the system unit case for a desktop computer; until used these are typically hidden from view with a faceplate. *Also called* drive bays.

Expansion bus The segment of the data bus that transports data between RAM and peripheral devices.

Expansion card A circuit board that is plugged into a slot on a motherboard to add extra functions, devices, or ports.

Expansion port A socket into which the user plugs a cable from a peripheral device, allowing data to pass between the computer and the peripheral device.

Expansion slot A socket or slot on a motherboard designed to hold a circuit board called an expansion card.

Fair use The right to use portions of copyrighted material without the permission of the copyright holder for purposes such as review, criticism, or parody.

Fake Web site A Web site that has been created by a third party to be a clever replica of a legitimate Web site; many are bogus storefronts designed exclusively for collecting credit card numbers from unwary shoppers.

Favorites A list of URLs for Web sites that you can create for your browser to store so that you can revisit those sites easily. *Also called* bookmarks.

Fiber-optic cable A bundle of thin tubes of glass used to transmit data as pulses of light.

Field The smallest meaningful unit of information contained in a data file.

File A named collection of data (such as a computer program, document, or graphic) that exists on a storage medium, such as a hard drive, flash drive, CD, or DVD. *Also called* computer file or data file.

File compression software A category of data compression software that shrinks one or more files into a single file that occupies less storage space than the separate files.

File date The date on which a file was created or last modified and saved as part of the file information; useful if you have created several versions of a file and want to make sure that you know which version is the most recent.

File extension A set of letters and/or numbers added to the end of a filename following a period that helps to identify the file contents or file type.

File format The method of organization used to encode and store data in a computer. Text formats include DOCX and TXT. Graphics formats include BMP, TIFF, and GIF.

File management To organize files and folders on storage media.

File management program A category of software, such as Windows Explorer or Mac OS Finder, that helps users find files and folders on their hard drives or other storage media, as well as, rename, move, copy, and delete files.

File management utility *See* File management program.

File path A combination of the drive letter, subdirectory, filename, and extension that identifies a file (for example, C:\Documents\filename.docx). *Also called* file specification or path.

File server A server that stores files and supplies them to network computers on request.

File size The physical size of a file on a storage medium, usually measured in kilobytes (KB) or megabytes (MB).

File specification *See* File path.

File tag Information that helps describe contents of a file; for example the location, camera settings, and people pictured in a photograph. Tags can be added manually or automatically and appear when viewing file lists in Windows Explorer, as well as in the file's Properties dialog box.

File virus A computer virus that infects executable files, such as programs with .exe filename extensions.

Filename A set of letters or numbers that identifies a file. Consists of a name followed by a period, followed by a file extension. *See also* File extension.

Filename extension *See* File extension.

Filenaming conventions A set of rules established by the operating system that must be followed to create a valid filename.

Finance software A category of software to help you keep a record of monetary transactions and investments.

Finder The file management utility on computers running Mac OS that helps users manage their files.

Firewall Software and/or hardware designed to filter out suspicious packets attempting to enter or leave a computer.

FireWire port A port on a digital camera or computer used to transfer photo data. *Also called* IEEE-1394 port.

Fixed Internet access Links your computer to an ISP from a stationary point, such as a wall socket or roof-mounted antenna.

Fixed wireless access Technology used to connect a computer to the Internet using wireless technology. *Also called* wireless broadband service.

Flash cookie A cookie created by Adobe Flash Player that tracks and targets consumers to collect and store personal data, such as the user's name or progress in a game. *Also called* local shared object. *See also* Cookie.

Flash graphic A popular vector graphics format developed by Adobe that can be used for still images or animations.

Flash memory A type of memory module that can store data without power consumption. It can be reused, making it popular for memory used with digital cameras.

Flash video A popular video format for the PC and Mac platforms; can be used for complex animations.

Folder The subdirectory, or subdivision, of a directory that can contain files or other folders.

Font A typeface or style of lettering, such as Arial, Times New Roman, and Gothic.

Form factor The physical attributes, such as size and dimensions, and intended use, of a component; refers to outer appearance and inner contents.

Format Refers to how all text, pictures, titles, and page numbers appear on the page.

Format shifting The process of converting media files from a format suitable to one device to a format suitable for a different kind of device.

Frame rate Refers to the number of frames displayed per second in a video or film.

Freeware Copyrighted software that is given away by the author or owner.

Frequency The number of times that a wave oscillates (moves back and forth between two points) per second. Short wave lengths have high frequencies.

Front Side Bus (FSB) Refers to the circuitry that transports data to and from the processor.

FTP (File Transfer Protocol) An Internet protocol that transfers files between local and remote host computers.

Full backup A copy of all the files for a specified backup job. *Also called* full-system backup.

Full-system backup *See* Full backup.

Fully qualified domain name (FQDN) An easy-to-remember Web page name that translates directly to the computer's unique IP address. *Also called* domain name.

Function key One of the keys numbered F1 through F12 located at the top of the computer keyboard that activates program-specific commands.

Gadget A utility program on a computer's desktop used to display information such as a clock, calendar, calculator, news aggregators, notes, and weather. *Also called* desktop gadget.

Gateway An electronic link that connects one computer system to another.

General Public License (GPL) Software created under this licensing policy allows people to make copies of software for their own use, to give it to others, or to sell it.

GIF (Graphics Interchange Format) A bitmap graphics file format popularized by CompuServe for use on the Web.

Giga- Prefix for billion.

Gigabit (Gb) Approximately one billion bits.

Gigabyte (GB) Approximately one billion bytes, typically used to refer to RAM and hard drive capacity.

Gigahertz (GHz) A measure of frequency equivalent to one billion cycles per second, usually used to measure speed.

Gradient A smooth blending of shades of different colors from light to dark.

Graphical user interface (GUI) A type of user interface that features on-screen objects, such as menus and icons, manipulated by a mouse. The GUI acronym is pronounced "gooey."

Graphics Any pictures, photographs, or images that can be manipulated or viewed on a computer.

Graphics card A circuit board inserted into a computer to handle the display of text, graphics, animation, and videos. *Also called* video card.

Graphics software A category of software for creating, editing, and manipulating images.

Graphics tablet A device that accepts input from a pressure-sensitive stylus and converts strokes into images on the screen.

Grayscale palette Digital images that are displayed in shades of gray, black, and white.

Grid computing system A network of diverse computers, such as PCs, Macs, workstations, and servers, in which each computer contributes processing resources to solving a single problem.

Groupware A category of business software designed to help several people collaborate on a single project using network or Internet connections.

Hacker A person who creates malicious computer programs sometimes to steal or damage your data or hardware or to assume your identity for financial gain. *Also called* cracker, black hat, or cybercriminal.

Handheld computer A small, pocket-sized computer such as the Apple iPhone, the BlackBerry Smartphone, and the Hewlett-Packard iPAQ, designed to run on its own power supply and provide users with basic applications.

Hard disk drive *See* Hard drive.

Hard drive A computer storage device that contains a large-capacity hard disk sealed inside the drive case.

Hard drive partition A section of a hard drive that is treated as a separate storage unit.

Hard drive platter The component of a hard disk drive on which data is stored. It is a flat, rigid disk made of aluminum or glass and coated with a magnetic oxide.

Hardware The electronic and mechanical devices in a computer system.

Head crash A collision between the read-write head and the surface of the hard disk drive platter, resulting in damage to some of the data on the disk.

History list A list that is created by your browser of the sites you visited so that you can display and track your sessions or revisit the site by clicking the URL in the list.

Hit A list of results in response to a search or query.

Homegroup In Windows 7, a collection of trusted networked computers that automatically share files and folders; access to the homegroup can be protected by a password.

Home page In a Web site, the page that is the first page you see when you go to the site. On an individual computer, the Web page that a browser opens each time it is started.

Host computer A computer system that stores and processes data accessed by multiple terminals from remote locations. In Internet terminology, any computer connected to the Internet.

Hotspot The range of network coverage in a public Wi-Fi network that provides open Internet access to the public. Any Wi-Fi-equipped device that enters a hotspot can gain access to the network's services, although sometimes a password is required or specific terms must be accepted before gaining access.

HTML (Hypertext Markup Language) A standardized format used to specify the format for Web page documents.

HTML document A plain text or ASCII document with embedded HTML tags that dictate formatting and are interpreted by a browser.

HTML form An HTML document containing blank boxes prompting users to enter information that can be sent to a Web server. Commonly used for e-commerce transactions.

HTML script A series of program instructions embedded in the text of an HTML document or in a file referenced from an HTML document; allows Web pages to be interactive and enables e-commerce sites to verify credit card information.

HTML tag An instruction, such as ..., inserted into an HTML document to provide formatting and display information to a Web browser.

HTTP (Hypertext Transfer Protocol) A communications standard that is used to transport Web pages over the Internet.

HTTP status code A code used by Web servers to report the status of a browser's request.

Hub A network device that connects several nodes of a local area network.

Human error A mistake made by a computer operator or programmer. *Also called* operator error.

Hyperlink The fundamental tool for navigating Web pages; you click a text or graphic link to jump to a location in the same Web page, open a different Web page, or go to a different Web site. *Also called* link.

Hypertext A way of linking information through the use of text and multimedia.

Hypertext link An underlined word or phrase that, when clicked, takes you to its designated URL. *Also called* link.

Hypertext Transfer Protocol (HTTP) *See* HTTP.

ICANN (Internet Corporation for Assigned Names and Numbers) A global organization that coordinates the management of the Internet's domain name system, IP addresses, and protocol parameters.

Identity theft When someone steals your personal data, such as your password, and uses it illegally to gain access to a Social Security number, credit card numbers, bank account numbers, health data, and other private details.

Image editing software A category of software that provides a set of electronic pens, brushes, and paints for drawing, creating, or editing graphics such as drawings and photographs. *Also called* paint software.

Incremental backup A backup of the computer files that were added or changed since the last backup—not necessarily the files that changed from the last full backup, but the files that changed since any full or differential backup.

Indexer A search engine component that processes information gathered by a crawler into a list of key words and URLs stored in a database; makes pages easy to find based on their content.

Information The words, numbers, and graphics used as the basis for human actions and decisions.

Information systems degree programs Programs that focus on applying computers to business problems.

Information systems (IS) department The department in a business or organization responsible for developing and maintaining the computers, data, and programs for an information system. *Also called* Information technology (IT) department.

Information technology degree programs Programs that focus on securing, upgrading, and maintaining the computer equipment and software businesses use.

Information technology (IT) department The department in a business or organization that is responsible for the computers, data, software, and support services. *Also called* Information Systems (IS) department.

Information technology (IT) industry Companies involved in the development, production, sales, and support of computers and software.

Information theft Unauthorized access to a computer system, such as military or government computers, to gain restricted information.

Infrared light A wireless transmission technology that uses a frequency range just below the visible light spectrum to transport data signals for short distances with a clear line of sight.

Infrared port Device that accepts infrared light containing photo data that was beamed by a camera to a computer. This method, though slow, eliminates the need for a cable.

Infrared signals Signals that carry data for short distances and with a clear line of sight, such as between a notebook computer and a printer.

Ink jet printer A nonimpact printer that creates characters or graphics by spraying liquid ink onto paper or other media.

Input (n) The information that is conveyed to a computer.

Input (v) The process of entering data into a computer.

Input device A device, such as a keyboard or mouse, that gathers input and transforms it into a series of electronic signals for the computer.

Insertion point Appears on the screen as a flashing vertical bar or flashing underline and indicates where the characters you type will appear on the screen. *Also called* cursor.

Install The process by which programs and data are copied to the hard drive of a computer system and otherwise prepared for access and use.

Installation agreement A version of the license agreement that appears on the computer screen when software is being installed and prompts the user to accept or decline.

Instant messaging (IM) A private chat in which users can communicate with each other using the computer to type messages in real time.

Integrated audio Sound card circuitry that is built into the motherboard of a computer or digital electronic device.

Integrated circuit (IC) A thin slice of silicon crystal containing microscopic circuit elements, such as transistors, wires, capacitors, and resistors. *Also called* chips, computer chips, or microchips.

Intellectual property Refers to the ownership of certain types of information, ideas, or representations. Includes patents, trademarks, and copyrighted material, such as music, photos, software, books, and films.

Intelligent agent Any software that can automate a task or autonomously execute a task when commanded to do so. *Also called* bot.

Internet The worldwide communication infrastructure that links computer networks using TCP/IP protocol.

Internet backbone The major communications links that form the core of the Internet.

Internet forum A Web site where people post comments to discussion threads (topics) which can be read at any time by others who visit the forum.

Internet Service Provider (ISP) A company that maintains Internet computers and telecommunications equipment in order to provide Internet access to businesses, organizations, and individuals.

Internet telephony A set of hardware and software that allows users to make phone calls over the Internet, usually without a long-distance charge. *Also called* Voice over IP (VoIP).

Interpage link A hyperlink that links to a different location on the same Web page.

Interpreter A program that converts high-level instructions in a computer program into machine language instructions, one instruction at a time.

IP (Internet Protocol) One of the main protocols of TCP/IP that is responsible for addressing packets so they can be routed to their destination.

IP address A unique identifying number assigned to each computer connected to the Internet.

ISP (Internet Service Provider) *See* Internet Service Provider.

Java A high-level programming language for Web-based projects.

Java applet Small Java applications that a browser downloads and runs on a computer to perform specialized tasks.

JavaScript Popular scripting language for Web-based applications.

Job search agent An automated program that searches one or more databases and notifies you when it finds a lead on a specific job type.

Joystick A pointing input device often used in gaming as an alternative to a mouse.

JPEG (Joint Photographic Experts Group) A file format that uses compression to store bitmap images. JPEG files have a .jpg filename extension.

Kbps *See* Kilobits per second.

KBps *See* Kilobytes per second.

Kernel The core module of an operating system that typically manages memory, processes, tasks, and files.

Keyboard An arrangement of letter, number, and special function keys that acts as the primary input device to the computer.

Keylogger A type of program that records your keystrokes; notorious for stealing passwords.

Keyword A word or term used as the basis for a database or Web-page search. *See* Search term.

Keyword stuffing An unethical practice in which meta keywords are manipulated to gain high relevancy rankings. Search engines take steps to foil such practices.

Kilo- A prefix for thousand.

Kilobit (Kb or Kbit) Approximately 1,000 bits; exactly 1,024 bits.

Kilobits per second (Kbps) A measurement of connection speed that refers to the amount of data that travels between a subscriber's computer and an ISP within a given time period.

Kilobyte (KB or Kbyte) Approximately 1,000 bytes; exactly 1,024 bytes.

Kilobytes per second (KBps) A measurement based on how many bytes per second are downloaded.

Label In a worksheet, any text that is used to describe data.

LAN (local area network) An interconnected group of computers and peripherals located within a relatively limited geographic area, such as a home office, building, or campus.

LANjacking A practice that occurs when hackers cruise around with a Wi-Fi-equipped computer set up to search for Wi-Fi signals coming from home and corporate Wi-Fi networks so they can access and use unsecured Wi-Fi networks to hack into files and gain unauthorized access to larger, wired networks. *Also called* war driving.

Laptop *See* Notebook computer.

Laptop computer A type of portable computer that is small and light enough to be carried from one location to another. *See also* Notebook computer.

Laser light A focused beam of light that, with a clear line of sight, can transmit data over long distances.

Laser mouse A pointing device that uses a laser as the light source to track movement.

Laser printer A printer that uses laser-based technology, similar to that used by photocopiers, to produce text and graphics.

Layout The physical position of each element on a page, in a spreadsheet, slide, or any report from a database.

LCD (liquid crystal display) monitor A type of flat panel computer screen that produces an image by manipulating light within a layer of liquid crystal cells.

LCD screen *See* LCD.

Library In Windows 7, used to organize files and folders on the storage media by containing links to files that are a similar type, such as document files or photo files; default libraries in Windows 7 are Documents, Music, Pictures, and Videos.

License agreement A legal contract that defines the ways in which you may use a computer program. For personal computer software, you will find the license on the outside of the package, on a separate card inside the package, on the CD/DVD packaging, or in one of the program files.

Linear editing A video editing technique that records segments of video from one tape to another.

Link The fundamental tool for navigating Web pages; you click a text or graphic link to jump to a location in the same Web page, open a different Web page, or go to a different Web site. *Also called* hyperlink.

Link popularity A measure of the quality and quantity of links from one Web page to others; pages with links to and from popular sites tend to get high relevancy ratings.

Linux A server operating system that is a derivative of UNIX and available as freeware.

Local application Software that is intended to be installed on a computer's hard disk.

Logical address A network address that is assigned to a network device when the physical address is in an incorrect format.

Mac (Macintosh computer) A personal computer platform designed and manufactured by Apple Computer.

MAC address A physical address, a unique number assigned to a network interface card when it is manufactured; used for some low-level network functions and can also be used to establish network security.

Mac OS The operating system software designed for use on Apple Macintosh and iMac computers.

Machine language A low-level language written in binary code that the computer can execute directly.

Magnetic storage The recording of data onto disks or tape by magnetizing particles of an oxide-based surface coating.

Mailbox Any storage location for email, such as the Inbox or Outbox.

Mailto link A link on a Web page that automatically opens a pre-addressed email form.

Main executable file A program that is used to start and run software, usually with a .exe file extension.

Mainframe computer A large, fast, and expensive computer used by businesses or government agencies to provide centralized storage, processing, and management for large amounts of data.

Malicious code *See* Malicious software.

Malicious software Any program or set of program instructions that is designed to surreptitiously enter a computer and disrupt its normal operations. Malicious software, including viruses, worms, and Trojan horses, is created and unleashed by individuals referred to as "hackers" or "crackers." *Also called* malware or malicious code.

Malware *See* Malicious software.

MAN (metropolitan area network) A public, high-speed network that can transmit voice and data within a range of 50 miles.

Markup language A language that provides text and graphics formatting through the use of tags. Examples include HTML, XHTML, and XML.

Mass-mailing worm A software program that often includes an attachment containing a worm and is difficult to track; spreads by sending itself to every address in the address book of an infected computer and can cause havoc on personal computers, LANs, and Internet servers.

Mathematical modeling software A category of software that provides tools for solving a wide range of math, science, and engineering problems.

Mbps *See* Megabits per second.

MBps *See* Megabytes per second.

Mechanical mouse Pointing device that reads its position based on the movement of a ball that rolls over a mouse pad placed on a desk.

Media player *See* Digital media player.

Mega- Prefix for million.

Megabit (Mb or **Mbit)** Approximately 1 million bits; exactly 1,048,576 bits.

Megabits per second (Mbps) A measurement of connection speed that refers to the amount of data that travels between a subscriber's computer and an ISP within a given time period.

Megabyte (MB) Approximately 1 million bytes; exactly 1,048,576 bytes.

Megabytes per second (Mbps) A measurement used to define data transfer rates.

Megahertz (MHz) A measure of frequency equivalent to 1 million cycles per second.

Megapixel A million pixels; used to express the resolution and quality of an image.

Memory The computer circuitry that holds data waiting to be processed, stored, or output.

Memory card reader A device that connects to a PC via a USB or serial cable that reads data from a flash memory module.

Memory stick A type of portable solid-state memory card that can store up to 2 TB of storage with very fast data transfer rates.

Meta keyword A keyword entered into a Web page header section when it is created and describes the page contents.

Metafile Graphics file that contains both vector and bitmap data.

Metasearch engine A program that performs broad-based Web searches, such as searching more than one job database at a time.

Microcomputer A category of computer that is built around a single processor chip.

Microprocessor *See* Processor.

Microsoft Windows An operating system developed by Microsoft Corporation that provides a graphical interface. Current version is Microsoft Windows 8. Previous versions include Windows 3.1, Windows 95, Windows 98, Windows ME, Windows 2000, Windows XP, Windows NT, Windows Vista, and Windows 7.

Microwave Electromagnetic wave with a frequency of at least 1 gigahertz.

Microwave signals Signals that transport data for large corporate networks and form part of the Internet backbone.

MIDI (Musical Instrument Digital Interface) A standardized way in which sound and music are encoded and transmitted between devices that play music.

MIDI sequence Digitally encoded music stored on a computer. Usually a file with a .mid, .cmf, or .rol file extension.

MIDI sequencing software A category of software used for creating sound effects and for controlling keyboards and other digital instruments.

Millisecond (ms) A thousandth of a second; used to measure access time, the time it takes a computer to find data on a storage medium and read it.

MIMO (multiple-input multiple-output) technology A technology that uses two or more antennae to essentially send multiple sets of signals between network devices.

Mobile app A program (such as a game, calendar, stock market tracker, traffic or weather monitor, or news feed) designed to run on mobile devices (such as smartphones and tablet computers). *Also called* mobile application.

Mobile broadband A data service offered by cellular service providers; requires a fast connection, a data service subscription, and mobile broadband equipment.

Mobile Internet Access Technologies, such as Mobile WiMAX, that offer a continuous Internet connection as you are walking or in transit; similar in concept to cellular phone service that allows you to move freely within the coverage area as it seamlessly hands off your signal from one tower to the next.

Mobile WiMAX A wireless communication option designed to offer Internet access with seamless handoff from the coverage area of one tower to the coverage area of another tower.

Modem A device that sends and receives data to and from computers over cable, satellite, or telephone lines.

Modifier key The [Ctrl], [Alt], or [Shift] key, used in conjunction with another key to expand the repertoire of available commands.

Modulate The process of changing the characteristics of a signal, such as when a modem changes a digital pulse into an analog signal.

Monitor A display device that forms an image by converting electrical signals from the computer into points of colored light on the screen; usually a computer's primary output device.

Motherboard The main circuit board in a computer that houses chips and other electronic components.

Mouse An input device that allows the user to select and move objects on the screen by moving it on a surface. *Also called* pointing device.

MP3 A file format that provides highly compressed audio files with very little loss of sound quality.

MP3 encoder Software that compresses a WAV file into an MP3 file.

MP3 player Software that plays MP3 music files.

MPEG (Moving Pictures Expert Group) A highly compressed file format for digital videos. Files in this format have a .mpg extension.

ms *See* Millisecond.

Multi-core processor A single chip containing the circuitry for multiple processors; faster than a processor with a single core.

Multifunction device Hardware that works both as an input and output device to combine the functions of a printer, scanner, copier, fax, and answering machine.

MultiMedia card (MMC) Solid state storage that includes a built-in controller in a package about the size of a postage stamp that was initially used in mobile phones and pagers but that is now also used in digital cameras and portable media players.

Multimedia Messaging Service (MMS) Messages sent using a smartphone or mobile device that can include text of up to 140 to 160 characters and include video, audio, and graphics.

Multiple-user license A software license that allows more than one person to use the software; priced per user and allows the allocated number of people to use the software at any time.

Multitasking Provides processor and memory management services that allow two or more tasks, jobs, or programs to run at the same time. Most of today's operating systems offer multitasking services.

NAN (neighborhood area network) A public, high-speed network that can transmit voice and data within a limited geographical area, usually spread over several buildings.

Nanosecond A unit of time representing 1 billionth of a second.

Narrowband A term that refers to communications channels that have low bandwidth.

Native file format A file format that is unique to a program or group of programs and has a unique file extension.

Navigation keypad The keypad on a keyboard with the Home, End, and arrow keys; used to efficiently move the screen-based insertion point or cursor.

Nested *See* Nested folders.

Nested folders A method of file management whereby folders are created within folders to hold folders as well as files. *Also called* subfolders.

Netbook A type of portable computer that is smaller than a notebook or a laptop computer. Classified as subnotebooks, these small computers are scaled-down versions of standard clamshell-style notebook computers.

Network A collection of computers and related devices, connected in a way that allows them to share data, hardware, and software. *Also called* computer network.

Network access point (NAP) A device that connects network service provider equipment and links.

Network-attached storage (NAS) A storage device that directly connects to a network.

Network card An expansion board mounted inside a computer to allow access to a local area network. *Also called* network interface card or NIC.

Network device An electronic device that broadcasts network data, boosts signals, or routes data to its destination.

Network-enabled printer A printer that connects directly to the network, rather than to one of the computers on a network.

Network hub A device that links two or more nodes of a wired network; accepts data from one of the computers and then broadcasts it to all of the other network nodes.

Network interface card (NIC) A small circuit board that sends data from and collects incoming data for a workstation over a network. *Also called* network card.

Network print server device A device that allows a workstation to be connected to the network without going through a workstation.

Network router A device that can transmit data from one network to another; used to connect LANs to WANs, it is useful for connecting a home network to the Internet. *Also called* router.

Network service provider (NSP) Company that maintains a series of nationwide Internet links.

Network specialist/administrator A person typically responsible for day-to-day operations and system maintenance in an information system that is centered on a network. *Also called* network manager.

Network switch A connection device that sends data only to network devices specified as the destination; used instead of a hub, it can increase a network's performance and security because data isn't flowing to every device on the network. *Also called* switch.

Networked peripheral A device, such as a printer or scanner, directly connected to a network rather than to a workstation.

News aggregator Downloaded software used to view the RSS feeds on your computer.

NIC *See* Network interface card.

Node Each hardware device on a network, including computers, servers, and printers; in a hierarchical database, a segment or record type.

Nonlinear editing A digital, video editing technique that uses a random-access device, such as a hard drive, to hold both the original footage and finished video.

Notation software A category of software used to help musicians compose, edit, and print musical scores.

Notebook computer Small, lightweight, portable computer that usually runs on batteries. *Also called* laptop or laptop computer.

Numeric data Numbers that represent quantities and can be used in arithmetic operations.

Numeric keypad Calculator-style input device for numbers located toward the right side of a keyboard.

Object code The low-level instructions that result from compiling source code.

Office productivity software A category of software that integrates word processing, spreadsheet, database, drawing, and presentation capabilities.

Offshoring Relocating business processes, such as development and production, to lower-cost locations in other countries.

OLED (organic light emitting diodes) A technology used on electronic device screens that features a crisp image and a faster response rate than a standard LCD screen; it also uses less power.

Online Refers to being connected to the Internet.

Online auction The electronic equivalent to home-based yard sales, rummage sales, and auctions; hosted by an Internet auction site, such as eBay, sellers post their merchandise or services and buyers bid for the posted items.

Online job bank An online database of job opening announcements that spans many industries or just one industry.

Online payment A system for payment that offers an alternative to credit cards to pay for auction items and to wire money over the Internet. *See also* Person-to-person payment.

Online shopping bag *See* Online shopping cart.

Online shopping cart An e-commerce cookie that stores information about items selected and collected for purchase. *Also called* online shopping bag.

Open source software A category of software, such as Linux, that includes its uncompiled source code, which can be modified and distributed by programmers.

Operating system (OS) System software that controls the computer's use of its hardware resources, such as memory and disk storage space.

Operator error The most common cause of lost and/or inaccurate data; mistakes made by a computer user, such as entering the wrong data or deleting a needed file. *Also called* human error.

Optical drive A CD drive, a DVD drive, a Blu-ray Disc (BD) drive, or a combination drive that is usually mounted inside the system unit.

Optical mouse Pointing device that uses an LED light and computer chip to track a light beam as it bounces off a surface, such as a desk or mouse pad.

Optical storage A means of recording data as light and dark spots on a CD, DVD, BD, or other optical media.

Organic light emitting diode *See* OLED.

Output The results produced by a computer (for example, reports, graphs, documents, pictures, and music).

Output device A device, such as a monitor or printer, that displays, prints, or transmits the results of processing from the computer memory.

Outsourcing The use of independent contractors, such as service and consulting firms, to perform specific tasks.

P2P filesharing The use of P2P (peer-to-peer) protocols that allow users to exchange files from one computer directly with another computer over the Internet.

Packet A small unit of data transmitted over the Internet.

Packet sniffer A computer program that monitors data as it travels over networks to observe and open any packet traveling on the network. *Also called* protocol analyzer.

Pages per minute (ppm) A measure of printer speed; most personal or small business printers are rated 15–30 ppm.

Paint software A category of software that provides a set of electronic pens, brushes, and paints for painting images on the screen. *Also called* image editing software.

PAN (personal area network) A term used to refer to the interconnection of personal digital devices within a range of about 30 feet (10 meters) and without the use of wires or cables.

Password A special set of characters used to restrict access to a computer or network.

Password manager Utility software that generates secure passwords and stores them along with user IDs and their corresponding sites.

Patch A small program or programs designed to correct, secure, or enhance an existing program.

Path *See* File path.

PC A microcomputer that uses Windows software and contains an Intel-compatible processor.

PC card A type of expansion card, such as for memory, a modem, sound card, or network card, and devices such as a hard drive that fit in a slot on a notebook computer.

Peer-to-peer network (P2P) The arrangement in which one workstation/server shares resources with another workstation/server; each computer on such a network must act as both a file server and workstation.

Peripheral device A component or equipment, such as a printer or scanner, that expands a computer's input, output, or storage capabilities.

Personal computer (PC) A microcomputer designed for use by an individual user for applications such as Internet browsing, graphics, email, and word processing; the term PC is often used to refer to personal computers running the Windows platform.

Personal finance software A category of software designed to help manage individual finances.

Personal firewall software A category of software designed to analyze and control incoming and outgoing packets.

Person-to-person payment An e-commerce method of payment that bypasses credit cards and instead uses an automatic electronic payment service. *See also* Online payment.

Peta- Prefix for thousand trillion.

Petabyte (PB) Used to identify vast amounts of data; approximately equal to 1,000 terabytes.

PGA (pin-grid array) A common chip design used for processors.

Pharming A method used by hackers to redirect a Web site's traffic to another (bogus) Web site.

Phishing A way that hackers steal passwords by posing as a legitimate representative of an official organization, such as your ISP, your bank, or an online payment service, in order to persuade you to disclose highly confidential information.

Phoneme Unit of sound that is a basic component of words; can be produced by speech synthesizers.

Photo editing software A category of software that provides tools that simplify common photo editing tasks; includes features specially designed to fix poor-quality photos by modifying contrast and brightness, cropping out unwanted objects, and removing red eye.

Photo printer Uses ink jet technology to produce photographic quality images.

Photosites A grid of tiny light-sensitive diodes on a digital camera's CCD. Photosites correspond to pixels, and determine the resolution of the image.

Physical address An address built into the circuitry of a network device at the time of its manufacture.

Physical topology The actual layout of network devices, wires, and cables.

Piconet A Bluetooth network that forms automatically when two or more Bluetooth devices come within range of each other.

Pixel (picture element) The smallest unit in a graphic image. Computer display devices use a matrix of pixels to display text and graphics.

Pixel interpolation A process used by graphics software to average the color of adjacent pixels in an image.

Place shifting Allows media that originates in one place to be accessed from another place without changing the device on which it is stored.

Platform A family or category of computers based on the same underlying software and hardware.

Player *See* Plug-in.

Plug and Play (PnP) The ability of a computer to recognize and adjust the system configuration for a newly added device automatically.

Plug-in A software module that adds a specific feature to a system. For example, in the context of the Web, a plug-in adds a feature to the user's browser, such as the ability to read PDF files. *Also called* helper application, add-on, or player.

PNG (Portable Network Graphics) A type of graphics file format similar to, but newer than, GIF or JPEG.

Podcast Downloadable Internet broadcast that includes newscasts, radio shows, and teleconferences; typically downloaded to a portable media player. *See also* Webcast.

Podcasting A way to deliver a podcast audio file through RSS feed technology.

Pointing device An input device, such as a mouse, that you use to manipulate an on-screen pointer and other screen-based graphical controls.

Pointing stick Pointing device typically used with notebook computers as an alternative to a mouse that looks like a pencil eraser and is embedded in the keyboard of a notebook computer. Push up, down, or sideways to move the on-screen pointer. *Also called* TrackPoint.

POP (Post Office Protocol) A protocol that is used to retrieve email messages from an email server.

Pop-up ad An advertisement that appears in a separate window when you enter a Web site or connect to Web pages.

Port probe The use of automated software to locate computers that have open ports and are vulnerable to unauthorized access. *Also called* port scan.

Port scan *See* Port probe.

Portable application A category of software designed to run from removable storage such as a CD, a DVD, or a USB flash drive. *Also called* Portable software.

Portable computer Computer that is small and light enough to be carried from one place to another, including notebook computers, laptop computers, netbooks, and tablet computers.

Portable Internet access The ability to easily move your Internet service from one location to another. Portable Internet access services include Wi-Fi, portable satellite, and portable wireless.

Portable media player *See* Digital media player.

Portable satellite Internet service A mobile option for Internet service in which a satellite dish can be quickly deployed from a stopped vehicle; transmits signals to and receives signals from a geostationary satellite.

Portable software A category of software designed to run from removable storage such as a CD, a DVD, or a USB flash drive. *Also called* portable application.

Power failure A complete loss of power to the computer system, usually caused by something over which you have no control.

Power-on self-test (POST) A diagnostic process that runs during startup to check components of the computer, such as the graphics card, RAM, keyboard, and disk drives.

Power spike An increase in power that lasts only a short time—less than one millionth of a second. Spikes can be caused by malfunctions in the local generating plant or the power distribution network, and they are potentially more damaging to your computer system and data than a power failure. *Also called* voltage spike.

Power strip A device that provides additional outlets for power but provides no protection against power spikes, surges, or failures.

Power surge A fluctuation in power that lasts a little longer than a power spike—a few millionths of a second. Surges can be caused by malfunctions in the local generating plant or the power distribution network, and they are potentially more damaging to your computer system and data than a power failure.

Ppm *See* Pages per minute.

Presentation software A category of software that provides tools to combine text, graphics, graphs, animation, and sound into a series of electronic slides that can be output on a projector, or as overhead transparencies, paper copies, or 35-millimeter slides.

Print server A server that handles jobs sent to network printers.

Printer A peripheral output device that creates hard copy output, including text, photographs, and graphic images.

Printer resolution Determines the quality or sharpness of printed images and text.

Processing The manipulation of data (symbols that represent facts, objects, and ideas) using a systematic series of actions.

Processor An integrated circuit that contains the circuitry for processing data. It is a single-chip version of the central processing unit (CPU) found in all computers. *Also called* microprocessor.

Processor clock A device on the motherboard of a computer responsible for setting the pace of executing instructions.

Productivity software A category of software that has the potential to help people do their work more efficiently.

Professional ethics On-the-job choices and activities that reflect our values.

Program The instructions that tell a computer how to perform a specific task such as word processing, graphics, or email. *Also called* application software or software.

Program data file Supplied with a software package, contains any data that is necessary for a task, but that is not supplied by the user, for example, a dictionary file. Program data files have filename extensions, such as .txt, .bmp, and .hlp.

Programming language Provides the tools that a programmer uses to create software. *Also called* computer language.

Project management software A category of software specifically designed as a tool for planning, scheduling, and tracking projects and their costs.

Proprietary software A software program that has restrictions on its use that are delineated by copyright, patents, or license agreements. Might be free or distributed commercially and includes commercial software, demoware, shareware, freeware, and open source software.

Protocol analyzer A computer program that monitors data as it travels over networks; can observe and open any packet traveling on the network. *Also called* packet sniffer.

Protocols Rules that ensure the orderly and accurate transmission and reception of data. Protocols start and end transmissions, recognize errors, send data at the appropriate speed, and identify the correct senders and recipients.

Prototype An experimental or trial version of a device or system.

Public domain software A category of software that is available for use by the public without restriction, except that it cannot be copyrighted.

Public Wi-Fi network A wireless LAN that provides open Internet access to the public.

Quality assurance specialist A computer professional who participates in alpha and beta test cycles of software. Also refers to a person who examines and tests computer chips and devices.

Query processor A Web browser component that looks for search terms in a search engine's indexed database and displays a list of relevant Web sites in the browser.

QuickTime A video and animation file format developed by Apple Computer that can also be run on PCs. QuickTime files have a .mov extension.

RAM (random access memory) A type of computer memory circuit that holds data, program instructions, and the operating system while the computer is on.

RAM cache Special high-speed memory that gives the CPU rapid access to data that would otherwise be accessed from memory elsewhere on the motherboard. *Also called* cache.

Random access The ability of a storage device (such as a hard drive) to go directly to a specific storage location without having to search sequentially from a beginning location. *Also called* direct access.

Ransomware Malicious code that encrypts documents and other files, then demands payment for the decryption key.

Rasterization The process of superimposing a grid over a vector image and determining the color depth for each pixel.

RAW A graphics format used by professional and semi-professional photographers to capture images before they are stored in other formats.

Ray tracing A technique by which light and shadow are added to a 3D image.

Read-only (ROM) technology Data stamped on the CD or DVD surface when it was manufactured, such as commercial software, music, and movies.

Read-write head The mechanism in a hard drive that magnetizes particles on the storage disk surface to write data, or senses the bits that are present to read data.

RealAudio (.ra) An audio file format developed by Real Networks especially for streaming audio data over the Web.

Really Simple Syndication *See* RSS.

Record In the context of database management, a record is the set of fields of data that pertain to a single entity in a database.

Recordable technology Optical storage technology used to create CDs, DVDs, and BDs.

Recovery CD A CD that contains all the operating system files and application software files necessary to restore a computer to its original state. *Also called* recovery disk.

Recovery disk *See* Recovery CD.

Reference software A category of software that provides a collection of information and a way to access that information.

Remote Access Trojan (RAT) A Trojan that allows remote hackers to transmit files to victims' computers, search for data, run programs, and use a victim's computer as a relay station for breaking into other computers. *See also* Trojan horse.

Rendering In graphics software, the process of creating a 3D solid image by covering a wireframe drawing and applying computer-generated highlights and shadows.

Repeater A network device that receives and retransmits amplified signals so that they can retain the necessary strength to reach their destinations.

Resolution The density of the grid used to display or print text and graphics, usually expressed in pixels; the greater the horizontal and vertical density, the higher the resolution.

Resolution dependent Graphics, such as bitmaps, for which the quality of the image is dependent on the number of pixels that make up the image.

Resource In the context of a computer system, refers to any component that is required to perform work such as the processor, RAM, storage space, and peripherals.

Response rate In the context of display device technology, response rate is how fast a screen updates the information being displayed.

Restore The act of moving data from a backup storage medium to a hard drive in the event original data has been lost.

Restore point A snapshot of your computer settings created by a Windows utility either automatically when you install new software or manually, which you can use if you have a hard drive failure or instability.

Rewritable technology (RW) An optical storage technology that uses phase change technology to alter a crystal structure on the disc surface to create patterns of light and dark spots, making it possible for stored data to be recorded and erased or modified multiple times.

RF (radio frequency) signals Data that is broadcast and received via radio waves with a transceiver.

Rich Site Summary *See* RSS.

Risk management The process of weighing threats to computer data against the amount of expendable data and the cost of protecting crucial data.

ROM (read-only memory) One or more integrated circuits that contain permanent instructions the computer uses during the boot process.

ROM BIOS (basic input/output system) A small set of basic input/output system instructions stored in ROM that causes the computer system to load critical operating files when the user turns on the computer.

Root directory The main directory of a disk or other storage medium.

Router A device used by LANs and found at each intersection on the Internet backbone that examines the IP address of incoming data and forwards the data toward its destination. *Also called* network router.

RSS (Rich Site Summary or **Really Simple Syndication)** A format for feeding or syndicating news or any content from Web sites to your computer.

RSS feeds Software that provides subscribers with summaries that link to the full versions of the RSS content.

Run-length encoding A graphics file compression technique that looks for patterns of bytes and replaces them with messages that describe the patterns.

Safe Mode A menu option that appears when Windows is unable to complete the boot sequence. By entering Safe Mode, a user can shut down the computer and then try to reboot it.

Salami shaving Redirecting small, unnoticeable amounts of money from large amounts.

Sampling rate The number of times per second a sound is measured during the recording process; a higher sampling rate means higher-quality sound.

Scanner An input device that converts a printed page of text or images into a digital format.

Screen size On a display device, the measurement in inches from one corner of the screen diagonally across to the opposite corner.

Script Program that contains a list of commands that are automatically executed as needed.

Scripting error An error that occurs when a browser or server cannot execute a statement in a script.

SDRAM (synchronous dynamic RAM) A type of RAM that synchronizes itself with the CPU, thus enabling it to run at much higher clock speeds than conventional RAM.

Search engine Program that uses keywords to find information on the Internet and return a list of relevant documents.

Search operator A word or symbol that has a specific function within a search, such as "AND" or "+." *Also called* Boolean operator.

Search site A Web site that provides a variety of tools to help you find information on the Web based on keyword searches.

Search term A word or phrase you enter into a search engine that is related to the information you want to find. *Also called* keyword.

SEC (single edge contact) cartridge A common, cassette-like chip designed for processors.

Secure connection Technology that encrypts data transmitted between a computer and a Web site to protect the data during electronic transactions so that the data must be decrypted before it can be used. Technologies that create secure connections include SSL and S-HTTP.

Secure Digital (SD) card Solid state storage device popular for MP3 and digital imaging storage that features fast data transfer rates.

Security software A category of software designed to protect computers from various forms of destructive software and unauthorized intrusions.

Security specialist A computer professional who analyzes security threats, implements solutions, and develops policies and procedures to protect computer equipment and data.

Security suite Integrates several security modules, such as antivirus, firewall, and privacy modules, that are used to protect against the most common types of malware, unauthorized access, and spam; might include additional features, such as Wi-Fi detection that warns of possible intrusions into your wireless network, and parental controls for monitoring and controlling children's Internet usage.

Security utility Protects and secures the computer. Helps control nuisance ads, intrusion attempts, and spam; also provides file-encryption and antivirus software.

Semiconducting material Materials such as silicon and germanium that are used to make chips. The conductive properties create miniature electronic pathways and components, such as transistors. *Also called* semiconductors.

Sequential access A form of data storage, usually on computer tape, that requires a device to read or write data one record after another, starting at the beginning of the medium.

Server A computer on a network that supplies the network with shared data and storage.

Server operating system Provides communications and routing services that allow computers to share data, programs, and peripheral devices by routing data and programs to each user's local computer, where the actual processing takes place.

Server-side script A series of statements that runs on a server; enables the server to accept data submitted by a form, processes that data, and then generates a custom HTML document that is sent to the browser for display.

Server software The software used by servers to locate and distribute data requested by a network or Internet users.

Service pack A collection of updates, fixes, and/or enhancements to a software program delivered in the form of a single installable package usually distributed over the Internet.

SET (Secure Electronic Transaction) A system that ensures the security of financial transactions on the Web.

Setup program A program module supplied with a software package for the purpose of installing the software.

Shared resource Hardware, software, and data on a network made available for authorized network users to access.

Shareware Copyrighted software marketed under a license that allows users to use the software for a trial period and then send in a registration fee if they wish to continue to use it.

Shopping bag An e-commerce cookie that stores information about items selected and collected for purchase. *Also called* online shopping cart.

Shrink-wrap license A software license usually sealed in an envelope, plastic box, or shrink wrapping that goes into effect as soon as you open the packaging.

S-HTTP (Secure HTTP) A method of encrypting data transmitted between a computer and a Web server by encrypting individual packets of data as they are transmitted.

Signal scrambling Term commonly used for obscuring cable or satellite television images until they are unscrambled by a set-top box or other authorized mechanism.

Single-user license A license that limits use of the software to only one person at a time.

Site license A software license generally priced at a flat rate and allows software to be used on all computers at a specific location.

Skins utility Used to customize screen-based desktops with screensavers that display clever graphics when the machine is idle.

Slide A component of presentation software that combines text, graphics, graphs, animations, and sound; a series of electronic slides can be displayed on a monitor for a one-on-one presentation or on a computer projection device for group presentations.

Smartphone A handheld digital communications device that usually has many features such as removable storage, email, Web access, voice communications, built-in camera, and GPS.

SMS (Short Message Service) System used to send text messages of 140 to 160 characters or less using your smartphone or mobile device. *See also* Text messaging.

SMTP An Internet protocol that transfers email messages from client computers to an email server.

Sniffing A technique used by hackers to guess a password by intercepting information sent out over computer networks.

Social networking An online networking activity through Web sites that offer registered members security in knowing that they are interacting with friends of friends rather than with strangers. Examples include LinkedIn and Facebook.

Socket A communication path between two remote programs.

Software The instructions that tell a computer how to perform tasks, such as system software and application software.

Software engineering A systematic approach to the design, creation, and retirement of computer software.

Software license A legal contract that defines the ways in which you may use a computer program. For personal computer software, the license is on the outside of the package, on a separate card inside the package, on the CD packaging, or in one of the program files. *Also called* license agreement.

Software publisher A company that produces computer software, including applications, operating systems, and programming languages.

Software suite A collection of application software sold as a single package.

Software upgrade Improvements or enhancements to existing installed software that is available to consumers who already have a software program installed.

Solid-state drive (SSD) A storage device that can be internal or external to a computer that has no moving parts.

Solid-state storage A variety of compact storage cards, pens, and sticks that stores data in a nonvolatile, erasable, low-power chip in a microscopic grid of cells.

Solid-state technology Data storage technology that stores data in a durable, erasable, low-power chip with no moving parts.

Sound card A small circuit board that gives the computer the ability to accept audio input from a microphone, play sound files stored on disks and CD-ROMs, and produce audio output through speakers or headphones. Required for high-quality music, narration, and sound effects.

Sound system Speakers and a circuit board (sound card) used to create high-quality music, narration, and sound effects using a computer.

Source code Computer instructions written in a high-level language.

Spam Unwanted electronic junk mail that arrives in your Inbox.

Spam filter Software that automatically routes advertisements and other junk mail to the Deleted Items folder maintained by your email client; can be effective for blocking unwanted emails.

Speakers Output devices that receive signals for the computer's sound card to play music, narration, or sound effects.

Speech recognition A category of software that analyzes voice sounds and converts them into phonemes.

Speech recognition software The process by which computers recognize voice patterns and words and convert them to digital data.

Speech synthesis The process by which computers produce sound that resembles spoken words.

Spotlight One of the file management utilities included with Mac OS.

Spreadsheet An electronic worksheet for numerical calculations presented in the form of a grid of columns and rows. Each cell in the grid has a unique cell reference, or address, that is based on its column and row location. *Also called* worksheet.

Spreadsheet software The software for creating electronic worksheets that hold data in cells and perform calculations based on that data.

Spyware Any technology on the Web that secretly gathers information and relays it to advertisers or other interested parties.

SSID (service set identifier) The name that identifies a particular LAN in areas where there are overlapping wireless networks, such as in a city or on a college campus; SSIDs help you log into the right network.

SSL (Secure Sockets Layer) A security protocol that uses encryption to establish a secure connection between a computer and a Web server.

Static IP address A permanently assigned and unique IP address, used by hosts or servers.

Statistical software A category of software that helps you analyze large sets of data to discover relationships and patterns, summarize survey results, test scores, experiment results, or population data.

Stealth virus A virus that can escape detection from antivirus software by removing its own signature and hiding in memory.

Storage The area in a computer that holds data on a permanent basis when it is not immediately needed for processing.

Storage capacity The amount of data that can be stored on a storage medium.

Storage device A mechanical apparatus that records data to and retrieves data from a storage medium.

Storage medium The physical material used to store computer data, such as a flash drive, a hard drive, USB flash drive, or an optical disc.

Storage technology Defines the data storage systems (storage media and storage devices) used by computers to store data and program files.

Store-and-forward technology A technology used by communications networks in which an email message is temporarily held in storage on a server until it is requested by a client computer.

Stored program A set of instructions that resides on a storage device, such as a hard drive, and can be loaded into memory and executed.

Streaming audio An Internet sound technology that sends a small segment of an audio file to a user's computer and begins to play it while the next segment is sent.

Streaming video An Internet video technology that sends a small segment of a video file to a user's computer and begins to play it while the next segment is sent.

Streaming video technology *See* Streaming video.

Strong encryption Encryption that is difficult to decrypt without the encryption key.

Style A combination of attributes—colors, sizes, and fonts—that specifies the way text is displayed.

Subdirectory A directory found under the root directory.

Subfolder A method of file management whereby folders are created within another folder. *Also called* nested folder.

Supercomputer The fastest and most expensive type of computer. At the time it is built, one of the fastest computers in the world; can tackle tasks that would not be practical for other computers such as breaking codes and modeling worldwide weather systems.

Surge protector *See* Surge strip.

Surge strip A low-cost device used to protect computer systems from power spikes and surges. *Also called* surge protector or surge suppressor.

Surge suppressor *See* Surge strip.

SVG (Scalable Vector Graphics) A graphics format designed specifically for Web display that automatically resizes when displayed on different screens.

Swap file The data that has been moved from RAM to virtual memory.

SWF graphic A popular vector graphics format created with Adobe Flash software that requires a browser plug-in to be viewed. SWF files use the .swf extensions and can be static or animated. *See also* Flash graphics.

Synthesized sound Artificially created sound, usually found in MIDI music or synthesized speech.

System palette A selection of colors that is used by an operating system to display graphic elements.

System requirements Specifications for the operating system and hardware configuration necessary for a software product to work correctly.

System software Computer programs that help the computer carry out essential operating tasks, such as an operating system.

System unit The case or box that contains the computer's power supply, storage devices, main circuit board, processor, and memory.

System utility Software that provides disk maintenance, such as tracking down and fixing disk errors or corrupted files. *Also called* utility software or utilities.

Systems analyst A computer professional responsible for analyzing information requirements, designing new information systems, and supervising the implementation of new information systems.

Table (database) An arrangement of data in a grid of rows and columns. In a relational database, a collection of record types with their data.

Table (layout) Gridlike structure that can hold text or pictures.

Tablet computer A portable computing device featuring a touch-sensitive screen that can be used as a writing or a drawing pad.

Tape A sequential magnetic storage technology that consists of a tape for the storage medium and a tape drive for the storage device.

Tape cartridge A removable magnetic tape module similar to a cassette tape.

Tape storage A sequential magnetic storage technology that consists of a tape for the storage medium and a tape drive for the storage device. Data is arranged as a long sequence of bits that begins at one end of the tape and stretches to the other end.

Tax preparation software A specialized type of personal finance software designed to help gather annual income and expense data, identify deductions, and calculate tax payments.

TCP (Transmission Control Protocol) One of the main protocols of TCP/IP that is responsible for establishing a data connection between two hosts and breaking data into packets.

TCP/IP (Transmission Control Protocol/Internet Protocol) A standard set of communication rules used by every computer that connects to the Internet.

Technical support specialist A computer professional who provides phone or online help to customers of computer companies and software publishers.

Technical writer A person who specializes in writing explanations of technical concepts and procedures.

Telecommute To use available technology to work from home or another off-site location.

Tera- Prefix for trillion.

Terabyte Used to identify a large amount of data; approximately equal to one trillion bytes.

Text editor A program with the basic functionality of a word processor that is used to create plain, unformatted simple text documents.

Text messaging A system used to send messages of 140 to 160 characters or less using your smartphone or mobile device. *See also* SMS (Short Message Service).

Text-to-speech software A category of software that generates speech, based on written text, that is played back through a computer's sound card.

Third-party utility Utility purchased from a third-party vendor.

Thumbnail A graphical link that expands in size when clicked.

TIFF (Tag Image File Format) A file format (.tif extension) for bitmap images that automatically compresses the file data.

Time shifting The process of recording a broadcast, such as a television show, so that it can be played back at a more convenient time.

TLS (Transport Layer Security) Protocols that encrypt data traveling between a client computer and an HTTP server; a successor to SSL.

Toner The fine powder in the cartridges used in laser printers that creates the image on the page.

Top-level domain The major domain categories into which groups of computers on the Internet are divided: com, edu, gov, int, mil, net, and org.

Touch screen technology Display device technology that makes it possible for touch or handwriting to be used to input data.

Touchpad An alternative input device often found on notebook computers. *Also called* trackpad.

Tracing software A category of software that locates the edges of objects in a bitmap graphic and converts the resulting shape into a vector graphic.

Trackball Pointing input device used as an alternative to a mouse.

Trackpad An alternative input device often found on notebook computers. *Also called* touchpad.

TrackPoint An alternative input pointing device often found on notebook computers. *Also called* pointing stick.

Tracks A series of concentric or spiral storage areas created on a storage medium during the formatting process.

Transceiver A combined transmitter/receiver used to send and receive data in the form of radio frequencies.

Transistor Key component in all integrated circuits; smaller, cheaper, and more reliable than vacuum tubes.

Trojan horse A computer program that appears to perform one function while actually doing something else, such as inserting a virus into a computer system or stealing a password. *Also called* Trojan virus.

Trojan virus *See* Trojan horse.

True Color bitmap graphic A color image with a color depth of 24 bits or 32 bits where each pixel can be displayed using any of 16.7 million different colors.

Two-factor authentication A form of user verification that verifies identity using two independent elements of confirmation, such as an ATM card and a PIN.

Unicode A 16-bit character representation code that can represent more than 65,000 characters.

Uninstall To remove software files, references, and Windows Registry entries from a computer's hard drive.

UNIX A multi-user, multitasking server operating system developed by AT&T's Bell Laboratories in 1969.

Unzipped Refers to files that have been uncompressed.

Uploading The process of sending a copy of a file from a local computer to a remote computer.

UPS (uninterruptible power supply) A device containing a battery that provides a continuous supply of power and other circuitry to prevent spikes and surges from reaching your computer.

Upstream speed The rate of data that is transmitted from your computer to the Internet.

URL (Uniform Resource Locator) The unique address of a Web page.

USB drive *See* USB flash drive.

USB flash drive A portable solid state storage device featuring a built-in connector that plugs directly into a computer's USB port. *Also called* USB drive.

USB (universal serial bus) port Popular ports for connecting peripheral devices including mice, cameras, mp3 players, scanners, and printers, that have USB connections.

User ID A combination of letters and numbers that identifies a user on a computer. *Also called* username.

User interface The software and hardware that enable people to interact with computers.

User rights Rules that limit the directories and files that each user can access; they can restrict the ability to erase, create, write, read, and find files.

Username *See* User ID.

Utility software A subcategory of system software designed to augment the operating system by providing ways for a user to control the allocation and use of hardware resources. *Also called* utilities.

V

alidation code Series of alphanumeric characters supplied by the software publisher that is required to complete the installation of software.

Value A number used in a calculation.

Vandalism Intentional defacement of Web sites.

Vector graphic Image generated from descriptions that determine the position, length, and direction in which lines and shapes are drawn.

Video A recorded series of images that displays motion with sound.

Video capture The process of converting analog video signals into digital format.

Video capture device A device that is used to convert analog video signals into digital data stored on a hard drive.

Video capture software Used with a video capture device to convert analog video signals into digital format.

Video card *See* Graphics card.

Video clip A small video file in a video format; large video files are often composed of many video clips.

Video editing software A category of software that provides a set of tools for transferring video footage from a camcorder to a computer, clipping out unwanted footage, assembling video

segments in any sequence, adding special visual effects, and adding a sound track.

Videocasting A video file that is distributed through downloads or the use of a feed, such as RSS; used to distribute news, sports, music, educational tutorials, and blogs.

Videoconferencing camera *See* Web cam.

Viewing angle width Measurement of a monitor or display device that indicates how far to the side you can still clearly see the screen image.

Virtual memory A computer's use of hard drive storage to simulate RAM.

Virtual private network (VPN) A way for users to access corporate networks by using a remote connection from home or a customer's office.

Virus A set of program instructions that attaches itself to a file, reproduces itself, and spreads to other files. It can corrupt files, destroy data, display an irritating message, or otherwise disrupt computer operations. *Also called* computer virus.

Virus definition A file that stores the information that your antivirus software uses to identify and eradicate viruses, Trojan horses, and worms.

Virus distribution Launching viruses, worms, and Trojan horses.

Virus hoax A message, usually email, that makes claims about a virus problem that doesn't actually exist.

Virus signature The unique computer code contained in a virus that helps with its identification. Antivirus software searches for known virus signatures.

VOB (Video Object) Industry-standard format for stand-alone DVD players.

Voice over IP (VoIP) Technology used to send and receive voice conversations over the Internet. *Also called* Internet telephony.

Voiceband modem The type of modem that would typically be used to connect a computer to a telephone line. *See also* Modem.

VoIP *See* Voice over IP (VoIP).

Volatile Data that can exist only with a constant power supply.

Voltage spike *See* Power spike.

VPN *See* Virtual private network.

W

AN (wide area network) An interconnected group of computers and peripherals that covers a large geographical area, such as multiple branches of a corporation.

War driving A practice that occurs when hackers cruise around with a Wi-Fi-equipped notebook computer to search for unsecured Wi-Fi network signals so they can access and hack into files to gain unauthorized access to larger, wired networks. *Also called* LANjacking.

Wave (.wav) An audio file format created as Windows native sound format.

Waveform audio A digital representation of sound in which a sound wave is represented by a series of samples taken of the wave height.

Wavetable A set of prerecorded musical instrument sounds in MIDI format.

Weak encryption Encryption that is relatively simple to decrypt without the encryption key.

Web (World Wide Web) An Internet service that links documents and information from computers distributed all over the world using the HTTP protocol. *Also called* World Wide Web.

Web 2.0 Refers to new and innovative ways of using the Web, such as social networking sites, wikis, blogs, and Web-based applications.

Web app *See* Web application.

Web application (Web app) A category of software that, instead of being installed on a local computer, is accessed with a Web browser; runs on a remote computer connected to the Internet.

Web authoring software A category of software that provides easy-to-use tools for composing, assembling, and generating HTML to develop Web pages.

Web-based email An email account that stores, sends, and receives email on a Web site rather than a user's computer.

Web browser A software program that runs on your computer and helps you access Web pages. *Also called* browser.

Web cache A stored collection of temporary files from previously viewed Web pages. *Also called* browser cache.

Web cam A camera that captures digital images using a computer.

Web crawler A search engine component that combs the Web to gather data that's representative of the contents of Web pages; downloads Web pages and submits them to an indexing utility for processing.

Web page A document on the World Wide Web that consists of a specially coded HTML file with associated text, audio, video, graphics, and links to other Web pages.

Web palette A standard selection of colors that all Internet browsers can display.

Web portfolio A hypertext version of a résumé that contains links to information and details referenced in the résumé, such as Web sites of former employers or schools and online projects. *Also called* electronic portfolio or ePortfolio.

Web resource Any data file that has a URL, such as an HTML document, a graphic, or a sound file.

Web search engine A program designed to help people locate information on the Web by formulating simple keyword queries; the search engine displays results or hits as a list of relevant Web sites. *Also called* search engine.

Web server A computer and software that stores and transmits Web pages to computers connected to the Internet.

Web site Location on the World Wide Web that contains information relating to specific topics.

Web site designer A computer professional who creates, tests, posts, and modifies Web pages.

Webcast A Web file that can contain audio as well as video used to distribute information that is distributed through downloads or the use of a feed, such as RSS. *See also* Podcast.

Whistleblower Someone in an organization who decides to speak out against on-the-job activities that are contrary to the mission of the organization or threaten the public interest.

Whistleblowing The disclosure by an employee (or professional) of confidential information that relates to some danger, fraud, or other illegal or unethical conduct connected with the workplace.

Widget A term used to define a utility program on an Apple computer's desktop used to display information such as a clock, calendar, calculator, news aggregators, notes, and weather. *Also called* dashboard widget.

Wi-Fi (Wireless Fidelity) A set of wireless networking technologies defined by IEEE 802.11 standards. Wi-Fi networks operate at 2.4 or 5.8 GHz.

Wi-Fi adapter *See* Wi-Fi card.

Wi-Fi card Required for transmission on a Wi-Fi network, required by every workstation and network peripheral; includes a transceiver (transmitter and receiver) and an antenna to transmit signals. *Also called* Wi-Fi adapter or transceiver.

Wi-Fi hotspot The range of network coverage where any Wi-Fi-equipped device that enters a hotspot can gain access to the network's services.

Wi-Fi network A wireless network that transmits data as radio waves over predefined frequencies, much like cordless telephones.

Wiki A collaborative document posted on the Web that can be viewed and changed by users.

WiMAX (Worldwide Interoperability for Microwave Access) An Ethernet-compatible network technology that is essentially wide-area Wi-Fi, with a range of 30 miles and data transmission rates of 70 Mbps.

Windows *See* Microsoft Windows.

Windows Explorer A file management utility included with most Windows operating systems that helps users manage their files.

Windows Media Audio (WMA) A compressed audio format with good sound quality; used on music download sites.

Windows Media DRM Developed by Microsoft to provide secure delivery of digital content over networks.

Windows Media Video A video format that offers sophisticated compression options for high-quality images; used for desktop video, PDA video, and streaming video over the Web.

Windows Phone A version of the Windows operating system designed for portable or mobile computers and smartphones.

Windows Registry A crucial data file maintained by the Windows operating system that contains the settings for hardware and software that has been installed on the system. *Also called* Registry.

Wired network A type of network in which the data travels over cables or wires from one device to another.

Wireframe A representation of a 3D object using separate lines, which resemble wire, to create a model.

Wireless access point Provides a central point for data transmitted over a wireless network by broadcasting signals to any devices with compatible Wi-Fi cards.

Wireless encryption Scrambles the data transmitted between wireless devices and then unscrambles the data only on devices that have a valid encryption key.

Wireless infrastructure network A network that uses a centralized broadcasting device, such as a wireless access point or router.

Wireless network A type of network that uses radio or infrared signals, instead of cables, to transmit data from one network device to another.

Wireless network key The basis for scrambling and unscrambling the data transmitted between wireless devices, similar to a password, only longer.

Wireless router A wireless access point that includes routing circuitry that can connect a Wi-Fi network to the Internet.

WMA *See* Windows Media Audio (WMA).

WMV *See* Windows Media Video.

Word processing software A category of software that assists the user in producing documents, such as reports, letters, papers, and manuscripts.

Word size The number of bits a CPU can manipulate at one time, which is dependent on the size of the registers in the CPU and the number of data lines in the bus.

Workgroup A group of computers that communicate with each other to share resources on a network.

Worksheet A computerized, or electronic, spreadsheet, based on a grid of columns and rows.

Workstation (1) A computer connected to a local area network. (2) A powerful desktop computer designed for specific tasks.

World Wide Web Consortium (W3C) An international consortium of companies involved with the Internet and developing open standards.

Worm A software program designed to enter a computer system, usually a network, through security "holes" and then replicate itself. *Also called* computer worm.

WPA (Wi-Fi Protected Access) Addresses some of WEP's weaknesses; utilizes TKIP (Temporal Key Integrity Protocol) to encrypt data based on the user's password.

WPA2 A secure way to encrypt data; uses the same kind of strong encryption required by government agencies and businesses.

X

XHTML The follow-up version to HTML 4, a set of specifications for creating HTML documents that a browser can display as a Web page.

XML (eXtensible Markup Language) A document format similar to HTML; allows the Web page developer to define customized tags for the purpose of creating more interactivity.

Z

Zeta- Prefix for sextillion.

Zettabyte Used to identify vast amounts of data; approximately equal to 1,000 exabytes (270 bytes).

Zipped Refers to files that have been compressed.

Zombie A computer controlled by a bad bot that carries out instructions from a malicious leader without the knowledge of the computer owner.

Index

Getting Started with Excel 2013

CASE ▶ You have been hired as an assistant at Quest Specialty Travel (QST), a company offering tours that immerse travelers in regional culture. You report to Grace Wong, the vice president of finance. As Grace's assistant, you create worksheets to analyze data from various divisions of the company, so you can help her make sound decisions on company expansion and investments.

Unit Objectives

After completing this unit, you will be able to:

- Understand spreadsheet software
- Identify Excel 2013 window components
- Understand formulas
- Enter labels and values and use the AutoSum button

- Edit cell entries
- Enter and edit a simple formula
- Switch worksheet views
- Choose print options

Files You Will Need

EX A-1.xlsx
EX A-2.xlsx
EX A-3.xlsx
EX A-4.xlsx
EX A-5.xlsx

Learning
Outcomes
• Describe the
 uses of Excel
• Define key spread-
 sheet terms

Understand Spreadsheet Software

Microsoft Excel is the electronic spreadsheet program within the Microsoft Office suite. An **electronic spreadsheet** is an application you use to perform numeric calculations and to analyze and present numeric data. One advantage of a spreadsheet program over pencil and paper is that your calculations are updated automatically, so you can change entries without having to manually recalculate. TABLE A-1 shows some of the common business tasks people accomplish using Excel. In Excel, the electronic spreadsheet you work in is called a **worksheet**, and it is contained in a file called a **workbook**, which has the file extension .xlsx. **CASE** ▸ *At Quest Specialty Travel, you use Excel extensively to track finances and manage corporate data.*

DETAILS

When you use Excel, you have the ability to:

- **Enter data quickly and accurately**

 With Excel, you can enter information faster and more accurately than with pencil and paper. FIGURE A-1 shows a payroll worksheet created using pencil and paper. FIGURE A-2 shows the same worksheet created using Excel. Equations were added to calculate the hours and pay. You can use Excel to recreate this information for each week by copying the worksheet's structure and the information that doesn't change from week to week, then entering unique data and formulas for each week.

- **Recalculate data easily**

 Fixing typing errors or updating data is easy in Excel. In the payroll example, if you receive updated hours for an employee, you just enter the new hours and Excel recalculates the pay.

- **Perform what-if analysis**

 The ability to change data and quickly view the recalculated results gives you the power to make informed business decisions. For instance, if you're considering raising the hourly rate for an entry-level tour guide from $12.50 to $15.00, you can enter the new value in the worksheet and immediately see the impact on the overall payroll as well as on the individual employee. Any time you use a worksheet to ask the question "What if?" you are performing **what-if analysis**. Excel also includes a Scenario Manager where you can name and save different what-if versions of your worksheet.

- **Change the appearance of information**

 Excel provides powerful features, such as the Quick Analysis tool, for making information visually appealing and easier to understand. Format text and numbers in different fonts, colors, and styles to make it stand out.

- **Create charts**

 Excel makes it easy to create charts based on worksheet information. Charts are updated automatically in Excel whenever data changes. The worksheet in FIGURE A-2 includes a 3-D pie chart.

- **Share information**

 It's easy for everyone at QST to collaborate in Excel using the company intranet, the Internet, or a network storage device. For example, you can complete the weekly payroll that your boss, Grace Wong, started creating. You can also take advantage of collaboration tools such as shared workbooks, so that multiple people can edit a workbook simultaneously.

- **Build on previous work**

 Instead of creating a new worksheet for every project, it's easy to modify an existing Excel worksheet. When you are ready to create next week's payroll, you can open the file for last week's payroll, save it with a new filename, and modify the information as necessary. You can also use predesigned, formatted files called **templates** to create new worksheets quickly. Excel comes with many templates that you can customize.

Quest Specialty Travel
Trip Advisor Division Payroll Calculator

Name	Hours	O/T Hrs	Hrly Rate	Reg Pay	O/T Pay	Gross Pay
Brueghel, Pieter	40	4	16.50	660–	132–	792–
Cortona, Livia	35	0	11–	385–	0–	385–
Klimt, Gustave	40	2	13–	520–	52–	572–
Le Pen, Jean-Marie	29	0	15–	435–	0–	435–
Martinez, Juan	37	0	13–	481–	0–	461–
Mioshi, Keiko	39	0	20.50	799.50	0–	799.50
Sherwood, Burton	40	0	16.50	660–	0–	660–
Strano, Riccardo	40	8	16–	640–	256–	896–
Wadsworth, Alicia	40	5	13–	520–	130–	650–
Yamamoto, Johji	38	0	15–	570–	0–	570–

FIGURE A-2: Excel worksheet

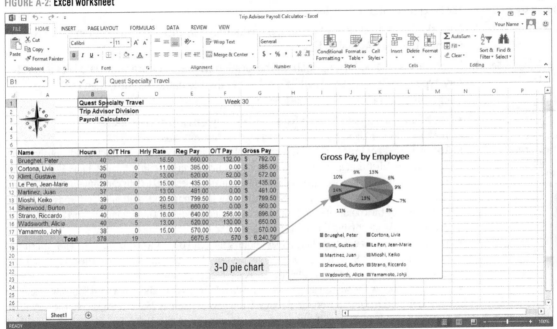

TABLE A-1: Business tasks you can accomplish using Excel

you can use spreadsheets to	by
Perform calculations	Adding formulas and functions to worksheet data; for example, adding a list of sales results or calculating a car payment
Represent values graphically	Creating charts based on worksheet data; for example, creating a chart that displays expenses
Generate reports	Creating workbooks that combine information from multiple worksheets, such as summarized sales information from multiple stores
Organize data	Sorting data in ascending or descending order; for example, alphabetizing a list of products or customer names, or prioritizing orders by date
Analyze data	Creating data summaries and short lists using PivotTables or AutoFilters; for example, making a list of the top 10 customers based on spending habits
Create what-if data scenarios	Using variable values to investigate and sample different outcomes, such as changing the interest rate or payment schedule on a loan

Identify Excel 2013 Window Components

Learning
Outcomes
• Open and save an
Excel file
• Identify Excel
window elements

To start Excel, Microsoft Windows must be running. Similar to starting any program in Office, you can use the Start screen thumbnail on the Windows taskbar, the Start button on your keyboard, or you may have a shortcut on your desktop you prefer to use. If you need additional assistance, ask your instructor or technical support person. **CASE** ▸ *You decide to start Excel and familiarize yourself with the worksheet window.*

1. **Start Excel, click** Open Other Workbooks **on the navigation bar, click** Computer, **then click** Browse **to open the Open dialog box**

2. **In the Open dialog box, navigate to the location where you store your Data Files, click** EX A-1.xlsx, **click** Open

 The file opens in the Excel window.

3. **Click the** FILE **tab, click** Save As **on the navigation bar, click** Computer, **then click** Browse **to open the Save As dialog box**

4. **In the Save As dialog box, navigate to the location where you store your Data Files if necessary, type** EX A-Trip Advisor Payroll Calculator **in the File name text box, then click** Save

 Using FIGURE A-3 as a guide, identify the following items:

 • The **Name box** displays the active cell address. "A1" appears in the Name box.
 • The **formula bar** allows you to enter or edit data in the worksheet.
 • The **worksheet window** contains a grid of columns and rows. Columns are labeled alphabetically and rows are labeled numerically. The worksheet window can contain a total of 1,048,576 rows and 16,384 columns. The intersection of a column and a row is called a **cell**. Cells can contain text, numbers, formulas, or a combination of all three. Every cell has its own unique location or **cell address**, which is identified by the coordinates of the intersecting column and row. The column and row indicators are shaded to make identifying the cell address easy.
 • The **cell pointer** is a dark rectangle that outlines the cell you are working in. This cell is called the **active cell**. In FIGURE A-3, the cell pointer outlines cell A1, so A1 is the active cell. The column and row headings for the active cell are highlighted, making it easier to locate.
 • **Sheet tabs** below the worksheet grid let you switch from sheet to sheet in a workbook. By default, a workbook file contains one worksheet—but you can have as many as 255, in a workbook. The New sheet button to the right of Sheet 1 allows you to add worksheets to a workbook. **Sheet tab scrolling buttons** let you navigate to additional sheet tabs when available.
 • You can use the **scroll bars** to move around in a worksheet that is too large to fit on the screen at once.
 • The **status bar** is located at the bottom of the Excel window. It provides a brief description of the active command or task in progress. **The mode indicator** in the lower-left corner of the status bar provides additional information about certain tasks.

5. **Click cell** A4

 Cell A4 becomes the active cell. To activate a different cell, you can click the cell or press the arrow keys on your keyboard to move to it.

6. **Click cell** B5, **press and hold the mouse button, drag** ⇗ **to cell** B14, **then release the mouse button**

 You selected a group of cells and they are highlighted, as shown in FIGURE A-4. A selection of two or more cells such as B5:B14 is called a **range**; you select a range when you want to perform an action on a group of cells at once, such as moving them or formatting them. When you select a range, the status bar displays the average, count (or number of items selected), and sum of the selected cells as a quick reference.

FIGURE A-3: Open workbook

FIGURE A-4: Selected range

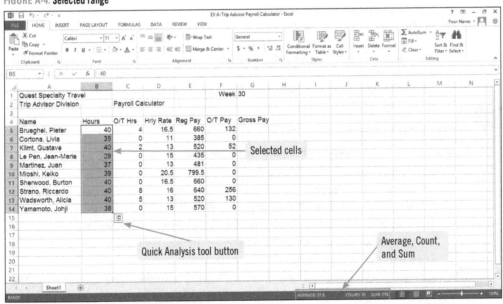

Using SkyDrive and Web Apps

If you have a free Microsoft account, you can save your Excel files to SkyDrive, a free cloud-based service from Microsoft. When you save files to SkyDrive, you can access them on other devices—such as a tablet or smart phone. SkyDrive is available as an app on smart phones, which makes access very easy. You can open files to view them on any device and

you can even make edits to them using **Office Web Apps**, which are simplified versions of the apps found in the Office 2013 suite. Because the Web Apps are online, they take up no computer disk space, and you can use them on any Internet-connected device. You can find more information in the "Working in the Cloud" appendix.

Understand Formulas

Learning
Outcomes
• Explain how a
formula works
• Identify Excel arith-
metic operators

Excel is a truly powerful program because users at every level of mathematical expertise can make calculations with accuracy. To do so, you use formulas. A **formula** is an equation in a worksheet. You use formulas to make calculations as simple as adding a column of numbers, or as complex as creating profit-and-loss projections for a global corporation. To tap into the power of Excel, you should understand how formulas work. **CASE** *Managers at QST use the Trip Advisor Payroll Calculator workbook to keep track of employee hours prior to submitting them to the Payroll Department. You'll be using this workbook regularly, so you need to understand the formulas it contains and how Excel calculates the results.*

STEPS

1. **Click cell E5**

 The active cell contains a formula, which appears on the formula bar. All Excel formulas begin with the equal sign (=). If you want a cell to show the result of adding 4 plus 2, the formula in the cell would look like this: =4+2. If you want a cell to show the result of multiplying two values in your worksheet, such as the values in cells B5 and D5, the formula would look like this: =B5*D5, as shown in FIGURE A-5. While you're entering a formula in a cell, the cell references and arithmetic operators appear on the formula bar. See TABLE A-2 for a list of commonly used arithmetic operators. When you're finished entering the formula, you can either click the Enter button on the formula bar or press [Enter].

2. **Click cell F5**

 An example of a more complex formula is the calculation of overtime pay. At QST, overtime pay is calculated at twice the regular hourly rate times the number of overtime hours. The formula used to calculate overtime pay for the employee in row 5 is:

 O/T Hrs times (2 times Hrly Rate)

 In the worksheet cell, you would enter: =C5*(2*D5), as shown in FIGURE A-6. The use of parentheses creates groups within the formula and indicates which calculations to complete first—an important consideration in complex formulas. In this formula, first the hourly rate is multiplied by 2, because that calculation is within the parentheses. Next, that value is multiplied by the number of overtime hours. Because overtime is calculated at twice the hourly rate, managers are aware that they need to closely watch this expense.

DETAILS

In creating calculations in Excel, it is important to:

• **Know where the formulas should be**

 An Excel formula is created in the cell where the formula's results should appear. This means that the formula calculating Gross Pay for the employee in row 5 will be entered in cell G5.

• **Know exactly what cells and arithmetic operations are needed**

 Don't guess; make sure you know exactly what cells are involved before creating a formula.

• **Create formulas with care**

 Make sure you know exactly what you want a formula to accomplish before it is created. An inaccurate formula may have far-reaching effects if the formula or its results are referenced by other formulas, as shown in the payroll example in FIGURE A-6.

• **Use cell references rather than values**

 The beauty of Excel is that whenever you change a value in a cell, any formula containing a reference to that cell is automatically updated. For this reason, it's important that you use cell references in formulas, rather than actual values, whenever possible.

• **Determine what calculations will be needed**

 Sometimes it's difficult to predict what data will be needed within a worksheet, but you should try to anticipate what statistical information may be required. For example, if there are columns of numbers, chances are good that both column and row totals should be present.

FIGURE A-5: **Viewing a formula**

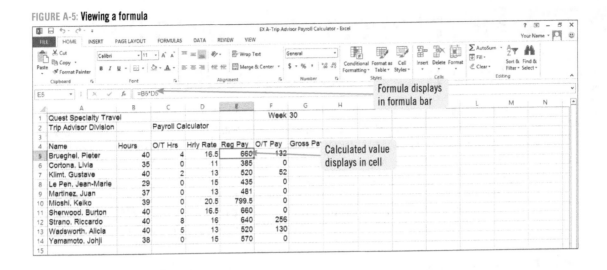

Formula displays in formula bar

E5 =B5*D5

	A	B	C	D	E	F	G	H
1	Quest Specialty Travel					Week 30		
2	Trip Advisor Division		Payroll Calculator					
3								
4	Name	Hours	O/T Hrs	Hrly Rate	Reg Pay	O/T Pay	Gross Pa	
5	Brueghel, Pieter	40	4	16.5	660	132		
6	Cortona, Livia	35	0	11	385	0		
7	Klimt, Gustave	40	2	13	520	52		
8	Le Pen, Jean-Marie	29	0	15	435	0		
9	Martinez, Juan	37	0	13	481	0		
10	Mioshi, Keiko	39	0	20.5	799.5	0		
11	Sherwood, Burton	40	0	16.5	660	0		
12	Strano, Riccardo	40	8	16	640	256		
13	Wadsworth, Alicia	40	5	13	520	130		
14	Yamamoto, Johji	38	0	15	570	0		
15								

Calculated value displays in cell

FIGURE A-6: **Formula with multiple operators**

Formula to calculate overtime pay

F5 =C5*(2*D5)

	A	B	C	D	E	F	G	H
1	Quest Specialty Travel					Week 30		
2	Trip Advisor Division		Payroll Calculator					
3								
4	Name	Hours	O/T Hrs	Hrly Rate	Reg Pay	O/T Pay	Gross Pay	
5	Brueghel, Pieter	40	4	16.5	660	132		
6	Cortona, Livia	35	0	11	385	0		
7	Klimt, Gustave	40	2	13	520	52		
8	Le Pen, Jean-Marie	29	0	15	435	0		
9	Martinez, Juan	37	0	13	481	0		
10	Mioshi, Keiko	39	0	20.5	799.5	0		
11	Sherwood, Burton	40	0	16.5	660	0		
12	Strano, Riccardo	40	8	16	640	256		
13	Wadsworth, Alicia	40	5	13	520	130		
14	Yamamoto, Johji	38	0	15	570	0		
15								

TABLE A-2: **Excel arithmetic operators**

operator	purpose	example
+	Addition	=A5+A7
-	Subtraction or negation	=A5-10
*	Multiplication	=A5*A7
/	Division	=A5/A7
%	Percent	=35%
^ (caret)	Exponent	=6^2 (same as 6^2)

Enter Labels and Values and Use the AutoSum Button

Learning
Outcomes
• Build formulas with
 the AutoSum
 button
• Copy formulas
 with the fill handle

To enter content in a cell, you can type in the formula bar or directly in the cell itself. When entering content in a worksheet, you should start by entering all the labels first. **Labels** are entries that contain text and numerical information not used in calculations, such as "2012 Sales" or "Travel Expenses". Labels help you identify data in worksheet rows and columns, making your worksheet easier to understand. **Values** are numbers, formulas, and functions that can be used in calculations. To enter a calculation, you type an equal sign (=) plus the formula for the calculation; some examples of an Excel calculation are "=2+2" and "=C5+C6". Functions are Excel's built-in formulas; you learn more about them in the next unit. **CASE** *You want to enter some information in the Trip Advisor Payroll Calculator workbook, and use a very simple function to total a range of cells.*

STEPS

1. **Click cell** A15, **then click in the** formula bar

 Notice that the **mode indicator** on the status bar now reads "Edit," indicating you are in Edit mode. You are in Edit mode any time you are entering or changing the contents of a cell.

QUICK TIP
If you change your mind and want to cancel an entry in the formula bar, click the Cancel button ✕ on the formula bar.

2. **Type** Totals, **then click the** Enter button ✓ **on the formula bar**

 Clicking the Enter button accepts the entry. The new text is left-aligned in the cell. Labels are left-aligned by default, and values are right-aligned by default. Excel recognizes an entry as a value if it is a number or it begins with one of these symbols: +, -, =, @, #, or $. When a cell contains both text and numbers, Excel recognizes it as a label.

3. **Click cell** B15

 You want this cell to total the hours worked by all the trip advisors. You might think you need to create a formula that looks like this: =B5+B6+B7+B8+B9+B10+B11+B12+B13+B14. However, there's an easier way to achieve this result.

4. **Click the** AutoSum button ∑ **in the Editing group on the HOME tab on the Ribbon**

 The SUM function is inserted in the cell, and a suggested range appears in parentheses, as shown in FIGURE A-7. A **function** is a built-in formula; it includes the **arguments** (the information necessary to calculate an answer) as well as cell references and other unique information. Clicking the AutoSum button sums the adjacent range (that is, the cells next to the active cell) above or to the left, although you can adjust the range if necessary by selecting a different range before accepting the cell entry. Using the SUM function is quicker than entering a formula, and using the range B5:B14 is more efficient than entering individual cell references.

QUICK TIP
You can create formulas in a cell even before you enter the values to be calculated; the results will be recalculated as soon as the data is entered.

5. **Click** ✓ **on the formula bar**

 Excel calculates the total contained in cells B5:B14 and displays the result, 378, in cell B15. The cell actually contains the formula =SUM(B5:B14), and the result is displayed.

6. **Click cell** C13, **type** 6, **then press** [Enter]

 The number 6 replaces the cell's contents, the cell pointer moves to cell C14, and the value in cell F13 changes.

7. **Click cell** C18, **type** Average Gross Pay, **then press** [Enter]

 The new label is entered in cell C18. The contents appear to spill into the empty cells to the right.

QUICK TIP
You can also press [Tab] to complete a cell entry and move the cell pointer to the right.

8. **Click cell** B15, **position the pointer on the** lower-right corner of the cell **(the fill handle) so that the pointer changes to** +, **drag the** + **to cell** G15, **then release the mouse button**

 Dragging the fill handle across a range of cells copies the contents of the first cell into the other cells in the range. In the range B15:G15, each filled cell now contains a function that sums the range of cells above, as shown in FIGURE A-8.

9. **Save your work**

FIGURE A-7: Creating a formula using the AutoSum button

FIGURE A-8: Results of copied SUM functions

Navigating a worksheet

With over a million cells available in a worksheet, it is important to know how to move around in, or **navigate**, a worksheet. You can use the arrow keys on the keyboard ↑ , ↓ , → or ← to move one cell at a time, or press [Page Up] or [Page Down] to move one screen at a time. To move one screen to the left press [Alt][Page Up]; to move one screen to the right press

[Alt][Page Down]. You can also use the mouse pointer to click the desired cell. If the desired cell is not visible in the worksheet window, use the scroll bars or use the Go To command by clicking the Find & Select button in the Editing group on the HOME tab on the Ribbon. To quickly jump to the first cell in a worksheet press [Ctrl][Home]; to jump to the last cell, press [Ctrl][End].

Excel 2013

Edit Cell Entries

Learning
Outcomes
• Edit cell entries in
 the formula bar
• Edit cell entries in
 the cell

You can change, or **edit**, the contents of an active cell at any time. To do so, double-click the cell, click in the formula bar, or just start typing. Excel switches to Edit mode when you are making cell entries. Different pointers, shown in TABLE A-3, guide you through the editing process. **CASE** *You noticed some errors in the worksheet and want to make corrections. The first error is in cell A5, which contains a misspelled name.*

STEPS

1. **Click cell A5, then click to the right of P in the formula bar**

 As soon as you click in the formula bar, a blinking vertical line called the **insertion point** appears on the formula bar at the location where new text will be inserted. See FIGURE A-9. The mouse pointer changes to $\bar{I}$ when you point anywhere in the formula bar.

2. **Press [Delete], then click the Enter button ✓ on the formula bar**

 Clicking the Enter button accepts the edit, and the spelling of the employee's first name is corrected. You can also press [Enter] or [Tab] to accept an edit. Pressing [Enter] to accept an edit moves the cell pointer down one cell, and pressing [Tab] to accept an edit moves the cell pointer one cell to the right.

3. **Click cell B6, then press [F2]**

 Excel switches to Edit mode, and the insertion point blinks in the cell. Pressing [F2] activates the cell for editing directly in the cell instead of the formula bar. Whether you edit in the cell or the formula bar is simply a matter of preference; the results in the worksheet are the same.

4. **Press [Backspace], type 8, then press [Enter]**

 The value in the cell changes from 35 to 38, and cell B7 becomes the active cell. Did you notice that the calculations in cells B15 and E15 also changed? That's because those cells contain formulas that include cell B6 in their calculations. If you make a mistake when editing, you can click the Cancel button ✕ on the formula bar *before* pressing [Enter] to confirm the cell entry. The Enter and Cancel buttons appear only when you're in Edit mode. If you notice the mistake *after* you have confirmed the cell entry, click the Undo button ↺ on the Quick Access toolbar.

5. **Click cell A9, then double-click the word Juan in the formula bar**

 Double-clicking a word in a cell selects it. When you selected the word, the Mini toolbar automatically displayed.

6. **Type Javier, then press [Enter]**

 When text is selected, typing deletes it and replaces it with the new text.

7. **Double-click cell C12, press [Delete], type 4, then click ✓**

 Double-clicking a cell activates it for editing directly in the cell. Compare your screen to FIGURE A-10.

8. **Save your work**

 Your changes to the workbook are saved.

Recovering unsaved changes to a workbook file

You can use Excel's AutoRecover feature to automatically save (Autosave) your work as often as you want. This means that if you suddenly lose power or if Excel closes unexpectedly while you're working, you can recover all or some of the changes you made since you saved it last. (Of course, this is no substitute for regularly saving your work: this is just added insurance.) To customize the AutoRecover settings, click the FILE tab, click Options, then click Save. AutoRecover lets you decide how often and into which location it should Autosave files. When you restart Excel after losing power, a Document Recovery pane opens and provides access to the saved and Autosaved versions of the files that were open when Excel closed. You can also click the FILE tab, click Open on the navigation bar, then click any file in the Recent Workbooks list to open Autosaved workbooks.

FIGURE A-9: **Worksheet in Edit mode**

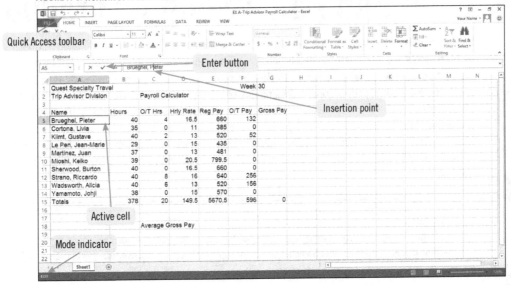

Quick Access toolbar

Enter button

Insertion point

Active cell

Mode indicator

FIGURE A-10: **Edited worksheet**

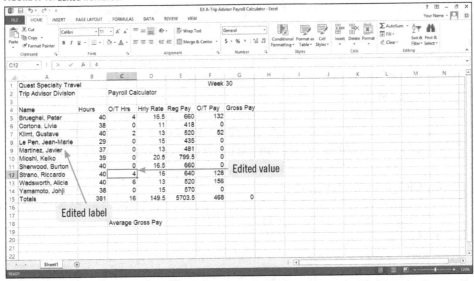

Edited value

Edited label

TABLE A-3: **Common pointers in Excel**

name	pointer	use to	visible over the
Normal	▷	Select a cell or range; indicates Ready mode	Active worksheet
Fill handle	+	Copy cell contents to adjacent cells	Lower-right corner of the active cell or range
I-beam	I	Edit cell contents in active cell or formula bar	Active cell in Edit mode or over the formula bar
Move	⇱	Change the location of the selected cell(s)	Perimeter of the active cell(s)
Copy	▷⁺	Create a duplicate of the selected cell(s)	Perimeter of the active cell(s) when [Ctrl] is pressed
Column resize	↔	Change the width of a column	Border between column heading indicators

© 2014 Cengage Learning

Enter and Edit a Simple Formula

Learning
Outcomes
• Enter a formula
• Use cell references
 to create a formula

You use formulas in Excel to perform calculations such as adding, multiplying, and averaging. Formulas in an Excel worksheet start with the equal sign (=), also called the **formula prefix**, followed by cell addresses, range names, values, and **calculation operators**. Calculation operators indicate what type of calculation you want to perform on the cells, ranges, or values. They can include **arithmetic operators**, which perform mathematical calculations (see TABLE A-2 in the "Understand Formulas" lesson); **comparison operators**, which compare values for the purpose of true/false results; **text concatenation operators**, which join strings of text in different cells; and **reference operators**, which enable you to use ranges in calculations. **CASE** ▸ *You want to create a formula in the worksheet that calculates gross pay for each employee.*

STEPS

1. **Click cell G5**

 This is the first cell where you want to insert the formula. To calculate gross pay, you need to add regular pay and overtime pay. For employee Peter Brueghel, regular pay appears in cell E5 and overtime pay appears in cell F5.

2. **Type =, click cell E5, type +, then click cell F5**

 Compare your formula bar to FIGURE A-11. The blue and red cell references in cell G5 correspond to the colored cell outlines. When entering a formula, it's a good idea to use cell references instead of values whenever you can. That way, if you later change a value in a cell (if, for example, Peter's regular pay changes to 690), any formula that includes this information reflects accurate, up-to-date results.

3. **Click the Enter button ✓ on the formula bar**

 The result of the formula =E5+F5, 792, appears in cell G5. This same value appears in cell G15 because cell G15 contains a formula that totals the values in cells G5:G14, and there are no other values at this time.

4. **Click cell F5**

 The formula in this cell calculates overtime pay by multiplying overtime hours (C5) times twice the regular hourly rate (2*D5). You want to edit this formula to reflect a new overtime pay rate.

5. **Click to the right of 2 in the formula bar, then type .5 as shown in FIGURE A-12**

 The formula that calculates overtime pay has been edited.

6. **Click ✓ on the formula bar**

 Compare your screen to FIGURE A-13. Notice that the calculated values in cells G5, F15, and G15 have all changed to reflect your edits to cell F5.

7. **Save your work**

Understanding named ranges

It can be difficult to remember the cell locations of critical information in a worksheet, but using cell names can make this task much easier. You can name a single cell or range of contiguous, or touching, cells. For example, you might name a cell that contains data on average gross pay "AVG_GP" instead of trying to remember the cell address C18. A named range must begin with a letter or an underscore. It cannot contain any spaces or be the same as a built-in name, such as a function or another object (such as a different named range) in the workbook. To name a range, select the cell(s) you want to name, click the Name box in the formula bar, type the name you want to use, then press

[Enter]. You can also name a range by clicking the FORMULAS tab, then clicking the Define Name button in the Defined Names group. Type the new range name in the Name text box in the New Name dialog box, verify the selected range, then click OK. When you use a named range in a formula, the named range appears instead of the cell address. You can also create a named range using the contents of a cell already in the range. Select the range containing the text you want to use as a name, then click the Create from Selection button in the Defined Names group. The Create Names from Selection dialog box opens. Choose the location of the name you want to use, then click OK.

FIGURE A-11: Simple formula in a worksheet

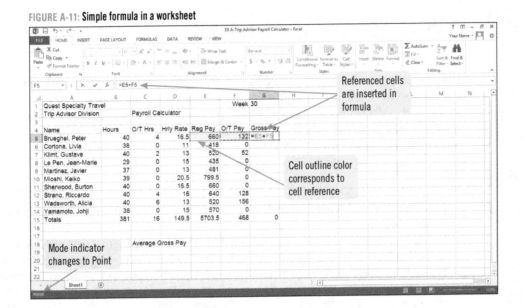

FIGURE A-12: Edited formula in a worksheet

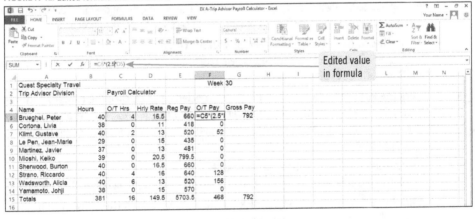

FIGURE A-13: Edited formula with changes

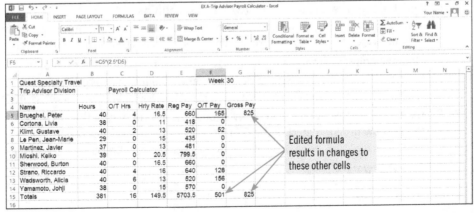

Switch Worksheet Views

Learning
Outcomes
• Change worksheet
views
• Create a header/
footer
• Select a range

You can change your view of the worksheet window at any time, using either the VIEW tab on the Ribbon or the View buttons on the status bar. Changing your view does not affect the contents of a worksheet; it just makes it easier for you to focus on different tasks, such as entering content or preparing a worksheet for printing. The VIEW tab includes a variety of viewing options, such as View buttons, zoom controls, and the ability to show or hide worksheet elements such as gridlines. The status bar offers fewer View options but can be more convenient to use. **CASE** *You want to make some final adjustments to your worksheet, including adding a header so the document looks more polished.*

STEPS

1. **Click the VIEW tab on the Ribbon, then click the Page Layout button in the Workbook Views group**

 The view switches from the default view, Normal, to Page Layout view. **Normal view** shows the worksheet without including certain details like headers and footers, or tools like rulers and a page number indicator; it's great for creating and editing a worksheet, but may not be detailed enough when you want to put the finishing touches on a document. **Page Layout view** provides a more accurate view of how a worksheet will look when printed, as shown in FIGURE A-14. The margins of the page are displayed, along with a text box for the header. A footer text box appears at the bottom of the page, but your screen may not be large enough to view it without scrolling. Above and to the left of the page are rulers. Part of an additional page appears to the right of this page, but it is dimmed, indicating that it does not contain any data. A page number indicator on the status bar tells you the current page and the total number of pages in this worksheet.

2. **Move the pointer ▷ over the header *without clicking***

 The header is made up of three text boxes: left, center, and right. Each text box is outlined in green as you pass over it with the pointer.

3. **Click the left header text box, type Quest Specialty Travel, click the center header text box, type Trip Advisor Payroll Calculator, click the right header text box, then type Week 30**

 The new text appears in the text boxes, as shown in FIGURE A-15. You can also press the [Tab] key to advance from one header box to the next.

4. **Select the range A1:G2, then press [Delete]**

 The duplicate information you just entered in the header is deleted from cells in the worksheet.

5. **Click the VIEW tab if necessary, click the Ruler check box in the Show group, then click the Gridlines check box in the Show group**

 The rulers and the gridlines are hidden. By default, gridlines in a worksheet do not print, so hiding them gives you a more accurate image of your final document.

6. **Click the Page Break Preview button 🔲 on the status bar**

 Your view changes to Page Break Preview, which displays a reduced view of each page of your worksheet, along with page break indicators that you can drag to include more or less information on a page.

7. **Drag the pointer ↕ from the bottom page break indicator to the bottom of row 20**

 See FIGURE A-16. When you're working on a large worksheet with multiple pages, sometimes you need to adjust where pages break; in this worksheet, however, the information all fits comfortably on one page.

8. **Click the Page Layout button in the Workbook Views group, click the Ruler check box in the Show group, then click the Gridlines check box in the Show group**

 The rulers and gridlines are no longer hidden. You can show or hide VIEW tab items in any view.

9. **Save your work**

FIGURE A-14: **Page Layout view**

Turns ruler on/off

Workbook Views group

Turns gridlines on/off

Vertical ruler

Header text box

Horizontal ruler

Additional dimmed page

Current page and total number of pages

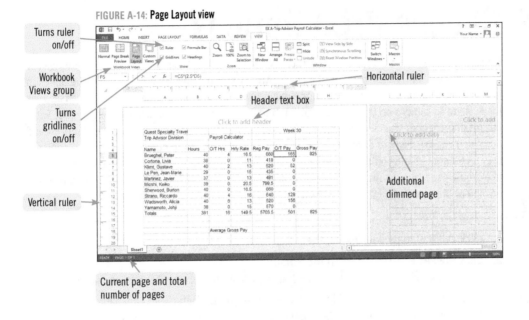

FIGURE A-15: **Header text entered**

HEADER & FOOTER TOOLS tab

Header text boxes

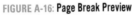

FIGURE A-16: **Page Break Preview**

Blue outline indicates print area

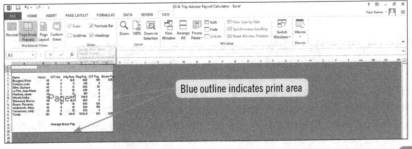

Choose Print Options

Learning
Outcomes
• Change the page
 orientation
• Hide/view gridlines
 when printing
• Preview and print
 a worksheet

Before printing a document, you may want to review it using the PAGE LAYOUT tab to fine-tune your printed output. You can use tools on the PAGE LAYOUT tab to adjust print orientation (the direction in which the content prints across the page), paper size, and location of page breaks. You can also use the Scale to Fit options on the PAGE LAYOUT tab to fit a large amount of data on a single page without making changes to individual margins, and to turn gridlines and column/row headings on and off. When you are ready to print, you can set print options such as the number of copies to print and the correct printer, and you can preview your document in Backstage view using the FILE tab. You can also adjust page layout settings from within Backstage view and immediately see the results in the document preview. **CASE** You are ready to prepare your worksheet for printing.

STEPS

1. **Click cell A20, type your name, then click** ✓

2. **Click the PAGE LAYOUT tab on the Ribbon**
 Compare your screen to FIGURE A-17. The solid outline indicates the default **print area**, the area to be printed.

QUICK TIP
You can use the
Zoom slider on the
status bar at any
time to enlarge your
view of specific areas
of your worksheet.

3. **Click the Orientation button in the Page Setup group, then click Landscape**
 The paper orientation changes to **landscape**, so the contents will print across the length of the page instead of across the width.

4. **Click the Orientation button in the Page Setup group, then click Portrait**
 The orientation returns to **portrait**, so the contents will print across the width of the page.

5. **Click the Gridlines View check box in the Sheet Options group on the PAGE LAYOUT tab, click the Gridlines Print check box to select it if necessary, then save your work**
 Printing gridlines makes the data easier to read, but the gridlines will not print unless the Gridlines Print check box is checked.

QUICK TIP
To change the active
printer, click the cur-
rent printer in the
Printer section in
Backstage view, then
choose a different
printer.

6. **Click the FILE tab, then click Print on the navigation bar**
 The Print tab in Backstage view displays a preview of your worksheet exactly as it will look when it is printed. To the left of the worksheet preview, you can also change a number of document settings and print options. To open the Page Setup dialog box and adjust page layout options, click the Page Setup link in the Settings section. Compare your preview screen to FIGURE A-18. You can print from this view by clicking the Print button, or return to the worksheet without printing by clicking the Back button ⬅. You can also print an entire workbook from the Backstage view by clicking the Print button in the Settings section, then selecting the active sheet or entire workbook.

QUICK TIP
If the Quick Print
button 🖨 appears
on the Quick Access
Toolbar, you can
print your worksheet
using the default set-
tings by clicking it.

7. **Compare your settings to FIGURE A-18, then click the Print button**
 One copy of the worksheet prints.

8. **Submit your work to your instructor as directed, then exit Excel**

Printing worksheet formulas

Sometimes you need to keep a record of all the formulas in a worksheet. You might want to do this to see exactly how you came up with a complex calculation, so you can explain it to others. To prepare a worksheet to show formulas rather than results when printed, open the workbook containing the formulas you want to print. Click the FORMULAS tab, then click the Show Formulas button in the Formula Auditing group to select it. When the Show Formulas button is selected, formulas rather than resulting values are displayed in the worksheet on screen and when printed. (The Show Formulas button is a *toggle*: click it again to hide the formulas.)

FIGURE A-17: **Worksheet with Portrait orientation**

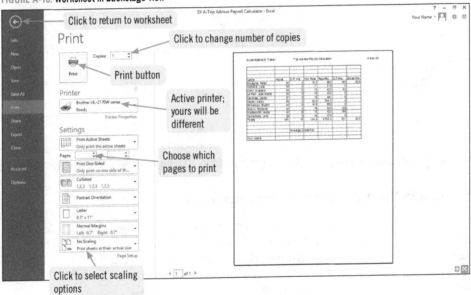

Outline surrounds print area

Your name appears here

FIGURE A-18: **Worksheet in Backstage view**

Click to return to worksheet

Print

Click to change number of copies

Print button

Printer

Active printer; yours will be different

Settings

Choose which pages to print

Click to select scaling options

Scaling to fit

If you have a large amount of data that you want to fit to a single sheet of paper, but you don't want to spend a lot of time trying to adjust the margins and other settings, you have several options. You can easily print your work on a single sheet by clicking the No Scaling list arrow in the Settings section on the Print button in Backstage view, then clicking Fit Sheet on One Page. Another method for fitting worksheet content onto one page is to click the PAGE LAYOUT tab, then change the Width and Height settings in the Scale to Fit group each to 1 Page. You can also use the Fit to option in the Page Setup dialog box to fit a worksheet on one page. To open the Page Setup dialog box, click the dialog box launcher in the Scale to Fit group on the PAGE LAYOUT tab, or click the Page Setup link on the Print tab in Backstage view. Make sure the Page tab is selected in the Page Setup dialog box, then click the Fit to option button.

Practice

Put your skills into practice with **SAM Projects!** SAM Projects for this unit can be found online. If you have a SAM account, go to www.cengage.com/sam2013 to download the most recent Project Instruction and Start Files.

Concepts Review

Label the elements of the Excel worksheet window shown in FIGURE A-19.

FIGURE A-19

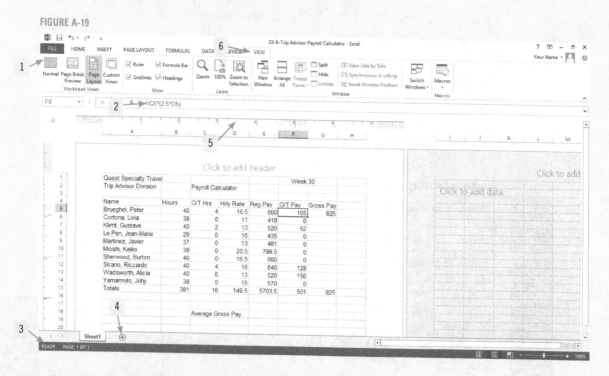

Match each term with the statement that best describes it.

7. Cell
8. Orientation
9. Normal view
10. Formula prefix
11. Workbook
12. Name box

a. Part of the Excel program window that displays the active cell address
b. Default view in Excel
c. Direction in which contents of page will print
d. Equal sign preceding a formula
e. File consisting of one or more worksheets
f. Intersection of a column and a row

Select the best answer from the list of choices.

13. The maximum number of worksheets you can include in a workbook is:
 a. 3.
 b. 250.
 c. 255.
 d. Unlimited.

14. Which feature could be used to print a very long worksheet on a single sheet of paper?
 a. Show Formulas
 b. Scale to fit
 c. Page Break Preview
 d. Named Ranges

15. Using a cell address in a formula is known as:
 a. Formularizing.
 b. Prefixing.
 c. Cell referencing.
 d. Cell mathematics.

16. A selection of multiple cells is called a:
 a. Group.
 b. Range.
 c. Reference.
 d. Package.

17. In which area can you see a preview of your worksheet?
 a. Page Setup
 b. Backstage view
 c. Printer Setup
 d. VIEW tab

18. Which worksheet view shows how your worksheet will look when printed?
 a. Page Layout
 b. Data
 c. Review
 d. View

19. Which key can you press to switch to Edit mode?
 a. [F1]
 b. [F2]
 c. [F4]
 d. [F6]

20. In which view can you see the header and footer areas of a worksheet?
 a. Normal view
 b. Page Layout view
 c. Page Break Preview
 d. Header/Footer view

21. Which view shows you a reduced view of each page of your worksheet?
 a. Normal
 b. Page Layout
 c. Thumbnail
 d. Page Break Preview

Skills Review

1. **Understand spreadsheet software.**
 a. What is the difference between a workbook and a worksheet?
 b. Identify five common business uses for electronic spreadsheets.
 c. What is what-if analysis?

2. **Identify Excel 2013 window components.**
 a. Start Excel.
 b. Open the file EX A-2.xlsx from the location where you store your Data Files, then save it as
 EX A-Weather Statistics.
 c. Locate the formula bar, the Sheet tabs, the mode indicator, and the cell pointer.

3. **Understand formulas.**
 a. What is the average high temperature of the listed cities? (*Hint*: Select the range B5:G5 and use the status bar.)
 b. What formula would you create to calculate the difference in altitude between Atlanta and Phoenix? Enter your answer (as an equation) in cell D13.

Skills Review (continued)

4. Enter labels and values and use the AutoSum button.
 a. Click cell H8, then use the AutoSum button to calculate the total snowfall.
 b. Click cell H7, then use the AutoSum button to calculate the total rainfall.
 c. Save your changes to the file.

5. Edit cell entries.
 a. Use [F2] to correct the spelling of SanteFe in cell G3 (the correct spelling is Santa Fe).
 b. Click cell A17, then type your name.
 c. Save your changes.

6. Enter and edit a simple formula.
 a. Change the value 41 in cell C8 to **52**.
 b. Change the value 37 in cell D6 to **35.4**.
 c. Select cell J4, then use the fill handle to copy the formula in cell J4 to cells J5:J8.
 d. Save your changes.

7. Switch worksheet views.
 a. Click the VIEW tab on the Ribbon, then switch to Page Layout view.
 b. Add the header **Average Annual Weather Statistics** to the center header text box.
 c. Add your name to the right header box.
 d. Delete the contents of cell A17.
 e. Delete the contents of cell A1.
 f. Save your changes.

8. Choose print options.
 a. Use the PAGE LAYOUT tab to change the orientation to Portrait.
 b. Turn off gridlines by deselecting both the Gridlines View and Gridlines Print check boxes (if necessary) in the Sheet Options group.
 c. Scale the worksheet so all the information fits on one page. If necessary, scale the worksheet so all the information fits on one page. (*Hint*: Click the Width list arrow in the Scale to Fit group, click 1 page, click the Height list arrow in the Scale to Fit group, then click 1 page.) Compare your screen to FIGURE A-20.
 d. Preview the worksheet in Backstage view, then print the worksheet.
 e. Save your changes, submit your work to your instructor as directed, then close the workbook and exit Excel.

FIGURE A-20

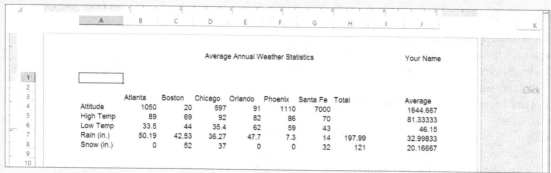

Independent Challenge 1

A local executive relocation company has hired you to help them make the transition to using Excel in their office. They would like to list their properties in a workbook. You've started a worksheet for this project that contains labels but no data.

a. Open the file EX A-3.xlsx from the location where you store your Data Files, then save it as **EX A-Property Listings**.

b. Enter the data shown in TABLE A-4 in columns A, C, D, and E (the property address information should spill into column B).

TABLE A-4

Property Address	Price	Bedrooms	Bathrooms
1507 Pinon Lane	525000	4	2.5
32 Zanzibar Way	325000	3	4
60 Pottery Lane	475500	2	2
902 Excelsior Drive	310000	4	3

© 2014 Cengage Learning

c. Use Page Layout view to create a header with the following components: the title **Property Listings** in the center and your name on the right.

d. Create formulas for totals in cells C6:E6.

e. Save your changes, then compare your worksheet to FIGURE A-21.

f. Submit your work to your instructor as directed.

g. Close the worksheet and exit Excel.

FIGURE A-21

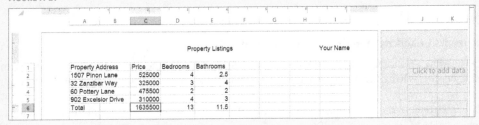

Independent Challenge 2

You are the General Manager for Prestige Import Motors, a small auto parts supplier. Although the company is just five years old, it is expanding rapidly, and you are continually looking for ways to save time. You recently began using Excel to manage and maintain data on inventory and sales, which has greatly helped you to track information accurately and efficiently.

a. Start Excel.

b. Save a new workbook as **EX A-Prestige Import Motors** in the location where you store your Data Files.

c. Switch to an appropriate view, then add a header that contains your name in the left header text box and the title **Prestige Import Motors** in the center header text box.

Independent Challenge 2 (continued)

d. Using FIGURE A-22 as a guide, create labels for at least seven car manufacturers and sales for three months. Include other labels as appropriate. The car make should be in column A and the months should be in columns B, C, and D. A Total row should be beneath the data, and a Total column should be in column E.

FIGURE A-22

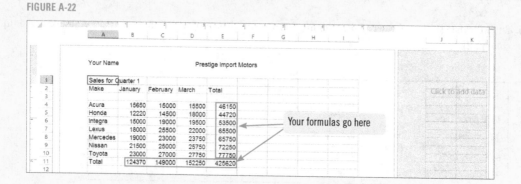

e. Enter values of your choice for the monthly sales for each make.

f. Add formulas in the Total column to calculate total quarterly sales for each make. Add formulas at the bottom of each column of values to calculate the total for that column. Remember that you can use the AutoSum button and the fill handle to save time.

g. Save your changes, preview the worksheet in Backstage view, then submit your work to your instructor as directed.

h. Close the workbook and exit Excel.

Independent Challenge 3

This Independent Challenge requires an Internet connection.

Your office is starting a branch in Paris, and you think it would be helpful to create a worksheet that can be used to convert Fahrenheit temperatures to Celsius, to help employees who are unfamiliar with this type of temperature measurement.

a. Start Excel, then save a blank workbook as **EX A-Temperature Conversions** in the location where you store your Data Files.

b. Create column headings using FIGURE A-23 as a guide. (*Hint*: You can widen column B by clicking cell B1, clicking the Format button in the Cells group on the HOME tab, then clicking AutoFit Column Width.)

c. Create row labels for each of the seasons.

d. In the appropriate cells, enter what you determine to be a reasonable indoor temperature for each season.

e. Use your Web browser to find out the conversion rate for Fahrenheit to Celsius. (*Hint*: Use your favorite search engine to search on a term such as **temperature conversion formula**.)

f. In the appropriate cells, create a formula that calculates the conversion of the Fahrenheit temperature you entered into a Celsius temperature.

g. In Page Layout View, add your name and the title **Temperature Conversions** to the header.

h. Save your work, then submit your work to your instructor as directed.

i. Close the file, then exit Excel.

Independent Challenge 3 (continued)

FIGURE A-23

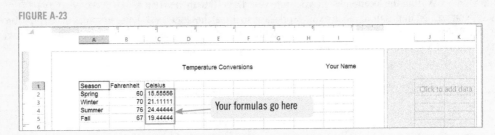

Independent Challenge 4: Explore

You've been asked to take over a project started by a co-worker whose Excel skills are not as good as your own. The assignment was to create a sample invoice for a prospective client. The invoice will include personnel, supplies, and sales tax. Your predecessor started the project, including layout and initial calculations, but she has not made good use of Excel features and has made errors in her calculations. Complete the worksheet by correcting the errors and improving the design. Be prepared to discuss what is wrong with all the items in the worksheet that you change.

a. Start Excel, open the file EX A-4.xlsx from the location where you store your Data Files, then save it as **EX A-Sample Invoice**.

b. There is an error in cell E5: please use the Help feature to find out what is wrong. If you need additional assistance, search Help on *overview of formulas*.

c. Correct the error in the formula in cell E5, then copy the corrected formula into cells E6:E7.

d. Correct the error in the formula in cell E11: then copy the corrected formula into cells E12 and E13.

e. Cells E8 and E14 each contain incorrect formulas. Cell E8 should contain a formula that calculates the total personnel expense and cell E14 should calculate the total supplies used.

f. Cell F17 should contain a formula that adds the Invoice subtotal (total personnel and total supplies).

g. Cell F18 should calculate the sales tax by multiplying the Subtotal (F17) and the sales tax (cell B18).

h. The Invoice Total (cell F19) should contain a formula that adds the Invoice subtotal (cell F17) and Sales tax (cell F18).

i. Switch to the Page Layout view and make the following changes to the Header: Sample Invoice for Week 22 (in the left header box), Client ABC (in the center header box), and your name (in the right header box).

j. Delete the contents of A1:A2, switch to the Normal view, then compare your worksheet to FIGURE A-24.

k. Save your work.

FIGURE A-24

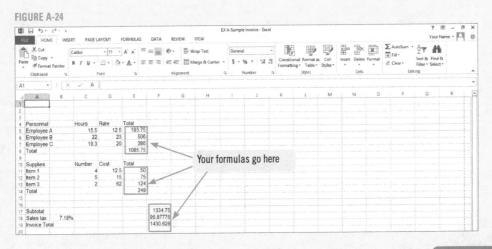

Visual Workshop

Open the file EX A-5.xlsx from the location where you store your Data Files, then save it as **EX A-Inventory Items**. Using the skills you learned in this unit, modify your worksheet so it matches FIGURE A-25. Enter formulas in cells D4 through D13 and in cells B14 and C14. Use the AutoSum button and fill handle to make entering your formulas easier. Add your name in the left header text box, then print one copy of the worksheet with the formulas displayed.

FIGURE A-25

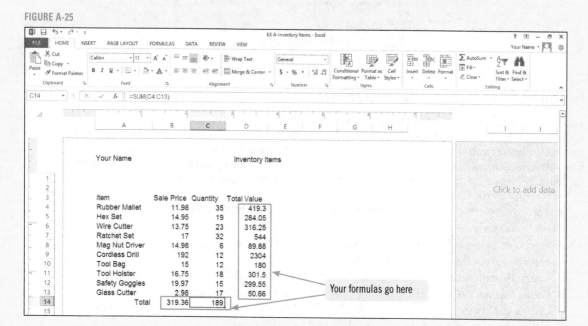

Getting Started with Excel 2013

Working with Formulas and Functions

CASE ▶ Grace Wong, vice president of finance at Quest Specialty Travel, needs to analyze tour expenses for the current year. She has asked you to prepare a worksheet that summarizes this expense data and includes some statistical analysis. She would also like you to perform some what-if analysis, to see what quarterly expenses would look like with various projected increases.

Unit Objectives

After completing this unit, you will be able to:

- Create a complex formula
- Insert a function
- Type a function
- Copy and move cell entries
- Understand relative and absolute cell references

- Copy formulas with relative cell references
- Copy formulas with absolute cell references
- Round a value with a function

Files You Will Need

EX B-1.xlsx
EX B-2.xlsx
EX B-3.xlsx
EX B-4.xlsx

Create a Complex Formula

Learning
Outcomes
• Create a complex
 formula by
 pointing
• Use the fill handle
 and Auto Fill

A **complex formula** is one that uses more than one arithmetic operator. You might, for example, need to create a formula that uses addition and multiplication. In formulas containing more than one arithmetic operator, Excel uses the standard **order of precedence** rules to determine which operation to perform first. You can change the order of precedence in a formula by using parentheses around the part you want to calculate first. For example, the formula =4+2*5 equals 14, because the order of precedence dictates that multiplication is performed before addition. However, the formula =(4+2)*5 equals 30, because the parentheses cause 4+2 to be calculated first. **CASE** ► *You want to create a formula that calculates a 20% increase in tour expenses.*

STEPS

1. **Start Excel, open the file** EX B-1.xlsx **from the location where you store your Data Files, then save it as** EX B-Tour Expense Analysis

2. **Select the range** B4:B11, **click the** Quick Analysis tool 🔲, **then click the** Totals tab
 The Totals tab in the Quick Analysis tool displays commonly used functions, as seen in FIGURE B-1.

3. **Click the** AutoSum button 🔲 **in the Quick Analysis tool**
 The newly calculated value displays in cell B12 and has a darker appearance than the figures in the selected range.

4. **Click cell** B12, **then drag the** fill handle **to cell** E12
 The formula in cell B12 is copied to cells C12:E12. The copied cells have the same dark appearance as that of cell B12.

5. **Click cell** B14, **type** =, **click cell** B12, **then type** +
 In this first part of the formula, you are using a reference to the total expenses for Quarter 1.

6. **Click cell** B12, **then type** *.2
 The second part of this formula adds a 20% increase (B12*.2) to the original value of the cell (the total expenses for Quarter 1).

7. **Click the** Enter button ☑ **on the formula bar**
 The result, 41789.556, appears in cell B14.

8. **Press [Tab], type** =, **click cell** C12, **type** +, **click cell** C12, **type** *.2, **then click** ☑
 The result, 41352.912, appears in cell C14.

9. **Drag the fill handle from cell** C14 **to cell** E14
 The calculated values appear in the selected range, as shown in FIGURE B-2. Dragging the fill handle on a cell copies the cell's contents or continues a series of data (such as Quarter 1, Quarter 2, etc.) into adjacent cells. This option is called **Auto Fill**.

10. **Save your work**

Using Apps for Office to improve worksheet functionality

Excel has more functionality than simple and complex math computations. Using the Apps for Office feature (found in the Apps group in the INSERT tab), you can insert an app into your worksheet that accesses the web and adds functionality to your work. Many of the available apps are free and can be used to create an email, appointment, meeting, contact, or task, or be a reference source, such as the Mini Calendar and Date Picker. When you click the Apps for Office button, you'll see any Recently Used Apps. Click

See All to display the featured apps and to go to the Office store to view available apps. When you find an app you want, make sure you're logged in to Office.com (you may need to log in again), click the app, click Add, then follow the prompts to download the app. Click the Apps for Office button, click See All, click the app you just added, then click Insert. The app will display as an embedded object in your worksheet and will also appear in the Recently Used Apps palette when you click the Apps for Office button.

FIGURE B-1: **Totals tab in the Quick Analysis tool**

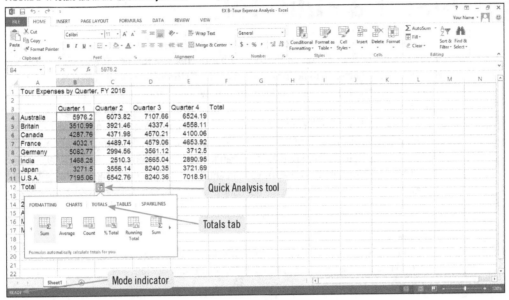

FIGURE B-2: **Complex formulas in worksheet**

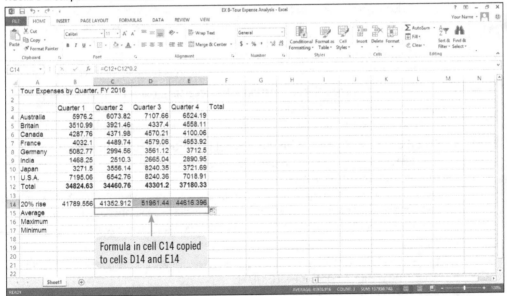

Reviewing the order of precedence

When you work with formulas that contain more than one operator, the order of precedence is very important because it affects the final value. If a formula contains two or more operators, such as 4+.55/4000*25, Excel performs the calculations in a particular sequence based on the following rules: Operations inside parentheses are calculated before any other operations. Reference operators (such as ranges) are calculated first. Exponents are calculated next, then any multiplication and

division—progressing from left to right. Finally, addition and subtraction are calculated from left to right. In the example 4+.55/4000*25, Excel performs the arithmetic operations by first dividing .55 by 4000, then multiplying the result by 25, then adding 4. You can change the order of calculations by using parentheses. For example, in the formula (4+.55)/4000*25, Excel would first add 4 and .55, then divide that amount by 4000, then finally multiply by 25.

Insert a Function

Learning
Outcomes
• Use the Insert
Function button
• Select a range for
use in a function
• Select a function
from the AutoSum
list arrow

Functions are predefined worksheet formulas that enable you to perform complex calculations easily. You can use the Insert Function button on the formula bar to choose a function from a dialog box. You can quickly insert the SUM function using the AutoSum button on the Ribbon, or you can click the AutoSum list arrow to enter other frequently used functions, such as AVERAGE. You can also use the Quick Analysis tool to calculate commonly used functions. Functions are organized into categories, such as Financial, Date & Time, and Statistical, based on their purposes. You can insert a function on its own or as part of another formula. For example, you have used the SUM function on its own to add a range of cells. You could also use the SUM function within a formula that adds a range of cells and then multiplies the total by a decimal. If you use a function alone, it always begins with an equal sign (=) as the formula prefix. **CASE** *You need to calculate the average expenses for the first quarter of the year, and decide to use a function to do so.*

STEPS

1. **Click cell B15**

 This is the cell where you want to enter the calculation that averages expenses per country for the first quarter. You want to use the Insert Function dialog box to enter this function.

QUICK TIP
When using the
Insert Function button
or the AutoSum list
arrow, it is not
necessary to type the
equal sign (=); Excel
adds it as necessary.

2. **Click the Insert Function button 𝑓ₓ on the formula bar**

 An equal sign (=) is inserted in the active cell and in the formula bar, and the Insert Function dialog box opens, as shown in FIGURE B-3. In this dialog box, you specify the function you want to use by clicking it in the Select a function list. The Select a function list initially displays recently used functions. If you don't see the function you want, you can click the Or select a category list arrow to choose the desired category. If you're not sure which category to choose, you can type the function name or a description in the Search for a function field. The AVERAGE function is a statistical function, but you don't need to open the Statistical category because this function already appears in the Most Recently Used category.

QUICK TIP
To learn about a
function, click it in
the Select a function
list. The arguments
and format required
for the function
appear below the list.

3. **Click AVERAGE in the Select a function list if necessary, read the information that appears under the list, then click OK**

 The Function Arguments dialog box opens, in which you define the range of cells you want to average.

QUICK TIP
When selecting a
range, remember to
select all the cells
between and includ-
ing the two refer-
ences in the range.

4. **Click the Collapse button 🔲 in the Number1 field of the Function Arguments dialog box, select the range B4:B11 in the worksheet, then click the Expand button 🔲 in the Function Arguments dialog box**

 Clicking the Collapse button minimizes the dialog box so you can select cells in the worksheet. When you click the Expand button, the dialog box is restored, as shown in FIGURE B-4. You can also begin dragging in the worksheet to automatically minimize the dialog box; after you select the desired range, the dialog box is restored.

5. **Click OK**

 The Function Arguments dialog box closes, and the calculated value is displayed in cell B15. The average expenses per country for Quarter 1 is 4353.0788.

6. **Click cell C15, click the AutoSum list arrow ∑ in the Editing group on the HOME tab, then click Average**

 A ScreenTip beneath cell C15 displays the arguments needed to complete the function. The text "number1" is shown in boldface type, telling you that the next step is to supply the first cell in the group you want to average. You want to average a range of cells.

7. **Select the range C4:C11 in the worksheet, then click the Enter button ✓ on the formula bar**

 The average expenses per country for the second quarter appears in cell C15.

8. **Drag the fill handle from cell C15 to cell E15**

 The formula in cell C15 is copied to the rest of the selected range, as shown in FIGURE B-5.

9. **Save your work**

Working with Formulas and Functions

FIGURE B-3: **Insert Function dialog box**

Search for a function field

Your list of recently used functions may differ

Or select a category list arrow

Description of selected function

FIGURE B-4: **Expanded Function Arguments dialog box**

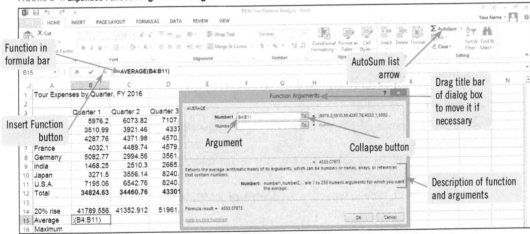

Function in formula bar

Insert Function button

Argument

AutoSum list arrow

Drag title bar of dialog box to move it if necessary

Collapse button

Description of function and arguments

FIGURE B-5: **Average functions used in worksheet**

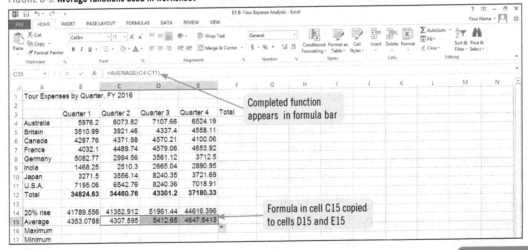

Completed function appears in formula bar

Formula in cell C15 copied to cells D15 and E15

Working with Formulas and Functions

Type a Function

Learning
Outcomes
• Select a function
 by typing
• Use AutoComplete
 to copy formulas

In addition to using the Insert Function dialog box, the AutoSum button, or the AutoSum list arrow on the Ribbon to enter a function, you can manually type the function into a cell and then complete the arguments needed. This method requires that you know the name and initial characters of the function, but it can be faster than opening several dialog boxes. Experienced Excel users often prefer this method, but it is only an alternative, not better or more correct than any other method. Excel's Formula AutoComplete feature makes it easier to enter function names by typing, because it suggests functions depending on the first letters you type. **CASE** *You want to calculate the maximum and minimum quarterly expenses in your worksheet, and you decide to manually enter these statistical functions.*

STEPS

1. **Click cell B16, type =, then type m**

 Because you are manually typing this function, it is necessary to begin with the equal sign (=). The Formula AutoComplete feature displays a list of function names beginning with "M" beneath cell B16. Once you type an equal sign in a cell, each letter you type acts as a trigger to activate the Formula AutoComplete feature. This feature minimizes the amount of typing you need to do to enter a function and reduces typing and syntax errors.

2. **Click MAX in the list**

 Clicking any function in the Formula AutoComplete list opens a ScreenTip next to the list that describes the function.

3. **Double-click MAX**

 The function is inserted in the cell, and a ScreenTip appears beneath the cell to help you complete the formula. See FIGURE B-6.

4. **Select the range B4:B11, as shown in FIGURE B-7, then click the Enter button ✓ on the formula bar**

 The result, 7195.06, appears in cell B16. When you completed the entry, the closing parenthesis was automatically added to the formula.

5. **Click cell B17, type =, type m, then double-click MIN in the list of function names**

 The MIN function appears in the cell.

6. **Select the range B4:B11, then press [Enter]**

 The result, 1468.25, appears in cell B17.

7. **Select the range B16:B17, then drag the fill handle from cell B17 to cell E17**

 The maximum and minimum values for all of the quarters appear in the selected range, as shown in FIGURE B-8.

8. **Save your work**

Using the COUNT and COUNTA functions

When you select a range, a count of cells in the range that are not blank appears in the status bar. For example, if you select the range A1:A5 and only cells A1, A4 and A5 contain data, the status bar displays "Count: 3." To count nonblank cells more precisely, or to incorporate these calculations in a worksheet, you can use the COUNT and COUNTA functions. The COUNT function returns the number of cells in a range that contain numeric data, including numbers, dates, and formulas. The COUNTA function returns the number of cells in a range that contain any data at all, including numeric data, labels, and even a blank space. For example, the formula =COUNT(A1:A5) returns the number of cells in the range that contain numeric data, and the formula =COUNTA(A1:A5) returns the number of cells in the range that are not empty. If you use the COUNT functions in the Quick Analysis tool, the calculation is entered in the cell immediately beneath the selected range.

Working with Formulas and Functions

FIGURE B-6: **MAX function in progress**

13					
14	20% rise	41789.556	41352.912	51961.44	44616.396
15	Average	4353.0788	4307.595	5412.65	4647.5413
16	Maximum	=MAX(			
17	Minimum	MAX(**number1**, [number2], ...)			

FIGURE B-7: **Completing the MAX function**

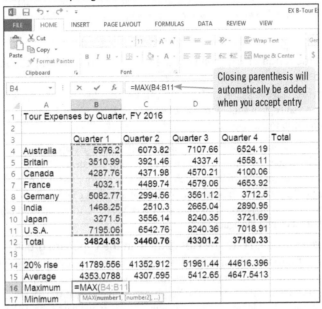

FIGURE B-8: **Completed MAX and MIN functions**

Excel 2013

Copy and Move Cell Entries

Learning
Outcomes
• Copy a range to
 the Clipboard
• Paste a Clipboard
 entry
• Empty cell contents
• Copy cell contents

There are three ways you can copy or move cells and ranges (or the contents within them) from one location to another: the Cut, Copy, and Paste buttons on the HOME tab on the Ribbon; the fill handle in the lower-right corner of the active cell or range; or the drag-and-drop feature. When you copy cells, the original data remains in the original location; when you cut or move cells, the original data is deleted from its original location. You can also cut, copy, and paste cells or ranges from one worksheet to another. **CASE** ➤ *In addition to the 20% rise in tour expenses, you also want to show a 30% rise. Rather than retype this information, you copy and move the labels in these cells.*

STEPS

QUICK TIP
To cut or copy
selected cell con-
tents, activate the
cell, then select the
characters within
the cell that you
want to cut or copy.

1. **Select the range B3:E3, then click the Copy button 🖹 in the Clipboard group on the HOME tab**

 The selected range (B3:E3) is copied to the **Clipboard**, a temporary Windows storage area that holds the selections you copy or cut. A moving border surrounds the selected range until you press [Esc] or copy an additional item to the Clipboard.

2. **Click the dialog box launcher 🔽 in the Clipboard group**

 The Office Clipboard opens in the Clipboard task pane, as shown in FIGURE B-9. When you copy or cut an item, it is cut or copied both to the Clipboard provided by Windows and to the Office Clipboard. Unlike the Windows Clipboard, which holds just one item at a time, the Office Clipboard contains up to 24 of the most recently cut or copied items from any Office program. Your Clipboard task pane may contain more items than shown in the figure.

QUICK TIP
Once the Office
Clipboard contains
24 items, the oldest
existing item is auto-
matically deleted
each time you add
an item.

3. **Click cell B19, then click the Paste button in the Clipboard group**

 A copy of the contents of range B3:E3 is pasted into the range B19:E19. When pasting an item from the Office Clipboard or Clipboard into a worksheet, you only need to specify the upper-left cell of the range where you want to paste the selection. Notice that the information you copied remains in the original range B3:E3; if you had cut instead of copied, the information would have been deleted from its original location once it was pasted.

4. **Press [Delete]**

 The selected cells are empty. You have decided to paste the cells in a different row. You can repeatedly paste an item from the Office Clipboard as many times as you like, as long as the item remains in the Office Clipboard.

QUICK TIP
You can also close
the Office Clipboard
pane by clicking the
dialog box launcher
in the Clipboard
group.

5. **Click cell B20, click the first item in the Office Clipboard, then click the Close button ✕ on the Clipboard task pane**

 Cells B20:E20 contain the copied labels.

6. **Click cell A14, press and hold [Ctrl], point to any edge of the cell until the pointer changes to ⤢, drag cell A14 to cell A21, release the mouse button, then release [Ctrl]**

 The copy pointer ⤢ continues to appear as you drag, as shown in FIGURE B-10. When you release the mouse button, the contents of cell A14 are copied to cell A21.

7. **Click to the right of 2 in the formula bar, press [Backspace], type 3, then press [Enter]**

8. **Click cell B21, type =, click cell B12, type *1.3, click the Enter button ✓ on the formula bar, then save your work**

 This new formula calculates a 30% increase of the expenses for Quarter 1, though using a different method from what you previously used. Anything you multiply by 1.3 returns an amount that is 130% of the original amount, or a 30% increase. Compare your screen to FIGURE B-11.

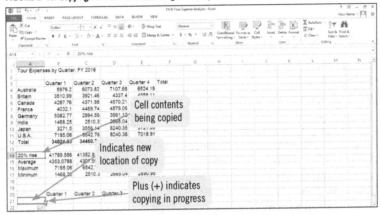

FIGURE B-9: Copied data in Office Clipboard

FIGURE B-10: Copying cell contents with drag-and-drop

FIGURE B-11: Formula entered to calculate a 30% increase

Inserting and deleting selected cells

As you add formulas to your workbook, you may need to insert or delete cells. When you do this, Excel automatically adjusts cell references to reflect their new locations. To insert cells, click the Insert list arrow in the Cells group on the HOME tab, then click Insert Cells. The Insert dialog box opens, asking if you want to insert a cell and move the current active cell down or to the right of the new one. To delete one or more selected cells, click the Delete list arrow in the Cells group, click Delete Cells, and in the Delete dialog box, indicate which way you want to move the adjacent cells. When using this option, be careful not to disturb row or column alignment that may be necessary to maintain the accuracy of cell references in the worksheet. Click the Insert button or Delete button in the Cells group to insert or delete a single cell.

Understand Relative and Absolute Cell References

Learning
Outcomes
• Identify cell refer-
encing
• Identify when to
use absolute or rel-
ative cell references

As you work in Excel, you may want to reuse formulas in different parts of a worksheet to reduce the amount of data you have to retype. For example, you might want to include a what-if analysis in one part of a worksheet showing a set of sales projections if sales increase by 10%. To include another analysis in another part of the worksheet showing projections if sales increase by 50%, you can copy the formulas from one section to another and simply change the "1" to a "5". But when you copy formulas, it is impor-
tant to make sure that they refer to the correct cells. To do this, you need to understand the difference between relative and absolute cell references. **CASE** ▶ *You plan to reuse formulas in different parts of your worksheets, so you want to understand relative and absolute cell references.*

DETAILS

Consider the following when using relative and absolute cell references:

• **Use relative references when you want to preserve the relationship to the formula location**

When you create a formula that references another cell, Excel normally does not "record" the exact cell address for the cell being referenced in the formula. Instead, it looks at the relationship that cell has to the cell containing the formula. For example, in FIGURE B-12, cell F5 contains the formula: =SUM(B5:E5). When Excel retrieves values to calculate the formula in cell F5, it actually looks for "the four cells to the left of the formula," which in this case is cells B5:E5. This way, if you copy the cell to a new location, such as cell F6, the results will reflect the new formula location, and will automatically retrieve the values in cells B6, C6, D6, and E6. These are **relative cell references**, because Excel is recording the input cells *in relation to* or *relative to* the formula cell.

In most cases, you want to use relative cell references when copying or moving, so this is the Excel default. In FIGURE B-12, the formulas in F5:F12 and in B13:F13 contain relative cell references. They total the "four cells to the left of" or the "eight cells above" the formulas.

• **Use absolute cell references when you want to preserve the exact cell address in a formula**

There are times when you want Excel to retrieve formula information from a specific cell, and you don't want the cell address in the formula to change when you copy it to a new location. For example, you might have a price in a specific cell that you want to use in all formulas, regardless of their location. If you use relative cell referencing, the formula results would be incorrect, because Excel would use a different cell every time you copy the formula. Therefore you need to use an **absolute cell reference**, which is a refer-
ence that does not change when you copy the formula.

You create an absolute cell reference by placing a $ (dollar sign) in front of both the column letter and the row number of the cell address. You can either type the dollar sign when typing the cell address in a formula (for example, "=C12*B16"), or you can select a cell address on the formula bar and then press [F4] and the dollar signs are added automatically. FIGURE B-13 shows formulas containing both absolute and relative references. The formulas in cells B19 to E26 use absolute cell references to refer to a potential sales increase of 50%, shown in cell B16.

FIGURE B-12: Formulas containing relative references

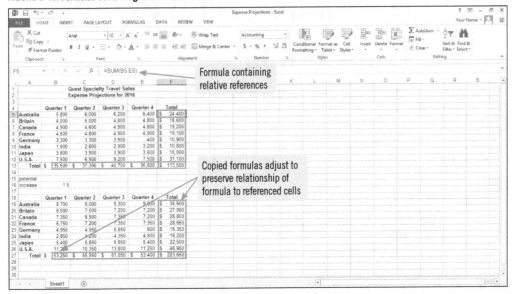

FIGURE B-13: Formulas containing absolute and relative references

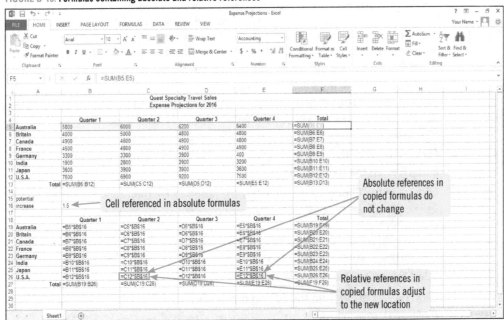

Using a mixed reference

Sometimes when you copy a formula, you want to change the row reference, but keep the column reference the same. This type of cell referencing combines elements of both absolute and relative referencing and is called a **mixed reference**. For example, when copied, a formula containing the mixed reference C$14 would change the column letter relative to its new location, but not the row number. In the mixed reference $C14, the column letter would not change, but the row number would be updated relative to its location. Like an absolute reference, a mixed reference can be created by pressing the [F4] function key with the cell reference selected. With each press of the [F4] key, you cycle through all the possible combinations of relative, absolute, and mixed references (C14, C14, C$14, and $C14).

Copy Formulas with Relative Cell References

Learning
Outcomes
• Copy and Paste
formulas with rela-
tive cell references
• Examine Auto Fill
and Paste Options
• Use the Fill button

Copying and moving a cell allows you to reuse a formula you've already created. Copying cells is usually faster than retyping the formulas in them and helps to prevent typing errors. If the cells you are copying contain relative cell references and you want to maintain the relative referencing, you don't need to make any changes to the cells before copying them. **CASE** ▶ *You want to copy the formula in cell B21, which calculates the 30% increase in quarterly expenses for Quarter 1, to cells C21 through E21. You also want to create formulas to calculate total expenses for each tour country.*

STEPS

1. **Click cell B21, if necessary, then click the Copy button** 🖼 **in the Clipboard group on the HOME tab**

 The formula for calculating the 30% expense increase during Quarter 1 is copied to the Clipboard. Notice that the formula =B12*1.3 appears in the formula bar, and a moving border surrounds the active cell.

QUICK TIP
To paste only specific
components of a
copied cell or range,
click the Paste list
arrow in the Clipboard
group, then click
Paste Special. You
can selectively copy
formats, formulas,
values, comments,
validation rules, trans-
pose columns and
rows, paste a link, or
add, subtract, multi-
ply, or divide using
the Paste Special
dialog box.

2. **Click cell C21, then click the Paste button** *(not the list arrow)* **in the Clipboard group**

 The formula from cell B21 is copied into cell C21, where the new result of 44798.988 appears. Notice in the formula bar that the cell references have changed, so that cell C12 is referenced in the formula. This formula contains a relative cell reference, which tells Excel to substitute new cell references within the copied formulas as necessary. This maintains the same relationship between the new cell containing the formula and the cell references within the formula. In this case, Excel adjusted the formula so that cell C12—the cell reference nine rows above C21—replaced cell B12, the cell reference nine rows above B21.

3. **Drag the fill handle from cell C21 to cell E21**

 A formula similar to the one in cell C21 now appears in cells D21 and E21. After you use the fill handle to copy cell contents, the **Auto Fill Options button** appears, as seen in FIGURE B-14. You can use the Auto Fill Options button to fill the cells with only specific elements of the copied cell if you wish.

4. **Click cell F4, click the AutoSum button** Σ **in the Editing group, then click the Enter button** ✓ **on the formula bar**

5. **Click** 🖼 **in the Clipboard group, select the range F5:F6, then click the Paste button**

 See FIGURE B-15. After you click the Paste button, the **Paste Options button** appears, which you can use to paste only specific elements of the copied selection if you wish. The formula for calculating total expenses for tours in Britain appears in the formula bar. You would like totals to appear in cells F7:F11. The Fill button in the Editing group can be used to copy the formula into the remaining cells.

6. **Select the range F6:F11**

7. **Click the Fill button** 🔽 **in the Editing group, then click Down**

 The formulas containing relative references are copied to each cell. Compare your worksheet to FIGURE B-16.

8. **Save your work**

FIGURE B-14: Formula copied using the fill handle

	Quarter 1	Quarter 2	Quarter 3	Quarter 4	
19					
20					
21	30% rise	45272.019	44798.988	56291.56	48334.429
22					

AutoFill Options button

Sheet1

FIGURE B-15: Formulas pasted in the range F5:F6

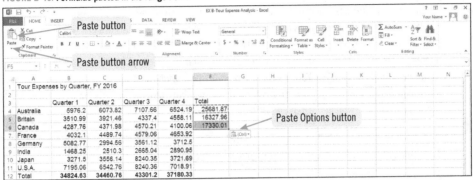

Paste button
Paste button arrow
Paste Options button

Tour Expenses by Quarter, FY 2016

	A	Quarter 1	Quarter 2	Quarter 3	Quarter 4	Total
4	Australia	5976.2	6073.82	7107.66	6524.19	25681.87
5	Britain	3510.99	3921.46	4337.4	4558.11	16327.96
6	Canada	4287.76	4371.98	4570.21	4100.06	17330.01
7	France	4032.1	4489.74	4579.06	4653.92	
8	Germany	5082.77	2994.56	3561.12	3712.5	
9	India	1468.25	2510.3	2665.04	2890.95	
10	Japan	3271.5	3556.14	8240.35	3721.69	
11	U.S.A.	7195.06	6542.76	8240.36	7018.91	
12	Total	34824.63	34460.76	43301.2	37180.33	

FIGURE B-16: Formula copied using Fill Down

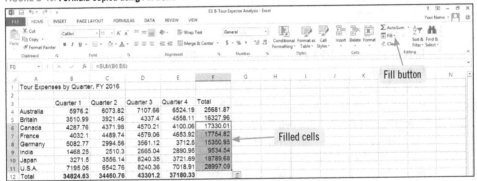

F6 =SUM(B6:E6)

Fill button

Tour Expenses by Quarter, FY 2016

	A	Quarter 1	Quarter 2	Quarter 3	Quarter 4	Total
4	Australia	5976.2	6073.82	7107.66	6524.19	25681.87
5	Britain	3510.99	3921.46	4337.4	4558.11	16327.96
6	Canada	4287.76	4371.98	4570.21	4100.06	17330.01
7	France	4032.1	4489.74	4579.06	4653.92	17754.82
8	Germany	5082.77	2994.56	3561.12	3712.5	15350.95
9	India	1468.25	2510.3	2665.04	2890.95	9534.54
10	Japan	3271.5	3556.14	8240.35	3721.69	18789.68
11	U.S.A.	7195.06	6542.76	8240.36	7018.91	28997.09
12	Total	34824.63	34460.76	43301.2	37180.33	

Filled cells

Using Paste Preview

You can selectively copy formulas, values, or other choices using the Paste list arrow, and you can see how the pasted contents will look using the Paste Preview feature. When you click the Paste list arrow, a gallery of paste option icons opens. When you point to an icon, a preview of how the content will be pasted using that option is shown in the worksheet. Options include pasting values only, pasting values with number formatting, pasting formulas only, pasting formatting only, pasting transposed data so that column data appears in rows and row data appears in columns, and pasting with no borders (to remove any borders around pasted cells).

Using Auto Fill options

When you use the fill handle to copy cells, the Auto Fill Options button appears. Auto Fill options differ depending on what you are copying. If you had selected cells containing a series (such as "Monday" and "Tuesday") and then used the fill handle, you would see options for continuing the series (such as "Wednesday" and "Thursday") or for simply pasting the copied cells. Clicking the Auto Fill Options button opens a list that lets you choose from the following options: Copy Cells, Fill Series (if applicable), Fill Formatting Only, Fill Without Formatting, or Flash Fill. Choosing Copy Cells means that the cell's contents and its formatting will be copied. The Fill Formatting Only option copies only the formatting attributes, but not cell contents. The Fill Without Formatting option copies the cell contents, but no formatting attributes. Copy Cells is the default option when using the fill handle to copy a cell, so if you want to copy the cell's contents and its formatting, you can ignore the Auto Fill Options button. The Flash Fill option allows you to create customized fill ranges on the fly, such as 2, 4, 6, 8, 10 by entering at least two values in a pattern: Excel automatically senses the pattern.

Copy Formulas with Absolute Cell References

Learning
Outcomes
• Create an absolute
 cell reference
• Use the fill handle
 to copy absolute
 cell references

When copying formulas, you might want one or more cell references in the formula to remain unchanged in relation to the formula. In such an instance, you need to apply an absolute cell reference before copying the formula to preserve the specific cell address when the formula is copied. You create an absolute reference by placing a dollar sign ($) before the column letter and row number of the address (for example, A1). **CASE** ▶ *You need to do some what-if analysis to see how various percentage increases might affect total expenses. You decide to add a column that calculates a possible increase in the total tour expenses, and then change the percentage to see various potential results.*

STEPS

1. **Click cell G1, type Change, then press [Enter]**

2. **Type 1.1, then press [Enter]**

 You store the increase factor that will be used in the what-if analysis in this cell (G2). The value 1.1 can be used to calculate a 10% increase: anything you multiply by 1.1 returns an amount that is 110% of the original amount.

3. **Click cell H3, type What if?, then press [Enter]**

4. **In cell H4, type =, click cell F4, type *, click cell G2, then click the Enter button ✓ on the formula bar**

 The result, 28250.1, appears in cell H4. This value represents the total annual expenses for Australia if there is a 10% increase. You want to perform a what-if analysis for all the tour countries.

5. **Drag the fill handle from cell H4 to cell H11**

 The resulting values in the range H5:H11 are all zeros, which is not the result you wanted. Because you used relative cell addressing in cell H4, the copied formula adjusted so that the formula in cell H5 is =F5*G3. Because there is no value in cell G3, the result is 0, an error. You need to use an absolute reference in the formula to keep the formula from adjusting itself. That way, it will always reference cell G2.

6. **Click cell H4, press [F2] to change to Edit mode, then press [F4]**

 When you press [F2], the range finder outlines the arguments of the equation in blue and red. The insertion point appears next to the G2 cell reference in cell H4. When you press [F4], dollar signs are inserted in the G2 cell reference, making it an absolute reference. See FIGURE B-17.

7. **Click ✓, then drag the fill handle from cell H4 to cell H11**

 Because the formula correctly contains an absolute cell reference, the correct values for a 10% increase appear in cells H4:H11. You now want to see what a 20% increase in expenses looks like.

8. **Click cell G2, type 1.2, then click ✓**

 The values in the range H4:H11 change to reflect the 20% increase. Compare your worksheet to FIGURE B-18.

9. **Save your work**

FIGURE B-17: **Absolute reference created in formula**

Absolute cell reference in formula

	A	B	C	D	E	F	G	H
1	Tour Expenses by Quarter, FY 2016						Change	
2								1.1
3		Quarter 1	Quarter 2	Quarter 3	Quarter 4	Total		What if?
4	Australia	5976.2	6073.82	7107.66	6524.19	25681.87		=F4*G2
5	Britain	3510.99	3921.46	4337.4	4558.11	16327.96		0
6	Canada	4287.76	4371.98	4570.21	4100.06	17330.01		0
7	France	4032.1	4489.74	4579.06	4653.92	17754.82		0
8	Germany	5082.77	2994.56	3561.12	3712.5	15350.95		0
9	India	1468.25	2510.3	2665.04	2890.95	9534.54		0
10	Japan	3271.5	3556.14	8240.35	3721.69	18789.68		0
11	U.S.A.	7195.06	6542.76	8240.36	7018.91	28997.09		0
12	Total	34824.63	34460.76	43301.2	37180.33			
13								
14	20% rise	41789.556	41352.912	51961.44	44616.3			
15	Average	4353.0788	4307.595	5412.65	4647.54			
16	Maximum	7195.06	6542.76	8240.36	7018.			
17	Minimum	1468.25	2510.3	2665.04	2890.			
18								
19								
20		Quarter 1	Quarter 2	Quarter 3	Quarter 4			
21	30% rise	45272.019	44798.988	56291.56	48334.429			
22								

Incorrect values from relative referencing in previously copied formulas

FIGURE B-18: **What-if analysis with modified change factor**

Modified change factor

	A	B	C	D	E	F	G	H
1	Tour Expenses by Quarter, FY 2016						Change	
2								1.2
3		Quarter 1	Quarter 2	Quarter 3	Quarter 4	Total		What if?
4	Australia	5976.2	6073.82	7107.66	6524.19	25681.87		30818.2
5	Britain	3510.99	3921.46	4337.4	4558.11	16327.96		19593.6
6	Canada	4287.76	4371.98	4570.21	4100.06	17330.01		20796
7	France	4032.1	4489.74	4579.06	4653.92	17754.82		21305.8
8	Germany	5082.77	2994.56	3561.12	3712.5	15350.95		18421.1
9	India	1468.25	2510.3	2665.04	2890.95	9534.54		11441.4
10	Japan	3271.5	3556.14	8240.35	3721.69	18789.68		22547.6
11	U.S.A.	7195.06	6542.76	8240.36	7018.91	28997.09		34796.5
12	Total	34824.63	34460.76	43301.2	37180.33			
13								
14	20% rise	41789.556	41352.912	51961.44	44616.396			
15	Average	4353.0788	4307.595	5412.65	4647.5413			
16	Maximum	7195.06	6542.76	8240.36	7018.91			
17	Minimum	1468.25	2510.3	2665.04	2890.95			
18								
19								
20		Quarter 1	Quarter 2	Quarter 3	Quarter 4			
21	30% rise	45272.019	44798.988	56291.56	48334.429			
22								

Using the fill handle for sequential text or values

Often, you need to fill cells with sequential text: months of the year, days of the week, years, or text plus a number (Quarter 1, Quarter 2,...). For example, you might want to create a worksheet that calculates data for every month of the year. Using the fill handle, you can quickly and easily create labels for the months of the year just by typing "January" in a cell. Drag the fill handle from the cell containing "January" until you have all the monthly labels you need. You can also easily fill cells with a date sequence by dragging the fill handle on a single cell containing a date. You can fill cells with a number sequence (such as 1, 2, 3,...) by dragging the fill handle on a selection of two or more cells that contain the sequence. To create a number sequence using the value in a single cell, press and hold [Ctrl] as you drag the fill handle of the cell. As you drag the fill handle, Excel automatically extends the existing sequence into the additional cells. (The content of the last filled cell appears in the ScreenTip.) To examine all the fill series options for the current selection, click the Fill button in the Editing group on the HOME tab, then click Series to open the Series dialog box.

Round a Value with a Function

The more you explore features and tools in Excel, the more ways you'll find to simplify your work and convey information more efficiently. For example, cells containing financial data are often easier to read if they contain fewer decimal places than those that appear by default. You can round a value or formula result to a specific number of decimal places by using the ROUND function. **CASE** ▶ *In your worksheet, you'd like to round the cells showing the 20% rise in expenses to show fewer digits; after all, it's not important to show cents in the projections, only whole dollars. You want Excel to round the calculated value to the nearest integer. You decide to edit cell B14 so it includes the ROUND function, and then copy the edited formula into the other formulas in this row.*

STEPS

1. **Click cell B14, then click to the right of = in the formula bar**

 You want to position the function at the beginning of the formula, before any values or arguments.

2. **Type RO**

 Formula AutoComplete displays a list of functions beginning with RO beneath the formula bar.

3. **Double-click ROUND in the functions list**

 The new function and an opening parenthesis are added to the formula, as shown in FIGURE B-19. A few additional modifications are needed to complete your edit of the formula. You need to indicate the number of decimal places to which the function should round numbers and you also need to add a closing parenthesis around the set of arguments that comes after the ROUND function.

4. **Press [END], type ,0), then click the Enter button ✓ on the formula bar**

 The comma separates the arguments within the formula, and 0 indicates that you don't want any decimal places to appear in the calculated value. When you complete the edit, the parentheses at either end of the formula briefly become bold, indicating that the formula has the correct number of open and closed parentheses and is balanced.

5. **Drag the fill handle from cell B14 to cell E14**

 The formula in cell B14 is copied to the range C14:E14. All the values are rounded to display no decimal places. Compare your worksheet to FIGURE B-20.

6. **Scroll down so row 25 is visible, click cell A25, type your name, then click ✓ on the formula bar**

7. **Save your work, preview the worksheet in Backstage view, then submit your work to your Instructor as directed**

8. **Exit Excel**

FIGURE B-19: **ROUND function added to an existing formula**

Tour Expenses by Quarter, FY 2016

	Quarter 1	Quarter 2	Quarter 3	Quarter 4	Total		What if?
Australia	5976.2	6073.82	7107.66	6524.19	25681.87		30818.2
Britain	3510.99	3921.46	4337.4	4558.11	16327.96		19593.6
Canada	4287.76	4371.98	4570.21	4100.06	17330.01		20796
France	4032.1	4489.74	4579.06	4653.92	17754.82		21305.8
Germany	5082.77	2994.56	3561.12	3712.5	15350.95		18421.1
India	1468.25	2510.3	2665.04	2890.95	9534.54		11441.4
Japan	3271.5	3556.14	8240.35	3721.69	18789.68		22547.6
U.S.A.	7195.06	6542.76	8240.36	7018.91	28997.09		34796.5
Total	34824.63	34460.76	43301.2	37180.33			
20% rise	=ROUND(B	41352.912	51961.44	44616.396			
Average	4353.0788	4307.595	5412.65	4647.5413			
Maximum	7195.06	6542.76	8240.36	7018.91			
Minimum	1468.25	2510.3	2665.04	2890.95			
	Quarter 1	Quarter 2	Quarter 3	Quarter 4			
30% rise	45272.019	44798.988	56291.56	48334.429			

Change 1.2

=ROUND(B12+B12*0.2

ROUND(number, num_digits)

ROUND function and opening parenthesis inserted in formula

Screentip indicates needed arguments

FIGURE B-20: **Completed worksheet**

Tour Expenses by Quarter, FY 2016

	Quarter 1	Quarter 2	Quarter 3	Quarter 4	Total		What if?
Australia	5976.2	6073.82	7107.66	6524.19	25681.87		30818.2
Britain	3510.99	3921.46	4337.4	4558.11	16327.96		19593.6
Canada	4287.76	4371.98	4570.21	4100.06	17330.01		20796
France	4032.1	4489.74	4579.06	4653.92	17754.82		21305.8
Germany	5082.77	2994.56	3561.12	3712.5	15350.95		18421.1
India	1468.25	2510.3	2665.04	2890.95	9534.54		11441.4
Japan	3271.5	3556.14	8240.35	3721.69	18789.68		22547.6
U.S.A.	7195.06	6542.76	8240.36	7018.91	28997.09		34796.5
Total	34824.63	34460.76	43301.2	37180.33			
20% rise	41790	41353	51961	44616			
Average	4353.0788	4307.595	5412.65	4647.5413			
Maximum	7195.06	6542.76	8240.36	7018.91			
Minimum	1468.25	2510.3	2665.04	2890.95			
	Quarter 1	Quarter 2	Quarter 3	Quarter 4			
30% rise	45272.019	44798.988	56291.56	48334.429			

=ROUND(B12+B12*0.2,0)

Function surrounds existing formula

Calculated values with no decimals

Excel 2013

Creating a new workbook using a template

Excel **templates** are predesigned workbook files intended to save time when you create common documents such as balance sheets, budgets, or time cards. Templates contain labels, values, formulas, and formatting, so all you have to do is customize them with your own information. Excel comes with many templates, and you can also create your own or find additional templates on the Web. Unlike a typical workbook, which has the file extension .xlsx, a template has the extension .xltx. To create a workbook using a template, click the FILE tab, then click New on the navigation bar. The New pane in Backstage view lists templates available through Office.com. The Blank workbook template is selected by default and is used to create a blank workbook with no content or special formatting. A preview of the selected template appears in a separate window on top of the New pane. To select a template, click one of the selections in the New pane, then click Create. FIGURE B-21 shows an Office.com template. (Your list of templates may differ.) When you click Create, a new

workbook is created based on the template; when you save the new file in the default format, it has the regular .xlsx extension. To save a workbook of your own as a template, open the Save As dialog box, click the Save as type list arrow, then change the file type to Excel Template.

FIGURE B-21: **EXPENSE TRENDS template selected in Backstage view**

Working with Formulas and Functions

Practice

Put your skills into practice with **SAM Projects!** SAM Projects for this unit can be found online. If you have a SAM account, go to www.cengage.com/sam2013 to download the most recent Project Instruction and Start Files.

Concepts Review

Label each element of the Excel worksheet window shown in FIGURE B-22.

FIGURE B-22

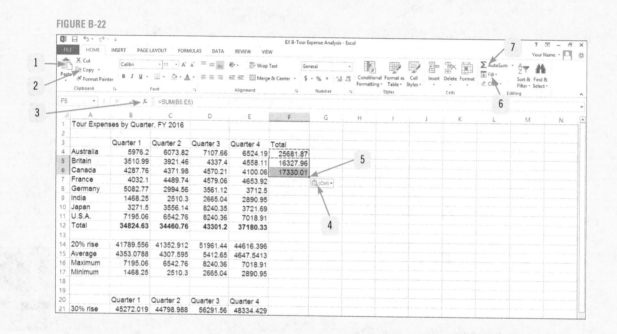

Match each term or button with the statement that best describes it.

8. Fill handle
9. [Delete]
10. Dialog box launcher
11. Formula AutoComplete
12. Drag-and-drop method

a. Clears the contents of selected cells
b. Item on the Ribbon that opens a dialog box or task pane
c. Lets you move or copy data from one cell to another without using the Clipboard
d. Displays an alphabetical list of functions from which you can choose
e. Lets you copy cell contents or continue a series of data into a range of selected cells

Select the best answer from the list of choices.

13. What type of cell reference changes when it is copied?

 a. Circular **c.** Relative

 b. Absolute **d.** Specified

14. What type of cell reference is C$19?

 a. Relative **c.** Mixed

 b. Absolute **d.** Certain

15. Which key do you press to copy while dragging and dropping selected cells?

 a. [Alt] **c.** [F2]

 b. [Ctrl] **d.** [Tab]

16. You can use any of the following features to enter a function *except*:

 a. Insert Function button. **c.** AutoSum list arrow.

 b. Formula AutoComplete. **d.** Clipboard.

17. Which key do you press to convert a relative cell reference to an absolute cell reference?

 a. [F2] **c.** [F5]

 b. [F4] **d.** [F6]

Skills Review

1. Create a complex formula.

 a. Open the file EX B-2.xlsx from the location where you store your Data Files, then save it as **EX B-Baking Supply Company Inventory**.

 b. Select the range B4:B8, click the Totals tab in the Quick Analysis tool, then click the AutoSum button.

 c. Use the fill handle to copy the formula in cell B9 to cells C9:E9

 d. In cell B11, create a complex formula that calculates a 30% decrease in the total number of cases of cake pans.

 e. Use the fill handle to copy this formula into cell C11 through cell E11.

 f. Save your work.

2. Insert a function.

 a. Use the AutoSum list arrow to create a formula in cell B13 that averages the number of cases of cake pans in each storage area.

 b. Use the Insert Function button to create a formula in cell B14 that calculates the maximum number of cases of cake pans in a storage area.

 c. Use the AutoSum list arrow to create a formula in cell B15 that calculates the minimum number of cases of cake pans in a storage area.

 d. Save your work.

3. Type a function.

 a. In cell C13, type a formula that includes a function to average the number of cases of pie pans in each storage area. (*Hint*: Use Formula AutoComplete to enter the function.)

 b. In cell C14, type a formula that includes a function to calculate the maximum number of cases of pie pans in a storage area.

 c. In cell C15, type a formula that includes a function to calculate the minimum number of cases of pie pans in a storage area.

 d. Save your work.

Skills Review (continued)

4. Copy and move cell entries.

 a. Select the range B3:F3.
 b. Copy the selection to the Clipboard.
 c. Open the Clipboard task pane, then paste the selection into cell B17.
 d. Close the Clipboard task pane, then select the range A4:A9.
 e. Use the drag-and-drop method to copy the selection to cell A18. (*Hint*: The results should fill the range A18:A23.)
 f. Save your work.

5. Understand relative and absolute cell references.

 a. Write a brief description of the difference between relative and absolute references.
 b. List at least three situations in which you think a business might use an absolute reference in its calculations. Examples can include calculations for different types of worksheets, such as time cards, invoices, and budgets.

6. Copy formulas with relative cell references.

 a. Calculate the total in cell F4.
 b. Use the Fill button to copy the formula in cell F4 down to cells F5:F8.
 c. Select the range C13:C15.
 d. Use the fill handle to copy these cells to the range D13:F15.
 e. Save your work.

7. Copy formulas with absolute cell references.

 a. In cell H1, enter the value **1.575**.
 b. In cell H4, create a formula that multiplies F4 and an absolute reference to cell H1.
 c. Use the fill handle to copy the formula in cell H4 to cells H5 and H6.
 d. Use the Copy and Paste buttons to copy the formula in cell H4 to cells H7 and H8.
 e. Change the amount in cell H1 to **2.5**.
 f. Save your work.

8. Round a value with a function.

 a. Click cell H4.
 b. Edit this formula to include the ROUND function showing zero decimal places.
 c. Use the fill handle to copy the formula in cell H4 to the range H5:H8.
 d. Enter your name in cell A25, then compare your work to FIGURE B-23.
 e. Save your work, preview the worksheet in Backstage view, then submit your work to your instructor as directed.
 f. Close the workbook, then exit Excel.

FIGURE B-23

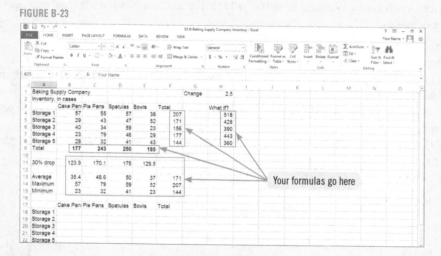

Independent Challenge 1

You are thinking of starting a small express oil change service center. Before you begin, you need to evaluate what you think your monthly expenses will be. You've started a workbook, but need to complete the entries and add formulas.

a. Open the file EX B-3.xlsx from the location where you store your Data Files, then save it as **EX B-Express Oil Change Expenses**.

b. Make up your own expense data, and enter it in cells B4:B10. (Monthly sales are already included in the worksheet.)

c. Create a formula in cell C4 that calculates the annual rent.

d. Copy the formula in cell C4 to the range C5:C10.

e. Move the label in cell A15 to cell A14.

f. Create formulas in cells B11 and C11 that total the monthly and annual expenses.

g. Create a formula in cell C13 that calculates annual sales.

h. Create a formula in cell B14 that determines whether you will make a profit or loss, then copy the formula into cell C14.

i. Copy the labels in cells B3:C3 to cells E3:F3.

j. Type **Projected Increase** in cell G1, then type **.2** in cell H2.

k. Create a formula in cell E4 that calculates an increase in the monthly rent by the amount in cell H2. You will be copying this formula to other cells, so you'll need to use an absolute reference.

l. Create a formula in cell F4 that calculates the increased annual rent expense based on the calculation in cell E4.

m. Copy the formulas in cells E4:F4 into cells E5:F10 to calculate the remaining monthly and annual expenses.

n. Create a formula in cell E11 that calculates the total monthly expenses, then copy that formula to cell F11.

o. Copy the contents of cells B13:C13 into cells E13:F13.

p. Create formulas in cells E14 and F14 that calculate profit/loss based on the projected increase in monthly and annual expenses.

q. Change the projected increase to **.17**, then compare your work to the sample in FIGURE B-24.

r. Enter your name in a cell in the worksheet.

s. Save your work, preview the worksheet in Backstage view, submit your work to your instructor as directed, close the workbook, and exit Excel.

FIGURE B-24

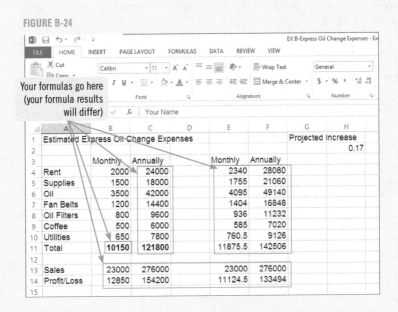

Excel 2013

Independent Challenge 2

The Dog Days Daycare Center is a small, growing pet care center that has hired you to organize its accounting records using Excel. The owners want you to track the company's expenses. Before you were hired, one of the bookkeepers began entering last year's expenses in a workbook, but the analysis was never completed.

a. Start Excel, open the file EX B-4.xlsx from the location where you store your Data Files, then save it as **EX B-Dog Days Daycare Center Finances**. The worksheet includes labels for functions such as the average, maximum, and minimum amounts of each of the expenses in the worksheet.

b. Think about what information would be important for the bookkeeping staff to know.

c. Using the Quick Analysis tool, create a formula in the Quarter 1 column that uses the SUM function, then copy that formula into the Total row for the remaining Quarters.

d. Use the SUM function to create formulas for each expense in the Total column.

e. Create formulas for each expense and each quarter in the Average, Maximum, and Minimum columns and rows using the method of your choice.

f. Compare your worksheet to the sample shown in FIGURE B-25.

g. Enter your name in cell A25, then save your work.

h. Preview the worksheet, then submit your work to your instructor as directed.

i. Close the workbook and exit Excel.

FIGURE B-25

	A	B	C	D	E	F	G	H	I
1	Dog Days Daycare Center								
2									
3	Operating Expenses for 2016								
4									
5	Expense	Quarter 1	Quarter 2	Quarter 3	Quarter 4	Total	Average	Maximum	Minimum
6	Rent	9240	9240	9240	9240	36960	9240	9240	9240
7	Utilities	9000	7982	7229	8096	32307	8076.75	9000	7229
8	Payroll	23456	26922	25876	29415	105669	26417.3	29415	23456
9	Insurance	8550	8194	8225	8327	33296	8324	8550	8194
10	Education	3000	3081	6552	4006	16639	4159.75	6552	3000
11	Inventory	29986	27115	25641	32465	115207	28801.8	32465	25641
12	Total	83232	82534	82763	91549				
13									
14	Average	13872	13755.7	13793.8	15258.2		Your formulas go here		
15	Maximum	29986	27115	25876	32465				
16	Minimum	3000	3081	6552	4006				

Independent Challenge 3

As the accounting manager of a locally owned business, it is your responsibility to calculate accrued sales tax payments on a monthly basis and then submit the payments to the state government. You've decided to use an Excel workbook to make these calculations.

a. Start Excel, then save a new, blank workbook to the drive and folder where you store your Data Files as **EX B-Sales Tax Calculations**.

b. Decide on the layout for all columns and rows. The worksheet will contain data for six stores, which you can name by store number, neighborhood, or another method of your choice. For each store, you will calculate total sales tax based on the local sales tax rate. You'll also calculate total tax owed for all six stores.

c. Make up sales data for all six stores.

d. Enter the rate to be used to calculate the sales tax, using your own local rate.

e. Create formulas to calculate the sales tax owed for each store. If you don't know the local tax rate, use **6.5%**.

f. Create a formula to total all the accrued sales tax.

g. Use the ROUND function to eliminate any decimal places in the sales tax figures for each store and the total due.

h. Add your name to the header, then compare your work to the sample shown in FIGURE B-26.

i. Save your work, preview the worksheet, and submit your work to your instructor as directed.

j. Close the workbook and exit Excel.

FIGURE B-26

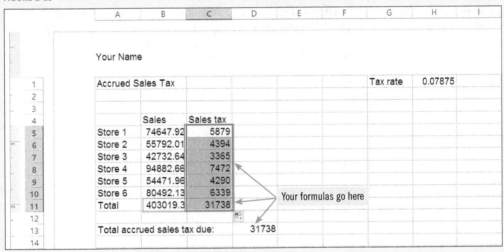

Independent Challenge 4: Explore

Since your recent promotion at work, you have started thinking about purchasing a home. As you begin the round of open houses and realtors' listings, you notice that there are many fees associated with buying a home. Some fees are based on a percentage of the purchase price, and others are a flat fee; overall, they seem to represent a substantial amount above the purchase prices you see listed. You've seen five houses so far that interest you; one is easily affordable, and the remaining four are all nice, but increasingly more expensive. Although you will be financing the home, the bottom line is still important to you, so you decide to create an Excel workbook to figure out the real cost of buying each one.

a. Find out the typical cost or percentage rate of at least three fees that are usually charged when buying a home and taking out a mortgage. (*Hint*: If you have access to the Internet you can research the topic of home buying on the Web, or you can ask friends about standard rates or percentages for items such as title insurance, credit reports, and inspection fees.)

b. Start Excel, then save a new, blank workbook to the location where you store your Data Files as **EX B-Home Purchase Costs**.

c. Create labels and enter data for at least three homes. If you enter this information across the columns in your worksheet, you should have one column for each house, with the purchase price in the cell below each label. Be sure to enter a different purchase price for each house.

d. Create labels for the Fees column and for an Amount or Rate column. Enter the information for each of the fees you have researched.

e. In each house column, enter formulas that calculate the fee for each item. The formulas (and use of absolute or relative referencing) will vary depending on whether the charges are a flat fee or based on a percentage of the purchase price. Make sure that the formulas for items that are based on a percentage of the purchase price (such as the fees for the Title Insurance Policy, Loan Origination, and Underwriter) contain absolute references.

Independent Challenge 4: Explore (continued)

f. Total the fees for each house, then create formulas that add the total fees to the purchase price. A sample of what your workbook might look like is shown in FIGURE B-27.

g. Enter a title for the worksheet in the header.

h. Enter your name in the header, save your work, preview the worksheet, then submit your work to your instructor as directed.

i. Close the file and exit Excel.

FIGURE B-27

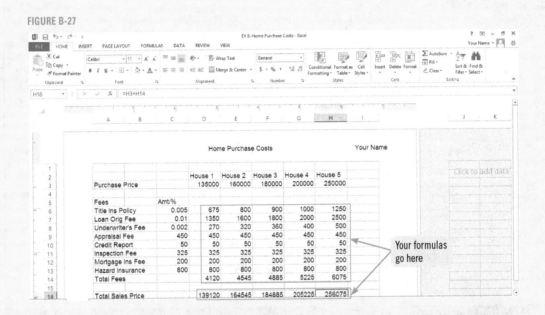

Visual Workshop

Create the worksheet shown in FIGURE B-28 using the skills you learned in this unit. Save the workbook as **EX B-Expense Analysis** to the location where you store your Data Files. Enter your name and worksheet title in the header as shown, hide the gridlines, preview the worksheet, and then submit your work to your instructor as directed. (*Hint:* Change the Zoom factor to 100% by clicking the Zoom out button twice.)

FIGURE B-28

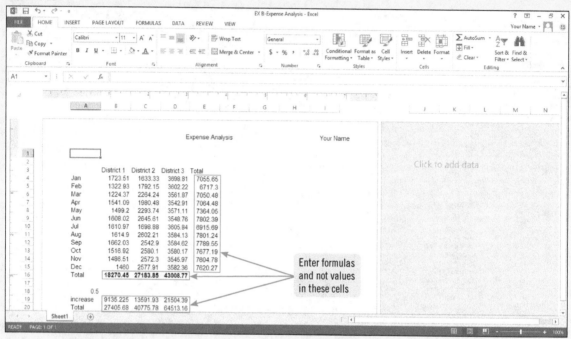

Working with Formulas and Functions

Formatting a Worksheet

CASE The corporate marketing managers at QST have requested data from all QST locations for advertising expenses incurred during the first quarter of this year. Grace Wong has created a worksheet listing this information. She asks you to format the worksheet to make it easier to read and to call attention to important data.

Unit Objectives

After completing this unit, you will be able to:

- Format values
- Change font and font size
- Change font styles and alignment
- Adjust the column width
- Insert and delete rows and columns

- Apply colors, patterns, and borders
- Apply conditional formatting
- Rename and move a worksheet
- Check spelling

Files You Will Need

EX C-1.xlsx
EX C-2.xlsx
EX C-3.xlsx
EX C-4.xlsx
EX C-5.xlsx

Format Values

Learning
Outcomes
• Format a number
• Format a date
• Increase/decrease
 decimals

The **format** of a cell determines how the labels and values look—for example, whether the contents appear boldfaced, italicized, or with dollar signs and commas. Formatting changes only the appearance of a value or label; it does not alter the actual data in any way. To format a cell or range, first you select it, then you apply the formatting using the Ribbon, Mini toolbar, or a keyboard shortcut. You can apply formatting before or after you enter data in a cell or range. **CASE** *Grace has provided you with a worksheet that details advertising expenses, and you're ready to improve its appearance and readability. You start by formatting some of the values so they are displayed as currency, percentages, and dates.*

STEPS

1. **Start Excel, open the file** EX C-1.xlsx **from the location where you store your Data Files, then save it as** EX C-QST Advertising Expenses

 This worksheet is difficult to interpret because all the information is crowded and looks the same. In some columns, the contents appear cut off because there is too much data to fit given the current column width. You decide not to widen the columns yet, because the other changes you plan to make might affect column width and row height. The first thing you want to do is format the data showing the cost of each ad.

2. **Select the range** D4:D32, **then click the** Accounting Number Format button $ **in the Number group on the HOME tab**

 The default Accounting **number format** adds dollar signs and two decimal places to the data, as shown in FIGURE C-1. Formatting this data in Accounting format makes it clear that its values are monetary values. Excel automatically resizes the column to display the new formatting. The Accounting and Currency number formats are both used for monetary values, but the Accounting format aligns currency symbols and decimal points of numbers in a column.

3. **Select the range** F4:H32, **then click the** Comma Style button ▪ **in the Number group**

 The values in columns F, G, and H display the Comma Style format, which does not include a dollar sign but can be useful for some types of accounting data.

4. **Select the range** J4:J32, **click the** Number Format list arrow, **click** Percentage, **then click the** Increase Decimal button **in the Number group**

 The data in the % of Total column is now formatted with a percent sign (%) and three decimal places. The Number Format list arrow lets you choose from popular number formats and shows an example of what the selected cell or cells would look like in each format (when multiple cells are selected, the example is based on the first cell in the range). Each time you click the Increase Decimal button, you add one decimal place; clicking the button twice would add two decimal places.

5. **Click the** Decrease Decimal button **in the Number group** twice

 Two decimal places are removed from the percentage values in column J.

6. **Select the range** B4:B31, **then click the** dialog box launcher **in the Number group**

 The Format Cells dialog box opens with the Date category already selected on the Number tab.

7. **Select the first** 14-Mar-12 format **in the Type list box as shown in** FIGURE C-2, **then click** OK

 The dates in column B appear in the 14-Mar-12 format. The second 14-Mar-12 format in the list (visible if you scroll down the list) displays all days in two digits (it adds a leading zero if the day is only a single-digit number), while the one you chose displays single-digit days without a leading zero.

8. **Select the range** C4:C31, **right-click the** range, **click** Format Cells **on the shortcut menu, click** 14-Mar **in the Type list box in the Format Cells dialog box, then click** OK

 Compare your worksheet to FIGURE C-3.

9. **Press** [Ctrl][Home], **then save your work**

Formatting a Worksheet

FIGURE C-1: **Accounting number format applied to range**

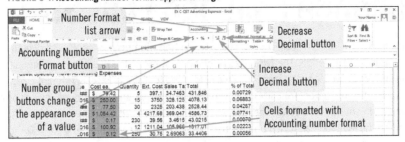

FIGURE C-2: **Format Cells dialog box**

FIGURE C-3: **Worksheet with formatted values**

Formatting as a table

Excel includes 60 predefined **table styles** to make it easy to format selected worksheet cells as a table. You can apply table styles to any range of cells that you want to format quickly, or even to an entire worksheet, but they're especially useful for those ranges with labels in the left column and top row, and totals in the bottom row or right column. To apply a table style, select the data to be formatted or click anywhere within the intended range (Excel can automatically detect a range of cells filled with data), click the Format as Table button in the Styles group on the HOME tab, then click a style in the gallery, as shown in FIGURE C-4. Table styles are organized in three categories: Light, Medium, and Dark. Once you click a style, Excel asks you to confirm the range selection, then applies the style. Once you have formatted a range as a table, you can use Live Preview to preview the table in other styles by pointing to any style in the Table Styles gallery.

FIGURE C-4: **Table Styles gallery**

Change Font and Font Size

Learning Outcomes
• Change a font
• Change a font size
• Use the Mini toolbar

A **font** is the name for a collection of characters (letters, numbers, symbols, and punctuation marks) with a similar, specific design. The **font size** is the physical size of the text, measured in units called points. A **point** is equal to 1/72 of an inch. The default font and font size in Excel is 11-point Calibri. TABLE C-1 shows several fonts in different font sizes. You can change the font and font size of any cell or range using the Font and Font Size list arrows. The Font and Font Size list arrows appear on the HOME tab on the Ribbon and on the Mini toolbar, which opens when you right-click a cell or range. **CASE** ▶ *You want to change the font and font size of the labels and the worksheet title so that they stand out more from the data.*

STEPS

1. **Click the** Font list arrow **in the Font group on the HOME tab, scroll down in the Font list to see an alphabetical listing of the fonts available on your computer, then click** Times New Roman, **as shown in** FIGURE C-5

 The font in cell A1 changes to Times New Roman. Notice that the font names on the list are displayed in the font they represent.

2. **Click the** Font Size list arrow **in the Font group, then click** 20

 The worksheet title appears in 20-point Times New Roman, and the Font and Font Size list boxes on the HOME tab display the new font and font size information.

3. **Click the** Increase Font Size button A^ **in the Font group twice**

 The font size of the title increases to 24 point.

4. **Select the range** A3:J3, **right-click, then click the** Font list arrow **on the Mini toolbar**

 The Mini toolbar includes the most commonly used formatting tools, so it's great for making quick formatting changes.

5. **Scroll down in the Font list and click** Times New Roman, **click the** Font Size list arrow **on the Mini toolbar, then click** 14

 The Mini toolbar closes when you move the pointer away from the selection. Compare your worksheet to FIGURE C-6. Notice that some of the column labels are now too wide to appear fully in the column. Excel does not automatically adjust column widths to accommodate cell formatting; you have to adjust column widths manually. You'll learn to do this in a later lesson.

6. **Save your work**

TABLE C-1: **Examples of fonts and font sizes**

font	12 point	24 point
Calibri	Excel	Excel
Playbill	Excel	Excel
Comic Sans MS	Excel	Excel
Times New Roman	Excel	Excel

© 2014 Cengage Learning

FIGURE C-5: Font list

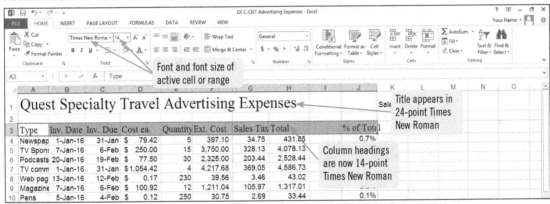

FIGURE C-6: Worksheet with formatted title and column labels

Inserting and adjusting online pictures and other images

You can illustrate your worksheets using online pictures and other images. Office.com makes many photos and animations available for your use. To add a picture to a worksheet, click the Online Pictures button in the Illustrations group on the INSERT tab. The Insert Pictures window opens. Here you can search for online pictures (or Clip Art) in Office.com, through the Bing search engine, or on your SkyDrive by typing one or more **keywords** (words related to your subject) in the appropriate Search text box, then click [Enter]. For example, pictures that relate to the keyword house in a search of Office.com appear in the Office.com window, as shown in FIGURE C-7. When you double-click the image you want in the window, the image is inserted at the location of the active cell. To add images on your computer (or computers on your network) to a worksheet, click the INSERT tab on the Ribbon, then click the Pictures button in the Illustrations group. Navigate to the file you want, then click Insert. To resize an

image, drag any corner sizing handle. To move an image, point inside the clip until the pointer changes to ⌖, then drag it to a new location.

FIGURE C-7: Results of Online Picture search

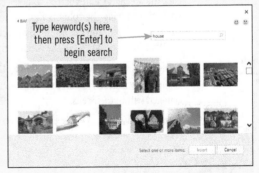

Change Font Styles and Alignment

Learning
Outcomes
• Apply formatting
• Use the Format
 Painter
• Change cell
 alignment

Font styles are formats such as bold, italic, and underlining that you can apply to affect the way text and numbers look in a worksheet. You can also change the **alignment** of labels and values in cells to position them in relation to the cells' edges—such as left-aligned, right-aligned, or centered. You can apply font styles and alignment options using the HOME tab, the Format Cells dialog box, or the Mini toolbar. See TABLE C-2 for a description of common font style and alignment buttons that are available on the HOME tab and the Mini toolbar. Once you have formatted a cell the way you want it, you can "paint" or copy the cell's formats into other cells by using the Format Painter button in the Clipboard group on the HOME tab. This is similar to using copy and paste, but instead of copying cell contents, it copies only the cell's formatting. **CASE** *You want to further enhance the worksheet's appearance by adding bold and underline formatting and centering some of the labels.*

STEPS

QUICK TIP

You can use the following keyboard shortcuts to format a selected cell or range: [Ctrl][B] to bold, [Ctrl][I] to italicize, and [Ctrl][U] to underline.

1. **Press [Ctrl][Home], then click the Bold button** B **in the Font group on the HOME tab**
 The title in cell A1 appears in bold.

2. **Click cell A3, then click the Underline button** U **in the Font group**
 The column label is now underlined, though this may be difficult to see with the cell selected.

3. **Click the Italic button** I **in the Font group, then click** B
 The heading now appears in boldface, underlined, italic type. Notice that the Bold, Italic, and Underline buttons in the Font group are all selected.

QUICK TIP

Overuse of any font style and random formatting can make a workbook difficult to read. Be consistent and add the same formatting to similar items throughout a worksheet or in related worksheets.

4. **Click the Italic button** I **to deselect it**
 The italic font style is removed from cell A3, but the bold and underline font styles remain.

5. **Click the Format Painter button** ✧ **in the Clipboard group, then select the range B3:J3**
 The formatting in cell A3 is copied to the rest of the column labels. To paint the formats on more than one selection, double-click the Format Painter button to keep it activated until you turn it off. You can turn off the Format Painter by pressing [Esc] or by clicking ✧. You decide the title would look better if it were centered over the data columns.

6. **Select the range A1:H1, then click the Merge & Center button** ▤ **in the Alignment group**
 The Merge & Center button creates one cell out of the eight cells across the row, then centers the text in that newly created, merged cell. The title "Quest Specialty Travel Advertising Expenses" is centered across the eight columns you selected. To split a merged cell into its original components, select the merged cell, then click the Merge & Center button to deselect it. The merged and centered text might look awkward now, but you'll be changing the column widths shortly. Occasionally, you may find that you want cell contents to wrap within a cell. You can do this by selecting the cells containing the text you want to wrap, then clicking the Wrap Text button ▤ in the Alignment group on the HOME tab on the Ribbon.

QUICK TIP

To clear all formatting from a selected range, click the Clear button ✧ in the Editing group on the HOME tab, then click Clear Formats.

7. **Select the range A3:J3, right-click, then click the Center button** ▤ **on the Mini toolbar**
 Compare your screen to FIGURE C-8. Although they may be difficult to read, notice that all the headings are centered within their cells.

8. **Save your work**

FIGURE C-8: **Worksheet with font styles and alignment applied**

TABLE C-2: **Common font style and alignment buttons**

button	description
B	Bolds text
I	Italicizes text
U	Underlines text
	Centers text across columns, and combines two or more selected, adjacent cells into one cell
	Aligns text at the left edge of the cell
	Centers text horizontally within the cell
	Aligns text at the right edge of the cell
	Wraps long text into multiple lines

Rotating and indenting cell entries

In addition to applying fonts and font styles, you can rotate or indent data within a cell to further change its appearance. You can rotate text within a cell by altering its alignment. To change alignment, select the cells you want to modify, then click the dialog box launcher in the Alignment group to open the Alignment tab of the Format Cells dialog box. Click a position in the Orientation box or type a number in the Degrees text box to rotate text from its default horizontal orientation, then click OK. You can indent cell contents using the Increase Indent button in the Alignment group, which moves cell contents to the right one space, or the Decrease Indent button, which moves cell contents to the left one space.

Adjust the Column Width

Learning
Outcomes
• Change a column
 width by dragging
• Resize a column
 with AutoFit
• Change the
 width of multiple
 columns

As you format a worksheet, you might need to adjust the width of one or more columns to accommodate changes in the amount of text, the font size, or font style. The default column width is 8.43 characters, a little less than 1". With Excel, you can adjust the width of one or more columns by using the mouse, the Format button in the Cells group on the HOME tab, or the shortcut menu. Using the mouse, you can drag or double-click the right edge of a column heading. The Format button and shortcut menu include commands for making more precise width adjustments. TABLE C-3 describes common column formatting commands. **CASE** ▶ *You have noticed that some of the labels in columns A through J don't fit in the cells. You want to adjust the widths of the columns so that the labels appear in their entirety.*

STEPS

1. **Position the mouse pointer on the line between the column A and column B headings until it changes to ↔**

 See FIGURE C-9. The **column heading** is the box at the top of each column containing a letter. Before you can adjust column width using the mouse, you need to position the pointer on the right edge of the column heading for the column you want to adjust. The cell entry "TV commercials" is the widest in the column.

2. **Click and drag the ↔ to the right until the column displays the "TV commercials" cell entries fully (approximately 15.29 characters, 1.23", or 112 pixels)**

 As you change the column width, a ScreenTip is displayed listing the column width. In Normal view, the ScreenTip lists the width in characters and pixels; in Page Layout view, the ScreenTip lists the width in inches and pixels.

3. **Position the pointer on the line between columns B and C until it changes to ↔, then double-click**

 Double-clicking the right edge of a column heading activates the **AutoFit** feature, which automatically resizes the column to accommodate the widest entry in the column. Column B automatically widens to fit the widest entry, which is the column label "Inv. Date".

4. **Use AutoFit to resize columns C, D, and J**

5. **Select the range E5:H5**

 You can change the width of multiple columns at once, by first selecting either the column headings or at least one cell in each column.

6. **Click the Format button in the Cells group, then click Column Width**

 The Column Width dialog box opens. Column width measurement is based on the number of characters that will fit in the column when formatted in the Normal font and font size (in this case, 11 pt Calibri).

7. **Drag the dialog box by its title bar if its placement obscures your view of the worksheet, type 11 in the Column width text box, then click OK**

 The widths of columns E, F, G, and H change to reflect the new setting. See FIGURE C-10.

8. **Save your work**

FIGURE C-9: Preparing to change the column width

FIGURE C-9: Preparing to change the column width

FIGURE C-10: Worksheet with column widths adjusted

TABLE C-3: Common column formatting commands

command	description	available using
Column Width	Sets the width to a specific number of characters	Format button; shortcut menu
AutoFit Column Width	Fits to the widest entry in a column	Format button; mouse
Hide & Unhide	Hides or displays hidden column(s)	Format button; shortcut menu
Default Width	Resets column to worksheet's default column width	Format button

Changing row height

Changing row height is as easy as changing column width. Row height is calculated in points, the same units of measure used for fonts. The row height must exceed the size of the font you are using. Normally, you don't need to adjust row heights manually, because row heights adjust automatically to accommodate font size changes. If you format something in a row to be a larger point size, Excel adjusts the row to fit the largest point size in the row. However, you have just as many options for changing row height as you do column width. Using the mouse, you can place the ✚ pointer on the line dividing a row heading from the heading below, and then drag to the desired height; double-clicking the line AutoFits the row height where necessary. You can also select one or more rows, then use the Row Height command on the shortcut menu, or click the Format button on the HOME tab and click the Row Height or AutoFit Row Height command.

Excel 2013

Insert and Delete Rows and Columns

Learning
Outcomes
• Use the Insert
 dialog box
• Use column and
 row heading
 buttons to insert
 and delete

As you modify a worksheet, you might find it necessary to insert or delete rows and columns to keep your worksheet current. For example, you might need to insert rows to accommodate new inventory products or remove a column of yearly totals that are no longer necessary. When you insert a new row, the row is inserted above the cell pointer and the contents of the worksheet shift down from the newly inserted row. When you insert a new column, the column is inserted to the left of the cell pointer and the contents of the worksheet shift to the right of the new column. To insert multiple rows, select the same number of row headings as you want to insert before using the Insert command. **CASE** ▶ *You want to improve the overall appearance of the worksheet by inserting a row between the last row of data and the totals. Also, you have learned that row 27 and column J need to be deleted from the worksheet.*

STEPS

1. **Right-click cell** A32, **then click** Insert **on the shortcut menu**

 The Insert dialog box opens. See FIGURE C-11. You can choose to insert a column or a row; insert a single cell and shift the cells in the active column to the right; or insert a single cell and shift the cells in the active row down. An additional row between the last row of data and the totals will visually separate the totals.

 QUICK TIP
 To insert a single row or column, right-click the row heading immediately below where you want the new row, or right-click the column heading to the right of where you want the new column, then click Insert on the shortcut menu.

2. **Click the** Entire row option button, **then click** OK

 A blank row appears between the Billboard data and the totals, and the formula result in cell E33 has not changed. The Insert Options button ⬦ appears beside cell A33. Pointing to the button displays a list arrow, which you can click and then choose from the following options: Format Same As Above (the default setting, already selected), Format Same As Below, or Clear Formatting.

3. **Click the** row 27 heading

 All of row 27 is selected, as shown in FIGURE C-12.

4. **Click the** Delete button **in the Cells group;** *do not click the list arrow*

 Excel deletes row 27, and all rows below it shift up one row. You must use the Delete button or the Delete command on the shortcut menu to delete a row or column; pressing [Delete] on the keyboard removes only the *contents* of a selected row or column.

 QUICK TIP
 If you inadvertently click the Delete list arrow instead of the button itself, click Delete Sheet Rows in the menu that opens.

5. **Click the** column J heading

 The percentage information is calculated elsewhere and is no longer necessary in this worksheet.

6. **Click the** Delete button **in the Cells group**

 Excel deletes column J. The remaining columns to the right shift left one column.

 QUICK TIP
 After inserting or deleting rows or columns in a worksheet, be sure to proof formulas that contain relative cell references.

7. **Use AutoFit to resize columns F and H, then save your work**

FIGURE C-11: Insert dialog box

Entire row
option button

FIGURE C-12: Worksheet with row 27 selected

	A	B	C	D	E	F	G	H	I	J	K	L	M	N
15	T-Shirts	3-Feb-16	4-Mar	$ 5.67	200	1,134.00	99.23	1,233.23		2.1%				
16	TV commercials	1-Feb-16	2-Mar	$1,054.42	4	4,217.68	369.05	4,586.73		7.7%				
17	Newspaper	1-Mar-16	31-Mar	$ 23.91	2	47.82	4.18	52.00		0.1%				
18	Web page ads	28-Feb-16	29-Mar	$ 0.17	275	47.30	4.14	51.44		0.1%				
19	Magazine	27-Feb-16	28-Mar	$ 100.92	12	1,211.04	105.97	1,317.01		2.2%				
20	Podcasts	22-Feb-16	23-Mar	$ 77.50	30	2,325.00	203.44	2,528.44		4.3%				
21	TV Sponsor	1-Feb-16	2-Mar	$ 250.00	30	7,500.00	656.25	8,156.25		13.8%				
22	Newspaper	25-Feb-16	26-Mar	$ 79.42	6	476.52	41.70	518.22		0.9%				
23	W		ar-16	9-Apr	$ 0.17	275	47.30	4.14	51.44		0.1%			
24	T		ab-16	16-Mar	$ 250.00	25	6,250.00	546.88	6,796.88		11.5%			
25	Pens	15-Mar-16	14-Apr	$ 0.12	250	30.75	2.69	33.44		0.1%				
26	TV commercials	1-Mar-16	31-Mar	$1,054.44	4	4,217.76	369.05	4,586.81		7.7%				
27	Hats	20-Mar-16	19-Apr	$ 7.20	250	1,800.00	157.50	1,957.50		3.3%				
28	Podcasts	20-Mar-16	19-Apr	$ 75.50	30	2,265.00	198.19	2,463.19		4.2%				
29	Newspaper		-Apr	$ 79.42	2	158.84	13.90	172.74		0.3%				
30	Podcasts		-Apr	$ 77.50	30	2,325.00	203.44	2,528.44		4.3%				
31	Billboard	28-Mar-16	27-Apr	$ 101.87	20	2,037.40	178.27	2,215.67		3.7%				
32														
33						2034	########	4,767.46	########		100.0%			

Delete button

Row 27 heading

Inserted row

Insert Options button

Hiding and unhiding columns and rows

When you don't want data in a column or row to be visible, but you don't want to delete it, you can hide the column or row. To hide a selected column, click the Format button in the Cells group on the HOME tab, point to Hide & Unhide, then click Hide Columns. A hidden column is indicated by a dark green vertical line in its original position. This green line disappears when you click elsewhere in the worksheet. You can display a hidden column by selecting the columns on either side of the hidden column, clicking the Format button in the Cells group, pointing to Hide & Unhide, and then clicking Unhide Columns. (To hide or unhide one or more rows, substitute Hide Rows and Unhide Rows for the Hide Columns and Unhide Columns commands.)

Adding and editing comments

Much of your work in Excel may be in collaboration with teammates with whom you share worksheets. You can share ideas with other worksheet users by adding comments within selected cells. To include a comment in a worksheet, click the cell where you want to place the comment, click the REVIEW tab on the Ribbon, then click the New Comment button in the Comments group. You can type your comments in the resizable text box that opens containing the computer user's name. A small, red triangle appears in the upper-right corner of a cell containing a comment. If comments are not already displayed in a workbook, other users can point to the triangle to display the comment. To see all worksheet comments, as shown in FIGURE C-13, click the Show All Comments button in the Comments group. To edit a

comment, click the cell containing the comment, then click the Edit Comment button in the Comments group. To delete a comment, click the cell containing the comment, then click the Delete button in the Comments group.

FIGURE C-13: Comments displayed in a worksheet

20	Podcasts	22-Feb-16	23-Mar	iPodAds	$ 75.50
21	TV Sponsor	1-Feb-16	2-Mar	Food Network	
22	Newspaper	25-Feb-16	26-Mar	Village Read	
23	Web page ads			9-Apr Advertising C	
24	TV Sponsor	15-Feb-16	16-Mar	Food Network	
25	Pens	15-Mar-16	14-Apr	Mass Appeal, Inc.	$ 0.12
26	TV commercial	1-Mar-16	31-Mar	Discovery Channel	$1,054.44
27	Podcasts	20-Mar-16	19-Apr	iPodAds	
28	Newspaper		1-Apr	1-May University Vo	
29	Podcasts	10-Apr-16	10-May	iPodAds	
30	Billboard	28-Mar-16	27-Apr	Advertising Concepts	$ 101.87
31					
32					$5,166.04
33					
34					

Grace Wong:
Should we continue with this market, or expand to other publications?

Grace Wong:
I think this will turn out to be a very good decision.

Excel 61

Excel 2013

Apply Colors, Patterns, and Borders

Learning Outcomes
- Use Live Preview to apply color to cells
- Format cells using the shortcut menu
- Apply a border and pattern to a cell

You can use colors, patterns, and borders to enhance the overall appearance of a worksheet and make it easier to read. You can add these enhancements by using the Borders, Font Color, and Fill Color buttons in the Font group on the HOME tab of the Ribbon and on the Mini toolbar, or by using the Fill tab and the Border tab in the Format Cells dialog box. You can open the Format Cells dialog box by clicking the dialog box launcher in the Font, Alignment, or Number group on the HOME tab, or by right-clicking a selection, then clicking Format Cells on the shortcut menu. You can apply a color to the background of a cell or a range or to cell contents (such as letters and numbers), and you can apply a pattern to a cell or range. You can apply borders to all the cells in a worksheet or only to selected cells to call attention to selected information. To save time, you can also apply **cell styles**, predesigned combinations of formats. **CASE** *You want to add a pattern, a border, and color to the title of the worksheet to give the worksheet a more professional appearance.*

STEPS

1. **Select cell A1, click the** Fill Color list arrow ⬛ ▾ **in the Font group, then hover the pointer over the** Turquoise, Accent 2 color **(first row, sixth column from the left)**

 See FIGURE C-14. Live Preview shows you how the color will look *before* you apply it. (Remember that cell A1 spans columns A through H because the Merge & Center command was applied.)

2. **Click the** Turquoise, Accent 2 color

 The color is applied to the background (or fill) of this cell. When you change fill or font color, the color on the Fill Color or Font Color button changes to the last color you selected.

3. **Right-click cell A1, then click** Format Cells **on the shortcut menu**

 The Format Cells dialog box opens.

4. **Click the** Fill tab, **click the** Pattern Style list arrow, **click the** 6.25% Gray style **(first row, sixth column from the left), then click** OK

5. **Click the** Borders list arrow ⬛ ▾ **in the Font group, then click** Thick Bottom Border

 Unlike underlining, which is a text-formatting tool, borders extend to the width of the cell, and can appear at the bottom of the cell, at the top, on either side, or on any combination of the four sides. It can be difficult to see a border when the cell is selected.

6. **Select the range A3:H3, click the** Font Color list arrow ⬛ ▾ **in the Font group, then click the** Blue, Accent 1 color **(first Theme color row, fifth column from the left) on the palette**

 The new color is applied to the labels in the selected range.

7. **Select the range J1:K1, click the** Cell Styles button **in the Styles group, click the** Neutral cell style **(first row, fourth column from the left) in the gallery, then AutoFit column J**

 The font and color change in the range is shown in FIGURE C-15.

8. **Save your work**

Formatting a Worksheet

FIGURE C-14: **Live Preview of fill color**

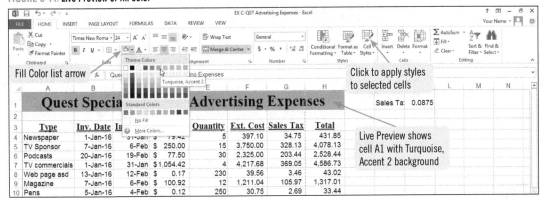

FIGURE C-15: **Worksheet with color, patterns, border, and cell style applied**

	A	B	C	D	E	F	G	H	I	J	K
1	Quest Specialty Travel Advertising Expenses									Sales Tax	0.0875
2											
3	Type	Inv. Date	Inv. Due	Cost ea.	Quantity	Ext. Cost	Sales Tax	Total			
4	Newspaper	1-Jan-16	31-Jan	$ 79.42	5	397.10	34.75	431.85			
5	TV Sponsor	7-Jan-16	6-Feb	$ 250.00	15	3,750.00	328.13	4,078.13			
6	Podcasts	20-Jan-16	19-Feb	$ 77.50	30	2,325.00	203.44	2,528.44			
7	TV commercials	1-Jan-16	31-Jan	$1,054.42	4	4,217.68	369.05	4,586.73			
8	Web page asd	13-Jan-16	12-Feb	$ 0.17	230	39.56	3.46	43.02			
9	Magazine	7-Jan-16	6-Feb	$ 100.92	12	1,211.04	105.97	1,317.01			
10	Pens	5-Jan-16	4-Feb	$ 0.12	250	30.75	2.69	33.44			
11	TV Sponsor	15-Jan-16	14-Feb	$ 250.00	15	3,750.00	328.13	4,078.13			
12	Billboard	12-Jan-16	11-Feb	$ 101.87	20	2,037.40	178.27	2,215.67			
13	Newspaper	25-Jan-16	24-Feb	$ 79.42	6	476.52	41.70	518.22			
14	Newspaper	1-Feb-16	2-Mar	$ 79.42	2	158.84	13.90	172.74			
15	T-Shirts	3-Feb-16	4-Mar	$ 5.67	200	1,134.00	99.23	1,233.23			
16	TV commercials	1-Feb-16	2-Mar	$1,054.42	4	4,217.68	369.05	4,586.73			

Working with themes and cell styles

Using themes and cell styles makes it easier to ensure that your worksheets are consistent. A **theme** is a predefined set of formats that gives your Excel worksheet a professional look. Formatting choices included in a theme are colors, fonts, and line and fill effects. To apply a theme, click the Themes button in the Themes group on the PAGE LAYOUT tab to open the Themes gallery, as shown in FIGURE C-16, then click a theme in the gallery. **Cell styles** are sets of cell formats based on themes, so they are automatically updated if you change a theme. For example, if you apply the 20% - Accent1 cell style to cell A1 in a worksheet that has no theme applied, the fill color changes to light blue with no pattern, and the font changes to Constantia. If you change the theme of the worksheet to Ion Boardroom, cell A1's fill color changes to red and the font changes to Century Gothic, because these are the new theme's associated formats.

FIGURE C-16: **Themes gallery**

Apply Conditional Formatting

Learning
Outcomes
• Create conditional
formatting in a
range
• Change format-
ting and parame-
ters in conditional
formatting

So far, you've used formatting to change the appearance of different types of data, but you can also use formatting to highlight important aspects of the data itself. For example, you can apply formatting that changes the font color to red for any cells where ad costs exceed $100 and to green where ad costs are below $50. This is called **conditional formatting** because Excel automatically applies different formats to data if the data meets conditions you specify. The formatting is updated if you change data in the work-sheet. You can also copy conditional formats the same way you copy other formats. **CASE** *Grace is concerned about advertising costs exceeding the yearly budget. You decide to use conditional formatting to highlight certain trends and patterns in the data so that it's easy to spot the most expensive advertising.*

STEPS

QUICK TIP
You can also use the
Quick Analysis tool
to create data bars,
but with fewer
choices.

1. **Select the range** H4:H30, **click the** Conditional Formatting button **in the Styles group on the HOME tab, point to** Data Bars, **then point to the** Light Blue Data Bar **(second row, second from left)**

 Data bars are colored horizontal bars that visually illustrate differences between values in a range of cells. Live Preview shows how this formatting will appear in the worksheet, as shown in FIGURE C-17.

QUICK TIP
You can apply an
Icon Set to a selected
range by clicking the
Conditional Format-
ting button in the
Styles group, then
pointing to Icon Sets;
icons appear within
the cells to illustrate
differences in values.

2. **Point to the** Green Data Bar **(first row, second from left), then click it**

3. **Select the range** F4:F30, **click the** Conditional Formatting button **in the Styles group, then point to** Highlight Cells Rules

 The Highlight Cells Rules submenu displays choices for creating different formatting conditions. For exam-ple, you can create a rule for values that are greater than or less than a certain amount, or between two amounts.

4. **Click** Between **on the submenu**

 The Between dialog box opens, displaying input boxes you can use to define the condition and a default format (Light Red Fill with Dark Red Text) selected for cells that meet that condition. Depending on the condition you select in the Highlight Cells Rules submenu (such as "Greater Than" or "Less Than"), this dialog box displays different input boxes. You define the condition using the input boxes and then assign the formatting you want to use for cells that meet that condition. Values used in input boxes for a condi-tion can be constants, formulas, cell references, or dates.

QUICK TIP
To define custom for-
matting for data that
meets the condition,
click Custom Format
at the bottom of the
with list, and then
use the Format Cells
dialog box to set the
formatting to be
applied.

5. **Type** 2000 **in the first text box, type** 4000 **in the second text box, click the** with list arrow, **click** Light Red Fill, **compare your settings to** FIGURE C-18, **then click** OK

 All cells with values between 2000 and 4000 in column F appear with a light red fill.

6. **Click cell** F7, **type** 3975.55, **then press** [Enter]

 When the value in cell F7 changes, the formatting also changes because the new value meets the condition you set. Compare your results to FIGURE C-19.

7. **Press** [Ctrl][Home] **to select cell A1, then save your work**

FIGURE C-17: Previewing data bars in a range

Data bars displayed
in selected range

FIGURE C-18: Between dialog box

Input boxes

Format for cells
meeting the condition

FIGURE C-19: Worksheet with conditional formatting

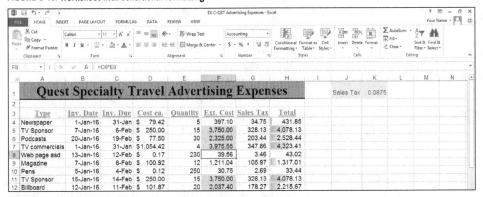

Managing conditional formatting rules

If you create a conditional formatting rule and then want to change the condition to reflect a different value or format, you don't need to create a new rule; instead, you can modify the rule using the Rules Manager. Select the cell(s) containing conditional formatting, click the Conditional Formatting button in the Styles group, then click Manage Rules. The Conditional Formatting Rules Manager dialog box opens. Select the rule you want to edit, click Edit Rule, and then modify the settings in the Edit the Rule Description area in the Edit Formatting Rule dialog box. To change the formatting for a rule, click the Format button in the Edit the Rule Description area, select the formatting styles you want the text to have, then click OK three times to close the Format Cells dialog box, the Edit Formatting Rule dialog box, and then the Conditional Formatting Rules Manager dialog box. The rule is modified, and the new conditional formatting is applied to the selected cells. To delete a rule, select the rule in the Conditional Formatting Rules Manager dialog box, then click the Delete Rule button.

Rename and Move a Worksheet

Learning Outcomes
- Rename a sheet
- Apply color to a sheet tab
- Reorder sheets in a workbook

By default, an Excel workbook initially contains one worksheet named Sheet1, although you can add sheets at any time. Each sheet name appears on a sheet tab at the bottom of the worksheet. When you open a new workbook, the first worksheet, Sheet1, is the active sheet. To move from sheet to sheet, you can click any sheet tab at the bottom of the worksheet window. The sheet tab scrolling buttons, located to the left of the sheet tabs, are useful when a workbook contains too many sheet tabs to display at once. To make it easier to identify the sheets in a workbook, you can rename each sheet and add color to the tabs. You can also organize them in a logical way. For instance, to better track performance goals, you could name each workbook sheet for an individual salesperson, and you could move the sheets so they appear in alphabetical order. **CASE** ▶ *In the current worksheet, Sheet1 contains information about actual advertising expenses. Sheet2 contains an advertising budget, and Sheet3 contains no data. You want to rename the two sheets in the workbook to reflect their contents, add color to a sheet tab to easily distinguish one from the other, and change their order.*

STEPS

1. **Click the** Sheet2 tab

 Sheet2 becomes active, appearing in front of the Sheet1 tab; this is the worksheet that contains the budgeted advertising expenses. See FIGURE C-20.

2. **Click the** Sheet1 tab

 Sheet1, which contains the actual advertising expenses, becomes active again.

3. **Double-click the** Sheet2 tab, **type** Budget, **then press** [Enter]

 The new name for Sheet2 automatically replaces the default name on the tab. Worksheet names can have up to 31 characters, including spaces and punctuation.

4. **Right-click the** Budget tab, **point to** Tab Color **on the shortcut menu, then click the** Bright Green, Accent 4, Lighter 40% color **(fourth row, third column from the right) as shown in** FIGURE C-21

5. **Double-click the** Sheet1 tab, **type** Actual, **then press** [Enter]

 Notice that the color of the Budget tab changes depending on whether it is the active tab; when the Actual tab is active, the color of the Budget tab changes to the green tab color you selected. You decide to rearrange the order of the sheets, so that the Budget tab is to the left of the Actual tab.

6. **Click the** Budget tab, **hold down the mouse button, drag it to the left of the** Actual tab, **as shown in** FIGURE C-22, **then release the mouse button**

 As you drag, the pointer changes to ▭, the sheet relocation pointer, and a small, black triangle just above the tabs shows the position the moved sheet will be in when you release the mouse button. The first sheet in the workbook is now the Budget sheet. See FIGURE C-23. You can move multiple sheets by pressing and holding [Shift] while clicking the sheets you want to move, then dragging the sheets to their new location.

7. **Click the** Actual sheet tab, **click the** Page Layout button 🔳 **on the status bar to open Page Layout view, enter your name in the left header text box, then click anywhere in the worksheet to deselect the header**

8. **Click the** PAGE LAYOUT tab **on the Ribbon, click the** Orientation button **in the Page Setup group, then click** Landscape

9. **Right-click the** Sheet3 tab, **click** Delete **on the shortcut menu, press** [Ctrl][Home], **then save your work**

Formatting a Worksheet

FIGURE C-20: **Sheet tabs in workbook**

Sheet1 tab Sheet2 tab

FIGURE C-21: **Tab Color palette**

Sheet2 renamed

FIGURE C-22: **Moving the Budget sheet**

Sheet relocation pointer

FIGURE C-23: **Reordered sheets**

Budget sheet comes
before Actual sheet

Excel 2013

Copying, Adding, and Deleting worksheets

There are times when you may want to copy a worksheet. For example, a workbook might contain a sheet with Quarter 1 expenses, and you want to use that sheet as the basis for a sheet containing Quarter 2 expenses. To copy a sheet within the same workbook, press and hold [Ctrl], drag the sheet tab to the desired tab location, release the mouse button, then release [Ctrl]. A duplicate sheet appears with the same name as the copied sheet followed by "(2)" indicating it is a copy. You can then rename the sheet to a more meaningful name. To copy a sheet to a different workbook, both the source and destination workbooks must be open. Select the sheet to copy or move, right-click the sheet tab, then click Move or Copy in the shortcut menu. Complete the information in the Move or Copy dialog

box. Be sure to click the Create a copy check box if you are copying rather than moving the worksheet. Carefully check your calculation results whenever you move or copy a worksheet. You can add multiple worksheets to a workbook by clicking the HOME tab on the Ribbon, pressing and holding [Shift], then clicking the number of existing worksheet tabs that correspond with the number of sheets you want to add, clicking the Insert list arrow in the Cells group on the HOME tab, then clicking Insert Sheet. You can delete multiple worksheets from a workbook by clicking the HOME tab on the Ribbon, pressing and holding [Shift], clicking the sheet tabs of the worksheets you want to delete, clicking the Delete list arrow in the Cells group on the HOME tab, then clicking Delete Sheet.

Check Spelling

Learning
Outcomes
• Describe how spell
 checking works
• Change the
 spelling using
 a suggestion
• Replace a word
 using Find & Select

Excel includes a spell checker to help you ensure that the words in your worksheet are spelled correctly. The spell checker scans your worksheet, displays words it doesn't find in its built-in dictionary, and suggests replacements when they are available. To check all of the sheets in a multiple-sheet workbook, you need to display each sheet individually and run the spell checker for each one. Because the built-in dictionary cannot possibly include all the words that anyone needs, you can add words to the dictionary, such as your company name, an acronym, or an unusual technical term. Once you add a word or term, the spell checker no longer considers that word misspelled. Any words you've added to the dictionary using Word, Access, or PowerPoint are also available in Excel. **CASE** ➤ *Before you distribute this workbook to Grace and the marketing managers, you check its spelling.*

STEPS

QUICK TIP
The Spelling dialog box lists the name of the language currently being used in its title bar.

1. **Click the** REVIEW **tab on the Ribbon, then click the** Spelling **button in the Proofing group**

 The Spelling: English (U.S.) dialog box opens, as shown in FIGURE C-24, with "asd" selected as the first misspelled word in the worksheet, and with "ads" selected in the Suggestions list as a possible replacement. For any word, you have the option to Ignore this case of the flagged word, Ignore All cases of the flagged word, Change the word to the selected suggestion, Change All instances of the flagged word to the selected suggestion, or add the flagged word to the dictionary using Add to Dictionary.

2. **Click** Change

 Next, the spell checker finds the word "Podacsts" and suggests "Podcasts" as an alternative.

3. **Verify that the word** Podcasts **is selected in the Suggestions list, then click** Change

 When no more incorrect words are found, Excel displays a message indicating that the spell check is complete.

4. **Click** OK

5. **Click the** HOME **tab, click** Find & Select **in the Editing group, then click** Replace

 The Find and Replace dialog box opens. You can use this dialog box to replace a word or phrase. It might be a misspelling of a proper name that the spell checker didn't recognize as misspelled, or it could simply be a term that you want to change throughout the worksheet. Grace has just told you that each instance of "Billboard" in the worksheet should be changed to "Sign."

6. **Type** Billboard **in the Find what text box, press [Tab], then type** Sign **in the Replace with text box**

 Compare your dialog box to FIGURE C-25.

7. **Click** Replace All, **click** OK **to close the Microsoft Excel dialog box, then click** Close **to close the Find and Replace dialog box**

 Excel has made two replacements.

8. **Click the** FILE **tab, click** Print **on the navigation bar, click the** No Scaling setting **in the Settings section on the Print tab, then click** Fit Sheet on One Page

9. **Click the** Return button **to return to your worksheet, save your work, submit it to your instructor as directed, close the workbook, then exit Excel**

 The completed worksheet is shown in FIGURE C-26.

Emailing a workbook

You can send an entire workbook from within Excel using your installed email program, such as Microsoft Outlook. To send a workbook as an email message attachment, open the workbook, click the FILE tab, then click Share on the navigation bar. With the Email option selected in the Share section in Backstage view, click Send as Attachment in the right pane. An email message opens in your default email program with the workbook automatically attached; the filename appears in the Attached field. Complete the To and optional Cc fields, include a message if you wish, then click Send.

FIGURE C-24: **Spelling: English (U.S.) dialog box**

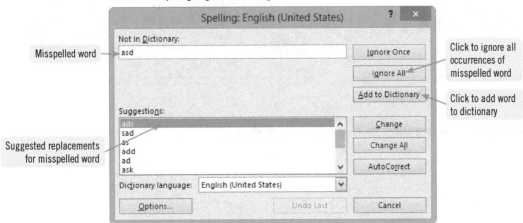

Misspelled word — asd

Click to ignore all occurrences of misspelled word

Click to add word to dictionary

Suggested replacements for misspelled word

FIGURE C-25: **Find and Replace dialog box**

Find and Replace

Find | Replace

Find what: Billboard

Replace with: Sign

Options >>

Replace All | Replace | Find All | Find Next | Close

FIGURE C-26: **Completed worksheet**

Your Name

Quest Specialty Travel Advertising Expenses

Sales Tax

Type	Inv. Date	Inv. Due	Cost ea.	Quantity	Ext. Cost	Sales Tax	Total
Newspaper	1-Jan-16	31-Jan	$ 79.42	5	397.10	34.75	431.85
TV Sponsor	7-Jan-16	6-Feb	$ 250.00	15	3,750.00	328.13	4,078.13
Podcasts	20-Jan-16	19-Feb	$ 77.50	30	2,325.00	203.44	2,528.44
TV commercials	1-Jan-16	31-Jan	$ 1,054.42	4	3,975.55	347.86	4,323.41
Web page ads	13-Jan-16	12-Feb	$ 0.17	230	39.56	3.46	43.02
Magazine	7-Jan-16	6-Feb	$ 100.92	12	1,211.04	105.97	1,317.01
Pens	5-Jan-16	4-Feb	$ 0.12	250	30.75	2.69	33.44
TV Sponsor	15-Jan-16	14-Feb	$ 250.00	15	3,750.00	328.13	4,078.13
Sign	12-Jan-16	11-Feb	$ 101.87	20	2,037.40	178.27	2,215.67
Newspaper	25-Jan-16	24-Feb	$ 79.42	6	476.52	41.70	518.22
Newspaper	1-Feb-16	2-Mar	$ 79.42	2	158.84	13.90	172.74
T-Shirts	3-Feb-16	4-Mar	$ 5.67	200	1,134.00	99.23	1,233.23
TV commercials	1-Feb-16	2-Mar	$ 1,054.42	4	4,217.68	369.05	4,586.73
Newspaper	1-Mar-16	31-Mar	$ 23.91	2	47.82	4.18	52.00
Web page ads	28-Feb-16	29-Mar	$ 0.17	275	47.30	4.14	51.44
Magazine	27-Feb-16	28-Mar	$ 100.92	12	1,211.04	105.97	1,317.01
Podcasts	22-Feb-16	23-Mar	$ 77.50	30	2,325.00	203.44	2,528.44
TV Sponsor	1-Feb-16	2-Mar	$ 250.00	30	7,500.00	656.25	8,156.25
Newspaper	25-Feb-16	26-Mar	$ 79.42	6	476.52	41.70	518.22
Web page ads	10-Mar-16	9-Apr	$ 0.17	275	47.30	4.14	51.44
TV Sponsor	15-Feb-16	16-Mar	$ 250.00	25	6,250.00	546.88	6,796.88
Pens	15-Mar-16	14-Apr	$ 0.12	250	30.75	2.69	33.44
TV commercials	1-Mar-16	31-Mar	$ 1,054.42	4	4,217.76	369.05	4,586.81
Podcasts	20-Mar-16	19-Apr	$ 75.50	30	2,265.00	198.19	2,463.19
Newspaper	21-Mar-16	20-Apr	$ 79.42	2	158.84	13.90	172.74
Podcasts	23-Mar-16	22-Apr	$ 77.50	30	2,325.00	203.44	2,528.44
Sign	28-Mar-16	27-Apr	$ 101.87	20	2,037.40	178.27	2,215.67
			$ 5,304.30	1784	52,443.17	4,588.78	57,031.95

Practice

Put your skills into practice with **SAM Projects!** SAM Projects for this unit can be found online. If you have a SAM account, go to www.cengage.com/sam2013 to download the most recent Project Instruction and Start Files.

Concepts Review

Label each element of the Excel worksheet window shown in FIGURE C-27.

FIGURE C-27

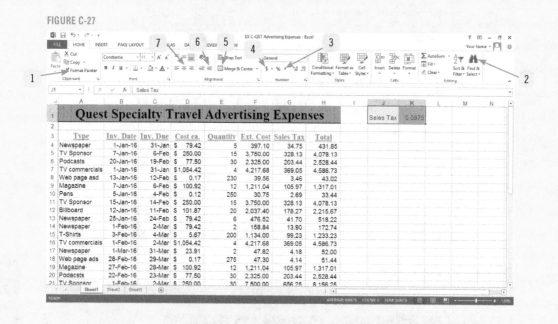

Match each command or button with the statement that best describes it.

8. **Conditional formatting**

9. $

10. **Spelling button**

11. **[Ctrl][Home]**

12. ▦

13. ◇ ▾

a. Checks for apparent misspellings in a worksheet

b. Adds dollar signs and two decimal places to selected data

c. Centers cell contents over multiple cells

d. Changes formatting of a cell that meets a certain rule

e. Moves cell pointer to cell A1

f. Displays background color options for a cell

Select the best answer from the list of choices.

14. Which button increases the number of decimal places in selected cells?

a. [icon]

b. [icon]

c. [icon]

d. [icon]

15. What feature is used to delete a conditional formatting rule?

a. Rules Reminder

b. Conditional Formatting Rules Manager

c. Condition Manager

d. Format Manager

16. Which button removes the italic font style from selected cells?

a. [I icon]

b. [B icon]

c. [I icon]

d. [U icon]

17. Which button copies multiple formats from selected cells to other cells?

a. [icon]

b. [icon]

c. [A icon]

d. [icon]

18. What is the name of the feature used to resize a column to accommodate its widest entry?

a. AutoFormat

b. AutoFit

c. AutoResize

d. AutoRefit

19. Which of the following is an example of Accounting number format?

a. 5555

b. $5,555.55

c. 55.55%

d. 5,555.55

Skills Review

1. Format values.

a. Start Excel, open the file EX C-2.xlsx from the location where you store your Data Files, then save it as **EX C-Life Insurance Premiums**.

b. Use the Sum function to enter a formula in cell B10 that totals the number of employees.

c. Create a formula in cell C5 that calculates the monthly insurance premium for the accounting department. (*Hint*: Make sure you use the correct type of cell reference in the formula. To calculate the department's monthly premium, multiply the number of employees by the monthly premium in cell B14.)

d. Copy the formula in cell C5 to the range C6:C10.

e. Format the range C5:C10 using Accounting number format.

f. Change the format of the range C6:C9 to the Comma Style.

g. Reduce the number of decimals in cell B14 to 0 using a button in the Number group on the HOME tab.

h. Save your work.

2. Change font and font sizes.

a. Select the range of cells containing the column labels (in row 4).

b. Change the font of the selection to Times New Roman.

c. Increase the font size of the selection to 12 points.

d. Increase the font size of the label in cell A1 to 14 points.

e. Save your changes.

3. Change font styles and alignment.

a. Apply the bold and italic font styles to the worksheet title in cell A1.

b. Use the Merge & Center button to center the Life Insurance Premiums label over columns A through C.

c. Apply the italic font style to the Life Insurance Premiums label.

d. Add the bold font style to the labels in row 4.

e. Use the Format Painter to copy the format in cell A4 to the range A5:A10.

f. Apply the format in cell C10 to cell B14.

g. Change the alignment of cell A10 to Align Right using a button in the Alignment group.

Skills Review (continued)

 h. Select the range of cells containing the column labels, then center them.

 i. Remove the italic font style from the Life Insurance Premiums label, then increase the font size to 14.

 j. Move the Life Insurance Premiums label to cell A3, then add the bold and underline font styles.

 k. Save your changes.

4. Adjust the column width.

 a. Resize column C to a width of 10.71 characters.

 b. Use the AutoFit feature to resize columns A and B.

 c. Clear the contents of cell A13 (do not delete the cell).

 d. Change the text in cell A14 to **Monthly Premium**, then change the width of the column to 25 characters.

 e. Save your changes.

5. Insert and delete rows and columns.

 a. Insert a new row between rows 5 and 6.

 b. Add a new department, **Charity**, in the newly inserted row. Enter **6** as the number of employees in the department.

 c. Copy the formula in cell C7 to C6.

 d. Add the following comment to cell A6: **New department**. Display the comment, then drag to move it out of the way, if necessary.

 e. Add a new column between the Department and Employees columns with the title **Family Coverage**, then resize the column using AutoFit.

 f. Delete the Legal row from the worksheet.

 g. Move the value in cell C14 to cell B14.

 h. Save your changes.

6. Apply colors, patterns, and borders.

 a. Add Outside Borders around the range A4:D10.

 b. Add a Bottom Double Border to cells C9 and D9 (above the calculated employee and premium totals).

 c. Apply the Aqua, Accent 5, Lighter 80% fill color to the labels in the Department column (do not include the Total label).

 d. Apply the Orange, Accent 6, Lighter 60% fill color to the range A4:D4.

 e. Change the color of the font in the range A4:D4 to Red, Accent 2, Darker 25%.

 f. Add a 12.5% Gray pattern style to cell A1.

 g. Format the range A14:B14 with a fill color of Dark Blue, Text 2, Lighter 40%, change the font color to White, Background 1, then apply the bold font style.

 h. Save your changes.

7. Apply conditional formatting.

 a. Select the range D5:D9, then create a conditional format that changes cell contents to green fill with dark green text if the value is between 150 and 275.

 b. Select the range C5:C9, then create a conditional format that changes cell contents to red text if the number of employees exceeds 10.

 c. Apply a purple gradient-filled data bar to the range C5:C9. (*Hint*: Click Purple Data Bar in the Gradient Fill section.)

 d. Use the Rules Manager to modify the conditional format in cells C5:C9 to display values greater than 10 in bold dark red text.

 e. Merge and center the title (cell A1) over columns A through D.

 f. Save your changes.

8. Rename and move a worksheet.

 a. Name the Sheet1 tab **Insurance Data**.

 b. Add a sheet to the workbook, then name the new sheet **Employee Data**.

 c. Change the Insurance Data tab color to Red, Accent 2, Lighter 40%.

Skills Review (continued)

d. Change the Employee Data tab color to Aqua, Accent 5, Lighter 40%.

e. Move the Employee Data sheet so it comes before (to the left of) the Insurance Data sheet.

f. Make the Insurance Data sheet active, enter your name in cell A20, then save your work.

9. Check spelling.

a. Move the cell pointer to cell A1.

b. Use the Find & Select feature to replace the Accounting label in cell A5 with Accounting/Legal.

c. Check the spelling in the worksheet using the spell checker, and correct any spelling errors if necessary.

d. Save your changes, then compare your Insurance Data sheet to FIGURE C-28.

e. Preview the Insurance Data sheet in Backstage view, submit your work to your instructor as directed, then close the workbook and exit Excel.

FIGURE C-28

Independent Challenge 1

You run a freelance accounting business, and one of your newest clients is Pen & Paper, a small office supply store. Now that you've converted the store's accounting records to Excel, the manager would like you to work on an analysis of the inventory. Although more items will be added later, the worksheet has enough items for you to begin your modifications.

a. Start Excel, open the file EX C-3.xlsx from the location where you store your Data Files, then save it as **EX C-Pen & Paper Office Supply Inventory**.

b. Create a formula in cell E4 that calculates the value of the items in stock based on the price paid per item in cell B4. Format the cell in the Comma Style.

c. In cell F4, calculate the sale price of the items in stock using an absolute reference to the markup value shown in cell H1.

d. Copy the formulas created above into the range E5:F14; first convert any necessary cell references to absolute so that the formulas work correctly.

e. Apply bold to the column labels, and italicize the inventory items in column A.

f. Make sure all columns are wide enough to display the data and labels.

g. Format the values in the Sale Price column as Accounting number format with two decimal places.

h. Format the values in the Price Paid column as Comma Style with two decimal places.

Independent Challenge 1 (continued)

i. Add a row under #2 Pencils for **Digital cordless telephones**, price paid **53.45**, sold individually (**each**), with **23** on hand. Copy the appropriate formulas to cells E7:F7.

j. Verify that all the data in the worksheet is visible and formulas are correct. Adjust any items as needed, and check the spelling of the entire worksheet.

k. Use conditional formatting to apply yellow fill with dark yellow text to items with a quantity of less than 25 on hand.

l. Use an icon set of your choosing in the range D4:D15 to illustrate the relative differences between values in the range.

m. Add an outside border around the data in the Item column (*do not* include the Item column label).

n. Delete the row containing the Thumb tacks entry.

o. Enter your name in an empty cell below the data, then save the file. Compare your worksheet to the sample in FIGURE C-29.

p. Preview the worksheet in Backstage view, submit your work to your instructor as directed, close the workbook, then exit Excel.

FIGURE C-29

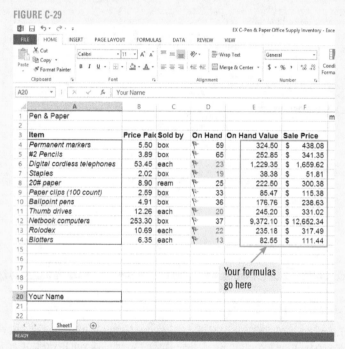

Independent Challenge 2

You volunteer several hours each week with the Assistance League of San Antonio, and you are in charge of maintaining the membership list. You're currently planning a mailing campaign to members in certain regions of the city. You also want to create renewal letters for members whose membership expires soon. You decide to format the list to enhance the appearance of the worksheet and make your upcoming tasks easier to plan.

a. Start Excel, open the file EX C-4.xlsx from the location where you store your Data Files, then save it as **EX C-San Antonio Assistance League**.

b. Remove any blank columns.

c. Create a conditional format in the Zip Code column so that entries greater than 78249 appear in light red fill with dark red text.

d. Make all columns wide enough to fit their data and labels. (*Hint:* You can use any method to size the columns.)

e. Use formatting enhancements, such as fonts, font sizes, font styles, and fill colors, to make the worksheet more attractive.

Independent Challenge 2 (continued)

f. Center the column labels.

g. Use conditional formatting so that entries for Year of Membership Expiration that are between 2017 and 2019 appear in green fill with bold black text. (*Hint*: Create a custom format for cells that meet the condition.)

h. Adjust any items as necessary, then check the spelling.

i. Change the name of the Sheet1 tab to one that reflects the sheet's contents, then add a tab color of your choice.

j. Enter your name in an empty cell, then save your work.

k. Preview the worksheet in Backstage view, make any final changes you think necessary, then submit your work to your instructor as directed. Compare your work to the sample shown in FIGURE C-30.

l. Close the workbook, then exit Excel.

FIGURE C-30

Member	Zip Code	Number of Employees	Year of Membership Expiration	Code	Year 2016
Candy's Candy Shop	78256	23	2020	3	
Chip Technology	78251	175	2021	3	
Computer Attic	78263	14	**2018**	2	
Deluxe Auto Shop	78245	17	**2017**	1	
Dental Associates	78287	15	**2018**	5	
Dr. Mary Terese	78263	12	2021	2	
Dunkin' Donuts	78278	10	**2018**	4	
Earl's Restaurant	78235	45	**2019**	3	
First Federal Bank	78267	36	2021	3	
Friendly Chevy	78286	17	2023	3	
From Office	78211	25	2022	5	
General Hospital	78225	538	2020	4	
Grande Table	78246	31	**2019**	4	
Holiday Inn	78221	75	**2018**	4	
Ken's Florist Shop	78241	10	**2017**	2	
Lisa's Photo Studio	78202	5	2020	4	
Meineke Muffler	78256	24	**2019**	1	
Midas Muffler	78221	22	2023	3	
Mill Shoppe	78205	165	2020	2	

Independent Challenge 3

Prestige Press is a Boston-based publisher that manufactures children's books. As the finance manager for the company, one of your responsibilities is to analyze the monthly reports from the five district sales offices. Your boss, Joanne Bennington, has just asked you to prepare a quarterly sales report for an upcoming meeting. Because several top executives will be attending this meeting, Joanne reminds you that the report must look professional. In particular, she asks you to emphasize the company's surge in profits during the last month and to highlight the fact that the Northeastern district continues to outpace the other districts.

a. Plan a worksheet that shows the company's sales during the first quarter. Assume that all books are the same price. Make sure you include the following:

• The number of books sold (units sold) and the associated revenues (total sales) for each of the five district sales offices. The five sales districts are Northeastern, Midwestern, Southeastern, Southern, and Western.

• Calculations that show month-by-month totals for January, February, and March, and a 3-month cumulative total.

• Calculations that show each district's share of sales (percent of Total Sales).

• Labels that reflect the month-by-month data as well as the cumulative data.

• Formatting enhancements such as data bars that emphasize the recent month's sales surge and the Northeastern district's sales leadership.

b. Ask yourself the following questions about the organization and formatting of the worksheet: What worksheet title and labels do you need, and where should they appear? How can you calculate the totals? What formulas can you copy to save time and keystrokes? Do any of these formulas need to use an absolute reference? How do you show dollar amounts? What information should be shown in bold? Do you need to use more than one font? Should you use more than one point size?

c. Start Excel, then save a new, blank workbook as **EX C-Prestige Press** to the location where you store your Data Files.

Independent Challenge 3 (continued)

d. Build the worksheet with your own price and sales data. Enter the titles and labels first, then enter the numbers and formulas. You can use the information in TABLE C-4 to get started.

TABLE C-4

Prestige Press										
1st Quarter Sales Report										
		January		February		March		Total		
Office	Price	Units Sold	Sales	Units Sold	Sales	Units Sold	Sales	Units Sold	Sales	Total % of Sales
Northeastern										
Midwestern										
Southeastern										
Southern										
Western										

© 2014 Cengage Learning

e. Add a row beneath the data containing the totals for each column.

f. Adjust the column widths as necessary.

g. Change the height of row 1 to 33 points.

h. Format labels and values to enhance the look of the worksheet, and change the font styles and alignment if necessary.

i. Resize columns and adjust the formatting as necessary.

j. Add data bars for the monthly Units Sold columns.

k. Add a column that calculates a 25% increase in total sales dollars. Use an absolute cell reference in this calculation. (*Hint*: Make sure the current formatting is applied to the new information.)

l. Delete the contents of cells J4:K4 if necessary, then merge and center cell I4 over column I:K.

m. Add a bottom double border to cells I10:L10.

n. Enter your name in an empty cell.

o. Check the spelling in the workbook, change to a landscape orientation, save your work, then compare your work to FIGURE C-31.

p. Preview the worksheet in Backstage view, then submit your work to your instructor as directed.

q. Close the workbook file, then exit Excel.

FIGURE C-31

Your formulas
go here

Independent Challenge 4: Explore

This Independent Challenge requires an Internet connection.

You are saving money to take the international trip you have always dreamed about. You plan to visit seven different countries over the course of 2 months, and you have budgeted an identical spending allowance in each country. You want to create a worksheet that calculates the amount of native currency you will have in each country based on the budgeted amount. You want the workbook to reflect the currency information for each country.

a. Start Excel, then save a new, blank workbook as **EX C-World Tour Budget** to the location where you store your Data Files.

b. Add a title at the top of the worksheet.

c. Think of seven countries you would like to visit, then enter column and row labels for your worksheet. (*Hint*: You may wish to include row labels for each country, plus column labels for the country, the $1 equivalent in native currency, the total amount of native currency you'll have in each country, and the name of each country's monetary unit.)

d. Decide how much money you want to bring to each country (for example, $1,000), and enter that in the worksheet.

e. Use your favorite search engine to find your own information sources on currency conversions for the countries you plan to visit.

f. Enter the cash equivalent to $1 in U.S. dollars for each country in your list.

g. Create an equation that calculates the amount of native currency you will have in each country, using an absolute cell reference in the formula.

h. Format the entries in the column containing the native currency $1 equivalent as Number number format with three decimal places, and format the column containing the total native currency budget with two decimal places, using the correct currency number format for each country. (*Hint*: Use the Number tab in the Format cells dialog box; choose the appropriate currency number format from the Symbol list.)

i. Create a conditional format that changes the font style and color of the calculated amount in the $1,000 US column to light red fill with dark red text if the amount exceeds **1000** units of the local currency.

j. Merge and center the worksheet title over the column headings.

k. Add any formatting you want to the column headings, and resize the columns as necessary.

l. Add a background color to the title and change the font color if you choose.

m. Enter your name in the header of the worksheet.

n. Spell check the worksheet, save your changes, compare your work to FIGURE C-32, then preview the worksheet in Backstage view, and submit your work to your instructor as directed.

o. Close the workbook and exit Excel.

FIGURE C-32

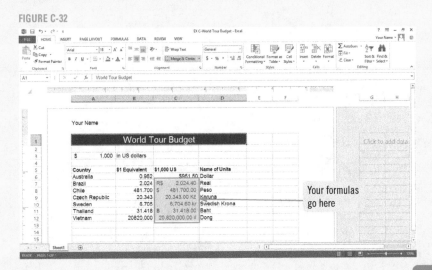

Visual Workshop

Open the file EX C-5.xlsx from the location where you store your Data Files, then save it as **EX C-Tip-Top Temps**. Use the skills you learned in this unit to format the worksheet so it looks like the one shown in FIGURE C-33. Create a conditional format in the Level column so that entries greater than 3 appear in light red fill with dark red text. Create an additional conditional format in the Review Cycle column so that any value equal to 3 appears in black fill with white bold text. Replace the Accounting department label with **Legal**. (*Hint*: The only additional font used in this exercise is 18-point Times New Roman in row 1.) Enter your name in the upper-right part of the header, check the spelling in the worksheet, save your changes, then submit your work to your instructor as directed. (*Hint*: Zoom out until the Zoom level is 100%.)

FIGURE C-33

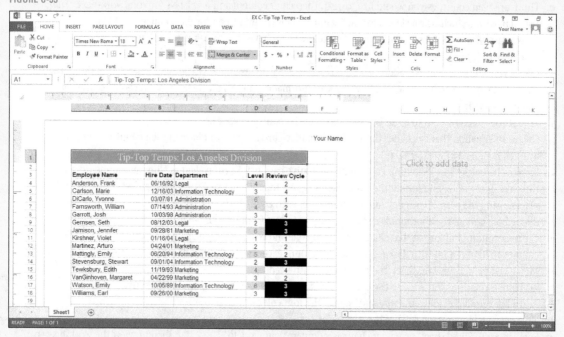

Working with Charts

CASE At the upcoming annual meeting, Grace Wong wants to emphasize spending patterns at Quest Specialty Travel. She asks you to create a chart showing the trends in company expenses over the past four quarters.

Unit Objectives

After completing this unit, you will be able to:

- Plan a chart
- Create a chart
- Move and resize a chart
- Change the chart design
- Change the chart format
- Format a chart
- Annotate and draw on a chart
- Create a pie chart

Files You Will Need

EX D-1.xlsx	EX D-4.xlsx
EX D-2.xlsx	EX D-5.xlsx
EX D-3.xlsx	EX D-6.xlsx

Plan a Chart

Learning
Outcomes
• Prepare to create
 a chart
• Identify chart
 elements
• Explore common
 chart types

Before creating a chart, you need to plan the information you want your chart to show and how you want it to look. Planning ahead helps you decide what type of chart to create and how to organize the data. Understanding the parts of a chart makes it easier to format and to change specific elements so that the chart best illustrates your data. **CASE** ▸ *In preparation for creating the chart for Grace's presentation, you identify your goals for the chart and plan its layout.*

DETAILS

Use the following guidelines to plan the chart:

• **Determine the purpose of the chart, and identify the data relationships you want to communicate graphically**

You want to create a chart that shows quarterly tour expenses for each country where Quest Specialty Travel provides tours. This worksheet data is shown in FIGURE D-1. You also want the chart to illustrate whether the quarterly expenses for each country increased or decreased from quarter to quarter.

• **Determine the results you want to see, and decide which chart type is most appropriate**

Different chart types display data in distinctive ways. For example, a pie chart compares parts to the whole, so it's useful for showing what proportion of a budget amount was spent on tours in one country relative to what was spent on tours in other countries. A line chart, in contrast, is best for showing trends over time. To choose the best chart type for your data, you should first decide how you want your data displayed and interpreted. TABLE D-1 describes several different types of charts you can create in Excel and their corresponding buttons on the INSERT tab on the Ribbon. Because you want to compare QST tour expenses in multiple countries over a period of four quarters, you decide to use a column chart.

• **Identify the worksheet data you want the chart to illustrate**

Sometimes you use all the data in a worksheet to create a chart, while at other times you may need to select a range within the sheet. The worksheet from which you are creating your chart contains expense data for each of the past four quarters and the totals for the past year. You will need to use all the quarterly data contained in the worksheet except the quarterly totals.

• **Understand the elements of a chart**

The chart shown in FIGURE D-2 contains basic elements of a chart. In the figure, QST tour countries are on the horizontal axis (also called the **x-axis**) and expense dollar amounts are on the vertical axis (also called the **y-axis**). The horizontal axis is also called the **category axis** because it often contains the names of data groups, such as locations, months, or years. The vertical axis is also called the **value axis** because it often contains numerical values that help you interpret the size of chart elements. (3-D charts also contain a **z-axis**, for comparing data across both categories and values.) The area inside the horizontal and vertical axes is the **plot area**. The **tick marks**, on the vertical axis, and **gridlines** (extending across the plot area) create a scale of measure for each value. Each value in a cell you select for your chart is a **data point**. In any chart, a **data marker** visually represents each data point, which in this case is a column. A collection of related data points is a **data series**. In this chart, there are four data series (Quarter 1, Quarter 2, Quarter 3, and Quarter 4). Each is made up of column data markers of a different color, so a **legend** is included to make it easy to identify them.

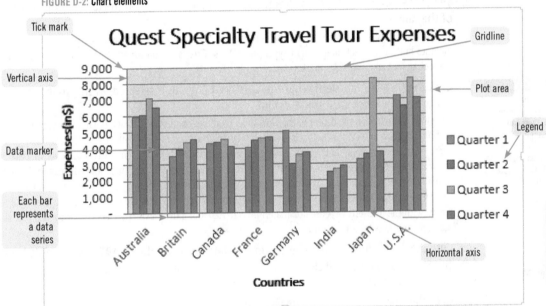

FIGURE D-2: Chart elements

Quest Specialty Travel Tour Expenses

Tick mark

Gridline

Vertical axis

Plot area

Data marker

Legend

Quarter 1

Quarter 2

Quarter 3

Quarter 4

Each bar represents a data series

Horizontal axis

Countries

TABLE D-1: Common chart types

type	button	description
Column		Compares data using columns; the Excel default; sometimes referred to as a bar chart in other spreadsheet programs
Line		Compares trends over even time intervals; looks similar to an area chart, but does not emphasize total
Pie		Compares sizes of pieces as part of a whole; used for a single series of numbers
Bar		Compares data using horizontal bars; sometimes referred to as a horizontal bar chart in other spreadsheet programs
Area		Shows how individual volume changes over time in relation to total volume
Scatter		Compares trends over uneven time or measurement intervals; used in scientific and engineering disciplines for trend spotting and extrapolation

Create a Chart

Learning
Outcomes
• Create a chart
• Switch a chart's
 columns/rows
• Add a chart title

To create a chart in Excel, you first select the range in a worksheet containing the data you want to chart. Once you've selected a range, you can use buttons on the INSERT tab on the Ribbon to create a chart based on the data in the range. **CASE** ▶ *Using the worksheet containing the quarterly expense data, you create a chart that shows how the expenses in each country varied across the quarters.*

STEPS

1. **Start Excel, open the file** EX D-1.xlsx **from the location where you store your Data Files, then save it as** EX D-Quarterly Tour Expenses

 You want the chart to include the quarterly tour expenses values, as well as quarter and country labels. You don't include the Total column and row because the figures in these cells would skew the chart.

2. **Select the range** A4:E12, **then click the** Quick Analysis tool ▤ **in the lower-right corner of the range**

 The Quick Analysis tool contains a tab that lets you quickly insert commonly used charts. The CHARTS tab includes buttons for each major chart type, plus a More Charts button for additional chart types, such as stock charts for charting stock market data.

3. **Click the** CHARTS tab, **verify that the** Clustered Column **is selected, as shown in** FIGURE D-3, **then click** Clustered Column

 The chart is inserted in the center of the worksheet, and two contextual CHART TOOLS tabs appear on the Ribbon: DESIGN, and FORMAT. On the DESIGN tab, which is currently in front, you can quickly change the chart type, chart layout, and chart style, and you can swap how the columns and rows of data in the worksheet are represented in the chart. When seen in the Normal view, three tools display to the right of the chart: these enable you to add, remove, or change chart elements ➕, set a style and color scheme ✎, and filter the results shown in a chart ▼. Currently, the countries are charted along the horizontal x-axis, with the quarterly expense dollar amounts charted along the y-axis. This lets you easily compare the quarterly expenses for each country.

4. **Click the** Switch Row/Column button **in the Data group on the CHART TOOLS DESIGN tab**

 The quarters are now charted along the x-axis. The expense amounts per country are charted along the y-axis, as indicated by the updated legend. See FIGURE D-4.

5. **Click the** Undo button ↺ **on the Quick Access toolbar**

 The chart returns to its original design.

6. **Click the** Chart Title placeholder **to show the text box, click anywhere in the** Chart Title text box, **press [Ctrl][A] to select the text, type** Quarterly Tour Expenses, **then click anywhere in the chart to deselect the title**

 Adding a title helps identify the chart. The border around the chart and the chart's **sizing handles**, the small series of dots at the corners and sides of the chart's border, indicate that the chart is selected. See FIGURE D-5. Your chart might be in a different location on the worksheet and may look slightly different; you will move and resize it in the next lesson. Any time a chart is selected, as it is now, a blue border surrounds the worksheet data range on which the chart is based, a purple border surrounds the cells containing the category axis labels, and a red border surrounds the cells containing the data series labels. This chart is known as an **embedded chart** because it is inserted directly in the current worksheet and doesn't exist in a separate file. Embedding a chart in the current sheet is the default selection when creating a chart, but you can also embed a chart on a different sheet in the workbook, or on a newly created chart sheet. A **chart sheet** is a sheet in a workbook that contains only a chart that is linked to the workbook data.

7. **Save your work**

FIGURE D-3: **CHARTS tab in Quick Analysis tool**

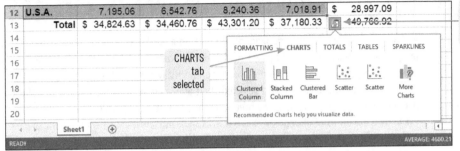

Quick Analysis Tool

FIGURE D-4: **Clustered Column chart with different presentation of data**

FIGURE D-5: **Chart with rows and columns restored and title added**

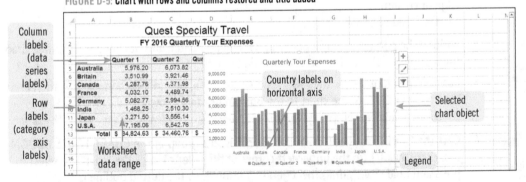

Excel 2013

Creating sparklines

You can quickly create a miniature chart called a **sparkline** that serves as a visual indicator of data trends. You can create a sparkline by selecting a range of data, clicking the Quick Analysis tool, clicking the SPARKLINES tab, then clicking the type of sparkline you want. (The sparkline appears in the cell immediately adjacent to the selected range.) You can also select a range, click the INSERT tab, then click the Line, Column, or Win/Loss button in the Sparklines group. In the Create Sparklines dialog box that opens, enter the cell in which you want the sparkline to appear, then click OK.

FIGURE D-6 shows a sparkline created in a cell. Any changes to data in the range are reflected in the sparkline. To delete a selected sparkline from a cell, click the Clear button in the Group group on the SPARKLINE TOOLS DESIGN tab.

FIGURE D-6: **Sparkline in a cell**

Move and Resize a Chart

Learning
Outcomes
• Reposition a chart
• Resize a chart
• Modify a legend
• Modify chart data

A chart is an **object**, or an independent element on a worksheet, and is not located in a specific cell or range. You can select an object by clicking it; sizing handles around the object indicate it is selected. (When a chart is selected in Excel, the Name box, which normally tells you the address of the active cell, tells you the chart number.) You can move a selected chart anywhere on a worksheet without affecting formulas or data in the worksheet. Any data changed in the worksheet is automatically updated in the chart. You can even move a chart to a different sheet in the workbook and it will still reflect the original data. You can resize a chart to improve its appearance by dragging its sizing handles. You can reposition chart objects (such as a title or legend) to predefined locations using commands using the Chart Elements button or the Add Chart Element button on the CHART TOOLS DESIGN tab, or you can freely move any chart object by dragging it or by cutting and pasting it to a new location. When you point to a chart object, the name of the object appears as a ScreenTip. **CASE** ▶ *You want to resize the chart, position it below the worksheet data, and move the legend.*

STEPS

1. **Make sure the chart is still selected, then position the pointer over the chart**

 The pointer shape ⁺�ℝ indicates that you can move the chart. For a table of commonly used object pointers, refer to TABLE D-2.

2. **Position ⁺ℝ on a blank area near the upper-left edge of the chart, press and hold the left mouse button, drag the chart until its upper-left corner is at the upper-left corner of cell A16, then release the mouse button**

 As you drag the chart, you can see the chart being dragged. When you release the mouse button, the chart appears in the new location.

3. **Scroll down so you can see the whole chart, position the pointer on the right-middle sizing handle until it changes to ⟷, then drag the right border of the chart to the right edge of column G**

 The chart is widened. See FIGURE D-7.

4. **Position the pointer over the upper-middle sizing handle until it changes to ↕, then drag the top border of the chart to the top edge of row 15**

5. **Position the pointer over the lower-middle sizing handle until it changes to ↕, then drag the bottom border of the chart to the bottom border of row 26**

 You can move any object on a chart. You want to align the top of the legend with the top of the plot area.

6. **Click the Quick Layout button in the Chart Layouts group of the CHART TOOLS DESIGN tab, click Layout 1 (in the upper-left corner of the palette), click the legend to select it, press and hold [Shift], drag the legend up using ⁺ℝ so the dotted outline is approximately ¼" above the top of the plot area, then release [Shift]**

 When you click the legend, sizing handles appear around it and "Legend" appears as a ScreenTip when the pointer hovers over the object. As you drag, a dotted outline of the legend border appears. Pressing and holding the [Shift] key holds the horizontal position of the legend as you move it vertically. Although the sizing handles on objects within a chart look different from the sizing handles that surround a chart, they function the same way.

7. **Click cell A12, type United States, click the Enter button ✔ on the formula bar, use AutoFit to resize column A, then save your work**

 The axis label changes to reflect the updated cell contents, as shown in FIGURE D-8. Changing any data in the worksheet modifies corresponding text or values in the chart. Because the chart is no longer selected, the CHART TOOLS tabs no longer appear on the Ribbon.

FIGURE D-7: **Moved and resized chart**

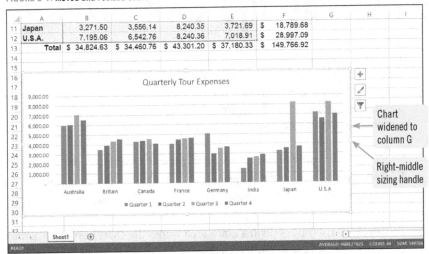

FIGURE D-8: **Worksheet with modified legend and label**

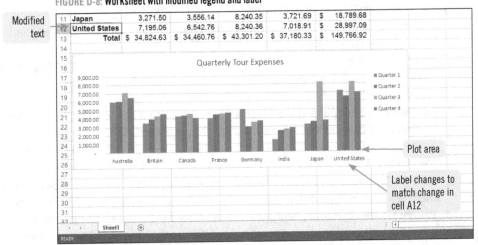

TABLE D-2: **Common object pointers**

name	pointer	use	name	pointer	use
Diagonal resizing	⤢ or ⤡	Change chart shape from corners	I-beam	I	Edit object text
Draw	+	Draw an object	Move	✛	Move object
Horizontal resizing	↔	Change object width	Vertical resizing	↕	Change object height

Moving an embedded chart to a sheet

Suppose you have created an embedded chart that you decide would look better on a chart sheet or in a different worksheet. You can make this change without recreating the entire chart. To do so, first select the chart, click the CHART TOOLS DESIGN tab, then click the Move Chart button in the Location group. The Move Chart dialog box opens. To move the chart to its own chart sheet, click the New sheet option button, type a name for the new sheet if desired, then click OK. If the chart is already on its own sheet, click the Object in option button, select the worksheet to where you want to move it, then click OK.

Change the Chart Design

Learning
Outcomes
• Change the chart
design
• Change the chart
type
• Apply a chart style

Once you've created a chart, you can change the chart type, modify the data range and column/row configuration, apply a different chart style, and change the layout of objects in the chart. The layouts in the Chart Layouts group on the CHART TOOLS DESIGN tab offer arrangements of objects in your chart, such as its legend, title, or gridlines; choosing one of these layouts is an alternative to manually changing how objects are arranged in a chart. **CASE** ▶ *You discovered the data for Japan and the United States in Quarter 3 is incorrect. After the correction, you want to see how the data looks using different chart layouts and types.*

STEPS

1. **Click cell D11, type 4568.92, press [Enter], type 6107.09, then press [Enter]**
 In the chart, the Quarter 3 data markers for Japan and the United States reflect the adjusted expense figures. See FIGURE D-9.

2. **Select the chart by clicking a blank area within the chart border, click the CHART TOOLS DESIGN tab on the Ribbon, click the Quick Layout button in the Chart Layouts group, then click Layout 3**
 The legend moves to the bottom of the chart. You prefer the original layout.

3. **Click the Undo button 🔄 on the Quick Access toolbar, then click the Change Chart Type button in the Type group**
 The Change Chart Type dialog box opens, as shown in FIGURE D-10. The left pane of the dialog box lists the available categories, and the right pane shows the individual chart types. A pale green border surrounds the currently selected chart type.

4. **Click Bar in the left pane of the Change Chart Type dialog box, confirm that the first Clustered Bar chart type is selected in the right pane, then click OK**
 The column chart changes to a clustered bar chart. See FIGURE D-11. You look at the bar chart, then decide to see how the data looks in a three-dimensional column chart.

5. **Click the Change Chart Type button in the Type group, click Column in the left pane of the Change Chart Type dialog box, click 3-D Clustered Column (fourth from the left in the top row) in the right pane, verify that the left-most 3-D chart is selected, then click OK**
 A three-dimensional column chart appears. You notice that the three-dimensional column format gives you a sense of volume, but it is more crowded than the two-dimensional column format.

6. **Click the Change Chart Type button in the Type group, click Clustered Column (first from the left in the top row) in the right pane of the Change Chart Type dialog box, then click OK**

7. **Click the Style 3 chart style in the Chart Styles group**
 The columns change to lighter shades of color. You prefer the previous chart style's color scheme.

8. **Click 🔄 on the Quick Access toolbar, then save your work**

Creating a combination chart

A **combination chart** is two charts in one; a column chart with a line chart, for example. This type of chart is helpful when charting dissimilar but related data. For example, you can create a combination chart based on home price and home size data, showing home prices in a column chart, and related home sizes in a line chart. Here a **secondary axis** (such as a vertical axis on the right side of the chart) would supply the scale for the home sizes. To create a combination chart, select all the data you want to plot, click Recommended Charts in the Charts group in the INSERT tab, click the All Charts tab, select Combo, supply the series information that conforms to the chart you want to create, then click OK. To change an existing chart to a combination chart, select the chart , then click Change Chart Type in the Type group on the CHART TOOLS DESIGN tab. Click Combo in the Change Chart Type dialog box, select the Secondary Axis box for each data series you want to plot, change the chart type to Line, then click OK.

FIGURE D-9: **Worksheet with modified data**

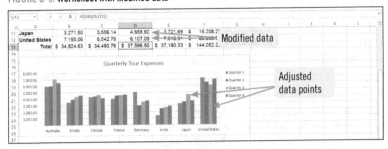

Modified data

Adjusted
data points

FIGURE D-10: **Change Chart Type dialog box**

Chart type
categories

Bar chart
type category

Currently
selected
chart type

FIGURE D-11: **Column chart changed to bar chart**

Click More button
to see additional
chart styles

Change Chart
Type button

Chart Elements button

Working with a 3-D chart

Excel includes two kinds of 3-D chart types. In a true 3-D chart, a third axis, called the **z-axis**, lets you compare data points across both categories and values. The z-axis runs along the depth of the chart, so it appears to advance from the back of the chart. To create a true 3-D chart, look for chart types that begin with "3-D," such as 3-D Column. In a 3-D chart, data series can sometimes obscure other columns or bars in the same chart, but you can rotate the chart to obtain a better view. Right-click the chart, then click 3-D Rotation. The Format Chart Area pane opens with the 3-D Rotation category active. The 3-D Rotation options let you change the orientation and perspective of the chart area, plot area, walls, and floor. The 3-D Format category lets you apply three-dimensional effects to selected chart objects. (Not all 3-D Rotation and 3-D Format options are available on all charts.)

Change the Chart Format

Learning
Outcomes
• Change the
 gridlines display
• Add axis titles
• Change the
 border color
• Add a shadow
 to an object

While the CHART TOOLS DESIGN tab contains preconfigured chart layouts you can apply to a chart, the Chart Elements button makes it easy to add, remove, and modify individual chart objects such as a chart title or legend. Using options on this shortcut menu (or using the Add Chart Element button on the CHART TOOLS DESIGN tab), you can also add text to a chart, add and modify labels, change the display of axes, modify the fill behind the plot area, create titles for the horizontal and vertical axes, and eliminate or change the look of gridlines. You can format the text in a chart object using the HOME tab or the Mini toolbar, just as you would the text in a worksheet. **CASE** *You want to change the layout of the chart by creating titles for the horizontal and vertical axes. To improve the chart's appearance, you'll add a drop shadow to the chart title.*

STEPS

1. **With the chart still selected, click the Add Chart Element button in the Chart Layouts group on the CHART TOOLS DESIGN tab, point to Gridlines, then click Primary Major Horizontal to deselect it**

 The gridlines that extend from the value axis tick marks across the chart's plot area are removed from the chart, as shown in FIGURE D-12.

2. **Click the Chart Elements button ⊞ in the upper-right corner *outside* the chart border, click the Gridlines arrow, click Primary Major Horizontal, click Primary Minor Horizontal, then click ⊞ to close the Chart Elements fly-out menu**

 Both major and minor gridlines now appear in the chart. **Major gridlines** represent the values at the value axis tick marks, and **minor gridlines** represent the values between the tick marks.

3. **Click ⊞, click the Axis Titles checkbox to select all the axis titles options, triple-click the vertical axis title on the chart, then type Expenses (in $)**

 Descriptive text on the category axis helps readers understand the chart.

4. **Triple-click the horizontal axis title on the chart, then type Tour Countries**

 The text "Tour Countries" appears on the horizontal axis, as shown in FIGURE D-13.

5. **Right-click the horizontal axis labels ("Australia", "Britain", etc.), click Font on the shortcut menu, click the Latin text font list arrow in the Font dialog box, click Times New Roman, click the Size down arrow, click until 8 is displayed, then click OK**

 The font of the horizontal axis labels changes to Times New Roman, and the font size decreases, making more of the plot area visible.

6. **With the horizontal axis labels still selected, click the HOME tab, click the Format Painter button 🖌 in the Clipboard group, then click the area within the vertical axis labels**

7. **Right-click the Chart Title ("Quarterly Tour Expenses"), click Format Chart Title on the shortcut menu, click the BORDER arrow ▷ in the Format Chart Title pane to display the options if necessary, then click the Solid line option button in the Format Chart Title pane**

 A solid border will appear around the chart title with the default blue color.

8. **Click the Effects button ◻ in the Format Chart Title pane, click Shadow, click the Presets list arrow, click Offset Diagonal Bottom Right in the Outer group (first row, first from the left), click the Format Chart Title pane Close button ✕, then save your work**

 A blue border with a drop shadow surrounds the title. Compare your work to FIGURE D-14.

Excel 2013

Adding data labels to a chart

There are times when your audience might benefit by seeing data labels on a chart. These labels appear next to the data markers in the chart and can indicate the series name, category name, and/or the value of one or more data points. Once your chart is selected, you can add this information to your chart by clicking the Chart Elements button in the upper-right corner outside the selected chart, clicking the Data Labels arrow, and then clicking a display option for the data labels. Once you have added the data labels, you can format them or delete individual data labels. To delete a data label, select it and then press [Delete].

Format a Chart

Learning
Outcomes
• Change the fill of
 a data series
• Use Live Preview
 to see a new data
 series color
• Apply a style to a
 data series

Formatting a chart can make it easier to read and understand. Many formatting enhancements can be made using the CHART TOOLS FORMAT tab. You can change the fill color for a specific data series, or you can apply a shape style to a title or a data series using the Shape Styles group. Shape styles make it possible to apply multiple formats, such as an outline, fill color, and text color, all with a single click. You can also apply different fill colors, outlines, and effects to chart objects using arrows and buttons in the Shape Styles group. **CASE** *You want to use a different color for one data series in the chart and apply a shape style to another to enhance the look of the chart.*

STEPS

1. **With the chart selected, click the** CHART TOOLS FORMAT **tab on the Ribbon, then click any column in the** Quarter 4 data series

 The CHART TOOLS FORMAT tab opens, and handles appear on each column in the Quarter 4 data series, indicating that the entire series is selected.

2. **Click the** Shape Fill list arrow **in the Shape Styles group on the CHART TOOLS FORMAT tab**

3. **Click** Orange, Accent 6 **(first row, 10th from the left) as shown in** FIGURE D-15

 All the columns for the series become orange, and the legend changes to match the new color. You can also change the color of selected objects by applying a shape style.

4. **Click any** column **in the** Quarter 3 data series

 Handles appear on each column in the Quarter 3 data series.

QUICK TIP
To apply a WordArt
style to a text object
(such as the chart
title), select the
object, then click a
style in the WordArt
Styles group on the
CHART TOOLS
FORMAT tab.

5. **Click the** More button ⏷ **on the Shape Styles gallery, then** *hover the pointer* **over the** Moderate Effect – Olive Green, Accent 3 shape style **(fifth row, fourth from the left) in the gallery, as shown in** FIGURE D-16

 Live Preview shows the data series in the chart with the shape style applied.

6. **Click the** Subtle Effect – Olive Green, Accent 3 shape style **(fourth row, fourth from the left) in the gallery**

 The style for the data series changes, as shown in FIGURE D-17.

7. **Save your work**

Previewing a chart

To print or preview just a chart, select the chart (or make the chart sheet active), click the FILE tab, then click Print on the navigation bar. To reposition a chart by changing the page's margins, click the Show Margins button ▦ in the lower-right corner of the Print tab to display the margins in the preview. You can drag the margin lines to the exact settings you want; as the margins change, the size and placement of the chart on the page changes too.

FIGURE D-15: **New shape fill applied to data series**

FIGURE D-16: **Live Preview of new style applied to data series**

FIGURE D-17: **Style of data series changed**

Changing alignment and angle in axis labels and titles

The buttons on the CHART TOOLS DESIGN tab provide a few options for positioning axis labels and titles, but you can customize their position and rotation to exact specifications using the Format Axis pane or Format Axis Title pane. With a chart selected, right-click the axis text you want to modify, then click Format Axis or Format Axis Title on the shortcut menu. In the pane that is displayed, click the Size & Properties button, then select the appropriate Text layout option. You can also create a custom angle by clicking the Custom angle up and down arrows. When you have made the desired changes, close the pane.

Annotate and Draw on a Chart

Learning
Outcomes
• Type text in a text box
• Draw an arrow on a chart
• Modify a drawn object

You can use text annotations and graphics to point out critical information in a chart. **Text annotations** are labels that further describe your data. You can also draw lines and arrows that point to the exact locations you want to emphasize. Shapes such as arrows and boxes can be added from the Illustrations group on the INSERT tab or from the Insert Shapes group on the CHART TOOLS FORMAT tab on the Ribbon. The INSERT group is also used to insert pictures into worksheets and charts. **CASE** *You want to call attention to the Germany tour expense decrease, so you decide to add a text annotation and an arrow to this information in the chart.*

STEPS

1. **Make sure the chart is selected with the CHART TOOLS FORMAT tab selected, click the Text Box button in the Insert Shapes group, then move the pointer over the worksheet**

 The pointer changes to ↓, indicating that you will insert a text box where you next click.

2. **Click to the right of the chart (anywhere *outside* the chart boundary)**

 A text box is added to the worksheet, and the DRAWING TOOLS FORMAT tab appears on the Ribbon so that you can format the new object. First you need to type the text.

3. **Type Great Improvement**

 The text appears in a selected text box on the worksheet, and the chart is no longer selected, as shown in FIGURE D-18. Your text box may be in a different location; this is not important, because you'll move the annotation in the next step.

4. **Point to an edge of the text box so that the pointer changes to ⁺⁺ₖ, drag the text box into the chart to the left of the chart title, as shown in FIGURE D-19, then release the mouse button**

 The text box is a text annotation for the chart. You also want to add a simple arrow shape in the chart.

5. **Click the chart to select it, click the CHART TOOLS FORMAT tab, click the Arrow button in the Insert Shapes group, then move the pointer over the text box on the chart**

 The pointer changes to ✚, and the status bar displays "Click and drag to insert an AutoShape." When ✚ is over the text box, black handles appear around the text in the text box. A black handle can act as an anchor for the arrow.

6. **Position ✚ on the black handle to the right of the "t" in the word "improvement" (in the text box), press and hold the left mouse button, drag the line to the Quarter 2 column for the Germany category in the chart, then release the mouse button**

 An arrow points to the Quarter 2 expense for Germany, and the DRAWING TOOLS FORMAT tab displays options for working with the new arrow object. You can resize, format, or delete it just like any other object in a chart.

7. **Click the Shape Outline list arrow in the Shape Styles group, click the Automatic color, click the Shape Outline list arrow again, point to Weight, then click 1½ pt**

 Compare your finished chart to FIGURE D-20.

8. **Save your work**

FIGURE D-18: **Text box added**

DRAWING
TOOLS
FORMAT tab

Text annotation

FIGURE D-19: **Text annotation on the chart**

Text annotation

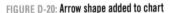

FIGURE D-20: **Arrow shape added to chart**

Arrow drawn and
formatted

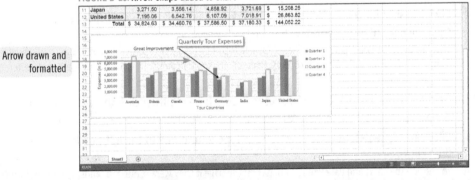

Adding SmartArt graphics

In addition to charts, annotations, and drawn objects, you can create a variety of diagrams using SmartArt graphics. **SmartArt graphics** are available in List, Process, Cycle, Hierarchy, Relationship, Matrix, and Pyramid categories. To insert SmartArt, click the Insert a SmartArt Graphic button in the Illustrations group on the INSERT tab to open the Choose a SmartArt Graphic dialog box. Click a SmartArt category in the left pane, then click the layout for the graphic in the right pane. The right pane shows a sample of the selected SmartArt layout, as shown in FIGURE D-21. The SmartArt graphic appears in the worksheet as an embedded object with sizing handles. Click the Text Pane button on the SmartArt Tools Design tab to open a text pane next to the graphic; you can

enter text into the graphic using the text pane or by typing directly in the shapes in the diagram.

FIGURE D-21: **Choose a SmartArt Graphic dialog box**

Create a Pie Chart

Learning
Outcomes
• Create a pie chart
• Explode a pie
 chart slice

You can create multiple charts based on the same worksheet data. While a column chart may illustrate certain important aspects of your worksheet data, you may find you want to create an additional chart to emphasize a different point. Depending on the type of chart you create, you have additional options for calling attention to trends and patterns. For example, if you create a pie chart, you can emphasize one data point by **exploding**, or pulling that slice away from, the pie chart. When you're ready to print a chart, you can preview it just as you do a worksheet to check the output before committing it to paper. You can print a chart by itself or as part of the worksheet. **CASE** ▸ *At an upcoming meeting, Grace plans to discuss the total tour expenses and which countries need improvement. You want to create a pie chart she can use to illustrate total expenses. Finally, you want to fit the worksheet and the charts onto one worksheet page.*

STEPS

1. **Select the range** A5:A12, **press and hold [Ctrl], select the range** F5:F12, **click the** INSERT tab, **click the** Insert Pie or Doughnut Chart button **in the Charts group, then click** 3-D Pie **in the chart gallery**

 The new chart appears in the center of the worksheet. You can move the chart and quickly format it using a chart layout.

2. **Drag the** chart **so its upper-left corner is at the upper-left corner of cell** G1, **click the** Quick Layout button **in the Chart Layouts group of the CHART TOOLS DESIGN tab, then click** Layout 2

 The chart is repositioned on the page, and its layout changes so that a chart title is added, the percentages display on each slice, and the legend appears just below the chart title.

3. **Select the** Chart Title text, **then type** Total Expenses, by Country

4. **Click the slice for the** India data point, **click it again so it is the only slice selected, right-click it, then click** Format Data Point

 The Format Data Point pane opens, as shown in FIGURE D-22. You can use the Point Explosion slider to control the distance a pie slice moves away from the pie, or you can type a value in the Point Explosion text box.

5. **Double-click** 0 **in the** Point Explosion text box, **type** 40, **then click the** Close button ✖

 Compare your chart to FIGURE D-23. You decide to preview the chart and data before you print.

6. **Click cell** A1, **switch to** Page Layout view, **type your name in the left header text box, then click cell** A1

 You decide the chart and data would fit better on the page if they were printed in landscape orientation.

7. **Click the** PAGE LAYOUT tab, **click the** Orientation button **in the Page Setup group, then click** Landscape

8. **Click the** FILE tab, **click** Print **on the navigation bar, click the** No Scaling setting **in the Settings section on the Print tab, then click** Fit Sheet on One Page

 The data and chart are positioned horizontally on a single page, as shown in FIGURE D-24. The printer you have selected may affect the appearance of your preview screen.

9. **Save and close the workbook, submit your work to your instructor as directed, then exit Excel**

FIGURE D-22: **Format Data Point pane**

Point Explosion slider

Point Explosion text box

FIGURE D-23: **Exploded pie slice**

FIGURE D-24: **Preview of worksheet with charts in Backstage view**

Fit Sheet on One Page setting

Show Margins button

Practice

Concepts Review

Label each element of the Excel chart shown in FIGURE D-25.

FIGURE D-25

Match each chart type with the statement that best describes it.

7. **Area**
8. **Line**
9. **Column**
10. **Combination**
11. **Pie**

a. Displays a column and line chart using different scales of measurement
b. Compares trends over even time intervals
c. Compares data using columns
d. Compares data as parts of a whole
e. Shows how volume changes over time

Select the best answer from the list of choices.

12. **Which tab appears only when a chart is selected?**
 a. INSERT
 b. CHART TOOLS FORMAT
 c. REVIEW
 d. PAGE LAYOUT

13. **Which is *not* an example of a SmartArt graphic?**
 a. Sparkline
 b. Basic Matrix
 c. Organization Chart
 d. Basic Pyramid

14. **How do you move an embedded chart to a chart sheet?**
 a. Click a button on the CHART TOOLS DESIGN tab.
 b. Drag the chart to the sheet tab.
 c. Delete the chart, switch to a different sheet, then create a new chart.
 d. Use the Copy and Paste buttons on the Ribbon.

15. **The object in a chart that identifies the colors used for each data series is a(n):**
 a. Data marker.
 b. Data point.
 c. Organizer.
 d. Legend.

16. **A collection of related data points in a chart is called a:**
 a. Data series.
 b. Data tick.
 c. Cell address.
 d. Value title.

17. **Which tab on the Ribbon do you use to create a chart?**
 a. DESIGN
 b. INSERT
 c. PAGE LAYOUT
 d. FORMAT

Skills Review

1. **Plan a chart.**
 a. Start Excel, open the Data File EX D-2.xlsx from the location where you store your Data Files, then save it as **EX D-Departmental Software Usage**.
 b. Describe the type of chart you would use to plot this data.
 c. What chart type would you use to compare the number of Excel users in each department?

2. **Create a chart.**
 a. In the worksheet, select the range containing all the data and headings.
 b. Click the Quick Analysis tool.
 c. Create a Clustered Column chart, then add the chart title **Software Usage, by Department** above the chart.
 d. If necessary, click the Switch Row/Column button so the Department appears as the x-axis.
 e. Save your work.

Skills Review (continued)

3. **Move and resize a chart.**

 a. Make sure the chart is still selected, and close any open panes if necessary.

 b. Move the chart beneath the worksheet data.

 c. Widen the chart so it extends to the right edge of column H.

 d. Use the Quick Layout button in the CHART TOOLS DESIGN tab to move the legend to the right of the charted data. (*Hint*: Use Layout 1.)

 e. Resize the chart so its bottom edge is at the top of row 25.

 f. Save your work.

4. **Change the chart design.**

 a. Change the value in cell B3 to **15**. Observe the change in the chart.

 b. Select the chart.

 c. Use the Quick Layout button in the Chart Layouts group on the CHART TOOLS DESIGN tab to apply the Layout 10 layout to the chart, then undo the change.

 d. Use the Change Chart Type button on the CHART TOOLS DESIGN tab to change the chart to a Clustered Bar chart.

 e. Change the chart to a 3-D Clustered Column chart, then change it back to a Clustered Column chart.

 f. Save your work.

5. **Change the chart layout.**

 a. Use the CHART ELEMENTS button to turn off the primary major horizontal gridlines in the chart.

 b. Change the font used in the horizontal and vertical axes labels to Times New Roman.

 c. Turn on the primary major gridlines for both the horizontal and vertical axes.

 d. Change the chart title's font to Times New Roman if necessary, with a font size of 20.

 e. Insert **Departments** as the primary horizontal axis title.

 f. Insert **Number of Users** as the primary vertical axis title.

 g. Change the font size of the horizontal and vertical axis titles to 10 and the font to Times New Roman, if necessary.

 h. Change "Personnel" in the worksheet column heading to **Human Resources**, then AutoFit column E.

 i. Change the font size of the legend to 14.

 j. Add a solid line border in the default color and a (preset) Offset Diagonal Bottom Right shadow to the chart title.

 k. Save your work.

6. **Format a chart.**

 a. Make sure the chart is selected, then select the CHART TOOLS FORMAT tab, if necessary.

 b. Change the shape fill of the Excel data series to Dark Blue, Text 2.

 c. Change the shape style of the Excel data series to Subtle Effect – Orange, Accent 6.

 d. Save your work.

7. **Annotate and draw on a chart.**

 a. Make sure the chart is selected, then create the text annotation **Needs more users**.

 b. Position the text annotation so the word "Needs" is just below the word "Software" in the chart title.

 c. Select the chart, then use the CHART TOOLS FORMAT tab to create a 1½ pt weight dark blue arrow that points from the bottom center of the text box to the Excel users in the Design department.

 d. Deselect the chart.

 e. Save your work.

Skills Review (continued)

8. Create a pie chart.

a. Select the range A1:F2, then create a 3-D Pie chart.

b. Drag the 3-D pie chart beneath the existing chart.

c. Change the chart title to **Excel Users**.

d. Apply the Style 7 chart style to the chart, then apply Layout 6 using the Quick Layout button.

e. Explode the Human Resources slice from the pie chart at **25%**.

f. In Page Layout view, enter your name in the left section of the worksheet header.

g. Preview the worksheet and charts in Backstage view, make sure all the contents fit on one page, then submit your work to your instructor as directed. When printed, the worksheet should look like FIGURE D-26.

h. Save your work, close the workbook, then exit Excel.

FIGURE D-26

Your Name

	Accounting	Marketing	Design	Human Resources	Purchasing
Excel	37	16	5	11	38
Word	15	35	17	15	10
PowerPoint	17	5	12	5	3
Access	20	25	8	10	15
Publisher	2	15	22	15	25

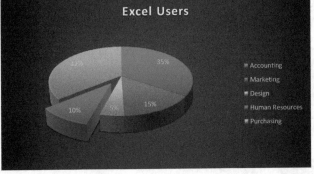

Independent Challenge 1

You are the operations manager for the Tulsa Arts Alliance in Oklahoma. Each year the group applies to various state and federal agencies for matching funds. For this year's funding proposal, you need to create charts to document the number of productions in previous years.

a. Start Excel, open the file EX D-3.xlsx from the location where you store your Data Files, then save it as **EX D-Tulsa Arts Alliance**.

b. Take some time to plan your charts. Which type of chart or charts might best illustrate the information you need to display? What kind of chart enhancements do you want to use? Will a 3-D effect make your chart easier to understand?

c. Create a Clustered Column chart for the data.

d. Change at least one of the colors used in a data series.

e. Make the appropriate modifications to the chart to make it visually attractive and easier to read and understand. Include a legend to the right of the chart, and add chart titles and horizontal and vertical axis titles using the text shown in TABLE D-3.

TABLE D-3

title	text
Chart title	Tulsa Arts Alliance Events
Vertical axis title	Number of Events
Horizontal axis title	Types of Events

© 2014 Cengage Learning

f. Create at least two additional charts for the same data to show how different chart types display the same data. Reposition each new chart so that all charts are visible in the worksheet. One of the additional charts should be a pie chart; the other is up to you.

g. Modify each chart as necessary to improve its appearance and effectiveness. A sample worksheet containing three charts based on the worksheet data is shown in FIGURE D-27.

h. Enter your name in the worksheet header.

i. Save your work. Before printing, preview the worksheet in Backstage view, then adjust any settings as necessary so that all the worksheet data and charts print on a single page.

j. Submit your work to your instructor as directed.

k. Close the workbook, then exit Excel.

FIGURE D-27

Working with Charts

Independent Challenge 2

You work at Bark Bark Bark, a locally owned day spa for dogs. One of your responsibilities at the day spa is to manage the company's sales and expenses using Excel. Another is to convince the current staff that Excel can help them make daily operating decisions more easily and efficiently. To do this, you've decided to create charts using the previous year's operating expenses including rent, utilities, and payroll. The manager will use these charts at the next monthly meeting.

a. Start Excel, open the Data File EX D-4.xlsx from the location where you store your Data Files, then save it as **EX D-Bark Bark Bark Doggie Day Spa Analysis**.

b. Decide which data in the worksheet should be charted. What chart types are best suited for the information you need to show? What kinds of chart enhancements are necessary?

c. Create a 3-D Clustered Column chart in the worksheet showing the expense data for all four quarters. (*Hint*: The expense categories should appear on the x-axis. Do not include the totals.)

d. Change the vertical axis labels (Expenses data) so that no decimals are displayed. (*Hint*: Right-click the axis labels you want to modify, click Format Axis, click the Number category in the Format Axis pane, change the number of decimal places, then close the Format Axis pane.)

e. Using the sales data, create two charts on this worksheet that compare the sales amounts. (*Hint*: Move each chart to a new location on the worksheet, then deselect it before creating the next one.)

f. In one chart of the sales data, add data labels, then add chart titles as you see fit.

g. Make any necessary formatting changes to make the charts look more attractive, then enter your name in a worksheet cell.

h. Save your work.

i. Preview each chart in Backstage view, and adjust any items as needed. Fit the worksheet to a single page, then submit your work to your instructor as directed. A sample of a printed worksheet is shown in FIGURE D-28.

j. Close the workbook, then exit Excel.

FIGURE D-28

Independent Challenge 3

You are working as an account representative at a magazine called *Creativity*. You have been examining the expenses incurred recently. The CEO wants to examine expenses designed to increase circulation and has asked you to prepare charts that can be used in this evaluation. In particular, you want to see how dollar amounts compare among the different expenses, and you also want to see how expenses compare with each other proportional to the total budget.

a. Start Excel, open the Data File EX D-5.xlsx from the location where you store your Data Files, then save it as **EX D-Creativity Magazine**.

b. Identify three types of charts that seem best suited to illustrate the data in the range A16:B24. What kinds of chart enhancements are necessary?

c. Create at least two different types of charts that show the distribution of circulation expenses. (*Hint*: Move each chart to a new location on the same worksheet.) One of the charts should be a 3-D pie chart.

d. In at least one of the charts, add annotated text and arrows highlighting important data, such as the largest expense.

e. Change the color of at least one data series in at least one of the charts.

f. Add chart titles and category and value axis titles where appropriate. Format the titles with a font of your choice. Apply a shadow to the chart title in at least one chart.

g. Add your name to a section of the header, then save your work.

h. Explode a slice from the 3-D pie chart.

i. Add a data label to the exploded pie slice.

j. Preview the worksheet in Backstage view. Adjust any items as needed. Be sure the charts are all visible on one page. Compare your work to the sample in FIGURE D-29.

k. Submit your work to your instructor as directed, close the workbook, then exit Excel.

FIGURE D-29

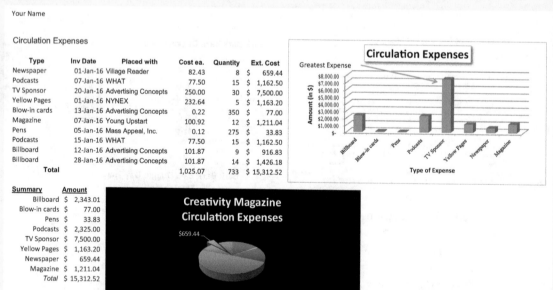

Independent Challenge 4: Explore

This Independent Challenge requires an Internet connection.

A cash inheritance from a distant relative has finally been deposited in your bank account, and you have decided to purchase a home. You have a good idea where you'd like to live, and you decide to use the web to find out more about houses that are currently available.

a. Start Excel, then save a new, blank workbook as **EX D-My Dream House** to the location where you save your Data Files.

b. Decide on where you would like to live, and use your favorite search engine to find information sources on homes for sale in that area. (*Hint*: Try using realtor.com or other realtor-sponsored sites.)

c. Determine a price range and features within the home. Find data for at least five homes that meet your location and price requirements, and enter them in the worksheet. See TABLE D-4 for a suggested data layout.

d. Format the data so it looks attractive and professional.

e. Create any type of column chart using only the House and Asking Price data. Place it on the same worksheet as the data. Include a descriptive title.

f. Change the colors in the chart using the chart style of your choice.

g. Enter your name in a section of the header.

h. Create an additional chart: a combo chart that plots the asking price on one axis and the size of the home on the other axis. (*Hint*: Use Help to get tips on how to chart with a secondary axis.)

i. Save the workbook. Preview the worksheet in Backstage view and make adjustments if necessary to fit all of the information on one page. See FIGURE D-30 for an example of what your worksheet might look like.

j. Submit your work to your instructor as directed.

k. Close the workbook, then exit Excel.

TABLE D-4

suggested data layout					
Location					
Price range					
	House 1	House 2	House 3	House 4	House 5
Asking price					
Bedrooms					
Bathrooms					
Year built					
Size (in sq. ft.)					

© 2014 Cengage Learning

FIGURE D-30

Visual Workshop

Open the Data File EX D-6.xlsx from the location where you store your Data Files, then save it as **EX D-Projected Project Expenses**. Format the worksheet data so it looks like FIGURE D-31, then create and modify two charts to match the ones shown in the figure. You will need to make formatting, layout, and design changes once you create the charts. (*Hint*: The shadow used in the 3-D pie chart title is made using the Outer Offset Diagonal Top Right shadow.) Enter your name in the left text box of the header, then save and preview the worksheet. Submit your work to your instructor as directed, then close the workbook and exit Excel.

FIGURE D-31

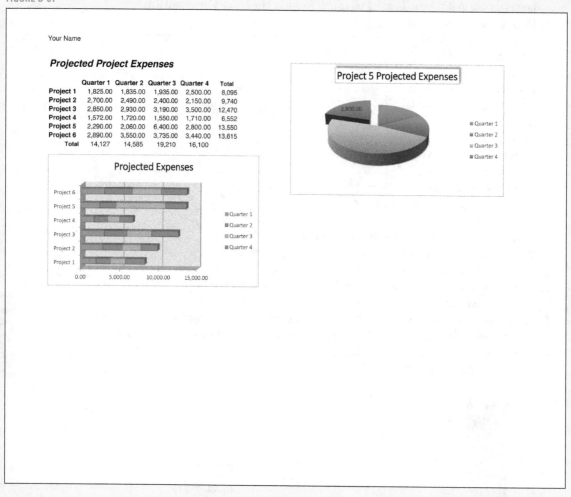

Getting Started with Access 2013

CASE ▶ Samantha Hooper is the tour developer for United States group travel at Quest Specialty Travel (QST), a tour company that specializes in customized group travel packages. Samantha uses Microsoft Access 2013 to store, maintain, and analyze customer and tour information.

Unit Objectives

After completing this unit, you will be able to:

- Understand relational databases
- Explore a database
- Create a database
- Create a table

- Create primary keys
- Relate two tables
- Enter data
- Edit data

Files You Will Need

QuestTravel-A.accdb
RealEstate-A.accdb
Recycle-A.accdb
BusinessContacts-A.accdb
Basketball-A.accdb

Learning
Outcomes
• Describe relational
database concepts
• Explain when to
use a database

Understand Relational Databases

Microsoft Access 2013 is relational database software that runs on the Windows operating system. You use **relational database software** to manage data that is organized into lists, such as information about customers, products, vendors, employees, projects, or sales. Many small companies track customer, inventory, and sales information in a spreadsheet program such as Microsoft Excel. Although Excel offers some list management features and is more commonly used than Access, Access provides many more tools and advantages for managing data. The advantages are mainly due to the "relational" nature of the lists that Access manages. TABLE A-1 compares the two programs. **CASE** *You and Samantha Hooper review the advantages of database software over spreadsheets for managing lists of information.*

DETAILS

The advantages of using Access for database management include:

- **Duplicate data is minimized**

 FIGURES A-1 and A-2 compare how you might store sales data in a single Excel spreadsheet list versus three related Access tables. With Access, you do not have to reenter information such as a customer's name and address or tour name every time a sale is made, because lists can be linked, or "related," in relational database software.

- **Information is more accurate, reliable, and consistent because duplicate data is minimized**

 The relational nature of data stored in an Access database allows you to minimize duplicate data entry, which creates more accurate, reliable, and consistent information. For example, customer data in a Customers table is entered only once, not every time a customer makes a purchase.

- **Data entry is faster and easier using Access forms**

 Data entry forms (screen layouts) make data entry faster, easier, and more accurate than entering data in a spreadsheet.

- **Information can be viewed and sorted in many ways using Access queries, forms, and reports**

 In Access, you can save queries (questions about the data), data entry forms, and reports, allowing you to use them over and over without performing extra work to re-create a particular view of the data.

- **Information is more secure using Access passwords and security features**

 Access databases can be encrypted and password protected.

- **Several users can share and edit information at the same time**

 Unlike spreadsheets or word-processing documents, more than one person can enter, update, and analyze data in an Access database at the same time.

FIGURE A-1: **Using a spreadsheet to organize sales data**

Tour information is duplicated when the same tour is purchased by multiple customers

Customer information is duplicated when the same customer purchases multiple tours

	A	B	C	D	E	F	G	H	I
1	CustNo	FName	LName	SalesNo	SaleDate	TourName	TourStartDate	City	Price
2	1	Gracita	Mayberry	35	7/1/2014	Red Reef Scuba	7/6/2014	Islamadora	1,500.00
3	2	Jacob	Alman	34	7/1/2014	Red Reef Scuba	7/6/2014	Islamadora	1,500.00
4	3	Julia	Bouchart	33	7/1/2014	Red Reef Scuba	7/6/2014	Islamadora	1,500.00
5	3	Julia	Bouchart	7	5/1/2014	Piper-Heitman Wedding	5/30/2014	Captiva	825.00
6	4	Jane	Taylor	13	5/11/2014	Red Reef Scuba	7/6/2014	Islamadora	1,500.00
7	4	Jane	Taylor	20	6/1/2014	American Heritage Tour	8/24/2014	Philadelphia	1,200.00
8	5	Samantha	Braven	30	7/1/2014	Red Reef Scuba	7/6/2014	Islamadora	1,500.00
9	5	Samantha	Braven	52	7/11/2014	Bright Lights Expo	12/1/2014	Branson	200.00
10	6	Kristen	Collins	3	4/30/2014	Ames Ski Club	1/2/2015	Breckenridge	850.00
11	6	Kristen	Collins	21	6/1/2014	Yosemite National Park Great Cleanup	7/20/2014	Sacramento	1,100.00
12	6	Kristen	Collins	29	7/1/2014	American Heritage Tour	8/24/2014	Philadelphia	1,200.00
13	6	Kristen	Collins	40	7/7/2014	Bright Lights Expo	12/1/2014	Branson	200.00
14	7	Tom	Camel	41	7/7/2014	Bright Lights Expo	12/1/2014	Branson	200.00
15	7	Tom	Camel	36	7/1/2014	American Heritage Tour	8/24/2014	Philadelphia	1,200.00
16	7	Tom	Camel	8	5/1/2014	Ames Ski Club	1/2/2015	Breckenridge	850.00
17	7	Tom	Camel	19	6/1/2014	Yosemite National Park Great Cleanup	7/20/2014	Sacramento	1,100.00
18	8	Dick	Tracy	43	7/8/2014	Bright Lights Expo	12/1/2014	Branson	200.00
19	9	Daniel	Cabriella	45	7/9/2014	American Heritage Tour	8/24/2014	Philadelphia	1,200.00
20	9	Daniel	Cabriella	46	7/9/2014	Bright Lights Expo	12/1/2014	Branson	200.00
21	10	Brad	Eahlie	66	7/14/2014	Boy Scout Jamboree	1/13/2015	Vail	1,900.00
22	11	Nancy	Diverman	32	7/1/2014	Red Reef Scuba	7/6/2014	Islamadora	1,500.00

FIGURE A-2: **Using a relational database to organize sales data**

Customers table

Cust No	First	Last	Street	City	State	Zip	Phone
1	Gracita	Mayberry	52411 Oakmont Rd	Kansas City	MO	64144	(555) 444-1234
2	Jacob	Alman	2505 McGee St	Des Moines	IA	50288	(555) 111-6931
3	Julia	Bouchart	5200 Main St	Kansas City	MO	64105	(555) 111-3081

Sales table

Cust No	TourNo	Date	SalesNo
1	2	7/1/14	35
2	2	7/1/14	34
3	2	7/1/14	33

Tours table

TourNo	TourName	TourStartDate	Duration	City	Cost
1	Stanley Bay Shelling	07/06/2014	3	Captiva	$750.00
2	Red Reef Scuba	07/06/2014	3	Islamadora	$1,500.00
3	Ames Ski Club	01/02/2015	7	Breckenridge	$850.00

TABLE A-1: **Comparing Excel with Access**

feature	Excel	Access
Layout	Provides a natural tabular layout for easy data entry	Provides a natural tabular layout as well as the ability to create customized data entry screens called forms
Storage	Restricted to a file's limitations	Virtually unlimited when coupled with the ability to use Microsoft SQL Server to store data
Linked tables	Manages single lists of information—no relational database capabilities	Relates lists of information to reduce data redundancy and create a relational database
Reporting	Limited	Provides the ability to create an unlimited number of reports
Security	Limited to file security options such as marking the file "read-only" or protecting a range of cells	When used with SQL Server, provides extensive security down to the user and data level
Multiuser capabilities	Not allowed	Allows multiple users to simultaneously enter and update data
Data entry	Provides limited data entry screens	Provides the ability to create an unlimited number of data entry forms

Explore a Database

Learning
Outcomes
• Start Access and
 open a database
• Identify Access
 components
• Open and define
 Access objects

You can start Access in many ways. If you double-click an existing Access *database* icon or shortcut, that specific database will open directly within Access. This is the fastest way to open an *existing* Access database. If you start Access on its own, however, you see a window that requires you to make a choice between opening a database and creating a new database. **CASE** ▶ *Samantha Hooper has developed a database called QuestTravel-A, which contains tour information. She asks you to start Access 2013 and review this database.*

STEPS

1. **Start Access**

 Access starts, as shown in FIGURE A-3. This window allows you to open an existing database, create a new database from a template, or create a new blank database.

 TROUBLE
 If a yellow Security
 Warning bar appears
 below the Ribbon,
 click Enable Content.

2. **Click the Open Other Files link, navigate to the location where you store your Data Files, click the QuestTravel-A.accdb database, click Open, then click the Maximize button ▢ if the Access window is not already maximized**

 The QuestTravel-A.accdb database contains five tables of data named Customers, Sales, States, TourCategories, and Tours. It also contains six queries, six forms, and four reports. Each of these items (table, query, form, and report) is a different type of **object** in an Access database and is displayed in the **Navigation Pane**. The purpose of each object is defined in TABLE A-2. To learn about an Access database, you explore its objects.

 TROUBLE
 If the Navigation
 Pane is not open,
 click the Shutter Bar
 Open/Close button
 ⏵⏵ to open it and
 view the database
 objects.

3. **In the Navigation Pane, double-click the Tours table to open it, then double-click the Customers table to open it**

 The Tours and Customers tables open to display the data they store. A **table** is the fundamental building block of a relational database because it stores all of the data. You can enter or edit data in a table.

4. **In the Navigation Pane, double-click the TourSales query to open it, double-click any occurrence of Heritage (as in American Heritage Tour), type Legacy, then click any other row**

 A **query** selects a subset of data from one or more tables. In this case, the TourSales query selects data from the Tours, Sales, and Customers tables. Editing data in one object changes that information in every other object of the database, demonstrating the power and productivity of a relational database.

5. **Double-click the CustomerRoster form to open it, double-click Tour in "American Legacy Tour," type Rally, then click any name in the middle part of the window**

 An Access **form** is a data entry screen. Users prefer forms for data entry (rather than editing and entering data in tables and queries) because information can be presented in an easy-to-use layout.

6. **Double-click the TourSales report to open it**

 An Access **report** is a professional printout. A report is for printing purposes only, not data entry. As shown in FIGURE A-4, the edits made to the American Legacy Rally tour name have carried through to the report.

7. **Click the Close button ⊠ in the upper-right corner of the window**

 Clicking the Close button in the upper-right corner of the window closes Access as well as the database on which you are working. Changes to data, such as the edits you made to the American Legacy Rally tour, are automatically saved as you work. Access will prompt you to save *design* changes to objects before it closes.

Use Custom web app to create a Web-enabled database

Use Blank desktop database to create a new, local Access database

Click a database name to open a recently used database; your list will differ

Use Templates to create a new Access database based on a template

Click to browse for an Access database

FIGURE A-4: Objects in the QuestTravel-A database

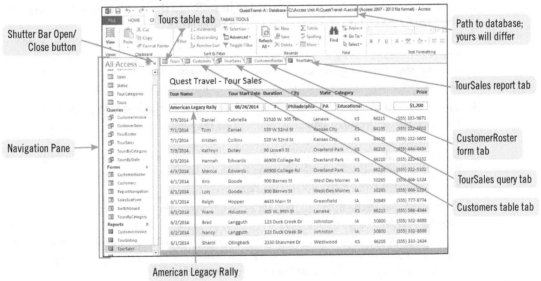

Shutter Bar Open/Close button

Path to database; yours will differ

Tours table tab

TourSales report tab

CustomerRoster form tab

Navigation Pane

TourSales query tab

Customers table tab

American Legacy Rally

TABLE A-2: Access objects and their purpose

object	icon	purpose
Table		Contains all of the raw data within the database in a spreadsheet-like view; tables are linked with a common field to create a relational database, which minimizes redundant data
Query		Allows you to select a subset of fields or records from one or more tables; queries are created when you have a question about the data
Form		Provides an easy-to-use data entry screen
Report		Provides a professional printout of data that can contain enhancements such as headers, footers, graphics, and calculations on groups of records

Access 2013

Create a Database

Learning
Outcomes
• Create a database
• Create a table
• Define key data-
 base terms

You can create a database using an Access **template**, a sample database provided within the Microsoft Access program, or you can start with a blank database to create a database from scratch. Your decision depends on whether Access has a template that closely resembles the type of data you plan to manage. If it does, building your own database from a template might be faster than creating the database from scratch. Regardless of which method you use, you can always modify the database later, tailoring it to meet your specific needs. **CASE** *Samantha Hooper reasons that the best way for you to learn Access is to start a new database from scratch, so she asks you to create a new database that will track customer communication.*

STEPS

1. **Start Access**

2. **Click the** Blank desktop database **icon, click the** Browse button 🗀**, navigate to the location where you store your Data Files, type** Quest **in the File name box, click** OK**, then click the** Create button

 A new, blank database file with a single table named Table1 is created, as shown in FIGURE A-5. Although you might be tempted to start entering data into the table, a better way to build a table is to first define the columns, or **fields**, of data that the table will store. **Table Design View** provides the most options for defining fields.

3. **Click the** View button ⊠ **on the FIELDS tab to switch to Design View, type** Customers **in the Save As dialog box as the new table name, then click** OK

 The table name changes from Table1 to Customers, and you are positioned in Table Design View, a window you use to name and define the fields of a table. Access created a field named ID with an AutoNumber data type. The **data type** is a significant characteristic of a field because it determines what type of data the field can store such as text, dates, or numbers. See TABLE A-3 for more information about data types.

4. **Type** CustID **to rename ID to CustID, press [↓] to move to the first blank Field Name cell, type** FirstName**, press [↓], type** LastName**, press [↓], type** Phone**, press [↓], type** Birthday**, then press [↓]**

 Be sure to separate the first and last names into two fields so that you can easily sort, find, and filter on either part of the name later. The Birthday field will only contain dates, so you should change its data type from Short Text (the default data type) to Date/Time.

5. **Click** Short Text **in the Birthday row, click the** list arrow**, then click** Date/Time

 With these five fields properly defined for the new Customers table, as shown in FIGURE A-6, you're ready to enter data. You switch back to Datasheet View to enter or edit data. **Datasheet View** is a spreadsheet-like view of the data in a table. A **datasheet** is a grid that displays fields as columns and records as rows. The new **field names** you just defined are listed at the top of each column.

6. **Click the** View button ▦ **to switch to Datasheet View, click** Yes **when prompted to save the table, press [Tab] to move to the FirstName field, type** *your* **first name, press [Tab] to move to the LastName field, type** *your* **last name, press [Tab] to move to the Phone field, type** 111-222-3333**, press [Tab], type** 1/32/1980**, then press [Tab]**

 Because 1/32/1980 is not a valid date, Access does not allow you to make that entry and displays an error message, as shown in FIGURE A-7. This shows that selecting the best data type for each field in Table Design View before entering data in Datasheet View helps prevent data entry errors.

TROUBLE
Tab through the
CustID field rather
than typing a value.
The CustID value
automatically incre-
ments to the next
number.

7. **Press [Esc], edit the Birthday entry for the first record to** 1/31/1980**, press [Tab], enter two more sample records using realistic data, right-click the** Customers table tab**, then click** Close **to close the Customers table**

FIGURE A-5: **Creating a database with a new table**

FIGURE A-6: **Defining field names and data types for the Customers table in Table Design View**

FIGURE A-7: **Entering your first record in the Customers table**

TABLE A-3: **Data types**

data type	description of data
Short Text	Text or numbers not used in calculations such as a name, zip code, or phone number
Long Text	Lengthy text greater than 255 characters, such as comments or notes
Number	Numeric data that can be used in calculations, such as quantities
Date/Time	Dates and times
Currency	Monetary values
AutoNumber	Sequential integers controlled by Access
Yes/No	Only two values: Yes or No
OLE Object	OLE (Object Linking and Embedding) objects such as an Excel spreadsheet or Word document
Hyperlink	Web and e-mail addresses
Attachment	External files such as .jpg images, spreadsheets, and documents
Calculated	Result of a calculation based on other fields in the table
Lookup Wizard	The Lookup Wizard helps you set Lookup properties, which display a drop-down list of values for the field; after using the Lookup Wizard, the final data type for the field is either Short Text or Number depending on the values in the drop-down list

Create a Table

Learning
Outcomes
• Create a table in
 Table Design View
• Set appropriate
 data types for
 fields

After creating your database and first table, you need to create new, related tables to build a relational database. Creating a table consists of these essential tasks: defining the fields in the table, selecting an appropriate data type for each field, naming the table, and determining how the table will participate in the relational database. **CASE** ▶ *Samantha Hooper asks you to create another table to store customer comments. The new table will eventually be connected to the Customers table so each customer record in the Customers table may be related to many records in the Comments table.*

STEPS

1. **Click the CREATE tab on the Ribbon, then click the Table Design button in the Tables group**
 Design View is a view in which you create and manipulate the structure of an object.

2. **Enter the field names and data types, as shown in FIGURE A-8**
 The Comments table will contain four fields. CommentID is set with an AutoNumber data type so each record is automatically numbered by Access. The Comment field has a Long Text data type so a long comment can be recorded. CommentDate is a Date/Time field to identify the date of the comment. CustID has a Number data type and will be used to link the Comments table to the Customers table later.

TROUBLE
To rename an object,
close it, right-click it
in the Navigation
Pane, and then click
Rename.

3. **Click the View button ▦ to switch to Datasheet View, click Yes when prompted to save the table, type Comments as the table name, click OK, then click No when prompted to create a primary key**
 A **primary key field** contains unique data for each record. You'll identify a primary key field for the Comments table later. For now, you'll enter the first record in the Comments table in Datasheet View. A **record** is a row of data in a table. Refer to TABLE A-4 for a summary of important database terminology.

4. **Press [Tab] to move to the Comment field, type Interested in future tours to New Zealand, press [Tab], type 1/7/15 in the CommentDate field, press [Tab], then type 1 in the CustID field**
 You entered 1 in the CustID field to connect this comment with the customer in the Customers table that has a CustID value of 1. Knowing which CustID value to enter for each comment is difficult. After you relate the tables properly (a task you have not yet performed), Access can make it easier to link each comment to the correct customer.

TROUBLE
The CommentID field
is an AutoNumber
field, which will auto-
matically increment
to provide a unique
value. If the number
has already incre-
mented beyond 1
for the first record,
AutoNumber still
works as intended.

5. **Point to the divider line between the Comment and CommentDate field names, and then drag the ┿ pointer to the right to widen the Comment field to read the entire comment, as shown in FIGURE A-9**

6. **Right-click the Comments table tab, click Close, then click Yes if prompted to save the table**

Creating a table in Datasheet View

You can also create a new table in Datasheet View using the commands on the FIELDS tab of the Ribbon. But if you use Design View to design your table before starting the data entry process, you will probably avoid some common data entry errors. Design View helps you focus on the appropriate data type for each field.

Selecting the best data type for each field before entering any data into that field helps prevent incorrect data and unintended typos. For example, if a field is given a Number, Currency, or Date/Time data type, you will not be able to enter text into that field by mistake.

FIGURE A-8: **Creating the Comments table**

Enter these field names → | Enter these data types →

FIGURE A-9: **Entering the first record in the Comments table**

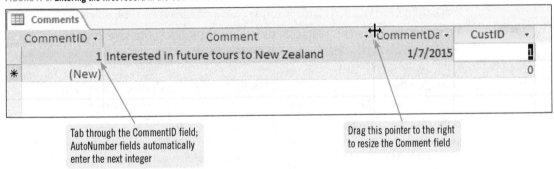

Tab through the CommentID field; AutoNumber fields automatically enter the next integer

Drag this pointer to the right to resize the Comment field

TABLE A-4: **Important database terminology**

term	description
Field	A specific piece or category of data such as a first name, last name, city, state, or phone number
Record	A group of related fields that describes a person, place, thing, or transaction such as a customer, location, product, or sale
Key field	A field that contains unique information for each record, such as a customer number for a customer
Table	A collection of records for a single subject such as Customers, Products, or Sales
Relational database	Multiple tables that are linked together to address a business process such as managing tours, sales, and customers at Quest Specialty Travel
Objects	The parts of an Access database that help you view, edit, manage, and analyze the data: **tables, queries, forms, reports, macros,** and **modules**

Create Primary Keys

Learning
Outcomes
• Set the primary
 key field
• Define one-to-
 many relationships

The **primary key field** of a table serves two important purposes. First, it contains data that uniquely identifies each record. No two records can have the exact same entry in the field designated as the primary key field. Second, the primary key field helps relate one table to another in a **one-to-many relationship**, where one record from one table may be related to many records in the second table. For example, one record in the Customers table may be related to many records in the Comments table. (One customer may have many comments.) The primary key field is always on the "one" side of a one-to-many relationship between two tables. **CASE** *Samantha Hooper asks you to check that a primary key field has been appropriately identified for each table in the new Quest database.*

1. **Right-click the** Comments table **in the Navigation Pane, then click** Design View

 Table Design View for the Comments table opens. The field with the AutoNumber data type is generally the best candidate for the primary key field in a table because it automatically contains a unique number for each record.

TROUBLE
Make sure the
DESIGN tab is
selected on the
Ribbon.

2. **Click the** CommentID field **if it is not already selected, then click the** Primary Key button **in the Tools group on the DESIGN tab**

 The CommentID field is now set as the primary key field for the Comments table, as shown in FIGURE A-10.

QUICK TIP
You can also click the
Save button 🖫 on
the Quick Access tool-
bar to save a table.

3. **Right-click the** Comments table tab, **click** Close, **then click** Yes **to save the table**

 Any time you must save design changes to an Access object such as a table, Access displays a dialog box to remind you to save the object.

4. **Right-click the** Customers table **in the Navigation Pane, then click** Design View

 Access has already set CustID as the primary key field for the Customers table, as shown in FIGURE A-11.

5. **Right-click the** Customers table tab, **then click** Close

 You were not prompted to save the Customers table because you did not make any design changes. Now that you're sure that each table in the Quest database has an appropriate primary key field, you're ready to link the tables. The primary key field plays a critical role in this relationship.

FIGURE A-10: **Creating a primary key field for the Comments table**

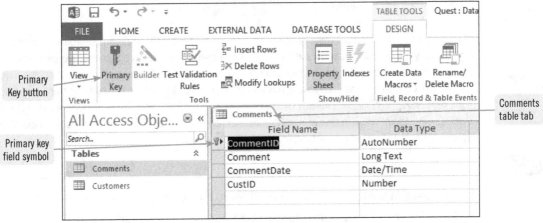

Primary Key button

Comments table tab

Primary key field symbol

FIGURE A-11: **Confirming the primary key field for the Customers table**

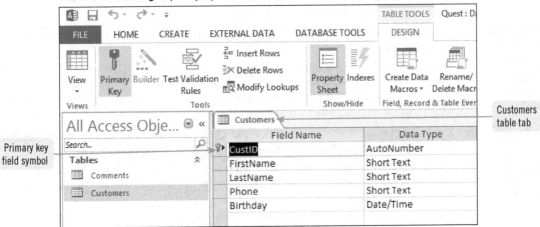

Customers table tab

Primary key field symbol

Learning about field properties

Properties are the characteristics that define the field. Two properties are required for every field: Field Name and Data Type. Many other properties, such as Field Size, Format, Caption, and Default Value, are defined in the Field Properties pane in the lower half of a table's Design View. As you add more property entries, you are generally restricting the amount or type of data that can be entered in the field, which increases data entry accuracy. For example, you might change the Field Size property for a State field to 2 to eliminate an incorrect entry such as FLL. Field properties change depending on the data type of the selected field. For example, date fields do not have a Field Size property because Access controls the size of fields with a Date/Time data type.

Relate Two Tables

Learning
Outcomes
• Define common
 field and foreign
 key field
• Create one-to-
 many relationships
• Set referential
 integrity

After you create tables and set primary key fields, you must connect the tables in one-to-many relationships to enjoy the benefits of a relational database. A one-to-many relationship between two tables means that one record from the first table is related to many records in the second table. You use a common field to make this connection. The common field is always the primary key field in the table on the "one" side of the relationship. **CASE** ▶ *Samantha Hooper explains that she has new comments to enter into the Quest database. To identify which customer is related to each comment, you define a one-to-many relationship between the Customers and Comments tables.*

STEPS

1. **Click the** DATABASE TOOLS tab **on the Ribbon, then click the** Relationships button

2. **In the Show Table dialog box, double-click** Customers, **double-click** Comments, **then click** Close

 Each table is represented by a small **field list** window that displays the table's field names. A key symbol identifies the primary key field in each table. To relate the two tables in a one-to-many relationship, you connect them using a common field, which is always the primary key field on the "one" side of the relationship.

3. **Drag** CustID **in the Customers field list to the** CustID field **in the Comments field list**

 The Edit Relationships dialog box opens, as shown in FIGURE A-12. **Referential integrity**, a set of Access rules that governs data entry, helps ensure data accuracy.

4. **Click the** Enforce Referential Integrity check box **in the Edit Relationships dialog box, then click** Create

 The **one-to-many line** shows the link between the CustID field of the Customers table (the "one" side) and the CustID field of the Comments table (the "many" side, indicated by the **infinity symbol**), as shown in FIGURE A-13. The linking field on the "many" side is called the **foreign key field**. Now that these tables are related, it is much easier to enter comments for the correct customer.

5. **Right-click the** Relationships tab, **click** Close, **click** Yes **to save changes, then double-click the** Customers table **in the Navigation Pane to open it in Datasheet View**

 When you relate two tables in a one-to-many relationship, expand buttons ➕ appear to the left of each record in the table on the "one" side of the relationship. In this case, the Customers table is on the "one" side of the relationship.

6. **Click the** expand button ➕ **to the left of the first record**

 A **subdatasheet** shows the related comment records for each customer. In other words, the subdatasheet shows the records on the "many" side of a one-to-many relationship. The expand button ➕ also changed to the collapse button ➖ for the first customer. Widening the Comment field allows you to see the entire entry in the Comments subdatasheet. Now the task of entering comments for the correct customer is much more straightforward.

7. **Enter two more comments, as shown in** FIGURE A-14

 Interestingly, the CustID field in the Comments table (the foreign key field) is not displayed in the subdatasheet. Behind the scenes, Access is entering the correct CustID value in the Comments table, which is the glue that ties each comment to the correct customer.

8. **Close the Customers table, then click** Yes **if prompted to save changes**

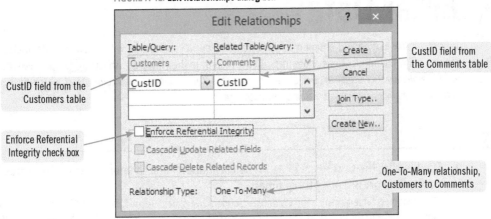
FIGURE A-12: **Edit Relationships dialog box**

CustID field from the Customers table

CustID field from the Comments table

Enforce Referential Integrity check box

One-To-Many relationship, Customers to Comments

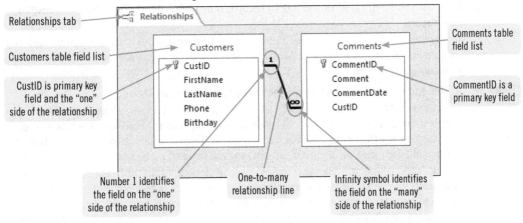
FIGURE A-13: **Linking the Customers and Comments tables**

Relationships tab

Customers table field list

CustID is primary key field and the "one" side of the relationship

Comments table field list

CommentID is a primary key field

Number 1 identifies the field on the "one" side of the relationship

One-to-many relationship line

Infinity symbol identifies the field on the "many" side of the relationship

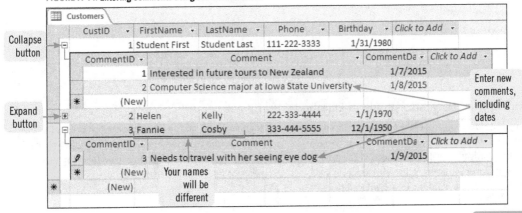
FIGURE A-14: **Entering comments using the subdatasheet**

Collapse button

Expand button

Enter new comments, including dates

Your names will be different

Enter Data

Learning
Outcomes
• Navigate records
 in a datasheet
• Enter records in a
 datasheet

Your skill in navigating and entering new records is a key to your success with a relational database. You can use many techniques to navigate through the records in the table's datasheet. **CASE** ▶ *Even though you have already successfully entered some records, Samantha Hooper asks you to master this essential skill by entering several more customers in the Quest database.*

STEPS

1. **Double-click the Customers table in the Navigation Pane to open it, press [Tab] three times, then press [Enter] three times**

 The Customers table reopens. The Comments subdatasheets are collapsed. Both the [Tab] and [Enter] keys move the focus to the next field. The **focus** refers to which data you would edit if you started typing. When you navigate to the last field of the record, pressing [Tab] or [Enter] advances the focus to the first field of the next record. You can also use the Next record ▶ and Previous record ◀ **navigation buttons** on the navigation bar in the lower-left corner of the datasheet to navigate through the records. The **Current record** text box on the navigation bar tells you the number of the current record as well as the total number of records in the datasheet.

QUICK TIP
Press [Tab] in the
CustID AutoNumber
field.

2. **Click the FirstName field of the fourth record to position the insertion point to enter a new record**

 You can also use the New (blank) record button ▶* on the navigation bar to move to a new record. You enter new records at the end of the datasheet. You learn how to sort and reorder records later. A complete list of navigation keystrokes is shown in TABLE A-5.

QUICK TIP
Access databases are
multiuser with one
important limitation:
two users cannot edit
the same *record* at
the same time. In
that case, a message
explains that the
second user must
wait until the first
user moves to a
different record.

3. **At the end of the datasheet, enter the three records shown in** FIGURE A-15

 The **edit record symbol** 🖉 appears to the left of the record you are currently editing. When you move to a different record, Access saves the data. Therefore, Access never prompts you to save *data* because it performs that task automatically. Saving data automatically allows Access databases to be **multiuser** databases, which means that more than one person can enter and edit data in the same database at the same time.

 Your CustID values might differ from those in FIGURE A-15. Because the CustID field is an **AutoNumber** field, Access automatically enters the next consecutive number into the field as it creates the record. If you delete a record or are interrupted when entering a record, Access discards the value in the AutoNumber field and does not reuse it. Therefore, AutoNumber values do not represent the number of records in your table. Instead, they provide a unique value per record, similar to check numbers.

Changing from Navigation mode to Edit mode

If you navigate to another area of the datasheet by clicking with the mouse pointer instead of pressing [Tab] or [Enter], you change from **Navigation mode** to Edit mode. In **Edit mode**, Access assumes that you are trying to make changes to the current field value, so keystrokes such as [Ctrl][End], [Ctrl][Home], [◀], and [▶] move the insertion point within the field. To return to Navigation mode, press [Tab] or [Enter] (thus moving the focus to the next field), or press [▲] or [▼] (thus moving the focus to a different record).

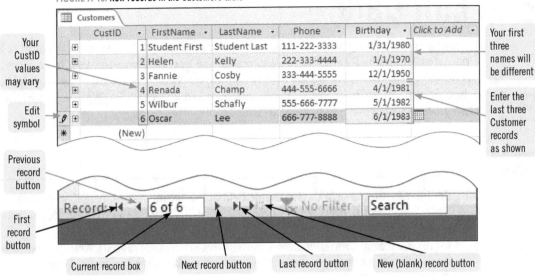

Your CustID values may vary

Edit symbol

Your first three names will be different

Enter the last three Customer records as shown

Previous record button

First record button

Current record box

Next record button

Last record button

New (blank) record button

TABLE A-5: **Navigation mode keyboard shortcuts**

shortcut key	moves to the
[Tab], [Enter], or [→]	Next field of the current record
[Shift][Tab] or [←]	Previous field of the current record
[Home]	First field of the current record
[End]	Last field of the current record
[Ctrl][Home] or [F5]	First field of the first record
[Ctrl][End]	Last field of the last record
[↑]	Current field of the previous record
[↓]	Current field of the next record

© 2014 Cengage Learning

Cloud computing

Using SkyDrive, a free service from Microsoft, you can store files in the "cloud" and retrieve them anytime you are connected to the Internet. Saving your files to the SkyDrive is one example of cloud computing. **Cloud computing** means you are using an Internet resource to complete your work. You can find more information in the "Working in the Cloud" appendix.

Edit Data

Learning
Outcomes
• Edit data in a data-
 sheet
• Delete records in a
 datasheet
• Preview and print
 a datasheet

Updating existing data in a database is another critical database task. To change the contents of an exist-ing record, navigate to the field you want to change and type the new information. You can delete unwanted data by clicking the field and using [Backspace] or [Delete] to delete text to the left or right of the insertion point. Other data entry keystrokes are summarized in TABLE A-6. **CASE** *Samantha Hooper asks you to correct two records in the Customers table.*

STEPS

1. **Double-click the** name **in the FirstName field of the second record, type** Kelsey, **press [Enter], type** Barker, **press [Enter], type** 111-222-4444, **press [Enter], type** 2/15/84, **then press [Enter]**

 You changed the name, telephone number, and birth date of the second customer. When you entered the last two digits of the year value, Access inserted the first two digits after you pressed [Enter]. You'll also change the third customer.

 QUICK TIP
 The ScreenTip for
 the Undo button
 ↺ displays the
 action you can undo.

2. **Press [Enter] to move to the FirstName field of the third record, type** Joshua, **press [Enter], type** Lang, **press [Enter], type** 222-333-4444, **then press [Esc]**

 Pressing [Esc] once removes the current field's editing changes, so the Phone value changes back to the pre-vious entry. Pressing [Esc] twice removes all changes to the current record. When you move to another record, Access saves your edits, so you can no longer use [Esc] to remove editing changes to the current record. You can, however, click the Undo button ↺ on the Quick Access toolbar to undo changes to a previous record.

3. **Retype** 222-333-4444, **press [Enter], type** 12/1/50 **in the Birthday field, press [Enter], click the** 12/1/50 **date you just entered, click the** Calendar icon 🗓, **then click** April 14, 1951, **as shown in** FIGURE A-16

 When you are working in the Birthday field, which has a Date/Time data type, you can enter a date from the keyboard or use the **Calendar Picker**, a pop-up calendar to find and select a date.

4. **Click the** record selector **for the last record (Oscar Lee), click the** Delete button **in the Records group on the HOME tab, then click** Yes

 A message warns that you cannot undo a record deletion. The Undo button is dimmed, indicating that you cannot use it. The Customers table now has five records, as shown in FIGURE A-17. Keep in mind that your CustID values might differ from those in the figure because they are controlled by Access.

 QUICK TIP
 If requested to print
 the Customers data-
 sheet by your
 instructor, click the
 Print button, then
 click OK.

5. **Click the** FILE **tab, click** Print, **then click** Print Preview **to review the printout of the Customers table before printing**

6. **Click the** Close Print Preview button, **click the** Close button **in the upper-right corner of the window to close the Quest.accdb database and Access 2013, then click** Yes **if prompted to save design changes to the Customers table**

FIGURE A-16: **Editing customer records**

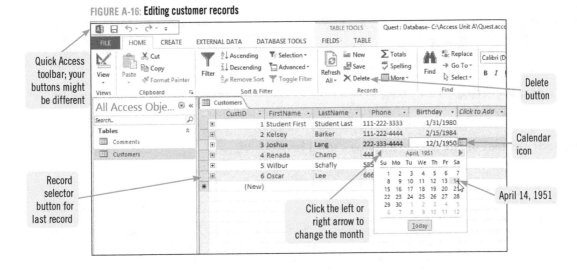

FIGURE A-17: **Final Customers datasheet**

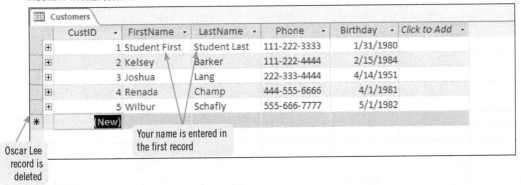

TABLE A-6: **Edit mode keyboard shortcuts**

editing keystroke	action
[Backspace]	Deletes one character to the left of the insertion point
[Delete]	Deletes one character to the right of the insertion point
[F2]	Switches between Edit and Navigation mode
[Esc]	Undoes the change to the current field
[Esc][Esc]	Undoes all changes to the current record
[F7]	Starts the spell-check feature
[Ctrl][']	Inserts the value from the same field in the previous record into the current field
[Ctrl][;]	Inserts the current date in a Date field

Resizing and moving datasheet columns

You can resize the width of a field in a datasheet by dragging the column separator, the thin line that separates the field names to the left or right. The pointer changes to ↔ as you make the field wider or narrower. Release the mouse button when you have resized the field. To adjust the column width to accommodate the widest entry in the field, double-click the column separator. To move a column, click the field name to select the entire column, then drag the field name left or right.

Access 2013

Practice

Put your skills into practice with **SAM Projects**! SAM Projects for this unit can be found online. If you have a SAM account, go to www.cengage.com/sam2013 to download the most recent Project Instruction and Start Files.

Concepts Review

Label each element of the Access window shown in FIGURE A-18.

FIGURE A-18

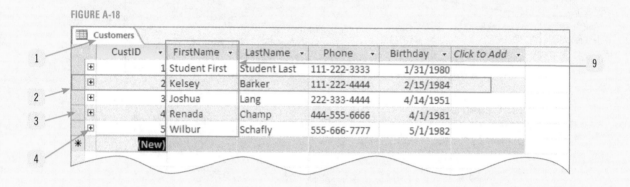

Match each term with the statement that best describes it.

10. Field
11. Record
12. Table
13. Datasheet
14. Query
15. Form
16. Report

a. A subset of data from one or more tables
b. A collection of records for a single subject, such as all the customer records
c. A professional printout of database information
d. A spreadsheet-like grid that displays fields as columns and records as rows
e. A group of related fields for one item, such as all of the information for one customer
f. A category of information in a table, such as a company name, city, or state
g. An easy-to-use data entry screen

Select the best answer from the list of choices.

17. Which of the following is *not* a typical benefit of relational databases?
 a. Minimized duplicate data entry
 b. More accurate data
 c. Faster information retrieval
 d. More common than spreadsheets

18. Which of the following is *not* an advantage of managing data with relational database software such as Access versus spreadsheet software such as Excel?

 a. Allows multiple users to enter data simultaneously

 b. Uses a single table to store all data

 c. Provides data entry forms

 d. Reduces duplicate data entry

19. When you create a new database, which object is created first?

 a. Form **c.** Module

 b. Query **d.** Table

Skills Review

1. **Understand relational databases.**

 a. Write down five advantages of managing database information in Access versus using a spreadsheet.

 b. Write a sentence to explain how the terms *field*, *record*, *table*, and *relational database* relate to one another.

2. **Explore a database.**

 a. Start Access.

 b. Open the RealEstate-A.accdb database from the location where you store your Data Files. Click Enable Content if a yellow Security Warning message appears.

 c. Open each of the four tables to study the data they contain. Complete the following table:

table name	number of records	number of fields

 d. Double-click the ListingsByRealtor query in the Navigation Pane to open it. Change any occurrence of Gordon Bono to *your* name. Move to another record to save your changes.

 e. Double-click the RealtorsMainForm in the Navigation Pane to open it. Use the navigation buttons to navigate through the 11 realtors to observe each realtor's listings.

 f. Double-click the RealtorListingReport in the Navigation Pane to open it. The records are listed in ascending order by last name. Scroll through the report to make sure your name is positioned correctly.

 g. Close the RealEstate-A database, and then close Access 2013.

3. **Create a database.**

 a. Start Access, click the Blank desktop database icon, use the Browse button to navigate to the location where you store your Data Files, type **RealEstateMarketing** as the filename, click OK, and then click Create to create a new database named RealEstateMarketing.accdb.

b. Switch to Table Design View, name the table **Prospects**, then enter the following fields and data types:

field name	data type
ProspectID	AutoNumber
ProspectFirst	Short Text
ProspectLast	Short Text
Phone	Short Text
Email	Hyperlink
Street	Short Text
City	Short Text
State	Short Text
Zip	Short Text

c. Save the table, switch to Datasheet View, and enter two records using *your* name in the first record and your instructor's name in the second. Tab through the ProspectID field, an AutoNumber field.

d. Enter **TX** (Texas) as the value in the State field for both records. Use school or fictitious (rather than personal) data for all other field data, and be sure to fill out each record completely.

e. Widen each column in the Prospects table so that all data is visible, then save and close the Prospects table.

4. Create a table.

a. Click the CREATE tab on the Ribbon, click the Table Design button in the Tables group, then create a new table with the following two fields and data types:

field name	data type
StateAbbrev	Short Text
StateName	Short Text

b. Save the table with the name **States**. Click No when asked if you want Access to create the primary key field.

5. Create primary keys.

a. In Table Design View of the States table, set the StateAbbrev as the primary key field.

b. Save the States table and open it in Datasheet View.

c. Enter one state record, using **TX** for the StateAbbrev value and **Texas** for the StateName value to match the State value of TX that you entered for both records in the Prospects table.

d. Close the States table.

6. Relate two tables.

a. From the DATABASE TOOLS tab, open the Relationships window.

b. Add the States, then the Prospects table to the Relationships window.

FIGURE A-19

c. Drag the bottom edge of the Prospects table to expand the field list to display all of the fields.

d. Drag the StateAbbrev field from the States table to the State field of the Prospects table.

e. In the Edit Relationships dialog box, click the Enforce Referential Integrity check box, then click Create. Your Relationships window should look similar to FIGURE A-19. If you connect the wrong fields by mistake, right-click the line connecting the two fields, click Delete, then try again.

f. Close the Relationships window, and save changes when prompted.

Skills Review (continued)

7. Enter data.

 a. Open the States table and enter the following records:

StateAbbrev field	StateName field
CO	Colorado
IA	Iowa
KS	Kansas
MO	Missouri
NE	Nebraska
OK	Oklahoma
WI	Wisconsin

 b. Add three more state records of your choice for a total of 11 records in the States table using the correct two-character abbreviation for the state and the correctly spelled state name.

 c. Close and reopen the States table. Notice that Access automatically sorts the records by the values in the primary key field, the StateAbbrev field.

8. Edit data.

 a. Click the Expand button for the TX record to see the two related records from the Prospects table.

 b. Enter two more prospects in the TX subdatasheet using any fictitious but realistic data, as shown in FIGURE A-20. Notice that you are not required to enter a value for the State field, the foreign key field in the subdatasheet.

FIGURE A-20

 c. If required by your instructor, print the States datasheet and the Prospects datasheet.

 d. Click the Close button in the upper-right corner of the Access window to close all open objects as well as the RealEstateMarketing.accdb database and Access 2013. If prompted to save any design changes, click Yes.

Independent Challenge 1

Consider the following twelve subject areas:

- Telephone directory
- College course offerings
- Restaurant menu items
- Vehicles
- Movie listings
- Islands of the Caribbean
- Physical activities
- Shopping catalog items
- Conventions
- Party guest list
- Members of the U.S. House
- Ancient wonders of the world of Representatives

a. For each subject, build a Word table with 4–7 columns and three rows. In the first row, enter field names that you would expect to see in a table used to manage that subject.

b. In the second and third rows of each table, enter two realistic records. The first table, Telephone Directory, is completed as an example to follow.

TABLE: **Telephone Directory**

FirstName	LastName	Street	Zip	Phone
Marco	Lopez	100 Main Street	88715	555-612-3312
Christopher	Stafford	253 Maple Lane	77824	555-612-1179

Independent Challenge 2

You are working with several civic groups to coordinate a community-wide cleanup effort. You have started a database called Recycle-A, which tracks the clubs, their trash deposits, and the trash collection centers that are participating.

a. Start Access, then open the Recycle-A.accdb database from the location where you store your Data Files. Enable content if prompted.

b. Open each table's datasheet to study the number of fields and records per table. Notice that there are no expand buttons to the left of any records because relationships have not yet been established between these tables.

c. In a Word document, re-create the following table and fill in the blanks:

d. Close all table datasheets, then open the Relationships window and create the following one-to-many relationships. Drag the tables from the Navigation Pane to the Relationships window, and drag the title bars and borders of the field lists to position them as shown in FIGURE A-21.

table name	number of fields	number of records

field on the "one" side of the relationship	field on the "many" side of the relationship
ClubNumber in Clubs table	ClubNumber in Deposits table
CenterNumber in Centers table	CenterNumber in Deposits table

e. Be sure to enforce referential integrity on all relationships. If you create an incorrect relationship, right-click the line linking the fields, click Delete, and try again. Your final Relationships window should look like FIGURE A-21.

f. Click the Relationship Report button on the DESIGN tab, and if required by your instructor, click Print to print a copy of the Relationships for Recycle-A report. To close the report, right-click the Relationships for Recycle-A tab and click Close. Click Yes when prompted to save changes to the report with the name **Relationships for Recycle-A**. Save and close the Relationships window.

FIGURE A-21

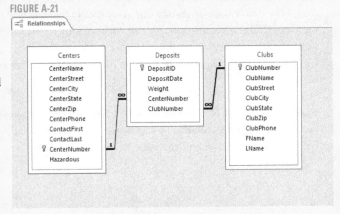

g. Open the Clubs table and add a new record with fictitious but realistic data in all of the fields. Enter **8** as the ClubNumber value and *your* name in the FName (first name) and LName (last name) fields.

h. Expand the subdatasheets for each record in the Clubs table to see the related records from the Deposits table. Which club made the most deposits? Be ready to answer in class. Close the Clubs table.

i. Open the Centers table and add a new record with fictitious but realistic data in all of the fields. Enter *your* first and last names in the CenterName field and **5** as the CenterNumber.

j. Expand the subdatasheets for each record in the Centers table to see the related records from the Deposits table. Which center made the most deposits? Be ready to answer in class. Close the Centers table.

k. Close the Recycle-A.accdb database, then exit Access 2013.

Independent Challenge 3

You are working for an advertising agency that provides advertising media for small and large businesses in the midwestern United States. You have started a database called BusinessContacts-A, which tracks your company's customers. (*Note: To complete this Independent Challenge, make sure you are connected to the Internet.*)

a. Start Access and open the BusinessContacts-A.accdb database from the location where you store your Data Files. Enable content if prompted.

b. Add a new record to the Customers table, using any local business name, *your* first and last names, **$7,788.99** in the YTDSales field, and fictitious but reasonable entries for the rest of the fields.

c. Edit the Sprint Systems record (ID 1). The Company name should be changed to **MTB Mobile**, and the Street value should be changed to **4455 College St**.

d. Delete the record for St Luke's Hospital (ID 20), then close the Customers table.

e. Create a new table with two fields, **State2** and **StateName**. Assign both fields a Short Text data type. The State2 field will contain the two-letter abbreviation for state names. The StateName field will contain the full state name.

f. Set the State2 field as the primary key field, then save the table as **States**.

g. Enter at least three records into the States table, making sure that all of the states used in the Customers datasheet are entered in the States table. This includes **KS Kansas**, **MO Missouri**, and any other state you entered in Step b when you added a new record to the Customers table.

h. Close all open tables. Open the Relationships window, add both the States and Customers field lists to the window, then expand the size of the Customers field list so that all fields are visible.

i. Build a one-to-many relationship between the States and Customers tables by dragging the State2 field from the States table to the State field of the Customers table to create a one-to-many relationship between the two tables. Enforce referential integrity on the relationship. If you are unable to enforce referential integrity, it means that a value in the State field of the Customers table doesn't have a perfect match in the State2 field of the States table. Open both table datasheets, making sure every state in the State field of the Customers table is also represented in the State2 field of the States table, close all datasheets, then reestablish the one-to-many relationship between the two tables with referential integrity.

j. Click the Relationship Report button on the DESIGN tab, then if requested by your instructor, click Print to print the report.

k. Right-click the Relationships for BusinessContacts-A tab, then click Close. Click Yes when prompted to save the report with the name **Relationships for BusinessContacts-A**.

l. Close the Relationships window, saving changes as prompted.

m. Close BusinessContacts-A.accdb database, and exit Access 2013.

Independent Challenge 4: Explore

Now that you've learned about Microsoft Access and relational databases, brainstorm how you might use an Access database in your daily life or career. Start by visiting the Microsoft Web site, and explore what's new about Access 2013.

(*Note:* To complete this Independent Challenge, make sure you are connected to the Internet.)

a. Using your favorite search engine, look up the keywords *benefits of a relational database* or *benefits of Microsoft Access* to find articles that discuss the benefits of organizing data in a relational database.

b. Read several articles about the benefits of organizing data in a relational database such as Access, identifying three distinct benefits. Use a Word document to record those three benefits. Also, copy and paste the Web site address of the article you are referencing for each benefit you have identified.

c. In addition, as you read the articles that describe relational database benefits, list any terminology unfamiliar to you, identifying at least five new terms.

d. Using a search engine or a Web site that provides a computer glossary such as *www.whatis.com* or *www.webopedia. com*, look up the definition of the new terms, and enter both the term and the definition of the term in your document as well as the Web site address where your definition was found.

e. Finally, based on your research and growing understanding of Access 2013, list three ways you could use an Access database to organize, enhance, or support the activities and responsibilities of your daily life or career. Type your name at the top of the document, and submit it to your instructor as requested.

Visual Workshop

Open the Basketball-A.accdb database from the location where you store your Data Files, then enable content if prompted. Open the Offense query datasheet, which lists offensive statistics by player by game. Modify any of the Ellyse Howard records to contain *your* first and last names, then move to a different record, observing the power of a relational database to modify every occurrence of that name throughout the database. Close the Offense query, then open the Players table. Note that there are no expand buttons to the left of the records indicating that this table does not participate on the "one" side of a one-to-many relationship. Close the Players table and open the Relationships window. Drag the tables from the Navigation Pane and create the relationships with referential integrity, as shown in FIGURE A-22. Note the one-to-many relationship between the Players and Stats table. Print the Relationships report if requested by your instructor and save it with the name **Relationships for Basketball-A**. Close the report and close and save the Relationships window. Now reopen the Players table noting the expand buttons to the left of each record. Expand the subdatasheet for your name and for several other players to observe the "many" records from the Stats table that are now related to each record in the Players table.

FIGURE A-22

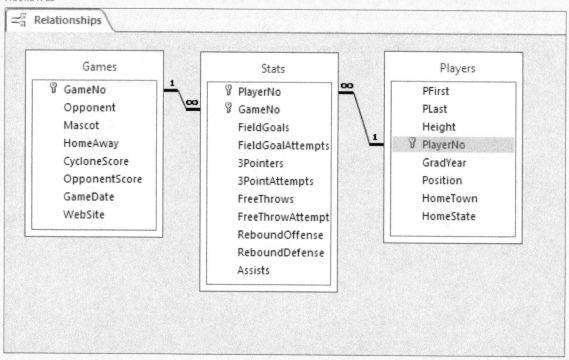

Building and Using Queries

CASE ▶ Samantha Hooper, tour developer for U.S. group travel at Quest Specialty Travel, has several questions about the customer and tour information in the Quest database. You'll develop queries to provide Samantha with up-to-date answers.

Unit Objectives

After completing this unit, you will be able to:

- Use the Query Wizard
- Work with data in a query
- Use Query Design View
- Sort and find data

- Filter data
- Apply AND criteria
- Apply OR criteria
- Format a datasheet

Files You Will Need

QuestTravel-B.accdb
Recycle-B.accdb
Membership-B.accdb
Congress-B.accdb
Vet-B.accdb
Baseball-B.accdb

Use the Query Wizard

Learning
Outcomes
• Describe the
 purpose for
 a query
• Create a query
 with the Simple
 Query Wizard

A **query** answers a question about the information in the database. A query allows you to select a subset of fields and records from one or more tables and then present the selected data as a single datasheet. A major benefit of working with data through a query is that you can focus on only the specific information you need to answer a question, rather than navigating through all the fields and records from many large tables. You can enter, edit, and navigate data in a query datasheet just like a table datasheet. However, keep in mind that Access data is physically stored only in tables, even though you can select, view, and edit it through other Access objects such as queries and forms. Because a query doesn't physically store the data, a query datasheet is sometimes called a **logical view** of the data. Technically, a query is a set of **SQL (Structured Query Language)** instructions, but because you can use Access query tools such as Query Design View to create and modify the query, you are not required to know SQL to build or use Access queries. **CASE** *You use the Simple Query Wizard to create a query that displays fields from the Tours and Customers tables in one datasheet.*

STEPS

1. **Start Access, open the** QuestTravel-B.accdb database, **enable content if prompted, then maximize the window**

 Access provides several tools to create a new query. One way is to use the **Simple Query Wizard**, which prompts you for the information it needs to create a new query.

2. **Click the** CREATE **tab on the Ribbon, click the** Query Wizard button **in the Queries group, then click** OK **to start the Simple Query Wizard**

 The Simple Query Wizard dialog box opens, prompting you to select the fields you want to view in the new query. You can select fields from one or more existing tables or queries.

3. **Click the** Tables/Queries list arrow, **click** Table: Tours, **double-click** TourName, **double-click** City, **double-click** Category, **then double-click** Price

 So far, you've selected four fields from the Tours table to display basic tour information in this query. You also want to add the first and last name information from the Customers table so you know which customers purchased each tour.

TROUBLE
Click the Remove
Single Field button
[<] if you need
to remove a field
from the Selected
Fields list.

4. **Click the** Tables/Queries list arrow, **click** Table: Customers, **double-click** FName, **then double-click** LName

 You've selected four fields from the Tours table and two from the Customers table for your new query, as shown in FIGURE B-1.

5. **Click** Next, **click** Next **to select Detail, select** Tours Query **in the title text box, type** TourCustomerList **as the name of the query, then click** Finish

 The TourCustomerList datasheet opens, displaying four fields from the Tours table and two from the Customers table, as shown in FIGURE B-2. The query can show which customers have purchased which tours because of the one-to-many table relationships established in the Relationships window.

FIGURE B-1: Selecting fields using the Simple Query Wizard

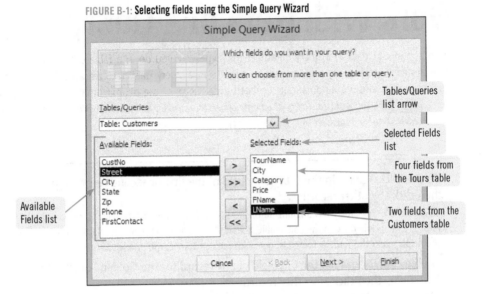

Tables/Queries list arrow

Selected Fields list

Four fields from the Tours table

Two fields from the Customers table

Available Fields list

FIGURE B-2: TourCustomerList datasheet

Four fields from Tours table

Two fields from Customers table

102 records

Work with Data in a Query

Learning
Outcomes
• Edit records in
 a query
• Delete records in
 a query

You enter and edit data in a query datasheet the same way you do in a table datasheet. Because all data is stored in tables, any edits you make to data in a query datasheet are actually stored in the underlying tables and are automatically updated in all views of the data in other queries, forms, and reports. **CASE** *You want to change the name of one tour and update a customer name. You can use the TourCustomerList query datasheet to make these edits.*

STEPS

1. **Double-click** Stanley **in the TourName field of the first or second record, type** Breeze, **then click any other record**

 All occurrences of Stanley Bay Shelling automatically update to Breeze Bay Shelling because this tour name value is stored only once in the Tours table. See FIGURE B-3. The tour name is selected from the Tours table and displayed in the TourCustomerList query for each customer who purchased this tour.

2. **Double-click** Orlando **in the City field of any record for the Golden Footsteps tour, type** Kissimmee, **then click any other record**

 All occurrences of Orlando automatically update to Kissimmee because this value is stored only once in the City field of the Tours table for the Golden Footsteps record. The Golden Footsteps tour is displayed in the TourCustomerList query for each customer who purchased the tour.

3. **Click the** record selector button **to the left of the first record, click the** HOME **tab, click the** Delete button **in the Records group, then click** Yes

 You can delete records from a query datasheet the same way you delete them from a table datasheet. Notice that the navigation bar now indicates you have 101 records in the datasheet, as shown in FIGURE B-4.

4. **Right-click the** TourCustomerList query tab, **then click** Close

 Each time a query is opened, it shows a current view of the data. This means that as new tours, customers, or sales are recorded in the database, the next time you open this query, the information will include all updates.

FIGURE B-3: Working with data in a query datasheet

Record selector button for first record

Updating Stanley to Breeze in one record updates all records

TourName	City	Category	Price	FName	LName
Breeze Bay Shelling	Captiva	Adventure	$750	Ralph	Hopper
Breeze Bay Shelling	Captiva	Adventure	$750	Lisa	Wilson
Ames Ski Club	Breckenridge	Adventure	$850	Kristen	Collins
Breeze Bay Shelling	Captiva	Adventure	$750	Kris	Goode
Breeze Bay Shelling	Captiva	Adventure	$750	Lois	Goode
Breeze Bay Shelling	Captiva	Adventure	$750	Naresh	Hubert
Piper-Heitman Wedding	Captiva	Family	$550	Julia	Bouchart
Ames Ski Club	Breckenridge	Adventure	$850	Tom	Camel
Golden Footsteps	Orlando	Site Seeing	$550	Shirley	Walker
Golden Footsteps	Orlando	Site Seeing	$550	Zohra	Vogue
Golden Footsteps	Orlando	Site Seeing	$550	Kathryn	Dotey
Golden Footsteps	Orlando	Site Seeing	$550	Jose	Hammer
Red Reef Scuba	Islamadora	Adventure	$1,500	Jane	Taylor
Breeze Bay Shelling	Captiva	Adventure	$750	Kori	Yode
American Heritage Tour	Philadelphia	Educational	$1,200	Sharol	Olingback

FIGURE B-4: Final TourCustomerList datasheet

(Design) View button

Delete button

101 records in the datasheet

Updating Orlando to Kissimmee in one record updates all records

Hiding and unhiding fields in a datasheet

To hide a field in a datasheet, right-click the field name at the top of the datasheet and click the Hide Fields option on the shortcut menu. To unhide a field, right-click any field name, click Unhide Fields, and check the hidden field's check box in the Unhide Columns dialog box.

Freezing and unfreezing fields in a datasheet

In large datasheets, you may want to freeze certain fields so that they remain on the screen at all times. To freeze a field, right-click its field name in the datasheet, and then click Freeze Fields. To unfreeze a field, right-click any field name and click Unfreeze All Fields.

Use Query Design View

Learning
Outcomes
• Work in Query
 Design View
• Add criteria to
 a query

You use **Query Design View** to add, delete, or move the fields in an existing query; to specify sort orders; or to add **criteria** to limit the number of records shown in the resulting datasheet. You can also use Query Design View to create a new query from scratch. Query Design View presents the fields you can use for that query in small windows called **field lists**. If you use the fields of two or more related tables in the query, the relationship between two tables is displayed with a **join line** (also called a **link line**) identifying which fields are used to establish the relationship. **CASE** ▶ *Samantha Hooper asks you to produce a list of tours in Florida. You use Query Design View to modify the existing ToursByState query to meet her request.*

STEPS

1. **Double-click the** ToursByState query **in the Navigation Pane to review the datasheet**

 The ToursByState query contains the StateName field from the States table and the TourName, TourStartDate, and Price fields from the Tours table. This query contains two ascending sort orders: StateName and TourName. All records in California, for example, are further sorted by the TourName value.

QUICK TIP
Drag the lower edge
of the field list to
view more fields.

2. **Click the** View button ☒ **on the HOME tab to switch to Query Design View**

 Query Design View displays the tables used in the query in the upper pane of the window. The link line shows that one record in the States table may be related to many records in the Tours table. The lower pane of the window, called the **query design grid** (or query grid for short), displays the field names, sort orders, and criteria used within the query.

QUICK TIP
Query criteria
are not case
sensitive, so Florida
equals FLORIDA
equals florida.

3. **Click the** first Criteria cell for the StateName field, **then type** Florida **as shown in** FIGURE B-5

 Criteria are limiting conditions you set in the query design grid. In this case, the condition limits the selected records to only those with "Florida" in the StateName field.

4. **Click the** View button ▦ **in the Results group to switch to Datasheet View**

 Now only nine records are selected, because only nine of the tours have "Florida" in the StateName field, as shown in FIGURE B-6. You want to save this query with a different name.

5. **Click the** FILE tab, **click** Save As, **click** Save Object As, **click the** Save As button, **type** FloridaTours, **then click** OK

 In Access, the **Save As command** on the FILE tab allows you to save the entire database (and all objects it contains) or just the current object with a new name. Recall that Access saves *data* automatically as you move from record to record.

6. **Right-click the** FloridaTours query tab, **then click** Close

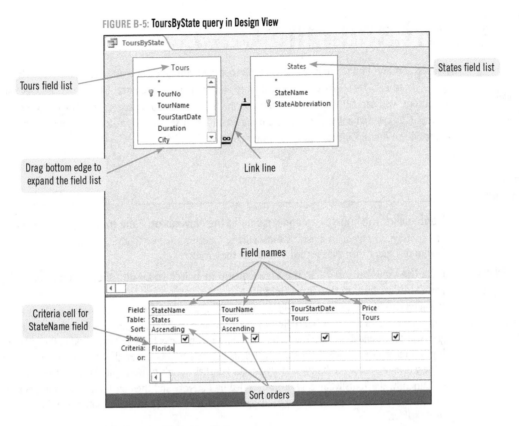

FIGURE B-5: **ToursByState query in Design View**

Tours field list

States field list

Tours

*
🔑 TourNo
TourName
TourStartDate
Duration
City

States

*
StateName
🔑 StateAbbreviation

Drag bottom edge to expand the field list

Link line

Field names

Criteria cell for StateName field

Field:	StateName	TourName	TourStartDate	Price
Table:	States	Tours	Tours	Tours
Sort:	Ascending	Ascending		
Show:	☑	☑	☑	☑
Criteria:	Florida			
or:				

Sort orders

FIGURE B-6: **ToursByState query with Florida criterion**

ToursByState

StateName	TourName	TourStartDate	Price
Florida	Breeze Bay Shelling	07/06/2014	$750
Florida	Golden Footsteps	05/23/2014	$550
Florida	Gulfside Birdwatchers	06/29/2014	$700
Florida	High Adventurers	06/05/2014	$575
Florida	Hummer Trail	05/30/2014	$725
Florida	Patriot Debate Club	06/12/2014	$605
Florida	Piper-Heitman Wedding	05/30/2014	$550
Florida	Red Reef Scuba	07/06/2014	$1,500
Florida	Tropical Sailboats	06/19/2014	$655

TourName values are in ascending order

Only nine Florida records are selected

Adding or deleting a table in a query

You might want to add a table's field list to the upper pane of Query Design View to select fields from that table for the query. To add a new table to Query Design View, drag it from the Navigation Pane to Query Design View, or click the Show Table button on the Design tab, then add the desired table(s). To delete an unneeded table from Query Design View, click its title bar, then press [Delete].

Sort and Find Data

Learning
Outcomes
• Apply sort orders
 to a query
• Find and replace
 data in a query
• Undo edits in
 a query

The Access sort and find features are handy tools that help you quickly organize and find data in a table or query datasheet. TABLE B-1 describes the Sort and Find buttons on the HOME tab. Besides using these buttons, you can also click the list arrow on the field name in a datasheet, and then click a sorting option. **CASE** *Samantha asks you to provide a list of tours sorted by TourStartDate, and then by Price. You'll modify the ToursByCategory query to answer this query.*

STEPS

1. **Double-click the** ToursByCategory query **in the Navigation Pane to open its datasheet**

 The ToursByCategory query currently sorts tours by Category, then by TourName. You'll add the Duration field to this query, then change the sort order for the records.

QUICK TIP
Drag a selected field
selector right or left
to move the column
to a new position in
the query grid.

2. **Click the** View button ☑ **in the Views group to switch to Design View, then double-click the** Duration field **in the Tours field list**

 When you double-click a field in a field list, Access inserts it in the next available column in the query grid. You can also drag a field from a field list to a specific column of the query grid. To select a field in the query grid, you click its field selector. The **field selector** is the thin gray bar above each field in the query grid. If you want to delete a field from a query, click its field selector, then press [Delete]. Deleting a field from a query does not delete it from the underlying table; the field is only deleted from the query's logical view.

 Currently, the ToursByCategory query is sorted by Category and then by TourName. Access evaluates sort orders from left to right. You want to change the sort order so that the records sort first by TourStartDate then by Price.

3. **Click** Ascending **in the Category Sort cell, click the** list arrow, **click** (not sorted), **click** Ascending **in the TourName Sort cell, click the** list arrow, **click** (not sorted), **double-click the** TourStartDate Sort cell **to specify an Ascending sort, then double-click the** Price Sort cell **to specify an Ascending sort**

 The records are now set to be sorted in ascending order, first by TourStartDate, then by the values in the Price field, as shown in FIGURE B-7. Because sort orders always work from left to right, you might need to rearrange the fields before applying a sort order that uses more than one field. To move a field in the query design grid, click its field selector, then drag it left or right.

4. **Click the** View button ▦ **in the Results group**

 The new datasheet shows the Duration field in the fifth column. The records are now sorted in ascending order by the TourStartDate field. If two records have the same TourStartDate, they are further sorted by Price. Your next task is to replace all occurrences of "Site Seeing" with "Cultural" in the Category field.

5. **Click the** Find button **on the HOME tab, type** Site Seeing **in the Find What box, click the** Replace tab, **click in the** Replace With box, **then type** Cultural

 The Find and Replace dialog box is shown in FIGURE B-8.

TROUBLE
If your find-and-
replace effort did not
work correctly, click
the Undo button
↺ and repeat
Steps 5 and 6.

6. **Click the** Replace All button **in the Find and Replace dialog box, click** Yes **to continue, then click** Cancel **to close the Find and Replace dialog box**

 Access replaced all occurrences of "Site Seeing" with "Cultural" in the Category field, as shown in FIGURE B-9.

7. **Right-click the** ToursByCategory query tab, **click** Close, **then click** Yes **to save changes**

FIGURE B-7: **Changing sort orders for the ToursByCategory query**

Duration field in Tours field list

Field selectors for Price and Duration fields

Sort orders for Category and TourName are removed

Ascending sort orders for TourStartDate and Price are added

FIGURE B-8: **Find and Replace dialog box**

Site Seeing in the Find What text box

Cultural in the Replace With text box

Additional Find and Replace options to fine-tune the search

Replace All button

FIGURE B-9: **Final ToursByCategory datasheet with new sort orders**

Cultural replaces Site Seeing in the Category field

Find button

Records with the same TourStartDate are further sorted by the Price field

TABLE B-1: **Sort and Find buttons**

name	button	purpose
Ascending		Sorts records based on the selected field in ascending order (0 to 9, A to Z)
Descending		Sorts records based on the selected field in descending order (Z to A, 9 to 0)
Remove Sort		Removes the current sort order
Find		Opens the Find and Replace dialog box, which allows you to find data in a single field or in the entire datasheet
Replace		Opens the Find and Replace dialog box, which allows you to find and replace data
Go To		Helps you navigate to the first, previous, next, last, or new record
Select		Helps you select a single record or all records in a datasheet

Filter Data

Learning
Outcomes
• Apply and remove
 filters in a query
• Use wildcards in
 criteria

Filtering a table or query datasheet *temporarily* displays only those records that match given criteria. Recall that criteria are limiting conditions you set. For example, you might want to show only tours in the state of California, or only tours with a duration of 14 days. Although filters provide a quick and easy way to display a temporary subset of records in the current datasheet, they are not as powerful or flexible as queries. Most important, a query is a saved object within the database, whereas filters are temporary because Access removes them when you close the datasheet. TABLE B-2 compares filters and queries. **CASE** *Samantha asks you to find all Adventure tours offered in the month of July. You can filter the Tours table datasheet to provide this information.*

QUICK TIP
You can also apply a
sort or filter by click-
ing the Sort and filter
arrow to the right of
the field name and
choosing the sort
order or filter values
you want.

1. **Double-click the** Tours table **to open it, click any occurrence of** Adventure **in the** Category field, **click the** Selection button **in the Sort & Filter group on the HOME tab, then click** Equals "Adventure"

 Eighteen records are selected, some of which are shown in FIGURE B-10. A filter icon appears to the right of the Category field. Filtering by the selected field value, called **Filter By Selection**, is a fast and easy way to filter the records for an exact match. To filter for comparative data (for example, where TourStartDate is *equal to* or *greater than* 7/1/2014), you must use the **Filter By Form** feature. Filter buttons are summarized in TABLE B-3.

2. **Click the** Advanced button **in the Sort & Filter group, then click** Filter By Form

 The Filter by Form window opens. The previous Filter By Selection criterion, "Adventure" in the Category field, is still in the grid. Access distinguishes between text and numeric entries by placing "quotation marks" around text criteria.

QUICK TIP
To clear previous
criteria, click the
Advanced button,
then click Clear
All Filters.

3. **Click the** TourStartDate cell, **then type** 7/*/2014 **as shown in** FIGURE B-11

 Filter By Form also allows you to apply two or more criteria at the same time. An asterisk (*) in the day position of the date criterion works as a wildcard, selecting any date in the month of July (the 7th month) in the year 2014.

QUICK TIP
Be sure to remove
existing filters before
applying a new filter,
or the new filter will
apply to the current
subset of records
instead of the entire
datasheet.

4. **Click the** Toggle Filter button **in the Sort & Filter group**

 The datasheet selects two records that match both filter criteria, as shown in FIGURE B-12. Note that filter icons appear next to the TourStartDate and Category field names as both fields are involved in the filter.

5. **Close the Tours datasheet, then click** Yes **when prompted to save the changes**

 Saving changes to the datasheet saves the last sort order and column width changes. Filters are not saved.

Using wildcard characters

To search for a pattern, you can use a **wildcard** character to represent any character in the condition entry. Use a question mark (?) to search for any single character and an asterisk (*) to search for any number of characters. Wildcard characters are often used with the **Like** operator. For example, the criterion Like "12/*/13" would find all dates in December of 2013, and the criterion Like "F*" would find all entries that start with the letter F.

FIGURE B-10: Filtering the Tours table

Selection button

Advanced button

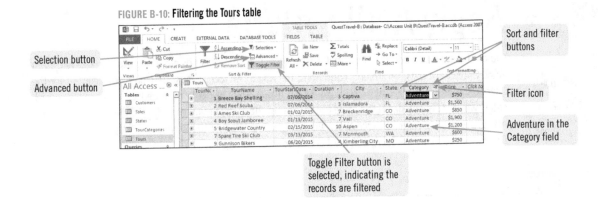

Sort and filter buttons

Filter icon

Adventure in the Category field

Toggle Filter button is selected, indicating the records are filtered

FIGURE B-11: Filtering By Form criteria

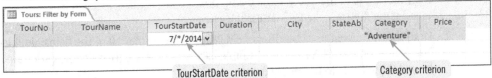

TourStartDate criterion

Category criterion

FIGURE B-12: Results of filtering by form

TourStartDate values are in July 2014

Filter icons

Category is equal to Adventure

TABLE B-2: Filters vs. queries

characteristics	filters	queries
Are saved as an object in the database		•
Can be used to select a subset of records in a datasheet	•	•
Can be used to select a subset of fields in a datasheet		•
Resulting datasheet used to enter and edit data	•	•
Resulting datasheet used to sort, filter, and find records	•	•
Commonly used as the source of data for a form or report		•
Can calculate sums, averages, counts, and other types of summary statistics across records		•
Can be used to create calculated fields		•

© 2014 Cengage Learning

TABLE B-3: Filter buttons

name	button	purpose
Filter		Provides a list of values in the selected field that can be used to customize a filter
Selection		Filters records that equal, do not equal, or are otherwise compared with the current value
Advanced		Provides advanced filter features such as Filter By Form, Save As Query, and Clear All Filters
Toggle Filter		Applies or removes the current filter

© 2014 Cengage Learning

Apply AND Criteria

Learning
Outcomes
• Enter AND criteria
in a query
• Define criteria
syntax
• Use comparison
operators with
criteria

You can limit the number of records that appear on a query datasheet by entering criteria in Query Design View. Criteria are tests, or limiting conditions, for which the record must be true to be selected for the query datasheet. To create **AND criteria**, which means that *all* criteria must be true to select the record, enter two or more criteria on the *same* Criteria row of the query design grid. **CASE** ▶ *Samantha Hooper asks you to provide a list of all Adventure tours in the state of Florida with a duration of 7 days or less. Use Query Design View to create the query with AND criteria to meet her request.*

STEPS

1. **Click the** CREATE **tab on the Ribbon, click the** Query Design button, **double-click** Tours, **then click** Close **in the Show Table dialog box**

 You want four fields from the Tours table in this query.

2. **Drag the** bottom edge of the Tours field list **down to display all of the fields, double-click** TourName, **double-click** Duration, **double-click** StateAbbrev, **then double-click** Category **to add these fields to the query grid**

 First add criteria to select only those records in Florida. Because you are using the StateAbbrev field, you need to use the two-letter state abbreviation for Florida, FL, as the Criteria entry.

3. **Click the** first Criteria cell for the StateAbbrev field, **type** FL, **then click the** View button 📷 **to display the results**

 Querying for only those tours in the state of Florida selects nine records. Next, you add criteria to select only the tours in Florida in the Adventure category.

4. **Click the** View button 📐, **click the** first Criteria cell for the Category field, **type** Adventure, **then click the** View button 📷 **in the Results group**

 Criteria added to the same line of the query design grid are AND criteria. When entered on the same line, each criterion must be true for the record to appear in the resulting datasheet. Querying for both FL and Adventure tours narrows the selection to five records. Every time you add AND criteria, you *narrow* the number of records that are selected because the record must be true for *all* criteria.

5. **Click the** View button 📐, **click the** first Criteria cell for the Duration field, **then type** <=7, **as shown in** FIGURE B-13

 Access assists you with **criteria syntax**, rules that specify how to enter criteria. Access automatically adds "quotation marks" around text criteria in Short Text and Long Text fields ("FL" and "Adventure") and pound signs (#) around date criteria in Date/Time fields. The criteria in Number, Currency, and Yes/No fields are not surrounded by any characters. See TABLE B-4 for more information about comparison operators such as > (greater than).

6. **Click the** View button 📷

TROUBLE
If your datasheet
doesn't match
FIGURE B-14, return
to Query Design View
and compare your
criteria with that of
FIGURE B-13.

 The third AND criterion further narrows the number of records selected to four, as shown in FIGURE B-14.

7. **Click the** Save button 💾 **on the Quick Access toolbar, type** AdventureFL **as the query name, click** OK, **then close the query**

 The query is saved with the new name, AdventureFL, as a new object in the QuestTravel-B database. Criteria entered in Query Design View are permanently saved with the query (as compared with filters in the previous lesson, which are temporary and not saved with the object).

FIGURE B-13: Query Design View with AND criteria

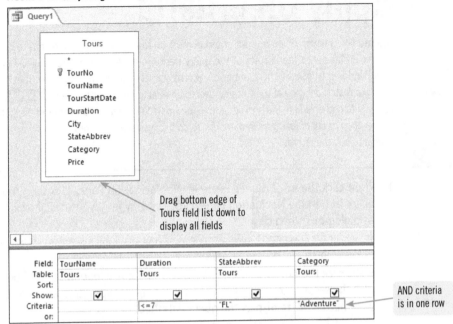

Drag bottom edge of
Tours field list down to
display all fields

Field:	TourName	Duration	StateAbbrev	Category
Table:	Tours	Tours	Tours	Tours
Sort:				
Show:	☑	☑	☑	☑
Criteria:		<=7	"FL"	"Adventure"
or:				

AND criteria
is in one row

FIGURE B-14: Final datasheet of AdventureFL query

TourName ▾	Duration ▾	State. ▾	Category ▾
Breeze Bay Shelling	3	FL	Adventure
Red Reef Scuba	3	FL	Adventure
High Adventurers	7	FL	Adventure
Gulfside Birdwatchers	7	FL	Adventure
✳			

Records meet all three criteria:
Duration <=7
State = "FL"
Category = "Adventure"

TABLE B-4: Comparison operators

operator	description	expression	meaning
>	Greater than	>500	Numbers greater than 500
>=	Greater than or equal to	>=500	Numbers greater than or equal to 500
<	Less than	<"Braveheart"	Names from A to Braveheart, but not Braveheart
<=	Less than or equal to	<="Bridgewater"	Names from A through Bridgewater, inclusive
<>	Not equal to	<>"Fontanelle"	Any name except for Fontanelle

Searching for blank fields

Is Null and Is Not Null are two other types of common criteria. The **Is Null** criterion finds all records where no entry has been made in the field. **Is Not Null** finds all records where there is any entry in the field, even if the entry is 0. Primary key fields cannot have a null entry.

Apply OR Criteria

Learning
Outcomes
• Enter OR criteria in
 a query
• Rename a query

You use **OR criteria** when *any one* criterion must be true in order for the record to be selected. Enter OR criteria on *different* Criteria rows of the query design grid. As you add rows of OR criteria to the query design grid, you *increase* the number of records selected for the resulting datasheet because the record needs to match *only one* of the Criteria rows to be selected for the datasheet. **CASE** *Samantha Hooper asks you to add criteria to the previous query. She wants to include Cultural tours in the state of Florida that are shorter than or equal to 7 days in duration. To do this, you modify a copy of the AdventureFL query to use OR criteria to add the records.*

STEPS

1. **Right-click the** AdventureFL query **in the Navigation Pane, click** Copy, **right-click a** blank spot **in the Navigation Pane, click** Paste, **type** AdventureCulturalFL **in the Paste As dialog box, then click** OK

 By copying the AdventureFL query before starting your modifications, you avoid changing the AdventureFL query by mistake.

2. **Right-click the** AdventureCulturalFL query **in the Navigation Pane, click** Design View, **click the** second Criteria cell in the Category field, **type** Cultural, **then click the** View button ▦ to display the query datasheet

 The query selected 11 records including all of the tours with Cultural in the Category field. Note that some of the Duration values are greater than 7 and some of the StateAbbrev values are not FL. Because each row of the query grid is evaluated separately, all Cultural tours are selected regardless of criteria in any other row. In other words, the criteria in one row have no effect on the criteria of other rows. To make sure that the Cultural tours are also in Florida and have a duration of less than or equal to 7 days, you need to modify the second row of the query grid (the "or" row) to specify that criteria.

3. **Click the** View button ▨, **click the** second Criteria cell in the Duration field, **type** <=7, **click the** second Criteria cell in the StateAbbrev field, **type** FL, **then click in any other cell of the grid**

 Query Design View should look like FIGURE B-15.

4. **Click the** View button ▦

 Six records are selected that meet all three criteria as entered in row one *or* row two of the query grid, as shown in FIGURE B-16.

5. **Right-click the** AdventureCulturalFL query tab, **click** Close, **then click** Yes **to save and close the query datasheet**

FIGURE B-15: **Query Design View with OR criteria**

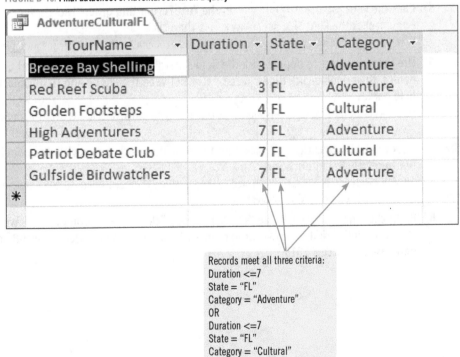

OR criteria is on
multiple rows

FIGURE B-16: **Final datasheet of AdventureCulturalFL query**

TourName	Duration	State	Category
Breeze Bay Shelling	3	FL	Adventure
Red Reef Scuba	3	FL	Adventure
Golden Footsteps	4	FL	Cultural
High Adventurers	7	FL	Adventure
Patriot Debate Club	7	FL	Cultural
Gulfside Birdwatchers	7	FL	Adventure

Records meet all three criteria:
Duration <=7
State = "FL"
Category = "Adventure"
OR
Duration <=7
State = "FL"
Category = "Cultural"

Format a Datasheet

Learning
Outcomes
• Zoom in print
 preview
• Format a datasheet
• Change page
 orientation

A report is the primary Access tool to create a professional printout, but you can print a datasheet as well. A datasheet allows you to apply some basic formatting modifications such as changing the font size, font face, colors, and gridlines. **CASE** *Samantha Hooper asks you to print a list of customers. You decide to format the Customers table datasheet before printing it for her.*

STEPS

1. **In the Navigation Pane, double-click the** Customers table **to open it in Datasheet View**

 Before applying new formatting enhancements, you preview the default printout.

2. **Click the** FILE tab, **click** Print, **click** Print Preview, **then click the** header **of the printout to zoom in**

 The preview window displays the layout of the printout, as shown in FIGURE B-17. By default, the printout of a datasheet contains the object name and current date in the header. The page number is in the footer.

3. **Click the** Next Page button ▶ **in the navigation bar to move to the next page of the printout**

 The last two fields print on the second page because the first is not wide enough to accommodate them. You decide to switch the report to landscape orientation so that all of the fields print on one page, and then increase the size of the font before printing to make the text easier to read.

4. **Click the** Landscape button **on the PRINT PREVIEW tab to switch the report to landscape orientation, then click the** Close Print Preview button

 You return to Datasheet View where you can make font face, font size, font color, gridline color, and background color choices.

5. **Click the** Font list arrow [Calibri (Body) ▾] **in the Text Formatting group, click** Times New Roman, **click the** Font Size list arrow [11 ▾]**, then click** 12

 With the larger font size applied, you need to resize some columns to accommodate the widest entries.

6. **Use the** ✛ **pointer to double-click the** field separator **between the Street and City field names, then double-click the** field separator **between the Phone and FirstContact field names**

 Double-clicking the field separators widens the columns as needed to display every entry in those fields, as shown in FIGURE B-18.

QUICK TIP
If you need a print-
out of this datasheet,
click the Print button
on the PRINT PREVIEW
tab, then click OK.

7. **Click the** FILE tab, **click** Print, **click** Print Preview, **then click the preview to zoom in and out to review the information**

 All of the fields now fit across a page in landscape orientation. The preview of the printout is still two pages, but with the larger font size, it is easier to read.

8. **Right-click the** Customers table tab, **click** Close, **click** Yes **when prompted to save changes, then click the** Close button **on the title bar to close the QuestTravel-B.accdb database and Access 2013**

FIGURE B-17: **Preview of Customers datasheet**

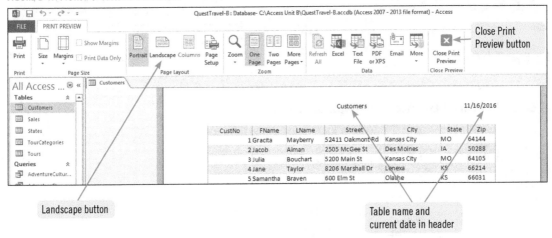

Landscape button

Close Print Preview button

Table name and current date in header

FIGURE B-18: **Formatting the Customers datasheet**

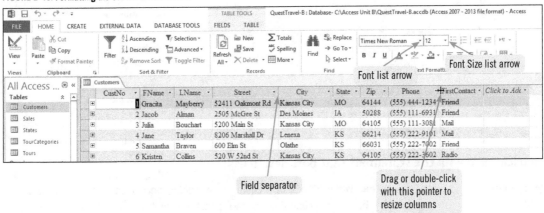

Font list arrow

Font Size list arrow

Field separator

Drag or double-click with this pointer to resize columns

Practice

Concepts Review

Label each element of the Access window shown in FIGURE B-19.

FIGURE B-19

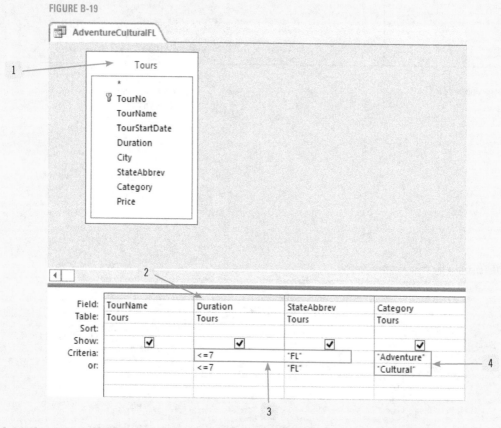

Match each term with the statement that best describes it.

5. Query grid
6. Field selector
7. Filter
8. Filter By Selection
9. Field lists
10. Sorting
11. Join line
12. Is Null
13. Criteria
14. Syntax
15. Wildcard

a. Putting records in ascending or descending order based on the values of a field
b. Limiting conditions used to restrict the number of records that are selected in a query
c. Creates a temporary subset of records
d. Small windows that display field names
e. Rules that determine how criteria are entered
f. Used to search for a pattern of characters
g. Criterion that finds all records where no entry has been made in the field
h. The lower pane in Query Design View
i. Identifies which fields are used to establish a relationship between two tables
j. A fast and easy way to filter the records for an exact match
k. The thin gray bar above each field in the query grid

Select the best answer from the list of choices.

16. **AND criteria:**
 a. Determine sort orders.
 b. Must all be true for the record to be selected.
 c. Determine fields selected for a query.
 d. Help set link lines between tables in a query.

17. **SQL stands for which of the following?**
 a. Structured Query Language
 b. Standard Query Language
 c. Special Query Listing
 d. Simple Query Listing

18. **A query is sometimes called a logical view of data because:**
 a. You can create queries with the Logical Query Wizard.
 b. Queries contain logical criteria.
 c. Query naming conventions are logical.
 d. Queries do not store data—they only display a view of data.

19. **Which of the following describes OR criteria?**
 a. Selecting a subset of fields and/or records to view as a datasheet from one or more tables
 b. Using two or more rows of the query grid to select only those records that meet given criteria
 c. Reorganizing the records in either ascending or descending order based on the contents of one or more fields
 d. Using multiple fields in the query design grid

20. **Which of the following is *not* true about a query?**
 a. A query is the same thing as a filter.
 b. A query can select fields from one or more tables in a relational database.
 c. A query can be created using different tools.
 d. An existing query can be modified in Query Design View.

Skills Review

1. **Use the Query Wizard.**
 a. Open the Recycle-B.accdb database from the location where you store your Data Files. Enable content if prompted.
 b. Create a new query using the Simple Query Wizard. Select the CenterName field from the Centers table, the DepositDate and Weight fields from the Deposits table, and the ClubName field from the Clubs table. Select Detail, and enter **CenterDeposits** as the name of the query.
 c. Open the query in Datasheet View, then change any record with the Barker Trash value to a center name that includes *your* last name.

2. **Work with data in a query.**
 a. Delete the first record (Hugo Trash Can with a DepositDate value of 2/4/2014).
 b. Change any occurrence of Lions of Fontanelle in the ClubName field to **Lions of Bridgewater**.
 c. Click any value in the DepositDate field, then click the Descending button on the HOME tab to sort the records in descending order on the DepositDate field.
 d. Use the Calendar Picker to choose the date of **12/16/2016** for the first record.
 e. Save and close the CenterDeposits query.

3. **Use Query Design View.**
 a. Click the CREATE tab, click the Query Design button, double-click Clubs, double-click Deposits, and then click Close to add the Clubs and Deposits tables to Query Design View.
 b. Drag the bottom edge of both field lists down to display all of the field names in both tables.
 c. Add the following fields from the Clubs table to the query design grid in the following order: FName, LName, ClubName. Add the following fields from the Deposits table in the following order: DepositDate, Weight. View the results in Datasheet View observing the number of records that are selected.
 d. In Design View, enter criteria to display only those records with a Weight value of **greater than or equal to 100**, then observe the number of records that are selected in Datasheet View.
 e. Save the query with the name **HeavyDeposits**.

4. **Sort and find data.**
 a. In Query Design View of the HeavyDeposits query, choose an ascending sort order for the ClubName field and a descending sort order for the Weight field.
 b. Display the query in Datasheet View noting how the records have been resorted.
 c. In the ClubName field, change any occurrence of Jaycees to **Dallas Jaycees**.
 d. In the FName field, change any occurrence of Tara to *your* initials.

5. **Filter data.**
 a. Filter the HeavyDeposits datasheet for only those records where the ClubName equals **Dallas Jaycees**.
 b. Apply an advanced Filter By Form and use the >= operator to further narrow the records so that only the deposits with a DepositDate value on or after 1/1/2015 are selected.
 c. Apply the filter to see the datasheet and if requested by your instructor, print the filtered HeavyDeposits datasheet.
 d. Save and close the HeavyDeposits query. Reopen the HeavyDeposits query to confirm that filters are temporary (not saved), and then close the HeavyDeposits query again.

Skills Review (continued)

6. Apply AND criteria.

 a. Right-click the HeavyDeposits query, copy it, and then paste it as **Heavy2014Deposits**.

 b. Open the Heavy2014Deposits query in Query Design View.

 c. Modify the criteria to select all of the records with a DepositDate in **2014** and a Weight value **greater than or equal to 100**.

 d. If requested by your instructor, print the Heavy2014Deposits datasheet, then save and close it.

7. Apply OR criteria.

 a. Right-click the HeavyDeposits query, copy it, then paste it as **HeavyDeposits2Clubs**.

 b. Open the HeavyDeposits2Clubs query in Design View, then add criteria to select the records with a ClubName of **Ice Kings** and a Weight value **greater than or equal to 100**.

 c. Add criteria to also include the records with a ClubName of **Junior League** with a Weight value **greater than or equal to 100**. FIGURE B-20 shows the results.

 d. If requested by your instructor, print the HeavyDeposits2Clubs datasheet, then save and close it.

8. Format a datasheet.

 a. In the Clubs table datasheet, apply an Arial Narrow font and a 14-point font size.

 b. Resize all columns so that all data and field names are visible.

 c. Display the Clubs datasheet in Print Preview, switch the orientation to landscape, click the Margins button in the Page Size group, then click Narrow to fit the printout on a single sheet of paper.

 d. If requested by your instructor, print the Clubs datasheet.

 e. Save and close the Clubs table, then close Access 2013.

FIGURE B-20

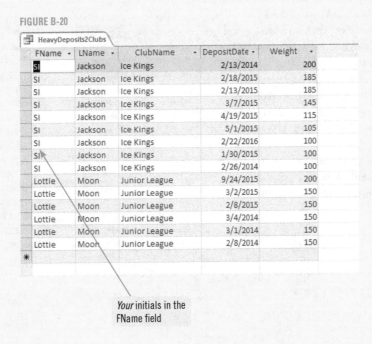

Your initials in the FName field

Independent Challenge 1

You have built an Access database to track membership in a community service club. The database tracks member names and addresses as well as their community service hours.

a. Open the Membership-B.accdb database from the location where you store your Data Files, enable content if prompted, then open the Activities, Members, and Zips tables to review their datasheets.

b. In the Zips table, click the expand button to the left of the 64131, Overland Park, KS, record to display the two members linked to that zip code. Click the expand button to the left of the Gabriel Hammer record to display the three activity records linked to Gabriel.

c. Close all three datasheets, click the DATABASE TOOLS tab, then click the Relationships button. The Relationships window also shows you that one record in the Zips table is related to many records in the Members table through the common ZipCode field, and that one record in the Members table is related to many records in the Activities table through the common MemberNo field.

d. Click the Relationship Report button, then if requested by your instructor, print the Relationship report. Close and save the report with the default name **Relationships for Membership-B**. Close the Relationships window.

e. Using Query Design View, build a query with the following fields: FirstName and LastName from the Members table and ActivityDate and HoursWorked from the Activities table.

f. View the datasheet, observe the number of records selected, then return to Query Design View.

g. Add criteria to select only those records where the ActivityDate is in March of 2014.

h. In Query Design View, apply an ascending sort order to the LastName and ActivityDate fields, then view the datasheet.

i. Change the name Quentin Garden to *your* name, widen all columns so that all data and field names are visible, and save the query with the name **March2014**, as shown in FIGURE B-21.

j. If requested by your instructor, print the March2014 datasheet, then close the March2014 query and close Access 2013.

FIGURE B-21

FirstName	LastName	ActivityDate	HoursWorked
Bart	Bouchart	3/29/2014	4
Golga	Collins	3/31/2014	8
Martha	Duman	3/27/2014	4
Allie	Eahlie	3/29/2014	4
Jana	Eckert	3/29/2014	5
Student First	Student Last	3/29/2014	4
Student First	Student Last	3/30/2014	8
Loraine	Goode	3/29/2014	5
Gabriel	Hammer	3/29/2014	5
Jeremiah	Hopper	3/27/2014	4
Helen	Hubert	3/29/2014	5
Heidi	Kalvert	3/29/2014	4
Harvey	Mackintosh	3/30/2014	4
Jon	Maxim	3/30/2014	4
Micah	Mayberry	3/29/2014	4
Patch	Mullins	3/30/2014	8
Patch	Mullins	3/31/2014	8
Young	Nelson	3/30/2014	10
Mallory	Olson	3/31/2014	8
Su	Vogue	3/30/2014	8
Sherry	Walker	3/29/2014	4
Taney	Wilson	3/30/2014	8

Record: 7 of 22 No Filter Search

Independent Challenge 2

You work for a nonprofit agency that tracks the voting patterns of Congress. You have developed an Access database with contact information for members of the House of Representatives. The director of the agency has asked you to create several state lists of representatives. You will use queries to extract this information.

a. Open the Congress-B.accdb database from the location where you store your Data Files, then enable content if prompted.

b. Open the Representatives and the States tables. Notice that one state is related to many representatives as evidenced by the expand buttons to the left of the records in the States tables.

c. Close both datasheets, then using Query Design View, create a query with the StateAbbrev, StateName, and Capital fields from the States table (in that order) as well as the LName field from the Representatives table.

d. Sort the records in ascending order on the StateName field, then in ascending order on the LName field.

e. Add criteria to select the representatives from Arizona or New Mexico. Use the StateAbbrev field to enter your criteria, using the two-character state abbreviations of **AZ** and **NM**.

f. Save the query with the name **ArizonaAndNewMexico** as shown in FIGURE B-22, view the results, then change the last name of Upton in the last record to *your* last name. Resize the columns as needed to view all the data and field names.

g. Print the ArizonaAndNewMexico datasheet if requested by your instructor, then close it and exit Access 2013.

FIGURE B-22

StateAbbrev	StateName	Capital	LName
AZ	Arizona	Phoenix	Christian
AZ	Arizona	Phoenix	Drake
AZ	Arizona	Phoenix	Gohmert
AZ	Arizona	Phoenix	Gonzalez
AZ	Arizona	Phoenix	Matheson
AZ	Arizona	Phoenix	McCaul
AZ	Arizona	Phoenix	Sanders
AZ	Arizona	Phoenix	Wolf
NM	New Mexico	Santa Fe	Miller
NM	New Mexico	Santa Fe	Student Last Name
NM	New Mexico	Santa Fe	Stupak

Independent Challenge 3

You have built an Access database to track the veterinarians and clinics in your area.

a. Open the Vet-B.accdb database from the location where you store your Data Files, then enable content if prompted.

b. Open the Vets table and then the Clinics table to review the data in both datasheets.

c. Click the expand button next to the Veterinary Specialists record in the Clinics table, then add *your* name as a new record to the Vets subdatasheet.

d. Close both datasheets.

e. Using the Simple Query Wizard, select the VetLast and VetFirst fields from the Vets table, and select the ClinicName and Phone fields from the Clinics table. Title the query **ClinicListing**, then view the datasheet.

f. Update any occurrence of Leawood Animal Clinic in the ClinicName field by changing Leawood to **Emergency** so the ClinicName is **Emergency Animal Clinic**.

g. In Query Design View, add criteria to select only **Emergency Animal Clinic** or **Veterinary Specialists** in the ClinicName field, then view the datasheet.

h. In Query Design View, move the ClinicName field to the first column, then add an ascending sort order on the ClinicName and VetLast fields.

i. Display the ClinicListing query in Datasheet View, resize the fields as shown in FIGURE B-23, then print the datasheet if requested by your instructor.

j. Save and close the ClinicListing datasheet, then exit Access 2013.

FIGURE B-23

ClinicName	VetLast	VetFirst	Phone
Emergency Animal Clinic	Ridwell	Kirk	(555) 555-1311
Emergency Animal Clinic	Rosenheim	Howard	(555) 555-1311
Emergency Animal Clinic	Salamander	Stephen	(555) 555-1311
Veterinary Specialists	Garver	Mark	(555) 555-4000
Veterinary Specialists	Major	Mark	(555) 555-4000
Veterinary Specialists	Manheim	Thomas	(555) 555-4000
Veterinary Specialists	Stewart	Frank	(555) 555-4000
Veterinary Specialists	Student Last	Student First	(555) 555-4000

Independent Challenge 4: Explore

An Access database is an excellent tool to help record and track job opportunities. For this exercise, you'll create a database from scratch that you can use to enter, edit, and query data in pursuit of a new job or career.

a. Create a new desktop database named **Jobs.accdb**.

b. Create a table named **Positions** with the following field names, data types, and descriptions:

Field name	Data type	Description
PositionID	AutoNumber	Primary key field
Title	Short Text	Title of position such as Accountant, Assistant Court Clerk, or Web Developer
CareerArea	Short Text	Area of the career field such as Accounting, Government, or Information Systems
AnnualSalary	Currency	Annual salary
Desirability	Number	Desirability rating of 1 = low to 5 = high to show how desirable the position is to you
EmployerID	Number	Foreign key field to the Employers table

c. Create a table named **Employers** with the following field names, data types, and descriptions:

Field name	Data type	Description
EmployerID	AutoNumber	Primary key field
CompanyName	Short Text	Company name of the employer
EmpStreet	Short Text	Employer's street address
EmpCity	Short Text	Employer's city
EmpState	Short Text	Employer's state
EmpZip	Short Text	Employer's zip code
EmpPhone	Short Text	Employer's phone, such as 913-555-8888

d. Be sure to set EmployerID as the primary key field in the Employers table and the PositionID as the primary key field in the Positions table.

e. Link the Employers and Positions tables together in a one-to-many relationship using the common EmployerID field. One employer record will be linked to many position records. Be sure to enforce referential integrity.

f. Using any valid source of potential employer data, enter five records into the Employers table.

g. Using any valid source of job information, enter five records into the Positions table by using the subdatasheets from within the Employers datasheet.
Because one employer may have many positions, all five of your Positions records may be linked to the same employer, you may have one position record per employer, or any other combination.

h. Build a query that selects CompanyName from the Employers table, and the Title, CareerArea, AnnualSalary, and Desirability fields from the Positions table. Sort the records in descending order based on Desirability. Save the query as **JobList**, and print it if requested by your instructor.

i. Close the JobList datasheet, then exit Access 2013.

Visual Workshop

Open the Baseball-B.accdb database from the location where you store your Data Files, and enable content if prompted. Create a query based on the Players and Teams tables, as shown in FIGURE B-24. Add criteria to select only those records where the PlayerPosition field values are equal to 1 or 2 (representing pitchers and catchers). In Query Design View, set an ascending sort order on the TeamName and PlayerPosition fields. In the results, change the name of Roy Campanella to *your* name. Save the query with the name **PitchersAndCatchers**, then compare the results with FIGURE B-24, making changes and widening columns to see all of the data. Print the datasheet if requested by your instructor. Save and close the query and the Baseball-B.accdb database, then exit Access 2013.

FIGURE B-24

TeamName	PlayerLast	PlayerFirst	Position
Brooklyn Beetles	Student Last Name	Student First Name	1
Brooklyn Beetles	Young	Cycylie	2
Mayfair Monarchs	Durocher	Luis	1
Mayfair Monarchs	Mathewson	Carl	2
Rocky's Rockets	Spalding	Andrew	1
Rocky's Rockets	Koufax	Sanford	2
Snapping Turtles	Ford	Charles	1
Snapping Turtles	Perry	Greg	2

Using Forms

CASE Samantha Hooper, a tour developer at Quest Specialty Travel, asks you to create forms to make tour information easier to access, enter, and update.

Unit Objectives

After completing this unit, you will be able to:

- Use the Form Wizard
- Create a split form
- Use Form Layout View
- Add fields to a form

- Modify form controls
- Create calculations
- Modify tab order
- Insert an image

Files You Will Need

QuestTravel-C.accdb
QuestLogo.bmp
RealEstate-C.accdb
ForSale.bmp
Dives-C.accdb

Membership-C.accdb
People.jpg
Recycle-C.accdb
Jobs-C.accdb
Baseball-C.accdb

©Tumanyan/Shutterstock

Use the Form Wizard

Learning
Outcomes
• Create a form with
 the Form Wizard
• Sort data in a form
• Describe form
 terminology
 and views

A **form** is an easy-to-use data entry and navigation screen. A form allows you to arrange the fields of a record in any layout so a **database user** can quickly and easily find, enter, edit, and analyze data. The **database designer** is the person responsible for building and maintaining tables, queries, forms, and reports for all of the database users. **CASE** *Samantha Hooper asks you to build a form to enter and maintain tour information.*

STEPS

1. **Start Access, open the** QuestTravel-C.accdb database **from the location where you store your Data Files, then enable content if prompted**

 You can use many methods to create a new form, but the Form Wizard is a fast and popular tool that helps you get started. The **Form Wizard** prompts you for information it needs to create a form, such as the fields, layout, and title for the form.

2. **Click the** CREATE tab **on the Ribbon, then click the** Form Wizard button **in the Forms group**

 The Form Wizard starts, prompting you to select the fields for this form. You want to create a form to enter and update data in the Tours table.

3. **Click the** Tables/Queries list arrow, **click** Table: Tours, **then click the** Select All Fields button >>

 You could now select fields from other tables, if necessary, but in this case, you have all of the fields you need.

4. **Click** Next, **click the** Columnar option button, **click** Next, **type** Tours Entry Form **as the title, then click** Finish

 The Tours Entry Form opens in **Form View**, as shown in FIGURE C-1. Access provides three different views of forms, as summarized in TABLE C-1. Each item on the form is called a **control**. A **label control** is used to *describe* the data shown in other controls such as text boxes. A label is also used for the title of the form, Tours Entry Form. A **text box** is used to *display* the data as well as enter, edit, find, sort, and also filter the data. A **combo box** is a combination of two controls: a text box and a list. The Category data is displayed in a combo box control. You click the arrow button on a combo box control to display a list of values, or you can edit data directly in the combo box itself.

QUICK TIP
Click in the text box
of the field you want
to sort *before* clicking
a sort button.

5. **Click** Breeze Bay Shelling **in the TourName text box, click the** Ascending button **in the Sort & Filter group, then click the** Next record button ▶ **in the navigation bar to move to the second record**

 The Ames Ski Club is the second record when the records are sorted in ascending order on the TourName data. Information about the current record number and total number of records appears in the navigation bar, just as it does in a datasheet.

6. **Click the** Previous record button ◀ **in the navigation bar to move back to the first record, click the** TourName text box, **then change American Heritage Tour to** Washington DC History Tour

 Your screen should look like FIGURE C-2. Forms displayed in Form View are the primary tool for database users to enter, edit, and delete data in an Access database.

7. **Right-click the** Tours Entry Form tab, **then click** Close

 When a form is closed, Access automatically saves any edits made to the current record.

FIGURE C-1: **Tours Entry Form in Form View**

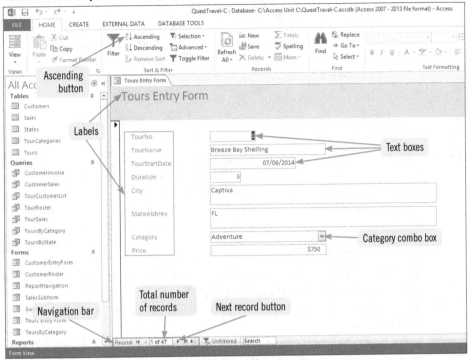

FIGURE C-2: **Displaying the results of a calculation in Form View**

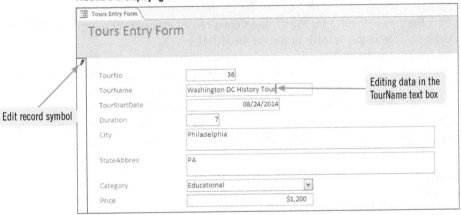

TABLE C-1: **Form views**

view	primary purpose
Form	To find, sort, enter, and edit data
Layout	To modify the size, position, or formatting of controls; shows data as you modify the form, making it the tool of choice when you want to change the appearance and usability of the form while viewing live data
Design	To modify the Form Header, Detail, and Footer section, or to access the complete range of controls and form properties; Design View does not display data

Create a Split Form

Learning
Outcomes
• Create a split form
• Enter and edit
 data in a form

In addition to the Form Wizard, you should be familiar with several other form creation tools. TABLE C-2 identifies those tools and the purpose for each. **CASE** *Samantha Hooper asks you to create another form to manage customer data. You'll work with the Split Form tool for this task.*

STEPS

QUICK TIP
Layout View allows
you to view and filter
the data, but not
edit it.

1. **Click the** Customers table **in the Navigation Pane, click the** CREATE **tab, click the** More Forms **button, click** Split Form, **then click the** Add Existing Fields **button in the Tools group on the DESIGN tab to close the Field List if it opens**

 The Customers data appears in a split form with the top half in **Layout View**, as shown in FIGURE C-3. The benefit of a **split form** is that the upper pane allows you to display the fields of one record in any arrangement, and the lower pane maintains a datasheet view of the first few records. If you edit, sort, or filter records in the upper pane, the lower pane is automatically updated, and vice versa.

2. **Click** MO **in the State text box in the upper pane, click the** HOME **tab, click the** Selection **button in the Sort & Filter group, then click** Does Not Equal "MO"

 Thirty-seven records are filtered where the State field is not equal to MO. You also need to change a value in the Jacob Alman record.

TROUBLE
Make sure you edit
the record in the
datasheet in the
lower pane.

3. **In the lower pane, select** Des Moines **in the City field of the first record, edit the entry to read** Dallas Center, **click any other record in the lower pane, then click** Jacob **in the first record of the lower pane**

 Moving from record to record automatically saves data. Note that "Dallas Center" is now the entry in the City field in both the upper and lower panes, as shown in FIGURE C-4.

4. **Click the** record selector **for the Kristen Collins record in the lower pane, then click the** Delete **button in the Records group on the HOME tab**

 You cannot delete this record because it contains related records in the Sales table. This is a benefit of referential integrity on the one-to-many relationship between the Customers and Sales tables. Referential integrity prevents the creation of **orphan records**, records on the *many* side of a relationship (in this case, the Sales table) that do not have a match on the *one* side (in this case, the Customers table).

5. **Click** OK, **right-click the** Customers form tab, **click** Close, **click** Yes **when prompted to save changes, then click** OK **to save the form with the name** Customers

TABLE C-2: Form creation tools

tool	icon	creates a form
Form		with one click based on the selected table or query
Form Design		from scratch in Form Design View
Blank Form		from scratch in Form Layout View
Form Wizard		by answering a series of questions provided by the Form Wizard dialog boxes
Navigation		used to navigate or move between different areas of the database
More Forms		based on Multiple Items, Datasheet, Split Form, Modal Dialog, PivotChart, or PivotTable arrangements
Split Form		with two panes, the upper showing one record at a time and the lower displaying a datasheet of many records

FIGURE C-3: **Customers table in a split form**

FIGURE C-4: **Editing data in a split form**

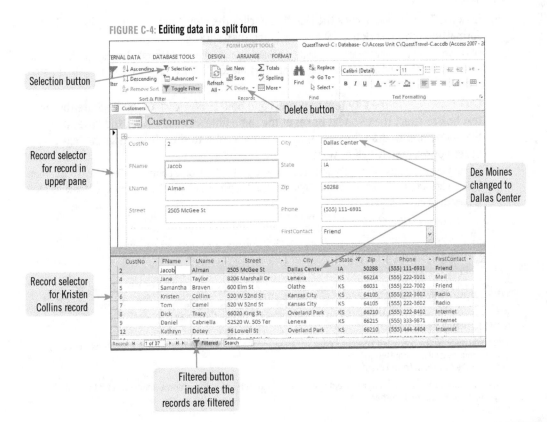

Use Form Layout View

Learning Outcomes
- Resize controls in Layout View
- Format controls in Layout View

Layout View lets you make some design changes to a form while you are browsing the data. For example, you can move and resize controls, add or delete a field on the form, filter and sort data, or change formatting characteristics, such as fonts and colors. **CASE** ▶ *Samantha Hooper asks you to make several design changes to the Tours Entry Form. You can make these changes in Layout View.*

STEPS

1. **Right-click** Tours Entry Form **in the Navigation Pane, then click** Layout View

 In Layout View, you can move through the records, but you cannot enter or edit the data as you can in Form View.

 > **TROUBLE**
 > If your third record is not Bigfoot Rafting Club, sort the records in ascending order on the TourName field.

2. **Click the** Next record button **in the navigation bar twice to move to the third record, Bigfoot Rafting Club**

 You often use Layout View to make minor design changes, such as editing labels and changing formatting characteristics.

3. **Click the** TourNo label **to select it if it is not already selected, click between the words Tour and No, then press** [Spacebar]

 You also want to edit a few more labels.

 > **TROUBLE**
 > Be sure to modify the *labels in the left column* instead of the text boxes on the right.

4. **Continue editing the labels, as shown in** FIGURE C-5

 You also want to change the text color of the first two labels, Tour No and Tour Name, to red to make them more noticeable.

5. **Click the** Tour No label, **click the** HOME tab, **click the** Font Color button ▣ **in the Text Formatting group, click the** Tour Name label, **then click** ▣

 Often, you want to apply the same formatting enhancement to multiple controls. For example, you decide to narrow the City and StateAbbrev text boxes. Select the text boxes at the same time to make the same change to both.

 > **TROUBLE**
 > Be sure to modify the *text boxes in the right column* instead of the labels on the left.

6. **Click** Placerville **in the City text box, press and hold** [Shift], **click** CA **in the StateAbbrev text box to select the two text boxes at the same time, release** [Shift], **then use the** ↔ **pointer to drag the** right edge of the selection **to the left to make the text boxes approximately half as wide**

 Layout View for the Tours Entry Form should look like FIGURE C-6. Mouse pointers in Form Layout and Form Design View are very important as they indicate what happens when you drag the mouse. Mouse pointers are described in TABLE C-3.

TABLE C-3: Mouse pointer shapes

shape	when does this shape appear?	action
⌖	When you point to any unselected control on the form (the default mouse pointer)	Single-clicking with this mouse pointer *selects* a control
✛	When you point to the upper-left corner or edge of a selected control in Form Design View or the middle of the control in Form Layout View	Dragging with this mouse pointer *moves* the selected control(s)
↕↔	When you point to any sizing handle (except the larger one in the upper-left corner in Form Design View)	Dragging with one of these mouse pointers *resizes* the control

FIGURE C-5: **Using Layout View to modify form labels on the Tours Entry Form**

Edit these labels to include a space between the words

FIGURE C-6: **Layout View for the Tours Entry Form**

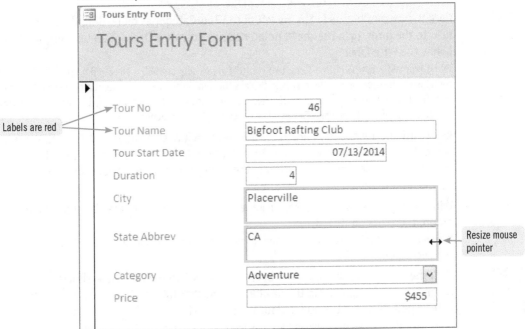

Labels are red

Resize mouse pointer

Table layouts

Layouts provide a way to group several controls together on a form or report to more quickly add, delete, rearrange, resize, or align controls. To insert a layout into a form or report, select the controls you want to group together, then choose the Stacked or Tabular button on the ARRANGE tab. Each option applies a table layout to the controls so that you can insert, delete, merge, or split the cells in the layout to quickly rearrange or edit the controls in the layout. To remove a layout, use the Remove Layout button on the ARRANGE tab in Form Design View.

Add Fields to a Form

Learning
Outcomes
• Add fields to a
 form
• Align controls
• Resize controls

Adding and deleting fields in an existing form is a common activity. You can add or delete fields in a form in either Layout View or Design View using the Field List. The **Field List** lists the database tables and the fields they contain. To add a field to the form, drag it from the Field List to the desired location on the form. To delete a field on a form, click the field to select it, then press the [Delete] key. Deleting a field from a form does not delete it from the underlying table or have any effect on the data contained in the field. You can toggle the Field List on and off using the Add Existing Fields button on the DESIGN tab. **CASE** *Samantha Hooper asks you to add the tour description from the TourCategories table to the Tours Entry Form. You can use Layout View and the Field List to accomplish this goal.*

STEPS

1. **Click the** DESIGN tab **on the Ribbon, click the** Add Existing Fields button **in the Tools group, then click the** Show all tables link **in the Field List**

 The Field List opens in Layout View, as shown in FIGURE C-7. Notice that the Field List is divided into sections. The upper section shows the tables currently used by the form, the middle section shows directly related tables, and the lower section shows other tables in the database. The expand/collapse button to the left of the table names allows you to expand (show) the fields within the table or collapse (hide) them. The Description field is in the TourCategories table in the middle section.

QUICK TIP
If you make a
mistake, click the
Undo button ↰
and try again.

2. **Click the** expand button ⊞ **to the left of the TourCategories table, drag the** Description field **to the form, then use the** ⛶ **pointer to drag the new Description text box and label below the Price label**

 When you add a new field to a form, two controls are usually created: a label and a text box. The label contains the field name and the text box displays the data in the field. The TourCategories table moved from the middle to the top section of the Field List. You also want to align and size the new controls with others already on the form. Form Design View works well for alignment activities.

3. **Right-click the** Tours Entry Form tab, **click** Design View, **click the** Description label, **press and hold** [Shift], **click the** Price label **to select both labels, release** [Shift], **click the** ARRANGE tab, **click the** Align button **in the Sizing & Ordering group, then click** Left

 Now resize the labels.

4. **With the two labels still selected, click the** Size/Space button **in the Sizing & Ordering group, then click** To Widest

 With the new controls in position, you want to enter a new record. You must switch to Form View to edit, enter, or delete data.

TROUBLE
Don't worry if your
Tour No value
doesn't match
FIGURE C-8. As an
AutoNumber value,
the value is inserted
automatically and is
controlled by Access.

5. **Click the** HOME tab, **click the** View button ▦ **to switch to Form View, click the** New (blank) record button ▶✱ **in the navigation bar, click the** TourName text box, **then enter a new record in the updated form, as shown in** FIGURE C-8

 Note that when you select a value in the Category combo box, the Description is automatically updated. This is due to the one-to-many relationship between the TourCategories and Tours tables in the Relationships window.

FIGURE C-7: **Field List in Form Layout View**

FIGURE C-8: **Entering a record in the updated Tours Entry Form in Form View**

Bound versus unbound controls

Controls are either bound or unbound. **Bound controls** display values from a field such as text boxes and combo boxes. **Unbound controls** do not display data; unbound controls describe data or enhance the appearance of the form. Labels are the most common type of unbound control, but other types include lines, images, tabs, and command buttons. Another way to distinguish bound from unbound controls is to observe the form as you move from record to record. Because bound controls display data, their contents change as you move through the records, displaying the entry in the field of the current record. Unbound controls such as labels and lines do not change as you move through the records in a form.

Modify Form Controls

Learning
Outcomes
• Modify control
properties
• Define bound and
unbound controls

You have already made many modifications to form controls, such as changing the font color of labels and the size of text boxes. Labels and text boxes are the two most popular form controls. Other common controls are listed in TABLE C-4. When you modify controls, you change their **properties** (characteristics). All of the control characteristics you can modify are stored in the control's **Property Sheet**. **CASE** ▶ *Because Quest offers more Adventure tours than any other type of tour, you decide to use the Property Sheet of the Category field to modify the default value to be "Adventure." You also use the Property Sheet to make other control modifications to better size and align the controls.*

STEPS

1. **Click the** Layout View button 🖳 **on the HOME tab, then click the** Property Sheet button **in the Tools group**

 The Property Sheet opens, showing you all of the properties for the selected item.

2. **Click the** Category combo box, **click the** Data tab **in the Property Sheet (if it is not already selected), click the** Default Value box, **type** Adventure, **then press** [Enter]

 The Property Sheet should look like FIGURE C-9. Access often helps you with the **syntax** (rules) of entering property values. In this case, Access added quotation marks around "Adventure" to indicate that the default entry is text. Properties are categorized in the Property Sheet with the Format, Data, Event, and Other tabs. The All tab is a complete list of all the control's properties. You can use the Property Sheet to make all control modifications, although you'll probably find that some changes are easier to make using the Ribbon. The property values change in the Property Sheet as you modify a control using the Ribbon.

TROUBLE
Be sure to click the
Tour No label on the
left, not the TourNo
text box on the right.

3. **Click the** Format tab **in the Property Sheet, click the** Tour No label **in the form to select it, click the** HOME tab **on the Ribbon, then click the** Align Right button ≣ **in the Text Formatting group**

 Notice that the **Text Align property** on the Format tab in the Property Sheet is automatically updated from Left to Right even though you changed the property using the Ribbon instead of within the Property Sheet.

4. **Click the** Tour Name label, **press and hold** [Shift], **then click** each other label **in the first column on the form**

 With all the labels selected, you can modify their Text Align property at the same time.

TROUBLE
You may need to
click ≣ twice.

5. **Click** ≣ **in the Text Formatting group**

 Don't be overwhelmed by the number of properties available for each control on the form or the number of ways to modify each property. Over time, you will learn about most of these properties. At this point, it's only important to know the purpose of the Property Sheet and understand that properties are modified in various ways.

TROUBLE
Don't worry if your
Tour No value
doesn't match
FIGURE C-10. It
is an AutoNumber
value, controlled
by Access.

6. **Click the** Save button 🖫 **on the Quick Access toolbar, click the** Form View button 🖳 **to switch to Form View, click the** New (blank) record button ▶✳ **in the navigation bar, then enter the record shown in** FIGURE C-10

 For new records, "Adventure" is provided as the default value for the Category combo box, but you can change it by typing a new value or selecting one from the list. With the labels right-aligned, they are much closer to the data in the text boxes that they describe.

FIGURE C-9: Using the Property Sheet

FIGURE C-10: Modified Tours Entry Form

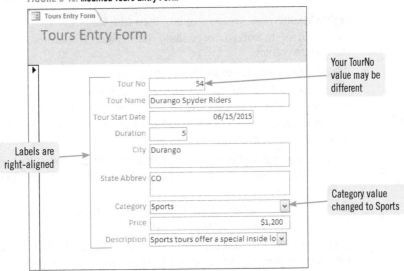

TABLE C-4: Common form controls

name	used to	bound	unbound
Label	Provide consistent descriptive text as you navigate from record to record; the label is the most common type of unbound control and can also be used as a hyperlink to another database object, external file, or Web page		•
Text box	Display, edit, or enter data for each record from an underlying record source; the text box is the most common type of bound control	•	
List box	Display a list of possible data entries	•	
Combo box	Display a list of possible data entries for a field, and provide a text box for an entry from the keyboard; combines the list box and text box controls	•	
Tab control	Create a three-dimensional aspect on a form		•
Check box	Display "yes" or "no" answers for a field; if the box is checked, it means "yes"	•	
Toggle button	Display "yes" or "no" answers for a field; if the button is pressed, it means "yes"	•	
Option button	Display a choice for a field	•	
Option group	Display and organize choices (usually presented as option buttons) for a field	•	
Line and Rectangle	Draw lines and rectangles on the form		•
Command button	Provide an easy way to initiate a command or run a macro		•

Access 2013

Create Calculations

Learning
Outcomes
• Build calculations
 on a form
• Move controls on
 a form

Text boxes are generally used to display data from underlying fields. The connection between the text box and field is defined by the **Control Source property** on the Data tab of the Property Sheet for that text box. A text box control can also display a calculation. To create a calculation in a text box, you enter an expression instead of a field name in the Control Source property. An **expression** is a combination of field names, operators (such as +, –, /, and *), and functions (such as Sum, Count, or Avg) that results in a single value. Sample expressions are shown in TABLE C-5. **CASE** ▶ *Samantha Hooper asks you to add a text box to the Tours Entry Form to calculate the tour end date. You can add a text box in Form Design View to accomplish this.*

STEPS

1. **Right-click the** Tours Entry Form tab, **then click** Design View
 You want to add the tour end date calculation just below the Duration text box. First, you'll resize the City and StateAbbrev fields.

2. **Click the** City label, **press and hold** [Shift], **click the** City text box, **click the** State Abbrev label, **click the** StateAbbrev text box **to select the four controls together, release** [Shift], **click the** ARRANGE tab, **click the** Size/Space button, **then click** To Shortest
 With the City and StateAbbrev fields resized, you're ready to move them to make room for the new control to calculate the tour end date.

QUICK TIP
You can also press an arrow key to move a selected control.

TROUBLE
If you position the new text box incorrectly, click ↰ on the Quick Access toolbar and try again.

3. **Click a blank spot on the form to deselect the four controls, click the** StateAbbrev text box, **use the** ⛭ **pointer to move it down, click the** City text box, **then use the** ⛭ **pointer to move it down**
 To add the calculation to determine the tour end date (the tour start date plus the duration), start by adding a new text box to the form between the Duration and City text boxes.

4. **Click the** DESIGN tab, **click the** Text Box button [abl] **in the Controls group, then click between the Duration and City text boxes to insert the new text box**
 Adding a new text box automatically adds a new label to the left of the text box.

TROUBLE
The number in your label is based on previous work done to the form, so it might vary.

5. **Click the new** Text20 label **on the left, double-click** Text20, **type** Tour End Date, **then press** [Enter]
 With the label updated to correctly identify the text box to the right, you're ready to enter the expression to calculate the tour end date.

QUICK TIP
Move the Property Sheet by dragging its title bar.

6. **Click the** new text box **to select it, click the** Data tab **in the Property Sheet, click the** Control Source property, **type** =[TourStartDate]+[Duration], **then press** [Enter] **to update the form, as shown in** FIGURE C-11
 All expressions entered in a control start with an equal sign (=). When referencing a field name within an expression, [square brackets]—(not parentheses) and not {curly braces}—surround the field name. In an expression, you must type the field name exactly as it was created in Table Design View, but you do not need to match the capitalization.

7. **Click the** View button ▦ **to switch to Form View, click the** value in the Tour Name text box, **click the** Ascending button, **select** 7 in the Duration text box, **type** 5, **then press** [Enter]
 Note that the tour end date, calculated by an expression, automatically changed to five days after the tour start date to reflect the new duration value. The updated Tours Entry Form with the tour date end calculation for the Ames Ski Club is shown in FIGURE C-12.

FIGURE C-11: **Adding a text box to calculate a value**

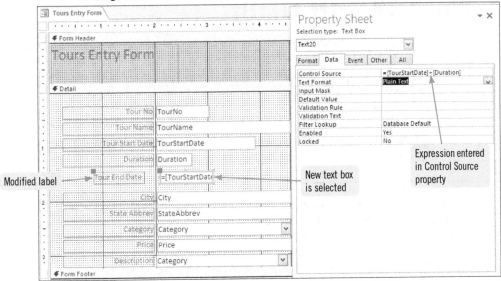

FIGURE C-12: **Displaying the results of a calculation in Form View**

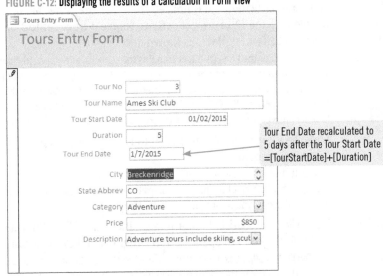

TABLE C-5: **Sample expressions**

sample expression	description
=Sum([Salary])	Uses the **Sum function** to add the values in the Salary field
=[Price] * 1.05	Multiplies the Price field by 1.05 (adds 5% to the Price field)
=[Subtotal] + [Shipping]	Adds the value of the Subtotal field to the value of the Shipping field
=Avg([Freight])	Uses the **Avg function** to display an average of the values in the Freight field
=Date()	Uses the **Date function** to display the current date in the form of mm-dd-yy
="Page " &[Page]	Displays the word Page, a space, and the result of the [Page] field, an Access field that contains the current page number
=[FirstName]& " " &[LastName]	Displays the value of the FirstName and LastName fields in one control, separated by a space
=Left([ProductNumber],2)	Uses the **Left function** to display the first two characters in the ProductNumber field

Modify Tab Order

Learning
Outcomes
• Modify tab order
 properties

After positioning all of the controls on the form, you should check the tab order and tab stops. **Tab order** is the order the focus moves as you press [Tab] in Form View. A **tab stop** refers to whether a control can receive the focus in the first place. By default, the Tab Stop property for all text boxes and combo boxes is set to Yes, but some text boxes, such as those that contain expressions, will not be used for data entry. Therefore, the Tab Stop property for a text box that contains a calculation should be set to No. Unbound controls such as labels and lines do not have a Tab Stop property because they cannot be used to enter or edit data. **CASE** ▶ *You plan to check the tab order of the Tours Entry Form, then change tab stops and tab order as necessary.*

STEPS

1. **Press [Tab] enough times to move through several records, watching the focus move through the bound controls of the form**

 Because the Tour End Date text box is a calculated field, you don't want it to receive the focus. To prevent the Tour End Date text box from receiving the focus, you set its Tab Stop property to No using its Property Sheet. You can work with the Property Sheet in either Layout or Design View.

QUICK TIP
You can also switch between views using the View buttons in the lower-right corner of the window.

2. **Right-click the** Tours Entry Form tab, **click** Design View, **click the** text box **with the Tour End Date calculation if it is not selected, click the** Other tab **in the Property Sheet, double-click the** Tab Stop property **to toggle it from Yes to** No, **then change the Name property to** TourEndDate, **as shown in** FIGURE C-13

 The Other tab of the Property Sheet contains the properties you need to change the tab stop and tab order. The **Tab Stop property** determines whether the field accepts focus, and the **Tab Index property** indicates the numeric tab order for all controls on the form that have the Tab Stop property set to Yes. The **Name property** on the Other tab is also important as it identifies the name of the control, which is used in other areas of the database. To review your tab stop changes, return to Form View.

QUICK TIP
In Form Design View, press [Ctrl][.] to switch to Form View. In Form View, press [Ctrl][,] to switch to Form Design View.

3. **Click the** View button 📇 **to switch to Form View, then press [Tab] nine times to move to the next record**

 Now that the tab stop has been removed from the TourEndDate text box, the tab order flows correctly from the top to the bottom of the form, but skips the calculated field. To review the tab order for the entire form in one dialog box, you must switch to Form Design View.

TROUBLE
If the order of your fields does not match those in FIGURE C-14, move a field by clicking the field selector and then dragging the field up or down.

4. **Right-click the** Tours Entry Form tab, **click** Design View, **then click the** Tab Order button **in the Tools group to open the Tab Order dialog box, as shown in** FIGURE C-14

 The Tab Order dialog box allows you to view and change the tab order by dragging fields up or down using the **field selector** to the left of the field name. Moving fields up and down in this list also renumbers the Tab Index property for the controls in their respective Property Sheets. If you want Access to create a top-to-bottom and left-to-right tab order, click **Auto Order**.

5. **Click** OK **to close the Tab Order dialog box, click the** Property Sheet button **to toggle it off, then click the** Save button 💾 **on the Quick Access toolbar to save your work**

FIGURE C-13: **Using the Property Sheet to set tab properties**

FIGURE C-14: **Tab Order dialog box**

Layout positioning

If the controls on a form are organized in a layout, you can quickly modify that layout by modifying the margins, padding, and anchoring options of the layout. Each of these features is found in the Position group on the ARRANGE tab in Form Design View. **Margin** refers to the space between the outer edge of the control and the data displayed inside the control. **Padding** is the space between the controls. **Anchoring** allows you to tie controls together so you can work with them as a group.

Insert an Image

Learning
Outcomes
• Insert an image on
 a form
• Modify form
 sections
• Print a selected
 record

Graphic images, such as pictures, logos, or clip art, can add style and professionalism to a form. The form section in which you place the images is significant. **Form sections** determine where controls are displayed and printed; they are described in TABLE C-6. For example, if you add a company logo to the Form Header section, the image appears at the top of the form in Form View as well as at the top of a printout. If you add the same image to the Detail section, it prints next to each record in the printout because the Detail section is printed for every record. **CASE** *Samantha Hooper suggests that you add the Quest logo to the top of the Tours Entry Form. You can add the control in either Layout or Design View, but if you want to place it in the Form Header section, you have to work in Design View.*

STEPS

1. **Click the** Form Header section bar, **click the** Insert Image button **in the Controls group, click** Browse, **then navigate to the location where you store your Data Files**
 The Insert Picture dialog box opens, prompting you for the location of the image.

2. **Double-click** QuestLogo.bmp, **then click in the Form Header section at about the 3" mark on the horizontal ruler**
 The QuestLogo image is added to the right side of the Form Header. You want to resize it to about 1" × 1".

3. **With the QuestLogo image still selected, use the** ↖ **pointer to drag the** lower-right corner **of the image up and to the left so that the image is about 1" × 1", then drag the top edge of the Detail section up using the** ⊕ **pointer, as shown in** FIGURE C-15
 When an image or control is selected in Design View, you can use **sizing handles,** which are small squares at the corners of the selection box. Drag a handle to resize the image or control. With the form completed, you open it in Form View to observe the changes.

4. **Click the** Save button 🖫 **on the Quick Access toolbar, then click the** View button 🖳 **to switch to Form View**
 You decide to add one more record with your final Tours Entry Form.

5. **Click the** New (blank) record button ▶⁎ **in the navigation bar, then enter the new record shown in** FIGURE C-16, **using your last name in the TourName field**
 Now print only this single new record.

6. **Click the** FILE **tab, click** Print **in the navigation bar, click** Print, **click the** Selected Record(s) **option button, then click** OK

7. **Close the Tours Entry Form, click** Yes **if prompted to save it, close the QuestTravel-C.accdb database, then exit Access 2013**

TABLE C-6: Form sections

section	controls placed in this section print:
Form Header	Only once at the top of the first page of the printout
Detail	Once for every record
Form Footer	Only once at the end of the last page of the printout

FIGURE C-15: **Adding an image to the Form Header section**

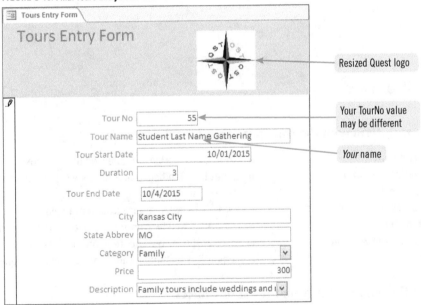

Form Header section bar

Insert Image button

3" mark on the ruler

Resize the Quest logo to be about 1" × 1"

Resize the Detail section

FIGURE C-16: **Final Tours Entry Form with new record**

Resized Quest logo

Your TourNo value may be different

Your name

Applying a background image

A **background image** is an image that fills the entire form or report, appearing "behind" the other controls. A background image is sometimes called a watermark image. To add a background image, use the Picture property for the form or report to browse for the image that you want to use in the background.

Practice

Concepts Review

Label each element of Form Design View shown in FIGURE C-17.

FIGURE C-17

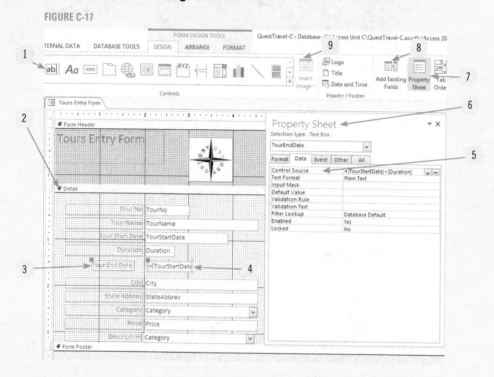

Match each term with the statement that best describes it.

10. **Bound control**
11. **Calculated control**
12. **Detail section**
13. **Database designer**
14. **Tab order**
15. **Form Footer section**

a. Created by entering an expression in a text box
b. Controls placed here print once for every record in the underlying record source
c. Used on a form to display data from a field
d. Controls placed here print only once at the end of the printout
e. The way the focus moves from one bound control to the next in Form View
f. Responsible for building and maintaining tables, queries, forms, and reports

Select the best answer from the list of choices.

16. **Every element on a form is called a(n):**
 a. Property.
 b. Control.
 c. Item.
 d. Tool.

17. **Which of the following is probably *not* a graphic image?**
 a. Logo
 b. Calculation
 c. Clip art
 d. Picture

18. **The most common bound control is the:**
 a. Text box.
 b. Label.
 c. Combo box.
 d. List box.

19. **The most common unbound control is the:**
 a. Combo box.
 b. Command button.
 c. Label.
 d. Text box.

20. **Which form view *cannot* be used to view data?**
 a. Datasheet
 b. Layout
 c. Preview
 d. Design

Skills Review

1. **Use the Form Wizard.**
 a. Start Access and open the RealEstate-C.accdb database from the location where you store your Data Files. Enable content if prompted.
 b. Click the CREATE tab, then use the Form Wizard to create a form based on all of the fields in the Realtors table. Use a Columnar layout and type **Realtor Entry Form** to title the form.
 c. Add a *new* record with *your* name in the RFirst and RLast text boxes. Note that the RealtorNo field is an AutoNumber field that is automatically incremented as you enter your first and last names. Enter your school's telephone number for the RPhone field value, and enter **4** as the AgencyNo field value.
 d. Save and close the Realtor Entry Form.

2. **Create a split form.**
 a. Click the Agencies table in the Navigation Pane, click the CREATE tab, click the More Forms button, then click Split Form.
 b. Switch to Form View and close the Property Sheet if it opens.
 c. Click the record selector in the lower pane for AgencyNo 3, Emerald Point Realtors, then click the Delete button in the Records group to delete this realtor. Click OK when prompted that you cannot delete this record because there are related records in the Realtors table.
 d. Navigate to the AgencyNo 4, Hollister Real Estate, record in either the upper or lower pane of the split form. Change 7744 Pokeberry Lane to **12345 Amanda Drive**.
 e. Right-click the Agencies form tab, click Close, click Yes when prompted to save changes, type **Agencies Split Form** as the name of the form, then click OK.

3. **Use Form Layout View.**
 a. Open the Realtor Entry Form in Layout View.
 b. Modify the labels on the left to read: **Realtor Number**, **Realtor First Name**, **Realtor Last Name**, **Realtor Phone**, **Agency Number**.
 c. Modify the text color of the labels to be black.
 d. Resize the RFirst, RLast, and RPhone text boxes on the right to be the same width as the RealtorNo and AgencyNo text boxes.
 e. Save the Realtor Entry Form.

4. **Add fields to a form.**
 a. Open the Field List, show all the tables, then expand the Agencies table to display its fields.
 b. Drag the AgencyName field to the form, then move the AgencyName label and combo box below the Agency Number controls.
 c. Modify the AgencyName label to read **Agency Name**.
 d. Modify the text color of the Agency Name label to black.
 e. Close the Field List and save and close the Realtor Entry Form.

Skills Review (continued)

5. Modify form controls.

a. Reopen the Realtor Entry Form in Layout View, then use the Align Right button on the HOME tab to right-align each of the labels in the left column.

b. Save the form, switch to Form View, then use the Agency Name combo box to change the Agency Name to **Marvin and Pam Realtors** for Realtor Number 1.

c. If the combo box is not wide enough to display the entire entry for Marvin and Pam Realtors, switch back to Layout View and widen the combo box as much as needed to display the entire entry.

d. In Layout View, resize and move all controls so that the labels are lined up on the left and the text boxes are lined up on the right, as shown in FIGURE C-18.

FIGURE C-18

6. Create calculations.

a. Switch to Form Design View, then add a text box below the Realtor Entry Form label in the Form Header section. Delete the Text14 label that is created when you add a new text box. The number in your label is based on previous work done to the form, so it might vary.

b. Widen the text box to be almost as wide as the entire form, then enter the following expression into the text box, which will add the words *Information for* to the realtor's first name, a space, and then the realtor's last name.
="Information for "&[RFirst]&" "&[RLast]

c. Save the form, then view it in Form View. Be sure the new text box correctly displays spaces in the text. Return to Design View to edit the expression if #Name? appears, which indicates that the expression was entered incorrectly.

d. In Form View, change the Realtor Last Name for Realtor Number 1 from West to **South**. Tab to the RPhone text box to observe how the expression in the Form Header automatically updates.

e. Tab through several records, observing the expression in the Form Header section.

7. Modify tab order.

a. Switch to Form Design View, then open the Property Sheet.

b. Select the new text box with the expression in the Form Header section, then change the Tab Stop property from Yes to No.

c. Select the RealtorNo text box in the Detail section, then change the Tab Stop property from Yes to No. (AutoNumber fields cannot be edited, so they do not need to have a tab stop.)

d. Close the Property Sheet.

e. Save the form and view it in Form View. Tab through the form to make sure that the tab order is sequential and skips the expression in the Form Header as well as the Realtor Number text box. Use the Tab Order button on the DESIGN tab in Form Design View to modify tab order, if necessary.

8. Insert an image.

a. Switch to Design View, then click the Form Header section bar.

b. Add the ForSale.bmp image to the right side of the Form Header, then resize the image to be about 1" × 1".

c. Remove extra blank space in the Form Header section by dragging the top edge of the Detail section up as far as possible.

d. Drag the right edge of the form as far as possible to the left.

e. Save the form, then switch to Form View. Move through the records, observing the calculated field from record to record to make sure it is calculating correctly.

f. Find the record with your name, as shown in FIGURE C-18, and if requested by your instructor, print only that record.

g. Close the Realtor Entry Form, close the RealEstate-C.accdb database, then exit Access.

Independent Challenge 1

As the manager of the scuba divers branch of the Quest Specialty Travel tour company, you have developed a database to help manage scuba dives. In this exercise, you'll create a data entry form to manage the dive trips.

a. Start Access, then open the Dives-C.accdb database from the location where you store your Data Files. Enable content if prompted.

b. Using the Form Wizard, create a form that includes all the fields in the DiveTrips table and uses the Columnar layout, then type **Dive Trip Entry** as the title of the form.

c. Switch to Layout View, then delete the ID text box and label.

d. Using Form Design View, use the [Shift] key to select all of the text boxes except the last one for TripReport, then resize them to the shortest size using the To Shortest option on the Size/Space button on the ARRANGE tab.

e. Using Form Design View, resize the Location, City, State/Province, Country, and Lodging text boxes to be no wider than the Rating text box.

f. Using Form Design View, move and resize the controls, as shown in FIGURE C-19. Once the controls are resized, drag the top of the Form Footer section up to remove the extra blank space in the Detail section.

g. Using Form Layout View, modify the labels and alignment of the labels, as shown in FIGURE C-19. Note that there are spaces between the words in the labels, the labels are right-aligned, and the text boxes are left-aligned. Use a dark blue color for the labels and black for the text in the text boxes.

h. In Form View, find the Great Barrier Reef tour. Edit the State/Province, Certification Diving, and Trip Report fields, as shown in FIGURE C-19 for the TripReport field using *your* name.

i. Save the form, then if requested by your instructor, print only the record with your name.

j. Close the Dive Trip Entry form, close the Dives-C.accdb database, then exit Access 2013.

FIGURE C-19

Access 2013

Independent Challenge 2

You have built an Access database to track membership in a community service club. The database tracks member names and addresses as well as their status in the club, which moves from rank to rank as the members contribute increased hours of service to the community.

a. Start Access, then open the Membership-C.accdb database from the location where you store your Data Files. Enable content if prompted.

b. Using the Form Wizard, create a form based on all of the fields of the Members table and only the DuesOwed field in the Status table.

c. View the data by Members, use a Columnar layout, then enter **Member Information** as the title of the form.

d. Enter a new record with *your* name and the school name, address, and phone number of your school for the Company and address fields. Give yourself a StatusNo entry of **1**. In the DuesPaid field, enter **75**. DuesOwed automatically displays 100 because that value is pulled from the Status table and is based on the entry in the StatusNo field, which links the Members table to the Status table.

e. In Layout View, add a text box to the form and move it below the DuesOwed text box.

f. Open the Property Sheet for the new text box, display the Data tab, and in the Control Source property of the new text box, enter the expression that calculates the balance between DuesOwed and DuesPaid: **=[DuesOwed]-[DuesPaid]**.

g. Open the Property Sheet for the new label, and change the Caption property on the Format tab for the new label to **Balance**.

h. Right-align all of the labels in the first column.

i. Set the Tab Stop property for the text box that contains the calculated Balance to **No**, then close the Property Sheet.

j. In Layout or Design View, resize DuesPaid and DuesOwed text boxes to be the same width as the new Balance text box, then right-align all data within the three text boxes.

FIGURE C-20

Member Information

FName	Student First
LName	Student Last
Company	JCCC
Street	12345 College Blvd
City	Overland Park
State	KS
Zip	66213
Phone	(444) 850-5555
StatusNo	1
DuesPaid	$85.00
DuesOwed	$100.00
Balance	$15.00

Independent Challenge 2 (continued)

k. Open the Property Sheet for the text box that contains the expression, and change the Format property on the Format tab to Currency. Close the Property Sheet.

l. Switch to Form Design View, then drag the right edge of the form to the 7" mark on the horizontal ruler. The horizontal ruler is located just above the Form Header section.

m. Click a blank spot on the right edge of the form, click the Insert Image button on the DESIGN tab, browse for the People.jpg image, then insert it on the right side of the form in the Detail section. (*Hint*: You will need to change the Web-Ready Image Files list in the Insert Picture dialog box to All Files to find .jpg images.)

n. Resize the picture to be about 2" × 2", then drag the right edge of the form to the left as far as possible. Also drag the top edge of the Form Footer up as far as possible to eliminate blank space in the Detail section.

o. Save the form, find the record with your name, change the DuesPaid value to **85**, then move and resize controls as necessary to match FIGURE C-20.

p. If requested by your instructor, print only the record with your name.

q. Save and close the Member Information form, then close the Membership-C.accdb database and exit Access 2013.

Independent Challenge 3

You have built an Access database to organize the deposits at a recycling center. Various clubs regularly deposit recyclable material, which is measured in pounds when the deposits are made.

a. Open the Recycle-C.accdb database from the location where you store your Data Files. Enable content if prompted.

b. Using the Form Wizard, create a form based on all of the fields in the CenterDeposits query. View the data by Deposits, use the Columnar layout, and title the form **Deposit Listing**.

c. Switch to Layout View, then make each label bold.

d. Modify the labels so that CenterName is **Center Name**, DepositDate is **Deposit Date**, and ClubName is **Club Name**.

e. Switch to Form Design View and resize the CenterName and ClubName text boxes so they are the same height and width as the Weight text box, as shown in FIGURE C-21.

f. Switch to Form View, find and change any entry of Dallas Jaycees in the ClubName field to *your* last name, then print one record with your name if requested by your instructor.

g. Using Form View of the Deposit Listing form, filter for all records with your last name in the ClubName field.

h. Using Form View of the Deposit Listing form, sort the filtered records in descending order on the DepositDate field.

i. Preview the first record, as shown in FIGURE C-21. If requested by your instructor, print the first record.

j. Save and close the Deposit Listing form, close the Recycle-C.accdb database, then exit Access.

FIGURE C-21

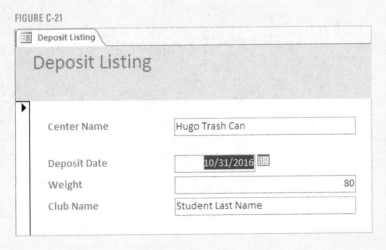

Independent Challenge 4: Explore

One way you can use an Access database on your own is to record and track your job search efforts. In this exercise, you will develop a form to help you enter data into your job-tracking database.

a. Start Access and open the Jobs-C.accdb database from the location where you store your Data Files. Enable content if prompted.

b. Click the CREATE tab, then use the Form Wizard to create a new form based on all the fields of both the Employers and Positions tables.

c. View the data by Employers, use a Datasheet layout for the subform, accept the default names for the form and subform, then open the form to view information.

d. Use Layout View and Design View to modify the form labels, text box positions, alignment, and sizes, as shown in FIGURE C-22. Note that the columns within the subform have been resized to display all of the data in the subform.

e. Change the CompanyName of IBM in the first record to *Your* **Last Name's Software**, and if instructed to create a printout, print only that record. Close the Employers form.

f. Click the Employers table in the Navigation Pane, then use the Split Form option on the More Forms button of the CREATE tab to create a split form on the Employers table. Close and save the split form with the name **Employers Split Form**.

FIGURE C-22

PositionID	Title	CareerArea	AnnualSalary	Desirability	EmployerID
1	Marketing Representative	Computers	$35,000.00	5	1
2	Systems Engineer	Computers	$37,000.00	5	1
* (New)					1

Using Forms

Independent Challenge 4: Explore (continued)

g. Open the Employers Split Form in Form View, and change the address and phone number information for EmployerID 1 to *your* school's address and phone information, as shown in FIGURE C-23.

h. Navigate through all five records, then back to EmployerID 1, observing both the upper and lower panes of the split form as you move from record to record.

i. Open the Employers form and navigate forward and backward through all five records to study the difference between the Employers form, which uses a form/subform versus the Employers Split Form. Even though both the Employers form and Employers Split Form show datasheets in the bottom halves of the forms, they are fundamentally very different. The split form is displaying the records of only the Employers table, whereas the Employers form is using a subform to display related records from the Positions table in the lower datasheet. You will learn more about forms and subforms in later units.

j. Close the Jobs-C.accdb database, then exit Access.

FIGURE C-23

Employers Split Form

Employers

EmployerID	1	EmpCity	Your School's City
CompanyName	Your Last Name's Software	EmpState	IA
EmpStreet	Your School's Street	EmpZip	99999
		EmpPhone	999-999-9999

EmployerID ▾	CompanyName ▾	EmpStreet ▾	EmpCity ▾	EmpState ▾	EmpZip ▾	EmpPhone ▾
1	Your Last Name's Sc	Your School's S	Your School's C	IA	99999	999-999-9999
2	EDS	500 Cricket St	Ames	IA	50010	515-555-3333
3	Google	600 Crocker St	Omaha	NE	66000	616-555-2222
4	Apple	700 Beetle St	Lincoln	NE	66110	616-555-1111
5	Bass Pro Shops	800 Ladybug St	Sioux City	NE	66220	616-555-3333
* (New)						

Record: I◄ ◄ 1 of 5 ► ►I ► ⛧ No Filter Search

Visual Workshop

Open the Baseball-C.accdb database, enable content if prompted, then use the Split Form tool to create a form named **Players**, as shown in FIGURE C-24, based on the Players table. Resize the PlayerLast text box as shown. Modify the labels as shown. View the data in Form View, and sort the records in ascending order by last name. Change the first, last, and nickname of the Henry Aaron record in the first record to *your* name, and if instructed to create a printout, print only that record. Save and close the Players form, close the Baseball-C.accdb database, then exit Access.

FIGURE C-24

Using Reports

CASE ▶ Samantha Hooper, a tour developer at Quest Specialty Travel, asks you to produce some reports to help her share and analyze data. A report is an Access object that creates a professional looking printout.

Unit Objectives

After completing this unit, you will be able to:

- Use the Report Wizard
- Use Report Layout View
- Review report sections
- Apply group and sort orders
- Add subtotals and counts
- Resize and align controls
- Format a report
- Create mailing labels

Files You Will Need

QuestTravel-D.accdb
RealEstate-D.accdb
Conventions-D.accdb
Membership-D.accdb

Recycle-D.accdb
JobSearch-D.accdb
Basketball-D.accdb

Use the Report Wizard

Learning
Outcomes
• Create a report
with the Report
Wizard
• Change page
orientation

A **report** is the primary object you use to print database content because it provides the most formatting, layout, and summary options. A report may include various fonts and colors, clip art and lines, and multiple headers and footers. A report can also calculate subtotals, averages, counts, and other statistics for groups of records. You can create reports in Access by using the **Report Wizard**, a tool that asks questions to guide you through the initial development of the report. Your responses to the Report Wizard determine the record source, style, and layout of the report. The **record source** is the table or query that defines the fields and records displayed on the report. The Report Wizard also helps you sort, group, and analyze the records. **CASE** *You use the Report Wizard to create a report to display the tours within each state.*

STEPS

1. **Start Access, open the** QuestTravel-D.accdb database, **enable content if prompted, click the** CREATE **tab on the Ribbon, then click the** Report Wizard button **in the Reports group**

 The Report Wizard starts, prompting you to select the fields you want on the report. You can select fields from one or more tables or queries.

2. **Click the** Tables/Queries list arrow, **click** Table: States, **double-click the** StateName field, **click the** Tables/Queries list arrow, **click** Table: Tours, **click the** Select All Fields button >> , **click** StateAbbrev **in the Selected Fields list, then click the** Remove Field button <

 By selecting the StateName field from the States table, and all fields from the Tours table except the StateAbbrev field, you have all of the fields you need for the report, as shown in FIGURE D-1.

3. **Click** Next, **then click** by States **if it is not already selected**

 Choosing "by States" groups together the records for each state. In addition to record-grouping options, the Report Wizard later asks if you want to sort the records within each group. You can use the Report Wizard to specify up to four fields to sort in either ascending or descending order.

4. **Click** Next, **click** Next **again to include no additional grouping levels, click the** first sort list arrow, **click** TourStartDate, **then click** Next

 The last questions in the Report Wizard deal with report appearance and the report title.

5. **Click the** Stepped option button, **click the** Landscape option button, **click** Next, **type** Tours by State **for the report title, then click** Finish

 The Tours by State report opens in **Print Preview**, which displays the report as it appears when printed, as shown in FIGURE D-2. The records are grouped by state, the first state being California, and then sorted in ascending order by the TourStartDate field within each state. Reports are **read-only objects**, meaning you can use them to read and display data but not to change (write to) data. As you change data using tables, queries, or forms, reports constantly display those up-to-date edits just like all of the other Access objects.

6. **Scroll down to see the second grouping section on the report for the state of Colorado, then click the** Next Page button ▶ **in the navigation bar to see the second page of the report**

 Even in **landscape orientation** (11" wide by 8.5" tall as opposed to **portrait orientation**, which is 8.5" wide by 11" tall), the fields on the Tours by State report may not fit on one sheet of paper. The labels in the column headings and the data in the columns need to be resized to improve the layout. Depending on your monitor, you might need to scroll to the right to display all the fields on this page.

FIGURE D-1: **Selecting fields for a report using the Report Wizard**

FIGURE D-2: **Tours by State report in Print Preview**

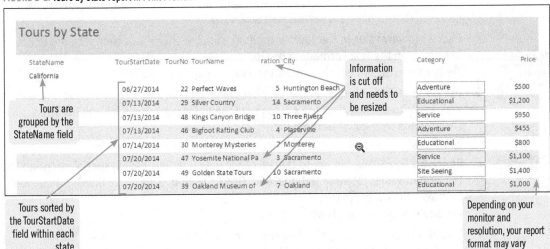

Changing page orientation

To change page orientation from Portrait (8.5" wide by 11" tall) to Landscape (11" wide by 8.5" tall) and vice versa, click the Portrait or Landscape button on the PRINT PREVIEW tab when viewing the report in Print Preview. To switch to Print Preview, right-click the report in the Navigation Pane, and then choose Print Preview on the shortcut menu.

Use Report Layout View

Learning
Outcomes
• Move and resize
 controls in Layout
 View
• Modify labels

Reports have multiple views that you use for various report-building and report-viewing activities. Although some tasks can be accomplished in more than one view, each view has a primary purpose to make your work with reports as easy and efficient as possible. The different report views are summarized in TABLE D-1. **CASE** *Samantha Hooper asks you to modify the Tours by State report so that all of the fields fit comfortably across one sheet of paper in landscape orientation.*

STEPS

TROUBLE
If the Field List window opens, close it.

1. **Right-click the** Tours by State report tab, **then click** Layout View
 Layout View opens and applies a grid to the report that helps you resize, move, and position controls. You decide to narrow the City column to make room for the Price data.

2. **Click** Huntington Beach **(or any value in the City column), then use the ↔ pointer to drag the right edge of the City column to the left to narrow it to about half of its current size, as shown in** FIGURE D-3
 By narrowing the City column, you create extra space in the report.

3. **Click** $500 **(or any value in the Price column), use the ⁺⃗ pointer to drag the Price values to the left of the Category column, click the** Price label, **then use ⁺⃗ to move the Price label to the left of the Category label**
 All the columns are now within the boundaries of a single sheet of paper in landscape orientation. You also notice that centering some data would make it easier to read.

4. **Click** 22 **(or any value in the TourNo column), click the** HOME **tab, then click the** Center button ▤ **in the Text Formatting group**
 The TourName column needs more space to completely display the tour names.

QUICK TIP
Resizing with ↔ instead of moving with ⁺⃗ maintains the vertical alignment of the controls.

5. **Use ↔ to resize both sides of the** TourStartDate, TourNo, **and** TourName **columns and their labels to the left, then use ↔ to resize the** Category, Price, City, **and** Duration **columns and their labels to the right**
 Now the report has enough room to resize the TourName column and the Duration label.

QUICK TIP
You can use the Undo button arrow ↶ ▾ to undo many actions in Layout View.

6. **Resize the** TourName **column so that all of the data is visible, paying special attention to the longest value, Yosemite National Park Great Cleanup, then resize the** Duration label **to display the complete text**
 You can also rename labels in Report Layout View.

7. **Click the** StateName label, **click between the words** State **and** Name, **press the** [Spacebar] **so that the label reads State Name, then modify the** TourStartDate, TourNo, **and** TourName **labels to contain spaces as well**

8. **Continue resizing the columns so that all of the data is visible and your report looks like** FIGURE D-4

FIGURE D-3: **Modifying the column width in Report Layout View**

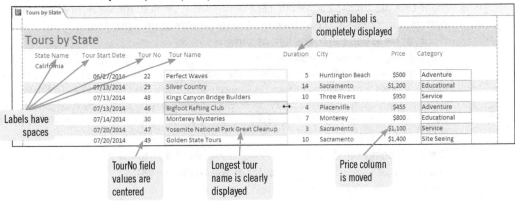

Resizing the City
field to make room
for other information

FIGURE D-4: **Final Tours by State report in Report Layout View**

Duration label is
completely displayed

Labels have
spaces

TourNo field
values are
centered

Longest tour
name is clearly
displayed

Price column
is moved

TABLE D-1: **Report views**

view	primary purpose
Report View	To quickly review the report without page breaks
Print Preview	To review each page of an entire report as it will appear if printed
Layout View	To modify the size, position, or formatting of controls; shows live data as you modify the report, making it the tool of choice when you want to change the appearance and positioning of controls on a report while also reviewing live data
Design View	To work with report sections or to access the complete range of controls and report properties; Design View does not display data

Review Report Sections

Learning
Outcomes
• Navigate through
 report sections
 and pages
• Resize the width of
 the report
• Work with error
 indicators

Report **sections** determine where and how often controls in that section print in the final report. For example, controls in the Report Header section print only once at the beginning of the report, but controls in the Detail section print once for every record the report displays. TABLE D-2 describes report sections. **CASE** ▶ *You and Samantha Hooper preview the Tours by State report to review and understand report sections.*

STEPS

1. **Right-click the** Tours by State tab, **click** Print Preview, **then scroll up and click the light blue bar at the top of the report if you need to zoom in to display the first page of the report, as shown in** FIGURE D-5

 The first page shows four sections: Report Header, Page Header, StateAbbreviation Header, and Detail.

2. **Click the** Next Page button ▶ **on the navigation bar to move to the second page of the report**

 If the second page of the report does not contain data, it means that the report may be too wide to fit on a single sheet of paper. You fix that problem in Report Design View.

QUICK TIP
If your report is too
wide, you will see a
green **error
indicator** in the
upper-left corner of
the report. Pointing
to the error icon ⬦
displays a message
about the error.

3. **Right-click the** Tours by State tab, **click** Design View, **scroll to the far right using the bottom horizontal scroll bar, then use the ↔ pointer to drag the** right edge of the report **as far as you can to the left, as shown in** FIGURE D-6

 In Report Design View, you can work with the report sections and make modifications to the report that you cannot make in other views, such as narrowing the width. Report Design View does not display any data, though. For your report to fit on one page in landscape orientation, you need to move all of the controls within the 10.5" mark on the horizontal **ruler** using the default 0.25" left and right margins. You will practice fixing this problem by moving all controls within the 10" mark on the ruler to make sure they all fit on the landscape printout.

TROUBLE
Be sure that the right
edge of the page
calculation is within
the 10" mark on
the ruler.

4. **Use the ⬧ pointer to drag the** page calculation **about 0.5" to the left, then use ↔ to drag the** right edge of the report **as far as you can to the left**

 To review your modifications, show the report in Print Preview.

QUICK TIP
You can also use
the View buttons in
the lower-right
corner of a report to
switch views.

5. **Right-click the** Tours by State tab, **click** Print Preview, **click** ▶ **to navigate to the last page of the report, then click the report to zoom in and out to examine the page, as shown in** FIGURE D-7

 Previewing each page of the report helps you confirm that no blank pages are created and allows you to examine how the different report sections print on each page.

TABLE D-2: Report sections

section	where does this section print?
Report Header	At the top of the first page
Page Header	At the top of every page (but below the Report Header on the first page)
Group Header	Before every group of records
Detail	Once for every record
Group Footer	After every group of records
Page Footer	At the bottom of every page
Report Footer	At the end of the report

© 2014 Cengage Learning

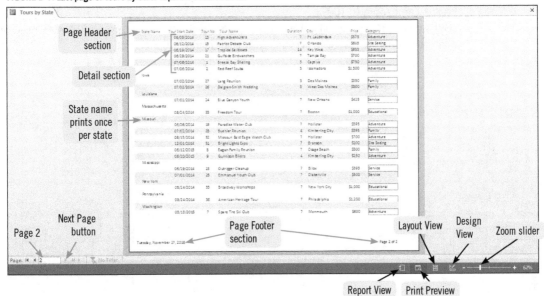

Apply Group and Sort Orders

Learning
Outcomes
• Group and sort
 records in a report
• Copy and paste
 controls

Grouping means to sort records by a particular field *plus* provide a header and/or footer section before or after each group of sorted records. For example, if you group records by the StateName field, the Group Header is called the StateName Header and the Group Footer is called the StateName Footer. The StateName Header section appears once for each state in the report, immediately before the records in that state. The StateName Footer section also appears once for each state in the report, immediately after the records for that state. **CASE** ▶ *The records in the Tours by State report are currently grouped by the StateAbbreviation field. Samantha Hooper asks you to further group the records by the Category field (Adventure, Educational, and Family, for example) within each state.*

STEPS

1. **Click the** Close Print Preview button **to return to Report Design View, then click the** Group & Sort button **in the Grouping & Totals group to open the Group, Sort, and Total pane**

 Currently, the records are grouped by the StateAbbreviation field and further sorted by the TourStartDate field. To add the Category field as a grouping field within each state, you work with the Group, Sort, and Total pane in Report Design View.

2. **Click the** Add a group button **in the Group, Sort, and Total pane, click** Category, **then click the** Move up button 🔼 **on the right side of the Group, Sort, and Total pane so that Category is positioned between StateAbbreviation and TourStartDate**

 A Category Header section is added to Report Design View just below the StateAbbreviation Header section. You move the Category control from the Detail section to the Category Header section so it prints only once for each new Category instead of once for each record in the Detail section.

3. **Right-click the** Category combo box **in the Detail section, click** Cut **on the shortcut menu, right-click the** Category Header section, **click** Paste, **then use the** ⌖ **pointer to drag the** Category combo box **to the right to position it as shown in** FIGURE D-8

 Now that you've moved the Category combo box to the Category Header, it will print only once per category within each state. You no longer need the Category label in the Page Header section.

4. **Click the** Category label **in the Page Header section, press [Delete], then switch to Print Preview and zoom to 100%**

 The Tours by State report should look like FIGURE D-9. Notice that the records are now grouped by category within state. Detail records are further sorted in ascending order by the tour start date.

FIGURE D-8: Group, Sort, and Total pane and new Category Header section

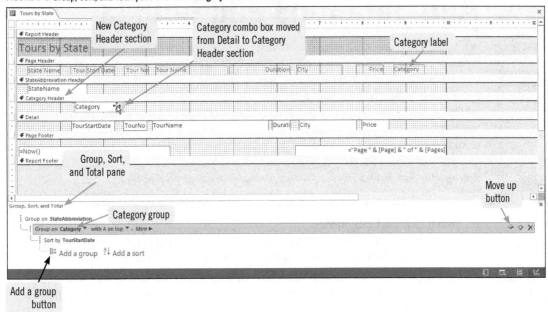

FIGURE D-9: Tours by State report grouped by category within state

Tours by State

StateAbbreviation Header section

State Name	Tour Start Date	Tour No	Tour Name		Duration	City	Price
California							

Category Header section

Adventure

	06/27/2014	22	Perfect Waves		5	Huntington Beach	$500
	07/13/2014	46	Bigfoot Rafting Club		4	Placerville	$455
	08/19/2014	44	Bear Valley Adventures		3	Sacramento	$725
	08/26/2014	45	Black Sheep Hiking Club		14	El Dorado Hills	$525

Detail records are sorted by TourStartDate

Educational

	07/13/2014	29	Silver Country		14	Sacramento	$1,200
	07/14/2014	30	Monterey Mysteries		7	Monterey	$800
	07/20/2014	39	Oakland Museum of Science		7	Oakland	$1,000
	09/14/2014	37	Cactus Language Exploration		7	San Diego	$800
	09/21/2014	38	Water Education Foundation		14	Fresno	$1,300
	09/29/2014	40	Redwood Forest Lab		14	Mill Valley	$1,500

Add Subtotals and Counts

Learning
Outcomes
• Create calculations
 to subtotal and
 count records
• Cut and paste
 controls

In a report, you create a **calculation** by entering an expression into a text box. When a report is previewed or printed, the expression is evaluated and the resulting calculation is placed on the report. An **expression** is a combination of field names, operators (such as +, −, /, and *), and functions that results in a single value. A **function** is a built-in formula, such as Sum or Count, that helps you quickly create a calculation. Notice that every expression starts with an equal sign (=), and when it uses a function, the arguments for the function are placed in (parentheses). **Arguments** are the pieces of information that the function needs to create the final answer. When an argument is a field name, the field name must be surrounded by [square brackets]. **CASE** *Samantha Hooper asks you to add a calculation to the Tours by State report to sum the total number of tour days within each category and within each state.*

STEPS

1. **Switch to Report Design View**

 A logical place to add subtotals for each group is right after that group of records prints, in the Group Footer section. You use the Group, Sort, and Total pane to open Group Footer sections.

TROUBLE
Click Category in the
Group, Sort, and
Total pane to display
the grouping options.

2. **Click the** More button **for the StateAbbreviation field in the Group, Sort, and Total pane, click the** without a footer section list arrow, **click** with a footer section, **then do the same for the** Category field, **as shown in** FIGURE D-10

 With the StateAbbreviation Footer and Category Footer sections open, you're ready to add controls to calculate the total number of tour days within each category and within each state. You use a text box control with an expression to make this calculation.

3. **Click the** Text Box button ⓐⓑⓘ **in the Controls group, then click just below the Duration text box in the Category Footer section**

 Adding a new text box automatically adds a new label to its left. First, you modify the label to identify the information, then you modify the text box to contain the correct expression to sum the number of tour days for that category.

TROUBLE
Depending on your
activity in Report
Design View, you
may see a different
number in the
Text##: label.

4. **Click the** Text19 label **to select it, double-click** Text19, **type** Total days:, **click the** Unbound text box **to select it, click** Unbound **again, type** =Sum([Duration]), **press [Enter], then widen the text box to view the entire expression**

 The expression =Sum([Duration]) uses the Sum function to add the days in the Duration field. Because the expression is entered in the Category Footer section, it will sum all Duration values for that category within that state. To sum the Duration values for each state, the expression needs to be inserted in the StateAbbreviation Footer.

QUICK TIP
Pasting the
expression in the
Report Footer section
would subtotal the
duration values for
the entire report.

5. **Right-click the** =Sum([Duration]) text box, **click** Copy, **right-click the** StateAbbreviation Footer section, **click** Paste, **then press [→] enough times to position the controls in the StateAbbreviation Footer section just below those in the Category Footer section, as shown in** FIGURE D-11

 With the expression copied to the StateAbbreviation Footer section, you're ready to preview your work.

TROUBLE
Drag the top edge of
all section bars up to
eliminate extra blank
space in the report.

6. **Switch to Print Preview, navigate to the last page of the report, then click to zoom so you can see all of the Washington tours**

 As shown in FIGURE D-12, 21 tour days are totaled for the Adventure category, and 3 for the Site Seeing category, which is a total of 24 tour days for the state of Washington. The summary data would look better if it were aligned more directly under the tour Duration values. You resize and align controls in the next lesson.

FIGURE D-10: Opening group footer sections

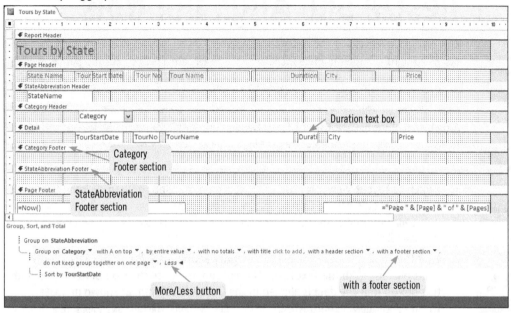

FIGURE D-11: Adding subtotals to group footer sections

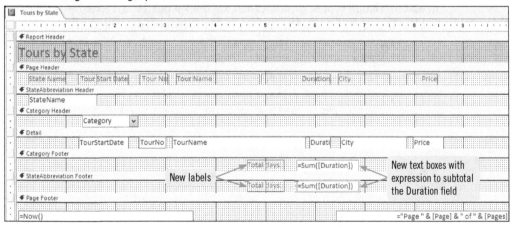

FIGURE D-12: Previewing the new group footer calculations

Resize and Align Controls

Learning
Outcomes
• Align data within
 a control
• Align the borders
 of controls

After you add information to the appropriate section of a report, you might also want to align the data in precise columns and rows to make the information easier to read. To do so, you can use two different types of **alignment** commands. You can left-, right-, or center-align a control *within its own border* using the Align Left ☰, Center ☰, and Align Right ☰ buttons on the HOME tab. You can also align the edges of controls *with respect to one another* using the Left, Right, Top, and Bottom commands on the Align button of the ARRANGE tab in Report Design View. **CASE** ▸ *You decide to resize and align several controls to improve the readability of the Tours by State report. Layout View is a good choice for these tasks.*

1. **Switch to Layout View, click the DESIGN tab on the Ribbon, then click the Group & Sort button to toggle off the Group, Sort, and Total pane**

 You decide to align the expressions that subtotal the number of tour days for each category within the Duration column.

QUICK TIP
You can also use the
buttons on the
FORMAT tab to align
and format text,
including applying
number formats and
increasing or
decreasing decimals.

2. **Click the Total days text box in the Category Footer, click the HOME tab, click the Align Right button ☰ in the Text Formatting group, then use the ↔ pointer to resize the text box so that the data is aligned in the Duration column, as shown in FIGURE D-13**

 With the calculation formatted as desired in the Category Footer, you can quickly apply those modifications to the calculation in the StateAbbreviation Footer as well.

TROUBLE
If you make a
mistake, click the
Undo button ↺
on the Quick Access
toolbar.

3. **Scroll down the report far enough to find and then click the Total days text box in the StateAbbreviation Footer, click ☰, then use the ↔ pointer to resize the text box so that it is the same width as the text box in the Category Footer section**

 With both expressions right-aligned and resized so they line up under the Duration values in the Detail section, they are easier to read on the report.

4. **Scroll the report so you can see all of the Colorado tours, as shown in FIGURE D-14**

 You can apply resize, alignment, or formatting commands to more than one control at a time. TABLE D-3 provides techniques for selecting more than one control at a time in Report Design View.

Precisely moving and resizing controls

You can move and resize controls using the mouse or other pointing device, but you can move controls more precisely using the keyboard. Pressing the arrow keys while holding [Ctrl] moves selected controls one **pixel (picture element)** at a time in the direction of the arrow. Pressing the arrow keys while holding [Shift] resizes selected controls one pixel at a time.

FIGURE D-14: Reviewing the aligned and resized controls

Colorado						
	Adventure					
	06/19/2014	18	Eagle Hiking Club	7	Aspen	$695
	06/29/2014	20	Team Discovery	5	Breckenridge	$550
	01/02/2015	3	Ames Ski Club	7	Breckenridge	$850
	01/13/2015	4	Boy Scout Jamboree	7	Vail	$1,900
	02/15/2015	5	Bridgewater Country	10	Aspen	$1,200
			Total days:	36		
	Family					
	03/11/2015	6	Franklin Family Reunion	3	Breckenridge	$700
			Total days:	3		Data is right-aligned
			Total days:	39		and text boxes are resized

TABLE D-3: Selecting more than one control at a time in Report Design View

technique	description
Click, [Shift]+click	Click a control, then press and hold [Shift] while clicking other controls; each one is selected
Drag a selection box	Drag a selection box (an outline box you create by dragging the pointer in Report Design View); every control that is in or is touched by the edges of the box is selected
Click in the ruler	Click in either the horizontal or vertical ruler to select all controls that intersect the selection line
Drag in the ruler	Drag through either the horizontal or vertical ruler to select all controls that intersect the selection line as it is dragged through the ruler

Format a Report

Learning
Outcomes
• Format controls
 and sections of a
 report
• Add labels to a
 report

Formatting refers to enhancing the appearance of the information. TABLE D-4 lists several of the most popular formatting commands found on the FORMAT tab when you are working in Layout or Report Design View. Although the Report Wizard automatically applies many formatting embellishments, you often want to change the appearance of the report to fit your particular needs. **CASE** *When reviewing the Tours by State report with Samantha, you decide to change the background color of some of the report sections to make the data easier to read. Your first change will be to shade each Category Header and Footer section (rather than alternating sections, the format initially provided by the Report Wizard). To make changes to entire report sections, you work in Report Design View.*

STEPS

QUICK TIP
The quick keystroke
for Undo is [Ctrl][Z].
The quick keystroke
for Redo is [Ctrl][Y].

1. **Switch to Design View, click the** Category Header section bar, **click the** FORMAT **tab on the Ribbon, click the** Alternate Row Color button arrow, **click** No Color, **click the** Shape Fill button, **then click the** Maroon 2 color square, **as shown in** FIGURE D-15

 Make a similar modification by applying a different fill color to the Category Footer section.

2. **Click the** Category Footer section bar, **click the** Alternate Row Color button arrow, **click** No Color, **click the** Shape Fill button, **then click the** Green 2 color square **(just to the right of Maroon 2 in the Standard Colors section)**

 When you use the Alternate Row Color and Shape Fill buttons, you're actually modifying the **Back Color** and **Alternate Back Color** properties in the Property Sheet of the section or control you selected. Background shades can help differentiate parts of the report, but be careful with dark colors as they may print as solid black on some printers and fax machines.

3. **Switch to Layout View to review your modifications**

 The category sections are clearer, but you decide to make one more modification to emphasize the report title.

4. **Click the** Tours by State label **in the Report Header section, click the** HOME **tab, then click the** Bold button **B in the Text Formatting group**

 The report in Layout View should look like FIGURE D-16. You also want to add a label to the Report Footer section to identify yourself.

5. **Switch to Report Design View, drag the** bottom edge of the Report Footer **down about 0.5", click the** Label button *Aa* **in the Controls group, click at the** 1" mark **in the Report Footer, type** Created by *your* name, **press** [Enter], **click the** HOME **tab, then click B in the Text Formatting group**

6. **Save and preview the Tours by State report**

7. **If required by your instructor, print the report, and then close it**

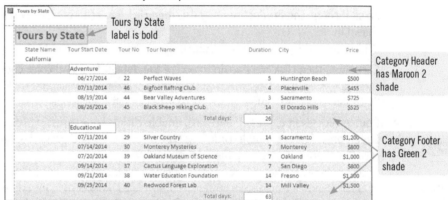

TABLE D-4: **Useful formatting commands**

button	button name	description
B	Bold	Toggles bold on or off for the selected control(s)
I	Italic	Toggles italic on or off for the selected control(s)
U	Underline	Toggles underline on or off for the selected control(s)
≡	Align Left	Left-aligns the selected control(s) within its own border
≡	Center	Centers the selected control(s) within its own border
≡	Align Right	Right-aligns the selected control(s) within its own border
▨	Background Color or Shape Fill	Changes the background color of the selected control(s)
▦	Alternate Row Color	Changes the background color of alternate records in the selected section
A	Font Color	Changes the text color of the selected control(s)
✎	Shape Outline Line Thickness option Line Type option	Changes the border color of the selected control(s) Changes the border style of the selected control(s) Changes the special visual effect of the selected control(s)

Create Mailing Labels

Learning
Outcomes
• Create a report of
labels
• Print specific
pages of a report

Mailing labels are often created to apply to envelopes, postcards, or letters when assembling a mass mailing. They have many other business purposes too, such as applying them to paper file folders or name tags. Any data in your Access database can be converted into labels using the **Label Wizard**, a special report wizard that precisely positions and sizes information for hundreds of standard business labels. **CASE** ▶ *Samantha Hooper asks you to create mailing labels for all of the addresses in the Customers table. You use the Label Wizard to handle this request.*

STEPS

1. **Click the** Customers table **in the Navigation Pane, click the** CREATE **tab, then click the** Labels button **in the Reports group**

 The first Label Wizard dialog box opens. The Filter by manufacturer list box provides over 30 manufacturers of labels. Because Avery is the most common, it is the default choice. With the manufacturer selected, your next task is to choose the product number of the labels you will feed through the printer. The cover on the box of labels you are using provides this information. In this case, you'll be using Avery 5160 labels, a common type of sheet labels used for mailings and other purposes.

2. **Scroll through the Product number list, then click** 5160 **(if not already selected), as shown in** FIGURE D-17

 Note that by selecting a product number, you also specify the dimensions of the label and number of columns.

3. **Click** Next**, then click** Next **again to accept the default font and color choices**

 The third question of the Label Wizard asks how you want to construct your label. You'll add the fields from the Customers table with spaces and line breaks to pattern a standard mailing format.

4. **Double-click** FName**, press [Spacebar], double-click** LName**, press [Enter], double-click** Street**, press [Enter], double-click** City**, type a** comma (,) **and press [Spacebar], double-click** State**, press [Spacebar], then double-click** Zip

 If your prototype label doesn't look exactly like FIGURE D-18, delete the fields in the Prototype label box and try again. Be careful to put a space between the FName and LName fields in the first row, a comma and a space between the City and State fields, and a space between the State and Zip fields.

QUICK TIP

In this case, all data is displayed. This message reminds you to carefully preview the data to make sure long names and addresses fully display within the constraints of the 5160 label dimensions.

5. **Click** Next**, double-click** LName **to select it as a sorting field, click** Next**, click** Finish **to accept the name** Labels Customers **for the new report, then click** OK **if prompted that some data may not be displayed**

 A portion of the new report is shown in FIGURE D-19. It is generally a good idea to print the first page of the report on standard paper to make sure everything is aligned correctly before printing on labels.

QUICK TIP

To include your name on the printout, change Aaron Alito's name to *your* own name in the Customers table, then close and reopen the Labels Customers report.

6. **If requested by your instructor, click the** Print button **on the PRINT PREVIEW tab, click the** From box**, type** 1**, click the** To box**, type** 1**, then click** OK **to print the first page of the report**

7. **Close the Labels Customers report, close the QuestTravel-D.accdb database, then exit Access 2013**

FIGURE D-17: **Label Wizard dialog box**

Product number 5160, dimensions, and number of columns

Avery is the manufacturer

FIGURE D-18: **Building a prototype label**

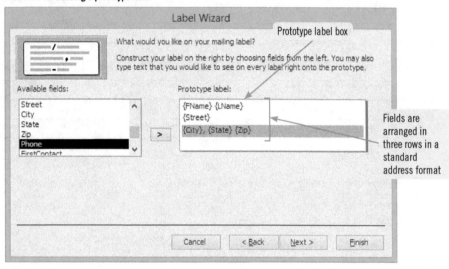

Prototype label box

Fields are arranged in three rows in a standard address format

FIGURE D-19: **Labels Customers report**

Aaron Alito 5989 Washington Ave Hollister, MO 67827	Jacob Alman 2505 McGee St Des Moines, IA 50288	Madison Bonocore 57 West 159th St Cushing, PA 87087
Julia Bouchart 5200 Main St Kansas City, MO 64105	Samantha Braven 600 Elm St Olathe, KS 66031	Daniel Cabriella 52520 W. 505 Ter Lenexa, KS 66215
Tom Camel 520 W 52nd St Kansas City, KS 64105	Kristen Collins 520 W 52nd St Kansas City, KS 64105	Nancy Diverman 466 Lincoln Rd Kansas City, MO 64105

Data is merged to a three-column Avery 5160 label format

Practice

Put your skills into practice with **SAM Projects!** SAM Projects for this unit can be found online. If you have a SAM account, go to www.cengage.com/sam2013 to download the most recent Project Instruction and Start Files.

Concepts Review

Label each element of the Report Design View window shown in FIGURE D-20.

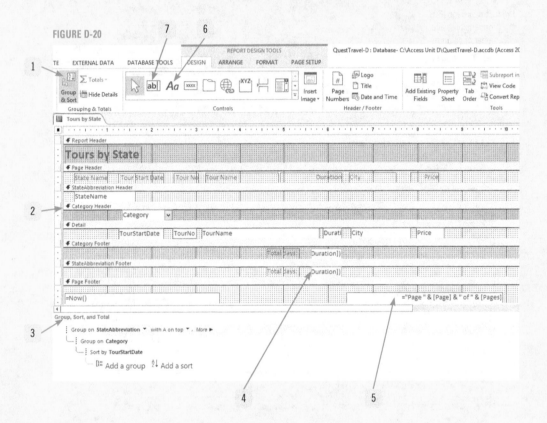

FIGURE D-20

Match each term with the statement that best describes it.

8. **Alignment**
9. **Expression**
10. **Grouping**
11. **Section**
12. **Detail section**
13. **Formatting**
14. **Record source**

a. Left, center, or right are common choices
b. Prints once for every record
c. Used to identify which fields and records are passed to the report
d. Sorting records *plus* providing a header or footer section
e. Determines how controls are positioned on the report
f. A combination of field names, operators, and functions that results in a single value
g. Enhancing the appearance of information displayed in the report

Select the best answer from the list of choices.

15. Which of the following is *not* a valid report view?
 a. Print Preview
 b. Section View
 c. Layout View
 d. Design View

16. Which type of control is most commonly placed in the Detail section?
 a. Image
 b. Line
 c. Text box
 d. Label

17. A title for a report would most commonly be placed in which report section?
 a. Group Footer
 b. Detail
 c. Report Header
 d. Report Footer

18. A calculated expression that presents page numbering information would probably be placed in which report section?
 a. Report Header
 b. Detail
 c. Group Footer
 d. Page Footer

19. Which of the following expressions counts the number of records using the FirstName field?
 a. =Count([FirstName])
 b. =Count[FirstName]
 c. =Count((FirstName))
 d. =Count{FirstName}

20. To align the edges of several controls with each other, you use the alignment commands on the:
 a. FORMATTING tab.
 b. DESIGN tab.
 c. PRINT PREVIEW tab.
 d. ARRANGE tab.

Skills Review

1. Use the Report Wizard.

a. Start Access and open the RealEstate-D.accdb database from the location where you store your Data Files. Enable content if prompted.

b. Use the Report Wizard to create a report based on the RLast and RPhone fields from the Realtors table, and the Type, SqFt, BR, Bath, and Asking fields from the Listings table.

c. View the data by Realtors, do not add any more grouping levels, and sort the records in descending order by the Asking field. (*Hint*: Click the Ascending button to toggle it to Descending.)

d. Use a Stepped layout and a Landscape orientation. Title the report **Realtor Listings**.

e. Preview the first and second pages of the new report.

2. Use Report Layout View.

a. Switch to Layout View and close the Field List and Property Sheet if they are open.

b. Narrow the RLast, RPhone, and Bath columns enough so they are only as wide as needed to display all data.

c. Modify the RLast label to read **Realtor**, the RPhone label to read **Phone**, the SqFt label to read **Square Feet**, the BR label to read **Bedrooms**, and the Bath label to read **Baths**.

d. Switch to Print Preview to review your changes.

3. Review report sections.

a. Switch to Report Design View.

b. Drag the text box that contains the Page calculation in the lower-right corner of the Page Footer section to the left so that it is to the left of the 9" mark on the horizontal ruler.

c. Drag the right edge of the entire report to the left so it ends within the 10" mark on the horizontal ruler. You may need to move or narrow the Baths label and Bath text box more than you did in Step 2b in order to accomplish this.

4. Apply group and sort orders.

a. Open the Group, Sort, and Total pane.

b. Add the Type field as a grouping field between the RealtorNo grouping field and Asking sort field. Make sure the sort order on the Asking field is in descending order (from largest to smallest).

c. Cut and paste the Type combo box from its current position in the Detail section to the Type Header section.

d. Move the Type combo box in the Type Header section so its left edge is at about the 1" mark on the horizontal ruler.

e. Delete the Type label in the Page Header section.

f. Switch to Layout View, and resize the Asking, Square Feet, Bedrooms, and Baths columns as needed so they are more evenly spaced across the page.

5. Add subtotals and counts.

a. Switch to Report Design View, then open the RealtorNo Footer section.

b. Add a text box control to the RealtorNo Footer section, just below the Asking text box in the Detail section. Change the label to read **Subtotal:**, and enter the expression **=Sum([Asking])** in the text box.

c. Drag the bottom edge of the Report Footer down about 0.25" to add space to the Report Footer.

d. Copy and paste the new expression in the RealtorNo Footer section to the Report Footer section. Position the new controls in the Report Footer section directly below the controls in the RealtorNo Footer section.

e. Modify the Subtotal: label in the Report Footer section to read **Grand Total:**.

f. Preview the last page of the report to view the new subtotals in the RealtorNo Footer and Report Footer sections.

6. Resize and align controls.

a. Switch to Layout View, click the Group & Sort button on the DESIGN tab to close the Group, Sort, and Total pane if it is open, and move to the last page of the report to view the Subtotal and Grand Total calculations at the same time.

b. Right-align the text within the Subtotal and Grand Total labels.

Skills Review (continued)

c. Switch to Design View, click the Asking text box, press and hold [Shift], and then click the text box in the RealtorNo and also the Report Footer sections to select all three text boxes at the same time. Click the ARRANGE tab, click the Align button, then click Right to right-align the edges of the Subtotal and Grand Total text boxes.

d. With all three text boxes still selected, click the FORMAT tab on the Ribbon, click the Apply Comma Number Format button, and click the Decrease Decimals button twice.

e. Preview the report to view the alignment and format on the Asking data and subtotals.

7. Format a report.

a. In Report Design View, change the Alternate Row Color of the Detail section to No Color.

b. Change the Alternate Row Color of the Type Header section as well as the RealtorNo Header section to No Color.

c. Change the Shape Fill color of the RealtorNo Header section to Green 2.

d. Select the RLast text box in the RealtorNo Header section, and change the Shape Fill color to Green 2 to match the RealtorNo Header section. Apply the Green 2 background color to the RPhone text box as well.

e. Bold the title of the report, the **Realtor Listings** label in the Report Header, and resize it to make it a little wider to accommodate the bold text.

f. Change the font color of each label in the Page Header section to black.

g. Save and preview the report in Report View. It should look like FIGURE D-21. The report should fit on two pages and the grand total for all Asking values should be 7,771,513. If there are blank pages between printed pages, return to Report Design View and drag the right edge of the report to the left.

FIGURE D-21

h. In Report Design View, add a label to the left side of the Report Footer section with your name.

i. Return to Print Preview, print the report if requested by your instructor, then save and close the Realtor Listings report.

8. Create mailing labels.

a. Click the Agencies table in the Navigation Pane, then start the Label Wizard.

b. Choose Avery 5160 labels and the default text appearance choices.

c. Build a prototype label with the AgencyName on the first line, Street on the second line, and City, State, and Zip on the third line with a comma and space between City and State, and a space between State and Zip.

d. Sort by AgencyName, and name the report **Labels Agencies**.

e. Preview then save and close the report. Click OK if a warning dialog box appears regarding horizontal space. The data in your label report does not exceed the dimensions of the labels.

f. If your instructor asks you to print the Labels Agencies report, open the Agencies table and change the name of Four Lakes Realtors to **Your LastName Realtors**. Close the Agencies table, reopen the Labels Agencies report, then print it.

g. Close the Labels Agencies report, close the RealEstate-D.accdb database, then exit Access 2013.

Independent Challenge 1

As the office manager of an international convention planning company, you have created a database to track convention, enrollment, and company data. Your goal is to create a report of up-to-date attendee enrollments.

a. Start Access, then open the Conventions-D.accdb database from the location where you store your Data Files. Enable content if prompted.

b. Use the Report Wizard to create a report with the AttendeeFirst and AttendeeLast fields from the Attendees table, the CompanyName field from the Companies table, and the ConventionName and CountryName from the Conventions table.

c. View your data by Conventions, do not add any more grouping levels, and sort in ascending order by CompanyName, then AttendeeLast.

d. Use the Block layout and Portrait orientation, then name the report **Convention Listing**.

e. In Layout View, change the labels in the Page Header section from ConventionName to **Convention** and AttendeeLast to **Attendee**. Delete the CountryName, CompanyName, and AttendeeFirst labels in the Page Header section.

f. In Report Design View, open the Group, Sort, and Total pane, then open the CompanyName Header and CompanyName Footer sections.

g. In Report Design View, expand the ConventionNo Header section about 0.25", then use the Cut and Paste commands to move the ConventionName text box from the Detail section to the left edge of the ConventionNo Header section.

h. Cut and paste the CountryName text box from the Detail section to the ConventionNo Header section. Move it to the right of the ConventionName text box.

i. Drag the top edge of the CompanyName Header section up to remove any extra blank space in the ConventionNo Header section.

j. Cut and paste the CompanyName text box from the Detail section to the CompanyName Header section. Move it to the right of the ConventionName text box in the ConventionNo Header section and to the left of the AttendeeLast text box in the Detail section.

k. Remove any extra blank space in the CompanyName Header section by dragging the top edge of the Detail section up as far as possible. Close the Group, Sort, and Total pane.

l. In Layout View, scroll through the entire report and resize the ConventionName, CountryName, and CompanyName text boxes as needed to show all of the data. Be careful, however, to not expand the report beyond the width of the portrait orientation of the report.

m. In Design View, expand the CompanyName Footer about 0.5", and add a new text box positioned below the AttendeeLast text box in the Detail section. Modify the new label in the Company Name Footer to read **Count:**. Enter an expression in a new text box to count the values in the AttendeeLast field, **=Count([AttendeeLast])**.

n. Format the text color of the Count: label to black and right-align the text within the label.

o. Change the color of the report title and the labels in the Page Header section to black. Preview the report. The subtotal count for the first convention should be 21.

p. Add a label with your name to the right side of the Report Header section, then print the first page if required by your instructor.

q. Save and close the Convention Listing report, close the Conventions-D.accdb database, then exit Access 2013.

Independent Challenge 2

You have built an Access database to track membership in a community service club. The database tracks member names and addresses as well as their status and rank in the club, and their hours of service to the community.

a. Start Access and open the Membership-D.accdb database from the location where you store your Data Files. Enable content if prompted.

b. Open the Members table, find and change the name of Traci Kalvert to *your* name, then close the Members table.

c. Use the Report Wizard to create a report using the Status and DuesOwed fields from the Status table, and the FName, LName, and DuesPaid fields from the Members table.

d. View the data by Status. Do not add any more grouping fields, and sort the records in ascending order by LName then FName.

e. Use a Stepped layout and Portrait orientation, title the report **Dues Report**, then preview the report.

f. Switch to Report Design View, then use the Group, Sort, and Total pane to open the StatusNo Footer section.

g. Add a text box to the StatusNo Footer section, just below the DuesPaid text box in the Detail section. Change the label to **Count:** and the expression in the text box to **=Count([DuesPaid])**.

h. Expand the StatusNo Footer section to provide more space, and add a second text box to the StatusNo Footer section, just below the first. Change the label to **Subtotal:** and the expression in the text box to **=Sum([DuesPaid])**.

i. Expand the StatusNo Footer section to provide more space, and add a third text box to the StatusNo Footer section, just below the second. Change the accompanying label to **Balance:**.

j. Change the text box expression to **=Count([DuesPaid])*[DuesOwed]–Sum([DuesPaid])**. This expression counts the number of values in the DuesPaid field, and multiplies it by the DuesOwed field. From that value, the sum of the DuesPaid field is subtracted. This calculates the balance between dues owed and dues paid.

k. Open the Property Sheet for the =Sum([DuesPaid]) text box. On the Format tab, set the Format property to **Currency** and the Decimal Places property to **2**. Repeat these property changes for the text box with the balance calculation.

l. Select the DuesPaid text box in the Detail section, press and hold [Shift], then select all three text boxes in the StatusNo Footer section. Align the right edges of all four controls using the Align button, then Right command on the ARRANGE tab of the Ribbon. Also, right-align the contents within the text boxes of the StatusNo Footer section using the Align Right button on the HOME tab of the Ribbon. Right-align the right edges of the three new labels in the StatusNo Footer section.

m. Save, then preview the Dues Report. Make sure the report does not contain blank pages and fix that in Report Design View if needed. Print the first page of the Dues Report if requested by your instructor. The StatusNo Footer section for the first status, New, is shown in FIGURE D-22.

n. Close the Dues Report, close the Membership-D.accdb database, then exit Access.

FIGURE D-22

Count:	7
Subtotal:	$375.00
Balance:	$325.00

Access 2013

Independent Challenge 3

You have built an Access database to organize the deposits at a recycling center. Various clubs regularly deposit recyclable material, which is measured in pounds when the deposits are made.

a. Start Access and open the Recycle-D.accdb database from the location where you store your Data Files. Enable content if prompted.

b. Open the Centers table, change **Trash Can** to *Your* **Last Name Recycling**, then close the table.

c. Use the Report Wizard to create a report with the CenterName field from the Centers table, the DepositDate and Weight fields from the Deposits table, and the ClubName field from the Clubs table.

d. View the data by Centers, do not add any more grouping levels, and sort the records in ascending order by DepositDate.

e. Use a Stepped layout and a Portrait orientation, then title the report **Deposit Listing**.

f. In Layout View, center the Weight label and Weight data within their controls. Resize the DepositDate label and data by dragging the left edge of the control farther to the left so the label text and all dates are clearly displayed.

g. Add spaces to the labels so that CenterName becomes **Center Name**, DepositDate becomes **Deposit Date**, and ClubName becomes **Club Name**.

h. In Report Design View, open the Group, Sort, and Total pane and then open the CenterNumber Footer section.

i. Add a text box to the CenterNumber Footer section just below the Weight text box with the expression =**Sum([Weight])**.

j. Rename the new label to be **Total Center Weight** and move and resize it as needed so that it doesn't overlap the text box.

k. Resize the =Sum([Weight]) text box in the CenterNumber Footer section to be the same size as the Weight text box in the Detail section. Align the right edges of the Weight text box in the Detail section with the =Sum([Weight]) text box in the CenterNumber Footer section. Center the data in the =Sum([Weight]) text box.

l. Expand the Report Footer section, then copy and paste the =Sum([Weight]) text box from the CenterNumber Footer section to the Report Footer section.

m. Move and align the controls in the Report Footer section to be positioned directly under their counterparts in the CenterNumber Footer section.

n. Change the label in the Report Footer section to **Grand Total Weight**.

o. Remove extra blank space in the report by dragging the bottom of the report as well as the section bars up, then preview a portion of the last page of the report, as shown in FIGURE D-23. The last Total Center Weight and Grand Total Weight values on your report should match the figure.

p. Save and close the Deposit Listing report, close the Recycle-D.accdb database, then exit Access.

FIGURE D-23

6/4/2013	90	Lions
6/20/2013	85	Junior League
8/31/2013	50	Girl Scouts #11
10/2/2013	90	Lions
Total Center Weight	2720	
Grand Total Weight	9365	

Independent Challenge 4: Explore

One way you can use an Access database on your own is to record and track your job search efforts. In this exercise, you create a report to help read and analyze data into your job-tracking database.

a. Start Access and open the JobSearch-D.accdb database from the location where you store your Data Files. Enable content if prompted.

b. Open the Employers table, and enter five more records to identify five more potential employers.

c. Use subdatasheets in the Employers table to enter five more potential jobs. You may enter all five jobs for one employer, one job for five different employers, or any combination thereof. Be sure to check the spelling of all data entered. For the Desirability field, enter a value from **1** to **5**, 1 being the least desirable and 5 the most desirable. Close the Employers table.

d. Use the Report Wizard to create a report that lists the CompanyName, EmpCity, and EmpState fields from the Employers table, and the Title, AnnualSalary, and Desirability fields from the Positions table.

e. View the data by Employers, do not add any more grouping levels, and sort the records in ascending order by Title.

f. Use an Outline layout and a Landscape orientation, then title the report **Job Opportunities**.

g. In Design View, revise the labels in the EmployerID Header section from CompanyName to **Company**, EmpCity to **City**, EmpState to **State**, and AnnualSalary to **Salary**.

h. In Design View, right-align the text within the Company, City, and State labels so they are closer to the text boxes they describe.

i. In Report Design View, move the Page expression in the Page Footer section and the right edge of the report to the left, within the 10.5" mark on the horizontal ruler, and then drag the right edge of the report to the left to make sure that the report fits within the margins of one sheet of paper in landscape orientation.

j. Open the EmployerID Footer section and use the Line control in the Controls group on the DESIGN tab to add a horizontal line across the width of the report in the EmployerID Footer section. (*Hint*: The Line control may be on the second row of the Controls box. Also, press and hold [Shift] while dragging the line to create a perfectly horizontal line.)

k. Click a green error indicator that appears on the labels in the EmployerID Header section, point to the warning button to read the ScreenTip, then click the drop-down arrow on the error indicator and click Ignore Error.

l. Preview and save the Job Opportunities report making sure that the report fits within one page wide, then print the first page if requested by your instructor.

m. Close the Job Opportunities report, close the JobSearch-D.accdb database, then exit Access 2013.

Visual Workshop

Open the Basketball-D.accdb database from the location where you store your Data Files and enable content if prompted. Open the Players table, enter *your* name instead of Kelsey Douglas, then close the table. Your goal is to create the report shown in FIGURE D-24. Use the Report Wizard, and select the PFirst, PLast, HomeTown, and HomeState fields from the Players table. Select the FieldGoals, 3Pointers, and FreeThrows fields from the Stats table. View the data by Players, do not add any more grouping levels, and do not add any more sorting levels. Use a Block layout and a Portrait orientation, then title the report **Scoring Report**. In Layout View, resize all of the columns so that they fit on a single piece of portrait paper, and change the labels in the Page Header section as shown. In Design View, open the PlayerNo Footer section and add text boxes with expressions to sum the FieldGoals, 3Pointers, and FreeThrow fields. Move, modify, align, and resize all controls as needed to match FIGURE D-24. Be sure to print preview the report to make sure that it fits within the width of one sheet of paper. Modify the report to narrow it in Report Design View if needed.

FIGURE D-24

Scoring Report

Player Name		Home Town	State	Field Goals	3 Pointers	Free Throws
Student First	Student Last	Linden	IA	4	1	3
				5	2	2
				5	3	3
				6	3	5
				4	1	1
				4	2	2
				3	2	1
				4	2	3
				4	2	3
				3	2	1
		Subtotals		42	20	24